INDUCING COMPLIANCE WITH INTERNATIONAL HUMANITARIAN LAW

The number of armed conflicts featuring extreme violence against the civilian population in areas with no or little State authority has risen significantly since the early 1990s. This phenomenon has been particularly prevalent in the African Great Lakes Region.

This collection of essays evaluates from an interdisciplinary perspective the various traditional and alternative instruments for inducing compliance with international humanitarian law. In particular, it explores the potential of persuasion as well as hierarchical means, such as criminal justice on the international and domestic level or quasi-judicial mechanisms by armed groups. Furthermore, it evaluates the role and potential of human rights bodies, peacekeeping missions and the UN Security Council's special compliance system for children and armed conflicts. It also considers how both Common Article 1 to the Geneva Conventions and the law of State responsibility could potentially increase compliance with international humanitarian law.

HEIKE KRIEGER is Professor of Public International Law at the Freie Universität Berlin. Between 2007 and 2014, she acted as Judge at the Constitutional Court of the State of Berlin.

INDUCING COMPLIANCE WITH INTERNATIONAL HUMANITARIAN LAW

Lessons from the African Great Lakes Region

Edited by

HEIKE KRIEGER

Assistant editor

JAN WILLMS

CAMBRIDGE
UNIVERSITY PRESS

CAMBRIDGE
UNIVERSITY PRESS

University Printing House, Cambridge CB2 8BS, United Kingdom

Cambridge University Press is part of the University of Cambridge.

It furthers the University's mission by disseminating knowledge in the pursuit of education, learning and research at the highest international levels of excellence.

www.cambridge.org
Information on this title: www.cambridge.org/9781107102057

First published 2015

A catalogue record for this publication is available from the British Library

Library of Congress Cataloguing in Publication data
Inducing compliance with international humanitarian law : lessons from the African Great Lakes region / edited by Heike Krieger, assistant editor Jan Willms
pages cm
ISBN 978-1-107-10205-7 (hardback)
1. International crimes – Great Lakes Region (Africa) – Prevention. 2. Humanitarian law – Africa. I. Krieger, Heike, editor. II. Willms, Jan
KQC982.I57I53 2015
341.6′7096761 – dc23 2015026255

ISBN 978-1-107-10205-7 Hardback

CONTENTS

CONTRIBUTORS

HELMUT PHILIPP AUST is a Senior Research Fellow at the Humboldt University, Berlin, where he teaches public international law and German constitutional law. Previously, he taught at the University of Munich and at the University of Federal Armed Forces, Munich. He was also a Visiting Fellow at the Lauterpacht Centre of International Law, University of Cambridge (2008) and a Visiting Scholar at Melbourne Law School (2014–2015). He is the author of 'Complicity and the Law of State Responsibility' (2011).

OLIVIER BANGERTER is a graduate in theology of both the University of Lausanne (master's) and the University of Geneva (PhD). He worked for the International Committee of the Red Cross (ICRC) between 2001 and 2011 and was the ICRC advisor for the dialogue with armed groups between 2008 and 2011. In this function, he met members and former members of around sixty armed groups around the world. Between October 2011 and January 2012, he worked for Small Arms Survey as a Senior Researcher. Between January 2012 and March 2014, he was the Lead at the Humanitarian Policy Team of the Federal Department of Foreign Affairs of Switzerland. Now he is the Thematic Team Leader of the team 'Serving the needs of people in conflict' in preparation of the 2016 World Humanitarian Summit at the United Nations Office for the Coordination of Humanitarian Affairs (OCHA).

ROBERT CRYER is Professor of International and Criminal Law at the University of Birmingham. In addition to writing a number of articles he is the author of 'Prosecuting International Crimes: Selectivity and the International Criminal Law Regime' (2005) and co-author (with Hakan Friman, Darryl Robinson and Elizabeth Wilmshurst) of 'An Introduction to International Criminal Law and Procedure' (2010) and (with Neil Boister) of 'The Tokyo International Military Tribunal: A Reappraisal' (2008). He is co-editor of the Journal of Conflict and Security Law and a member of the editorial board of the Journal of International Criminal Justice.

DIETER FLECK, formerly Director of the Department of International Agreements & Policy of the German Ministry of Defence, is Honorary President of the International Society for Military Law and the Law of War, member of the Advisory Board of the Amsterdam Center for International Law (ACIL) and member of the Editorial Board of the Journal of International Peacekeeping.

ROBIN GEIß is Professor of International Law and Security at the University of Glasgow. Previously, he was Professor of international and European law at the University of Potsdam. Prior to that, he worked as legal advisor for the International Committee of the Red Cross (ICRC) in Geneva and served as ICRC delegate to the United Nations Human Rights Council. He was conferred his doctorate for a thesis on failed States in 2003 and holds an LLM degree in International Legal Studies from New York University.

MATTHEW HAPPOLD is Professor in International Public Law at the University of Luxembourg, where he teaches public international law, international dispute settlement and international human rights law. He previously taught at the universities of Hull, Nottingham and Sussex, and worked at the British Institute of International and Comparative Law. He has been a Visiting Fellow at the Human Rights Program at Harvard Law School and a Visiting Professional in the Office of the Prosecutor of the International Criminal Court. His publications include 'International Law in a Multipolar World' (editor: 2011), 'Child Soldiers in International Law' (2005) and Constitutional Human Rights in the Commonwealth (co-editor with Michael Anderson, 2003). He is a member of the editorial board of the Human Rights Law Review and of the editorial advisory board of the Revue trimestrielle des droits de l'homme. In January 2014, he was appointed a member of the Luxembourg Commission consultative des droits de l'homme.

CLAUDIA HOFMANN is the Director of the Master in International Service (MIS) programme at the School of International Service at American University in Washington, DC. She is also an Associate Fellow at the Royal Institute of International Affairs, Chatham House. Dr Hofmann's research addresses the role of non-State actors in world politics, with a particular emphasis on rebels, insurgents and organized criminal groups as a challenge to foreign and security policy. Her recent research focuses on the interplay between drugs and organized criminal groups and national security. Dr Hofmann has a rich background in academic teaching and policy-oriented in-depth research on both sides of the Atlantic. Her work has resulted in a number of peer-reviewed academic publications, international policy papers, presentations and policy consultations.

BALINGENE KAHOMBO is a PhD candidate in public international law at Freie Universität Berlin. A graduate of higher studies in public law at the University of Kinshasa, he was also an assistant Lecturer at the University of Goma (Democratic Republic of the Congo) and is a collaborate researcher at the Institute for Democracy, Governance, Peace and Development in Africa (IDGPDA). He is a member of the international network of research, Rule of Law Program for sub-Saharan Africa, supported by the Konrad Adenauer Foundation and also a magistrate (judge) in the Democratic Republic of the Congo. He has commented on issues of the rule of law, elections and constitutional justice in Africa, African regional integration and peace and security in Africa, as well as international criminal law and the international judicial cooperation in criminal matters pertaining to Africa.

REGINA KLOSTERMANN has worked as a Research Associate at the Collaborative Research Center 700 (SFB) dealing with questions of enforcement of international humanitarian law. She is mainly focusing on the role of non-governmental organizations in ensuring compliance with international humanitarian law by non-State actors. She obtained the Maîtrise en droit with a focus on international law at Université Jean Moulin, Lyon III in France. She is currently working for an international law firm.

HEIKE KRIEGER is Professor of Law at the Freie Universität Berlin and has, inter alia, taught at the Universities of Göttingen and Nottingham and the Centre for Transnational Legal Studies, London. Between 2007 and 2014 she acted as Judge at the Constitutional Court of the State of Berlin. She has published extensively on issues of international humanitarian law, human rights law and general public international law. She is also Vice President of the German Society for Military Law and Humanitarian Law, and directs a research project on 'Legitimacy and Law-Making in International

Humanitarian Law' at the Collaborative Research Center 'Governance in Areas of Limited Statehood' funded by the German Research Foundation.

JEAN-MICHEL KUMBU is Professor of Law. He teaches, inter alia, employment law and economic legislation at the Université de Kinshasa and other universities in the Democratic Republic of the Congo. He also acts as a lawyer with a focus on business law. He is an expert in democratic governance at the United Nations Development Program in Kinshasa.

ZACHARIAH MAMPILLY is Associate Professor of Political Science and International Studies and Director of the Program in Africana Studies at Vassar College. He has also taught at the University of California, Los Angeles, Columbia University and the University of Dar es Salaam as a Fulbright Fellow. His research focuses on the nature of resistance, both violent and non-violent, with an emphasis on Africa and South Asia. His first book, 'Rebel Rulers: Insurgent Governance and Civilian Life during War', was published by Cornell University Press in 2011. His manuscript on popular protest in Africa ('Africa Uprising: Popular Politics and Political Change', co-written with Adam Branch) is forthcoming from Zed Press.

FAUSTIN ZACHARIE NTOUBANDI was Assistant Professor of Law at the Justus-Liebig University of Gießen and researcher at the Franz von Liszt Institute of International Law between 2004 and 2012. He has also taught at a number of universities, including the Université de Bretagne occidentale in Brest (France), the University of Wisconsin in Madison (USA) and UNICRI in Turin (Italy). He is presently Visiting Scholar at the Universitiy of Toronto. He has published extensively on various questions of public international law, human rights law and international humanitarian law.

KIRSTEN SCHMALENBACH is Professor of Public International Law and European Union Law at the University of Salzburg and Vice Dean of the law faculty of the University of Salzburg. She has, inter alia, taught at the universities of Cologne, Bayreuth, Graz and Rutgers (Camden). The focus of her academic writings lies on issues of the international law of treaties, international humanitarian and human rights law, institutional law of international organizations and EU external relations.

ULRICH SCHNECKENER is Professor of International Relations & Peace and Conflict studies at the University of Osnabrück and Director of the

Center for Democracy and Peace Research (ZeDF) of the University of Osnabrück. From 2002 to 2009 he worked as Senior Researcher at the German Institute for International and Security Affairs (SWP) in Berlin. His areas of research are international conflict management, State- and peace-building processes and the role of non-State armed actors in international politics.

SANDESH SIVAKUMARAN is Professor of Public International Law at the University of Nottingham. He has worked at the International Court of Justice, the International Criminal Tribunal for the former Yugoslavia and the Special Court for Sierra Leone, and acted as an expert or advisor for a number of States, UN entities and non-governmental organizations.

DOMINIK STEIGER works as a Senior Fellow and Lecturer at Freie Universität Berlin. Formerly, he has, inter alia, worked at the International Criminal Tribunal for Rwanda and has taught and researched at the University of Potsdam where he obtained his PhD as a scholarship holder of the Konrad-Adenauer-Stiftung. During the academic year 2014–2015, he is an Emile-Noël-Fellow at New York University. He has published on issues of human rights law, international humanitarian law, general public international law and public law.

DENIS M. TULL is a Senior Researcher at the German Institute for International and Security Affairs (SWP) in Berlin. He received his PhD in political science from the University of Hamburg in 2004. His articles on Africa's international relations, State transformation and State building in Africa, insurgencies and peacekeeping have appeared in International Security, International Peacekeeping, African Affairs and the Journal of Modern African Studies, among other journals.

JAN WILLMS is former Research Associate at the Collaborative Research Center 700 (SFB) and completed his doctoral thesis about the duty of extraterritorial military presences to cooperate with international criminal courts and tribunals. Previously, he worked for the Legal Division of the International Committee of the Red Cross and the International Criminal Tribunal for the former Yugoslavia. He holds an LLM in public international law from the University of Nottingham. Currently, he is a Reasearch Associate at the German Bundestag.

SIOBHÁN WILLS is a Professor of Law in the Transitional Justice Institute, University of Ulster. Prior to this, she was based at University College Cork where she was Co-Director of the Centre for Criminal Justice and Human Rights. Her research is mainly focused on international humanitarian law and human rights law, especially in relation to peacekeeping and protection of civilians. She is a member of the International Law Association's Committee on the Use of Force and is also a member of the Royal Irish Academy's Social Sciences Committee. In 2013, she held the Ariel Sallows Visiting Chair in Human Rights at the University of Saskatchewan. She has held visiting fellowships at Harvard Law School on the Human Rights Program as a Fulbright Fellow, at New York University Law School on the Hauser Global Fellowship Program, at St John's College (University of Oxford), at Australia National University and at the Human Rights Consortium, School of Advanced Studies, University of London. She obtained her LLB from the National University of Ireland Galway, her LLM from Yale Law School and her PhD from the University of Oxford.

REED M. WOOD (PhD, University of North Carolina, Chapel Hill) is Assistant Professor of political science at Arizona State University. His research interests include political violence, human rights and insurgency. His research has recently appeared in International Studies Quarterly, Human Rights Quarterly, the Journal of Peace Research and the Journal of Conflict Resolution. He is also Co-Manager of the Political Terror Scale (PTS).

PREFACE

At the time of finalizing this book, the focus of the international community has turned to the ongoing conflict in Syria. There are widespread violations of international humanitarian law committed by State and non-State actors. This book is intended to shed some light on the methods for inducing compliance with international humanitarian law in war-torn areas of limited statehood. While focusing on the African Great Lakes Region, the book's conclusions will hopefully contribute to a better understanding of compliance mechanisms for conflicts between State and non-State actors in other regions as well.

The book is part of a broader research project on compliance with international humanitarian law in areas of limited statehood. The project forms part of the Collaborative Research Center 700 at the Freie Universität Berlin – a coordinated research programme funded by the German Research Foundation (DFG). The Center focuses on the questions as to how effective and legitimate governance can be sustained in areas of limited statehood and which problems emerge under such conditions.

The volume is conceived as an edited collection because improving compliance with international humanitarian law requires an exchange of ideas and experiences between lawyers, social scientists and practitioners. A profound understanding of the reasons why armed groups and States' armed forces commit acts of violence against the civilian population is an important basis for evaluating the efficiency and legitimacy of the norms of international humanitarian law and for considerations of legal policy. On the other hand, legal analysis helps political scientists to apply the appropriate variables in their empirical research. For the book's coherence, the authors participated in a workshop, 'Enforcing International Humanitarian Law in Contemporary African Conflicts', which was funded by the DFG and the German Foundation for Peace Research (DSF).

As the editor I am grateful to the authors of the volume for engaging with the project, participating in the workshop and contributing to the book. The volume profited from the help and support of a number of people working at the Research Center and the law faculty of the Freie Universität Berlin. Special thanks are due to my assistant editor, Jan Willms, for his commitment and diligent work. My research assistants Björnstjern Baade, Anna Dieter, Anna Hankings-Evans, Linus Mührel, Yasemin Skowronek and Sebastian Walther conformed the text and the footnotes to the style guide. Anton Petrov and Moritz Thörner prepared the index. Kirsten Leube and Antonina Sanchez helped with the English language: thank you all for your work! Finally, I am grateful to Elizabeth Spicer and Richard Woodham at Cambridge University Press for their advice and support.

Heike Krieger

TABLE OF TREATIES

Short forms of treaty names appear in parentheses after the full title of the treaty, where applicable.

African Charter on Human and Peoples' Rights, Banjul, 27 June 1981, in force 21 October 1986, OAU Doc. CAB/LEG/67/3 rev.5; (1982) 21 I.L.M. 58 (African Charter)

American Convention on Human Rights, San José, 22 November 1969, in force 18 July 1978, 1144 U.N.T.S. 123 (ACHR)

Charter of the United Nations, San Francisco, 26 June 1945, in force 24 October 1945, 1 U.N.T.S. 16 (UN Charter)

Constitutive Act of the African Union, Lomé, 11 July 2000, in force 26 May 2001, 2158 U.N.T.S. 3

Convention (IV) Respecting the Laws and Customs of War on Land and Its Annex: Regulations Concerning the Laws and Customs of War on Land, The Hague, 18 October 1907, in force 26 January 1910, 3 Martens Nouveau Recueil (ser. 3) 461 (Hague Regulations)

Convention for the Protection of Human Rights and Fundamental Freedoms, Rome, 4 November 1950, entry into force 3 September 1953, E.T.S. No. 5 (European Convention on Human Rights, ECHR)

Convention on the Prevention and Punishment of the Crime of Genocide, New York, 9 December 1948, in force 12 January 1951, 78 U.N.T.S. 277 (Genocide Convention)

Convention on the Prohibition of the Use, Stockpiling, Production and Transfer of Anti-Personnel Mines and on Their Destruction, Oslo, 18 September 1997, in force 1 March 1999, 2056 U.N.T.S. 211

Convention on the Rights of the Child, New York, 20 November 1989, in force 2 September 1990, 1577 U.N.T.S. 3 (CRC)

Convention on the Safety of United Nations and Associated Personnel, New York, 9 December 1994, in force 15 January 1999, 2051 U.N.T.S. 391 (Safety Convention)

European Convention for the Prevention of Torture and Inhuman or Degrading Treatment or Punishment, Strasbourg, 26 November 1987, in force 1 February 1989, C.E.T.S. No. 126

consequently lacking'.[5] Instead of failed or failing States, the book uses the social science term 'limited statehood' because the term neither implies a normative judgment that a State has failed nor suggests that State failure would be the definite result of a process. It is also broader in that only parts of a country as well as areas spanning over parts of several countries might be affected, and it can cover transitional States.[6]

In war-torn areas of limited statehood, the rise of armed, violent non-State actors collides with the State-centric traditional nature of public international law with apparently detrimental consequences to (classical) compliance structures in international humanitarian law. Even though in military terms, armed groups might be on equal footing with State's armed forces or may even possess superior military capabilities, in legal terms, parties to the conflict are not equal; rights and obligations are thus asymmetrical. The most obvious example concerns the (national) criminal responsibility of members of the armed groups for their mere participation in hostilities against their government and their lack of a prisoner-of-war status. Thus, to put it in simple terms, non-State actors are expected to comply with not only norms in the creation of which they have never participated and to which they have never consented but also those which apparently do not even entail great benefits for them. This asymmetry directly affects the classically most important motive for compliance in international law – reciprocity – and seems to diminish the prospect of compliance based on the norm's legitimacy.[7]

[5] T. Risse and T. Börzel, 'Human Rights – The New Agenda' (Working Paper No. 7, Transworld: Transatlantic Relations and the Future Global Governance, December 2012), at 10; T. Risse and T. Börzel, 'Human Rights in Areas of Limited Statehood: the New Agenda', in T. Risse, S. Ropp and K. Sikkink (eds.), *The Persistent Power of Human Rights: From Commitment to Compliance* (Cambridge: Cambridge University Press, 2013) 63–84, at 63.

[6] T. Risse and U. Lehmkuhl, 'Governance in Areas of Limited Statehood – New Modes of Governance?', Research Program of the Research Center (SFB) 700 (SFB-Governance Working Paper Series No. 1, December 2006), at 9.

[7] N. Lamp, 'Conceptions of War and Paradigms of Compliance' (2011) 16 *Journal of Conflict and Security Law* 225, at 240–250, who bases his understanding of the characteristics of the so-called 'new wars' on the arguments of H. Münkler, *The New Wars* (Cambridge: Polity Press, 2005); R. Geiß, 'Asymmetric Conflict Structures' (2006) 88 *International Review of the Red Cross* 757, at 770, 773; C. Bassouni, 'The New Wars and the Crisis of Compliance with the Law of Armed Conflict by Non-State Actors' (2008) 98 *Journal of Criminal Law and Criminology* 711, at 765 et seq.; M. Sassòli, 'The Implementation of International Humanitarian Law: Current and Inherent Challenges' (2007) 10 *Yearbook of International Humanitarian Law* 45, at 49.

1

Introduction

HEIKE KRIEGER

Enforcement and compliance have always been the Achilles heel of international humanitarian law. Despite all efforts to minimize human suffering in wartime, atrocities seem to be an endemic component of warfare. This observation prompted Hersch Lauterpacht's famous statement that 'if international law is . . . at the vanishing point of law, the law of war is . . . at the vanishing point of international law'.[1] With the rise of the so-called 'new wars',[2] after the end of the Cold War, a wide-ranging perception crystallized that these wars pose an even stronger challenge to the enforcement of international humanitarian law than more traditional forms of armed conflicts. Already in 1999, in its first resolution on the protection of civilians in armed conflict, the Security Council expressed 'its deep concern at the erosion in respect for international humanitarian . . . law' in contemporary armed conflicts.[3]

Many of the perpetuated armed conflicts in the Great Lakes Region in Africa are considered to be representative of this phenomenon. Fragmented armed groups fight each other or armed forces of a government, which represents only the remainders of collapsed State structures. In addition, both sides might receive support from third States or armed groups based in third States. These kinds of conflicts typically occur in war-torn areas of limited statehood.[4] Political science has labelled areas of limited statehood as 'those parts of a country in which central authorities lack the ability to implement and enforce rules and decisions and in which the legitimate monopoly over the means of violence is

[1] H. Lauterpacht, 'The Problem of the Revision of the Law of War' (1952) 29 *British Yearbook of International Law* 360, at 382.

[2] M. Kaldor, *New and Old Wars*, 2d edn (Cambridge: Polity Press, 2006).

[3] UNSC Resolution 1265 (17 September 1999).

[4] S. Chojnacki and Z. Branovic, 'New Modes of Security – The Violent Making and Unmaking of Governance in Areas of Limited Statehood', in T. Risse (ed.), *Governance Without a State? Policies and Politics in Areas of Limited Statehood* (New York: Columbia University Press, 2011), 89–114.

Geneva Convention I for the Amelioration of the Condition of the Wounded and Sick in Armed Forces in the Field, Geneva, 12 August 1949, in force 21 October 1950, 75 U.N.T.S. 31 (Geneva Convention I, GC I)

Geneva Convention II for the Amelioration of the Condition of Wounded, Sick and Shipwrecked Members of the Armed Forces at Sea, Geneva, 12 August 1949, in force 21 October 1950, 75 U.N.T.S. 85 (Geneva Convention II, GC II)

Geneva Convention III Relative to the Treatment of Prisoners of War, Geneva, 12 August 1949, in force 21 October 1950, 75 U.N.T.S. 135 (Geneva Convention III, GC III)

Geneva Convention IV Relative to the Protection of Civilian Persons in Time of War, Geneva, 12 August 1949, in force 21 October 1950, 75 U.N.T.S. 287 (Geneva Convention IV, GC IV)

International Covenant on Civil and Political Rights, New York, 16 December 1966, in force 23 March 1976, 999 U.N.T.S. 171 (ICCPR)

Protocol Additional to the Geneva Conventions of 12 August 1949, and Relating to the Protection of Victims of International Armed Conflicts (Protocol I), Geneva, 8 June 1977, in force 7 December 1978, 1125 U.N.T.S. 3 (Additional Protocol I, AP I)

Protocol Additional to the Geneva Conventions of 12 August 1949, and Relating to the Protection of Victims of Non-International Armed Conflicts (Protocol II), Geneva, 8 June 1977, in force 7 December 1978, 1125 U.N.T.S. 609 (Additional Protocol II, AP II)

Protocol Additional to the Geneva Conventions of 12 August 1949, and Relating to the Adoption of an Additional Distinctive Emblem (Protocol III), Geneva, 8 December 2005, in force 14 January 2007, 2404 U.N.T.S. 19 (Additional Protocol III, AP III)

Protocol to the African Charter on Human and Peoples' Rights on the Rights of Women in Africa, Maputo, 11 July 2003, in force 25 November 2005, Doc. CAB/LEG/66.6

Statute of the International Criminal Court, Rome, 17 July 1998, in force 1 July 2002, 37 I.L.M. 1002 (ICC Statute)

Vienna Convention on the Law of Treaties, Vienna, 23 May 1969, in force 27 January 1980, 1155 U.N.T.S. 331

In these wars, it appears to be the case that warfare no longer aims at military victory. Parties to these conflicts '[are said] to rarely pursue their aims by attempting to defeat the military forces of the enemy; instead, a political or economic logic [is said] to infuse the conduct of war itself'.[8] Thus, civilian casualties are no longer an incidental side effect, but the actual essence of warfare in the form of ethnic cleansing or economic exploitation of civilians, for example, through slavery and trafficking,[9] sometimes even creating the impression that violence against civilians is used for no ostensible purpose at all. Therefore, assumptions about the so-called 'new wars' assert that the parties to these conflicts are only interested in preserving an endemic state of war. 'Perpetual warfare' is seen by some observers as a 'form of life' for many of its protagonists. If killing civilians is the actual goal of warfare, actors have no discernible interest in internalizing norms that prohibit such a use of force. Since their actions are illegal from the outset, the parties to the conflicts are considered unable to pursue their interest within the boundaries of international humanitarian law. It is argued that this inability leads to a lack of motives for voluntary compliance, which in turn makes persuasion to do so unfeasible and diminishes the influence which the public image of the conflict parties could exert on their behaviour. Thus, some observers hold that in places such as eastern parts of the Democratic Republic of the Congo (DRC) or in regard to the Lord's Resistance Army (LRA) in Northern Uganda, 'a paradigm of compliance which counts on the voluntary observance of the law by the warring parties and therefore has to presuppose that the law is compatible with their interests . . . becomes utterly inadequate under the circumstances of the "new wars"'.[10]

If reciprocity is really breaking away as a motive for compliance, classical enforcement instruments, such as reprisals, will lose their effectiveness. Moreover, the fragmentation of armed groups and their loose organizational structures appear to make enforcement through military hierarchy and discipline practically impossible. Where there are no strict military hierarchies and institutions, internalization of the laws of war is highly unlikely. In view of collapsing State structures, the same often holds true for remainders of the State's armed forces.[11] Likewise, in

[8] Lamp, 'Conceptions of War', above note 7, at 234.

[9] Ibid. 234–35; Sassòli, 'The Implementation of International Humanitarian Law', above note 7, at 59.

[10] Lamp, 'Conceptions of War', above note 7, at 245.

[11] Sassòli, 'The Implementation of International Humanitarian Law', above note 7, at 59.

areas of limited statehood, other State structures also fail to contribute to enforcing international humanitarian law. Corresponding national legislation, for instance, cannot be enforced through national institutions, such as criminal courts.[12]

This perspective indeed offers a bleak prospect for an effective compliance with international humanitarian law in conflicts such as those in the African Great Lakes Region. Against this backdrop, the present volume aims to inquire into traditional and alternative instruments for inducing compliance with the rules of international humanitarian law. In doing so, it concentrates on those compliance mechanisms which have been in the foreground of international efforts in recent years. This includes non-hierarchical instruments, such as persuasion, as well as hierarchical mechanisms, such as criminal prosecution and sanctions imposed by the United Nations Security Council. While these instruments predominantly rely on efforts of the international community, the book also inquires as to what responses might engage the actors in the war-torn areas of limited statehood themselves. Thus, by taking an interdisciplinary approach, the book challenges some of the assumptions underlying the concept of the so-called 'new wars' and its impact on compliance. It aims to shed some light on the different actors who must be involved in the process, as well as the extent to which their discretion is surrounded and curtailed by legal obligations.

The book's approach is to focus on a particular region which is dominated by war-torn areas of limited statehood: the African Great Lakes Region. While international humanitarian law as a legal regime must be conceived in such a manner as to be applicable to all contemporary forms of war, understanding compliance requires concentrating on particular conflicts. The regional focus is prompted by the nature of enforcement. Setting legal standards and inducing compliance differ in this respect. While the process of standard-setting calls mainly for generalization and a more universal approach, inducing compliance is closely related to the concrete circumstances on the ground. Actual decisions to obey a legal norm result from a complex mixture of diverse motivations. Power relations as well as historical, political, social and anthropological conditions determine these motivations so that compliance is

[12] For an overview of classical enforcement measures of international humanitarian law, see S. Vöneky, 'Implementation and Enforcement of International Humanitarian Law', in D. Fleck (ed.), *The Handbook of International Humanitarian Law*, 3d edn (Oxford: Oxford University Press, 2013), sections 1401–1436.

context-dependent.[13] Therefore, understanding the mechanisms of compliance and enforcement requires a close look at what is occurring on the ground in specific conflict constellations. Accordingly, this book is conceived as an interdisciplinary one. If the law shall preserve its function of directing the conduct of actors (*verhaltenssteuernde Funktion*), it is necessary to understand the dominant political and social circumstances.

Hence, the book starts with two contributions from a political science perspective, which challenge some of the assumptions of the theory of the 'new wars'. On the basis of the rational choice theory, Reed Wood addresses the phenomenon that violence against civilians fluctuates over time in perpetuated conflicts. Starting from the assumption that the 'new war' theories fail to explain this variation, Wood illustrates that insurgents are more likely to target civilians when they face major military setbacks by means of a case analysis of the LRA. Zachariah Mampilly focuses on insurgent governance in the DRC. Mampilly analyses under which conditions insurgencies are likely to establish governance structures and what governance practices are used for which reasons, and scrutinizes reactions of civilians and other actors to those efforts. Thus, he tests the common understanding of Congolese insurgent groups as appalling examples of warlordism and calls for a more nuanced approach by external actors towards armed groups so that insurgent governance systems can contribute to civilian welfare. The contributions by Ulrich Schneckener and Claudia Hofmann, Olivier Bangerter as well as Sandesh Sivakumaran directly build on these insights. Schneckener and Hofmann analyse how international non-governmental organizations and private individuals try to persuade armed groups by mediation and norm diffusion. By focusing on the International Committee of the Red Cross (ICRC), Geneva Call, the Centre for Humanitarian Dialogue and the Carter Center, they develop their thesis that such actors enjoy more freedom and flexibility to communicate with armed groups than with State actors. They conclude that such activities will contribute to norm transfer if armed groups are interested in their public image and struggle to become political actors. In his comment, Bangerter explains how this process of persuasion works in practice.

Part I closes with a suggestion as to how to address the deficits in the legitimacy of international humanitarian law from the perspective of

[13] M. Bothe, 'Compliance', in R Wolfrum (ed.), *The Max Planck Encyclopedia of Public International Law* (Oxford: Oxford University Press, 2008, online edition, www.mpepil.com).

armed groups. Since these legitimacy deficits are seen as a major obstacle to voluntary compliance, Sivakumaran looks for ways in which armed groups' accountability for international humanitarian law violations can be created. He favours allowing such groups to commit themselves to the norms by issuing unilateral declarations or by concluding ad hoc agreements and explores alternative options, such as participation in treaty creation or the use of their legally relevant practice in the process of creating international customary law.

Part II of the volume focuses on hierarchical enforcement of international humanitarian law and international criminal law through criminal prosecution. Criminal prosecution takes place on different levels: criminal courts operate at the national level established by the State as well as by armed groups (so-called rebel courts). Criminal prosecution can also occur at the international level, in particular before the International Criminal Court (ICC). Sivakumaran's suggestion that armed groups should at least be allowed to play a role in enforcing international humanitarian law is taken up by Jan Willms, who analyses rebel courts and their potential for law enforcement. If insurgent governance can be established even under the condition of armed conflict in areas of limited statehood, armed groups themselves may play a role in law enforcement. Though international law does not forbid such courts, their potential for enforcement and protection of civilians is impaired by the fear of the nation-State that these courts might legitimize insurgent governance. Based on a case study, Willms concludes that there is a limited potential for enforcement and suggests ways to improve it, thus stressing Sivakumaran's pledge for the need to create armed groups' accountability. Yet, in his comment, Dieter Fleck is more sceptical about the rebel courts' contribution to law enforcement.

The establishment of international criminal courts is one of the major responses through which the international community tried to address the challenge for compliance which stems from war-torn areas of limited statehood. It is telling that so far, all situations under investigation before the ICC deal with African non-international armed conflicts.[14] However, international criminal prosecution is criticized because it is difficult to demonstrate empirical evidence that it fulfils its deterrent and educative purposes in war-torn areas of limited statehood. Does this form of remote

[14] By 2014, situations under investigation before the ICC concern conflicts in the Central African Republic, Cote d' Ivoire, Dafur, Sudan, the Democratic Republic of the Congo, Kenya, Libya, Mali and Uganda.

and slow international prosecution really have any deterrent effect, or is the threat of criminal prosecution too abstract for an individual fighter in the DRC to comply with a set of legal rules he may never have heard of? Robert Cryer addresses this criticism in his contribution to the volume, stressing that the selective approach of international criminal prosecution challenges its legitimacy. On the other hand, according to the ICC Statute, jurisdiction of the ICC is only complementary to national criminal jurisdictions. Criminal prosecution by the State concerned also contributes to ownership and might thus increase compliance. Therefore, efforts are sustained to improve national criminal prosecution. However, the contributions by Jean-Michel Kumbu and Balingene Kahombo provide a candid firsthand insight into the diverse legal and political obstacles a State, such as the DRC, would have to overcome to effectively prosecute war crimes.

Criminal prosecution on the international or national level does not stand alone; it is accompanied by other new (hierarchical) enforcement mechanisms which the international community has developed especially since the late 1990s. Part III deals with the most important initiatives. First, there are at present numerous attempts to enforce international humanitarian law through human rights bodies, especially at the regional level of the European Convention on Human Rights, as well as the American Convention on Human Rights, but also the African Charter on Human and Peoples' Rights. Dominik Steiger argues in favour of such an approach, since human rights bodies may be able to step into the gap which is left by the lack of an individual complaints procedure in international humanitarian law. He tries to rebut the widespread interpretation that, at least for the conduct of hostilities, international humanitarian law should prevail over human rights law[15] because States have agreed to the applicability of human rights law even in times of war. In his comment, Faustin Ntoubandi adds the perspective of the African Union's human rights organs.

Second, there are the activities of the UN Security Council. Focusing on the regime on children and armed conflict, Regina Klostermann analyses the role of the UN Security Council in enforcing the pertinent international norms, in particular through imposing targeted sanctions. On the basis of an interdisciplinary approach, she arrives at the conclusion that

[15] For an overview of the diverging opinions on the relationship between international human rights law and international humanitarian law, see R. Kolb, 'Human Rights and Humanitarian Law', in R. Wolfrum (ed.), *The Max Planck Encyclopedia of Public International Law* (Oxford: Oxford University Press, 2008, online edition, www.mpepil.com), paras. 27 et seq.

the Security Council's special compliance system for children and armed conflict is a promising step towards inducing compliance since it basically fulfils the requirements that political theory has identified as motives for compliance. It is not only the UN Security Council's sanctions system which has undergone major changes. The parameters of UN peacekeeping have also fundamentally changed. Above all, mandates have become more robust. Since 1999, these mandates regularly include an undertaking to protect civilians coupled with expanding authorities to use force.[16] This development has been welcomed as 'the only way to prevent massive violations of IHL [international humanitarian law] in the short term' in many so-called 'new wars'.[17] However, Siobhán Wills takes a more sceptical view of these changes in UN peacekeeping. In her contribution, she stresses that the effectiveness of the mandate to protect civilians is determined by the resources of the mission, its other aims, its relation to the host State and other local stakeholders, as well as the interest of the troop-contributing nations. On the basis of a case study about peacekeeping in the DRC and other African States, she illustrates the dilatory effect of these variables. These findings are aggravated if UN peacekeepers' complicity with the host State's violations of international law is at stake, or if peacekeepers themselves violate international humanitarian law. Therefore, Wills suggests revising the understanding of peacekeepers' obligations under international humanitarian law through, inter alia, an extensive interpretation of Common Article 1 of the Geneva Convention which would require peacekeepers to react to violations of the Conventions by others, provided the peacekeepers are able to do so. In his comment, Matthew Happold criticizes this approach from a legal perspective, while Denis Tull's comment furthers the argument that the effectiveness of UN peacekeepers' civilian protection missions is doubtful. However, on the basis of a case study of the Chapter VII-based United Nations Organization Stabilization Mission in the Democratic Republic of the Congo (MONUSCO), he concludes that MONUSCO's failure might have positive impacts on organizational learning, probably improving the international practice of civilian protection.

[16] Starting with UNSC Resolution 1279 (30 November 1990), such a mandate is, inter alia, included in UNSC Resolution 1291 (24 February 2000); UNSC Resolution 1493 (28 July 2003); UNSC Resolution 1756 (15 May 2007); UNSC Resolution 1856 (22 December 2008); UNSC Resolution 2053 (27 June 2012); UNSC Resolution 2078 (28 November 2012).

[17] Lamp, 'Conceptions of War', above note 7, at 260 with reference to Münkler, *New Wars*, above note 7, at 84.

Not only is the effectiveness of UN peacekeeping hampered by third States' unwillingness to contribute troops, but all efforts to induce compliance from the outside require that the international community is willing to act at all. There is a widespread perception that the lack of a corresponding political will is a major reason for the lack of effective enforcement of international humanitarian law by some of the more powerful third States.[18] However, if there is no sufficient political will to act, the question arises whether the political discretion of third States may be curtailed by legal obligations. To curtail discretion is, after all, one of the aims of the concept of the duty to protect.[19] In Part IV, Robin Geiß, Helmut Aust and Kirsten Schmalenbach inquire as to whether there are other more forcefully binding legal obligations aiming in the same direction. Geiß starts by examining whether Common Article 1 to the four Geneva Conventions includes an external compliance dimension, that is, a duty to ensure respect vis-à-vis other States and/or non-State actors who violate the Conventions. On the basis of an analysis of the relevant State practice, the author submits that the obligation to ensure respect should be understood as a wide obligation which requires States to take positive measures whenever the Geneva Conventions are infringed. However, in the face of the perpetuated conflict in the Democratic Republic of the Congo, third States did not only refrain from taking meaningful measures to ensure compliance with the Geneva Conventions, but also even supported those committing wrongful acts. Aust addresses the question as to whether such States and international organizations could be held responsible under the law of State responsibility for their support. In response to the question, the author discusses the applicable international legal rules on complicity deriving from the law of international responsibility and its possible modifications which may stem from international humanitarian law. Aust's opinion that it can be seen as a new phenomenon to determine the responsibility of those aiding and assisting as much as the main actors' responsibility holds true even more when it comes to a State's support for armed groups. Kirsten Schmalenbach illustrates the responsibility gap that is created by the Draft Articles on the Law of State Responsibility, which start from the hypothesis that a State is only responsible for its own conduct and not for the conduct of non-State actors whose actions are in principle not attributable to the State. This responsibility gap works in

[18] Sassòli, 'The Implementation of International Humanitarian Law', above note 7, at 52.

[19] A. Peters, 'The Security Council's Responsibility to Protect' (2011) 8 *International Organizations Law Review* 15, at 31.

favour of those States which support armed groups who fight against their government, such as in the Great Lakes Region. Although Schmalenbach can ascertain some further developments, she ends on a pessimistic note.

In her concluding contribution, Heike Krieger submits that the international community addresses the challenges for compliance with international humanitarian law which arise from war-torn areas of limited statehood by shifting competences to actors other than the State concerned. In particular, international organizations have developed a mix of instruments in order to enforce international humanitarian law. However, since these organizations are dependent on their member States, who might be reluctant to accept engagement with armed groups, activities of humanitarian non-State actors have become an important element in efforts to induce compliance. Based on the overall results of the book, Heike Krieger investigates reasons for compliance in war-torn areas of limited statehood and arrives at the conclusion that traditional motives are still relevant and must therefore be addressed by the corresponding mechanisms.

PART I

Conditions for compliance by armed groups – focusing on non-hierarchical instruments

2

Understanding strategic motives for violence against civilians during civil conflict

REED M. WOOD

1. Introduction

Civilians have paid a particularly heavy toll in Africa's post-Cold War civil conflicts. Millions of civilians have died as the result of starvation, disease and battle-related violence, often euphemistically called 'collateral damage'. More disturbing still, both insurgents and government agents have intentionally killed tens of thousands of unarmed non-combatants in these conflicts. While accurate numbers of deaths are difficult to compile, available data suggest that since 1991, roughly half of all direct conflict-related deaths are non-combatants who were intentionally targeted by armed actors.[1] Figure 2.1 shows a comparison of 'one-sided' (direct and intentional) killings and battle-related deaths for African conflicts between 1991 and 2008.[2] Such direct, intentional violence is particularly disturbing because it reflects a concerted effort on the part of the perpetrator to victimize vulnerable, unarmed populations. While the most egregious abuses are attributable to African States and their allied militias (e.g., the 1994 Rwandan genocide) African rebels have demonstrated a similar willingness to brutalize civilians. As Figure 2.2 demonstrates, insurgent attacks on civilians often equal or outpace those by the government. Insurgent attacks against civilians are particularly perplexing. Conventional wisdom suggests that insurgents are at least partly reliant on the population for their survival. Civilians, after all, provide insurgents with intelligence, resources and camouflage and act as sources of recruitment. For exactly this reason, classical insurgency theorists such as Mao

1 Data come from the Uppsala Conflict Data Program (Uppsala Conflict Data Program), www.ucdp.uu.se/.

2 The Uppsala Conflict Data Program defines one-sided violence as deaths resulting from intentional and direct action by an armed actor against unarmed persons. These deaths occur outside of battles and therefore exclude civilians killed as a result of indirect actions and direct but unintentional actions such as crossfire and accidental targeting such as in artillery barrages or aerial bombardment where the civilians are not the explicit target.

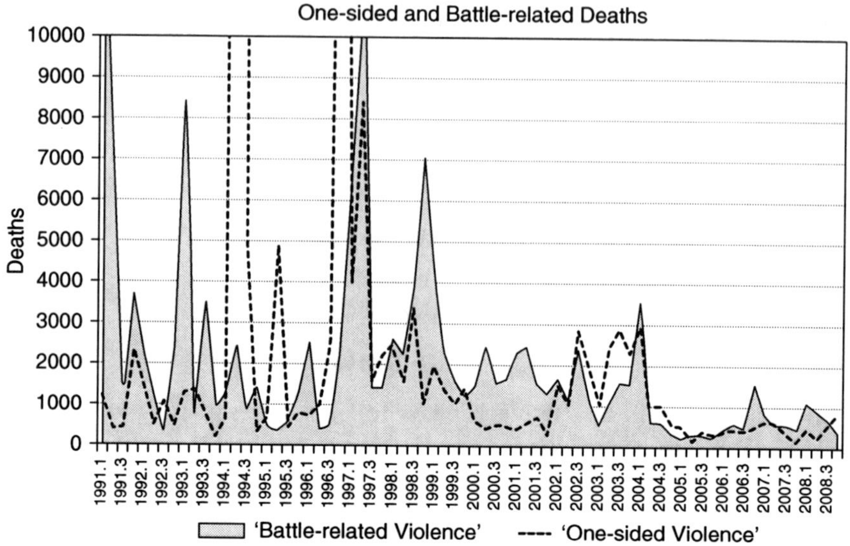

Figure 2.1 Comparison of quarterly deaths resulting from all one-sided violence and all battle related deaths for African conflicts between 1991 and 2008. Values on the vertical axis are constrained to 10000 in order to show variation in lower levels of deaths. Data are taken from the Uppsala Conflict Data Program (see above, note 1).

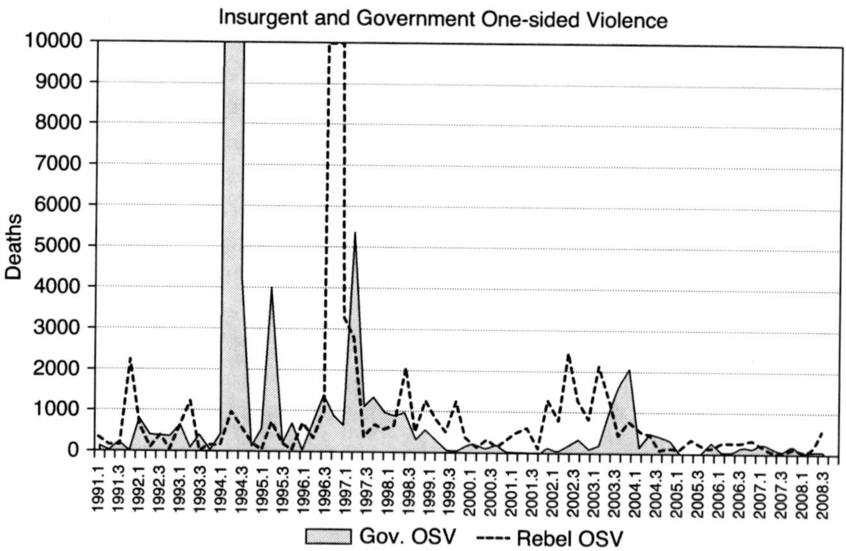

Figure 2.2 Comparison of quarterly deaths resulting from insurgent and government one-sided violence (OSV) for African conflicts between 1991 and 2008. Values on the vertical axis constrained to 10000 in order to show variation in lower levels of deaths. Data are taken from the Uppsala Conflict Data Program (see above, note 1).

Zedong and Ernesto 'Che' Guevara asserted that rebels should respect civilians and avoid violence towards them as it risked undermining the revolution.[3]

Given such admonitions against attacks on peasants, why do many insurgent groups engage in high levels of civilian victimization? The question presents a theoretical puzzle for scholars of political violence and a substantive policy problem for practitioners interested in ameliorating the human cost of civil conflict. This chapter therefore addresses the motives for insurgent violence against the civilian population. Herein, I argue that compared to other explanations, strategic approaches are better able to explain temporal variations in insurgent violence. I argue that violence intentionally directed against civilians is a short-term strategy that helps insurgents to recoup lost human and material resources. Civilian victimization is therefore 'rational' to the extent that it helps insurgents stave off collapse and denies victory to the government. Consequently, victimization is anticipated during moments in which the viability of the groups is threatened or when it faces significant military setbacks.

This chapter proceeds as follows. I first review recent literature on insurgent violence and argue that strategic approaches offer more explanatory power than those based on ideology, ethnic enmity or other non-strategic explanations. I then present the central argument – that violence is often a response to strategic setbacks and threats to group survival. I then examine this relationship empirically. I do so in two ways. First, I provide a brief, illustrative case analysis of the Lord's Resistance Army (LRA). Second, I conduct statistical analyses using a new data set on violence in African civil conflicts in the post-Cold War period. Both lend support to the hypotheses. I close by discussing the implication of the findings and assess the role of international humanitarian law in affecting insurgent behaviours towards civilians.

2. Motives for victimization

Popular accounts of civil wars frequently attribute the brutalization of the civilian population to nonstrategic motivations. According to these perspectives, the savagery that attends many post-Cold War conflicts seems devoid of strategic logic and appears prima facie to serve little rational

[3] E. Guevara, *Guerrilla Warfare* (New York: Vintage Books, 1969); M. Zedong, *On Guerrilla Warfare* (New York: Praeger, 1961).

purpose. In the wake of the mass killings in Rwanda, Somalia and Bosnia, some scholars and many journalists asserted that violence and terror against civilians among rival communal groups resulted from long simmering hatreds, ancient enmities and the desire to enact brutal vengeance for historically distant grievances.[4] In short, a pre-existing potential for mass violence was simply 'unleashed' by larger societal collapse. As order decays, old hatreds emerge and deterministically lead antagonistic ethnic communities to commit mass violence against one another in attempts to redress old grievances.

Other scholars locate the origins of mass killings not in extremist nationalism or ancient hatred but simply in the sadism of rogue actors. According to this line of reasoning, brutality and mass violence is largely blamed on the actions of a small group of 'bad apples'. John Mueller, for example, explained the 'banality of ethnic war' in Rwanda and Bosnia as the result of small groups of thugs and criminals for whom the conflicts represented bountiful opportunities to indulge in violence, looting, rape, free drugs and alcohol, all with the blessing of the authorities.[5] Mary Kaldor similarly attributes the victimization to thugs and profiteers, arguing that increased civilian victimization stems from a change in the nature of conflict in the post-Cold War period. Specifically, in the so-called 'new wars', ideologically driven revolutionary groups have been replaced with poorly organized, ill-trained, decentralized and profit-oriented criminal gangs, paramilitaries and local warlords.[6] Such 'thuggish', criminal rebels are viewed as inherently more brutal than their more ideological Cold War counterparts. Jeremy Weinstein presents a more nuanced and theoretically grounded extension of this argument. His political economy approach to insurgency suggests that organizations with access to large resource endowments are more likely to attract larger numbers of low quality recruits (e.g., thugs). This adverse selection process diminishes insurgent leaders' ability to screen potential recruits and allows 'thugs' to crowd out true believers. Consequently, loot-driven rebellions engage in more brutality towards the population both because lootable resources

[4] S. Huntington, *The Clash of Civilizations and the Remaking of World Order* (New York: Simon and Schuster, 1996); R. Kaplan, *Balkan Ghost: A Journey through History* (New York: St. Martin's Press, 1993); C. Kaufmann, 'Possible and Impossible Solutions to Ethnic Civil Wars' (1996) 4 *International Security* 136.

[5] J. Mueller, 'The Banality of Ethnic Conflict' (2000) 25 *International Security* 42.

[6] M. Kaldor, *New and Old Wars: Organized Violence in a Global Era* (Cambridge: Polity Press, 1999).

supplant reliance on the population and members are less interested in advancing political goals and more interested in short-term profit seeking and other selfish behaviours.[7]

While there is merit to these explanations, they all face significant shortcomings. For instance, theories rooted in the inherent violence of ethnic contests make monumental assumptions about both the rigidness of ethnic identity and individuals' 'inability' to defect during a conflict.[8] Moreover, many of the most-cited studies of the 'savagery' of ethnic wars draw heavily on a handful of select cases, namely the 1994 Rwandan genocide and the 1990s Balkans conflicts. The limited scope of such studies inhibits testing the validity of the hypothesis that ethnic wars are more violent than their non-ethnic counterparts. Cross-national statistical evaluations have found that conflicts organized around ethnicity more rapidly escalate to full-scale wars and that conflicts in States with high ethnic polarization generate higher battlefield costs. However, other recent studies suggest ethnic conflicts may produce fewer deaths overall or suggest little relationship between ethnic conflict and levels of civilian killing.[9]

Arguments that place the locus of control for violence in the hands of sadistic thugs and banal criminals face the limitation that such characters are nearly ubiquitous in wars. As such, these arguments provide no explanation for the variation in violence across conflicts because they fail to explain variation in the presence of sadists. Kaldor's 'New Wars' argument faces similar limitations. Principally, Kaldor neither provides any clear evidence that post-Cold War conflicts cause greater civilian casualties than earlier conflicts nor adequately explains variations in violence across contemporary conflicts. Weinstein's argument is the most theoretically sophisticated, and he provides comparative evidence that rebel groups with foreign sponsorship or access to lootable resources inflict more violence on the population. However, as with both identity-based

[7] J. Weinstein, *Inside Rebellion: The Politics of Insurgent Violence* (Cambridge: Cambridge University Press, 2007).

[8] S. Kalyvas, 'Ethnic Defection in Civil War' (2008) 41 *Comparative Political Studies* 1043.

[9] K. Eck, 'From Armed Conflict to War: Ethnic Mobilization and Conflict Intensification' (2009) 53 *International Studies Quarterly* 369; P. Lujala, 'Deadly Combat over Natural Resources: Gems, Petroleum, Drugs, and the Severity of Armed Civil Conflict' (2009) 53 *Journal of Conflict* 50; B. Lacina, 'Explaining the Severity of Civil Wars' (2006) 50 *Journal of Conflict Resolution* 276; R. Wood, 'Rebel Capability and Strategic Violence against Civilians' (2010) 47 *Journal of Peace Research* 601.

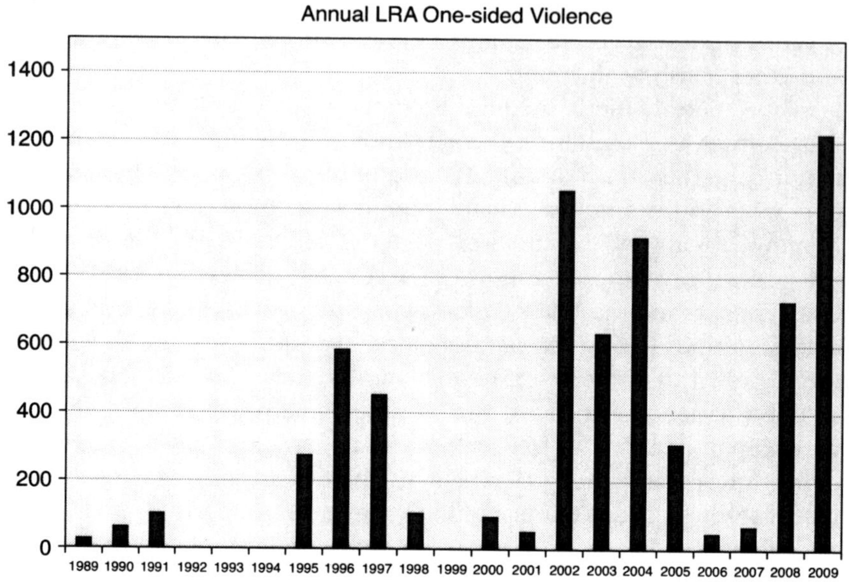

Figure 2.3 Annual LRA one-sided violence for years 1989 through 2009. Data are taken from Uppsala Conflict Data Program online database (see above, note 1).

explanations and other resource-based arguments, the theory assumes that violence is largely a predetermined outgrowth of specific conditions. As such, many non-strategic theories deny agency to the actor, overlook the dynamics of the conflict that are likely to influence violence and fail to provide a clear set of motives for inflicting violence on civilians.

However, the most significant limitation of much of the non-strategic theory is the inability to explicitly account for variations in violence over time. Group behaviour is seldom static. Even the most violent of insurgent groups rely heavily on violence at some moments yet act with comparative restraint at other. The case of the LRA illustrates the manner in which insurgent violence towards civilians varies over time. The notable variation in LRA violence depicted in Figure 2.3 provokes a key question, which is not so much why the LRA – or any guerrilla group – chooses violence, but rather, why do they resort to violence against the population at certain times, while at other times de-emphasize violence as a war strategy? Structural and organizational theories are unable to answer these questions because they focus on largely static components of an often dynamic conflict environment.

3. Strategy variation

Strategic theories address some of the shortcomings of structural or organizational theories. Rather than viewing violence as a by-product of specific historical or structural conditions, strategic choice explanations focus on the incentives and relevant constraints that lead armed actors to adopt one set of strategies rather than another. Violence against civilians is therefore instrumental to the armed group's strategy. In this sense, these armed actors follow Hannah Arendt's assertion that actors choose violence when they believe it will advance their goals.[10] Specifically, previous research has argued that belligerents employ violence to eliminate enemies, facilitate control over territory or populations or generate resources for the group.[11] Strategic theories also acknowledge that civil wars take place in constantly evolving environments and that conflict actors respond to changes in their environments by updating war strategies. Insurgents shed strategies deemed ineffective or inefficient given the context and adopt new strategies which they perceive as more likely to abet their goals. Principally, changes in resource availability, military capabilities and civilian support shape the incentives for violence.

3.1. Capabilities and war strategy

The strategies available to belligerents are in part a function of their capabilities. The type of warfare adopted and the strategies of violence employed are closely related to the war technologies available to belligerents and to the capability balance between them.[12] Yet, strategies are not

[10] H. Arendt, *On Violence* (New York: Harcourt, Brace & World, 1970).

[11] L. Balcells, 'Rivalry and Revenge: Violence against Civilians in Conventional Civil Wars' (2010) 54 *International Studies Quarterly* 291; D. Hoffman, 'The Civilian Target in Sierra Leone and Liberia: Political Power, Military Strategy, and Humanitarian Intervention' (2004) 103 *African Affairs* 211; L. Hultman, 'Keeping the Peace or Spurring Violence? Unintended Effects of Peace Operations on Violence against Civilians' (2010) 12 *Civil Wars* 29, at 32–34; L. Hultman, 'The Power to Hurt in Civil War: The Strategic Aim of RENAMO Violence' (2009) 35 *Journal of Southern African Studies* 821; A. Vinci, 'The Strategic Use of Fear by the Lord's Resistance Army' (2005) 16 *Small Wars and Insurgencies* 360; Wood, 'Rebel Capability', above note 9.

[12] Balcells, 'Rivalry and Revenge', above note 11, at 295–96; S. Kalyvas, *The Logic of Violence in Civil War* (Cambridge: Cambridge University Press, 2006); S. Kalyvas and L. Balcells, 'International System and Technologies of Rebellion: How the End of the Cold War Shaped Internal Conflict' (2010) 104 *American Political Science Review* 415; A. Lockyer, 'Foreign Intervention and Warfare in Civil Wars: The Effects of Exogenous Resources on the Course and Nature of the Angolan and Afghan Conflicts' (PhD thesis, University of Sydney, 2008); A. Lockyer, 'The Dynamics of Warfare in Civil War' (2010) 12 *Civil Wars* 91.

fixed but vary over the course of the conflict in response to changes in actors' capabilities.[13] For instance, small groups of armed insurgents that lack the recruits or military technologies necessary to fight the regime directly often adopt non-conventional tactics or terrorism; but as the group strengthens, they may adopt traditional guerrilla tactics and later still may employ more conventional tactics.[14]

Recent studies have begun to focus on the relationship between insurgent violence and changes in insurgent military capabilities. For example, Wood argues that violence is tied to both insurgent capabilities as well as the strategies adopted by the State.[15] Specifically, stronger insurgents who face particularly brutal regimes choose lower levels of violence against civilians. Kalyvas argues that selective violence is more likely to occur in areas where an actor has superior but incomplete control, while indiscriminate violence is most likely to occur in areas where the perpetrator has little to no control.[16] Although this theory primarily focuses on the spatial distribution of violence, the causal logic extends quite readily to explaining temporal variations in violence when aggregated to the macro level. Kalyvas's argument, however, dismisses the more macro-level changes that often influence general trends in insurgent violence. Violence is certainly localized, but aggregate shifts in the balance of power necessitate the reallocation of resources and the evolution of tactics to cope with the new strategic environment. For example, faltering control in specific locations often results from troop losses or other military setbacks at the macro level. This might occur as the direct result of battle loss and subsequent retreat, or it might result from the redistribution of troops from areas of firm control to weakening control. In either case, resource depletion serves as the underlying condition that drives changes in violence.

Adopting a more aggregate approach, Hultman argues that violence represents a strategic response to troop loss because it serves as a costly signal of resolve to the target regime.[17] The underlying logic posits that

[13] Lockyer, 'Foreign Intervention', above note 12.

[14] D. Byman, 'Understanding Proto-Insurgencies' (2008) 31 *Strategic Studies* 165; C. Butler and S. Gates, 'Asymmetry, Parity, and (Civil) War: Can International Relations Theories Help Us Understand Civil War?' (2010) 35 *International Interactions* 330. This variation of methods observed by the above authors is similar to the model proposed explicitly by classic leftist guerrilla strategists. See Guevara, *Guerrilla Warfare*, above note 3; Zedong, *On Guerrilla Warfare*, above note 3.

[15] Wood, 'Rebel Capability', above note 9.

[16] Kalyvas, *The Logic of Violence*, above note 12.

[17] L. Hultman, 'Battle Losses and Rebel Violence: Raising the Cost of Fighting' (2007) 19 *Terrorism and Political Violence* 205.

violence is intended primarily to impose costs on the government. By targeting civilians, insurgents demonstrate that the government cannot protect its population, which raises the political costs on the regime. In addition, the destabilization caused by civilian victimization increases the military costs to the regime. In both cases, violence is expected to pressure the government into negotiations and create a more favourable bargaining situation for the insurgents. The theory accurately addresses changes in violence in response to shifts in the strategic environment; however, it overlooks important relationships between civilians and insurgents. Therein, civilians serve only as means by which rebels convey resolve to the government. Furthermore, this theory neglects the role that violence plays in the acquisition of territory and control over the population. As I argue below, rather than augmenting the rebels' bargaining position, victimizing civilians represents an attempt by insurgents to reverse strategic setbacks and recoup lost resources. Thus, while I agree with Hultman's proposed relationship, I suggest a different causal mechanism to explain the incentive for targeting civilians.

3.2. *Civilian support, capabilities and control*

Controlling civilian behaviour is a central objective for insurgents (as well as States) in civil conflicts. While not all insurgents actively seek the support of the population, virtually all rebels desire to influence the actions of civilians. Insurgents need civilians to provide resources and camouflage, and at the very least, they attempt to deter civilian collaboration with adversaries.[18] Violence is, of course, just one strategy insurgents use to achieve these objectives. Yet when armed groups lack public support or alternative means through which to shape civilian behaviours, violence becomes an increasingly attractive option. This observation suggests that the violence illustrated in the LRA case is perhaps not as surprising. Lacking resources, support and territorial control, the LRA resorted to mass killing and abduction to feed its resource needs and terrorize the population into submission, allowing the group to acquire resources and to prevent defeat.[19]

18 Kalyvas, *The Logic of Violence*, above note 12.

19 J. Bevan, 'The Myth of Madness: Cold Rationality and Resource Plunder by the Lord's Resistance Army' (2007) 9 *Civil Wars* 343; A. Branch, 'Neither Peace nor Justice: Political Violence and the Peasantry in Northern Uganda, 1986–1998' (2005) 8 *African Studies Quarterly* 1; Vinci, 'The Strategic Use of Fear', above note 11.

Traditional insurgency theory posits that civilians are critical for the success of rebellion.[20] Even those who have access to other resources must rely on local populations for intelligence and benefit from the acquisition of local resources and fresh recruits from the population. Furthermore, the existence of a sympathetic population lowers the incentive for violence against it. High levels of latent support from the population ease recruitment and reduce the amount of coercion necessary to shape civilian behaviours. However, when civilians withhold support from rebels, incentives for violence increase. Mkandawire, for example, argues that the lack of congruence between the demands and aspirations of urban-based guerrilla groups and the interests of rural peasants partly explains the amount of violence African rebels inflict on civilians. Because these groups have little in common with the rural population and little to offer them, they find among them little support. Consequently, African rebels have frequently resorted to violence, intimidation and looting to acquire resources and to control the rural population.[21] Levels of civilian support and insurgent reliance on civilians vary over the course of a conflict. Changes in the strategic environment pressure belligerents to change their relationship with the population. At some points, insurgents may find it useful to incorporate civilians into their movement, to protect them from government violence or to implement policies that benefit civilians (e.g., land tenure, social welfare, etc.). At other times, however, they may ignore civilians, coerce them into assisting the insurgents (e.g., as porters or labourers), force them to flee or actively target them for violence. For instance, in Uganda, Museveni's National Resistance Army (NRA) altered its relations with civilians repeatedly during its five-year conflict with the Obote regime. At times, it incorporated civilians into governing structures; at other times, it expelled them from the conflict area.[22] In a similar vein, the Sudanese People's Liberation Army's (SPLA) relationship with the local population shifted notably over the course of the conflict. During periods in which the group faced high levels of competition from the Khartoum regime or other militant factions, its interest

[20] T. Wickham-Crowley, *Guerrillas and Revolution in Latin America: A Comparative Study of Insurgents and Regimes since 1956* (Princeton: Princeton University Press, 2002); Zedong, *On Guerrilla Warfare*, above note 3; Guevara, *Guerrilla Warfare*, above note 3.

[21] T. Mkandawire, 'The Terrible Toll of Post-Colonial Rebel Movements in Africa: Towards an Explanation of the Violence against the Peasantry' (2002) 40 *Journal of Modern African Studies* 181.

[22] N. Kasfir, 'Guerrillas and Civilian Participation: The National Resistance Army in Uganda, 1981–86' (2005) 43 *Journal of Modern African Affairs* 271.

in providing (and its ability to provide) services to civilians and incorporate them into governance structures declined. However, during periods in which it maintained a virtual monopoly on control in southern Sudan – particularly post-2001 – it worked on establishing itself as the legitimate ruler of the southern population and made serious efforts to provide services and governance structures to the population under its control.[23]

Claire Metelits argues that competition over resources drives insurgent violence.[24] Specifically, as competition increases, violence is likely to increase. Changes in civilian–insurgent relations are closely related to more general changes in a group's military capacity and the trajectory of the conflict. Competition may influence insurgent behaviour, but the underlying mechanism driving violence is the inability of insurgents to co-opt, control or contract with the local population. In addition, demand for resources influences the importance of achieving this goal. Insurgent resource demands as well as civilian's willingness to supply this support vary over the conflict. When demand is high yet support is weak, the incentive to employ coercive violence increases. As military capabilities decline, resources are burned and troops defect or are killed, the demand to rapidly replenish them increases. Significant losses place insurgents in a dire position in which the immediate acquisition of resources becomes critical to the continued survival of the group. Insurgents are therefore more likely to increase the level of coercion against the population in an attempt to quickly recoup lost resources.

The level of coercion necessary to accrue these resources is partly a function of extant support for the insurgents among the population. However, collaboration is endogenous to the conflict environment. Civilians are likely to support whichever side is in control, regardless of their true preferences.[25] Additionally, civilians' preferences are partially based on calculations about the expected victor in a conflict or which side can credibly provide a superior set of incentives (security, material goods, etc.).[26] When insurgents suffer major military defeats or appear to be losing the war, civilians are less likely to voluntarily offer their support.

[23] C. Metelits, *Inside Insurgency: Violence, Civilians, and Revolutionary Group Behavior* (New York: New York University Press, 2010); Z. Mampilly, *Rebel Rulers: Insurgent Governance and Civilian Life during War* (Ithaca, New York: Cornell University Press, 2011).

[24] Metelits, *Inside Insurgency*, above note 23.

[25] Kalyvas, *The Logic of Violence*, above note 12.

[26] E. Wood, *Insurgent Collective Action and Civil War in El Salvador* (Cambridge: Cambridge University Press, 2003); T. D. Mason, 'Insurgency, Counterinsurgency, and the Rational Peasant' (1996) 86 *Public Choice* 63.

Similarly, major setbacks such as significant troop loss, the destruction of bases or the collapse of control signal to civilians that insurgents are likely incapable of providing sufficient benefits to offset the cost of collaboration. In either case, civilian support wanes when insurgent capabilities are in rapid decline. Civilian collaboration and support are therefore decreasing at exactly the moment when demand for it by insurgents is at its greatest. When support is not forthcoming and civilians appear likely to defect to the regime, incentives for coercive violence increase.

The above discussion suggests that as insurgents weaken they are increasingly likely to brutalize the population as a short-term strategy of resource acquisition and a means to maintain control over civilians. The specific mechanisms driving this effect are the overall depletion of the group's resources (primarily troops), which raises the demand to acquire replacement resources, and the declining willingness of the population to provide support. First, as conflict becomes more costly and survival becomes more uncertain, insurgents are increasingly likely to target civilians. This occurs because of the combination of acute resource demands and the concomitant decline in civilian willingness to support a weakening group. Second, as discussed above, poor battlefield performance relative to the regime reduces civilian support, which in turn augments the incentive for violence. This produces the central hypothesis of this chapter:

H1: Insurgents are more likely to escalate violence against civilians when they face major military setbacks.

4. Examining violence dynamics

I rely on two methods to assess the hypothesis that adverse strategic shifts contribute to increased rebel violence. I first coarsely trace the military history of the LRA, paying particular attention to changes in the conflict environment that negatively impacted the group's military capabilities and the manner in which these events in turn relate to changes in violence against civilians. In order to assess the generalizability of the argument – that is, how well it accounts for violence across an array of cases – I use a simple statistical test. Both approaches provide support for the general argument.

4.1. A case illustration: LRA violence

Figure 2.4 illustrates graphically the yearly estimate of civilian deaths attributed to the LRA as well as the estimated proportion of insurgents

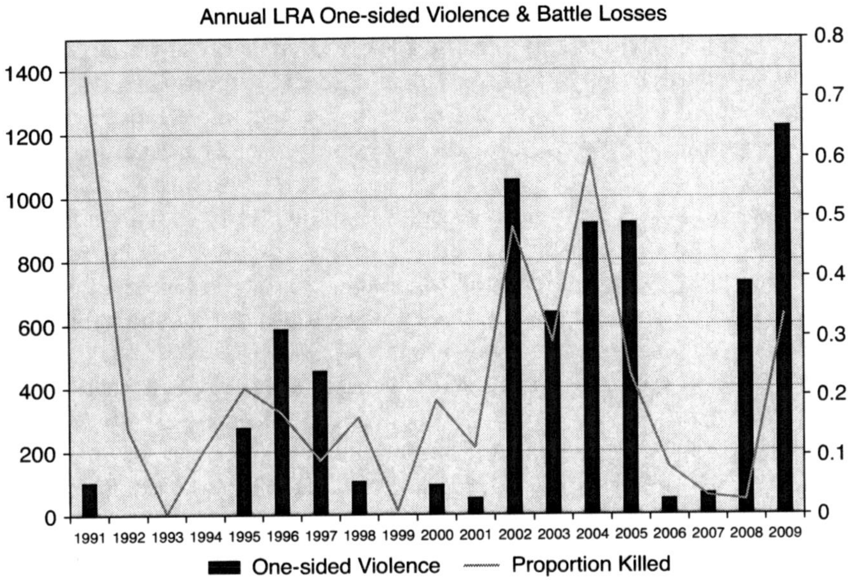

Figure 2.4 Comparison of annual LRA one-sided violence and proportion of troops killed for years 1991 through 2009. Data are taken from Uppsala Conflict Data Program online database (see above, note 1). Battle deaths are not available for the years 1989 and 1990.

killed in battle during the year. While the values are not a perfect match, the figure suggests that the troop loss sustained by the insurgents co-varies with their use of violence against civilians. During periods in which the insurgents sustained significant troop losses, they appeared to victimize civilians to a greater extent. A cursory narrative of the case provides additional support for the relationship between strategic setbacks and the group's willingness to target civilians.

Media reports often refer to LRA leader Joseph Kony as a 'madman' or imply that the group has no discernible political goals. While the LRA's political message may not necessarily reflect a high degree of political fluency, it would be largely incorrect to state that the LRA lacks any political motivations or coherent demands.[27] However, inferring madness

[27] K. Dunn, 'Killing for Christ? The Lord's Resistance Army of Uganda' (2004) 103 *Current History* 206; M. Schomerus, 'The Lord's Resistance Army in Sudan: A History and Overview' (Working Paper No. 8, Bachelor of Science in Business Administration, Graduate Institute of International Studies, 2007).

or lack of political goals from violence is problematic and overlooks the changing relationships between the LRA and civilians and other actors within the conflict. The longevity of the group, numerous shifts in the conflict environment over the period of the conflict and the high level of variance in the use of violence make the group a useful case for exploring the validity of the argument above. Moreover, the high levels of violence and common accusation of 'madness' make the group a challenging but important case for examining rational choice hypotheses generally. If strategic choice explanations help to explain the behaviours of highly violent, 'erratic' groups like the LRA, they should be transportable to a variety of other cases.

The LRA emerged around 1988 following the defeat of Alice Lakwena's Holy Spirit Movement and the conclusion of a peace deal between the Ugandan People's Democratic Army (UPDA) and the Ugandan government. While most of the Ugandan People's Democratic Army's forces complied with the terms of the peace agreement, a number of soldiers refused to surrender, choosing instead to continue guerrilla combat against the government. Many of these troops, including Odong Latek, joined forces with a small guerrilla force commanded by a relative of Alice Lakwena's named Joseph Kony. This force was known briefly as the Ugandan People's Democratic Force, but following Latek's death in 1990, Kony assumed command of the forces and renamed the movement the Lord's Resistance Army. By 1990, the LRA had become the only notable force fighting in the Acholi-dominated areas of Northern Uganda.

Initially, the group was able to garner at least nominal support from the local Acholi population by positioning itself as a counterforce to the Museveni-led government.[28] During this early period, the group committed relatively few abuses against civilians – especially considering the magnitude of violence observed in later periods. However, by the early 1990s popular support rapidly declined as the group proved unable to effectively challenge the government, war fatigue set in among the population, and LRA coercion led to civilian resentment.[29] In addition to a general decline in civilian support, the early 1990s witnessed significant military setbacks for the LRA. In 1991, the government launched a major counterinsurgency offensive against the group known as Operation North. Government attacks caused the deaths of hundreds of LRA soldiers and the formation of community defence organizations – which the rebels viewed as an extension of the Ugandan government and a betrayal

[28] Bevan, 'The Myth of Madness', above note 19, at 348. [29] Ibid. 348.

by the population – frustrated access to local communities.[30] According to Branch, this was the first time that the Acholi population had sufficient contact with the regime to engender any support for it.[31] Furthermore, the level of popular support for the LRA began to rapidly decline around this same time, eroding the group's resource base.[32] This decline in support therefore came during exactly the moment in which the group was most in needed of recouping resources. In response to its weakened military position and declining civilian support, the LRA shifted its war strategy, turning from guerrilla tactics to mass violence against the population.[33]

Following near defeat in Operation North, the LRA retreated into the forests of Northern Uganda and across the border into Sudan. During this period, both military engagements with the Ugandan government and violence against civilians entered a temporary period of decline. Two events partly explain this change. First, around this time, the LRA attained sponsorship from the government of Sudan.[34] The advent of foreign sponsorship and its expansion throughout the early 1990s increased the insurgent's military capacity, providing them with arms and access to sanctuary beyond the Ugandan government's reach. By 1994, the group had nearly fully relocated its base of operations to southern Sudan and aligned itself with other government-backed militias operating in the area. This situation placed the group largely beyond the reach of the government and provided time and resources with which to rebuild the movement. While Sudan's sponsorship may have reduced the group's reliance on the local population for resources, it did not seem to lead to a significant uptick in violence against civilians. In contrast to the behaviour predicted by organizational theories, during this period, the LRA focused most of its attention on battles with the SPLA and engaged in limited one-sided violence against civilians. A second factor that may explain the lull in violence is a notable shift in government counterinsurgency strategy. During this period, the government increasingly

30 T. Allen and K. Vlassenroot (eds.), *The Lord's Resistance Army: Myth and Reality* (London: Zed Books, 2010), at 11; R. Doom and K. Vlassenroot, 'Kony's Message: A New Koine? The Lord's Resistance Army in Northern Uganda' (1999) 98 *African Affairs* 5, at 23.

31 Branch, 'Neither Peace nor Justice', above note 19, at 16. 32 Ibid. 439.

33 Ibid.; R. Gersony, 'The Anguish of Northern Uganda: Results of a Field-Based Assessment of the Civil Conflicts in Northern Uganda' (Kampala: Report submitted to the United States Embassy, 1997); Doom and Vlassenroot, 'Kony's Message', above note 30, at 23–24; Uppsala Conflict Data Program, Conflict Encyclopedia, 'Uganda', www.ucdp.uu.se/gpdatabase/gpcountry.php?id=160&regionSelect=2-Southern_Africa#.

34 F. van Acker, 'Uganda and the Lord's Resistance Army: The New Order No One Ordered' (2004) 103 *African Affairs* 335, at 337.

supplemented military approaches with political solutions to resolve the conflict.[35] This strategy culminated in the government's effort to start formal peace talks with the insurgents in late 1993 and early 1994.

Peace talks collapsed in February 1994 following Kony's foot-dragging suspicion that Sudan might intervene on the LRA's behalf, and Museveni's ultimatum that the rebels lay down their weapons within one week or face renewed government attacks.[36] Following the collapse of peace talks and Museveni's deployment of reinforcements to the region, the LRA resumed attacks against the local population as the war escalated.[37] This second phase of the war witnessed another brutal evolution in LRA war strategy. Beginning in early 1995, the group faced a renewed counterinsurgency effort from the government; moreover, Kony believed that the Acholi community had failed to support him in the negotiations.[38] It was during this period that, in an effort to recoup losses sustained in fighting and to boost its human resources, the LRA began to engage the mass abductions for which it has become notorious.[39]

Between 1995 and 1996, the conflict quickly escalated as the LRA fought a war on two fronts – against the SPLA in Sudan and the Ugandan government in north Uganda. The relationship between the regime in Khartoum and the LRA reached its height in 1996 and began to wane thereafter.[40] In late 1995 and through early 1996, the SPLA engaged in a series of assaults on LRA positions in Sudan.[41] Early in 1997, the Ugandan government began to escalate its military efforts against the insurgents.[42] It also established a new series of 'protected camps', which were intended to separate the population from the insurgents. However, rather than defending the camps with regular military troops, the government again returned to training and arming local militias, training some 12,000 militia men in the region.[43] This proved disastrous for the population. It served to frustrate the LRA's ability to gather resources and reified Kony's perception of Acholi betrayal, but also left the population vulnerable to LRA attacks.

[35] Doom and Vlassenroot, 'Kony's Message', above note 30, at 23–24.

[36] Ibid. 24. [37] Branch, 'Neither Peace nor Justice', above note 19, at 18.

[38] Doom and Vlassenroot, 'Kony's Message', above note 30, at 25; E. Leonard, 'The Lord's Resistance Army: An African Terrorist Group?' (2010) 4 *Perspectives on Terrorism* 20, at 36.

[39] Leonard, 'The Lord's Resistance Army', above note 38, at 25.

[40] Schomerus, 'The Lord's Resistance Army', above note 27, at 25.

[41] Branch, 'Neither Peace nor Justice', above note 19, at 19.

[42] Uppsala Conflict Data Program, 'Uganda', above note 33.

[43] Branch, 'Neither Peace nor Justice', above note 19, at 19.

Later that year, the SPLA overran key LRA strongholds along the border with Uganda, forcing Kony and other LRA leaders to flee to Juba.[44] Ironically, the increased success of the counterinsurgency campaign during the period came at severe costs to unprotected civilians. As demonstrated by Figure 2.4, the series of adverse changes in the strategic environment correlates with a dramatic upswing in the annual number of intentional killings committed by the LRA.

By early 1999, the insurgents were forced back across the Sudanese border. Following a few engagements early in the year, the conflict remained relatively calm. The conflict emerged from nine months of relative peace largely as a result of transnational events and shifting support for the rebels. Increased pressure from the United States led to peace talks between Sudan and Uganda in late 1999. The Nairobi Agreement of 1999 formally committed both sides to cease support for cross-border insurgent organizations.[45] In addition, in early 2000, the Ugandan government adopted the Amnesty Act, which offered a blanket amnesty to all rebels willing to hand over their weapons and reintegrate into civilian life. Most of the LRA's top leadership rejected the offer; however, many mid-level officers and rank-and-file soldiers began to accept the amnesty offer and defected from the group, albeit slowly at first.[46] While conflict violence did not resurge to the levels observed in 1996–1998, both battle deaths and civilian killings increased relative to 1999.

The conflict entered a third distinctly violent phase beginning in 2002. In March of that year, the Museveni regime reached an agreement with Khartoum that allowed the armed forces of Uganda to pursue LRA insurgents across the border into Sudan, effectively eliminating the ability the group had previously enjoyed to fall back to jungle bases out of Uganda's reach and recoup lost resources. Operation 'Iron Fist', which involved more than 5,000 Ugandan troops, forces from the SPLA and logistical and material support from the United States, followed in April. The operation resulted in the destruction of multiple LRA bases and the deaths of hundreds of LRA troops (as well as thousands of abducted children and local civilians killed by Ugandan forces). Operation Iron Fist left the LRA

44 Branch, 'Neither Peace nor Justice', above note 19, at 21; Uppsala Conflict Data Program, 'Uganda', above note 33.

45 Schomerus, 'The Lord's Resistance Army', above note 27, at 26.

46 Conciliation Resources/Quaker Peace & Social Justice, 'Coming Home: Understanding Why Commanders of the Lord's Resistance Army Choose to Return to Civilian Life' (London, May 2006), at 8, www.c-r.org/sites/c-r.org/files/ComingHome_200605_ENG.pdf.

battered but was unable to completely dislodge them from southern Sudan and Northern Uganda. Indeed, the fragmented group managed to outflank the SPLA and Ugandan army force and expand into new territories.[47] During the months that followed, the group committed some of the worst atrocities of the conflict. According to reports from mid-year, the group killed hundreds of Sudanese civilians as it was pushed north by Ugandan forces.[48] This is consistent with the values reported in Figure 2.3, which show that insurgent violence against civilians increased dramatically in 2002 and remained high through 2005.

Three principal factors explain the persistence of violence against civilians during this period. First, support from the Khartoum continued to decline throughout the period as relations between the Sudanese and Ugandan regimes improved. Notably, in 2004, the governments expanded the deal initiated by the Nairobi Agreement, allowing Ugandan forces to penetrate farther into Sudanese territory. This exerted additional military pressure on the LRA, who, by that point, had few safe havens from which they could evade attacks and replenish resources. Second, the changing international climate that allowed the Ugandan armed forces to purse the LRA deep into Sudan permitted high levels of engagement between the insurgents and Ugandan government forces. Consequently, the group sustained significant troop losses throughout the period. Third, at least according to some sources, the amnesty programme introduced by the government in 2000 began to take a noticeable toll on LRA capacity. While defections from the group were slow at first, the pace quickened in subsequent years. According to one report, the number of LRA members taking advantage of the programme increased to nearly 1,100 in 2002 and to more than 3,600 at its peak in 2004.[49] Both factors further constrained the resources and fighting capacity of the group, making their ability to continue their war effort more difficult. As such, the group relied increasingly on large-scale abductions, the use of child soldiers and terror against the population as a whole to accrue the resources necessary for its survival. By the end of this period, the LRA's ranks had shrunk to just a few hundred soldiers, and it had been forced to break into smaller, more mobile units in order to evade opposing forces.[50]

[47] Allen and Vlassenroot, *The Lord's Resistance Army*, above note 30, at 14; K. Somerville, 'Uganda's Rebels Keep the Faith', *BBC News*, 3 July 2002, news.bbc.co.uk/2/hi/africa/2083241.stm.

[48] Somerville, 'Uganda's Rebels', above note 47.

[49] Conciliation Resources, 'Coming Home', above note 46, at 8.

[50] Uppsala Conflict Data Program, 'Uganda', above note 33.

Mid-2006 through mid-2008 saw another notable decline in violence as the government of Uganda and the LRA again entered into peace negotiations. The Juba peace process began in mid-2006 and was intended to serve as a comprehensive solution to the conflict. Negotiations continued at a staggered pace over the subsequent two years as the government and insurgents negotiated long-term solutions to economic and political issues as well as the return of internally displaced persons, redevelopment and reintegration plans as well as accountability and justice issues, including war crimes courts and the issue of indictments against LRA leadership recently issued by the International Criminal Court. The rebels and government signed an agreement on reconciliation and accountability in June 2007, and talks were scheduled to resume in August following consultations with civil society groups. Talks resumed in November but again stalled due to intra-LRA disputes. Kony sacked the leader and several members of the peace delegation after accusing them of profiting from the talks. More troubling, Kony apparently executed the LRA's second in command, Vincent Otti (as well as his wife and children), following disagreements over the direction of the peace talks.[51] Talks resumed yet again in January and entered into what should have been the final stage. All parties agreed to sign the Final Peace Agreement in April, but Kony failed to materialize. Despite Kony's continued insistence of his commitment to a peace agreement, he failed to appear at several prearranged meetings with negotiators. In September, mediators disbanded the monitoring team overseeing the talks and declared the talks dead. A final meeting was arranged between Kony and Ugandan officials in November, but Kony again failed to show. Analysts and observers largely speculated that the period of peace talks simply served as a ruse by which Kony could rebuild his forces and rearm for war.[52]

The events that followed closely mirrored those of 2002. In December 2008, the combined forces of Uganda and the Democratic Republic of the Congo (DRC), with logistical support from the US military, launched operation 'Lightning Thunder' against the LRA. According to media reports, the attacks destroyed Kony's camp, destroyed most of the group's supplies and caused heavy casualties.[53] As in previous episodes of

[51] 'Ugandan Rebel Deputy Feared Dead', *BBC News*, 7 November 2007, news.bbc.co.uk/2/hi/africa/7082437.stm.

[52] Uppsala Conflict Data Program, 'Uganda', above note 33.

[53] 'Armies "Strike at Uganda Rebels"', *BBC News*, 14 December 2008, news.bbc.co.uk/2/hi/africa/7782649.stm; 'Uganda "Strikes LRA Rebel Camps"', *BBC News*, 21 December 2008,

military pressure, the remnants of the guerrillas broke into small, highly mobile units that undertook a campaign of mass violence and abductions against peasant villages along the Uganda-DRC border. During these 'Christmas Massacres', the LRA killed as many as a 1,000 people and abducted hundreds or thousands of persons (primarily children) in an attempt to destabilize the region and stave off defeat by opposing forces.

The brief case history presented here, as well as the graph comparing yearly battle-related troop deaths and international civilians, suggests an observable patterning in the use of civilian victimization by the LRA: during periods in which the group was strained militarily, faced declining resources or endured military setbacks, it escalated its levels of violence against the population. This brief account of the LRA's military history illustrates the potential relationship between declining military capabilities and insurgent violence against civilians. However, it is difficult to generalize from a single case; moreover, the examination above did not attempt to control for other factors that may have influenced the group's decision-making. In order to further plumb this relationship, I conducted a statistical analysis using data on both civilian victimization and the magnitude of a group's military losses. The results allow me to better generalize about the relationships observed in the LRA case.

4.2. *Statistical analysis*

The statistical analysis is conducted using a sample of African conflicts adapted from the Uppsala Conflict Data Program's Geocoded Events Dataset, which includes Eck and Hultman's one-sided violence data temporally disaggregated by month.[54] This data set captures monthly violence data for the thirty-three African conflicts in twenty-four countries for the years 1991–2008.[55] The sample yields nearly 2,000 conflict months. The

news.bbc.co.uk/2/hi/africa/7794399.stm; 'LRA Rebels Fleeing Towards Central African Republic', *Agence France-Presse*, 2 January 2009.

[54] R. Sundberg, M. Lindgren and A. Padskocimaite, *Uppsala Conflict Data Program Georeferenced Event Dataset (GED) Codebook, Version 1.0* (Uppsala: Uppsala University, 2004); K. Eck and L. Hultman, 'One-Sided Violence against Civilians in War' (2007) 44 *Journal of Peace Research* 233; L. Hultman, J. Kathman and M. Shannon, 'United Nations Intervention and Violence against Civilians in Civil War' (unpublished manuscript, Swedish National Defence University and University of Mississippi, 2011).

[55] In some cases, conflicts involve multiple insurgent organizations. Ideally, all data would match a single rebel organization with a government rather than aggregating the violence related to multiple groups into a single measure.

data set includes monthly estimates of the number of battle deaths sustained by both the insurgents and State security forces as well as the number of one-sided deaths for which each group was responsible. The former reflects troops killed in active combat operations, while the latter captures non-combatants killed intentionally by combatants outside of the battlefield context, such as the massacre of civilians, the summary execution of non-combatants and terror attacks specifically targeting non-combatants. Although the measure does not fully capture all abuses of the civilian population, it serves as a reasonable proxy of the strategic use of violence against the civilian population by armed political actors.

One-sided rebel violence serves as the dependent variable in the regression analysis. The hypothesis presented above focuses on strategic setbacks as a cause of civilian victimization. Specifically, it posits that as insurgents lose ground to government forces – as they weaken militarily – they are more likely to escalate violence against civilians. In order to account for short-term changes in the trajectory of the conflict, I construct two variables measuring the extent of short-term strategic setbacks for insurgents. The first measure reflects the monthly balance of troop loss between the insurgents and the regime. It is constructed by dividing the number of battle deaths accruing to the insurgents by the number sustained by government forces in a given month. In this construction, values of the variable greater than 1 suggest greater losses by the insurgents relative to the government while values less than 1 reflect better performance relative to the government. A value near 1 would reflect an even distribution of battlefield losses. I use natural log of the ratio in the analysis in order to make the distribution more uniform and to dampen the influence of the extremes of the range. The value is then lagged by one period in order to capture the expected sequence of violence: civilian killing follows poor relative battlefield performance. The second measure reflects the estimated proportion of insurgent forces lost in a given year. It is constructed by dividing the number of troops lost in a given month by the yearly estimated total insurgent forces. The measure is somewhat limited because the denominator (insurgent forces) is constant throughout the year, while the numerator (insurgent losses) varies by month.[56] Ideally, monthly total troop levels would be provided, but such data are not available. The simple ratio ranges from 0 (no battle deaths) to 0.48 (or nearly half of the troops killed). On average, the rate of insurgent troop loss is approximately 0.7 percent, or about 1 soldier out of every 150.

[56] This method essentially assumes a 100% replacement rate during the year.

I employ a negative binomial regression model to test the relationship between the battle deaths ratio measure and the number of civilians killed by insurgents in the following month. I use several control variables in the model to account for other possible explanations for insurgent violence against civilians. State security forces and rebels engage in tit-for-tat killing that led to an escalation of violence; similarly, State repression generally has been noted as a cause of terror attacks against civilians.[57] As such, I control for the level of one-sided violence employed by the State. The variable is taken from the same data set as the dependent variable and is lagged for one period. I use the natural log of the count in order to constrain the effects of extreme outliers, such as the April 1994 mass killing conducted by the Hutu-led Rwandan government. I also control for the overall severity of the conflict in a given month. Previous studies have demonstrated that as the intensity of the conflict increases overall, both rebels and States increase violence against civilians.[58] The measure used here is a simple binary variable that measures whether or not the conflict reached a high level of combat intensity during the year – that is, whether the conflict exceeded 1,000 battlefield deaths for the year. The measure is code as '1' for conflicts that produced fewer than 1,000 battle deaths in a given year and '2' if the conflict reached or exceeded 1,000 deaths. It is taken from the Uppsala Conflict Data Program/Peace Research Institute Oslo Armed Conflict Dataset.[59]

Conflicts over territory may lead to more severe violence.[60] Territorial annexation or attempts at territorial independence may provoke genocide if the territory is considered integral to the State and to the leader's vision of it. The measure of territorial conflict is a binary variable coded '1' if the conflict was a secessionist conflict and '0' otherwise. It is taken from the Armed Conflict Dataset. I also control for the presence of lootable resources in the conflict area. Popular accounts of conflict violence, especially in Africa, have focused on the role of easily extractable resources such as so-called 'blood diamonds'; other empirical works find that conflicts in areas with such resources produce a greater number of conflict casualties.[61] I therefore include a dummy variable coded as '1' for conflicts in which lootable resources such as drugs (cannabis, coca, opium, etc.)

[57] Wood, 'Rebel Capability', above note 9. [58] Ibid.

[59] L. Harbom and P. Wallensteen, 'Armed Conflict, 1946–2009' (2010) 47 *Journal of Peace Research* 501.

[60] B. Valentino, *Final Solutions* (Ithaca, NY: Cornell University Press, 2004); B. Walter, *Reputation and Civil War* (Cambridge: Cambridge University Press, 2009).

[61] Weinstein, *Inside Insurgency*, above note 7; Lujala, 'Deadly Combat', above note 9.

and gemstones are present within the conflict area. Geospatial data on the location of gems is from Lujala and Gilmore et al.; drug data is from Lujala.[62]

I include two State-level controls in the analysis as well. First, I include a measure of the State's regime type. Recent analyses on terrorism and other violence against civilians suggest that such violence may be higher in democracies. Goodwin, for example, suggests that terrorists use more indiscriminate violence against civilians in democracies because voters are more easily seen as supportive of the State policies.[63] This measure is taken from the frequently used Polity IV data set, which measures regime type on a 21-point scale of autocracy to democracy.[64] I also control for the size of the population of the country. States with larger populations present greater opportunities for violence against civilians. Population size is taken from the Correlates of War National Capabilities data set. I use the log-transformation of the measure.[65]

Previous studies have also demonstrated that the duration of a conflict affects the level of violence. Lujala finds that longer conflicts increase the number of battle deaths.[66] However, Kalyvas contends that over time, indiscriminate violence against civilians should decline as actors learn that such tactics are counterproductive and switch to more selective forms of repression and killing.[67] To account or this potential effect, I include a measure of the duration of the conflict. The measure is the count in months of the duration of the conflict since the beginning and is taken from the Uppsala Conflict Data Program Conflict Termination Dataset.[68] Finally, I include a lagged dummy variable to account for the presence of one-sided violence by the insurgent group in the previous year. Civilian victimization tends to be self-perpetuating with groups continuing to employ violence towards civilians once they have adopted it as a strategy.

The results for the regression model are presented in Table 2.1. Model 1 shows the results for the regression using a simple one-month lag of the

62 Lujala, 'Deadly Combat', above note 9; E. Gilmore et al., 'Conflict Diamonds: A New dataset' (2005) 22 *Conflict Management and Peace Science* 257.

63 J. Goodwin, 'A Theory of Categorical Terrorism' (2006) 84 *Social Forces* 2027; R. Pape, *Dying to Win: The Strategic Logic of Suicide Terrorism* (New York: Random House, 2005).

64 M. Marshall and T. Gurr, 'Polity IV Project: Political Regime Characteristics and Transitions, 1800–2006' (last updated 6 June 2014), www.systemicpeace.org/polity/polity4.htm.

65 D. J. Singer et al., 'Capability Distribution, Uncertainty, and Major Power War, 1820–1965', in B. Russett (ed.), *Peace, War, and Numbers* (Beverly Hills: Sage Press, 1972), at 19–48.

66 Lujala, 'Deadly Combat', above note 9.

67 Kalyvas, *The Logic of Violence*, above note 12.

68 J. Kreutz, 'How and When Armed Conflicts End: Introducing the Uppsala Conflict Data Program Conflict Termination Dataset' (2010) 47 *Journal of Peace Research* 243.

Table 2.1 *Regression Results*

Variable	Model 1	Model 2
Battle Death Ratio$_{\ln (t-1)}$	0.113 (0.058)*	
Insurgent Loss$_{\ln (t-1)}$		13.611 (5.598)*
Government OSV$_{\ln (t-1)}$	0.435 (0.141)*	0.365 (0.118)*
Conflict Intensity	0.782 (0.327)*	0.567 (0.311)+
Territorial Conflict	−2.720 (0.680)*	−2.989 (0.668)*
Lootable Resources	−0.571 (0.460)	−0.674 (0.473)
Regime Type	−0.051 (0.050)	−0.019 (0.061)
Population$_{\ln}$	0.406 (0.278)	0.587 (0.264)*
Conflict Duration	0.000 (0.004)	0.001 (0.005)
Rebel OSV Dummy$_{(t-1)}$	1.814 (0.330)*	1.873 (0.325)*
Observations	1990	1699
Wald X^2	117.07	116.62
Prob. > X^2	0.000	0.000

Regression coefficients and standards errors from negative binomial models. Standard errors clustered on conflict in parentheses. * = p-value ≤ 0.05. + = p-value ≤ 0.1.

battle deaths ratio variable, while Model 2 shows the results for the model using the loss proportion variable. Both sets of results provide support for the general hypothesis that during periods in which the tide of battle turns against the insurgents, they increasingly victimize civilians. The coefficient on the variable accounting for the balance of conflict-related deaths is positive and significant. This suggests that as insurgents suffer more losses relative to the government, they increasingly target civilians for violence. In addition, the regression results in Model 2 show a similar statistical relationship between the proportion of the insurgent group killed in action per month and increases in violence against civilians. The coefficient for the variable accounting for the proportion of troops lost in a month is also positive and significant, suggesting that as insurgents weaken as a result of rising battlefield cost, they increasingly victimize civilians. Moreover, both mechanisms discussed in the theory section receive some support from the models. The deaths ratio measure captures the relationship between declining battlefield performance and increased reluctance on the part of civilians to provide support to an ineffective insurgency, thus indirectly leading to increased violence. The proportional loss variable, on the other hand, captures the more direct influence of

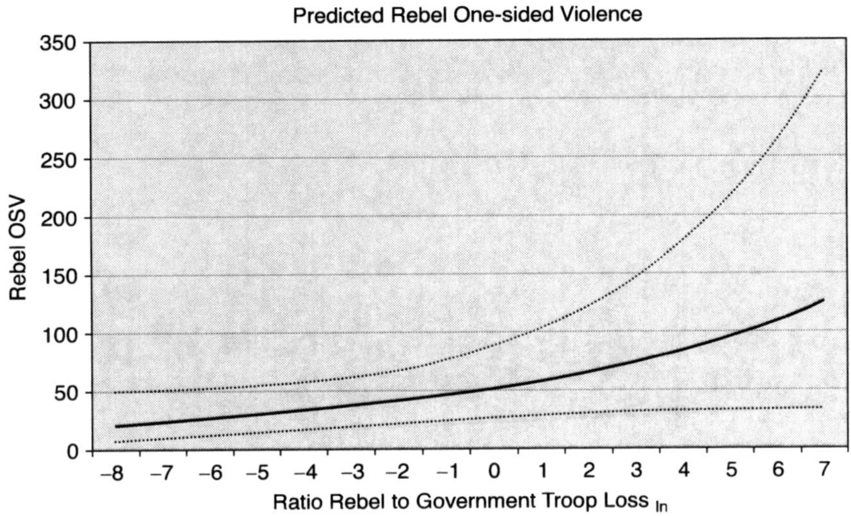

Figure 2.5 Predicted number of persons killed by rebel one-sided violence given varying values of the logged ratio of rebel to government battlefield troop losses accrued in the previous month. Predictions were conducted with Clarify software. Independent variables set at respective mean or median values. 95% confidence intervals denoted by dotted lines.

resource depletion on the incentive to target civilians. Moreover, the results match fairly well with the case narrative presented above, which illustrates a general relationship between years in which the LRA was engaged in heavy, costly fighting with the regime or suffered other types of military setbacks and their use of civilian victimization as a tool of warfare.

Because regression coefficients from negative binomials are rather difficult to interpret, I compute the predicted number of one-sided insurgent killings for varying levels of the relative loss and proportional loss variables using a series of simulations.[69] These predictions are shown in Figures 2.5 and 2.6, respectively. With respect to relative battlefield performance, the average insurgent group suffers about 1.3 times the troop loss of the government in the average month – in logarithmic terms, this equates to about 0.24. Thus, an average insurgency suffering an average level of loss

[69] G. King, M. Tomz and J. Wittenberg, 'Making the Most of Statistical Analyses: Improving Interpretation and Presentation' (2000) 44 *American Journal of Political Science* 347.

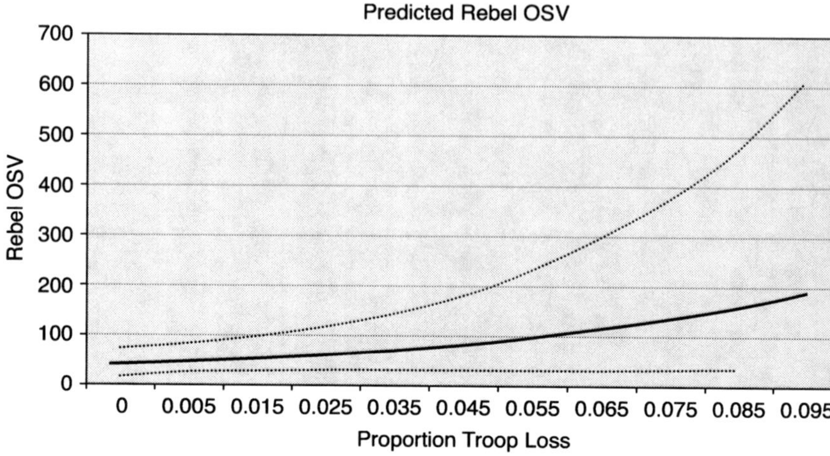

Figure 2.6 Predicted number of persons killed by rebel one-sided violence given varying values of proportion of rebel forces killed during the previous month. Predictions were conducted with Clarify software. Independent variables set at respective mean or median values. 95% confidence intervals denoted by dotted lines.

is expected to kill approximately fifty civilians in a given month (provided they engaged in any one-sided violence in the previous month). A one standard deviation increase in relative troop loss (at about '2' on the graph or approximately a 7:1 loss ratio in a given month) leads insurgents to kill approximately sixty-four civilians in the subsequent month – a 28 percent increase. A two standard deviation increase leads insurgents to kill roughly seventy-five civilians, which translates to approximately a 50 percent increase in civilian victimization.

Figure 2.6 shows the predictions based on the variable, estimating the proportion of insurgent troops lost in a given month. Like the previous predictions, the graph demonstrates how increasing battlefield costs that have a direct and negative impact on insurgents result in short-term increases in violence against civilians. Unlike the previous simulation, however, the ratio presented here is linear. As such, interpretation is much easier. According to the simulation, the average insurgent organization loses approximately 0.7 percent of its fighting force for each active combat month. Although this figure might seem low, it is important to recall that these are monthly figures. Thus, each year, the average African insurgency would lose roughly 8 percent of its combat troops to battle. Even given the rather high assumption on replacement used here, this suggests that insurgency is very costly indeed for those who participate. Based on these predictions, an insurgent organization sustaining an average level of monthly combat loss is expected to kill approximately forty-seven civilians in a given month (again supposing they engaged in killing in the previous period). A one standard deviation increase in loss – approximately 3.5 percent of the total force – increases the magnitude of civilian killing to roughly seventy civilians killed in the month following the loss. This represents a nearly 50 percent increase in civilian killings. A two standard deviation increase in proportional loss contributes to approximately ninety civilians killed, or about a 90 percent increase in killing. As the graph demonstrates, further losses radically increase insurgent killing. For instance, when an insurgent group suffers a 10 percent loss – a literal decimation of the force – it is anticipated to kill over 200 civilians in the subsequent month. This level of monthly loss is rare for insurgencies, but it illustrates the backlash created when insurgencies are significantly weakened as a result of battlefield defeats.

Turning to the control variables, the results are broadly consistent with previous research but return a few surprising and noteworthy results. First, the results validate previous findings that violence begets violence – as governments escalate violence in the current period, insurgents reciprocate in the following period. Similarly, high-intensity conflict is related to higher levels of insurgent violence. Not surprisingly, the model suggests that violence may be partially path dependent. Once a group chooses violence as a strategy, it is likely to continue to employ it. The results for the variable accounting for regime type fail to support theories about any relationship between the level of democracy in a State and insurgents' decision to use violence against civilians. This might be partly driven by the low number of non-democratic States in the sample – Africa is one of the least democratized regions. Regardless, we cannot infer from these results that insurgencies in democratic States are any more or less violent. The length of the conflict also appears to have little influence on the level of violence employed by insurgents. The variable for the population size of a country returns inconsistent results. In both models, the coefficient is positive, but it only achieves statistical significance in the second model.

Two results are quite surprising as they cut against popular arguments for insurgent violence. First, the results for the lootable resources variable are negative and statistically insignificant. The result therefore fails to support the argument that access to lootable resources encourages civilian victimization. This result should not necessarily be taken to mean that insurgencies that engage in gemstone or drug trade kill less civilians, but simply that the presence of such lootable resources does not predetermine violence by the groups. It does, however, suggest that greater emphasis should be placed on why some groups choose to rely on looting as a means to sustain themselves. The variable accounting for secessionist conflicts is also somewhat counterintuitive. While much of the literature posits that ethnically based conflicts and those surrounding breakaway territories are inherently more violent, these results suggest otherwise. The coefficient for the binary variable is both negative and statistically significant, suggesting that territorially oriented conflicts actually result in fewer civilian killings by insurgents. It is possible that the effect results from greater reliance on social networks among co-ethnics. That is, in such conflicts, insurgents may be more successful at rallying support from the civilian population, thus reducing the need to resort to violence as a mobilization tool. Indeed, Eck's research suggests that ethnic conflicts escalate to full-scale wars more quickly, demonstrating that such insurgents may be more successful at organizing among co-ethnics.[70] It might also be the case that following an initial wave of violence and ethnic cleansing, violence decreases because it has effectively succeeded in homogenizing the conflict area. Given that recent research shows that insurgents are more likely to target areas of perceived support for the opposition,[71] it follows that such homogenization would result in lower levels of violence.

5. Discussion and conclusion

As suggested by both the qualitative analysis and the statistical test, adverse changes in an insurgent group's strategic environment contribute to escalation in the group's use of violence against the civilian population. More specifically, during periods in which insurgents perform poorly on the battlefield relative to government forces, or when they lose significant troop strength as a result of combat, they are increasingly likely to escalate violence against civilians. This should not necessarily suggest that such changes fully explain variation in insurgent violence over the course of a conflict or which conflicts are most severe. Rather, these analyses highlight the importance of considering how rapidly changing battlefield conditions and alterations in the larger strategic landscape help shape the strategies employed by insurgents.

[70] Eck, 'From Armed Conflict to War', above note 9.

[71] Hultman, 'The Power to Hurt', above note 11.

What does this analysis suggest for the application of international humanitarian law in civil wars? This relationship observed above has important implications for policy-makers, practitioners and others interested in advancing international humanitarian law and related legal principles. Although the argument does not directly engage the issue of legality or the role of international law in altering insurgent behaviour, international humanitarian law can (and often does) play a central role in diminishing the costs associated with insurgent violence. Indeed, re-establishing order in a weak or anarchic environment, providing aid to the vulnerable or injured and sanctioning transgressors of international law are themselves valuable enterprises. However, international humanitarian law practitioners may wish to consider a number of potential implications from this manuscript in order to improve policies aimed at alleviating the suffering of war-stricken people.

First, international humanitarian law practitioners should be careful not to overestimate or misjudge the manner in which legal norms or institutions alter the incentive structure for insurgents to victimize civilians. Threats of prosecution in ad hoc international tribunals or the International Criminal Court are unlikely to alter insurgent behaviours in a meaningful manner. As the discussion above highlights, violence against civilians represents a short-term effort to ensure group survival. Insurgents often focus on the short-term because the future is highly unpredictable given the dynamic nature of conflict environment. As such, prosecution threats are unlikely to figure into the immediate strategy formulation of insurgent leaders. Moreover, to the extent the probability of prosecution might exert a marginal influence on insurgent behaviours, the impact is likely to be detrimental rather than beneficial because it reduces the incentive to resolve the conflict. Complications in peace talks between the LRA and the Ugandan government over the issue of Kony's indictment are a case in point. Insurgents are practical and rational enough to recognize that victors seldom face prosecution while the defeated may end up behind bars. Given this recognition, practitioners should seriously re-examine threats of prosecution and may need to consider the less palatable option of amnesty for insurgent leaders.

Second, practitioners should appreciate the underlying motives for violence. In line with the theory above, efforts to promote 'stability' or 'resolve' conflict may unintentionally lead to adverse outcomes. Militarized interventions that attempt to crush the rebellion may simply worsen attacks on civilians if they only partially succeed. The multi-national attempt to eliminate the LRA in 2008 provides a telling example. Although the intervention weakened the group, it failed to consider the ramifications of partial success, leading to the deaths of more than 1,000 civilians. Intervention by the Economic Community of West African States Monitoring Group (ECOMOG) in Sierra Leone produced a similar effect. After a year-long lull, violence by the Revolutionary United Front escalated dramatically as the combined forces of Nigerian troops and Kamajor militias succeeded in driving insurgents of the Armed Forces Revolutionary Council and Revolutionary United Front out of Freetown in early 1998. Severely weakening an insurgency may be the first step on the path to ending war. However, policy-makers should be aware of the potential for increased civilian causalities as the group weakens. This is not to suggest that foreign States and international organizations interested in ending conflict and protecting civilians refrain from intervention. Rather, organizations and policy-makers seeking to uphold or promote international humanitarian law should use these insights to better prepare for the possibility of backlash against civilians and pre-emptively design strategies to protect vulnerable populations from insurgent attacks and to establish adequate humanitarian services for victims. Furthermore, this analysis highlights the dangers of partial success. Intervention forces are often risk averse and unwilling to accept the material and human costs that come with concerted efforts to eradicate insurgents. States and international organizations dedicated to ending insurgency and protecting civilians may therefore need to absorb significant costs to achieve their goals. Ironically, democracies, the States most often interested in promoting international humanitarian law, may also be the most sensitive to these costs.

Even well-intentioned efforts, such as peacekeeping missions, may inadvertently trigger a humanitarian disaster. United Nations peacekeeping operations typically require the nominal approval of the sovereign State in which they are deployed. As such, the UN is likely to attend to the reservations and considerations of the host State while (inadvertently or intentionally) ignoring the interests of the insurgent group. Moreover, peacekeeping missions may produce short-term spikes in violence by rebels if they foresee that peacekeeping represents a threat to their likelihood of victory or to their continued profit from the conflict.[72] As with the issue of international prosecution, efforts to resolve conflicts through international intervention may require attending to the interests of rebels as much as to those of States. Groups enforcing international humanitarian law must therefore focus directly on the tension between

[72] Hultman, 'Keeping the Peace', above note 11.

an international legal system that assumes the sovereign State as the legitimate locus of legal power as well as politics and the reality of power dynamics in a fragile or collapsed State. Civil conflicts produce systems of segmented and overlapping sovereignty.[73] Over time, rebels can become the de facto rulers of territory and garner as much (if not more) legitimacy as the 'sovereign' governments they challenge.[74] Humanitarian law strategies that presume government sovereignty is inherently more legitimate may prove ineffective if they inadvertently reverse social and political developments in insurgent territory. Civilians often come to rely on the services and order insurgent control provides. Incorporating rebel governance structures into international humanitarian law-promotion efforts in order to maintain sufficient services and stability for significant segments of the population may therefore become a necessary part of those strategies. Moreover, international strategies of peacekeeping and post-conflict reconstructions should not overlook these features of civil war order in favour of preserving the sovereignty of nation-States.

The above discussion focuses on the rationale for insurgent violence towards civilians. In doing so, it reiterates that civilian victimization is rarely a product of madness but rather part of a calculated strategy of coercion, disruption and group survival. Moreover, it highlights a number of issues that international humanitarian law practitioners and policy-makers should consider before designing policies and strategies intended to halt insurgencies and protect civilians. Although these strategies may be well intentioned, they could have negative consequences for civilians if the strategies fail to anticipate the violence commensurate with group decay and setback or if they neglect to consider the legitimacy of rebel governance efforts. Counterinsurgency, peacekeeping, post-conflict stability, reconstruction efforts and the promotion of international law all are noble ventures. But specific strategies must reflect an acute understanding of conflict dynamics and conditions on the ground in order to succeed and to avoid inadvertently creating victims.

73 Kalyvas, *The Logic of Violence*, above note 12.

74 Mampilly, *Rebel Rulers*, above note 23.

3

Insurgent governance in the Democratic Republic of the Congo

ZACHARIAH MAMPILLY

1. Introduction

Many contemporary insurgencies[1] from across the ideological spectrum take over large territories for extended periods of time, establishing complex systems to regulate the social, political and economic life of civilians. Insurgent organizations regularly engage in a variety of governance activities including – but not limited to – providing security from violence; developing educational and health facilities; establishing a system of food production and distribution; allocating land and other resources to provide opportunities for civilians to engage in livelihood activities (agriculture, small business, etc.); providing shelter to the displaced; regulating market transactions; taxation of civilians and commercial actors; resolving civil disputes; and addressing other social problems that commonly accompany situations of internal war, such as theft, drug use and prostitution. In this chapter, I examine the development of governance systems by rebels in the Democratic Republic of the Congo (hereafter Congo). I first provide a general description of insurgent governance focusing on the negotiations of rebel leaders with a variety of actors that shape the governance outcomes observed. I outline a series of relevant propositions drawing on the framework developed in my 2011 book on rebel governance[2] and assess how well it accounts for the behaviour of several Congolese insurgencies with a particular focus on the Rassemblement Congolais pour la Démocratie (RCD) and its offshoots.

[1] I use the terms rebels and insurgents interchangeably. Rebels and insurgents are armed factions that use violence to challenge the state. I distinguish these from 'militia', which includes groups that work alongside government forces.

[2] Z. Mampilly, *Rebel Rulers: Insurgent Governance and Civilian Life During War* (New York: Cornell University Press, 2011).

2. Insurgent governance

At a basic level, governance can be characterized as a decision issued by one actor that a second is expected to obey.[3] As such, governance is not the sole province of recognized State governments. When speaking of an armed group, governance refers to the ability of an insurgency to both regulate life within a territory and provide public goods to a captive population through the establishment of a governance system, including formal and informal structures as well as practices of rule. As Kasfir explains,[4] rebel governance is 'the range of possibilities for organization, authority, and responsiveness created between guerrillas and civilians', which can range from 'elaborately patterned relationships as well as the absence of any patterned activity'.

Why do some rebels establish sophisticated systems of governance that provide extensive public goods to civilians under their control, while others do little, if anything, for their publics? I argue that insurgent governance systems are both a product of the initial preferences of the rebel command and a reflection of the opportunities and constraints that emerge through interactions between the rebellion and other political actors during the war. Therefore, a convincing explanation of governance variation must address initial conditions as well as the war-driven dynamics. Specifically, two conditions present at the onset of the rebellion – first, the type of pre-conflict relations between State and society and second, the strategic agenda of the group – are important initial indicators of insurgent interest in developing a governance system. But insurgent governance performance is not path dependent. Instead, it evolves over the life of the war due to interactions between rebels and various categories of political actors operating behind rebel lines.

All insurgencies face a similar dilemma, that is, how should they interact with the local populations that they come into contact with? Some groups seek to do away with the question of civilian governance by depopulating territory under their control. Others are content to rely solely on violence. Both types of armed groups often face the reality that, even when successful militarily, they may never transform into legitimate political actors.

[3] M. Kahler and D. A. Lake, 'Governance in a Global Economy: Political Authority in Transition' (2004) 37 *PS: Political Science and Politics* 409, at 409.

[4] N. Kasfir, 'Dilemmas of Popular Support in Guerilla War: The National Resistance Army in Uganda, 1981–1986' (paper presented to the Laboratory in Comparative Ethnic Processes 6, University of California, Los Angeles, 2002), at 4.

Many other insurgent leaders seek to control territory and establish governance systems in pursuit of their broader organizational agenda. Controlling territory can signal the relative strength of a rebellion to rivals and can increase their access to the local population – an essential source of support if sufficient inducements are provided. Failing to win over the local population can lead to defections or other direct challenges of the armed group's control. Thus, in order to ensure their viability, insurgencies often cannot rely on coercion alone, but work to gain a degree of consent from the civilian population. The question is: Why do some rebels decide to engage civilians in their political project? And relatedly, how do they go about doing so? Extrapolating from this formulation, it is by providing public goods and engaging in other ruling practices that an insurgency may be able to legitimize its political authority and receive support from the local population.

To better understand insurgent governance practices, I travelled to areas of rebel-control in the Congo, Sudan and Sri Lanka between 2004 and 2010. Three central concerns drove the field research process: (1) Under what conditions are insurgent leaders likely to take seriously the task of governing civilians? (2) Why do insurgents adopt certain ruling practices and how do they design their civil administrations?[5] (3) How do civilians and other actors perceive and respond to governance efforts by insurgents? Based on this research, I outline a framework for explaining the underlying factors that shape the differing ways rebel leaders interact with local populations through some sort of governance system. The next section draws on this framework.

3. A framework for assessing insurgent governance provision

An insurgent organization is a collection of men and women joining together at great risk to pursue a common agenda, with little chance of success. Most organizations tend to be top-down entities, with tremendous power invested in the command. All commands must decide when and how to divert resources away from the military battle and redirect them towards civilian governance. These resources not only are financial but also include the insurgent personnel who leave the battlefield to oversee the civil administration. Hence, the decision by a rebel command to devote resources to civilian governance is rarely made lightly.

[5] The formal structures of rebel governance systems are commonly referred to as 'civil administrations' or some variation thereof.

Throughout the following discussion, the rebel command is treated as the primary agent shaping the nature of the organization's governance efforts. However, a central assumption is that the command operates in a highly constrained political environment. Indeed, different commands respond to similar pressures from various actors that can determine the effectiveness of the civilian governance system they develop. As a result of these processes, many organizations develop complex relationships with local societies that go far beyond mere extraction. My intention is not to proclaim any laws of rebel behaviour, but rather to explore this political environment while also highlighting its exceedingly dynamic nature. The concern is to comprehend under what conditions insurgent organizations are more likely to take civilian governance seriously.

My approach diverges from foundational analyses by rebel theorists that assume the unconstrained agency of the command on questions of governance.[6] In this view, leaders develop governance systems in line with their ideological beliefs, a position that overemphasizes the capacities of the insurgent command. I also diverge from the political economy approach that ties insurgent behaviour directly to their particular resources base. According to this approach, resource endowments remain static over the course of the conflict. As such, they cannot account for rebel governance, which often exhibits considerable variation both temporally during different phases of the fighting and spatially based on the degree of territorial control.[7]

Governance provision in rebel-controlled areas often involves more than the formal structures of the insurgent civil administration. Since insurgents often interact with, or attempt to co-opt, other non-State actors engaging in service provision, it is essential to examine the whole set of relationships that shape the provision of public goods within a rebel zone of control. Thus, beyond the effectiveness of insurgent structures for distributing public goods, I am also concerned with the role of other political actors and their intersection with insurgent governance systems. These relationships may not always be formalized, thus requiring us to

[6] E. Guevara, *Guerrilla Warfare* (New York: Vintage Books, 1969); Z. Mao, *On Guerilla Warfare* (New York: Praeger, 1961).

[7] For example, J. Weinstein, *Inside Rebellion: The Politics of Insurgent Violence* (Cambridge: Cambridge University Press, 2007), at 26–27. It is also doubtful that the resource base is as fixed as this approach assumes as rebels frequently show considerable dexterity in shifting between various sources of funding. Critiques have been leveled by F. Sanín, 'Telling the Difference: Guerrillas and Paramilitaries in the Colombian War' (2008) 36 *Politics & Society* 3.

examine the complex practices of rule that create the bargaining context between insurgents, other political actors operating in conflict zones and civilians.[8]

The effectiveness of a rebel governance system can be assessed by examining several sectors that illustrate its ability to govern a civilian population: first, a police force and judicial mechanism; second, other public goods such as health and education; and third, the development of legislative bodies or other feedback mechanisms.[9] These sectors correspond with what are generally agreed upon as the three core functions of modern government – namely, security, welfare and representation.[10]

Despite a desire to demonstrate long-term horizons, rebel leaders engage in governance strategies that evince an instrumental understanding of the shifting terrain of the battlefield – and they adapt their efforts accordingly. Indeed, governance is rarely an immediate concern, because organizations only come into control of territory after the initial phases of the fighting. Generally, a sufficient period of relatively stable territorial control is a precondition for any insurgency attempting to construct a civilian governance system, though, as the National Transitional Council in Libya demonstrated, the window for establishing a system of civilian governance is increasingly smaller, particularly in the glare of international media.[11] Still, public welfare provision beyond security is rarely an immediate imperative for a rebel command.[12]

The establishment of a force capable of policing the population, followed by a broader judicial mechanism to regulate disputes, is often the primary concern for insurgencies upon taking control of territory. Regulating the means of violence is an essential precondition for the development of a broader system of governance. The establishment of security structures allows an insurgency to demonstrate its relative power to civilians, in addition to laying claim to a key component of Weberian sovereignty – the monopoly over the use of violence. Without a

[8] Kahler and Lake, 'Governance in a Global Economy', above note 3, at 412.

[9] T. Wickham-Crowley, 'The Rise (and Sometimes Fall) of Guerrilla Governments in Latin America' (1987) 2 *Sociological Forum* 473.

[10] Insurgents frequently levy taxes on the civilian population, an important component of governance. But data on most rebel taxation remain low quality, which makes it difficult to offer any substantive claims on its impact on rebel governance.

[11] This is why the universe of rebel governance cases is only a fraction of the total number of insurgencies: many groups either fail to take and hold territory for a sufficient period of time or choose to operate in a roving fashion.

[12] Wickham-Crowley, 'The Rise of Guerrilla Governments', above note 9, at 486.

functioning security system, it is difficult for rebels to gain the credibility from being recognized as the dominant force and to initiate a process of providing additional collective goods.[13] Furthermore, since the insurgency already possesses effective instruments of coercion, a police force is not nearly as cumbersome to establish as other public goods, like social welfare programmes or legislative bodies.

The provision of public welfare items is often viewed as a secondary concern, yet rebels have proven remarkably adept at providing a wide variety of services. As with security, the delivery of services can be ad hoc (informal) or bureaucratic (formal). Fostering civilian participation in governance decisions is rarely a priority for rebel commands because most tend to have an autocratic predisposition, though it has been known to happen. For example, the African Party for the Independence of Guinea and Cape Verde (PAIGC), under guerrilla leader Amílcar Cabral, held semi-democratic elections for its leadership council. More commonly, rebels work to incorporate civilians into the provision of specific services. For example, in the early phases of the conflict in Sri Lanka, the Tamil Tigers relied on the assistance of civilian committees to provide basic services like education.

4. Explaining variation in insurgent governance systems

Rebel leaders vary widely in the degree to which they have considered questions of civilian governance prior to the conflict. But regardless of their initial preferences, the construction of governance systems is more commonly an iterative process whereby the adoption of specific practices and structures is responsive to the behaviour of a number of diverse political actors, each operating within a specific local and international context. From below, organizations face pressure from the denizens of the areas under their control. From within, organizations must take into consideration factions representing oppositional perspectives, whether based on cultural or ideological differences or just greed. From above, organizations interact with transnational actors, including international agencies, foreign organizations – both commercial and charitable, religious groups, diasporas as well as other governments. At each step of the conflict, leaders refine their governance strategy in response to these conflict-induced dynamics, adopting or rejecting approaches in an evolutionary fashion.

[13] Weinstein, *Inside Rebellion*, above note 7, at 26–27.

5. From below: civilian demands affecting insurgent governance

Comparative analyses of rebel behaviour often treat populations as static, responsive solely to the behaviour of the rebels or other political actors, rather than constituting an active agent capable of influencing events. Thus, analyses of insurgent–civilian relations have emphasized such factors as resource endowments,[14] organizational capacity[15] and geographic surroundings.[16] Each of these approaches views the population as generic, malleable by external forces and incapable of influencing the command.

However, civilians are rarely passive actors and can manipulate the tenor of governance efforts through the explicit demands they make.[17] Civilians have a variety of ways of responding to rebel control, ranging from wholesale support, limited or coerced participation, public and private protest, disengagement (by fleeing rebel territory), covert and overt collaboration with the incumbent State and even violent rejection through the formation of local militias. An insurgency's most immediate tool for ensuring compliance is always its ability to deploy coercive tactics upon civilians. Still, civilians do not lack agency in their negotiations with insurgent leaders. Indeed, the decision by the population to either embrace or reject a specific organization is a strategic one that can affect the behaviour of insurgent leaders, who must design their governance systems to respond to civilian demands.

Another tendency is to separate the dynamics of civil wars from the social and historical conditions that precede the conflict. However, the pre-conflict relationship between the population and the incumbent government can affect the behaviour of rebel organizations, particularly as it pertains to questions of governance. Thus, it is problematic to treat civilians as cattle, responding herd-like to generic stimuli as pre-conflict patterns of behaviour often influence civilian responses to various insurgent initiatives.[18] The task is to determine a way to distinguish between those populations likely to make claims upon the political authority and the types of claims they are likely to make.

[14] Ibid. [15] Kasfir, 'Dilemmas of Popular Support in Guerilla War', above note 4.

[16] J. Herbst, *States and Power in Africa: Comparative Lessons in Authority and Control* (Princeton: Princeton University Press, 2000); T. Mkandawire, 'The Terrible Toll of Post-colonial "Rebel Groups" in Africa: Towards an Explanation of the Violence against the Peasantry' (2002) 40 *Journal of Modern African Studies* 181.

[17] S. Kalyvas, 'The Ontology of "Political Violence": Action and Identity in Civil Wars' (2003) 1 *Perspectives on Politics* 475, at 481.

[18] N. Kriger, *Zimbabwe's Guerrilla War: Peasant Voices* (Cambridge: Cambridge University Press, 1991), at 147.

Variations in civilian preferences are shaped by the pre-conflict governance practices of the incumbent government. Among other differences, governments have the power to determine whether the population is habituated to paying taxes, whether it has a say in politics and whether it views ethnicity or cultural markers as politically salient. I argue that the relationship between a government and the population has a determinative impact on the effectiveness of rebel governance systems as insurgent leaders respond to demands made by civilians conditioned in distinct ways by their relationship to the pre-conflict political authority.

5.1. *Rentier versus merchant populations*

Scholars have shown how the past lingers in reconfigurations of political order.[19] Prior interactions between State and society have important impacts on the development of new institutions and practices of rule triggered by the outbreak of violence.[20] Indeed, only by understanding the pre-conflict State–society relationship can we grasp the modalities that produce diverse insurgent governance systems across cases, as various civilian populations – politically habituated in differing ways – make distinct demands upon the rebel political authority. The history of the penetration of the State into society is one method for distinguishing between various categories of civilian behaviour that a rebel government is likely to encounter. Specifically, in order to understand the type of relationship a local community is likely to have with an insurgency, it is important to understand how and to what degree that community was integrated politically into the pre-conflict State through the expansion of the government bureaucracy.[21]

Leaders of many post-colonial States struggled to emulate the revenue-accumulation model based on taxation (hereafter referred to as *merchant* States) developed by their former colonial masters. Instead, they turned

[19] J. Migdal, *Strong States and Weak Societies: State-Society Relations and State Capabilities in the Third World* (Princeton: Princeton University Press, 1988).

[20] Mkandawire, 'The Terrible Toll', above note 16; D. North, *Institutions, Institutional Change and Economic Performance* (New York: Cambridge University Press, 1991).

[21] My usage of 'penetration' is meant to extend beyond the idea of 'governmental capacity', which is used to compare the relative capacity of governments in different states. Governmental capacity refers to the 'extent to which governmental agents control resources, activities, and populations within the government's territory', but does not take into consideration territorial variation in state capacity. C. Tilly, *The Politics of Collective Violence* (Cambridge: Cambridge University Press, 2003), 41; C. Tilly, *Coercion, Capital, and the European State, AD 990–1990* (Cambridge: Basil Blackwell, 1990).

to the quick financial rewards offered through the collection of rents from foreign investments in natural resources and from lucrative strategic political alliances. The rentier State emerged in response to a globalized world order that rewarded local political elites with large economic surpluses based on their control of native resources and their mutually profitable relationship with agents in more developed countries. These resources accrued to juridically empowered political elites, even if they lacked empirical control.[22] Scholars have argued that State authorities who rely on rents possess greater autonomy from the will of the public as the government has little need to develop a broad tax base, preferring to either buy off non-cooperative citizens or build a coercive apparatus capable of keeping the population in line.[23]

Two different political outlooks characterize popular attitudes about government based on the above discussion. In the rentier State, populations have no sense of ownership over decision-making as they are not required to fund the State through taxation.[24] Therefore, a disengaged government produces an apolitical population, disconnected from the local machinations of the often ineffective public bureaucracy. In contrast, in the merchant State, an active population is heavily invested in decision-making through its direct financial contributions. Citizens in these States aggressively seek to limit the behaviour of the political authority in a way that is beneficial for the well-being of the polity.

Put another way, civilians politically habituated by rentier State fiscal policies are unaware of their ability to influence the political authority, a condition that carries over to political formations that develop in the face of a conflict-produced State withdrawal. In merchant States where the bureaucratic structures penetrate deeply into the public psyche and are capable of both collecting taxes and providing public goods, civilians are habituated to having a say in political affairs. In both cases, it is up to a

[22] Herbst, *States and Power in Africa*, above note 16; R. Jackson, *Quasi-States: Sovereignty, International Relations and the Third World* (Cambridge: Cambridge University Press, 1990).

[23] Mkandawire, 'The Terrible Toll', above note 16; M. Moore, 'Revenues, State Formation, and the Quality of Governance in Developing Countries' (2004) 25 *International Political Science Review* 297.

[24] This is not to imply that no community within the State has dense relations with the State authority. Some communities are the favoured recipient of State largesse and enjoy considerable benefits from this relationship. However, without an underlying mechanism driving the state–society relationship, there is considerable variation between communities within these States, each of which may have distinct relationships with the central government.

rebel command to determine how to deal with the civilian population, and its ability to establish structures that respond to the demands articulated by the local community will determine the success or failure of its governance project. Failure to do so may open the group to internal challenges, both political and militaristic, from civilians.

State penetration also produces a secondary effect that shapes governance beyond civilian demands. To mitigate against civilian challenges, leaders often tap into and even co-opt pre-existing institutions and networks of power, which are themselves the direct product of the pre-conflict relationship between the incumbent State and political actors.[25] Merchant States are characterized by more effective social control resulting from the denser and hierarchically organized relations between the State and significant social groups that allow citizens to be more demanding in their interactions with the political authority. However, in the rentier State, the lack of a functional State bureaucracy opens up the path to alternate forms of governance by non-State actors often at odds with the formal government. Political and social order is likely to be provided by an ad hoc array of political actors including religious institutions, charitable organizations, private corporations, trade networks and traditional authorities.[26] Such a parcellized authority structure can create obstacles for rebel leaders as they seek to develop their own structures and practices of governance, forcing them to negotiate with many different actors in their efforts to build a governance system.[27] This compares with the legacy of a highly penetrated State, a situation in which rebels confront cohesive institutions and networks of power.

6. From within: internal dynamics affecting insurgent governance

6.1. Secessionist versus reformist insurgents

Elites seeking to mobilize a population often adopt ethnic claims, as compared to other societal cleavages such as class or gender.[28] Ethnic or nationalist appeals are considered to be more resonant than other

[25] J. Migdal, *Boundaries and Belonging: States and Societies in the Struggle to Shape Identities and Local Practices* (New York: Cambridge University Press, 2004).

[26] T. Bierschenk and J.-P. de Sardan, 'Local Powers and a Distant State in Rural Central African Republic' (1997) 35 *The Journal of Modern African Studies* 441.

[27] T. Raeymaekers, K. Menkhaus and K. Vlassenroot, 'State and non-State Regulation in African Protracted Crises: Governance without Government?' (2008) 21 *Afrika Focus* 7.

[28] S. Tambiah, *Leveling Crowds: Ethnonationalist Conflicts and Collective Violence in South Asia* (Berkeley and Los Angeles: University of California Press, 1996).

types of claims and hence more useful as the basis for any collective enterprise. Historical factors have contributed to ethnic claims taking on even greater salience in the post-colonial world. As colonial authorities openly manipulated ethnic identity as a tool of political control, the post-colonial State bureaucracies of many countries remained ethnicized.[29] As a result, counter-claims to State power also came to emanate primarily from ethno-nationalist subgroups.[30]

Through this process, ethnicity has taken on instrumental overtones. Access to political and civil rights, in addition to material benefits, continues to be determined by membership in the 'right' ethnic community. Since exclusion from political and economic opportunities is often ethnicized, appeals to ethnic solidarity often serve as the basis for insurgent collective action. But distinguishing a segment of the population from the rest of the society also generates its own expectations within an ethnic community. Unlike those who seek power at the national level, secessionists have a greater immediate need to prove their ability to improve the material welfare of their target populations. As Tambiah suggests, ethno-nationalism is the articulation of a desire by communities 'to achieve their own regional and local sociopolitical formations'.[31]

Insurgent organizations must frequently decide between various strategies in deciding how to interact with the different communities inhabiting their areas of control. All insurgencies that seek popular support treat some communities as potential collaborators requiring restraint and certain positive inducements, while other communities, for a variety of reasons, can be dealt with only with violence. Rebellions that seek to topple an established regime must seek to assuage, potentially, the entire population in order to avoid challenges to their authority once in power. In addition, reformist insurgents frequently have a longer time-horizon for improving civilian governance, frequently delaying expectations until after victory has been achieved.

In contrast, secessionist groups define the target audiences for their various actions (both violent and non-violent) more narrowly. As a result, leaders face a higher barrier as they draw from a more limited constituency for support. In addition, the targeted audience often expects improvements in their living conditions soon after the rebels take territory. Insurgent leaders must convince their ethnic kin of the

[29] M. Mamdani, *Citizen and Subject: Contemporary Africa and the Legacy of Late Colonialism* (Princeton: Princeton University Press, 1996).

[30] Tambiah, *Leveling Crowds*, above note 28.

[31] Ibid. 17.

potential payoffs likely to accrue in the short term, rendering them more susceptible to criticisms and demands from within. The ethnic population targeted for mobilization is also likely to face harassment on the basis of their collective ascriptive identity – rather than individual political allegiances – thereby further raising the costs to the community if the insurgency is unable to provide a degree of stability.

Secessionist leaders may also be positively influenced by the international communities clear preference for nation-State-like actors. International humanitarian law has long privileged struggles for national liberation over other types of violent movements.[32] This bias is echoed in the clear preference of transnational activist networks to throw their weight behind movements of cultural preservation that seek a degree of political autonomy[33] over the more messy 'reformist' insurgencies that seek to capture power at the centre. Thus, I argue that organizations with a secessionist or ethno-nationalist agenda have a vested interest in proving their ability to serve as de facto governments as their ability to garner support will be shaped by their governance performance.

As discussed earlier, many other factors that affect rebel behaviour around governance are endogenously driven by the conflict dynamics and emerging from a variety of locations only after the initiation of fighting. I turn to these now.

6.2. Ideology

The role of ideology and its relationship to governance provision has a commonly hypothesized positive correlation, that is, groups that espouse leftist political philosophies are more likely to evince greater concern for the well-being of the civilian population. However, the ideological agenda professed to an external audience is primarily rhetorical and has little direct influence on the behaviour of insurgents in their relations with civilian populations.

A more nuanced take recognizes that ideological influences do not solely find expression in outward articulations but can influence the internal organizational strategy adopted by the command. Leaders are

[32] M. Sassòli, 'Transnational Armed Groups and International Humanitarian Law' (Occasional Paper No. 6, Program on Humanitarian Policy and Conflict Research, Harvard University, 2006).

[33] C. Bob, *The Marketing of Rebellion: Insurgents, Media and International Activism* (Cambridge: Cambridge University Press, 2006).

not bound to any particular organizational strategy, and they can and do switch over time based on strategic considerations. Thus, ideology is only salient for an insurgency when it shapes the internal organizational strategy adopted by the command. In particular, leaders who take seriously Maoist ideas – specifically, Mao's emphasis on conventional warfare, disciplined cadre, a prolonged period of political mobilization and the development of broad-based civil administrative structures that function to incorporate the peasantry into the insurgent organization – must devote considerable resources to civilian governance. These organizational strategies are available to any group regardless of their public political position; hence, many ethno-nationalist groups have implemented a Maoist organizational strategy, and even right-wing groups like União Nacional para a Independência Total de Angola (UNITA) in Angola have done the same.

Insurgents who fight solely using hit-and-run tactics can only affect civilian livelihoods for the worse, as governance remains the preserve of the incumbent. In contrast, holding territory requires the development of a security force to demonstrate insurgent control, an elemental building block towards a broader system of governance. Ensuring troop discipline signals to the public that the organization has the ability to mediate the use of violence within its territory. And finally, devoting personnel to political mobilization is necessary to educate the public about the organization's intentions so as not to ostracize its potential base of support. But it also requires the organization to develop structures for this purpose – structures that can be put to use for other governance concerns such as providing education, delivering public health messages, delivering medications and so on.

6.3. Cleavages

Another internal factor is related to the composition of the local community and the cleavages that exist prior to the outbreak of conflict. Though desirable, full hierarchical control within any organization is never possible; instead, some degree of tension between internal factions is inevitable.[34] Factions may compete as a result of differences over how to allocate material resources, the political agenda for the group, the real or imagined cultural or ethnic orientation of the organization or some

[34] M. Barnett and M. Finnemore, 'The Politics, Power, and Pathologies of International Organizations' (1999) 53 *International Organization* 699, at 724.

combination of all three. Such internal divisions can lead each faction to perceive the organization's overall mission in fundamentally different ways with significant effects on governance efforts.[35] In the worst-case scenario, these divisions may even lead to the fracturing of the broader movement and the emergence of multiple militant rivals to the original organization.

There are two questions to address in regards to the above. First, how and why are some insurgent organizations able to suppress internal cleavages and forge a unified command, while others are ripped apart by similar tensions? Internal dynamics often reflect relationships between local communities and the command in constitutive ways. And the ability of rebel leaders to incorporate representatives from constituent factions within their organization is a key determinant of the type of command – either unified or divided – a group will have.

Pre-conflict cleavages at the local level tend to persist and affect rebel behaviour once fighting begins, regardless of the stated cause of the war.[36] If the movement is multi-ethnic, multi-religious or multi-regional, tensions between component factions can bubble to the surface due to perceived dominance or mistreatment on either side.[37] Such local-level economic, racial, ethnic, religious and regional differences all impact the behaviour of leaders as they attempt to cajole or coerce a governance system upon a less than complacent population. Any attempts at consolidating their rule requires leaders to assess the nature of the population they seek to control and devise strategies to mitigate potential cleavages that could emerge. Indeed, pre-existing internal cleavages can have a wide variety of consequences for organizations, and the command must devote attention and resources to ensure that they do not undermine the ability of the organization to pursue its goals effectively.

Second, it is critical to understand how a divided or unified command affects the internal organization of an insurgency and the impact on its ability to develop a system of civilian governance. More dramatically, if the command actually splits into multiple rival factions, how does contested territorial control shape insurgent governance efforts? Rebel leaders able to establish a unified command that exerts its control throughout the entire organization and corresponding territory – despite internal

[35] E. Wood, 'Variation in Sexual Violence during War' (2006) 34 *Politics & Society* 307.

[36] Kalyvas, 'The Ontology', above note 17, at 478–80.

[37] M. Jok and S. Hutchinson, 'Sudan's Prolonged Second Civil War and the Militarization of Nuer and Dinka Ethnic Identities' (1999) 42 *African Studies Review* 125.

competition – are more capable of implementing a cohesive system of governance than an organization divided into competing factions.[38] If the leadership can establish an undisputed political authority over its territory, it strengthens its ability to offer protection to its chief supporters, extract more resources and wage war.[39]

7. From above: transnational factors affecting insurgent governance

Civil wars are rarely contained within the territorial boundaries of a single State.[40] Despite reluctance from international organizations to legitimate non-State violent groups, the presence of different transnational actors within areas of rebel control serves to link such spaces to the formal world system. Thus, it is important to consider the impact of transnational actors on rebel behaviour as it pertains to civilian governance.

Transnational actors perform an array of essential functions in contemporary conflict zones, whether commercial, humanitarian or militaristic. Insurgent leaders are aware of the potential benefits and risks of aligning with transnational actors and often work to engage such actors in their political projects.[41] As a result, different categories of transnational actors produce distinctive effects on insurgent behaviour regarding civilian governance.

However, despite recognizing the integral role that the international community plays in fomenting and fostering contemporary violent conflicts, attention has generally focused on the economic agendas driving international actors to intervene in rebel-controlled territories and the resulting configurations of power that result.[42] Less attention has been devoted to the political interventions required on the ground to make such transactions possible. For insurgents, providing a modicum of political order on the ground both results from their interactions with

[38] E. Guevara, *The African Dream: The Diaries of the Revolutionary War in the Congo* (New York: Grove Press, 1999), at 79.

[39] Tilly, *Coercion, Capital, and the European State*, above note 21, at 181.

[40] T. Callaghy, R. Kassimir and R. Latham, (eds.), *Intervention and Transnationalism in Africa: Global Networks of Power* (Cambridge: Cambridge University Press, 2001); K. Gleditsch, 'Transnational Dimensions of Civil War' (2007) 44 *Journal of Peace Research* 293.

[41] Bob, *The Marketing of Rebellion*, above note 33.

[42] C. Nordstrom, *Shadows of War: Violence, Power, and International Profiteering in the Twenty-First Century* (Berkeley and Los Angeles: University of California Press, 2004); W. Reno, *Warlord Politics and African States* (Boulder: Lynne Rienner, 1998).

transnational actors, as well as being an effort undertaken to woo such actors to their territory in the first place.

Rebel leaders react to resources and constraints produced by an increasingly transnational world, going as far as 'marketing' their rebellion to actors in the international community.[43] However, analyses of rebel organizations' relationships with transnational actors fail to delineate the precise effects of such interactions on the primary insurgent interface with the civilian population, that is, the rebel civil administration. As a result, they tend to assume only a negative impact on civilian governance, an assumption that ignores the nuances of such complicated interactions. Not every transnational interaction will have the same effect on governance. Indeed, different categories of transnational actors have their own views regarding civilian treatment formed prior to their engagement with various militant groups. These preferences can include deep concern, passive disinterest or outright hostility towards local residents affecting how transnational actors engage with a particular organization and the concomitant effects of the intervention on civilian governance. The question is: When do such transnational relationships negatively affect insurgent civilian governance efforts? And when are they likely to have a more positive impact? The various categories of transnational actors play two important roles – as supporters or competitors – that have different effects on the behaviour of rebel leaders.

7.1. Supporters

Transnational actors may function as supporters of rebel organizations by providing resources that impact their ability and desire to grapple with civilian governance concerns. Insurgencies with a limited resource base have a strong incentive to develop relations with transnational actors in order to generate financial resources and take advantage of the credibility imbued through such associations.[44] Insurgencies are commonly assumed to draw such support from two types of transnational actors: private corporations and other States. Both types of actors are explicit about their self-interested engagement with rebel groups, offering leaders direct financial payments and other material support in exchange for

[43] Bob, *The Marketing of Rebellion*, above note 33.

[44] M.-J. Zahar, 'Protégés, Clients, Cannon Fodder: Civil-Militia Relations in Internal Conflicts' (2001) in S. Chesterman, ed., *Civilians in War* (Boulder: Lynne Rienner Publishers, 2001), at 43–65.

assistance in pursuit of material or strategic gains. In the early phases of a rebellion when such resources are essential, the effect is often to undermine civilian agency on governance by reducing the need for the organization to mobilize popular support.[45]

The source of funding, however, is not the sole determinant of governance outcomes. Variation in financing strategies over time is an important constraint on its impact. These can be caused by a shift in political alliances between States or by the collapse of a commodities market; and insurgencies must adjust their fiscal strategies to adapt to changing conditions, or risk collapse. When faced with a shift in their funding source, many groups do succumb, of course. But many others prove more durable, shifting between a mix of available funding strategies. Whether patronage from an external State, the sale of natural resources or more illicit goods or the extortion, smuggling and taxation of civilians and commercial or charitable organizations, insurgencies have a variety of strategies for raising funds, often combining a mix of approaches over their existence.

Equally important, States and commercial actors are not the only transnational actors that provide support to organizations. Many other transnational actors engage in conflict zones for ostensibly humanitarian purposes. The manner by which rebels can benefit from these relationships has been discussed, most prominently in the notion of a substitution effect that allows insurgent leaders to neglect civilian welfare in favour of more military concerns.[46] However, organizations concerned with civilian welfare issues, including foreign non-governmental organizations (NGOs), international agencies, diasporic organizations and religious institutions, may also have a positive impact on rebel governance, if an effective coordinating mechanism can be established by the insurgency. Incorporating humanitarian actors can stimulate the development of the governance system by providing resources, services and expertise that can supplement the organization's own capacity to meet civilian needs. For rebels, such collaborations may provide an effective way to address civilian welfare without diverting limited financial resources or personnel. For humanitarian organizations, working with insurgents can ease their access to populations affected by the fighting. Rebels may also

[45] Weinstein, *Inside Rebellion*, above note 7.

[46] M. Anderson, *Reflection on the Practice of Outside Assistance: Can We Know What Good We Do* (Berghoff Research Center, 2001); A. de Waal, *Famine Crimes: Politics and the Disaster Relief Industry in Africa* (Oxford: James Currey, 1997).

provide security for development and relief projects and offer their own local expertise to supplement these efforts.

For example, insurgents have successfully incorporated NGOs into their governance project. By forcing these organizations to work within a contractual framework that delineates the specific activities they will be allowed to engage in, the areas in which they can operate and any other requirements regarding the hiring of personnel or the payment of duty to the political authority, insurgents have inserted themselves between the aid organization and the population they seek to serve.[47]

7.2. *Competitors*

If the organization fails to co-opt transnational actors into its governance system, however, it may come to view such organizations and networks as competitors in the battle for the 'hearts and minds' of civilians. This can occur in one of three ways. First, governance provision can be negatively affected in situations in which insurgents fail to synchronize their actions with the needs of local trading networks and foreign corporations with commercial interests in rebel-controlled territory. Whether through the hiring of private security firms or shoring up government military forces, private actors have repeatedly shown their willingness to challenge insurgent control over territory, often to the detriment of the civilian population caught within. Second, by providing basic services to a receptive population, aid organizations that refuse to fall in line with the insurgent programme can undercut the revolutionary promises made by rebel leaders, offering immediate rewards instead of weak promises for a better future.[48] Third, human rights activists and journalists, both local and international, are tapped into transnational activists networks that can mobilize international public opinion against insurgencies that exploit civilians or that rely on excessive coercion to ensure civilian compliance. Similarly, religious institutions, with their transnational networks of believers, have proven effective in mobilizing public opinion against the behaviour of undisciplined violent groups.

[47] A. Branch and Z. Mampilly, 'Winning the War, but Losing the Peace? The Dilemma of SPLM/A Civil Administration and the Tasks Ahead' (2005) 43 *Journal of Modern African Studies* 1; de Waal, *Famine Crimes*, above note 46.

[48] In India, Naxalite insurgents expelled all charitable organizations operating in territories under their control out of fear that the NGOs were improving peasant welfare and hence reducing the salience of their violent appeals.

Though private competitors generally have a harmful effect on insurgent civilian governance efforts, the effect of non-commercial competitors is decidedly more mixed. In many cases, the activities of recalcitrant NGOs or critical human rights activists are likely to push the insurgent command to become defensive about their treatment of civilians. This can result in armed groups working to hide their abuses from the international community, to the detriment of affected communities. However, in certain cases, such pressure may push rebel leaders to take seriously the task of addressing civilian needs, particularly if they perceive that a change in behaviour will produce more positive coverage for the rebellion. The wording of this discussion is purposefully conditional as it relies on idiosyncratic factors that may push the organization to take governance more seriously. For example, positive coverage of a rival organization may pressure insurgents to devote more attention to civilian needs. In situations where insurgent control is complete, however, the same pressure from transnational actors may simply push the organization to imprison or expel any competitors in their midst. In the next section, I show how the framework can explain variation in insurgent governance systems by drawing on the case of Congo.

8. Insurgent governance in the Democratic Republic of the Congo

8.1. *Overview*

The conflict in the Congo has generated a bewildering array of armed groups across the country since 1996. More than forty rebel groups have existed with vastly different ethnic memberships, operational capacities, military strategies and political agendas – ranging from poorly equipped local community-based militias to large-scale conventional armies and everything in between.[49] As I discuss below, most of these organizations were largely incapable of meeting the challenge of civilian governance. But contrary to the received wisdom, this was not simply due to rebel leaders' lack of concern for civilian welfare. Several of the groups did make important efforts to develop civilian governance systems even if these efforts largely amounted to nothing. However, from their failure, we can learn much about the challenges of developing a suitable system of governance – particularly when conditions are not favourable. In

[49] L. E. Seay, 'The Advantage of State Failure? Why Congolese Armed Groups Don't Provide Health Care' (unpublished manuscript, 2011).

particular, groups like the RCD, the Mouvement de Libération du Congo (MLC) under Jean-Pierre Bemba, the Congrès National pour la Défense du Peuple (CNDP) of Laurent Nkunda and less well-known groups like the Forces Armées du Peuple Congolais (FAPC) under Commander Jérôme Kakwavu Bakonde and even segments of the Mai-Mai militias all attempted to develop civilian governance systems to varying degrees, drawing on distinct modalities of rule.

The framework offers important insights regarding both points of convergence and divergence between these Congolese insurgencies. Each of these groups faced several common challenges, which are necessary to take into consideration when examining the viability of insurgent governance systems in the Democratic Republic of the the Congo. Most important, despite variation in motivation, structure and capacity, each group faced a similarly convoluted political environment in areas they came to control. During the reign of Mobutu Sese Seko, the State withdrew from vast portions of the country's territory, leaving behind a minimalist bureaucratic apparatus that interacted with local actors in complex and unique political arrangements. As the State withered away, Zaireans were forced to turn towards civil society and other non-State actors, such as aid organizations, traditional authorities, business associations and religious institutions, all of which negotiated with the remnants of the Mobutuist State to provide a semblance of social order to their highly localized constituencies.

As a result, prior to the war, eastern Zaire was characterized by a complex arrangement that established a degree of social and political order through interactions between active agents of a distant State and multiple categories of non-State political and economic actors. Central and regional offices of the government continued to be staffed by personnel who generated income through fees and other kickbacks charged to civilians. Working hand in hand with private companies and regional trading networks, State agents ensured a steady extraction of the region's extensive resources with few benefits for the surrounding communities. Little was provided to residents in the way of meaningful public services, whether health, education, infrastructure or even a consistent legal system. Instead, aid organizations and religious institutions, in conjunction with local chiefs, stepped in to provide some public goods and construct other developmental projects.[50]

[50] C. Young, 'The Heart of the African Conflict Zone: Democratization, Ethnicity, Civil Conflict, and the Great Lakes Crisis' (2006) 9 *Annual Review of Political Science* 301.

Thus, from the start of the first war in 1996, Congolese insurgents confronted a parcellized system of governance in which social order was provided by a complex constellation of actors negotiating with agents of the State or the remnants of the Congolese bureaucracy, the legacy of Mobutu's rentier politics. As a result, once in control of territory each group had to negotiate with a wide variety of local and transnational social and political actors, including traditional chiefs, religious authorities, business people and local and transnational NGOs, ultimately rendering effective civilian governance an elusive pursuit.

All five insurgencies struggled to provide even basic public goods, but they varied in the degree to which they were able to achieve some degree of legitimacy among a specific population. The three groups that espoused reformist agendas (RCD, MLC, CNDP) struggled to legitimize their rule among the population, while those that targeted narrow, ethnically defined constituencies (Mai-Mai, FAPC) were able to gain considerably more popular legitimacy. Other differences in their operational capabilities, their political agendas, the cultural milieu from which they emerged and the set of political actors they negotiated with also shaped the variation between the different insurgent governance systems.

For example, the MLC did establish a civilian governance system in Equateur province during the second war. The organization appointed a representative assortment of individuals to ministerial positions, and it even paid some administrators for their services. By and large, however, the MLC relied on pre-existing institutions and personnel to continue handling the responsibilities of governing, an ineffective mode of civilian governance that was common among reformist insurgencies in the Democratic Republic of the Congo.[51] Still, despite his failure to provide effective governance, Bemba, the rebellion's leader, emerged as a popular civilian politician after the end of the war and was for a time the leading opposition figure, having transformed his organization into a political party.

The CNDP also established a parallel administration in areas of North Kivu under its control. The rebellion did get involved in aspects of civilian governance, establishing a system of taxation and interfering

[51] International Crisis Group, 'The Kivus: The Forgotten Crucible of the Congo Conflict' (Africa Report 56, Nairobi/Brussels, 24 January 2003); T. Carayannis, 'The Complex Wars of the Congo: Towards a New Analytic Approach' (2003) 38 *Journal of Asian and African Studies* 232; Z. Mampilly, 'Stationary Bandits: Understanding Rebel Governance' (PhD thesis, University of California, 2007).

in the structure of the education system,[52] though without offering much in the way of public goods. Under Nkunda, a Congolese Tutsi, the movement faced questions about its agenda from the local communities who have long been suspicious of the Tutsi community over its national allegiances.[53] In order to combat this perception, the CNDP government waded deeply into the fraught realm of nationalist symbology in Congo. What is striking about the CNDP was its success in improving perceptions of its political authority despite providing few public goods. By deploying a symbolic repertoire that included a new anthem to proclaim the movement's nationalist goals and a new flag that simply recoloured the Mobutu era version, the organization was able to overcome considerable suspicion among local Kivutiens. As a result, the CNDP was able to generate higher degrees of identification and compliance with its rule among a wide assortment of Kivutiens despite its upper echelon's being controlled by the Congolese Tutsi community.[54]

Similarly, a segment of the Mai-Mai under Commander Padiri used cultural appeals to legitimate its rule over a population in areas under its control in the Kivus.[55] This was an especially important strategy for the Mai-Mai, a diverse set of ethnic militias that sometimes aligned with the Kinshasa government but frequently operated autonomously, often holding territory and governing various 'indigenous' populations against what they perceived as foreign invasions. Padiri's group, the largest Mai-Mai faction in eastern Congo, established an administration, the *administration des forêts*, that attempted to provide a degree of public services as an inducement for greater civilian participation. Like the other groups discussed, Padiri's group did not attempt to develop an alternate bureaucratic arrangement to replace the State administration, preferring instead to retain the administrative practices and infrastructure that evolved in the Congo under Mobutu. Civilian administrators were put in place to continue managing certain public goods including education, policing and judicial functions, though under the surveillance of intelligence agents.

[52] Seay, 'The Advantage of State Failure', above note 49.

[53] J. Stearns, 'Laurent Nkunda and the National Congress for the Defence of the People (CNDP)', in S. Marysse, F. Reyntjens and S. Vandeginste (eds.), *L'Afrique des grandes lacs. Annuaire 2007–2008* (Paris: L'Harmattan, 2008), at 245.

[54] Ibid.; Z. Mampilly, 'Performing the Nation-State: Rebel Groups and Symbolic Processes', in A. Arjona, N. Kasfir and Z. Mampilly (eds.), *Rebel Governance* (New York: Cambridge University Press, forthcoming).

[55] This paragraph is largely drawn from K. Hoffmann, 'Myths Set in Motion: The Governance Practices of General Padiri's Maï-Maï Militia' in ibid.

Reflective of their indigenous appeals, the organization sought to legitimize its governance system by positioning Padiri as a mythico-religious figure and emphasizing its position as the defender of certain cosmological beliefs and practices. The effect of this positioning, according to Hoffmann, served 'to legitimize the group and induce civilians to comply with its orders'.[56]

One of the more interesting cases in the Democratic Republic of the Congo was that of the FAPC.[57] Based out of the northeastern towns of Aru and Ariwara along the Ugandan border, the organization seemingly controlled an ideal area for generating resources through smuggling and control of lucrative customs points. Instead of operating as a racketeering organization as a political-economy approach might predict, the group worked closely with non-State actors including powerful local trading networks to establish a semblance of social order within areas under its control. Titeca points out that this was necessary for a variety of reasons, including the reality that insurgent groups rarely have the expertise necessary to monetize natural resources without civilian cooperation. Tellingly, the FAPC territory even became a magnet for internally displaced civilians fleeing violence in neighbouring areas.

8.2. The RCD's governance system

In order to illustrate these dynamics more closely, the final section discusses[58] the behaviour of the RCD, the longest lasting of the many Congolese insurgencies, which controlled the largest population and territory during the war. As a reformist insurgency with a weak political wing plagued by multiple and often brutal internecine conflicts and operating within a rentier State characterized by multiple and competing nodes of power, the RCD was not particularly well suited to develop an effective governance system. Still, there is value in closely examining this case as it sheds light on the diverse factors that shape civilian governance outcomes.

The RCD emerged as one of several militant groups occupying vast portions of eastern Congo in the late 1990s. The organization attempted

[56] Ibid.

[57] K. Titeca, 'Access to Resources and Predictability in Armed Rebellion: The FAPC's Short-lived "Monaco" in Eastern Congo' (2011) 46 *Africa Spectrum* 2.

[58] This section is drawn from the chapter on the Democratic Republic of the Congo published in Mampilly, *Rebel Rulers*, above note 2.

to fight a conventional war with Kinshasa, building up a large army and holding a huge territorial enclave along the eastern border of the country in the Kivu provinces. During its reign, the organization failed to maintain security or provide public welfare goods to the civilian population. However, it is not true, as is often claimed, that the RCD cared little about civilian governance. Rather, multiple efforts to develop a system of governance consistently came up short, and the organization suffered a deep crisis of legitimacy as a result.

Most commentators tend to view the RCD and its offshoots harshly for their oppressive and frequent use of force against civilians under their control. But to characterize the behaviour of the rebels as driven solely by the engine of violence ignores their sustained attempts to address the extraordinarily complex political situation within the large territory they controlled. Focused on the capital Kinshasa but forced to confront a tangled political environment in the eastern provinces, the RCD made discernible efforts to forge a political hierarchy using a variety of strategies. These attempts may all be judged failures, but in their failure, they shed light on the strategies available to reformist insurgencies operating in conditions where the political authority is unclear, the population is non-supportive and even hostile, infrastructure is minimal, inter-ethnic tensions are high and involvement from the international community is either malicious, illicit or inconsequential.

In order to understand the trajectory of the RCD's civilian governance project, it must be situated within a broader narrative of neglect that characterized relations between the centre and the periphery since Mobutu. After the 1996 war first broke out, State retraction accelerated, leaving behind a multiplicity of diverse institutional arrangements that the RCD was forced to interact with – either by coercing these actors into submission or finding other ways to co-opt them. The failure of the rebellion's governance project resulted from the command's inability to negotiate with this alternate political and economic configuration. Instead, the insurgent organization too often resorted to coercion to subdue those who challenged its rule. I argue that three factors help explain this failure. First, the rebel leadership did not address concerns about the ethnic and national affiliation of the rebellion. Second, the command was unable to resolve internal tensions between different factions that undermined its ability to implement a coherent political agenda. And finally, focused on Kinshasa and reliant on foreign markets and governments for revenue, the leaders struggled to develop the local expertise required to achieve hegemony over territory far from the capital.

Two weeks after the start of the second Congo war in August 1998, the political wing of the RCD was formed in Goma.[59] Initially unified under Ernest Wamba dia Wamba, an exiled Congolese academic, at the helm, the RCD was really a collection of different factions.[60] Wamba dia Wamba was the most prominent member of a group of academics and exiles that became involved in the political wing, most with roots in other provinces outside of the Kivus. A second group comprised former cabinet ministers and army officers from the Mobutu regime who were anxious to return to power. Finally, a third group included leaders who participated in the first war, but had been marginalized by Laurent Kabila.

To accommodate the diversity of interests represented by its constituent factions and to prevent the emergence of a dominant figure, the new rebel command was organized with a consensus-based collective leadership. A complex political structure including a presidency, general assembly, political council and an executive council was established with close to 200 members split between the various branches. This arrangement led to internal disputes between the different structures and undermined Wamba dia Wamba's command over the RCD, eventually leading to the formation of multiple power centres.[61] In addition, Uganda and Rwanda preferred to deal with different factions, leading to a split early in the life of the rebel command. The stalemate produced by the entry of Angola and Zimbabwe into the conflict brought these internal divisions to the fore.

The academically oriented faction did initially go to great lengths to tout its adherence to an extended programme of peasant mobilization. However, the weakness of the political wing within the command meant that the more militarist component quickly came to the fore. Structures to generate civilian participation were never developed, demonstrating the relative lack of concern for popular support. The command also had notoriously poor control over its troops, and reports of civilian abuse were widespread. The organization's initial struggles to establish a governance system reflect these inadequacies.

[59] O. Afoaku, 'Congo's Rebels: Their Origins, Motivations and Strategies', in J. F. Clark (ed.), *The African Stakes of the Congo War* (New York: Palgrave Macmillan, 2002), 109–28.

[60] S. Kayunga, 'The Leadership Crisis within the Congolese Rally for Democracy (RCD) and Its Implications for the Peace Process in the Democratic Republic of Congo' (paper presented at the Conference on Conflict and Peace-Making in the Great Lakes Region, Entebbe, Uganda, July 10–12, 2000).

[61] Ibid.

As the war dragged on, the RCD command faced severe internal challenges to its control that led to multiple splits, as well as challenges from other violent militant groups, including those led by former RCD leaders. Internal challenges undermined the ability of the organization to develop its civilian governance system, constantly concerned, as it was, with putting down these inner revolts. Internal divisions within the command also tended to percolate throughout the organization, reducing the ability of the dominant faction to implement a single political agenda and maintain organizational discipline. At the same time, external rivals sought to legitimate their existence by expressing empathy with civilian discontent. This led the RCD-Goma, the reconstituted entity, to devote more and more resources to its military wing for the purpose of suppressing such challenges.

From the outbreak of hostilities in 1998, the leaders of the insurgency were ill prepared to handle the demands of establishing a governance system over the areas they controlled. Aspirations to portray the rebel command as a government-in-waiting were hindered by their failure to comprehend the harsh political environment they confronted upon taking power. Instead, the ensuing stalemate forced insurgent leaders to reluctantly face up to the reality of being little more than a localized rebellion with limited territory and extremely difficult relationships with its own public. In the words of the RCD Vice President Arthur Zahidi Ngoma: 'We hadn't realized that we would have to set up what is more or less a government so fast, but it's an obligation now'.[62] After the leadership split, these inadequacies became even more exposed, as those figures who had thought the most about civilian governance left the dominant faction, the RCD-Goma.

Perceptions and reality concerning the RCD-Goma diverge around the contentious subject of how the organization treated local residents of the Kivus during the conflict. Horrendous violence has come to typify the Congolese conflicts, and rough estimates for the number of war-related deaths ranges between 2 million and 6 million – a strikingly high number considering the short duration of the conflict, though it is impossible to place an exact number on the organization's share of the dead. Throughout the country, 2.3 million Congolese were internally displaced with the

[62] BBC Monitoring 1998, cited in D. Tull, 'The Reconfiguration of Political Order in Postcolonial Africa: A Case Study from North Kivu (DR Congo)' (PhD thesis, University of Hamburg, 2004), at 133.

two provinces of North and South Kivu that the RCD-Goma controlled accounting for 1 million of these. Over 400,000 Congolese also found refuge in neighbouring countries.[63] Although a startling indictment of the violence, these figures also represent the culmination of a gradual process of decline and disorder that began much earlier. Rather than representing a fundamental disjuncture, rebel rule over the Kivus reflects a high degree of continuity between the degraded pre-conflict State institutions and forms of political order that emerged in the absence of the State.[64]

The RCD sought to impose order over its territory through a variety of strategies, none of which succeeded. There were a number of reasons for this, largely related to the organization's reliance on international relationships. By providing the nascent insurgency easy access to weaponry and other military resources, Rwanda and Uganda undercut the need for a prolonged period of popular mobilization. Instead, pro-Rwandan forces in the leadership advocated for a quick military victory. It was assumed that challenges to insurgent rule could be contained through coercive means alone, a strategy whose weaknesses were demonstrated after the entry of foreign powers led to a military stalemate.

But reliance on Rwandan State patronage and intra-regional trade networks are not the sole reason for the failure of the RCD's governance project. Once the invasion stalled, a variety of actors operating from within rebel territory directly challenged the insurgents, driven by a xenophobic hostility to the organization's perceived Rwandan taint.[65] Even genuine efforts by the insurgents to develop governance structures ran into complications due to the complex political landscape the group was forced to navigate. Thus, viewing the insurgency's behaviour as warlordism is insufficient. Failure to implement political order is different than promoting disorder. And while the insurgents certainly contributed to the chaos, their minimalist approach to governance did comprise two discernible goals that were in line with the command's own agenda. First, they sought to limit violent challenges to their rule and reduce other sources of disorder within the territory they controlled. And second, they sought to co-opt pre-existing administrative structures, either by

[63] S. Autesserre, 'Local Violence, International Indifference? Post-Conflict "Settlement" in the Eastern D.R. Congo (2003–2005)' (PhD thesis, New York University, 2006), at 71.

[64] Tull, 'The Reconfiguration', above note 62, at 8.

[65] T. Longman, 'The Complex Reasons for Rwanda's Engagement in Congo', in Clark (ed.), *The African Stakes*, above note 59, 129–44.

replacing local administrators with rebel sympathizers or inducing local actors to support their agenda, through coercion or material benefits.

The diminution of the State under Mobutu and the emergence of an alternate political order prior to the war required the rebel leadership to develop relationships with a constellation of distinct local political actors, including the remnants of the State, private trading networks and civil society actors like churches, traditional authorities, aid organizations and human rights activists. Initially, the RCD attempted to take charge of the pre-existing bureaucratic institutions still operating in the east. Higher-ranking positions including provincial governorships were generally given to rebel loyalists. Personnel were often drawn from members of the Congolese Tutsi community, hence reinforcing the perception that the insurgency was a foreign-backed proxy of the local Rwandophone community.[66] But more often, local administrative positions were left in the hands of the same bureaucrats who manned those positions prior to the outbreak of the conflict, as long as they did not challenge the insurgency's military agenda.[67] Personnel from foreign aid organizations who had worked with both the Mobutu regime and the rebel civil administration testified that in the initial months after the invasion, the insurgents sought to reinvigorate State institutions and use them as a basis for their own governance system, with some success.

Eventually, the command recognized that these former State structures were incapable of being resuscitated, serving only as sources of patronage for local elites. Resources generated through the trade in natural resources or from foreign patrons might have productively been directed towards reviving the civil administration. However, their purpose was never to improve civilian livelihoods, but rather to pay for military expenses or line the pockets of individuals within the rebel organization. Instead, as with the situation prior to the war, bureaucrats operating in the rebel-controlled Kivus were left to their own devices to raise revenue through extraction from the local population.

Recognising the inadequacy of relying on the defunct State bureaucracy, the command sought to expand its governance project by working to co-opt the real sources of political order in the region. In the Kivus, this meant reaching out to civil society actors, including the churches, NGOs

[66] G. Prunier, 'The Catholic Church and the Kivu Conflict' (2001) 31 *Journal of Religion in Africa* 139, at 157.

[67] Tull, 'The Reconfiguration', above note 62, at 134.

engaged in human rights and developmental work, traditional authorities and unions. As discussed earlier, Mobutu's rule had created opportunities for these non-State actors to emerge as significant players in the region's social, political and economic life. Their centrality to the daily functioning of civilian life in the provinces was further bolstered in 1994 following the Rwandan genocide when huge amounts of international money flowed into the region to alleviate the refugee crisis.[68]

Following the outbreak of conflict, ethnicity came to play an increasingly important role in the realm of civil society. Civil society leaders tended to resist efforts by the rebels to support the insurgent political programme and openly challenged the group's control of the region. Community leaders that I spoke to in Bukavu openly condemned the rebels, portraying the RCD as a tool of Tutsi domination and expressing harsh, stereotypical views about the broader Tutsi community in the region.[69] The rebels fared better in Goma, the capital of North Kivu, as the Rwandophone community constituted a much higher percentage of the overall population than Bukavu. Indeed, this favourable population composition helped the RCD administrators to integrate their governance efforts with local civil society actors who were more sympathetic to the struggle of the Congolese Hutu and Tutsi communities. Below, I describe in greater detail rebel negotiations over civilian governance issues with a variety of societal actors, some of whom became supporters, though many others were competitors to the rebel government.

At the forefront of all civil society actors were various religious institutions, especially the Catholic Church. The Church's prominence in eastern Congo has roots in the colonial era when it was a favoured partner of the Belgian colonial regime. Under Mobutu, the relationship between Church leaders and the central government was often contentious. But the weakness of the Congolese State allowed the Church to emerge as a powerful social and economic force in many parts of the country. Often organized into an elaborate structure with multiple technical departments, churches filled in for the absence of State authority in providing public goods such as health, education and other developmental services.[70] Churches from all denominations were also the most

[68] H. Romkema, 'An Analysis of the Civil Society and Peace-Building Prospects in the North and South Kivu Provinces, Democratic Republic of Congo' (Bukavu DR Congo: Life & Peace Institute, 2001), at 36.

[69] Longman, 'The Complex Reasons', above note 65.

[70] Prunier, 'The Catholic Church', above note 66, at 156.

important employers in the region with each provincial office often hiring hundreds or thousands of salaried employees.[71]

Recognising that the churches were a potential rival centre of power, the rebel command initially hoped to co-opt church leaders into its governance efforts.[72] The fact that several prominent church leaders (Monsignors) in and around Goma were of Rwandophone descent gave the group some initial success and led many to question the loyalties of the churches.[73] However, the churches were also divided. And other Monsignors were more supportive of indigenous groups, including the powerful leaders of the Catholic Church in Bukavu, generally considered the 'most important site of resistance [to rebel rule] in South Kivu', in the words of one aid official who worked in the region at the time. In fact, the ethnic sympathies of Christian leaders often came to the fore when they discussed their opinion of the RCD-Goma, and several prominent church leaders, including the powerful Monsignor Monsengwo Pasinya of Kisangani, a leading figure of the anti-Mobutu opposition, openly attacked the insurgency in a variety of national and international forums.

The command's awkward attempts to pressure religious leaders into supporting the insurgency's governance project not only failed to co-opt these institutions but also exacerbated civilian resentment for what was rightly perceived as meddling by the insurgents. In response, the organization was forced to extricate itself from interference in the affairs of the churches, thereby returning them to the position they occupied prior to the conflict – that is, a source of social and economic stability with an antagonistic relationship to the local political authority – in this case, the RCD government.

The rebellion had more success with their attempts at co-opting 'tribal' authorities in the East. *Bami* (or traditional chiefs) were empowered throughout Congo's history by State authorities seeking to project their dominion across the country. Bami were thus habituated to accommodating a wide variety of political regimes that came to power in Kinshasa. Indeed, in regional capitals like Goma and Bukavu, Bami often found ways to manipulate the political authority to bring greater material benefits to their constituents. Insurgent leaders adopted the Mobutuist strategy of inducing cooperation among the traditional authorities through a mix

[71] Tull, 'The Reconfiguration', above note 62, at 253.

[72] Human Rights Watch, 'Eastern Congo Ravaged: Killing Civilians and Silencing Protest', at 12 (3A) (New York: Human Rights Watch, May 2000).

[73] Romkema, 'An Analysis of the Civil Society', above note 68, at 44.

of coercion and material incentives. Bami served a number of functions for the rebel leadership, including raising material support and recruits for the rebels and helping the group extend its authority into remote rural areas. They also helped collect information on other armed groups operating in the Kivus.[74] Thus, claiming their support was an important strategy for the insurgent leaders. To this end, in September 2001, the organization held an Inter-Kivutien Dialogue with an agenda of forcing traditional leaders to recognize its authority. During this meeting, a number of Bami were forcibly recruited into the rebel group.[75]

In cases where the Bami proved more recalcitrant, the insurgents would interfere in chiefly succession disputes with the intention of installing more sympathetic leaders. Unlike the Church, which could always call on transnational networks to publicize any harassment by the rebel army, traditional authorities had only two options for refusing the organization's overtures: they could either flee the area or resist violently. Many chose the latter option, especially those representing autochthonous groups, often forming alliances with the Mai-Mai militias in the region to challenge rebel rule, frequently with considerable success.[76]

The insurgency's attempts to forcibly co-opt societal actors extended to the ethnicized realm of NGOs. The organization early on saw the value of winning over personnel from the Kivus's dynamic civil society sector, hoping to piggyback off their significant influence in the urban areas. In both North and South Kivu, the organization relied on a familiar mix of sticks and carrots to induce support, or, at the least, to limit the challenge such actors could pose. It is important to distinguish between two categories of NGOs operating in the Kivus. On the one hand, there were the local branches of international humanitarian organizations engaged in relief and development work, such as World Vision and Médecins Sans Frontières (MSF), the presence of which escalated significantly following the migration of Rwandan Hutus to the region in 1994.[77] On the other hand were human rights organizations such as the Pole Institute in Goma or Héritiers de la Justice and the Initiative Congolaise pour la Justice et

[74] Tull, 'The Reconfiguration', above note 62, at 145–47.

[75] P. Englebert, 'Why Congo Persists: Globalization, Sovereignty, and the Violent Reproduction of a Weak State' (Queen Elizabeth House Working Paper No. 95, Oxford University, 2003).

[76] S. Jackson, 'Sons of Which Soil? The Language and Politics of Autochthony in Eastern D.R. Congo' (2006) 49 *African Studies Review* 95.

[77] S. K. Lischer, *Dangerous Sanctuaries: Refugee Camps, Civil Wars, and the Dilemmas of Humanitarian Aid* (Ithaca: Cornell University Press, 2005).

la Paix in Bukavu, which worked alongside international organizations like Human Rights Watch and had engaged in peace and democracy work in the region prior to the outbreak of conflict. Mirroring their respective positions vis-à-vis the debate on political neutrality, organizations that engaged in relief and development work had a more congenial relationship with the rebels than groups advocating human rights, whose personnel were often targeted for harassment.

Staff from relief and development organizations described their relationship with the insurgent civil administration as cordial, though they were aware of the politicized nature of their interactions and were accustomed to bribing the rebels with cash or other material items.[78] The insurgent command recognized the benefits of attracting such NGOs to their territory. For example, in a 2001 interview, the RCD-Goma Minister for Territorial Administration, Joseph Mudumbi, proclaimed: 'In our area, humanitarian agencies have always been free to work... We are doing what we can to facilitate the agencies because our people need help'.[79] Such organizations were expected to provide details to the rebellion about the work they intended to do so that the civil administration could regulate their behaviour.[80]

Informants related to me the ways in which the insurgents sought to channel aid to communities perceived as sympathetic to the insurgent cause, granting operating permission to NGOs only if they were willing to direct aid to these areas. Consistent with this logic, the rebel government did not hesitate to place restrictions on aid organizations operating in areas sympathetic to its perceived competitors, such as areas under the control of various Mai-Mai militias. However, in order to avoid accusations of favouritism and in order to maintain the façade that the civil administration was pro-development, the rebels would not restrict aid groups openly. Rather, they had a number of strategies to subvert their work. For example, noncompliant organizations would frequently be targeted with strategic checkpoints designed to impede mobility to certain areas. Or the rebels would simply refuse to provide security to areas perceived as non-supportive. More threateningly, the insurgency would

78 UN, 'Final Report of the Panel of Experts on the Illegal Exploitation of Natural Resources and Other Forms of Wealth of the Democratic Republic of the Congo' (New York: United Nations, 2002).

79 D. Gough, 'Congo War Blamed for 2 1/2 Million Deaths', *San Francisco Chronicle*, 5 May 2001.

80 Human Rights Watch, 'Eastern Congo Ravaged', above note 72.

engage in anonymous raids of aid resources that could not be traced back to a rebel cadre.

The relationship between human rights organizations and the rebellion exhibited considerably less congeniality. The leadership was acutely aware of the importance of these organizations in shaping opinions about the RCD-Goma in the international arena. Furthermore, many advocacy groups were actively tied into transnational human rights networks that sought to document the behaviour of the insurgency in ways that the command accurately assessed to be detrimental to its image.[81] Therefore, within areas clearly under its control, the organization often sought to restrict the activities of human rights activists. The insurgent command put into place travel restrictions on personnel from local advocacy groups in order to limit their interaction with colleagues in the West. This limited the fundraising and advocacy activities of local activists, both locally and abroad.[82] The insurgents also attempted to avoid perpetrating violence openly in urban areas under its control, preferring instead to use coercion away from the international spotlight, mostly in rural areas where human rights activists, both local and international, were less likely to go.

The NGO world was divided ethnically, and certain organizations did overtly align with the rebel leadership. This was more common in North Kivu where the demographic strength of the Rwandophone community meant that local Tutsis commonly played a role within various civil society organizations. In South Kivu, the demographic weakness of the Banyamulenge community allowed hostile civil society organizations to largely exclude the RCD-Goma from making inroads.

Considering the convoluted nature of the RCD-Goma's civilian governance efforts, it is hard to draw clear lines between the insurgency and the provision of even minimal services in the Kivus during the war. From the emergence of a second rebellion in 1998 to the official end of the war in 2002, when control of several non-strategic public services passed back to the central government in Kinshasa,[83] the organization did develop a civil administration divided between specific departments of education, health, social affairs and so on. Other departments such as taxation, security and immigration remained under rebel control even after the 2002 agreement. Ultimately, education and healthcare remained the preserve of religious and charitable institutions with little involvement from

[81] Romkema, 'An Analysis of the Civil Society', above note 68.
[82] Human Rights Watch, 'Eastern Congo Ravaged', above note 72.
[83] Autesserre, 'Local Violence', above note 63, at 123.

the insurgent government. More successfully, the insurgency did provide some degree of public order by working with traditional authorities and religious institutions to engage in a number of conflict reduction efforts.

9. Conclusion

How can international humanitarian law be leveraged to improve insurgent civilian governance efforts? Deeper engagement up to and including limited recognition of insurgent governance systems should be considered by those concerned with improving the welfare of populations trapped within contemporary conflict zones. However, as discussed in the framework, efforts to engage are particularly fraught as human rights interventions may have both positive and negative effects on civilian welfare. As challengers to the rebel claim of representing civilian interests, insurgencies may view international humanitarian law advocates as competitors in the war for hearts and minds and respond negatively. More positively, rebellions that make efforts to ensure civilian welfare by providing effective civilian governance appreciate and even solicit the attention of human rights actors for their initiatives. For example, encouraged by human rights advocates, the National Transitional Council in Libya publicly embraced the Geneva Conventions – an action that provided a mechanism by which to hold the organization accountable to international humanitarian law.

Not every or even most insurgencies warrant engagement or recognition. A deeper understanding of the civilian governance systems of rebel organizations is thus an important starting point for disaggregating those that deserve attention from those that are beyond the pale. In this context, the behaviour of Congolese insurgent groups regarding civilian governance is especially instructive due to the widespread vision of these groups as particularly heinous examples of warlordism. As the above discussion demonstrates, many of these groups did make sustained attempts to deal with governance issues, efforts that may have proved more effective with the right inducements from international actors.

Intervening effectively requires that human rights advocates adopt an independent position vis-à-vis non-State armed groups and enter into domestic conflicts with nuance and sophistication, conditions that have yet to be realized. The challenge is that while international humanitarian law is an evolving concern, it has yet to truly disconnect itself from the interests of States. And States are unlikely to appreciate the value (in terms of civilian welfare) of granting recognition to certain insurgents that meet a minimum threshold of civilian governance. The reality is that States, concerned with empowering domestic rivals, are unlikely to support – and are likely to actively prevent – efforts to extend even minimal advantages to insurgent organizations. Formally engaging rebel governance systems as a mechanism for ensuring civilian welfare would grant them the opportunity to openly engage with international society in ways that State governments have been loath to do and may actively resist. Still, advocates of international humanitarian law should centre civilian welfare as their primary focus and motivating force, even if they may find themselves caught uncomfortably between resentful State governments and opportunistic rebellions seeking to leverage their international relationships as a result.

4

The power of persuasion

The role of international non-governmental organizations in engaging armed groups

ULRICH SCHNECKENER AND CLAUDIA HOFMANN*

1. Introduction

Non-State armed groups shape the environment during and after armed conflict in many ways: they are responsible for violence against unarmed civilians, thus breaching international humanitarian law, and can facilitate the establishment of criminal and informal economies typically seen in post-war societies. However, they also may see themselves as representing distinct interests within the populace and may build on their broad support. Non-State armed actors – such as rebel groups, militias, warlords, clan chiefs, terrorists, criminals and mercenaries – can disturb, undermine or completely truncate State- and peace-building processes, leading to further violence that affects the efforts of humanitarian aid workers, representatives of governments and peacekeepers. Non-State armed actors can be defined as actors who are willing and able to use violence to pursue their objectives; are not integrated into formalized State institutions, such as regular armies, presidential guards, police or special forces; possess a certain degree of autonomy with regard to politics, military operations, resources and infrastructure; and have an organizational structure (unlike spontaneous riots). The definition encompasses both politically and ideologically motivated groups as well as profit-oriented actors (such as criminals or mercenaries).[1]

* This chapter is based on a research project funded by the German Foundation for Peace Research (DSF). See also U. Schneckener, *Zwischen Vermittlung und Normdiffusion. Möglichkeiten und Grenzen internationaler NGOs im Umgang mit nicht-staatlichen Gewaltakteuren* (Osnabrück: Forschung DSF Forschung, No. 35, 2013).

1 U. Schneckener, 'Spoilers or Governance Actors? Engaging Armed Non-State Groups in Areas of Limited Statehood' (SFB Working Paper No. 21, Berlin, October 2009), at 8–9.

A number of strategies have been employed by the international community when dealing with non-State armed actors, ranging from counterinsurgency and containment to negotiation and mediation to integration and co-optation.[2] However, these approaches reveal that State-actors, such as the affected government and third countries involved in the conflict, still have difficulties in dealing with non-State armed actors.[3] These difficulties are often based on States' commitments to international treaties, the decisions of the UN Security Council, diplomatic customs between sovereign States and other political considerations, such as the fear of legitimizing armed actors. International non-governmental organizations (INGOs) and private individuals – such as elder statesmen, influential persons and retired high officials – command more freedom and flexibility to contact armed groups or respond to their requests. In the conflict resolution literature, the assumption is often made that INGOs generally benefit from their reputation as non-partisan and independent actors. This puts them in the unique position of being able to act as an interlocutor and facilitator for certain issues and to communicate with non-State armed actors independent of political or diplomatic considerations.

Two approaches in particular have been employed by such specialized INGOs in engaging armed actors: *mediation* and *norm diffusion*. The first approach aims at the facilitation of dialogue and negotiations between conflicting parties as well as at peace processes through different forms of mediation and mediation support. The focus is on reducing violence, establishing ceasefires and peace agreements and assuring their sustainable implementation. INGOs in this field concentrate mainly on methods of unofficial diplomacy by linking Track I and Track II approaches and also on capacity building in order to strengthen conflict resolution skills. The second approach – norm diffusion – has

[2] See U. Schneckener, 'Dealing with Armed Non-State Actors in State- and Peacebuilding: Types and Strategies', in W. Benedek, C. Daase and P. van Dyne (eds.), *Transnational Terrorism, Organized Crime and Peacebuilding* (London: Palgrave, 2010), at 229–48; V. Dudouet, 'Mediating Peace with Proscribed Armed Groups' (Special Report No. 239, United States Institute of Peace, Washington, DC, 2010); C. Hofmann and U. Schneckener, How to Engage Armed Groups? Reviewing Options and Strategies for Third Parties (2011) 4 *Sicherheit und Frieden* 254.

[3] S. Sivakumaran, 'Implementing Humanitarian Norms through non-State Armed Groups', Chapter 6, in this volume, at 146; J. Willms, 'Courts of Armed Groups – a Tool for Inducing Higher Compliance with International Humanitarian Law', Chapter 7, in this volume, at 179–80; C. Hofmann, 'Engaging Non-State Armed Groups in Humanitarian Action' (2006) 13 *International Peacekeeping* 396.

worked on improving the dissemination of and general adherence to international norms among armed groups with the goal of persuading them to adapt and change their behaviour accordingly. Norm diffusion approaches employ different forms of strategic communication as well as capacity-building measures and knowledge transfer as means to alter and, eventually, to end violent behaviour.

Both approaches have a number of characteristics in common. They are norm-based and norm-oriented, that is, they refer to fundamental principles and norms in order to persuade conflicting parties either to stop violence and engage in a peace process (by mediation) or to respect humanitarian and human rights norms, which in turn will affect the way they use violence in a conflict. In both instances, specialized INGOs use similar strategies in engaging armed groups, such as social influence, dialogue, strategic argumentation, aspects of bargaining (about concrete issues or procedures), capacity building and knowledge transfer, monitoring as well as (public) naming and shaming (in cases of non-compliance or violations of norms). Given the nature of INGOs, both types of activity rely mainly on the 'power of persuasion'. INGOs may persuade armed groups to accept mediation efforts or humanitarian norms. Most often, these persuasion processes involve several rounds of talks and debates, the establishment of personal contacts, flexible arrangements, anticipation of the agenda and the interests of armed groups and long-term engagement.

This chapter analyses the approaches of international civil society organizations in mediating conflicts with and communicating international norms to non-State armed actors. It elaborates on the different methods as well as the basic favourable conditions for success of the approaches to evaluate the strengths and limits of INGOs in dealing with non-State armed actors. The chapter examines the Centre for Humanitarian Dialogue and the Carter Center regarding their work in mediation and mediation support and the International Committee of the Red Cross (ICRC)[4] and Geneva Call regarding their efforts towards the diffusion of international norms among armed groups.[5] It finds

[4] Legally, the ICRC is a private association formed under the Swiss Civil Code. Internationally, however, the ICRC enjoys the status of a legal entity under international humanitarian law and is, therefore, different from conventional INGOs.

[5] Detailed insight into the workings of the INGOs was gained during several rounds of interviews with representatives of the Centre for Humanitarian Dialogue, the Carter Center, Geneva Call and the ICRC in 2009 and 2010. Furthermore, first generalizations and findings were discussed with representatives of these INGOs as well as with academics and other experts in the field during a workshop on 4–5 March 2010 at the German Institute for International and Security Affairs (SWP) in Berlin, Germany.

that under specific circumstances, armed actors can be open-minded regarding international norms, especially if they are striving to become political actors governed by normative behaviour and are willing to be judged by this behaviour. This creates new avenues for internal and external actors when interacting with armed actors.

2. Mediation and mediation support: Centre for Humanitarian Dialogue and Carter Center

INGOs, active in the field of mediation and mediation support, are in close contact with the parties to a conflict, be it in an official or an unofficial role, with a view to facilitating, mediating and negotiating peace processes between them. They choose between two distinct roles as they engage either as direct mediators between the parties to the conflict or as support for an official mediator giving advice and logistical support and executing supplementary tasks. Accordingly, they are often involved in informal pre-negotiations, the preparation of non-papers and the direct mediation with armed actors during and after conflict. Their engagement in conflict resolution often rests on the assumption that in conflict, any kind of dialogue based on humanitarian principles is constructive and benefits a political agreement now or in the future. INGOs also assume that the initiatives of private organizations and individuals – such as elder statesmen, former high-ranking officials or prominent civil society activists – have the capacity to support official negotiations now or in the future.

In this field of activity, INGOs have a range of options at their disposal. For instance, they may offer 'good offices' (their reputation and connections to high-level diplomats and politicians) for the creation of dialogue and discussion, formally as well as informally. They can mobilize humanitarian, diplomatic and political reactions to such dialogue in order to increase the pressure on the parties to a conflict as well as the benefit they may gain from talks. They support the parties to the conflict with expertise on technical questions and facilitate support from specialized organizations, for example, with regard to mine clearance, project-specific financial support and logistical support. They recommend courses of action for decision-makers in the region as well as donors and intervening governments and carry out strategic planning for effective intervention. They support the education of local civil society organizations and the general public in the active and constructive participation in a peace process. They carry out monitoring and appraisals of the State of the conflict transformation. A long-term engagement with influential persons in the conflict in particular allows INGOs to capture specific indicators and early warning signs with regard to the conflict process, as well as fact-finding trips and verification missions. Through a combination of these efforts, INGOs attempt to loosen the hardened lines of conflict and achieve progress towards an agreement and resolution.[6]

Examples of the activities of the Centre for Humanitarian Dialogue and the Carter Center illustrate the achievements as well as the shortcomings and limitations of such approaches. Both INGOs offer 'good offices' and dialogue in view of supporting a mediation and negotiation process between armed groups and governments and, if promising, act as direct mediators in these processes.

The Centre for Humanitarian Dialogue, founded in August 1999, is a Swiss non-governmental organization that offers high-level mediation services and mediation support to State and non-State actors involved in international conflicts and disputes. Its aim is to 'reduce the consequences of the conflict, improve security and ultimately contribute to the conflict's peaceful resolution' through third-party mediation, driven by humanitarian values.[7] The activities of the Centre may be as diverse as the facilitation of informal talks between belligerents and the facilitation, negotiation and implementation of internationally monitored ceasefire agreements, assisting with the inclusion of representatives of non-State armed actors into a political opposition and a political process (in collaboration with the national United Nations Peace-building Office, among others). Moreover, the Centre's activities include offering good offices and technical assistance and providing opportunities for dialogue

[6] On the rationale as well as technique on formal conflict resolution, mediation and negotiation, see J. Bercovitch (ed.), *Studies in International Mediation. Essays in Honor of Jeffrey Z. Rubin* (London: Palgrave Macmillan Ltd., 2002); L. A. Dunn and L. Kriesberg, 'Mediating Intermediaries. Expanding Roles of Transnational Organisations', in Bercovitch (ed.), *Studies in International Mediation*, this note, at 194–212; S. Touval and I. W. Zartman (eds.), *International Mediation in Theory and Practice* (Boulder, CO: Westview Press, 1985). For a discussion of conflict resolution approaches of INGOs in particular, see T. Debiel and M. Sticht, *Towards a New Profile? Development, Humanitarian and Conflict-Resolution INGOs in the Age of Globalization* (Duisburg: Institut für Entwicklung und Frieden, 2005).

[7] C. Buchanan and J. Chávez, 'Guns and Violence in the El Salvador Peace Negotiations', Centre for Humanitarian Dialogue, Country Study No. 3 (London, March 2008), at 2, www.hdcentre.org/uploads/tx_news/84GunsandViolenceintheElSalvadorPeaceNegotiations.pdf.

with belligerents on humanitarian issues and attempting to create an environment conducive to inclusive dialogue, reform and the increase of humanitarian efforts. In its mediation support activities, the Centre for Humanitarian Dialogue assists mediation processes by other actors in armed conflicts. In cases where other mediators or facilitators are already involved, embedded or successful, the Centre for Humanitarian Dialogue offers advice, staff and logistical support; it shares its experience in the mediation sector, assists in developing new approaches to the respective issues and produces publications where the constraints of a mediator's confidentiality allow it to do so. An important element of its operational work is the Oslo Forum, a network of prominent mediators founded 2003 and organized by the Centre for Humanitarian Dialogue and the Norwegian Foreign Ministry. The Oslo Forum aims at increasing the international reputation and status of mediation procedures. Participants meet once a year to exchange their views and experiences in an informal setting.[8]

The aim of an involvement of the Centre for Humanitarian Dialogue is the reduction or ending of violence and the demobilization of the armed actors involved in the conflict. Beyond the provision of immediate security, the Centre aims at tackling process-related political issues in order to sustain any renunciation of violence. It attempts to balance the divide between the warring parties by offering advice as well as access to actors outside of the conflict to armed groups, who may find themselves in a novel situation and lack valuable connections to the political arena. Such actors may not be aware of political proceedings and may use the Centre for Humanitarian Dialogue as a source of information and knowledge, especially when operating in great secrecy. A starting point for the Centre's engagement is usually the reference to humanitarian aspects – in particular, improving the protection of civilians in conflict. When initiating contact with conflict actors, be they governments or armed groups, the Centre for Humanitarian Dialogue presents itself as a 'humanitarian actor' which aims at dialogue – and later at mediation – primarily on humanitarian issues, such as better access to the suffering population (see Darfur between 2008 and 2010) or brokering a ceasefire (see Aceh between 1999 and 2003). This approach is based on the conviction that dialogue 'literally humanises conflict' and that '[d]ialogue does not confer legitimacy, compromise principles or strategic interests, or presumes any

[8] Participants are, inter alia, prominent figures such as Martti Ahtisaari, Kofi Annan, Betty Bigombe, Lakdar Brahimi, Thabo Mbeki, Luis Moreno-Ocampo and Gareth Evans.

outcome'.[9] Also, as one interview partner pointed out, the Centre for Humanitarian Dialogue assumes that 'who talked once, will talk again'.

The Centre's own mediation work is well illustrated by its engagement with the Free Aceh Movement (Gerakan Aceh Merdeka) in Aceh, Indonesia (1999–2003). In late 1999, factors in internal Indonesian politics had led to a situation that weakened hardliners within the government and the Free Aceh Movement, creating circumstances under which mediation became an option for the parties.[10] The involvement of a small, relatively unknown organization such as Centre for Humanitarian Dialogue, coming from a country with a neutral reputation, seemed promising for bringing new commitment into the process, while keeping the issue an internal affair as much as possible. The Centre for Humanitarian Dialogue had established good contacts with the highest levels of Indonesian politics, communicating 'the organization's interest in Aceh, its ability to act in a facilitative role and its desire to submit a formal written proposal for the ways it could help with dialogue'.[11] As a result, '[i]n November 1999 Indonesia's President, Abdurrahman Wahid, suggested to the Centre for Humanitarian Dialogue that they work to solve the conflict in Aceh'.[12] Due to the novelty as well as internal fragility of the plan to find a solution with the Free Aceh Movement, the Centre agreed to maintain a low profile with only a minimum of expatriate staff on the ground and pledged to merely facilitate rather than mediate or arbitrate.[13] By 2000, the Centre for Humanitarian Dialogue had established an ongoing dialogue between the government of Indonesia and the Free Aceh Movement in the format of joint meetings in Switzerland as well as in Aceh, with no more than three expatriates from the Centre in Aceh at one time. In May 2000, the parties to the conflict signed an understanding for a three-month humanitarian

9 Centre for Humanitarian Dialogue, *Annual Report 2010* (Geneva, 2011), at 12; M. Griffiths and T. Whitfield, *Mediation Ten Years On. Challenges and Opportunities for Peacemaking* (Geneva: Centre for Humanitarian Dialogue, 2010), at 18.

10 The military was weakened by the secession of Timor-Leste, and the emergence of information on military atrocities against Timor-Leste and the Free Aceh Movement was politically weakened by the support of a referendum by the Acehnese civil society. See F. Heiduk, *Staateszerfall als Herrschaftsstrategie: Indonesien zwischen Desintegration und Demokratisierungsblockade am Beispiel des Aceh-Konflikts* (Baden-Baden: Nomos, 2010), at 91.

11 K. Huber, 'The Centre for Humanitarian Dialogue in Aceh: Promises and Pitfalls of INGO Mediation and Implementation' (2004) 9 *Policy Studies* 20.

12 T. Kivimäki and D. Gorman, *Non-Governmental Actors in Peace Processes: The Case of Aceh* (Geneva: Centre for Humanitarian Dialogue, 2008), at 8.

13 Ibid. 9.

pause in Aceh, which allowed for the secure delivery of humanitarian assistance to the local population. The pause came into effect on 2 June 2000, was renewed for another three months in September and ended in November 2000. It was followed by a return of violence between the military and the Free Aceh Movement in March 2001. Nevertheless, the dialogue was continued, and a number of joint committees between the government and the Free Aceh Movement, with representatives of the two parties, remained functional. In early 2001, the Centre realized that the role of a third party in the process would have to change from facilitation to mediation, which surpassed the capabilities of the INGO. As a response to the new demands, the Centre for Humanitarian Dialogue introduced a number of internationally known mediation advisors (or 'wise men') to the process.[14] They attended all future talks in Aceh and Jakarta on behalf of the Centre for Humanitarian Dialogue. Additionally, the 'Gang of Four' – consisting of the European Union, the Norwegian government, the United States and the World Bank – began to get involved in the process led by the Centre for Humanitarian Dialogue in the same year, which changed the Centre's involvement in the process as its efforts were now supported by representatives of the international community. In December 2002, the parties to the conflict signed a Cessation of Hostilities Agreement in Geneva, which provided for the establishment of a tripartite monitoring mission to oversee its implementation. Under the auspices of the Centre for Humanitarian Dialogue, the government of Indonesia permitted fifty active international military monitors from Norway, Thailand and the Philippines to oversee the monitoring mission. However, disagreements between the government and the Free Aceh Movement increased over subsequent months (especially over the issue of demilitarization), and a meeting in Tokyo in May 2003 of the Joint Council, the highest dispute resolution mechanism of the process, failed to resolve the issues. For instance, it remained unclear whether giving up arms by the Free Aceh Movement took precedence over the withdrawal of Indonesian troops and special forces, which areas in Aceh should be transformed into peace zones and what would be the specifics of the democratic elections envisaged for 2004. This lack of precision led to a delay in implementation, which was seen as a breach of the Agreement by the Indonesian government and used by the

[14] The team of mediation advisors consisted of Harvard Senior Fellow William Ury, retired US General Anthony Zinni, former Foreign Minister of Yugoslavia Budimir Loncar, former Foreign Minister of Thailand Surin Pitsuan, British Parliamentarian Lord Eric Avebury and Hurst Hannum, Professor of International Law at the Fletcher School, Tufts University.

Free Aceh Movement to build para-governmental structures in rural areas in Aceh.[15] The situation escalated further, and martial law was declared in Aceh shortly after the end of the Tokyo meeting. With the start of a military offensive, all international and local staff members were relieved of their official duties, and the Centre's engagement in Aceh ended.

Despite the ultimate failure of the agreement between the Free Aceh Movement and the Indonesian government, the Centre for Humanitarian Dialogue contributed to a resolution of the conflict in Aceh in two distinct ways. First, it started a process of dialogue and negotiation between two parties that were gridlocked for a long period before the engagement. Second, it opened the door for international intervention and demonstrated the opportunities and possibilities that such intervention could provide. Arguably, both contributions enabled much of the peace process that finally took place in 2004 after a deadly tsunami struck the country. The final peace talks were again facilitated by an INGO – this time the Finnish Crisis Management Initiative (CMI) under the leadership of former Finnish President Martti Ahtisaari – and resulted in the signing of a final peace agreement in August 2005. Under the agreement, Aceh received a special autonomy status, and government troops withdrew from the country in exchange for Free Aceh Movement's disarmament. Arguably, while the Centre's engagement did not result in an enduring cessation of hostilities, it created a history of negotiation and dialogue between the parties to the conflict as well as formal structures and previous agreements that renewed negotiations could build on.[16]

The Carter Center was founded in 1982 in Atlanta, Georgia, by former US President Jimmy Carter as a policy research centre in close connection with Emory University in Atlanta. The Center's largest programme with most of the personal and financial resources focuses on health and the fight against viral illnesses, such as Guinea worm disease, trachoma and river blindness. In its conflict resolution work, it aims at being a peace broker based on the assumption that neutral and independent INGOs are able to gain access, build relationships and offer mediation services in situations where formal actors, such as governments and international organizations, are not necessarily welcome.[17] In these situations, the Carter Center offers an alternative channel for dialogue as well as

[15] Heiduk, *Staateszerfall als Herrschaftsstrategie*, above note 10, at 95–96.

[16] Centre for Humanitarian Dialogue, Annual Report 2010, at 16, www.hdcentre.org/uploads/tx_news/15AnnualReport2010.pdf.

[17] The Carter Center, 'Resolving Conflicts, at 1, www.cartercenter.org/resources/pdfs/factsheets/conflicts-facts.pdf.

Table 4.1 *Centre for Humanitarian Dialogue: basic information*

Headquarter:	Geneva, Switzerland
Field Offices:	Singapore and Nairobi (regional offices)
Founded in:	August 1999
Mission:	Generating favourable conditions 'for the creation of a universal and multi-sectoral dialogue on humanitarian issues', improving the understanding of crises and conflicts and processing the practical experience in the field
Executive Director:	David Harland
Staff:	Approx. 20 in Geneva, approx. 70 worldwide
Key funders:	Approx. 25 different donors, including Norway, Switzerland, Sweden, the Netherlands, the European Union, Australia, Belgium, Canada, Denmark, Germany, Ireland, Liechtenstein, Singapore, the United Kingdom, the Open Society Institute, the Third Millennium Foundation and the Rockefellers Brothers Fund.
Budget:	20 million Swiss francs (in 2012)

assistance to warring parties by offering dispute resolution where other official and traditional mechanisms are unavailable or have failed. The Carter Center operates at the State level and above many other INGOs in the field. The involvement of former US President Jimmy Carter secures direct access to the level of heads of States and other high-level decision-makers in all relevant sections necessary for a conflict resolution process, such as foreign and defence ministers. It is, therefore, located influentially between countries' official diplomacy and unofficial peace-building efforts (semi-official mediation).

The Carter Center's work is guided by five general principles, which have an impact on its mediation efforts.[18] First, the Center emphasizes timely actions and results based on careful research and analysis. Second, the Center only engages in situations where there is no other effective engagement by others in order to avoid a duplication of efforts. Third, it recognizes the possibility of failure as an 'acceptable risk'. Fourth, it strives to remain impartial and neutral in its dispute resolution activities. And fifth, the Center believes in building capacities and knowledge transfer in order to improve the lives of peoples. These principles have

[18] The Carter Center, *Annual Report 2012–13*, at 1, www.cartercenter.org/resources/pdfs/news/annual_reports/annual-report-13.pdf.

been introduced to minimize the danger of being instrumentalized and generally from selecting an unsuitable mediation approach for a given conflict situation. According to the Carter Center, it aims at adapting to different circumstances in the field and uses different strategies for engagement dependent on the nature of the conflict itself.

Most important, based on prior consultations, the official mediation starts with an invitation in which all parties declare that they are committed to the process. This invitation is an important aspect of Carter's engagement since it constitutes a moral obligation for the parties not to undermine the process or to instrumentalize it for their own interests. If this is still the case, the Carter Center can point to the invitation and threaten to publicly blame the spoiling behaviour of one or both sides. As a rule, the mediation will be conducted by Carter personally, supported by a small team. Accordingly, the approach is very much shaped by the personality and experiences of Jimmy Carter. The former US president usually starts with a personal statement in which he reminds the parties of their moral responsibility for peace and human rights. His authority and reputation as a prominent and well-respected mediator allow him to guide the negotiations in a particular direction in order to achieve results. If an agreement is signed, the INGO will support the implementation process, including renewed negotiations, if necessary. In case of failure, the Carter Center will end its mission and will make that known to the public internationally. However, in the case of many States, such as Sudan, Uganda and the Middle East, the contact between Carter and leading actors may remain in place and can be revived for mediation if the situation changes.

The Carter Center mediates in conflicts between governments (for instance, in Bosnia and Herzegovina, Haiti and the Korean Peninsula in 1994 and the Great Lakes region in 1995) and supports regional mediators (for instance, the Economic Community of West African States (ECOWAS) in Liberia, 1991–1997), and, in a more basic approach, it aims at strengthening democratic foundations (for instance, in Nepal since 2004)[19] and advancing human rights, conflict prevention and

19 The Carter Center's engagement in Nepal presents an exception to the rule as it is the only project that resulted from the Center's own initiative. A staff member and later senior UN official prepared the project as a desk study to begin with. In 2004, the Center then approached royal and government officials and representatives from other national organizations to discuss viable solutions for conflicts and opportunities for mediation. Because the relevant decision-makers were not receptive to a possible mediation, however, the project transformed into a democracy-focused project.

reforms through trainings and workshops. Moreover, it mediates directly between States and non-State armed actors, as seen in its engagement with the Sudan People's Liberation Army/Movement (SPLA/M) and the Lord's Resistance Army (LRA) between 1989 and 2003.

Shortly after Omar al-Bashir's military coup in Sudan, Jimmy Carter attempted to mediate between Bashir and the SPLA/M, which sought to establish a democratic Sudan, with it (the SPLA/M) as the leading party in control of the southern areas. Although talks were broken off after only five days because of the imposition of Sharia and emergency laws, Carter remained in close personal contact with the leaders of the parties to the conflict. In 1995, Carter re-attempted to conduct mediation between the parties to the conflict and this time achieved a ceasefire that would allow health workers to access areas in which the Guinea worm disease and river blindness were endemic. This mediation had been comparatively straightforward as John Garang, leader of the SPLA/M, held a quasi-legitimate status within the United States, and, thus, meetings in Sudan as well as in the United States could take place relatively often, making communication comparatively easy. The ceasefire lasted for six months, and Carter and the Center had hoped that the ceasefire would lead to official peace talks resuming between the government of Sudan and the SPLA/M. Although this did not happen, Carter was invited back into the country in 1999 and was asked to mediate talks and assist in restoring diplomatic relations between Sudan and Uganda. Relations had previously been broken off because of Sudan's alleged support for the LRA, a sectarian religious and military group that has sought to overthrow the Ugandan government. However, due to unreliable and slow communication between the Carter Center and LRA leader Joseph Kony and a failed confidence-building measure resulting from this (an arrangement had been made for Kony to meet with his parents), Kony soon refused to actively partake in any mediation process. Overall, he participated in only three meetings with the Center but sent high-ranking officials in other cases. A large number of meetings with Kony had to be cancelled, and he proved to be an unreliable mediation partner. Generally, Northern Uganda was an unfortunate environment for high-level mediation because secrecy is very highly valued by the parties, which made arrangements for meetings more difficult. The entire mediation process relied on individuals taking risks when conveying messages. In response to this challenge, and anticipating any possible misuse, the Carter Center provided Kony with a telephone that could only dial specific numbers, but communication did not improve. Garang of the SPLA/M, who had been in close contact with President Museveni of Uganda rather than with the Carter Center, had altogether failed to respond to Carter's invitation to participate in the mediation process at this point. Accordingly, pre-negotiations as well as the mediation led by Jimmy Carter himself took place only between representatives of Sudan and Uganda and eventually the presidents of both countries, Al-Bashir and Museveni, respectively.[20] The relatively formal type and setting for the negotiations that the Carter Center offers, as well as an understanding of what could be gained through these negotiations, corresponded more directly to the two governments than with the leaderships of the armed groups.[21] Nevertheless, the Carter Center kept trying to initiate dialogue between the government of Uganda and the LRA. In their efforts, the Center cooperated with representatives of the United Nations Children's Fund (UNICEF), Uganda's Acholi community and the governments of Sudan, Uganda, Canada, Egypt and Libya.[22] Finally, in 2003, the Center decided to cease its efforts, concluding that no progress could be made in the current constellation.

Overall, the examples of the Centre for Humanitarian Dialogue and the Carter Center reveal the flexibility that INGOs dispose of when engaging conflict parties and armed groups. As small organizations, they are able to react quickly to requests from all sides with regard to meeting times, locations and format. It is also easier and more straightforward for INGOs – compared to large States' or international organizations' bureaucratic apparatuses – to keep the negotiations and aspects thereof

[20] The Nairobi Agreement, between the presidents of Sudan and Uganda, was reached within a day of the Center talking to both presidents, recording the mutual commitment of the parties to stop supporting forces against each other's governments and to re-establish full diplomatic relations between them. The Carter Center was asked to remain engaged and oversee the implementation process. It did so by convening various ministerial and security meetings to explain and re-negotiate smaller issues.

[21] Talks with the SPLA/M were taken up again in 2002, when Carter met in Rumbek in southwestern Sudan with President Al-Bashir in Khartoum and SPLA/M leaders, primarily SPLM Deputy Chairman and key negotiator for the South, Salva Kiir. Shortly after this visit, Garang also met with President Carter for further talks in Atlanta. However, by this time, a peace initiative led by the Intergovernmental Authority on Development (IGAD), begun in 1994 and supported by partners and a consortium of donor countries (including the United States), had become the focus of the peace process for both the government in Khartoum and the SPLA/M by 2002, so that Carter did not become directly involved. The negotiations, conducted by General Lazarus Sumbeiywo from Kenya, eventually led to the 2005 Comprehensive Peace Agreement (CPA) between the government of Sudan and the SPLA/M in Naivasha, Kenya, and did not involve any participation from Carter or the Center. See also The Carter Center, 'Africa Trip Report: March 2002' (2 March 2002), www.cartercenter.org/news/documents/doc449.html.

[22] The Carter Center, 'Uganda' (2010), cartercenter.org/countries/uganda.html.

Table 4.2 *Carter Center: basic information*

Headquarter:	Atlanta, Georgia, United States
Field Offices:	Subject to the Center's project work they change accordingly
Founded in:	1982
Mission:	Mediating conflicts and facilitating dialogue with the aim to ease tensions; assisting regional organizations in building conflict resolution capacities; and seeking to make a contribution to implementing peace agreements
President and CEO:	Amb. (Ret.) Mary Ann Peters
Staff:	175 employees in total, but only a dozen are associated with the Conflict Resolution Program
Key funders:	United States Agency for International Development (USAID); the UK Department for International Development (DfID); the governments of Norway, Sweden and the Netherlands; other governmental and multi-lateral actors, and corporations.
Budget:	198.1 million USD of total contributions and grants (in 2012/13), approx. 5% are related to the Conflict Resolution Program

secret. The same benefit may result from the personal and often individual relationships between the INGOs and the parties to a conflict. A case in point is the participation of Jimmy Carter in the negotiations. The clout that he delivers as a private individual allows him to push negotiations. And even during the negotiations themselves, INGOs may demonstrate more flexibility in dealing with certain issues at hand, identifying creative solutions and assisting in the realizations of the solutions with little delay. Both examples highlight the normative dimension of INGO's approaches in mediation and mediation support. The Centre for Humanitarian Dialogue as well as the Carter Center do not only act on specific norms, rules and principles, but they also aim at promoting international humanitarian or human rights norms in order to establish a basis for further dialogue. Particularly with regard to Jimmy Carter, this norm-based approach is further strengthened by a strong personal commitment and reputation.

3. Norm diffusion: ICRC and Geneva Call

INGOs and civil society organizations, which are active in the norm diffusion field, campaign primarily for the adherence to and diffusion of international humanitarian norms, such as universal human rights and the ban on landmines. They demand their anchoring as behavioural standards in international politics and the strengthening of international humanitarian law. They engage armed troops, police and security forces as well as non-State armed actors often over a long period of time to increase the knowledge about existing norms among them. Additionally, they observe their implementation through monitoring and verification processes.

INGOs' approach disposes of three distinct behavioural and implementation mechanisms in particular for which they often rely on the support of other local, regional and international organizations and which are usually interconnected: social pressure, persuasion and negotiation.[23] First, INGOs may exert social pressure on the relevant actors by challenging their conduct and increasing the support for international norms among the international community. In case of a violation of an international norm, INGOs often publish this knowledge internationally in an attempt to pressure third-party actors into denouncing the perpetrator and threatening isolation from the international community – for example, through the suspension of diplomatic, military and economic cooperation and, in the case of non-State armed actors, an increase of sanctions against them. The INGOs sampled here will decide strategically when to use their knowledge to pressure armed groups and when the retention of trust is more promising to their cause.[24] At the same time, INGOs increase incentives for an adherence to international norms by arguing that a change of behaviour will increase the acceptance and status of the actors and strengthen their image internationally. Second, INGOs interact with armed actors directly and make arguments with regard to content for the adherence to international norms. In campaigns, workshops and facilitated meetings with experts, INGOs publicize their 'better arguments' and illustrate different avenues of action. Third, INGOs bargain with armed groups using incentives such as technical support (for example, with regard to demining, explosive ordnance disposal, mine risk education and victim assistance) that will be accessible to them once they

[23] For the role of human rights INGOs in norm diffusion and socialization regarding State actors, see T. Risse, K. Sikkink and S. C. Ropp (eds.), *The Power of Human Rights: International Norms and Domestic Change* (Cambridge: Cambridge University Press, 1999); T. Risse, A. Jetschke and H. P. Schmitz, *Die Macht der Menschenrechte* (Baden-Baden: Nomos, 2002).

[24] The ICRC is a noted exception in this area, since, by principle, it will not make violations public so as to maintain the trust that it has with the armed group.

have subscribed to the norm in question. Two prominent organizations active in the norm diffusion field, the ICRC and Geneva Call, illustrate this approach.[25]

When the ICRC was founded as a civil organization in 1863 by Henry Dunant, its main concern was to bring relief to wounded soldiers on the battlefield and develop international treaties that would protect the wounded as well as the medical personnel assisting them. These principles still represent the foundation for the ICRC's work, though its scope has expanded considerably. The ICRC's specific mandate is anchored in the 1949 Geneva Conventions and the 1977 Additional Protocols, in which the organization is given specific rights and tasks during and after armed conflict, such as visiting prisoners of war, supplying food and other necessities for the civilian population, reuniting families and searching for missing persons. Furthermore, according to the Statutes of the International Red Cross and Red Crescent Movement, the ICRC also must 'work for the understanding and dissemination of knowledge of international humanitarian law applicable in armed conflicts and to prepare any development thereof'.[26] Legally, the ICRC is a private association formed under the Swiss civil code; the ICRC's Assembly is composed of a maximum of twenty-five Swiss citizens. Internationally, however, the ICRC enjoys the status of a legal entity under international humanitarian law and is, therefore, different from conventional INGOs. Accordingly, the organization possesses certain privileges – such as exemptions from taxes and customs – similar to those of other international organizations. Most important, however, are the ICRC's immunities and its right not to disclose evidence to international criminal tribunals and the International Criminal Court.

The ICRC strongly values impartiality, neutrality and independence and thus does not distinguish between State and non-State conflict actors systematically or normatively. In practice, this means that the ICRC seeks out direct contact with State and non-State armed actors, independent

[25] See in more detail C. Hofmann and U. Schneckener, 'NGOs and Nonstate Armed Actors: Improving Compliance with International Norms' (United States Institute of Peace Special Report No. 284, Washington, DC: United States Institute of Peace, 2011); C. Hofmann and U. Schneckener, 'Verhaltensänderung durch Normdiffusion? Die Ansätze von IKRK und Geneva Call im Umgang mit bewaffneten Gruppen' (2010) 85 *Die Friedens-Warte – Journal of International Peace and Organization* 73.

[26] See Article 4.1(g) of the Statutes of the International Red Cross and Red Crescent Movement (3 October 2013), www.icrc.org/eng/resources/documents/misc/icrc-statutes-080503.htm.

of whether they fight on the side of or against the government and offers each the same services. At the time of writing, the ICRC is engaged with more than 100 non-State armed actors in about thirty countries, concentrating particularly on the provisions encoded in Common Article 3 of the Geneva Conventions. Article 3 concerns the humane treatment of all persons in enemy hands; the prohibition of murder, mutilation and torture as well as cruel, humiliating and degrading treatment; and the taking of hostages and unfair trials.[27] The ICRC employs two mechanisms to increase respect for international humanitarian law in armed conflicts: formally expressing commitment to humanitarian norms and gradually implementing them. Ideally, these mechanisms are mutually supportive, and, practically, they are often pursued in parallel.

First, a range of legal tools give all actors in a conflict an opportunity to make an express commitment to international humanitarian norms. This not only instils the armed actor's leadership with a sense of self-determination and responsibility but also circumvents their feeling not to be bound by international law when they are neither involved in its creation nor allowed to sign the relevant international treaty. An express commitment may contain new legal obligations that go beyond the existing provisions (i.e., a constitutive agreement) or restate law that is already binding in non-international conflict (i.e., a declaratory agreement). In 1992, the parties to the conflict in Bosnia and Herzegovina concluded a declaratory agreement vowing respect for the provisions of Common Article 3 of the Geneva Conventions and adding provisions regulating the protection of the wounded, sick and shipwrecked; of hospitals and medical units; and of the civilian population. Similar agreements were made in Yemen in 1962 and Nigeria in 1967. Constitutive agreements were concluded with the government of El Salvador and the Frente Farabundo Martí para la Liberación Nacional (FMLN) in 1990 and between the government of the Philippines and the National Democratic Front of the Philippines (NDFP) in 1998, accepting human rights norms that went beyond the commitments of Common Article 3 of the Geneva Conventions and Additional Protocol II.

Unilateral declarations give armed actors another opportunity to express commitment to international humanitarian norms and human rights independent from any other party. In September 1987, the

[27] ICRC, *Integrating the Law* (Geneva: ICRC, 2007). See also L. Zegveld, *The Accountability of Armed Opposition Groups in International Law* (Cambridge: Cambridge University Press, 2002).

Coordinadora Guerrillera Simón Bolívar (CGSB), a short-lived umbrella organization of rebel groups in Colombia, declared its intention to respect international humanitarian norms. In 1991 and 1996, the ICRC received declarations from the National Democratic Front of the Philippines (NDFP). Such agreements have also been part of ceasefire or peace agreements. The 2002, ceasefire agreement between the government of Angola and the União Nacional para a Independência Total de Angola (UNITA) contained an additional section that guaranteed the halting of all force movements in the reinforcement or occupation of new military positions. The ceasefire agreement between the government of the Democratic Socialist Republic of Sri Lanka and the Liberation Tigers of Tamil Eelam (LTTE), also in 2002, included an additional Article on protecting the population against hostile acts, such as torture, intimidation, abduction, extortion and harassment.

The second mechanism represents the main part of the ICRC's concept. It follows the premise that, if violations are to be avoided, rules and regulations need to become an integral part of the behaviour of armed actors in military operations. Generally, the process begins by disseminating information about existing humanitarian regulations, as it cannot be assumed that armed actors have comprehensive knowledge of international law or its implications for their operations. Subsequent work addresses four dimensions in particular: doctrine, education and training, equipment and effective sanctions. Ideally, changes in these four dimensions are mutually reinforcing so that the entire process is a comprehensive approach requiring continual and long-term interaction with an armed actor, accounting for the time the actor needs to execute and implement all necessary organizational changes. To influence behaviour, international humanitarian norms have to become a common and integral part of an actor's doctrine. And for this to happen, the humanitarian norms have to be incorporated into all directives, procedures, rules of behaviour and handbooks concerning the training, terminology and decision-making processes of fighters – strategically and tactically. Special handbooks need to be compiled that speak to the relevant levels and specializations of the armed organization, such as different levels of command or fighters in populated areas. Even if no systematic curriculum exists, non-State armed actors have some form of educational system that at least covers weapons training, which can be used for humanitarian purposes. Additionally, the ICRC offers training courses for teachers, trainers and legal advisors of non-State armed actors. The highest level of command must equip fighters to minimize or avoid violations of international humanitarian norms, and the ICRC can inspect future combatants during training to determine whether they are equipped in accordance with the provisions of international humanitarian law. During these training situations, the ICRC also aims at demonstrating to fighters the effects their weapons have on civilian victims. Finally, the ICRC stresses that sanctions within the group itself must not violate international law and human rights: while commanders must be able to discipline fighters, especially to punish violations of rules and regulations, sanctions must be applied consistently and reasonably to demonstrate the earnestness of the leadership and their commitment to international humanitarian norms.

Independent from which particular engagement strategy is used for a particular armed actor, the ICRC focuses on strategic argumentation.[28] To be effective, discussions and dissemination sessions with armed actors must be adapted according to the motivations and interests of the actors. They need to explain why it is in the actors' best interests to adhere to international humanitarian law. The ICRC has pursued several lines of argument in the past. First, adhering to international humanitarian law might improve actors' reputations on the international and local levels and among their allies and constituency. Additionally, the actor may gain the moral high ground that could lead to political gains. Second, if an actor develops a reputation for treating prisoners of war well, people might surrender to it more easily. Third, while reciprocity is not necessary for international humanitarian law to apply, it is more likely that the other side will treat the actors' members well after taking them prisoner if it sees the actors treating their prisoners in a similar manner. Fourth, violations of international humanitarian law may be disadvantageous in the long run, in damage to an actor's reputation, loss of support, or ostracism by the population. By the same logic, compliance might benefit the actor. Adherence to international humanitarian norms also may help facilitate post-conflict reconciliation. Fifth, international humanitarian norms may preserve military interests; they were originally developed by military commanders, accounting for the balance between military needs and humanity. It is not only more humane, but also in the commander's interest to have well-disciplined troops and a functioning command structure. Sixth, the adherence to international humanitarian law may save resources, especially in keeping infrastructure intact. Finally, recent developments in the prosecution of violations of international law

[28] ICRC, *Increasing Respect for International Humanitarian Law in Non-International Armed Conflicts* (Geneva: ICRC, 2008), at 30–31.

Table 4.3 *ICRC: basic information*

Headquarter:	Geneva, Switzerland
Field Offices:	Engages non-State armed groups in approx. 30 countries
Founded in:	1863, internationally mandated by the 1949 Geneva Conventions and their Additional Protocols
Mission:	Takes measures to ensure respect for, promote, reaffirm and even clarify and develop international humanitarian law
President:	Peter Maurer
Staff:	10,100 local employees, 1,600 specialized staff and delegates and around 940 staff at the Geneva headquarters (in 2013)
Key funders:	States parties to the Geneva Conventions, national Red Cross and Red Crescent Societies, supranational organizations, funds from private sources and income from securities
Budget:	1,234.0 million Swiss Francs (in 2013), including 1.045.1 million Swiss Francs for field activities

occurring during conflict, such as setting up of the International Criminal Tribunal for Yugoslavia (ICTY), the International Criminal Tribunal for Rwanda (ICTR) and the International Criminal Court (ICC), have strengthened the international legal framework, making prosecution of violations more likely.

Whether the aforementioned mechanisms and arguments succeed in changing armed actors' behaviour depends mostly on whether the ICRC is granted access to actors' leadership and whether this contact can be maintained over a longer period of time. The ICRC's approach to armed actors is top down, relying on the cooperation of both political and military leadership. In its efforts, however, the ICRC is supported by its distinct status and reputation as a neutral humanitarian organization that engages non-State armed actors in the same way it engages State actors regarding their obligations under international humanitarian law. All weapon bearers are subject to the same normative demands. This transparency awards the ICRC with an exceptional credibility; at the same time, this credibility must be reaffirmed in each individual case through the personal interactions of ICRC delegates.

Geneva Call, founded in 2002, directly engages non-State armed actors to increase adherence to humanitarian norms, particularly concerning international humanitarian law and international human rights law. The INGO currently addresses three issues: adherence to the universal anti-personnel mine ban, respect for children in armed conflict and respect for the rights of women in conflict. The bulk of Geneva Call's work, however, focuses on landmines, specifically in territories that non-State armed actors control. Many non-State armed actors maintain anti-personnel landmines as a part of their standard arsenal due to their low cost, availability, uncomplicated production and simple use. Actors manufacture, trade, sell and use landmines to advance their goals. Today, more than seventy States are believed to be mine-affected; in the past ten years, landmines, explosive remnants of war (ERW) and victim-activated improvised explosive devices (IED) have caused approximately 74,000 casualties. An inquiry conducted in 2006 found that forty non-State armed actors in at least seven countries reportedly used landmines between 2003 and 2005.[29] Experts estimate that 10 to 40 percent of landmines fail to explode as intended, and then remain active and make access to certain areas highly dangerous. Landmines used by non-State armed actors in particular tend to be first-generation mines without activity limits, possibly remaining active for decades. Landmines can impede a country's development for multiple generations; simultaneously, they impair the non-State armed actor by killing and maiming its own fighters, restricting troop movements and diminishing support that they might otherwise enjoy from the affected population.

The 1997 Convention on the Prohibition of the Use, Stockpiling, Production and Transfer of Anti-Personnel Mines and on their Destruction – otherwise known as the Ottawa Treaty – internationally regulates the use of landmines. Non-State actors did not participate in the negotiation process and are not eligible to sign the international treaty for lack of appropriate status. They are subject to the provisions of the Ottawa Treaty if their home State is a signatory party, but in practice, they often do not know about their responsibilities regarding the landmines ban and do not feel bound by them because they did not expressly agree to the provisions. Without the active inclusion and assistance of non-State armed actors, however, the landmines problem is not being addressed in its entirety. For this reason, Geneva Call aims to persuade armed actors to change their behaviour and respect the international landmines ban. To this end, it has designed an innovative mechanism that allows

[29] International Campaign to Ban Landmines (ICBL), *Landmine Monitor Report 2009: Toward a Mine-Free World, Annual Report* (Ottawa: Mines Action Canada, 2009), www.the-monitor.org/lm/2009/res/Landmines_Report_2009.pdf; A. Sjöberg, *Armed Non-State Actors and Landmines: A Global Report Profiling NSAs and their Use, Acquisition, Production, Transfer and Stockpiling of Landmines* (Geneva: Geneva Call, 2006), vol. I.

armed actors to commit to the norms of the Ottawa Treaty by signing the Deed of Commitment for Adherence to a Total Ban on Anti-Personnel Mines and for Cooperation in Mine Action between Geneva Call and the armed actor. The mechanism attempts to balance the shortcomings of international law by offering a parallel process for non-State armed actors that enables them to actively enter a formal commitment to the ban of anti-personnel landmines. Under the Deed, the armed actor agrees to several conditions: first, to acknowledge the norm of a total ban on anti-personnel landmines established by the 1997 Ottawa Treaty; second, to adhere to a total ban of anti-personnel landmines, which includes the complete prohibition of all use, development, production, acquisition, stockpiling, retention and transfer of mines; third, to cooperate in and undertake stockpile destruction, mine clearance, victim assistance, mine awareness and various other forms of mine action; fourth, to allow and cooperate in the monitoring and verification of the commitment, which entails visits and inspections by Geneva Call and other independent international and national organizations, as well as the provision of necessary information to those organizations; and fifth, to issue the necessary orders and directives to commanders and fighters, including measures for information dissemination, training and disciplinary sanctions.

Additionally, Article 6 of the Deed explains that signing the Deed does not alter the legal status of the non-State armed actor, pursuant to Common Article 3 of the Geneva Conventions. The Deed itself is most commonly seen as a unilateral declaration by the armed actor, with Geneva Call and the government of the Republic and Canton of Geneva serving as witnesses. It is signed by an individual representing and acting in the name of the armed actor, often in the historic Alabama Room at the Hôtel-de-Ville in Geneva, where the Geneva Convention was signed in 1864.

Geneva Call currently engages approximately sixty armed actors. Until the end of 2013, forty-three armed actors from sixteen different countries have signed the Deed – seventeen groups from Somalia alone and six from Myanmar. The others are from Burundi, India, Iran, Iraq, the Philippines, Sudan, Turkey and Western Sahara.[30] Several other actors have not signed the Deed but have pledged to prohibit or limit the use of anti-personnel landmines, either through individual unilateral declarations or as a part of a ceasefire agreement with the government. Still others have undertaken

[30] See Geneva Call, *Landmine Ban*, www.genevacall.org/how-we-work/armed-non-state actors/.

mine clearance and victim assistance in areas under their control. The government of Somaliland refuses to sign the Deed because it considers itself to be a State and aspires to sign the Ottawa Treaty instead.

In most cases, the armed actors have already begun mine clearings and other action. Geneva Call supports the implementation of the Deed and monitors the progress made. In 2008, the INGO facilitated technical assistance through specialized organizations to destroy stockpiles held by two signatory groups in Western Sahara and Somalia. Two other signatories in Burundi and Sudan reported to Geneva Call the complete destruction of their stockpiles after having joined the respective government; a signatory in the Republic of Myanmar/Burma reported clearing all of its landmines and mine components; one signatory reported a stockpile located in Northern Iraq as destroyed. In Somalia, Geneva Call arranged for the assistance of a specialized organization to undertake explosive ordnance disposal (EOD) and to provide emergency support to mine victims. Additionally, Geneva Call organized workshops and mine risk education (MRE) seminars and surveys in areas under signatories' control in cooperation with partner organizations.

Geneva Call establishes contact with non-State armed actors in three possible ways. The first way is by direct contact, for the purpose of a dialogue on landmines, as with the Mouvement des Nigériens pour la Justice (MNJ), the Partiya Karkerên Kurdistan (PKK), the Partîya Demokrata Kurdistan (PDK), the Patriotic Union of Kurdistan (PUK) and Al Houtis in Yemen. Second, contact has been facilitated indirectly through third parties, most commonly through local NGOs or civil society groups but also through other non-State armed actors, as occurred with the Mouvement des Forces Démocratiques de Casamance (MFDC), Palipehutu-FNL in Burundi, the Ejército de Liberación Nacional (ELN) in Colombia, the Liberation Tigers of Tamil Eelam (LTTE) in Sri Lanka and the Partiya Jiyana Azad a Kurdistanê (PJAK). Third, some actors have contacted Geneva Call directly to begin a dialogue on anti-personnel landmines after having heard of Geneva Call's initiative, as did Chin National Front in Burma. Geneva Call does not begin a dialogue with an armed actor until it has thoroughly analysed the group's character, aims, leadership, internal structure, past practices and the like; assessed the dynamics of conflict and other factors, such as the capabilities of the armed actor and their assumed commitment, to assure maximum security; considered the probability of success; and developed the right arguments that persuade the particular non-State armed actor to give up landmines and adhere to a total ban. According to Geneva Call, armed actors are willing to sign and commit to the Deed for several reasons. These include improving the quality of life in the territory controlled by them, enabling mine action programmes and protecting their constituency; improving political stability; confirming for itself that it is respected as an organization and taken seriously by an international (non-governmental) actor, coming from an internationally highly respected country (i.e., the Swiss factor); demonstrating the ability to uphold the principles of international humanitarian law and, consequently, aspiring to gain international reputation and respect; and accepting the relatively limited military utility of anti-personnel mines, which may indiscriminately wound, maim and kill enemies, their constituencies and their own fighters and harm their military capacity.

To follow up allegations of Deed violations, Geneva Call has developed a monitoring mechanism that can, in practice, be difficult to employ, as the parties to a conflict may actually not have an interest in verifying claims. This is true for armed actors as well as governments if allegations are only made to discredit the opposition internationally. Monitoring, therefore, may involve self-reporting and progress reports (e.g., the Polisario Front), evaluation through local INGOs and civil society (e.g., PKK in Turkey) and following up on accusations (e.g., Moro Islamic Liberation Front in the Philippines). In practice, this method may not be entirely satisfying and convincing (see, e.g., Puntland, Somalia and the Philippines). Geneva Call maintains, however, that most non-State armed actors abide by the core of the prohibitions on the use, production, acquisition and transfer of landmines. Armed groups are also undertaking demining, stockpile destruction, mine risk education and victim assistance, and they often collaborate with specialized humanitarian organizations for this purpose. Moreover, their decisions to abstain from using landmines have in the past facilitated the accession of States to the 1997 Ottawa Treaty, as social pressure on the State government built up once a local non-State armed actor had signed the Deed of Commitment. This happened in Sudan after the signature of the Sudan People's Liberation Movement/Army (SPLA/M) and in Iraq after the accession of the Kurdistan Democratic Party (KDP) and regional governments led by the Patriotic Union of Kurdistan (PUK). Although not a party to the Ottawa Treaty, Morocco submitted a voluntary report to Geneva Call and invited the organization in 2008 to form recommendations for the government after Geneva Call had engaged the rebel movement Polisario Front (Western Sahara) successfully in 2005.[31]

[31] Geneva Call, *Annual Report 2008* (Geneva: Geneva Call, 2008), at 17, www.genevacall.org/resources/annual-reports/f-annual-reports/2001--2010/gc-annual-report-2008.pdf.

Table 4.4 *Geneva Call: basic information*

Headquarter:	Geneva, Switzerland
Founded in:	2000
Mission:	Engaging armed non-State actors to comply with the norms of international humanitarian law and human rights law
President:	Elisabeth Decrey Warner
Staff:	Approx. 25
Key funders:	Swiss Federal Department of Foreign Affairs (Political Division IV), the Swedish International Development Cooperation Agency (SIDA), the Republic and Canton of Geneva, the Australian Agency for International Development (AusAID), the British Department for International Development (DfID) and the European Commission
Budget:	3.59 million Swiss Francs (in 2013)

Efforts to ban landmines have a strong technical dimension, as armed actors often need more information to avoid mistakes when handling and disposing of these weapons. Unlike the ICRC, Geneva Call does not have special status; it depends on host governments to at least tolerate its activities. But even if governments attempt to obstruct Geneva Call's efforts and refuse to give access to territory controlled by the armed actors, even State actors have an interest in controlling and containing anti-personnel landmines. They are equally affected and responsible for protecting civilians. In recent years, Geneva Call aimed at transferring its particular approach to other thematic issues. Since 2010, the NGO has launched two new initiatives: first, a Deed of Commitment for the Protection of Children from the Effects of Armed Conflict (signed by nine armed groups by the end of 2013) and, second, a Deed of Commitment for the Prohibition of Sexual Violence in Situations of Armed Conflicts and Towards the Elimination of Gender Discrimination (signed by four armed groups by the end of 2013).

The contributions that both norm diffusion INGOs make is a dissemination and proliferation regarding international humanitarian and human rights law in general and the universalization of a mine ban in particular, by means of persuasion. Geneva Call's focus on a single issue makes mutual consent as well as the armed actor's concessions less complicated compared to dialogue concerning multiple issues, such as in a peace process. Concurrently, as the agreement is less complex because it is focused on a single issue, the access to armed actors is more straightforward. The goal Geneva Call pursues is clear, and it can be communicated in this way to non-State armed actors. In comparison, the ICRC's dialogue with armed groups attempts to – argumentatively – explain and disseminate all norms entailed in international humanitarian law and human rights law. If it has the 'better arguments', armed actors (in theory) will be persuaded to accept these norms as normatively 'right' and change their behaviour accordingly. This implies that the ICRC and to some extent also Geneva Call need to take into account the tactical and strategic considerations of the armed group and reflect on the overall military situation in which the group is acting.[32]

Yet, both approaches are not without limits, particularly if the armed actor emphasizes other priorities and preferences as being superior to the norms of international law. Both approaches are, therefore, very much dependent on the cooperation of the leadership of the non-State armed group. Therefore, if the armed actor sees anti-personnel landmines as a necessary means of warfare, Geneva Call may not have a working argument against this. Similarly, if 'ethnic cleansing' is part of the armed actor's strategy of violence (as was the case during the war in Bosnia 1992–1995, for example), the ICRC will have difficulties persuading the actor that it is in its interest to adhere to international norms. The conclusion of ad hoc agreements might still be possible to assist the wounded or elderly in specific circumstances, but matters of behaviour may not be changed in principle.

4. Strengths and limits of INGOs engaging armed groups

In general, INGOs employing mediation and norm diffusion approaches pursue different goals. For mediation, the aim is the facilitation of dialogue and peace processes. The rationale is that dialogue between the parties will eventually lead to a change of behaviour of the armed group. Overall, it aims at an agreement between the parties to a conflict that will end or reduce violence. At the same time, dialogue is seen to have inherent value in itself, particularly with regard to potential positive effects on future facilitations, mediations and negotiations. Accordingly, singular instances of conflict resolution approaches are of shorter duration and dependent on the willingness of parties to accept a facilitator and mediator.

[32] See O. Bangerter, 'Reasons Why Armed Groups Choose to Respect International Humanitarian Law or Not' (2011) 93 *International Review of the Red Cross* 353.

Norm diffusion approaches focus on the advancement of international humanitarian law, for instance, the Ottawa Treaty and the Geneva Conventions, respectively, as seen in the cases of Geneva Call and the ICRC. The aim is to achieve a change in the armed actor's behaviour based on norm diffusion. The means to achieve this aim include strategic communication, informational diffusion, procedural diffusion through institutionalized cooperation, transference through capacity building and knowledge transfer. Accordingly, the primary intent of such initiatives is not necessarily 'more peace' in the first place, but rather 'less violence', particularly regarding civilians and, more generally, the prevention of an increasing erosion of international humanitarian norms during conflicts.

The strengths of these approaches compared to State approaches and those of international organizations remain considerable. Summarizing, INGOs that are active in this field are not subject to the same diplomatic constraints and commitments as State actors and international organizations.[33] In this sense, their interactions with armed actors have potentially less consequences with regard to the status of armed actors and the credibility of their grievances, as well as the sovereignty, legitimacy and authority of the host State. Moreover, their perceived independence from States in particular often increases their credibility among armed actors because they are seen as being removed from the alleged interests of other intervening actors, such as strategic power, resources and business. Procedurally, INGOs' engagement is also often assumed to be more flexible and based on principles other than those of intervening State actors and international organizations. They tend to be small in number with a more informal organization and bureaucracy that allows them to be flexible and quick to react to changed circumstances. They will often be able to accommodate ad hoc meetings with armed actors as well as maintain personal contact with the leadership of an armed group. The vertical network form of organization appears to be a particular advantage as it avoids the need of feedback in a large hierarchical organization, resulting in lengthy periods of coordination before being able to proceed in the communication or mediation process with the armed actor.

Moreover, members of INGOs are more readily perceived as 'impartial' and 'altruistic'. Because of this perception of independence and the lack of a 'State bias', INGOs' approaches to engaging armed actors are often

[33] It is important to recognize that with regard to personal relationships, perception may become more important than factual conditions. This perception by armed groups is different for individual INGOs.

viewed as being more sincere and dedicated to a sustainable resolution of the conflict based on the demands and preferences of the parties to conflict rather than being interested in the maintenance of the status quo. Three characteristics in particular support this view of INGOs among non-State armed actors. First, the INGOs in question do not offer any 'take it or leave it' options but instead attempt to create options that are specifically tailored to the particular conflict situation and the parties involved. This can be seen in the Centre for Humanitarian Dialogue's negotiation between the government of Indonesia and the Free Aceh Movement that attempted to acknowledge both the security concerns of the government as well as the armed actor; the Carter Center's approach to mediation in Sudan and Uganda that aimed at including all stakeholders in a peace process; Geneva Call's strategic use of reasoning when persuading armed groups to cease to employ landmines; and the ICRC's argumentative approach to spreading the adherence to international humanitarian law. As such, while the INGOs may have preferences for solutions of their own – in peace processes as well as with regard to the application of international norms – they do not have any tangible leverage against the parties in conflict that would allow them to push or pressure them. Consequently, viable middle ground between the parties alone can lead to an agreement. Second, because of a lack of tangible leverage, dialogue, cooperation and concessions must become the basis of an INGO-led mediation or norm diffusion process. This may be different if powerful State actors are involved that may, implicitly or explicitly, compel the parties to a conflict to agree to a preferred compromise, which can only be sustained by outside pressure and the threat of sanctions. In addition, INGOs usually apply the same principles to all parties concerned. As shown by all four examples, they do not only ask armed groups to respect particular norms but also address the same issues with governments and State actors, which, in turn, increases the credibility of INGOs when engaging armed groups. Third, in order to gain a position of trust among the parties to a conflict that allows INGOs to mediate and persuade, they build on their reputation and personal integrity. The Centre for Humanitarian Dialogue tends to employ individuals with experience in government-level negotiations in order to be perceived as knowledgeable, competent and trustworthy, and the Carter Center builds heavily on the experience and clout of former President Jimmy Carter. Similarly, Geneva Call and the ICRC create relationships with armed groups in order to gain their trust and esteem. Again, with no tangible leverage to put pressure on the parties to the conflict, INGOs rely on the personal reputation of their staff as well as on the institutional integrity of their organization. Accordingly, it often takes INGOs a considerable amount of time to set up the personal and informal relationships that sustain a certain level of influence on armed actors and their decision-makers. Such relationships are generally built on empathy and an understanding of the issues at hand. Swiss organizations in particular, such as the Centre for Humanitarian Dialogue, Geneva Call and the ICRC, also benefit from a distinct 'Swiss factor' that grants an advance allocation of confidence and trust in these organizations based on the constructive reputation that Switzerland has built for itself in the field of international negotiations as well as on the country's historical neutrality.

A further advantage INGOs have in engaging armed actors is the inattention that is often paid to their efforts by State actors, international organizations and the media. Accordingly, they are subject to less pressure to succeed in the sense of producing concrete agreements, particularly compared to State actors. Instead, they are able to build long-term relationships with armed groups, concentrate on single issues rather than the entire peace process and link humanitarian issues with those of peace and security. For example, the Carter Center in the past has been able to negotiate short-term, fixed ceasefires that allowed for the eradication of specific illnesses. It has also been able to facilitate the necessary technical help needed to carry out the health mission and has attempted to use the opportunity to extend the ceasefire and start a long-term negotiation process. Leaders of armed groups experience a comparatively low-entry threshold for mediation and negotiation initiatives organized by INGOs and lose little by pulling out of a mediation or norm diffusion process. This may make it more likely for them to just attempt a dialogue. For INGOs, their reputation and credibility is at stake with every engagement with armed actors – a loss of which will negate their position with an individual armed actor and potentially others as well. As a safeguard, INGOs such as the Carter Center or the ICRC can use their solid contacts within local civil society organizations and networks to create social pressure for some armed groups to maintain the process. Depending on the degree of confidentiality in the process, they can also inform the public about the developments in the process and, thus, reveal spoiling behaviour. Moreover, they can incorporate a wider range of stakeholders into the process, such as diaspora groups, religious or traditional authorities and other civil society actors that may apply additional pressure on the parties as well as make a potential agreement more sustainable.

At the same time, INGOs display a number of shortcomings and even risks compared to State actors and international organizations. First, their lack of resources alone requires them to request international assistance at one point or another, provoking questions about the feasibility of INGO-led mediation and negotiation processes considering that such processes are often long and potentially protracted. Additionally, without the resources to sustain personal contacts in the field on a long-term basis, it may be difficult to maintain a commitment by the parties to the process. Even where these initial obstacles have been overcome and an INGO-brokered agreement has been reached – for example, in Aceh, Indonesia, in 2003 – the implementation and monitoring of the commitments in the agreement have surpassed the capacities of INGO. In Aceh, international peacekeepers were supporting the Centre for Humanitarian Dialogue when it encountered problems in implementing the peace agreement and lacked the resources and status to impose sanctions on the parties to the conflict to keep them committed to the process. Additionally, the INGO needed to extend its intellectual capacities to experts from the field and academia. Even in smaller projects, INGOs often lack the personnel and financial backing, particularly when their work is based largely on project-specific funding. In these cases, INGOs' lack of resources and capacities has required them to rely on external partners, such as local civil society organizations, local governments and third countries. Second, their credibility, legitimacy and mandate for engaging armed actors have been questioned vigorously. Their lack of supervision by an international body and the difficulty in monitoring their engagement of armed actors have severely increased apprehension towards an instrumentalization of INGOs by armed actors in general. Third, and most fundamentally, their ability to effectively influence the behaviour of political actors – State and non-State – at all has been challenged. Particularly the duration of engagement has been under scrutiny with establishing contacts and building relationships being long-term projects. Where the establishment of viable contacts with higher levels has failed, INGOs have proceeded to mediate and negotiate with lower-level officials, raising more questions on the sustainability of these processes. Moreover, the fragility of the personal, individual and empathetic connection between the INGO staff and the representatives of the armed actor has raised serious security concerns for INGO personnel and particularly local staff, who are usually among the first victims in cases of retaliation.

In addition to this, INGOs' work is often limited by general environmental factors, such as the course and history of the conflict, its dynamics and its levels of escalation. While these factors remain inconsequential in the systematic constitution of INGOs' efforts, in individual cases, a deteriorating security situation can lead personnel to temporarily withdraw from the process. Accordingly, Geneva Call, for example, regards ceasefires and phases of military cool down as particularly suitable for talks. Moreover, some INGOs identify specific factors regarding the relationship between the parties, the macro-political constellation in the conflict and the perception of external actors and INGOs as supportive for a negotiation process. For example, the Carter Center deems it necessary for negotiations that the parties to a conflict see a significant difference between the costs of a continuation of the conflict and the usefulness of dialogue with the opposing party. For this to occur, a mutually perceived stalemate between the parties is often seen as a beneficial starting point for dialogue stimulated by an external mediator who is acknowledged and seen as having integrity by all parties concerned. On the other hand, the Centre for Humanitarian Dialogue as well as the ICRC acknowledge that an engagement as early as possible in a violent conflict would be beneficial. Thus, as with other external actors, timing for engagement remains a crucial issue which is difficult to assess.

5. Conclusion

The examined INGOs' approaches towards mediation and norm diffusion are based on the general assumption that non-State armed actors by themselves are led by norms and values, to which the leaders constantly refer in their statements and declarations. The reason for this is that a number of armed groups are concerned with their public image and reputation, moral authority and source of legitimacy, as well as the expectations that are put on them, in particular by their own followers and constituencies. Therefore, INGOs argue that these normative statements should be taken seriously and the behaviour of armed groups should be evaluated accordingly. Armed groups can be held accountable to public statements concerning their desire to end a conflict, which represents a component of the Centre for Humanitarian Dialogue's and the Carter Center's efforts. And, moreover, the armed groups' self-image of norm-based actors can be an entry point for debates about international norms and standards which is part of both the ICRC and Geneva Call approaches. The mechanisms these organizations have developed aim at pressuring armed actors to justify their actions. On an argumentative level, this becomes more difficult for the actors the more they have committed themselves to humanitarian norms. For this reason, the declaratory acceptance of norms should be seen as a first step, opening the opportunity to entangle armed actors in an argument about the diffusion and internalization of norms – the same mechanism that is used to diffuse norms, such as non-violence and human rights, among State actors.

However, the limits of the 'power of persuasion' have also become apparent: it is more hazardous to employ a norms-driven mechanism with regard to non-State armed actors, who often need to take serious precautions for their security. Additionally, the mechanism appears particularly to affect a certain type of non-State armed actor, namely those actors and leaders who follow a political programme, see themselves as representatives of a distinct population (such as a tribe, a minority group or a social segment of the society) and are interested in providing governance in the territory they control. These actors already anticipate a future role in the State, either through revolution and regime change or separation and the establishment of a new State. They, therefore, may act as would-be State actors and would like to be seen as such by outsiders. This profile suggests that INGOs can be far more effective working with 'classic' rebel groups, clan chiefs and militias than with terrorists, warlords or criminals, who do not typically have such national-level political ambitions. Moreover, it appears that the effectiveness of both mediation and norm diffusion is heavily influenced by the way armed groups are organized internally. Not only the willingness of leaders to cooperate with INGOs and make concessions is crucial but also the ability of leaders to make sure that agreements are respected and kept by their rank and file is central. Thus, aspects such as loose forms of organization, internal rivalries and fragmentation, lack of stable headquarters or bases, lack of leadership skills and lack of military discipline will undermine any meaningful process of mediation and norm diffusion. Nevertheless, external actors dealing with non-State armed actors need to be aware of the existing range of approaches used by different actors in the field, as well as their possibilities and limits. In any particular case, they need to know about the capabilities of all possible external actors, such as INGOs, to develop a joint effort or at least a complementing approach towards armed groups. The activities of INGOs in engaging non-State armed groups in a humanitarian dialogue may facilitate a change of behaviour, make such groups more approachable and convey norms that other actors can build on, such as in future peace processes. In this respect, INGO activities may well work towards norm transfer and peace building even if they – in contrast to governments or international organizations – have to rely on persuasion only.

5

Comment – persuading armed groups to better respect international humanitarian law

OLIVIER BANGERTER

1. Introduction – where does persuasion fit?

Better respect[1] for international humanitarian law[2] is a question of life and death for people protected by this body of law. Commanders and fighters respecting international humanitarian law means that risks inherent to living in a conflict area will be significantly lowered. It incidentally also

[1] I use 'better respect' instead of the usual 'respect' because 'respect' on its own may convey the idea that armed groups do not respect international humanitarian law. Reality is much more complex: while some groups are known for gruesome atrocities including massacres, mass rapes, abduction of children and widespread amputations, one should not presume that all armed groups have a bad record. Most actually make some efforts to respect international humanitarian law already, and we may address their (real) shortcomings rather than a purported lack of will, which is a much better position to start from. In Africa, the Mouvement des Forces Démocratiques de la Casamance (MFDC), founded in 1982, is often quoted as an example of an armed group exercising restraint. For an example, see V. Foucher, 'The Resilient Weakness of Casamançais Separatists', in M. Bøås and K. C. Dunn (eds.), *African Guerrillas: Rage against the Machine* (London: Lienne Rynner Publishers, 2007), at 171. Quite surprisingly for a group active in the Mano River region, the Liberian United for Reconciliation and Democracy (LURD), active since 2000 and now defunct, has received some praise for its efforts to spare and protect civilians, be it from the International Crisis Group ('Liberia, The Key to Ending Regional Instability' (ICG Africa Report No. 43, 2002), at 9: 'the LURD have largely ceased serious human rights violations since June 2001') or Human Rights Watch – though grudgingly – ('Back to the Brink, War Crimes by Liberian Government and Rebels' (2002) at 2: 'Rebel abuses appear to be less widespread and systematic than those committed by government forces').

[2] Respect is not an absolute. It can vary within the group, with units or individuals behaving better than others, as well as within international humanitarian law, with some provisions respected more than others. For the sake of this chapter, we shall consider respect as a single process. The reader should however keep in mind that all that will be said also applies to partial improvements. Such results can also be attained through one-step-at-a-time tactics; even if intermediary results fall short of the ultimate goal (protection of lives and dignity of people affected by the armed conflict as stipulated by international humanitarian law), they may make a valuable difference on the ground.

means that the need for humanitarian assistance is likely to be lower as people feel secure enough to stay in their homes, where they have better coping mechanisms than they would if they were on the move.

A better respect for international humanitarian law is primarily the result of inside action, and no one can respect international humanitarian law in the stead of parties to a conflict. Outsiders, such as political actors, humanitarian players, non-governmental organizations, communities, the media or academics, can only have an indirect effect on respect for international humanitarian law.

Indirect does not mean insignificant, and there are many examples of armed groups taking positive action following an interaction with outsiders, who managed to induce them to better respect international humanitarian law. These processes encompass several actions, of which persuasion is only one. Prompting armed groups can be done through information, persuasion, monitoring, support and coercion. Information and persuasion target individuals primarily, while support, monitoring and coercion target mostly organizations.

1. *Information.* Numerous armed groups as organizations have little knowledge of the actual content of international humanitarian law beyond some general ideas such as the notion of protection of civilians. They may – and often do – have an understanding of their obligations that is fragmentary at best. It would be no fiction to state that a commander-in-chief of an armed group may be adamant on respecting his prisoners, but not know that it is also his responsibility to provide medical care to them. It would sadly be no fiction either to have groups ready to commit to the protection of civilians attacking civilians because 'they are not civilians' in their opinion.[3] Providing information is therefore essential, and often underestimated: only a relatively small circle of persons are well aware of legal concepts in any given society, and it is unlikely that leaders of armed groups will be recruited in this particular circle.

[3] In Revolutionary United Front ideology, 'civilians were required and expected to bear the costs of the revolution, for instance by providing food and labour. Consequently, those civilians who resisted the RUF [Revolutionary United Front] were enemies'. *Prosecutor v. Sesay, Kallon and Gbao* (Judgment) Case No. SCSL-04-15-T, (2 March 2009), para. 709. Yet, the Revolutionary United Front had adopted their 'eight codes of conduct' that prohibited plunder, sexual violence and ill-treatment of prisoners. For a longer discussion of this specific case, see O. Bangerter, *Internal Control: Codes of Conduct within Insurgent Armed Groups* (Geneva: Small Arms Survey, 2012), at 38–43, www.smallarmssurvey.org/fileadmin/docs/B-Occasional-papers/SAS-OP31-internal-control.pdf.

2. *Persuasion.* By persuasion, we mean interaction with armed groups aimed at convincing them to change their behaviour.[4] Groups who have knowledge of international humanitarian law – albeit basic – may not see why they should respect it. Persuading them to do so is the subject of this chapter. Although this chapter focuses on the role of humanitarian players at large, we must remember that much persuasion is done at the level of communities, negotiating various arrangements with armed groups.[5]
3. *Monitoring.* It is not unheard of that the same commander who politely listened to persuasion yesterday will burn a village or loot humanitarian aid tomorrow.[6] Violations may happen, even when the armed group has taken all possible measures to prevent and sanction them. Monitoring these violations and holding the group accountable is therefore the necessary complement to persuasion and support.[7] Bilateral dialogue far from the public eye or public reporting[8] – or a combination of both – may ensure that the group follows through on its prior commitments or decides to mend some of its ways.
4. *Support.* Armed groups may take a number of measures to improve their respect for international humanitarian law. These include political measures, such as unilateral declarations, and policy measures in areas like doctrine, education and teaching and sanctions.[9] These measures may seem straightforward, but some support from the outside may allow a group to adopt them with greater speed and efficiency.
5. *Coercion.* This can only be exerted with success by States. Coercion measures include sanctions on armed groups for certain actions,[10]

[4] For the sake of brevity, we shall exclude indirect methods of persuasion, including media campaigns and dialogue through intermediaries. These have great potential because they may change the opinion of armed groups' constituencies – an opinion that armed groups disregard at their own peril, but cannot be dealt with in the present article.

[5] In the Philippines, a number of communities have negotiated with both the Armed Forces of the Philippines and the Moro Islamic Liberation Front or the New People's Army to declare their village a 'peace zone', thus preventing access to it by the parties for military operations.

[6] The author is aware of specific cases involving *ninjas Nsilulus* in the Democratic Republic of the Congo and so-called *Janjaweed* in Sudan (Darfur). There are many others.

[7] As Sandesh Sivakumaran noted, armed groups themselves sometimes ask for external monitoring, an opportunity that should not be missed. See S. Sivakumaran, 'Implementing Humanitarian Norms through Non-State Armed Groups', Chapter 6 in this volume, at 126, 130–31.

[8] Organizations such as Human Rights Watch usually do this. The public loss of face for armed groups that such reports can represent is a powerful incentive to comply.

[9] I have described these measures in Bangerter, *Internal Control*, above note 3.

[10] Such actions are often based on lists, such as those of the United Nations Secretary-General naming parties that make use of child soldiers, or so-called terrorists lists.

prosecution by international tribunals and outright pressure. States that support armed groups have leverage proportional to the level of support they provide.[11] Should they request certain behaviour, it is unlikely that the armed group would be in a position to ignore this demand.[12]

Persuasion is only one of the elements of inducing armed groups to a better respect for international humanitarian law and should not be taken in isolation. At the very least, it must be coupled with information and monitoring if one hopes to get results.[13] The five elements we have outlined usually happen simultaneously, especially where a variety of players try to prompt armed groups to respect international humanitarian law better. None are fundamentally better or more important than the others;[14] they are merely different tools having different usage, which can reinforce each other.

2. Persuasion and its limitations

The opportunities and limitations of persuasion remain misunderstood. Many humanitarian workers – and some academics – yearn for some

[11] It can also lessen the interest in compliance when the external backer is ready to provide support regardless of the insurgents' track record, as was shown by South African support to the Resistencia Nacional Moçambicana (RENAMO) in the 1970s and 1980s. See J. Weinstein, *Inside Rebellion: The Politics of Insurgent Violence* (Cambridge: Cambridge University Press, 2007).

[12] The support given by NATO to the Libyan Transitional National Council in 2011 included providing air support, airdropping weapons and making funds confiscated from the Gaddafi regime available to the Transitional National Council, as well as diplomatic support up to recognition as legitimate representative of the people of Libya. Had the Transitional National Council not already adopted measures to ensure as much compliance as possible by its troops, NATO would have been in a prime position to demand it. For the Transitional National Council's March 2011 statement on treatment of prisoners and their 'frontline manual', that is, guidelines for fighters, see theirwords.org/?country=LBY&ansa=62 and www.ejiltalk.org/operationalising-the-law-of-armed-conflict-for-dissident-forces-in-libya/#more-3711 (with a description of the context of these guidelines, as well as a full copy). There are other examples of statements by the Transitional National Council regarding international humanitarian law. In their case, the issue was one of control of the local military councils, most notably of the Misrata Military Council whose fighters literally emptied the town of Tawergha of its population as revenge for their alleged support to Gaddafi forces.

[13] For a holistic view of these processes, see G. Zeender, 'Getting Non-State Actors to Protect IDPs', in *Forced Migration Review, Protection and Assisting the Internally Displaced: The Way Forward, Supplement* (Refugee Studies Centre: Oxford, 2005), at 22–23, www.fmreview.org/FMRpdfs/FMR24/IDP%20Supplement/full.pdf.

[14] For example, key individuals must be persuaded to accept or require support, while monitoring or coercion can lead to a greater demand for information.

magic formula that could work wonders in no time. Their unconscious image of success in persuasion terms is that of a war criminal suddenly seeing the light, through their crafty arguing, their force of conviction or the mere evidence of truth as they convey it. Beyond caricature, the recurrent demand for 'the argument that will win the day' shows that the dream is alive and widespread. Those who have such dreams are more often than not bitterly disappointed. There is no argument that will change commanders or fighters instantly. Unless there is an understanding that persuasion neither starts nor finishes with arguments, any persuasion attempt will likely be fruitless.

This applies to Africa as much as it does to all other continents. Members of armed groups live in a dangerous world and need more than a good-willed person with a few humanitarian and often shallow arguments to be persuaded to change their (potentially) faulty ways.

I will propose the main steps that can lead to persuading those armed groups that violate the law to change this situation and those that want to respect it to even improve their behaviour. Although some arguments carry more weight than others,[15] I will stop short of giving any here.[16]

Step 1 – earn the right to be heard

The first and main challenge in persuasion lies in being recognized as someone who has a legitimate right to talk on these issues. Without personal credibility, as well as some institutional credibility, even the best arguments will tend to fall on deaf ears.[17]

How could it be otherwise? Leaders, commanders and fighters of armed groups are engaged in a dangerous business that may well cost them their lives, their friends' lives and the lives of their families back home. Having a foreigner telling them what to do is unlikely to impress them, be it only because the foreigner is potentially asking fighters to have fewer chances of survival and victory. In addition, this foreigner

[15] The risk of international prosecution is not one of those most compelling, as the Lord's Resistance Army (LRA) and Darfur cases have shown.

[16] I have outlined the most common arguments in O. Bangerter, 'Talking to Armed Groups' (2011) 37 *Forced Migrations Review* 7. I have further developed reasons explaining respect and lack of respect in 'Reasons Why Armed Groups Choose to Respect IHL, or Not' (2011) 93 *International Review of the Red Cross* 353.

[17] This explains why it is easier for a humanitarian worker to persuade armed groups to give security guarantees to their organizations; the nearer one is to the proposed change, the more credible one is considered. Conversely, this explains why persuading armed groups to better respect international humanitarian law is more difficult.

may be part of an organization they do not respect for its achievements or they see as reneging on its promises.

Some armed groups even consider all foreign humanitarian organizations to be a threat, which should therefore not be allowed to work in their area of control; this seems to be the case with a number of players within Al Shabab in Somalia.[18] Groups refusing contact with foreign organizations present a difficult challenge, but their attitude remains the exception. In Africa, most groups are ready to talk to humanitarian organizations, researchers or journalists.[19] Whether they consider these persons credible enough to discuss sensitive issues – such as respect for international humanitarian law – is another question.

Any person and organization wanting to persuade an armed group to do something (or refrain from doing something) should aim to appear knowledgeable – as well as be trustworthy – about the situation. Unless one is considered to have a legitimate right to talk about such issues, one will not be heard, let alone listened to. To be fair with armed groups, a young humanitarian worker who has never fired a weapon in his life is not the best person to instruct a commander on how to lead an operation. Explaining one's credentials to talk about certain issues and listening to members of the armed group goes a long way in establishing credibility.[20]

One can discredit oneself very quickly by using arguments based on a wrong understanding of the armed group and its functioning, of the cultural and conflictual context, of the humanitarian issues or of the implications of the law for military reality. Some humanitarian

[18] In July 2011, realizing that they could not do without external relief, they lifted their 2009 ban on aid organizations; Sheikh Ali Mohamud Rage, an al-Shabab spokesperson, had stated, 'We have now decided to welcome all Muslim and non-Muslim aid agencies to assist the drought-stricken Somalis in our areas'. ('Somali Armed Group Lifts Aid Ban amid Drought', YouTube video, posted by Al Jazeera English on 7 July 2011, www.youtube .com/watch?v=lIY4GBdhbNo). They reinstated the ban a few days later, and at the time of writing, their exact position remains difficult to decipher ('Al Shabab Says Aid Group Ban Remains in Place', YouTube video, posted by Al Jazeera English on 22 July 2011, www .youtube.com/watch?v=ZtGF73dr-jk).

[19] The challenge may lie more in physically reaching areas under their control, but even this is less difficult than often thought. On 9 July 2011, Al Jazeera aired a feature on the situation in the Nuba Mountains, showing air bombings but also including an interview of Sudan People's Liberation Movement (SPLM) commander Abdul Aziz Adam Al-Hilu ('Bleak Future for People in Sudan's Southern Kordofan', YouTube video posted by Al Jazeera English on 9 July 2011, www.youtube.com/watch?v=sfhOHbu33Mg).

[20] Humanitarian workers often accomplish this by concentrating on humanitarian consequences of military operations and not on the operations themselves, as well as by listing countries where they have previously worked.

organizations in Darfur around 2005 considered all Africans as victims and all Arabs as 'Janjaweeds', allied with a repressive State (not realising that roughly half of all Arabic tribes, mostly in South Darfur, had not participated in actions in the war at that stage, and that some had fought against the government). Their ignorance of the ways Arabic populations were suffering from the situation, and their perceived lack of impartiality undermined their credibility when they tried to persuade Arab militia not to burn and loot villages.

Step 2 – have a realistic vision and goal

Armed groups are not blank pages that we can write on. They come with their history, with their worldview – sometimes articulated in political concepts – with their doctrine, with their practice and with pressure put on them by their foes, supporters and constituencies. They also come with different attitudes towards violations. The leadership can order them, they can condone[21] them, they can let them happen[22] or they can forbid, prevent and sanction them. Violations and measures to curb them are the result of complex processes. At the organizational level, compliance or non-compliance with international humanitarian law is the result of cumulative measures taken at the political level and at the policy level, that is, in doctrine, in training and education and in sanctions.[23]

In addition, armed groups are also seldom monolithic. Key individuals may have very different attitudes towards international humanitarian law and outsiders. Some are 'hawks' or hardliners, while others are 'doves' or more prone to compromise. Some may consider international humanitarian law a priority, while others may consider that it is not. Some will welcome foreigners coming to areas under their control, while others will be reluctant. These are only a few examples. Individuals and their attitude matter a lot in any organization and even more so in armed groups where individuals draw support from ethnic or tribal constituencies.

In addition, at the conceptual level, some armed groups choose to respect international humanitarian law or parts of it for reasons that are neither humanitarian nor legal. Former members of various Chadian rebel groups based in the country's east[24] all told me that they had received

[21] Not having given orders, they can still approve of the action post facto.

[22] Neither ordering nor approving violations, the leadership is passive when they are committed or is powerless to stop them.

[23] See Bangerter, *Internal Control*, above note 3.

[24] Active over a period of forty years, until 2009.

stringent orders not to harm civilians. The rationale behind this order – respected on the ground – was compelling, if slightly surprising: all of these groups feared that families and clans would take revenge against them for any incident involving their fighters, and they could not afford to fight both the government and the tribes. Other armed groups choose not to respect international humanitarian law, or parts of it, for a number of reasons. Random violence is an extremely rare occurrence. Even the Revolutionary United Front (RUF) in Sierra Leone – whose bad reputation is deserved – used the amputation of limbs in a calculated way, both to attract the international community's attention and to derail an election. There was no way to persuade the Revolutionary United Front to renounce such actions.

All of these elements will influence orders given and therefore fighters' behaviour. Hoping to obtain a complete and sudden change from such a system that may have taken years to develop is naïve at best. Persuasion must be seen realistically. It will not happen overnight and may require repetition of the same arguments to the same individuals. It must also be replicated with many key individuals unless the group itself takes action in this matter.

Improving respect for international humanitarian law is a lengthy process. There can be rapid and substantial progress in certain areas, but there usually is no quick solution to the whole problem. Realising that persuasion can only happen within a mid-term dialogue with both individuals within an organization (in this case an armed group) and with the organization itself is a prerequisite for success. Understanding that there is a complex history behind most decisions taken in war and that persuasion attempts are only one element in this system is the other one. Without understanding why and how violations occur, and without a mid-term engagement, there is no hope for significant success.

Step 3 – practise humility

Commanders often do not expect to hear foreigners' opinions on how the group is waging its war. At most, they may gladly accept advice stemming from a good knowledge of humanitarian or legal issues. Lack of knowledge coupled with arrogance telling commanders what to do destroy the potential of persuasion. Some have told Charles Taylor's fighters that they needed to treat the population better in order to win hearts and minds, arguing that this would help them win the war. They have discovered, to their dismay, that the National Patriotic Front of Liberia (NPFL) did not really care about winning hearts and minds and still came to power.

Arrogance is certainly the most obstructive character flaw in terms of dialogue with armed groups. This is manifested most often through people not listening seriously to armed groups. There is and must be a time to really listen to armed groups before we start speaking up for the respect of international humanitarian law.

Not doing this creates situations of stalemate, where humanitarian workers repeat ad nauseam that 'killing civilians is wrong because it is against the law and it is against the law because it is wrong'.[25] Yet, people are seldom ready to make concessions when they feel that whatever they may say will not even be heard. This basic rule of interpersonal negotiations seems to be overlooked too often when it comes to dialogue with armed groups.

Step 4 – understand the patterns

Violations do not simply happen and – like compliance – are the result of complex mechanisms. Without a thorough understanding of these processes, persuasion attempts are doomed to failure. This includes an understanding of what armed groups are actually doing. When armed groups are presumed guilty of all possible crimes, negotiations on partial ameliorations become impossible to the detriment of those persons protected by international humanitarian law. In the reality of modern armed conflicts, such partial ameliorations have, however, been negotiated with a measure of success even with groups which seemed unlikely to accept it. For instance, in the former Yugoslavia, militias conducting ethnic cleansing could be persuaded to allow humanitarian organizations to evacuate the wounded and sick from areas under their control.

This presumption of guilt must be challenged in itself. First, this is statistically wrong, as the best figures in our possession show that insurgents may be responsible in average for roughly half the violations committed in

[25] In Hugo Slim's very accurate words. The complete quote is: 'In a dialogue about civilians, it is not enough to repeat over and over again the standard chant that "killing civilians is wrong because it is against the law and it is against the law because it is wrong". This circular reasoning – which sums up the intellectual basis of most popular pro-civilian reasoning today – is obviously not enough of an argument to challenge and convince committed anti-civilian ideologues'. H. Slim and D. Mancini-Griffoli, *Interpreting Violence: Anti-civilian Thinking and Practice and How to Argue against It More Effectively* (Geneva: Centre for Humanitarian Dialogue, 2007), at 24.

the world.[26] Second, considering all violations as equal is misleading. The same action, for instance, the murder of a civilian, may have widely differing causes. An armed group may have the policy of murdering civilians in its areas of control if they are of the wrong ethnic group.[27] An armed group may also refrain from disciplining its fighters for fear of them defecting, or simply lack the command-and-control structure able to prevent local commanders from murdering, or a third party may use the guise of the armed group to commit the murder. To have an impact beyond individual cases,[28] we must discern patterns of violations. Even the most gruesome violence is seldom random, and even the most violent group usually has several reasons for committing the same crimes.[29] Disaggregating violations both by type and reason opens venues for persuasion as a group may be more open to discuss some issues than others.

Persuasion attempts only have a prospect of success if the true underlying causes can be addressed. If the issue is command and control over his fighters, it is useless to accuse a commander of genocide. The most this would achieve is antagonize the commander to no avail.

Understanding mechanisms also implies understanding mechanisms in place for compliance, as well as their limits. There may be no need to reinforce persuasion efforts in one area because the group has it covered quite well, leaving more time and energy for other problematic areas. The now-at-peace Mouvement des Nigériens pour la Justice (MNJ) in Niger had an oath that each recruit had to swear on the Quran, including the promise not to harm civilians. The MNJ's record of accomplishment in this regard was quite good, with notable exceptions, such as taking civilians hostage on various occasions. Some have simply discarded their efforts as incoherent or fruitless, which was a mistake. Lack of understanding of reasons of violations – and compliance – means lost opportunities. Arguing with the MNJ on the basis of their oath and showing the inconsistency between its oath and their taking hostages could have contributed to the amelioration of the situation.

[26] If anything, States may be responsible for slightly more violations across the board. For some statistics, see O. Bangerter, 'Reasons Why Armed Groups Choose to Respect International Humanitarian Law, or Not' (2011) 93 *International Review of the Red Cross* 353, at 356–57.

[27] An example of this is the infamous Interahamwe and Impuzamugambi in Rwanda.

[28] Most violations – and most consequences they have for people protected by international humanitarian law – are not the result of the whim of one single individual and are therefore likely to recur.

[29] K. Thams Olsen, 'Violence against Civilians in Civil War: Understanding Atrocities by the Lord's Resistance Army in Northern Uganda' (Conflict Research Group Working Paper No. 8, Ghent, 2007).

Taking stock of measures in place allows for some leverage in the discussion. After all, whatever the reasons motivating their public pronouncements on respect of international humanitarian law, armed groups expose themselves to criticism if they do not respect the standards they have set for themselves.[30] Whether their motivations in doing so are humanitarian or opportunistic matters much less than the fact they offer leverage for persuasion by doing so.

Step 5 – dialogue over time

Persuasion can only take place in the frame of a dialogue. Bashing arguments is not a good way forward. To have any prospect of success, one has to speak the same language as the armed group. Persuasion requires active listening,[31] asking questions, readiness to challenge what is said . . . and time.

Time spent is essential: persuasion is a lengthy process as well as a labour-intensive one. Sowing doubt first is often a better tactic than aiming for a quick breakthrough. This allows members of the armed group to rethink their position by themselves. Asking questions is a powerful tool to help this process, apart from the fact that it shows genuine interest. And time allows enhancing one's credibility. Persistence and coherence between words and deeds can only be experienced over time, and they are in the eye of the beholder, that is, the armed group.

Armed groups will often test people to make sure that they are indeed trustworthy interlocutors to begin with.[32] They may ask tricky questions

[30] In Afghanistan, the Taliban have taken some harsh criticism for the discrepancy between their codes of conduct and their actions. See K. Clark, 'The Lahya: Calling the Taleban to Account', *Afghanistan Analysts Network*, June 2011, aan-afghanistan.com/uploads/20110704_CKlark_The_Layha.pdf, and G. Kleponis, 'Throwing the Book at the Taliban: Undermining Taliban Legitimacy by Highlighting Their Own Hypocrisy' (2010) *Small Wars Journal*, smallwarsjournal.com/blog/journal/docs-temp/523-kleponis.pdf.

[31] One should take armed groups' rhetoric on norms seriously if only because their public positions provide either leverage for persuasion or a good view on why they refuse to abide by international humanitarian law.

[32] Many armed groups have been in action for years or decades (the Forces Démocratiques de Libération du Rwanda (FDLR) have been around in the Democratic Republic of the Congo for almost twenty years); their commanders and leaders may have changed positions within the group but still carry a memory of the interaction between themselves and foreign or local organizations. As they perceive to have time on their side, it is only natural that they use the test of time to differentiate between those who will come and go and those who want to establish a real dialogue.

to see how the other reacts; they may cancel appointments at short notice to see how persistent the other will be; they may use fake arguments to determine how much the other discerns reality. When trust is truly established, most issues can be discussed, although not always to our immediate satisfaction. Quick breakthroughs happen, but they are rarer than lengthy persuasion.

3. Conclusion – individuals matter

Armed groups are primarily constituted of individuals, and these persons matter. Persuasion is not a science but rather is the result of a relation, and individuals matter immensely in this domain. While this is true of an external player wanting to influence an armed group, it is even truer within the armed group. Not all individual leaders, commanders and fighters have the same importance or power. Some may exert influence over violations or compliance, while others may only have a limited voice in this debate.[33] Persuasion aimed at the wrong person may result in a commander doing what he is told by his superiors despite his personal feeling that it is not very good, or in a fighter executed for not following orders.

Understanding the individual's margin of decision is essential. Not all members of an armed group have the same responsibilities or freedom of action, but all have some decision-making power. The more centralized an armed group is, the more persuasion can be concentrated at the top with a group of key individuals. In this case, discussing issues beyond day-to-day business at a tactical or operational level is simply a waste of time. On the contrary, with a decentralized group – or a group unable to enforce its control – most issues must be discussed at all levels. Individuals are equal in dignity, but not in importance when it comes to a better respect of international humanitarian law.

Addressing the right issue with the right people, however, is only part of the story. Once one individual has been persuaded to better comply with international humanitarian law, there are still many others left to be convinced. Changing armed groups one fighter at a time is a never-ending process. It is much better to let the armed group as an organization persuade its own members, for instance, through a code of conduct or

[33] It obviously also works positively; those within the group who have signed documents regarding international humanitarian law become advocates of these rules.

military code coupled with political education.[34] But this only happens when key individuals in leadership positions have been persuaded beforehand.

[34] The Umkhonto we Sizwe (the armed wing of the South African National Congress (ANC)) military code is a good example of such measures. It was released at the ANC National Consultative Conference at Kabwe in June 1985 as part of a larger document titled 'Report of Commission on National Structures, Constitutional Guidelines and Codes of Conduct'. Among other elements, it states that:

3. All combatants shall act in such a manner that the people will put their trust in the army, recognise it as their protector, and accept the liberation movement as their legitimate and authentic representative. The following acts or omissions shall be an offence:

a) Conduct that weakens the people's trust, confidence and faith in the ANC and Umkhonto.
b) Theft from a comrade or the people, looting of property, or other forcible seizure of goods.
c) Abuse of authority and/or power.
d) Cruelty inflicted on a member of the army or public.
e) Assaults, rape, disorderly conduct, the use of insulting and/or obscene language, bullying and intimidation, whether against a comrade or member of the public.
f) Shameful conduct likely to disgrace the ANC, army or the offender, or bring them into disrepute, or 16 provoke indignation and contempt against them, such as violating the rights and dignity of the opposite sex, whether in operational or base areas.
g) Unjustifiable homicide.
h) Ill-treatment of prisoners of war or persons in custody.

ANC, Umkhonto we Sizwe Military Code, 1985, General Regulations, para. 3, www.anc.org.za/show.php?id=88.

6

Implementing humanitarian norms through non-State armed groups

SANDESH SIVAKUMARAN*

1. Introduction

This chapter is based on two self-evident propositions. First, only States may ratify international humanitarian law treaties. Second, non-international armed conflicts are fought between States and non-State armed groups or between armed groups. The disjunction between these two statements is apparent: one of the parties involved in armed conflicts, namely armed groups, cannot ratify international humanitarian law treaties. Yet – or because of this – armed groups frequently commit themselves to humanitarian norms in general and international humanitarian law norms in particular.

This chapter considers some of the issues that are raised by commitments of armed groups. In particular, it assesses ways in which the commitments could be utilized more effectively. Commitments, by themselves, are insufficient to create a climate of respect for humanitarian norms. At the very least, the norms have to be 'translated' into language that is understood by fighters. They must be internalized both within the group and by individual fighters. The commitments also need to be enforced by the group. Accordingly, there is a role to be played by armed groups at each of the stages following the issuance of a commitment. Their role at each of these stages forms the substance of this chapter.

2. Commitments to humanitarian norms

It is sometimes suggested that armed groups rarely commit to humanitarian norms. However, this is by no means the case. In the actual practice

* I am grateful to the British Academy for a research grant which allowed me to obtain some of the armed group commitments that are mentioned in this chapter. This chapter is based on a presentation given at the Enforcing International Humanitarian Law in Contemporary African Conflicts conference in September 2011 and was completed shortly thereafter.

of armed conflicts, armed groups frequently make ad hoc commitments. This is a worldwide phenomenon, and one that dates back to at least the 1800s. However, nowhere is it truer than in contemporary African conflicts.[1] It is also suggested, on occasion, that when armed groups do make commitments to respect humanitarian norms, they do so for political reasons and without any intention to comply with their commitments. However, just as States act for different reasons, so too do armed groups.

Accordingly, the importance of such commitments has long been recognized, with the International Committee of the Red Cross (ICRC) traditionally taking on the role of encouraging commitments.[2] More recently, two other organizations – Geneva Call and Human Rights Watch – have played a similar role, extracting commitments from armed groups. For example, during the 2011 conflict in Libya, the National Transitional Council issued a communiqué that prohibited the use of anti-personnel mines and anti-vehicle mines.[3] This followed a pledge that was made to Human Rights Watch one day earlier. Likewise, numerous armed non-State actors fighting in contemporary African conflicts have signed Geneva Call's Deed of Commitment on an anti-personnel mine ban.[4] As will be discussed below, for a number of reasons, these commitments must be taken seriously.[5]

2.1. *Unilateral declarations*

The usual form that a commitment takes is a unilateral declaration. Through such declarations, the group sets out its position on international humanitarian law, international human rights law and/or related bodies of law, such as the Guiding Principles on Internal Displacement. Declarations may be issued on the initiative of the group itself or may be solicited by organizations such as the ICRC, Geneva Call or Human Rights Watch. They might be drafted without any outside assistance, or they might benefit from the advice of specialists in the field.

1 See, for example, the compilation of commitments in C. Ewumbue-Monono, 'Respect for International Humanitarian Law by Armed Non-State Actors in Africa' (2006) 88 *International Review of the Red Cross* 905.

2 This is evident from a perusal of the ICRC archives.

3 Communiqué by the Libyan National Transitional Council Regarding Landmines, 28 April 2011, www.hrw.org/sites/default/files/related_material/Communique.pdf.

4 Examples of those who signed the commitment include the Conseil National pour la Défense de la Démocratie-Forces de Défense de la Démocratie (CNDD-FDD) of Burundi, the Polisario Front of Western Sahara and a variety of Somali groups.

5 See below, Section 2.3.

Unilateral declarations might relate to the full body of the applicable law or might deal with particular norms at issue in the conflict. The depth and complexity of unilateral declarations vary considerably. Some amount to no more than a couple of sentences or a few paragraphs. For example, the Justice and Equality Movement (JEM) and the Sudan Liberation Movement-Unity (SLM-Unity), both fighting in the conflict in Darfur, issued a statement in 2008, which provided in relevant part:

> We will do our utmost to guarantee the protection of civilian populations in accordance with the principles of human rights and international humanitarian law. In collaboration with UNICEF, we will adopt measures ensuring protection of children in Darfur. We also affirm the principles of freedom of movement.
>
> We reaffirm our commitment to refrain from targeting or forcibly displacing civilian populations, destroying civilian infrastructure, recruiting children for military operations, and to hold to account perpetrators of acts of rape and other forms of gender based violence. We recognize that placing military assets and personnel in close proximity to civilian areas increases the risk that civilians will be caught up in hostilities or even targeted. We will therefore continue our policy of maintaining a proper physical separation between our armed forces and the civilian population. We also continue to commit to curtailing the militarization of IDP/refugee camps.
>
> We reaffirm our commitment to clearly instructing our personnel on the ground regarding their obligations under human rights and international humanitarian law.[6]

By contrast, in the case of the Front de Libération Nationale (FLN), fighting for the independence of Algeria from France, numerous declarations were issued from 1956 onwards.[7] The FLN also published an eighty-five-page booklet relating to the application of the Geneva Conventions to the conflict.[8] The Provisional Government of the Algerian Republic later acceded to the Geneva Conventions, such accession being accepted by a

[6] Centre for Humanitarian Dialogue, 'The Geneva/Darfur Humanitarian Dialogue: Statement by the Opposition Movements [JEM and SLM-Unity]', press release, 11 July 2008, theirwords.org/media/transfer/doc/1_sd_jem_slm_a_unity_2008_18-9786ecfeda2b4605ff60bcdc4aab48b2.pdf.

[7] See, for example, the commitment of a representative of the FLN to the ICRC, Note de Dossier, 16 February 1956, ICRC Archives 225 008-002; Lettre de la Délégation Algérienne, représentant le Front de Libération Nationale et l'Armée de Libération Nationale à Monsieur David de Traz, Représentant Spécial du Comité International de la Croix-Rouge, 23 February 1956, ICRC Archives B AG 202 008–001.

[8] White Paper on the Application of the Geneva Conventions of 1949 to the French-Algerian Conflict (Algerian Office, New York, 1960).

number of States even though Algeria itself had not been formally recognized as a State.[9] The mere length of a declaration is thus relatively unimportant. Indeed, there is something to be said for a short, succinct statement that is understandable to all, rather than a lengthy excursus into different aspects of the law that are not at issue in the conflict.

2.2. *Ad hoc agreements*

Another means by which armed groups set out their position on humanitarian norms is through an ad hoc agreement that is concluded with one or more entities. Usually, this other entity will be the State against which the armed group is in conflict. However, agreements have also been concluded with UN entities, non-governmental organizations or a combination thereof. The classic example of an agreement concluded between a non-State armed group and a UN entity is the agreement concluded between South Sudanese armed groups and Operation Lifeline Sudan in the mid-1990s.[10]

Ad hoc agreements also relate to a variety of subject matters, including international humanitarian law, international human rights law and related issues, such as the protection of internally displaced persons. The most well-known example of an ad hoc agreement is the 22 May 1992 Agreement concluded between the various parties fighting in the conflict in Bosnia.[11] However, the 22 May 1992 Agreement is just an example of an ad hoc agreement. Other important agreements on international humanitarian law include the 2002 agreement concluded between the government of Sudan and the Sudan People's Liberation Movement (SPLM) on the protection of civilians. That agreement provided:

> The Government of the Republic of Sudan (GOS) and the Sudan People's Liberation Movement (SPLM) (hereafter referred to as the 'Parties') reconfirm their obligations under international law, including common Article 3 of the 1949 Geneva Conventions, to take constant care to protect

[9] Instruments of Accession of the Algerian Republic to the Geneva Conventions of 12 August 1949 (registered at Berne, 20 June 1960), reproduced in M. Bedjaoui, *Law and the Algerian Revolution* (Brussels: International Association of Democratic Lawyers, 1961), at 199.

[10] SPLM-United/Operation Lifeline Sudan, Agreement on Ground Rules, May 1996; SPLM/Operation Lifeline Sudan, Agreement on Ground Rules, 3 July 1995; South Sudan Independence Movement Operation/Lifeline Sudan, Agreement on Ground Rules, 5 August 1995.

[11] Agreement of 22 May 1992, reproduced in M. Sassòli, A. A. Bouvier and A. Quintin, *How Does Law Protect in War?*, 3 vols. (Geneva: ICRC, 2011), vol. III, at 1717.

> the civilian population, civilians and civilian objects against the dangers arising from military operations. In this context, the Parties specifically commit themselves:
> a) to refrain from targeting or intentionally attacking non-combatant civilians;
> b) to refrain from targeting or intentionally attacking civilian objects or facilities, such as schools, hospitals, religious premises, health and food distribution centres, or relief operations, or objects or facilities indispensable to the survival of the civilian population and of a civilian nature;
> c) to refrain from endangering the safety of civilians by intentionally using them as 'human shields' or by using civilian facilities such as hospitals or schools to shield otherwise lawful military targets; and
> d) to take all precautions feasible to avoid incidental loss of civilian life, injury to civilians, and danger to civilian objects.
>
> Military operations include, but are not limited to, air attacks, artillery attacks, ground attacks, ambushes and intentional military activity or other uses of force that could result in the killing or injury of persons or damage or destruction of property.[12]

Ceasefire agreements tend also to include provisions on humanitarian law, as was the case with the 2006 Cessation of Hostilities Agreement and the 2008 Ceasefire Agreement concluded between the government of Uganda and the Lord's Resistance Army (LRA).[13] Peace agreements might also include provisions on humanitarian law.[14] It may be thought that, by definition, peace agreements are concluded at a point in time that makes them inappropriate for binding parties by international humanitarian law. However, in the case of the 1996 Abidjan Peace Agreement that was concluded between the government of Sierra Leone and the Revolutionary United Front (RUF), the agreement provided that the parties are '[c]ommitted to promoting . . . full respect for human rights and humanitarian laws'.[15] Following the failure of the agreement and the subsequent return to violence, the RUF pointed to the provision and argued that both the government and the RUF 'had committed themselves to the

[12] Agreement between the Government of the Republic of Sudan and the Sudan People's Liberation Movement to Protect Non-Combatant Civilians and Civilian Facilities from Military Attack, 10 March 2002.

[13] Cessation of Hostilities Agreement, Addendum I, 1 November 2006; Agreement on a Permanent Ceasefire, 23 February 2008.

[14] See, for example, Peace Agreement between the Government of Liberia (GOL), The Liberians United for Reconciliation and Democracy (LURD), The Movement for Democracy in Liberia (MODEL) and the Political Parties, 18 August 2003, Article XII.

[15] Abidjan Peace Agreement, 30 November 1996.

promotion of popular participation in government and full respect for human rights and humanitarian laws'.[16]

Ad hoc agreements, ceasefire agreements and peace agreements also tend to contain provisions on human rights norms, lending support to the view that, at least in certain cases, armed groups may be bound by human rights obligations.[17] Such agreements include those concluded between the Government of Liberia, Liberians United for Reconciliation and Democracy (LURD) and Movement for Democracy in Liberia (MODEL) in 2003;[18] the government of Sudan and the Eastern Sudan Front in 2006;[19] and the government of Sudan and the Sudan Liberation Movement (SLM) and Justice and Equality Movement (JEM), also in 2006.[20]

Thus, it is not at all unusual for ad hoc agreements to be concluded between parties to a conflict and for them to include humanitarian norms.

2.3. *Importance of commitments*

Commitments that are issued by armed groups on an ad hoc basis are important for a number of reasons. First is the idea of ownership of norms.[21] One aspect of the idea of ownership is that involvement in a process may lead to greater compliance with the results of that process. In the specific context of armed groups and humanitarian norms, examples emerge, from time to time, of armed groups arguing that they are not bound by particular norms because they did not participate in the creation of those norms. The best example of such an argument – albeit in a non-African context – is the communication between the International Committee of the Red Cross and the Viet Cong during the conflict in

16 'Lasting Peace in Sierra Leone: The Revolutionary United Front Sierra Leone (RUF/SL) Perspective and Vision' (undated), theirwords.org/media/transfer/doc/sl_ruf_08-8b0383b426906a2602263d3afda2c66d.pdf.

17 See generally A. Clapham, *Human Rights Obligations of Non-State Actors* (Oxford: Oxford University Press, 2006).

18 Peace Agreement between the Government of Liberia (GOL), the Liberians United for Reconciliation and Democracy (LURD), the Movement for Democracy in Liberia (MODEL) and the Political Parties, 18 August 2003, Article XII.

19 Eastern Sudan Peace Agreement, 14 October 2006, Article 6.

20 Darfur Peace Agreement, 5 May 2006, Articles 1(7) and 3.

21 See, in particular, M. Sassòli, 'Possible Legal Mechanisms to Improve Compliance by Armed Groups with International Humanitarian Law and International Human Rights Law' (paper presented at the Armed Groups Conference, Vancouver, 13–15 November 2003).

Vietnam. Following an exhortation on the part of the ICRC to the Viet Cong in 1965 to respect international humanitarian law, the Viet Cong responded: 'the National Liberation Front of South Vietnam did not participate in the Geneva Conventions for the protection of war victims and is not bound by the Conventions'.[22] The Viet Cong went so far as to return the text of the ICRC appeal to the ICRC.[23]

The point should not be overstated, however. As will already be apparent, numerous armed groups do commit to humanitarian norms despite not being involved in the creation of those norms. Nonetheless, a related example in the context of a State's involvement in the creation of a norm illustrates the idea of ownership of norms. Following the 1974–1977 Diplomatic Conference, there was considerable debate as to whether the United States would ratify the Additional Protocols. Certain individuals, including leading figures within the US delegation to the Diplomatic Conference, were in favour of US ratification subject to the entry of a number of reservations. A leading US military lawyer, however, was more reticent and indicated that the support for ratification on the part of certain individuals resulted from their participation in the Diplomatic Conference and that a certain objectivity was thereby lost.[24] It is far less pertinent for the purposes of this chapter whether the US should have ratified the Protocols; more interesting is the suggestion that involvement in a process can lead to support for the results of that process. This is as true of armed groups as it is of States.

A second reason these commitments need to be taken seriously is the impact they can have on other actors. Commitments by one group may later be used as a model by other groups.[25] Commitments of armed groups also affect commitments of States. For example, the government of Sudan ratified the Ottawa Convention in 2003, after the SPLM signed the Geneva Call Deed of Commitment, which provides for similar obligations on the part of armed non-State actors.[26] High-level officials involved in

[22] Letter from Chef de la Représentation Permanente du FLN du Sud-Vietnam en URSS to Representative of the ICRC, 16 October 1965, ICRC Archives B AG 202 223–005. The French translation by the ICRC of the Russian original reads: 'le Front National de Libération du Vietnam du Sud n'ait pas participé aux Conventions de Genève pour la protection des victimes de la guerre et ne soit pas lié par ces Conventions . . . '.

[23] Ibid.

[24] W. H. Parks, 'Air War and the Law of War' (1990) 32 *Air Force Law Review* 1, at 87 fn. 279.

[25] See below, Section 3.

[26] On the Geneva Call Deed of Commitment, see www.genevacall.org/how-we-work/deed-of-commitment/. The SPLM signed the Deed in October 2001.

mine action in Sudan indicate that the government of Sudan would not have ratified the Ottawa Convention if not for the SPLM signature of the Geneva Call Deed.[27] Likewise, in 2011, when South Sudan became a new State and the SPLM became its government, it acceded to the Ottawa Convention.[28]

A third reason is that an analysis of ad hoc commitments, of States and of non-State armed groups alike leads to a more accurate reflection of the operation of humanitarian norms in practice. Consider the issue of prisoners of war. It is well known that prisoner-of-war status simply does not exist in the law of non-international armed conflict. Yet, in practice, things are rather more nuanced. In some large-scale non-international armed conflicts of an extended duration, captured fighters have been treated as prisoners of war. This was true, for example, during the latter part of the Algerian War of Independence (1954–1962)[29] and the conflict in Eritrea in the late 1980s.[30] During the attempted secession of Biafra, the Operational Code of Conduct issued by the federal government to the armed forces in 1967 provided that '[s]oldiers who surrender will not be killed. They are to be disarmed and treated as prisoners of war. They are entitled in all circumstances to humane treatment and respect for their person and their honour'.[31] On the Biafran side, de facto prisoner-of-war camps were also established and visits undertaken by the ICRC.[32] Thus, the situation on the ground is not always as the law would suggest.

Likewise, it is often thought that anti-personnel mines are a 'poor person's weapon', given that they are inexpensive and relatively easy to purchase or manufacture. Thus, armed groups will use them because they may be unable to get their hands on heavy weaponry. Yet, practice

27 M. Barber, 'Preface', in Geneva Call, *Armed Non-State Actors and Landmines: A Global Report Profiling NSAs and their Use, Acquisition, Production, Transfer and Stockpiling of Landmines* (Geneva: Geneva Call, 2005), vol. I, at 1.

28 Accession of 11 November 2011.

29 For the French treatment of detainees, see ICRC, *The ICRC and the Algerian Conflict* (Geneva: ICRC, 1962), at 6; A. Rosas, *The Legal Status of Prisoners of War* (Helsinki: Suomalainen Tiedeakatemia, 1976), at 149. For the Algerian treatment in this respect, see A. Fraleigh, 'The Algerian Revolution as a Case Study in International Law', in R. A. Falk (ed.), *The International Law of Civil War* (Baltimore: Johns Hopkins University Press, 1971), 179–243, at 196.

30 H. McCoubrey, *International Humanitarian Law: The Regulation of Armed Conflicts* (Aldershot: Dartmouth, 1990), at 181.

31 Operational Code of Conduct for the Nigerian Army, para. 4(e), July 1967, reproduced in A. H. M. Kirk-Greene, *Crisis and Conflict in Nigeria: A Documentary Sourcebook 1966–1969* (Oxford: Oxford University Press, 1971), vol. I, at 455–56.

32 See 'Help to War Victims in Nigeria' (1969) 9 *International Review of the Red Cross* 119, at 122.

relating to the Geneva Call Deed of Commitment suggests that many armed groups will accept a prohibition on the use of anti-personnel mines.

Ad hoc commitments may also assist in interpreting certain notions. For example, the notion of a civilian and the meaning of civilians who take a direct part in hostilities are complex issues and contested ones at that.[33] Armed groups may have their own interpretations of these terms, which present additional perspectives to the debate.

Fourth, in certain respects, ad hoc commitments of armed groups may be in advance of humanitarian standards. For example, the SPLM committed to apply the Convention on Certain Conventional Weapons at a time when the Convention was applicable to international armed conflicts alone.[34] The National Transitional Council of Libya prohibited the use of anti-vehicle mines and anti-personnel mines during the 2011 conflict in Libya.[35] However, it is equally true that ad hoc commitments can purport to derogate from existing humanitarian standards, making them particularly problematic for the reasons of ownership considered above.

Finally, the issuance of an ad hoc commitment creates an entry point within the group for further dialogue on related issues. When outside actors engage with the armed group, the engagement can take as a reference point the commitment of the group. This may also lead to the establishment of trust between the relevant parties. A representative of one government which is involved in a non-international armed conflict indicated along precisely theselines that the peace process was helped along by the conclusion of an earlier bilateral agreement on humanitarian norms.[36]

3. Translation of humanitarian norms

A mere commitment to respect the law, by itself, is entirely insufficient. Commitments of armed groups are often drafted by the political wing

[33] For an important statement by the ICRC on the subject, see ICRC, *Interpretive Guidance on the Notion of Direct Participation in Hostilities under International Law* (Geneva: ICRC, May 2009). However, this is itself controversial. See, for example, the symposium at (2010) 42 *New York University Journal of International Law and Politics* 637.

[34] Formation of New Sudan Authority on Landmines, 9 May 2004, referring to Doc.CM/1884(LX11) Annex II.

[35] Communiqué by the Libyan National Transitional Council Regarding Landmines, above note 3; compare Convention on the Prohibition of the Use, Stockpiling, Production and Transfer of Anti-Personnel Mines and on Their Destruction, Oslo, 18 September 1997, in force 1 March 1999, 2056 U.N.T.S. 211.

[36] Information provided confidentially to the author.

of the group rather than the military wing. The political wing may be based outside the State in which the conflict is fought. The influence of the political wing on the military wing will also vary from group to group. Furthermore, commitments tend to be made by the elites of the group, those who interact with representatives of the international community and who perhaps know what it is that the international community wishes to hear. For all of these reasons, ad hoc commitments may have a limited effect on fighters on the ground. In short, as is well known, the mere existence of a commitment cannot be equated with compliance with the law.

In particular, a certain 'translation' of the humanitarian norm is required. There must be translation from the political wing to the military wing and from the elite of the group to the rank and file. Technical legal language will also need to be translated into everyday language. For example, the important (and difficult) concept of proportionality, the contested notions of civilian and direct participation in hostilities and the detailed requirements stemming from the obligation to take all feasible precautions have to be understood by those who are actually doing the fighting. Hundreds of norms need to be whittled down to those that are relevant to the particular conflict and the specific group. Translation from a state-of-the-art humanitarian commitment into rules that are understandable and relevant to the armed group will also enable persons within the group to sit down with knowledgeable outside actors, to talk through ideas and to share concerns.

Another way in which the translation could take place – and to a limited extent already does take place – is through the drafting of codes of conduct and regulations that are internal to the group. Indeed, these very points have been recognized by one armed group – the Chin National Front (CNF) of Burma – in an internal regulation. That regulation provides:

> The objective of writing this law is to let all the CNF members understand it. In other words, this law is meant for the people who practice it. The Geneva [Conventions are] written by international legal experts using relevant legal terms. Therefore, translating the original version of the Geneva [Conventions] into Burmese and distributing among the CNF members would be lengthy and boring and would not help in practical usage. If the members are to be made aware of the precepts of the Geneva [Conventions] and made to follow it, then it is necessary to make it easy to read and understand and present it in a practicable way . . . [37]

[37] Chin National Front, Code, undated (unofficial translation).

For similar reasons, in the case of the National Transitional Council of Libya in 2011, outside experts drew up flowcharts and 'a set of fairly simple propositions' that could be used by untrained fighters on the ground.[38]

That this be done is nothing short of critical and, in many ways, is more important than the issuance of a unilateral declaration or the conclusion of a bilateral agreement. Unilateral declarations and bilateral agreements provide the normative framework; but that normative framework then needs to be implemented. If anything is to be enforced by the group, it will be the group's code of conduct or internal regulations.

The most well-known example of a contemporary code of conduct of an armed group again relates to a non-African conflict, namely the Layha for the Mujahadeen of the Taliban of Afghanistan, issued in 2006, again in 2009 and then again in 2010.[39] Again, however, the Layha is simply an example of a code of conduct. Most, if not all, armed groups will have some form of internal rules as this is the way in which discipline can be maintained and orders enforced. For example, the RUF of Sierra Leone and the National Resistance Army (NRA) of Uganda under Museveni had internal codes, both of which were based on the Three Main Rules of Discipline and Eight Points for Attention of the Chinese People's Liberation Army.[40]

Just as unilateral declarations and bilateral agreements take various forms, so too do codes of conduct and internal regulations. Some are purely humanitarian in nature. For example, the Eight Codes of Conduct of the RUF provided:

> To speak politely to masses
> To pay fairly for all you buy
> To return everything that you borrow
> To pay for everything that you demand or damage
> Do not damage crops

[38] See I. Scobbie, 'Operationalising the Law of Armed Conflict for Dissident Forces in Libya', *EJIL: Talk!* (blog), 31 August 2011, www.ejiltalk.org/operationalising-the-law-of-armed-conflict-for-dissident-forces-in-libya/.

[39] The 2009 version is reproduced in Sassòli, Bouvier and Quintin, *How Does Law Protect in War?*, above note 11, vol. III, at 2325. The 2010 version is reproduced in (2011) 93 *International Review of the Red Cross* 103.

[40] RUF, Eight Codes of Conduct, reproduced in *Prosecutor v. Sesay, Kallon and Gbao* (Judgment) Case No. SCSL-04-15-T (2 March 2009), para. 705; National Resistance Army Code of Conduct, reprinted in O. O. Amaza, *Museveni's Long March from Guerrilla to Statesman* (Kampala: Fountain Publishers, 1998), at 246; Chinese People's Liberation Army, Three Main Rules of Discipline (1927; reissued 1947); Eight Points for Attention (1947).

> Do not take liberty from women
> Do not ill-treat captives
> Do not hate or swear people.[41]

Others contain a combination of humanitarian norms and disciplinary norms, such as the Code of Conduct of the NRA of Uganda with its section on 'dealing with the public', 'relationship among the soldiers', 'punishments' and 'offences'.[42] More generally, it is important that military codes are combined with their humanitarian counterparts so that the military code is not seen as superior to the humanitarian code, trumping it in cases of emergency.[43] This would be akin to the position in international humanitarian law in which notions of humanity and military necessity are incorporated into the rules, with the effect that military necessity cannot override the application of a provision.

It has been suggested that armed groups that have codes of conduct are less likely to violate humanitarian norms than groups that do not have codes of conduct.[44] However, the issue must be considered on a case-by-case basis. To take but one example, the RUF had internal regulations, but they could hardly be said to have been respected. As the RUF Trial Judgment reveals, violations were rife, including looting, pillage and sexual violence, the very things that were prohibited by the Code of Conduct. Indeed, contrary to several rules of the Code, the RUF undertook actions such as Operation Pay Yourself, which, as the name suggests 'decreed that fighters were to "pay themselves" by looting civilian property'.[45]

Codes are important also for the broader impact that they may have. As already indicated, the NRA of Uganda, under the leadership of Museveni, adopted a code of conduct. That code formed the basis of the code of the State armed forces when the NRA gained power and Museveni became president. As already mentioned, the Three Main Rules of Discipline and the Eight Codes of Conduct of the Chinese People's Liberation Army under Mao Tse-Tung were adopted many years later by various groups, including the NRA and the RUF.[46] Accordingly, the importance of codes of conduct and internal regulations should not be underestimated.

41 Reproduced in *Prosecutor v. Sesay et al.*, above note 40, para. 705.

42 National Resistance Army Code of Conduct, above note 40.

43 I am grateful to Olivier Bangerter for this point.

44 International Council on Human Rights Policy, 'Ends and Means: Human Rights Approaches to Armed Groups' (2000), at 52.

45 *Prosecutor v. Sesay et al.*, above note 40, para. 783.

46 Ibid. para. 705.

However, certain difficulties emerge from this notion of translation of norms. A particular norm may be translated in such a manner as to depart from the international law understanding of the norm. This, in turn, will prove problematic if the norm is understood in a way that violates international law. The SPLM's understanding of persons who may be targeted is a case in point. Such persons included individuals who were 'directly or indirectly cooperating with the autocratic regime in Khartoum in order to sustain or consolidate its rule and to undermine the objectives and efforts of the People's Revolution' and individuals who 'propagate or advocate ideas, ideologies or philosophies or organize societies and organizations inside the country or abroad, that tend to uphold or perpetuate the oppression of the people or their exploitation by the Khartoum regime or by any other system of similar nature'.[47] This is considerably broader than, and contrary to, international humanitarian law understandings of legitimate targets. It will be particularly difficult for an outside observer to change the practice of an armed group if the group's code requires that the practice be undertaken.

Thus, translation of humanitarian norms presents a potentially useful means by which norms may be implemented. However, it also presents a potentially significant difficulty.

4. Utilization of commitments

So far, the focus has been on what armed groups could – or should – do in order to implement humanitarian norms. However, this is not the only factor to consider when implementing norms. The international community also has a role to play in implementing humanitarian norms through armed groups.

The high watermark relates to an involvement on the part of armed groups in the creation and development of international humanitarian law, an involvement that can take a variety of forms.[48] The strongest form relates to participation in treaty negotiations, whether through actual participation in a diplomatic conference; the feeding of views into the

[47] SPLM/A, Penal and Disciplinary Laws, section 29(1)(c), 4 July 1984 (quoted in J.-M. Henckaerts and L. Doswald-Beck, *Customary International Humanitarian Law*, 2 vols. (Cambridge: Cambridge University Press, 2005), vol. II, at 126–27).

[48] See generally A. Roberts and S. Sivakumaran, 'Lawmaking by Nonstate Actors: Engaging Armed Groups in the Creation of International Humanitarian Law' (2012) 37 *Yale Journal of International Law* 107, on which this section is based.

conference, for example, in the form of a background paper; or the convening of prior or concomitant meetings of armed groups. There are examples of this in practice. During the 1974–1977 Diplomatic Conference, various national liberation movements attended and took part in the work of the Conference.[49] Indeed, the Diplomatic Conference was 'convinced' that 'the progressive development and codification of international humanitarian law applicable in armed conflicts is a universal task in which the national liberation movements can contribute positively'.[50] Along different lines, prior to meetings of States parties to the Ottawa Convention, Geneva Call convenes meetings of signatories to its Deed of Commitment.[51]

Staying with the subject of humanitarian treaties, even if diplomatic conferences are limited to States, it may be that armed groups can be authorized to accede to treaties. Thus, the creation of the instrument is limited to States, but accession is open more broadly. Again, there is precedent to this effect, with the Provisional Government of the Algerian Republic acceding to the Geneva Conventions some years before it was recognized as a State.[52]

Despite the existence of these precedents, very real obstacles are evident. The precedent of national liberation movements is limited, given that they arose at a unique moment in history, namely, the period of decolonization. Furthermore, invitations were issued only to groups that had been recognized by regional intergovernmental organizations. Neither point applies in respect of armed groups; and States will likely be reluctant to allow armed groups a role at diplomatic conferences.

Turning to the second principal source of international law – customary international law – it may be that the practice and *opinio juris* of armed groups can be used in the formation of custom. This was the approach taken in the *Tadić* Decision on Interlocutory Appeal on Jurisdiction.[53]

[49] Resolution 3(I), 1 March 1974, in *Official Records of the Diplomatic Conference on the Reaffirmation and Development of International Humanitarian Law Applicable in Armed Conflicts, 1974–1977* (Berne: Federal Political Department, 1978), vol. 1, pt. II, at 5.

[50] Ibid.

[51] See, for example, Declaration by Signatories to the Deed of Commitment under Geneva Call for Adherence to a Total Ban on Anti-Personnel Mines and for Cooperation in Mine Action to the Cartagena Summit on a Mine-Free World, Nov. 30–Dec. 4 2009, 19 June 2009, www.genevacall.org/resources/nsas-statements/f-nsas-statements/2001–2010/2009–19jun-finalsign.pdf.

[52] Instruments of Accession of the Algerian Republic, above note 9.

[53] *Prosecutor v. Tadić*, Case No. IT-94-1-AR72, Decision on Defence Motion for Interlocutory Appeal on Jurisdiction (2 October 1995), paras. 102, 103, 107.

However, it has not since been followed by the International Criminal Tribunal for the former Yugoslavia (ICTY). The Customary International Humanitarian Law study, which was concluded under the auspices of the ICRC, collected some statements and practice of armed groups.[54] However, it listed this under the heading of 'other relevant practice' and did not use the category in the actual formulation of the rules.[55] Nonetheless, the study seemed to recognize that the practice was relevant, albeit unsure quite what to do with it. A second approach would thus be to create a category of practice that governs armed groups alone.[56] Insofar as this alternative is concerned, there is a danger of bifurcation of standards for States parties to conflicts and non-State armed group parties to conflicts. It could also go against the notion of equality of obligation of belligerents. A third alternative would thus be to establish a body of 'quasi-custom'.[57] Even here, difficulties arise in the precise manner in which the practice and *opinio juris* of armed groups would be used in the formation of the rules. Nonetheless, the difficulties could be successfully navigated.[58]

Were the involvement of armed groups in the conclusion of multilateral treaties and the creation of customary international law considered too much of an interference with the traditional architecture of international law, focus could be placed on the ad hoc commitments of armed groups and the normative weight to be given to them. Commitments would be treated as binding law only for the parties to the commitments with little impact on the wider legal framework.

Unilateral declarations of armed groups would be treated as binding upon them. Just as certain unilateral declarations of States are considered binding,[59] the same would be true of declarations of armed groups on humanitarian norms. Again, there is some practice to this effect. Pursuant to Security Council Resolution 1379 (2001), certain parties to armed conflicts or those involved in other situations of concern are required to conclude an action plan with local UN entities. These action plans, relating to the cessation of the recruitment and use of child soldiers,

54 J.-M. Henckaerts and L. Doswald-Beck, *Customary International Humanitarian Law*, above note 47, vol. II, at 64, 77, 115, 126, 356, 412, 778, 870, 2882, 3610.

55 Ibid. vol. I, at xxxvi.

56 Sassòli, 'Possible Legal Mechanisms', above note 21, at 7.

57 On this alternative, see Roberts and Sivakumaran, 'Lawmaking by Nonstate Actors', above note 48, at 149–51.

58 For ways in which this could be addressed, see Roberts and Sivakumaran, 'Lawmaking by Nonstate Actors', above note 48, at 137–41.

59 See *Nuclear Tests Case (Australia v. France)* (Merits) 1974 I.C.J. 253, paras. 43–46.

are binding on the armed group. Only if an action plan is concluded, and followed, will the party be delisted from the Security Council list.[60] Likewise, the Geneva Call Deed of Commitment is binding on armed non-State actor signatories, at least insofar as Geneva Call is concerned. Other examples exist in relation to ad hoc declarations. For example, the Palestine Liberation Organization (PLO) issued a declaration in relation to the Geneva Conventions. The Depositary considered this declaration 'valid', and it was referred to by the International Court of Justice in the *Wall* Advisory Opinion.[61]

Insofar as ad hoc agreements between armed groups and other actors are concerned, they could be considered akin to treaties – 'hybrid treaties' – and thus be binding on parties to the agreements.[62] Indeed, the 22 May 1992 Agreement has been utilized in a number of different ways by the ICTY,[63] all resulting from the idea that the Agreement was binding on the parties to it. Peace agreements are considered binding on the parties to them. Although various views exist on the nature of peace agreements – as treaties, not treaties, mini-constitutions, and the like[64] – their binding nature is rarely questioned. Indeed, the Security Council instituted sanctions against the União Nacional para a Independência Total de Angola (UNITA) for failing to implement the Acordos de Paz.[65] Given that a peace agreement is often not a single agreement, but a collection of previously concluded agreements, including agreements on humanitarian norms, these agreements would also be binding.[66]

60 UNSC Resolution 1539 (22 April 2004).

61 The Note from the Depositary is reprinted in 'Palestine and the Geneva Conventions' (1990) 74 *International Review of the Red Cross* 64. See *Legal Consequences of the Construction of a Wall in the Occupied Palestinian Territory* (Advisory Opinion) 2004 I.C.J. 136, para. 91.

62 See Roberts and Sivakumaran, 'Lawmaking by Nonstate Actors', above note 48, at 143–46.

63 See L. Vierucci, '"Special Agreements" between Conflicting Parties in the Case-Law of the ICTY', in B. Swart, A. Zahar and G. Sluiter (eds.), *The Legacy of the International Criminal Tribunal for the Former Yugoslavia* (Oxford: Oxford University Press, 2011), at 401–33.

64 See, for example, C. Bell, 'Peace Agreements: Their Nature and Legal Status' (2006) 100 *American Journal of International Law* 373; *Prosecutor v. Kallon and Kamara* (Decision on Challenge to Jurisdiction: Lomé Amnesty Accord) Case Nos. SCSL-2004-15-AR72(E) and SCSL-2004-16-AR72(E) (13 March 2004); A. Cassese, 'The Special Court and International Law: The Decision Concerning the Lomé Agreement Amnesty' (2004) 2 *Journal of International Criminal Justice* 1130, at 1134–35.

65 UNSC Resolution 864 (15 September 1993).

66 See generally C. Bell, *Peace Agreements and Human Rights* (Oxford: Oxford University Press, 2000); C. Bell, *On the Law of Peace* (Oxford: Oxford University Press, 2008).

5. Enforcement of humanitarian norms

Even if States are unwilling to allow armed groups to play a role in the creation or development of humanitarian norms, armed groups should still be able to play a role in the enforcement of the norms. Otherwise, the norms end up being considered something that is external to the group – created, enforced and even imposed by others.

5.1. Courts

A role for armed groups in the enforcement of international humanitarian law in particular can take different forms. The strongest form is the convening of courts on the part of the armed group to enforce the law.[67] This happens reasonably frequently in practice. To take but two examples of African conflicts, the Mouvement de Libération du Congo (MLC) operated a 'military judicial system'.[68] It adopted a Code of Conduct which contained rules on military discipline and outlined the framework of the Martial Court and Disciplinary Board system.[69] The Disciplinary Board had the competence to try junior officers for any offence except murder, theft, rape and certain others. Cases involving those offences were to be referred to the Martial Court.[70] A few years earlier, during the armed conflict in Sierra Leone (1991–2002), the RUF convened what it termed 'people's courts'. The RUF recounted:

> A few RUF fighters in the bush went on the rampage and as their own way of stating their objection to the planned elections, they proceeded on a campaign to cut off the hands of innocent villagers as a message that no voting should occur. This was how the amputation of hands started in Sierra Leone by desperate RUF men... Pa Foday Sankoh, the RUF leader was especially chagrined at the actions taken by these few RUF fighters. Our leader is aware that in war, atrocities occur especially when young disenfranchised men are revolting against an oppressive system.

[67] See generally S. Sivakumaran, 'Courts of Armed Opposition Groups: Fair Trials or Summary Justice?' (2009) 7 *Journal of International Criminal Justice* 489; J. Somer, 'Jungle Justice: Passing Sentence on the Equality of Belligerents in Non-international Armed Conflict' (2007) 89 *International Review of the Red Cross* 655; J. Willms, 'Courts of Armed Groups – A Tool for Inducing Higher Compliance with International Humanitarian Law?', Chapter 7 in this volume.

[68] *Prosecutor v. Bemba Gombo* (Decision Pursuant to Article 61(7)(a) and (b) of the Rome Statute on the Charges of the Prosecutor Against Jean-Pierre Bemba Gombo) Case No. ICC-01/05-01/08 (15 June 2009), para. 461.

[69] Ibid. para. 462. [70] Ibid.

> However, Pa Sankoh has never condoned acts of violence against civilians by RUF fighters. Pa Foday Sankoh immediately set up a special investigative Tribunal. This Tribunal was set up by the RUF War & Peace Council to look into the actions of and subsequently discipline the RUF fighters who performed these amputations. After the tribunal, all those fighters found guilty of this were publicly executed.[71]

The convening of courts on the part of armed groups is sometimes considered controversial.[72] However, it is unrealistic to tell an armed group that it is unable to enforce the law itself and that instead, it has to hand over the relevant individuals to the State for the State to try them. This is true regardless of whether the accused is a fighter of the armed group or a member of the State armed forces in the hands of the armed group. An armed group has indirectly handed over one of its members to the opposing State for trial on one occasion – the Mai-Mai of the Democratic Republic of the Congo in 2010. However, even then, the Mai-Mai handed over to the UN peacekeeping force an individual who was suspected of committing sexual violence; the UN peacekeeping force in turn handed him over to the government. However, it seems that the Mai-Mai was expecting the individual to be handed over to the International Criminal Court rather than to the State, with a spokesperson for the Mai-Mai stating that '[w]e gave [the accused] to the UN so that he can be investigated by the international criminal court for his actions against the local population'.[73]

The convening of courts is a sensitive issue insofar as States are concerned. The creation of courts and the function of law enforcement are considered intrinsic State functions. Accordingly, to extend them to non-State armed groups is sometimes considered to legitimize such groups and afford them a certain status. Even from the perspective of other actors, the matter is controversial. The International Council for Human Rights Policy, which is otherwise in favour of engaging armed groups on humanitarian norms, indicated that 'the fact that it is possible to work with armed groups (to improve their knowledge of international

[71] RUF Political Leadership-Kailahun District, 'RUF Calls for Independent Investigations', 15 January 1999.

[72] See, for example, the submission of Amnesty International to the *Bemba* Trial Chamber: *Prosecutor v. Bemba Gombo* (Amicus Curiae Observations on Superior Responsibility Submitted Pursuant to Rule 103 of the Rules of Procedure and Evidence) Case No. ICC-01/05-01/08–406 (20 April 2009).

[73] X. Rice, 'Milita Commander Mayele Arrested After Mass Rape of Congo Villagers', *The Guardian*, 6 October 2010.

standards, to advise them on "judicial" matters, and on training programmes for their military commanders) does not mean that it is desirable to do so'.[74] In the *Bemba Gombo* Case, Amnesty International submitted an amicus curiae brief arguing that superiors within a non-State armed group have to refer a matter to State or international authorities to satisfy their obligations under the principle of command responsibility and that referral to a non-State armed group authority would not suffice.[75] Importantly, the *Bemba Gombo* Pre-Trial Chamber did not agree with the proposition. In its decision confirming charges of command responsibility for war crimes in respect of Jean-Pierre Bemba Gombo, the Pre-Trial Chamber indicated that it had 'given particular weight to the availability of a functional military judicial system within the MLC through which [Bemba Gombo] could have punished crimes committed and prevented their future repetition during the period of intervention'.[76] This suggests that, in an appropriate situation, referral to an armed group judicial system may suffice.

5.2. *Fact-finding*

Aside from the convening of courts on the part of armed groups, there are a number of other ways in which armed groups could play a role in the enforcement of humanitarian norms. A less intrusive approach would be to include a member of the armed group on a particular fact-finding mission in addition to an official of the State. In this regard, the Taliban of Afghanistan made the interesting proposal in 2010 that a committee should be established to investigate civilian casualties resulting from the conflict in Afghanistan, which would comprise representatives from the Taliban, the International Security Assistance Force (ISAF) and the UN.[77]

An alternative would be to allow the armed group – again along with the State – the opportunity to select members of the fact-finding mission from a standing list drawn up by a relevant international body. Delicate issues may arise surrounding the modalities of the selection, confidentiality of

[74] International Council on Human Rights Policy, 'Ends and Means', above note 44 (emphases omitted).

[75] *Prosecutor v. Bemba Gombo* (Amicus Curiae Observations), above note 72, paras. 20–26.

[76] *Prosecutor v. Bemba Gombo* (Decision Pursuant to Article 61(7)(a) and (b)), above note 68, para. 501.

[77] Z. Mujahid, 'Response of the Spokesman of the Islamic Emirate of Afghanistan about Civilian Casualties' Survey', 15 August 2010.

witnesses and the like. However, with creative thinking, these difficulties could be overcome.

At the very least, invitations of armed groups to the international community to undertake a fact-finding mission should not be ignored. Unfortunately, this is not infrequently the case. During the attempted secession of Biafra from Nigeria, an observer team accepted an invitation from the government of Nigeria to assess its compliance with particular norms.[78] The same mission declined a similar invitation on the part of the Biafran authorities.[79] Today, in many cases, invitations on the part of armed groups are simply ignored. During the conflict in Sierra Leone, following the attribution of amputations of civilians to the RUF, the RUF issued a press release indicating that '[i]t is time the International Community set up an investigation into whom are the perpetrators of amputations'.[80] In an interview in 2008, Laurent Nkunda, then the leader of the National Congress for the Defence of the People (CNDP), stated that, after he heard accusations that the CNDP were recruiting child soldiers, 'I called for Unicef to come and verify it'.[81] Jean-Pierre Bemba Gombo indicated that he wrote to the Special Representative of the Secretary-General for the Democratic Republic of the Congo asking for UN involvement in conducting certain investigations.[82] The possibility certainly exists that, were these invitations to be accepted, the armed group would withdraw them or would find a way to obstruct the investigation. However, if that is the case, the bluff needs to be called. Otherwise, genuine offers are conflated with insincere ones, and none are acted upon.

5.3. *Self-reporting*

A distinct approach, which could be utilized in addition to either or both of the above, is to create a self-reporting mechanism through which armed groups would be required to report on the measures that they took to comply with humanitarian norms. This already exists in an attenuated

78 'Report of the Observer Team to Nigeria', 24 September–23 November 1968, Cmnd 3878 (HMSO, 1969).

79 A. H. M. Kirk-Greene, *Crisis and Conflict in Nigeria: A Documentary Sourcebook 1966–1969* (Oxford: Oxford University Press, 1971), vol. II, at 81.

80 RUF Political Leadership-Kailahun District, 'RUF Calls for Independent Investigations', 15 January 1999.

81 L. Nkunda, 'Fighting for Peace', *The Guardian Weekly*, 22 April 2008.

82 *Prosecutor v. Bemba Gombo* (Conclusions de la Défense en Réponse a l'acte d'Accusation, Amende du 30 Mars 2009) Case No. ICC-01/05-01/08 (24 April 2009), para. 239.

form, with armed groups that are signatories to Geneva Call's Deed of Commitment being required to report to Geneva Call on a range of matters, including challenges they have faced in complying with the Deed.[83] The advantage of a self-reporting mechanism is that armed groups are required to think about the issues, raise any difficulties they are experiencing and explain their response to allegations of violations. For Geneva Call:

> Self-monitoring and self-reporting have the advantage of ensuring that signatory NSAs take responsibility for their commitment. The responsibility for monitoring their own compliance and collecting information increases the sensitivity of signatories to their . . . obligations and creates a greater sense of ownership. Such cooperation in information sharing is not a mere formality; it is a significant indication of the will of the signatories to abide by their commitment.[84]

Following the reporting, dialogue should ensue so as to talk through issues, improve knowledge and understanding and resolve difficulties and violations. Otherwise, the process becomes a mere formality of simply submitting reports. As the experience with the human rights treaty bodies has shown, different actors treat their responsibilities with different levels of seriousness. There is also a danger of experiencing a backlog or of creating reporting fatigue. Nonetheless, the idea of self-reporting could prove to be a valuable one, particularly if it is linked to an instrument containing a compilation of key humanitarian norms which armed groups could sign,[85] or if it sits alongside an individual complaints procedure.[86]

6. Conclusion

There are a number of ways in which armed groups can play a greater role in the implementation of humanitarian norms while staying within the existing normative framework. The key point is that armed groups should

[83] See P. Bongard and J. Somer, 'Monitoring Armed Non-State Actor Compliance with Humanitarian Norms: A Look at International Mechanisms and the Geneva Call Deed of Commitment' (2011) 93 *International Review of the Red Cross* 673.

[84] Geneva Call, 'Engaging Armed Non-State Actors in a Landmine Ban: The Geneva Call Progress Report (2000–2007)', Geneva Call, 2007, at 25.

[85] See S. Sivakumaran, 'How to Improve upon the Faulty Legal Regime of Internal Armed Conflicts', in A. Cassese (ed.), *Realizing Utopia: The Future of International Law* (Oxford: Oxford University Press, 2012), at 525–37.

[86] See J. K. Kleffner and L. Zegveld, 'Establishing an Individual Complaints Procedure for Violations of International Humanitarian Law' (2000) 3 *Yearbook of International Humanitarian Law* 384.

have some sort of role in the creation, translation and enforcement of humanitarian norms in order to foster a sense of ownership and therefore improve levels of compliance. Aside from a few exceptions, that is not the case today. In this sense, there has been relatively little implementation of humanitarian norms through non-State armed groups.

At the time of writing, certain States had expressed their reluctance for outside bodies to engage with armed groups, even on humanitarian norms, for fear that this may imbue the group with a certain legal status or afford them a certain legitimacy. The issue of even engaging armed groups on humanitarian norms is a delicate one. Indeed, in 2010, the US Supreme Court held that providing advice or training on international humanitarian law to certain armed groups could amount to providing material support to terrorist groups in violation of US law.[87]

However, in decades past, the very regulation of non-international armed conflict led to concerns surrounding the legal status and legitimacy of armed groups. These concerns have been ameliorated significantly by the clause in Common Article 3 to the Geneva Conventions, also to be found in subsequent instruments, to the effect that application of the rules does not affect the legal status of the group. A clause to a similar effect may be needed to avoid criticism of engaging with armed groups on humanitarian norms.

[87] *Holder v. Humanitarian Law Project*, 130 S. Ct. 2705 (2010).

PART II

Criminal prosecution – hierarchical enforcement on different levels

7

Courts of armed groups – a tool for inducing higher compliance with international humanitarian law?

JAN WILLMS*

1. Introduction

The armed group[1] Mouvement de Libération du Congo (MLC), led by Jean-Pierre Bemba, controlled large parts of the north of the Democratic Republic of the Congo (DRC) between the late 1990s and 2003. In the beginning, the MLC acted fairly responsibly and installed a civilian administration. In 2002 and 2003, however, its members committed atrocities in the DRC and the Central African Republic. In February 2003, the MLC tried twenty-seven of its members for extortion, rape, assassination, looting and disobeying orders.[2] The trials took place in the headquarters of the MLC in the north of the DRC. The UN peace support operation MONUC would have provided airplanes for defence attorneys from Kinshasa to travel in, but the government of the DRC prevented them from boarding.[3] The verdicts were delivered one week after the beginning of the trial[4] and attracted serious criticism. In front of the Security Council, the United States condemned three aspects of the trial, namely:

* I am grateful to Dieter Fleck, Heike Krieger and Sandesh Sivakumaran for providing comments on earlier drafts of this chapter. I also owe thanks to the participants of the Conference on the Implementation of International Humanitarian Law in Contemporary African Conflicts in September 2011 in Potsdam, where I presented and discussed the issue. All possible errors remain, of course, mine.

[1] The term is used here for armed non-State actors that at least meet the requirements in Common Article 3 of the Geneva Conventions.

[2] Interview with MLC Leader Jean-Pierre Bemba, Integrated Regional Information Networks (IRIN), 6 February 2003, www.irinnews.org/fr/reportfrench.aspx?reportid=41456.

[3] IRIN, 'MLC Completes Ituri Rights Violations Trials', Subject to Appeal, 27 February 2003, www.irinnews.org/fr/report/41456/drc-interview-with-mlc-leader-jean-pierre-bemba.

[4] Ibid.

(1) 'inadequate' due process guarantees 'afforded to the defendants'
(2) 'disregard for the serious nature of the crimes, as reflected in the light sentences handed down'; and
(3) 'the failure to charge anyone with crimes against humanity or war crimes'.[5]

Similarly, Jean-Marie Guéhenno, Under-Secretary-General for Peace-keeping Operations, said that the trials had not achieved real accountability.[6] While the DRC simply obstructed the MLC's trial, the UN and the United States were more pragmatic. Their criticism was not that an armed group had used courts but only the manner in which the MLC had done so.

This example illustrates a basic dilemma. On the one hand, States are usually unwilling to accept the operation of an armed group's court on their territory because the administration of justice is considered to be a very important aspect of their sovereignty. On the other hand, the international community[7] has a strong interest in the enforcement of international humanitarian law, in which such rebel courts might play a role.

Can courts of armed groups be an effective tool for the implementation of the law of armed conflict[8] despite States' concerns about their sovereignty? In response to that question, it will first be addressed whether such courts are legal or even required under international humanitarian and human rights law (Section 2). Then this chapter will deal with the question of whether the prohibition of double jeopardy must be applied to 'judgments' issued by courts of armed groups (Section 3). This will be followed by a more empirical analysis whether such courts can contribute to the implementation of humanitarian law (Section 4) and to what extent they respect fair trial guarantees (Section 5). Subsequently, the effect of courts of armed groups on the empirical legitimacy of the armed groups possessing them will be analysed (Section 6). Finally, how the international community should react to these kinds of courts will be discussed (Section 7).

[5] United Nations Security Council, 4784th Meeting, S/PV.4784, Mr. Williamson (USA), at 19.

[6] Ibid. 3.

[7] The term 'international community' is used here to refer to the interests that are shared among the majority of international actors. For a good discussion of the term, see A. Paulus and B. Simma, 'The "International Community": Facing the Challenge of Globalization' (1998) 9 *European Journal of International Law* 266.

[8] The terms 'international humanitarian law' and 'law of armed conflict' are used here interchangeably.

2. The status of courts of armed groups

2.1. Are courts of armed groups prohibited?

Turning to their legal status, courts of armed groups are normally illegal under a State's domestic law. In light of the topic of this book, it is more important to focus on their legality under international law standards for the protection of individuals. If courts of armed groups were illegal under international law, this would compromise any positive effects such courts might have on the implementation of international humanitarian law rules.

2.1.1. International humanitarian law

There are two conventional provisions in the law of armed conflict relevant to courts of armed groups: Common Article 3(1)(d) of the 1949 Geneva Conventions (GC) and Article 6 of Additional Protocol II to the Geneva Conventions (Additional Protocol II, AP II). Moreover, Rule 100 of the Customary Law Study of the International Committee of the Red Cross (ICRC) also prescribes that fair trial guarantees apply by means of customary international law in non-international armed conflicts.[9]

Provided that the respective thresholds of application are met, these fair trial guarantees apply when courts of armed groups adjudicate violations of international humanitarian law, regardless of whether the defendant is a civilian or belongs to the party that conducts the trial or to the adverse party.[10] Indeed, violations of humanitarian law have, by definition, a nexus to the armed conflict.[11]

[9] J.-M. Henckaerts and L. Doswald-Beck, *Customary International Humanitarian Law* 2 vols. (Cambridge: Cambridge University Press, 2005), vol. I, at 352.

[10] S. Sivakumaran, *The Law of Non-International Armed Conflict* (Oxford: Oxford University Press, 2012), at 249. In non-international armed conflict, international humanitarian law also protects persons against the armed group to which they belong. *Prosecutor v. Ntaganda* (Decision Pursuant to Article 61(7)(a) and (b) of the Rome Statute on the Charges of the Prosecutor Against Bosco Ntaganda) Case No. ICC-01/04–02/06 (9 June 2014), paras. 76–82; Sivakumaran, *Law*, this note, at 246–49. Besides Sandesh Sivakumaran, I am also grateful to Jean-Marie Henckaerts, Krisztina Huszti-Orban, Jelena Pejic, Marco Sassòli, Jonathan Somer and Cornelius Wiesener for sharing their views with me on this issue.

[11] The application of international humanitarian law more generally presupposes a link to the armed conflict which follows from its conditions of application and which has been affirmed by international criminal tribunals on a number of occasions. See, for example, *Prosecutor v. Milutinovic* (Judgment) Case No. IT-05-87-T (26 February 2009), paras. 127–128. More specifically, Article 6(1) AP II restricts the application of Article 6 AP II to the 'prosecution and punishment of criminal offences related to the armed conflict'. By definition, this condition is also met if violations of international humanitarian law are adjudicated.

International humanitarian law contains no rule that explicitly prohibits courts by armed groups. Only Common Article 3 GC, which requires a 'judgment pronounced by a regularly constituted court', makes one hesitate. By its ordinary meaning, this would seem to mean something along the lines of the human rights standard 'established by law'. If 'law' is interpreted as State law only, this could be understood as prohibiting armed groups to operate courts.[12] In the context of humanitarian law, the term 'law' could also include law by an armed group. Similarly, a court could be 'regularly constituted' within the law of the armed group.

At any rate, according to the principles of effectiveness and good faith, it would not make sense to also apply a norm to non-State actors[13] which they cannot possibly comply with. The phrase 'regularly constituted court' has not been reused in Article 6 AP II which indicates that States did not place much emphasis on how a court of an armed group is established but were much more concerned about fair trial guarantees.

Customary international humanitarian law does not – according to the ICRC – prohibit courts of armed groups either. Rule 100 of the ICRC Customary Law Study is formulated in a general fashion and does not require a regularly constituted court. The Rule simply reads: 'No one may be convicted or sentenced, except pursuant to a fair trial affording all essential judicial guarantees'.[14] Similarly, the Manual of Non-International Armed Conflict sets out fair trial guarantees that armed groups in principle can meet.[15]

The above-mentioned U.S. condemnation of the MLC's too light punishment implicitly supports the conclusion that courts of armed groups are not illegal under international humanitarian law.[16] Otherwise, the United States would absurdly be demanding an act that violates humanitarian law in order to punish a violation of the same body of law. The same reasoning can be applied, *mutatis mutandis*, to the following statements.

[12] It will be discussed below whether this is actually the case under human rights law. See Section 2.1.3.

[13] It can hardly be doubted that Common Article 3 GC including its rules on courts formally applies to armed groups since the chapeau of that Article is addressed to 'each Party'. This formal application is dealt with in more detail by S. Sivakumaran, 'Courts of Armed Opposition Groups: Fair Trials or Summary Justice?' (2009) 7 *Journal of International Criminal Justice* 489, at 495–98.

[14] Henckaerts and Doswald-Beck, *Customary International Humanitarian Law*, above note 9, vol. I, at 352.

[15] Y. Dinstein, C. Garraway and M. Schmitt, 'The Manual on the Law of Non-International Armed Conflict' (2006) 36 *Israel Yearbook on Human Rights*, Special Supplement, at 51–52.

[16] See above note 5 and corresponding text.

The Security Council urged that 'RCD [Rally for Congolese Democracy]-GOMA must . . . ensure an end to all violations of human rights and to impunity in all areas under its control'.[17] The Special Rapporteur for of the UN Commission on Human Rights in Sudan demanded that two armed groups operating in South Sudan, long before it acquired independence, 'should take the necessary measures without delay to prevent future violations by investigating the cases brought to their attention and holding the perpetrators responsible'.[18] The Commission of Inquiry for Libya (at a time when the non-international armed conflict was still ongoing[19]) recommended to the Libyan National Transitional Council 'to conduct exhaustive, impartial and public investigations into all allegations of international human rights law and international humanitarian law violations . . . with full respect of judicial guarantees'.[20] These calls on consolidated armed groups to investigate crimes in situations of armed conflict support the conclusion that the law of armed conflict does not prohibit such courts.

2.1.2. Rome Statute of the International Criminal Court

Since Article 8(2)(c)(iv) of the Statute of the International Criminal Court (ICC) is, by and large, simply a criminalized version of common Article 3, it is not surprising that Article 8(2)(c)(iv) does not forbid courts of armed groups either. In the ICC Elements of Crimes, a 'regularly constituted court' is defined as a court 'affording the essential guarantees of independence and impartiality'; and independence and impartiality are standards that courts by armed groups are in principle able to meet.

[17] UNSC Presidential Statement 22 (23 July 2002), para. 4.

[18] Report of the Special Rapporteur on the Situation of Human Rights in Sudan (20 February 1996), UN Doc. E/CN.4/1996/62, para. 87.

[19] It is not necessary to dwell on the question of the qualification of the conflict. In order to identify the Commission's opinion on the applicability of human rights law to armed groups, it is sufficient to note that the Commission qualified the conflict as non-international and referred to the National Transitional Council as a 'dissident armed group' in the sense of Additional Protocol II to the Geneva Conventions. See Report of the International Commission of Inquiry to Investigate All Alleged Violations of International Human Rights Law in the Libyan Arab Jamahiriya (1 June 2011), UN Doc. A/HRC/17/44, paras. 60–65. At any rate, as Dapo Akande rightly pointed out, the recognition of the National Transitional Council as the 'legitimate governing authority in Libya' did not take place before 15 July 2011. Dapo Akande, 'Recognition of Libyan National Transitional Council as Government of Libya', *EJIL: Talk!*, 23 July 2011, www.ejiltalk.org/recognition-of-libyan-national-transitional-council-as-government-of-libya/.

[20] Commission of Inquiry – Libya, above note 19, para. 269.

Although this interpretation in the ICC Elements of Crimes fails to differentiate between regular constitution and fair trial guarantees,[21] it is an authoritative interpretation of the Rome Statute. The ICC's jurisprudence in the *Bemba* Case also confirms that courts of armed groups are not illegal. Before the decision on confirming or declining charges, Amnesty International submitted amicus curiae observations. Therein, Amnesty argued that Bemba could not use a court of an armed group in order to avoid command responsibility. Amnesty reasoned that such a court does not meet the human rights standard 'established by law' and is not able to provide for a fair trial.[22] Pre-Trial Chamber II did not share this view. On the contrary, it established command responsibility on the basis that Bemba's armed group had a 'functional military judicial system' which was not used.[23] This clearly confirms the interpretation that armed groups are able to meet the requirements in Article 8(2)(c)(iv) ICC Statute. Otherwise, the ICC would encourage war crimes.

2.1.3. Human rights law

Courts of armed groups are not prohibited under international humanitarian law. But what is the status of these courts under human rights law? The first question that arises is whether armed groups are bound by human rights law at all. Although still very controversial, there is growing international practice and an increasing tendency in the literature that speaks in favour of such an application, especially in cases where armed groups control territory and/or exercise quasi-governmental authority[24] or for *jus cogens* norms.[25] Fair trial guarantees would, in

21 J. Somer, 'Jungle Justice: Passing Sentence on the Equality of Belligerents in Non-international Armed Conflict' (2007) 89 *International Review of the Red Cross* 655, at 675.

22 *Prosecutor v. Bemba Gombo* (Amicus Curiae Observations on Superior Responsibility submitted pursuant to Rule 103 of the Rules of Procedure and Evidence) Case No. ICC-01/05–01/08–406 (20 April 2009), paras. 22–23.

23 *Prosecutor v. Bemba Gombo* (Decision Pursuant to Article 61(7)(a) and (b) of the Rome Statute) Case No. ICC-01/05–01/08 (15 June 2009), para. 501.

24 This view is found in a large number of UN reports. See, for example, Report of the United Nations Fact-Finding Mission on the Gaza Conflict (25 September 2009), UN Doc. A/HRC/12/48, para. 305; Report of the International Commission of Inquiry to Investigate All Alleged Violations of International Human Rights Law in the Libyan Arab Jamahiriya (1 June 2011), UN Doc. A/HRC/17/44, para. 72.

25 First Report of the Committee on Non State Actors, 'Non-State Actors in International Law: Aims, Approach and Scope of Project and Legal Issues', in International Law Association Report on the Seventy-Fourth Conference (The Hague, 2010), para. 3.2; A. Bellal,

the opinion of the Human Rights Committee, qualify as *jus cogens* norms.[26]

Arguments in support of the application of human rights law to non-State actors differ. One is in essence functional: '[A]s an insurrectionary movement takes control over territory and establishes an administration, it . . . automatically assumes the human rights obligations resting on the territory'.[27] Others primarily base themselves on State practice and *opinio juris*.[28] It cannot be said with certainty whether practice has crystallized into a clear-cut obligation of armed groups to respect human rights. However, such a duty is developing.[29]

Assuming that the right to a fair trial applies to courts of armed groups, the courts would have to be 'competent' or 'established by law'.[30] While the Human Rights Committee declined to pronounce itself on these terms,[31] Nowak interprets them as follows:

G. Giacca, and S. Casey-Maslen, 'International Law and Armed Non-State Actors in Afghanistan' (2011) 65 *International Review of the Red Cross* 47, at 72–73.

26 General Comment on States of Emergency (General Comment 29), Human Rights Committee, 31 August 2001, UN Doc. CCPR/C/21/Rev.1/Add.11 (stating that peremptory norms include 'fundamental principles of fair trial, including the presumption of innocence').

27 J. Hessbruegge, 'Human Rights Violations Arising from the Conduct of Non-State Actors' (2005) 11 *Buffalo Human Rights Law Review* 21, at 40–41. For his point, Hessbruegge relies on an expansive interpretation of General Comment 26. It is stated in the Comment that the 'rights enshrined in the Covenant belong to the people living in the territory of the State party'. However, the Human Rights Committee did not relate this statement to control by non-State actors. In fact, in all examples the Human Rights Committee puts forward (change of government, dismemberment, State succession), a State still has the authority. See General Comment on Issues Relating to the Continuity of Obligations to the International Covenant on Civil and Political Rights (General Comment 26), Human Rights Committee, 8 December 1997, UN Doc. CPR/C/21/Rev.1/Add.8/Rev. 1, para. 4.

28 C. Tomuschat, 'The Applicability of Human Rights Law to Insurgent Movements', in H. Fischer et al. (eds.), *Krisensicherung und Humanitärer Schutz – Crisis Management and Humanitarian Protection: Festschrift für Dieter Fleck* (Berliner Wissenschafts-Verlag: Berlin, 2004), 573–91; A. Clapham, 'Human Rights Obligations of Non-State Actors in Conflict Situations' (2006) 88 *International Review of the Red Cross* 491, at 495–508.

29 See the considerable amount of practice assembled by Tomuschat, Clapham (both in the preceding note) as well as Henckaerts and Wiesener. J.-M. Henckaerts and C. Wiesener, 'Human Rights Obligations of Non-State Armed Groups: A Possible Contribution from Customary International Law?, in R. Kolb and G. Gaggioli (eds.), *Research Handbook on Human Rights and Humanitarian Law* (Elgar: Cheltenham, 2013), 146–69.

30 Article 14(1) of the ICCPR; Article 7(1)(a) of the African Charter on Human and Peoples' Rights. The African Court for Human and Peoples' Rights has not yet dealt with the right to a competent court.

31 *Fals Borda et al. v. Colombia* (46/1979), Human Rights Committee, 27 July 1982, para. 13.3.

> Both conditions [competent and established by law] are to ensure that the jurisdictional power of a tribunal is determined generally and independent of the given case, i.e. not arbitrarily by a specific administrative act. The term 'law' is . . . to be understood in the strict sense of a parliamentary statute or an equivalent unwritten norm of common law, which must be accessible to all persons subject to it.[32]

Especially where armed groups wish to pass their own laws, most of them find it difficult to meet the requirement of a 'parliamentary statute'. However, if armed groups were bound by a human rights norm they were not able to comply with, 'such a rule . . . [would] not be complied with and it . . . [would] undermine the credibility and protecting effect of other rules'.[33] This would run counter to the principal reason that motivates deliberations on how armed groups could be bound by human rights law, that is, the protection gap for populations living under its control.[34] It would therefore seem reasonable to functionally interpret the requirement that a court must be established by law. Indeed, this condition has been flexibly interpreted outside the domestic law context.[35] The European Court of Human Rights held that courts of a non-State entity unrecognized by the international community could, in principle, meet the 'established by law' condition:

> In certain circumstances, a court belonging to the judicial system of an entity not recognised under international law may be regarded as a tribunal 'established by law' provided that it forms part of a judicial system operating on a 'constitutional and legal basis' reflecting a judicial tradition compatible with the Convention, in order to enable individuals to enjoy the Convention guarantees.[36]

32 M Nowak, *U.N. Covenant on Civil and Political Rights: CCPR Commentary* (Kehl: N.P. Engel Verlag, 2005), at 319. For a similar definition, see the jurisprudence of the European Court of Human Rights: *Coëme et al. v. Belgium* (Judgment) Application No. 32492/96 (18 October 2000) para. 98.

33 Sassòli makes this point in the context of international humanitarian law. M. Sassòli, 'Taking Armed Groups Seriously: Ways to Improve Their Compliance with International Humanitarian Law' (2010) 1 *International Humanitarian Legal Studies* 5, at 16.

34 See, for example, Bellal, Giacca and Casey-Maslen, 'Afghanistan', above note 25, at 70.

35 In *Tadić*, 'established by law' was held to mean 'established according to the rule of law' in an international law context. *Prosecutor v. Tadić* (Decision on the Defence Motion for Interlocutory Appeal on Jurisdiction) Case No. IT-94-1-AR72 (2 October 1995), para. 45.

36 *Ilaşcu et al. v. Moldova and Russia* (Judgment) Application No. 4877/99, European Court of Human Rights, 8 July 2004, paras. 455–464. See also *Cyprus v. Turkey* (Judgment) Application No. 25781/94, European Court of Human Rights, 10 May 2001, paras. 231, 236–237. For criticism of this interpretation, see in particular *Cyprus v. Turkey*, this note, Partly Dissenting Opinion of Judge Palm Joined by Judges Jungwiert, Levits, Pantiru, Kovler and Marcus-Helmons, 101, at 101–105, and *Cyprus v. Turkey*, this note, Partly Dissenting Opinion of Judge Marcus-Helmons, 119, at 119–124.

Admittedly, the European Court of Human Rights held this with regard to consolidated de facto regimes, such as the Turkish Republic of Northern Cyprus and the Moldavian Republic of Transnistria, which have a higher degree of organization than most armed groups. However, it is still remarkable that the European Court of Human Rights, which can only adjudicate human rights violations attributable to States, allows at all for that possibility. Moreover, the Commission of Inquiry for Libya[37] and the Security Council[38] considered that human rights law applied to the Libyan National Transitional Council and the Rally for Congolese Democracy GOMA, respectively, and called for accountability measures by these armed groups. Hence, if human rights law applied to armed groups, it would not per se prohibit that they have courts.

2.2. *The possible duty of armed groups to investigate and prosecute*

We have seen that international law rules regarding the protection of individuals do not prohibit armed groups to operate courts. The next question, then, is whether armed groups are obliged to investigate and prosecute war crimes. If armed groups were under a duty to investigate and prosecute, this would strengthen the role of their courts as a tool for implementation. The duty to investigate and prosecute is enshrined in international humanitarian and international criminal law but can also be deduced from human rights law.[39]

37 Commission of Inquiry – Libya, above note 19, paras. 72 (human rights), 269 (accountability).

38 UNSC Presidential Statement 22, above note 17 and corresponding text.

39 If we accepted that human rights law applied to armed groups, an obligation to investigate a certain human rights law violation could also be the basis for a duty to investigate a particular war crime if the two crimes had the same underlying offence. The Human Rights Committee has developed, for example, the obligation to investigate violations of the right to life. *Amirov v. Russian Federation* (1447/2006), Human Rights Committee, 2 April 2009, paras. 11.2–11.4. A violation of the right to life during armed conflict could at the same time be a violation of international humanitarian law. However, there is no obligation to investigate under human rights law that specifically encompasses all war crimes. Moreover, the relationship between international humanitarian and human rights law needs to be borne in mind, although there seem to be no inherent conflicts between the duties to investigate in both branches of law. For the last point, see the 'Report of the Committee of Independent Experts in International Humanitarian and Human Rights Law to Monitor and Assess any Domestic, Legal or Other Proceedings Undertaken by Both the Government of Israel and the Palestinian Side, in the light of General Assembly Resolution 64/254, Including the Independence, Effectiveness, Genuineness of these Investigations and their Conformity with International Standards' (23 September 2010), UN Doc. A/HRC/15/50, para. 29; M. Schmitt, 'Investigating Violations of International Law in Armed Conflict' (2011) 2 *Harvard National Security Journal* 31, at 54.

The treaty-based law of armed conflict only obliges States to investigate war crimes.[40] Similarly, it would be difficult to contend that customary international humanitarian law imposes a duty to investigate and prosecute for all armed groups. Even the ICRC in its Customary Law Study, which is sometimes criticized for demanding too much of non-State actors,[41] finds an obligation to investigate and prosecute in Rule 158 only for States.[42] George Abi-Saab's contention in his separate opinion in the *Tadić* Case that the grave breaches provisions applied in non-international armed conflict[43] did not include an explicit claim that armed groups should be bound by it. It might also be that he only considered States and de facto regimes, like those that operated in the former Yugoslavia, to be the addressees of the grave breaches provisions.

However, the examples quoted above[44] could indicate a trend towards an obligation to investigate and prosecute for well-consolidated armed groups that control territory. The Goldstone Report on the violations of international humanitarian and human rights law during the 2008–2009 Gaza Conflict even held (at least for Gaza) that any de facto authority exercising government-like functions was under an obligation to prosecute members of armed groups in the territory under its control, seemingly regardless of whether the members of the armed groups are affiliated to the de facto authority or not:

> The Gaza authorities are responsible for ensuring that effective measures for accountability for violations of IHRL [international human rights law] and IHL [international humanitarian law] committed by armed groups acting in or from the Gaza Strip are established. The Mission points out that such responsibility would continue to rest on *any* authority exercising government-like functions in the Gaza Strip.[45]

40 See, in particular, the grave breaches regime. Geneva Convention I, Article 49; Geneva Convention II, Article 50; Geneva Convention III, Article 129; Geneva Convention IV, Article 146.

41 Sassòli, 'Taking Armed Groups Seriously', above note 33, at 17.

42 Henckaerts and Doswald-Beck, *Customary International Humanitarian Law*, above note 9, vol. I, at 558. For support of the Rule, see Schmitt, 'Investigating Violations', above note 39, at 44–45.

43 *Prosecutor v. Tadić*, above note 35, Separate Opinion of Judge Abi-Saab. For a sceptical view of Abi Saab's opinion, see L. Moir, 'Grave Breaches and Internal Armed Conflicts' (2009) 7 *Journal of International Criminal Justice* 787.

44 See above notes 4 as well as 17 through 20 and corresponding text. Admittedly, the practice with regard to Libya (above note 19) and Sudan (above note 18) are only recommendations.

45 Report of the United Nations Fact-Finding Mission on the Gaza Conflict (25 September 2009), UN Doc. A/HRC/12/48, at 509 (emphasis added). It is not clear whether the Goldstone Report imposes a duty to investigate for all de facto authorities (or regimes). The case of Gaza is different, especially since the hostilities are often classified as an

This somewhat limited practice does not allow to claim with certainty whether or not an obligation to investigate and prosecute exists for armed groups, let alone whether armed groups are obliged to set up courts. Arguably, such a rule would not be realistic for all armed groups.[46]

Assuming that the ICRC is correct in claiming that States are always under an obligation to investigate in non-international armed conflicts, whereas armed groups are not necessarily obligated to do so, would that not violate the principle of equality of belligerents, disadvantage States and ultimately endanger the observance of international humanitarian law?[47] Not necessarily. If States engage in practice by which they bind themselves with a duty to investigate and prosecute in non-international armed conflict without at the same time compelling armed groups to do so, those States would be inconsistent when subsequently criticizing this variance in obligations. The risk that unequal obligations lead to an erosion of international humanitarian law seems marginal in this particular case. Indeed, it would not necessarily be detrimental to the observance of humanitarian law if a State were under a duty to investigate and prosecute, whereas an armed group that is unable to meet such an obligation were not. After all, States tend to oppose courts by armed groups on their territory.[48] However, it needs to be said that the principle of equality of belligerents is otherwise very important and should be defended against those who generally question its relevance.[49]

All in all, it is to date difficult to sustain that armed groups are under a duty to investigate and prosecute war crimes. Nonetheless, such an obligation to prosecute may exist on an individual level, that is, it may be incumbent on commanders of armed groups pursuant to the doctrine of

international armed conflict. The Goldstone Report is ambiguous in that regard and seems to acknowledge that the armed conflict has both international and non-international elements. Ibid. 87. However, the subsequent Tomuschat Report claims that the armed conflict had clearly been classified as international in nature. Report of the Committee of Independent Experts, above note 39, para. 18.

[46] In a similar context, Sassòli doubts whether armed groups are able to conduct habeas corpus proceedings. Sassòli, 'Taking Armed Groups Seriously', above note 33, at 17.

[47] For an affirmative answer, see ibid. 16–17, and Somer, 'Jungle Justice', above note 21, at 684. For the opinion that the principle of equality of belligerents does not apply to non-international armed conflicts, see L. Doswald-Beck, 'The Right to Life in Armed Conflict: Does International Humanitarian Law Provide all the Answers?' (2006) 88 *International Review of the Red Cross* 881, at 890.

[48] See above note 3.

[49] In the context of international armed conflict, see M. Mandel, 'Aggressors' Rights: The Doctrine of "Equality between Belligerents" and the Legacy of Nuremberg' (2011) 24 *Leiden Journal of International Law* 627 (in particular at 649 where Mandel simply overlooks that an aggressor has no incentive to respect international humanitarian law if every act in pursuance of armed conflict is illegal anyway).

command responsibility. Pursuant to Article 28 of the ICC Statute, military commanders in any kind of armed conflict incur responsibility for core crimes (genocide, crimes against humanity and war crimes) committed by their subordinates if the commander failed 'to take all necessary and reasonable measures within his or her power to prevent or repress' them and provided that the respective commander knew or ought to have known about these crimes.[50] This mode of liability is accepted as customary international law in Rule 153 of the ICRC Customary Law Study.[51]

How a subordinate must be punished depends on the gravity of the crime[52] and on what is materially possible.[53] Depending on the capacities of the armed group, it is not always reasonable to expect a criminal trial. Pre-Trial Chamber II of the ICC seems to have adopted such a functional approach. It considered 'the availability of a functional military judicial system' and that this system was not properly used as one aspect leading to a violation of Bemba's command responsibility.[54]

Hence, there does not seem to be a clear obligation to set up courts, either on the armed group or on the commander. Commanders only have to ensure prosecution if such courts are available. The *Bemba* decision may even be a disincentive for armed groups to set up courts because once a court is set up, a commander must ensure that subordinates are tried by these courts if that commander intends to avoid command responsibility for the subordinates' crimes.

3. Courts of armed groups and the *ne bis in idem* principle

Another argument that could be advanced against courts of armed groups is based on the *ne bis in idem* principle. The argument could run as follows: if after a sham trial by a court of an armed group, the *ne bis in idem*

50 See also Article 7(3) of the Statute of the International Tribunal for the Former Yugoslavia, annexed to UNSC Resolution 827 (25 May 1993) and Article 6(3) Statute of the International Tribunal for Rwanda, annexed to UNSC Resolution 955 (8 November 1994).

51 Henckaerts and Doswald-Beck, *Customary International Humanitarian Law*, above note 9, vol. I, at 607.

52 Even where it is materially possible, a criminal trial is not always necessary. An ICTY Trial Chamber held that disciplinary punishment was sufficient for pillage. *Prosecutor v. Hadžihasanović* (Judgment) Case No. IT-01-47-T (15 March 2006), paras. 2056–2058. On the other hand, the Appeals Chamber added that a disciplinary sanction not exceeding sixty days would have been insufficient to punish murder and cruel treatment. *Prosecutor v. Hadžihasanović* (Judgment) Case No. IT-01-47-A (22 April 2008), paras. 149–155.

53 *Prosecutor v. Bemba Gombo* (Decision), above note 23, para. 434.

54 *Prosecutor v. Bemba Gombo* (Decision), above note 23, para. 501.

principle makes a new trial for the same offence by a state or international court illegal,[55] this would undermine efforts towards accountability. However, is the basis for this argument actually correct? In other words, does international law oblige State and/or international courts to apply the *ne bis in idem* principle to trials by courts of armed groups?

Four bodies of law, which will be analysed in turn, speak against such an obligation: international humanitarian law (Section 3.1), customary international criminal law (Section 3.2), human rights law (Section 3.3) and the Rome Statute (Section 3.4).

3.1. International humanitarian law

None of the two instruments that regulate fair trial guarantees in non-international armed conflicts (Common Article 3 GC and Article 6 AP II) explicitly contain the *ne bis in idem* principle. Arguably, the principle could be subsumed under 'judicial guarantees which are recognized as indispensable by civilized peoples' in Common Article 3(1)(d) GC. However, this would be an expansive reading of Common Article 3 as there is no basis in the *travaux préparatoires* of the Geneva Conventions for such an interpretation.[56] Moreover, the European Convention on Human Rights in the form it was originally adopted only a year after the Geneva Conventions does not contain a prohibition of double jeopardy. Likewise, the fair trial guarantees enumerated in Additional Protocol II, which are used to interpret the meaning of indispensable judicial guarantees in Common Article 3 GC,[57] do not contain the *ne bis in idem* principle either.

Nonetheless, the *ne bis in idem* principle could apply as a norm of customary international law to non-international armed conflicts. In that regard, Article 75 of Additional Protocol I to the Geneva Conventions (Additional Protocol I, AP I), which comprises the prohibition of double jeopardy, is often considered a customary norm applicable to non-international armed conflicts.[58] Similarly, Rule 100 of the ICRC

55 Peter Rowe makes this point with regard to the ICC. P. Rowe, 'War Crimes', in D. McGoldrick, P. Rowe and E. Donnelly (eds.), *The Permanent International Criminal Court: Legal and Policy Issues* (Oxford: Hart Publishing, 2004), 203–32, at 227.

56 Final Record of the Diplomatic Conference of Geneva of 1949, Federal Political Department, Berne.

57 Sivakumaran, 'Courts of Armed Opposition Groups', above note 13, at 501–02.

58 See, for example, J. Pejic, 'The Protective Scope of Common Article 3: More than Meets the Eye' (2011) 93 *International Review of the Red Cross* 189, at 211–12; K. Dörmann and L. Colassis, 'International Humanitarian Law in the Iraq Conflict' (2004) 47 *German Yearbook of International Law* 293, at 323 (pronouncing themselves on international armed

Customary Law Study compels the parties to the conflict to observe the *ne bis in idem* principle in non-international armed conflicts.[59] It is therefore well arguable that the prohibition of double jeopardy in Article 75(4)(h) AP I applies as custom to non-international armed conflicts.

However, this does not mean that the *ne bis in idem* principle is applicable to trials conducted by the adverse party. This clearly follows from the ordinary meaning of Article 75(4)(h):

> [N]o one shall be prosecuted or punished *by the same Party* for an offence in respect of which a final judgment acquitting or convicting that person has been previously pronounced *under the same law and judicial procedure.*[60]

In sum, Article 75(4)(h) AP I, transposed to non-international armed conflicts, does not prohibit trials by a State or an international criminal court or tribunal for an offence which a court of an armed group has already adjudicated. Nor does, as has been shown, any other rule of international humanitarian law impose such a prohibition.

3.2. *Customary international criminal law*

In theory, an obligation of States to apply the principle of double jeopardy to trials by armed groups could have developed as a rule of customary international law from national criminal procedures or cases. Unsurprisingly, however, there is no significant amount of State practice to confirm this.[61] In fact, many States do not even recognize that the *ne bis in idem*

conflicts only); W.H. Taft, 'The Law of Armed Conflict After 9/11: Some Salient Features' (2003) 28 *Yale Journal of International Law* 319, at 322. Note that William H. Taft was the Legal Advisor to the US Department of State at the time and that he did not claim to reflect his personal opinion. Therefore, his article is often referred to as the official position of the US government, including by a plurality of four US Supreme Court Justices in the *Hamdan* case. *Hamdan v. Rumsfeld*, 548 U.S. 557, 633 (2006).

[59] See Henckaerts and Doswald-Beck, *Customary International Humanitarian Law*, above note 9, vol. I, at 352, 370–71. For the updated practice, see ICRC, 'Customary International Humanitarian Law -, Practice Relating to Rule 100', www.icrc.org/customary-ihl/eng/docs/v2_rul_rule100. The practice specifically pointing to a prohibition of double jeopardy in non-international armed conflict is not overwhelming. It is therefore not surprising that the Manual of Non-International Armed Conflict (above note 15, at 51–52) does not include the *ne bis in idem* principle in its list of fair trial guarantees.

[60] (emphases added). See also Yves Sandoz et al. (eds.), *Commentary on the Additional Protocols*, ICRC, (Martinus Nijhoff Publishers: Geneva, 1987), at 884.

[61] There does not seem to be any State practice which points to an international law obligation to take judgments by armed groups into consideration for the *ne bis in idem* principle. However, States have, of course, *discretion* to so recognize the judgments of armed non-State actors. Following the defeat of the Confederate States of the South in the American

principle applies to trials conducted in other States.[62] The Italian delegate to the discussion on the Draft Code of Offences against Peace and Security of Mankind explained why:

> [O]utside some bilateral or limited multilateral circles of States, there is not sufficient trust in the administration of justice by other States, especially when offences with political aspects are concerned. States are concerned that a person having committed a heinous crime against peace and security of mankind might find protection from prosecution in the rest of the world in an acquittal or a mild sentence given in a given State for reasons of political sympathy.[63]

Another rationale for not applying the prohibition of double jeopardy in international contexts is the sovereign right of a State (provided the State has jurisdiction) to try a suspect on its territory. If a State declined to prosecute a person because another State had already put that person on trial, this would undermine the former State's sovereignty.[64] The above-mentioned arguments apply *a fortiori* to trials conducted by armed groups because States are very well entitled to assert their sovereignty over such groups and usually do not trust them.

However, many States make use of the so-called *Anrechnungsprinzip* (the principle of deduction), meaning that a prison sentence already served for the same offence (or conduct) in another State is deducted from the sentence awarded in the second trial. This principle should, for humanitarian reasons, also be applied to sentences imposed by courts of armed groups.

Civil War, the Supreme Court developed a test according to which certain acts not 'in furtherance of the [Confederate] rebellion' continued to be valid. *Texas v. White*, 74 U.S. 700, 733 (1868).

62 See State practice quoted in C. van den Wyngaert and G. Stessens, 'The International Non bis in Idem Principle: Resolving Some of the Unanswered Questions' (1999) 48 *International and Comparative Law Quarterly* 779, at 783 et seq.; Antonio Cassese also holds that while the internal *ne bis in idem* principle is a rule of customary international law, it does not apply to trials in different States. However, he argues that such 'a customary rule is arguably evolving, *at least with regard to international crimes*'. He concedes, however, that he can only cite 'vertical' practice on the relations between international and national courts: A. Cassese, *International Criminal Law* (Oxford: Oxford University Press, 2003), at 319–21.

63 T. Treves, Sixth Committee of the United Nations General Assembly (XLII session), 10 November 1987, reproduced in M. Gestri et al. (eds.), 'Diplomatic and Parliamentary Practice (1988–1992)' (1996) 8 *Italian Yearbook of International Law* 157, at 196–97.

64 Van den Wyngaert and Stessens, 'Non bis in Idem', above note 62, at 782.

3.3. *Human rights law*

That most States do not apply the prohibition of double jeopardy to previous trials by other States (and *a fortiori* not to previous trials by armed groups) is in conformity with human rights law. In light of this volume's focus on the African Great Lakes Region, the African Charter for Human and Peoples' Rights and the International Covenant for Civil and Political Rights (ICCPR) are applicable. While the African Charter does not contain a prohibition of double jeopardy, Article 14(7) ICCPR reads:

> No one shall be liable to be tried or punished again for an offence for which he has already been finally convicted or acquitted in accordance with the law and penal procedure of each country.

Although the text is ambiguous, the reference to 'each country' only makes proper sense if understood to mean that the person may not be tried again under the jurisdiction of the same State.[65] The Human Rights Committee shares this interpretation and considers new trials in States other than that of the first trial to be in accordance with Article 14(7) ICCPR.[66] Hence, the Human Rights Committee would *a fortiori* consider that a trial by a court of an armed group does not bar a subsequent trial for the same conduct by a State court.

3.4. *The Rome Statute of the International Criminal Court*

Finally, is the ICC obliged to apply the prohibition of double jeopardy in relation to trials by armed groups? The relevant paragraph, Article 20(3) of the ICC Statute, reads as follows:

> No person who has been tried by another court for conduct also proscribed under Article 6, 7 or 8 shall be tried by the Court with respect to the same conduct unless the proceedings in the other court:

[65] The German translation refers to 'jeweiligen Landes' and hence supports this point (although German is not one of the authentic languages).

[66] *A.P. v. Italy*, (204/1986), Human Rights Committee, 1990, UN Doc. CCPR/C/OP/2 at 67, para 7.3: 'The Committee observes that this provision prohibits double jeopardy only with regard to an offence adjudicated in a given State'. The Committee confirmed this interpretation in *A.R.J. v. Australia*, Human Rights Committee, 11 August 1997, UN Doc. CCPR/C/60/D/692/1996. The Committee repeated this view in General Comment 32 but added that this should not 'undermine efforts by States to prevent retrial for the same criminal offence through international conventions'. General Comment on Article 14: The Right to Equality before Courts and Tribunals and to a Fair Trial (General Comment 32), Human Rights Committee, 24 July 2007, UN Doc. CCPR/C/GC/32, para. 57. Manfred Nowak criticized this approach as 'fairly general and too absolute'. Nowak, *CCPR Commentary*, above note 32, at 356.

(a) Were for the purpose of shielding the person concerned from criminal responsibility for crimes within the jurisdiction of the Court; or
(b) Otherwise were not conducted independently or impartially in accordance with the norms of due process recognized by international law and were conducted in a manner which, in the circumstances, was inconsistent with an intent to bring the person concerned to justice.

The term '(an)other court' in the *chapeau* of Article 20(3) on so-called 'upward' *ne bis in idem* (i.e., first trial by a national court, second trial by the ICC) could by its ordinary meaning apply to courts of armed groups.[67] However, many delegations at the 1998 Rome Conference implicitly ruled out such an interpretation (e.g., by referring to 'national' courts).[68] Moreover, participants never discussed whether a trial by a court of an armed group could trigger the *ne bis in idem* principle.[69] Since many States do not apply the prohibition of double jeopardy to previous trials by other States, one would at least expect a discussion about the even more controversial application of the principle to previous trials conducted by armed groups. At any rate, even if Article 20(3) of the ICC Statute applied to judgments by courts of armed groups, an armed group could not use this to shield a person from jurisdiction. Article 20(3) foresees a new trial based on the same conduct in case the previous trial was unfair or meant to protect the defendant from prosecution.

Concerning the principle of deduction, the second sentence of Article 78(2) ICC Statute states that the ICC 'may deduct any time otherwise spent in detention in connection with conduct underlying the crime'. The phrase 'otherwise spent in detention' is sufficiently broad to include prison sentences ordered by courts of armed groups. It is indeed regrettable that the deduction of sentence is only discretionary.[70]

67 This also seems to be the basis of Peter Rowe's conclusion. Rowe, 'War Crimes', above note 55, at 227.

68 United Nations Diplomatic Conference of Plenipotentiaries on the Establishment of an International Criminal Court, Official Records, UN Doc. A/CONF.183/13 (vol. II), at 73 (Mr. Muladi, Indonesia), at 214 (Mr. Holmes, Canada), at 215 (Mr. Corthout, Belgium). Recourse to the preparatory works may be had because the ordinary meaning is ambiguous. Article 32(a) Vienna Convention on the Law of Treaties.

69 Ibid.

70 C. Van den Wyngaert and T. Ogena, 'Ne bis in idem Principle, Including the Issue of Amnesty' in A. Cassese, P. Gaeta and J. Jones (eds.), *International Criminal Court: A Commentary*, 2 vols. (Oxford: Oxford University Press, 2002), vol. I, 705–29, at 724; L. Finlay, 'Does the International Criminal Court Protect against Double Jeopardy: An Analysis of Article 20 of the Rome Statute' (2008–2009) 15 *Davis Journal of International Law & Policy* 221, at 242–43.

To sum up, international or regional *ne bis in idem* standards in the constellations relevant for the African Great Lakes Region do not prohibit that persons already tried by a court of an armed group are retried in a State or international court. This is somewhat more ambiguous in the case of the ICC, but the ICC may retry persons whose previous processes were unfair or a sham. Hence, if courts of armed groups try persons with the intention to shield them from prosecution, they can subsequently still be held accountable.

4. Implementation of humanitarian law by courts of armed groups

So far, this chapter has dealt with the legal questions relevant to the role of courts of armed groups as a tool for implementation. Now, the contribution of armed groups' courts to the enforcement of humanitarian law will be assessed empirically on the basis of their codes (Section 4.1), their actual behaviour (Section 4.2) and their potential more generally (Section 4.3).

4.1. The purpose of courts established by armed groups

Even though this volume focuses on the African Great Lakes Region, all armed groups with courts in sub-Saharan Africa will be assessed. This will lead to a bigger sample and include other armed groups which operated in armed conflicts similar to those in the Great Lakes Region. Nevertheless, there is only a limited number of armed groups that operated courts in sub-Saharan Africa whose penal codes on military matters are available to the public. For example, Bemba's Mouvement de Libération du Congo (1998–2002) had courts but did not have a publicly available penal code. Others, such as the Revolutionary United Front (RUF) in Sierra Leone (1991–2002),[71] the Holy Spirit Movement (founded 1986)[72] and its successor, the Lord's Resistance Army,[73] only have codes of conduct but no courts. Members of the Mouvement des Nigériens pour la Justice (since 2007)[74] only swear an oath, again without a judicial mechanism. The only armed groups with publicized penal codes in sub-Saharan Africa were the armed wing of the African National Congress (ANC)

[71] Reproduced in O. Bangerter, *Internal Control: Codes of Conduct within Insurgent Armed Groups* (Geneva: Small Arms Survey, 2012), at 73, www.smallarmssurvey.org/fileadmin/docs/B-Occasional-papers/SAS-OP31-internal-control.pdf. The book also contains an excellent comment on codes of armed groups.

[72] Reproduced in ibid. 81. [73] Reproduced in ibid. 91. [74] Reproduced in ibid. 101.

(1961–1990),[75] Museveni's National Resistance Army (NRA) in Uganda (1981–1986) and the Sudanese People's Liberation Army (SPLA) in South Sudan (1983–2011).

Except for some provisions not directly related to fighting, such as political education, the codes established by these former armed groups are mandatory. Therein, mainly two types of laws are distinguishable: rules designed to protect individuals (including international humanitarian law) and, much more prominently, provisions aimed at enhancing the military capacity of the armed group. The rules on defections, desertions, disrespect for officers and mutiny are the greatest in number and sophistication, at least with regard to the SPLA and NRA.[76]

[75] Though not necessarily all activities of the armed wing of the ANC were governed by international humanitarian law, the Truth and Reconciliation Commission considered that the ANC was in an armed conflict with South Africa to which humanitarian law applied. The Report of the Truth and Reconciliation Commission, vol. II, Chapter 4, www.justice.gov.za/trc/report/finalreport/Volume%202.pdf. Before the end of apartheid, the ANC was also considered a national liberation movement. Since South Africa only acceded to Additional Protocol I in 1995, it is not clear whether the ANC had been such a movement in the sense of Article 1(4) AP I. This would only have been the case if Article 1(4) AP I and Article 96(3) AP I had been customary international law at the time of ANC's armed struggle. Antonio Cassese argued that this was indeed the case, but conceded that South Africa was not bound because it did not participate at the Diplomatic Conference preceding the adoption of the Protocols. A. Cassese, 'The Geneva Protocols of 1977 on the Humanitarian Law of Armed Conflict and Customary International Law' (1984) 3 *Pacific Basin Law Journal* 55, at 70–71. Even if South Africa were bound, the ANC's vague declaration did not formally give it the status of a national liberation movement in the sense of Article 1(4) AP I. Article 96(3) AP I requires that the declaration of adherence to the Geneva Conventions is deposited with the Swiss Federal Council, but the latter refused to accept the deposit. For these reasons, it is adequate to refer to the ANC's armed wing as an armed group.

[76] Umkhonto we Sizwe Military Code of the ANC, including General Regulations, released at the ANC National Consultative Conference at Kabwe in June 1985, full text available at www.anc.org.za/show.php?id=88&t=Umkhonto+we+Sizwe; the SPLA Act 2003, full text available at www.gurtong.net/LinkClick.aspx?fileticket=9bvQQGr4nD4%3D&tabid=342; Code of Conduct of the National Resistance Army, Legal Notice No. 1 (23 August 1986); Operational Code of Conduct of the National Resistance Army, Legal Notice No. 1 (23 August 1986). The NRA Code of Conduct has been reproduced in O. Amaza, *Museveni's Long March from Guerrilla to Statesman* (Kampala: Fountain, 1998), at 246–51. A slightly abridged version of the NRA code is found in Bangerter, *Internal Control*, above note 71, at 76. I am also very grateful to Olivier Bangerter for providing me with SPLA and ANC documents, which have (in parts) been reproduced in his book (at 88, 104).

Although published only after the NRA took over the power in Uganda, the Code of Conduct and the Operational Code were already in force before when the NRA still acted as an armed group. See, for example, N. Kasfir, 'Guerrillas and Civilian Participation: The National Resistance Army in Uganda, 1981–86' (2005) 43 *Journal of Modern African Studies* 271, at 284.

Before independence, the SPLA in South Sudan already had thirty-three sophisticated laws. This included the SPLA Act from 2003 with all sorts of rules on military discipline (e.g., insubordinate behaviour, intoxication, malingering) and procedural laws (composition, convening, powers, sentence of court martial; procedure in case of concurrent jurisdiction; oath by witnesses). Of almost 130 paragraphs, there is only one that in part contains rules on the protection of individuals. This paragraph somewhat vaguely penalizes pillage and 'cruel, indecent and unnatural' behaviour.[77] The annexed SPLA Code of Conduct contains more rules on good relations with the public, but they are not criminalized.[78]

Similarly, the NRA had a very basic code of conduct and a much more elaborate operational code of conduct. The operational code of conduct almost exclusively contained offences concerned with loyalty and commitment, such as leaking of operational information, mutiny, desertion and cowardice in action, which were all very broadly defined.[79] Only the offence of 'undermining the relationship with the civilian population' outlawed pillage and threats against the civilian population.[80]

The codes of conduct only contain very basic rules of the law of armed conflict, such as the prohibition to kill the adversary in custody[81] and the prohibition to pillage civilians.[82] Very importantly, all three of them prohibit attacks against civilians.[83] The ANC and the NRA prohibited rape explicitly,[84] whereas the SPLA did so implicitly.[85] However, none of the codes prohibits the recruitment of child soldiers. To be fair on the issue of child soldiers, the Ugandan NRA ceased to exist as an armed group in 1986, but Uganda only ratified Additional Protocol II in 1991.[86] Similarly,

[77] The SPLA Act 2003, Chapter V, Article 33(f), 33(g), above note 76.

[78] Code of Conduct for the SPLA, Articles 1–2, above note 76.

[79] NRA Operational Code of Conduct, above note 76, part III, Article 12.

[80] Ibid. part III, Article 12.

[81] ANC Military Code, General Regulations, Article 3(h); Code of Conduct for the SPLA, Article 2(h); NRA Code of Conduct, Article 4 (all three at above note 76).

[82] ANC Military Code, General Regulations, Article 3(b); Code of Conduct for the SPLA, Article 2(b); NRA Code of Conduct, Article 11(iv) (all three at above note 76).

[83] ANC Military Code, General Regulations, Article 3(e); Code of Conduct for the SPLA, Article 2(a); NRA Code of Conduct, Article 1 (all three at above note 76).

[84] ANC Military Code, General Regulations, Article 3(e); NRA Operational Code of Conduct, part III, Article 12 (both at above note 76).

[85] The prohibition of rape falls under the prohibition to 'abuse, insult, shout at, beat or in any way annoy any member of the public'. Code of Conduct for the SPLA, Article 2(a), above note 76.

[86] See ICRC, Treaties and States Parties to Such Treaties, www.icrc.org/applic/ihl/ihl.nsf/States.xsp?xp_viewStates=XPages_NORMStatesParties&xp_treatySelected=475.

the armed wing of the ANC became inactive in 1990, whereas South Africa acceded to Additional Protocol in 1995.[87] Therefore, both the NRA and the ANC were not bound by Article 4(3)(c) AP II, pursuant to which children below the age of 15 'shall neither be recruited . . . nor allowed to take part in hostilities'. According to the majority at the Special Court for Sierra Leone in the *Norman* decision on the issue, the prohibition on using child soldiers in customary international law began to develop between 1990 and 1994 and was criminalized at latest by November 1996,[88] that is, at a time when the NRA and ANC no longer qualified as armed groups. In contrast, the SPLA was, from the mid-1990s, bound by the customary duty not to recruit children under the age of 15 and not to use them to actively participate in hostilities.

Any conclusions derived from the codes must be treated with caution as it may well be that the codes are not properly enforced in the actual practice of armed groups. However, information on such practice of armed groups' courts is particularly scarce. There do not seem to be any written judgments by courts of armed groups, at least none that are public. However, there is some indication on the basis of NGO reports that courts of armed groups were very much resolved to enforce military discipline, loyalty, bravery and cohesion within the armed group. For example, a court martial of the SPLA sentenced thirty-three of its members to death for refusing to participate in an ambush.[89] At the same time, the SPLA did not hold its members accountable for violations of international humanitarian law committed in combat, such as indiscriminate shootings of civilians and looting and burning of civilian belongings. The SPLA record for trying non-combat-related offences was mixed and allegedly varied depending on the ethnic origin of the defendant.[90] The ANC sentenced persons to death who were suspected of mutiny.[91] Its members, including commanders, routinely tortured suspected spies without being held accountable.[92] However, the Truth and Reconciliation Commission reported that the ANC punished murder and rape with the death penalty.[93]

87 Ibid.

88 *Prosecutor v. Norman* (Decision on Preliminary Motion Based on Lack of Jurisdiction) (Child Recruitment) Case No. SCSL-2004–14-AR72 (E) (31 May 2004), para. 50. But see *Norman*, this note, Dissenting Opinion of Justice Robertson.

89 J. Prendergast, J. Rone and K. Sorensen (Human Rights Watch), *Civilian Devastation: Abuses by All Parties in the War in Southern Sudan* (New York: Human Rights Watch, 1994), at 327–28.

90 Ibid. 330–31.

91 Truth and Reconciliation Commission, above note 75, vol. II, Chapter 4, paras. 153–158.

92 Ibid. paras. 159–180.

93 Ibid. para. 158.

In light of the above, it is fair to say that the armed groups under discussion set up courts primarily to establish and maintain military discipline, loyalty, bravery and cohesion within the armed group. Ultimately, therefore, they were meant to enhance the military capacity of the armed group and, only to a lesser degree, to implement the law of armed conflict. However, in all fairness, the lack of humanitarian law in the codes of the NRA and ANC – both from the mid-1980s – can also be explained by the lacking criminalization of humanitarian law of non-international armed conflict at the time. The last version of the SPLA Act, however, is from 2003, when many international criminal law rules were already accepted as customary. At any rate, it should also be borne in mind that military discipline may well favour compliance with humanitarian law. Only through military discipline can the observance of the rules for the protection of the individual be ensured among the lower ranks.

4.2. *The level of compliance with humanitarian law by armed groups with courts*

It has been established in the last subsection that the codes of the ANC, NRA and SPLA contained some basic humanitarian law provisions. More decisively, however, is the *actual* degree of compliance with international humanitarian law (other than fair trial guarantees, which will be addressed in the next section) of these armed groups. In that regard, none of these three former armed groups under discussion attained a level of compliance that is fully satisfactory. All of them even violated basic prohibitions in Common Article 3 GC and other Geneva law provisions. The ANC was particularly harsh with suspected spies and tortured them.[94] The NRA[95]

[94] Ibid. paras. 158–180.

[95] There are various personal accounts of former child soldiers who were forcibly recruited and used by the NRA. For a summary of the account of China Keitetsi, see R. Meshberg, 'Commitment to Human Rights', alumnimagazine.uconn.edu/sprg2007/feature1.html. The account of Kassim Ouma, abducted at the age of five and forced to torture, is the subject of the film 'Kassim the Dream' and is summarized by M. Großekathöfer in 'Der Schattenboxer', *Der Spiegel*, 22 October 2007, www.spiegel.de/spiegel/print/d-53364545.html. The NRA introduced a severe torture method called *Kadoya* to Uganda in the early 1980s whereby the elbows are tightly tied behind the back. It causes damage to the neuromuscular function of the upper limbs; victims of *Kadoya* report extreme weakness in the upper arms and cannot work manually. International Rehabilitation Council for Torture Victims, Medical Aspects of Torture as Seen in Uganda, 2004, www.irct.org/Admin/Public/DWSDownload.aspx?File=%2fFiles%2fFiler%2fpublications%2fipip%2fNational-adaptation-Uganda-medical-material.pdf. After the NRA consolidated its

and SPLA[96] tortured and made use of child soldiers.[97] However, all of them showed a degree of respect for civilians that compares favourably to the outright disrespect for humanitarian law by other armed groups that are primarily made up of child soldiers and that commit systematic and widespread atrocities against the whole civilian population: mass rapes, burning down of entire villages, murder and often mutilations. Two of the most infamous examples of this kind of armed group are the Lord's Resistance Army (LRA) in its particularly violent years and the Revolutionary United Front (RUF). The blatant disregard for the law of armed conflict by these two armed groups, which systematically targeted civilians, is well documented.[98] In contrast thereto, the ANC, NRA and SPLA showed much more respect for civilians.

Admittedly, many armed groups respect international humanitarian law better than the RUF and the LRA, but even when the comparator spectrum is broadened, the SPLA, NRA and ANC are among those that committed fewer humanitarian law violations. In that regard, Jeremy Weinstein compares the NRA to the Resistência Nacional Moçambicana (RENAMO), which was also active in the 1980s, and finds that the NRA showed more respect for civilians and their property than RENAMO.[99] Concerning the SPLA, Human Rights Watch reported that '[s]ome observers rate the SPLA factions as more disciplined than many other

power in Uganda, human rights organizations started to take interest in its continuing violations. Amnesty International, 'Document – Uganda: Human Rights Violations by the National Resistance Army', 1991, www.amnesty.org/en/documents/AFR59/020/1991/en/.

96 Human Rights Watch, *Civilian Devastation*, above note 89, at 195–218, 226–27. Human Rights Watch, 'There Is No Protection: Insecurity and Human Rights in Southern Sudan', 2009, at 3, 24, 38, www.hrw.org/sites/default/files/reports/southsudan0209_webwcover.pdf.

97 The NRA and the SPLA were not bound by the prohibition to recruit child soldiers (see above notes 86 through 88 as well as the corresponding text). However, the forcible recruitment of children should be considered inhuman treatment in violation of Common Article 3(1) GC, by which the NRA and the armed wing of the ANC were bound at all times of their existence. South Africa acceded to Geneva Convention I in 1952, and Sudan acceded in 1957. www.icrc.org/applic/ihl/ihl.nsf/States.xsp?xp_viewStates=XPages_NORMStatesParties&xp_treatySelected=365.

98 For the RUF, see Bangerter, *Internal Control*, above note 71, at 38–43; for the LRA, see R. Wood, 'Understanding Strategic Motives for Violence', in Chapter 2 of this volume. While the degree of violence of the Lord's Resistance Army varies, it repeatedly engaged in extremely cruel practices against civilians, which included hacking persons to death or forcing children to do so.

99 J. Weinstein, 'Resources and the Information Problem in Rebel Recruitment' (2005) 49 *Journal of Conflict Resolution* 598, especially at 609–14.

African insurgents' but rightly added that 'this is not an acceptable standard'.[100] The ANC generally spared civilians, at least those on whose behalf it fought.[101]

In sum, the SPLA, NRA and ANC were more disciplined, pursued discernible military objectives and used violence against civilians more selectively than many other armed groups without courts. Is this behaviour due to the courts? There is a methodological problem for this claim because it cannot be ascertained whether factors other than the courts resulted in a higher standard of compliance. Indeed, if a responsible leadership installs courts to genuinely prosecute violations of the law of armed conflict, it is quite likely to also take other measures that are apt to lead to a higher degree of compliance, such as careful recruitment, training and close supervision of subordinates.[102]

The SPLA, ANC and NRA continuously pursued political goals and were ultimately successful in achieving them. In light of these aspirations, these groups needed to show that their power was to the local population's advantage, giving their leaders good reasons to ensure comparatively high respect for civilians. Hence, it would be an overstatement to explain the higher degree of discipline and respect for international humanitarian law exclusively with their operation of courts. However, it is plausible to assume that the courts were one factor that helped the leadership to instil more discipline and a relatively high respect for the civilian population.[103]

4.3. *The potential of courts of armed groups to implement humanitarian law*

The potential of a court of an armed group to implement humanitarian law depends largely on the armed group's current normative views. Indeed, a court is only a means to enforce a certain prescribed behaviour, a behaviour which might – depending on the 'law' of the armed group –

[100] Human Rights Watch, *Civilian Devastation*, above note 89, at 330.

[101] T. Lodge, 'State of Exile: The African National Congress of South Africa: 1976–86' (1987) 9 *Third World Quarterly* 1, at 11, fn. 37.

[102] Along these lines, Weinstein argues that the NRA's higher respect for civilians was due to the NRA's lack of resources, which meant that members were more strongly committed to the NRA's cause than the opportunistic joiners of RENAMO, who were primarily interested in financial gain. Weinstein, 'Resources', above note 99, especially at 609–14. While Weinstein's thesis is convincing, it is also plausible that the NRA's courts contributed to a higher degree of respect for the law of armed conflict.

[103] The ANC's relatively high respect for civilians has been attributed to its disciplinary system. Lodge, 'State of Exile', above note 101, at 11, fn. 37.

be incompatible with international humanitarian law. In other words, courts of armed groups are more likely to be a means rather than the cause for higher compliance.

However, in case the leadership of an armed group is willing to enforce the law of armed conflict, the potential of armed groups' courts to do so is comparatively high. Sanctions imposed by the armed group are likely to be more effective than sanctions by States or international criminal tribunals. This is because sanctions by armed groups are immediate, more visible to other members of the armed group and installed by an institution which members of the armed group ordinarily respect. Moreover, the deterrent effect of such sanctions may well be stronger because all members of the armed group know that the punishment may also be applied to them. After all, fighters of armed groups will usually be within the reach of the sanctioning system of the armed group, whereas they will not, in most cases, be within the direct reach of State or international prosecution authorities.

Apart from being more effective, courts of armed groups may also be the only reasonably available forum for prosecution. An armed group is unlikely to be willing to transfer its suspects to the State against which it fights. An armed group might also be unwilling to hand the person over to another State, and in many cases, no other State might even wish to open an investigation. International courts are not an option for prosecuting low-ranking fighters due to jurisdictional and resource limitations.[104]

Pre-Trial Chamber II of the ICC has implicitly taken the same view when confirming the charges of Jean-Pierre Bemba Gombo. Before the decision, Amnesty International submitted Amicus Curiae Observations and argued that Bemba had been obliged to submit the violations allegedly committed by his subordinates to a State court or the ICC.[105] However, when dealing with the command responsibility of Bemba, Pre-Trial Chamber II did not entertain these avenues for prosecution. Instead, it affirmed command responsibility inter alia on the basis that Bemba did not use the judicial system of the MLC.[106] Thus, the ICC considered in these circumstances a trial by a court of an armed group more plausible than a trial by a State jurisdiction.

Since it is often not realistic to expect that members of armed groups are tried by an international or State court, a trial by a court of an armed group can be the best alternative. Frequently, the only feasible alternative

[104] Sivakumaran, 'Courts of Armed Opposition Groups', above note 13, at 510.

[105] *Prosecutor v. Bemba Gombo* (Amicus Curiae), above note 22, paras. 21–25.

[106] *Prosecutor v. Bemba Gombo* (Decision), above note 23, para. 501.

for the armed groups is to punish an offender without a court trial. This would be a viable option in the case of small disciplinary infractions which attract lenient punishments. However, a lenient penalty would not be sufficient in the case of serious violations of humanitarian law where a penalty must be adequate to avoid command responsibility.[107] Since serious crimes require severe penalties, they should be adjudicated in a fair trial and not administratively. But do courts of armed groups offer sufficient procedural guarantees?

5. Fair trial guarantees

It has already been determined that due process standards enshrined in international humanitarian law,[108] and arguably in human rights law,[109] apply to courts of armed groups. Yet, why are fair trial guarantees even relevant for the question whether courts of armed groups can be a tool for inducing compliance with international humanitarian law? Admittedly, even an unfair trial may still enforce international humanitarian law effectively. However, the violation of due process guarantees laid down in humanitarian law undermines such contributions to higher compliance. In other words, if enforcing a humanitarian law rule means the violation of another such rule, the net humanitarian impact of the enforcement is questionable.

5.1. Fair trial guarantees granted by courts of sub-Saharan armed groups

The armed groups under discussion could hardly guarantee a fair trial. The criticism of the MLC for lacking procedural guarantees has already been mentioned.[110] The NRA Operational Code of Conduct comprised one article on procedure[111] but no fair trial guarantees. Similarly, the ANC General Regulations only contained one article on the punishments that

[107] In the *Hadžihasanović* Appeals Chamber Judgment (above note 52, para. 152), disciplinary punishment of a maximum of sixty days was not considered sufficient in light of the gravity of the crime of murder.

[108] See above notes 9–11 and corresponding text. For an excellent interpretation of fair trial guarantees applicable to courts of armed groups, see Sivakumaran, 'Courts of Armed Opposition Groups', above note 13, at 500–09.

[109] See above notes 24–28 and corresponding text.

[110] See above note 5 and corresponding text.

[111] NRA Operational Code of Conduct, above note 76, Article 25.

could be inflicted[112] but no fair trial guarantees. Indeed, the South African Truth and Reconciliation Commission deplored that court martials of the ANC were flawed and until 1986 held without any legal representation of the defendants.[113]

The SPLA Act 2003 sets out a procedure which is remarkably detailed for a non-State actor[114] but contains no right to a defence counsel, for example. Nevertheless, although the courts that operated in SPLA-held territory had serious faults, judges started to emancipate themselves more and more from the SPLA even before South Sudan attained statehood. Indeed, it was already a sign of growing independence of judges that they took legal action against SPLA soldiers, even though the judges' decisions were often not carried out in the end.[115] Admittedly, however, courts in South Sudan, especially after 2005, were not in all aspects representative for courts of armed groups anymore. This is because they received support from the UN and were tolerated by the North after the SPLA signed the Comprehensive Peace Agreement. Despite these caveats, the example of the SPLA shows that courts are able to slowly become independent from an armed group that controls the court's area of jurisdiction and hence fulfil an important requirement for a fair trial.

5.2. *The capability of courts by armed groups to respect fair trial guarantees*

Insufficient fair trial guarantees have been an issue with all armed groups discussed above. This raises the more general question of whether courts of armed groups are generally unable or unwilling to conduct fair trials.

Regarding their ability, most armed groups, in particular less organized ones, have less potential than States to guarantee a fair trial because armed groups tend to have fewer resources than States. Indeed, armed groups have to devote a lot of their existing resources to their military because States usually try to defeat armed groups on their territory. Foreign States and the UN are, in most cases, not willing to provide aid in order to improve the judiciary of armed groups.[116]

112 ANC General Regulations, above note 76, Article 8.

113 Truth and Reconciliation Commission, above note 91, vol. II, at 352.

114 SPLA Act 2003, above note 76, in particular Chapter IX.

115 Human Rights Watch, 'There is No Protection', above note 96, at 32.

116 This does not necessarily apply for more consolidated de facto regimes like Somaliland. UNDP in Somalia, 'Judiciary Strengthened as First Batch of Judges Graduate from Legal Training', www.so.undp.org/content/somalia/en/home/presscenter/articles/2010/3/1/Judiciary_strengthened_as_first_batch_of_judges_graduate_from_legal_training.html.

It can also be doubted whether leaders of armed groups are in all cases willing to observe due process guarantees. They are liable to consider their courts an instrument to implement their policies and are therefore prone to interfere with the trials. However, armed groups are more likely to be willing to conduct a fair trial in humanitarian law cases than in those concerning mutiny, defections or spying. The passing of sensitive military information to the enemy may seriously endanger the survival of the armed group, whereas a violation of the law of armed conflict by its own members will usually not have this effect. It is simply less risky to provide for a fair trial (which may result in an acquittal) to suspected humanitarian law offenders than to those who are suspected of not being loyal to the armed group.

6. Empirical legitimacy of armed groups

Closely connected to loyalty is empirical legitimacy.[117] Indeed, according to Max Weber, empirical legitimacy is the perceived obligation of the governed to follow a particular authority. Weber observed relationships of legitimacy not only between the authority and the population but also between the authority and its administration.[118] Transposed to our case, empirical legitimacy measures the degree to which the armed group's members feel obliged to follow the armed group's leadership. In case an armed group also seeks to rule over the local population, empirical legitimacy also describes whether the local population perceives a duty to follow the rule of the armed group.

The question that follows is in which way courts influence the empirical legitimacy of armed groups. Courts can help to secure justice and security,

[117] I am indebted to Zeljko Branovic, Anke Draude and Cord Schmelzle for discussing different concepts of legitimacy with me and for providing comments on this section.

[118] M. Weber, *Wirtschaft und Gesellschaft. Grundriss der Verstehenden Soziologie* (Frankfurt: Zweitausendeins, 2005), at 158–59. Weber's sociology of domination or authority laid the foundations for the empirical concept of legitimacy that is still favoured by political scientists and sociologists today. In contrast, political theorists and philosophers regard legitimacy not as the perceived but as the actual normative status of a political order, which can in their view be impartially determined. C. Schmelzle, 'Evaluating Governance: Effectiveness and Legitimacy in Areas of Limited Statehood' (SFB-Governance Working Paper Series, No. 26, November 2011), at 7, www.sfb-governance.de/en/publikationen/working_papers/wp26/SFB-Governance-Working-Paper-26.pdf. It seems that most law scholars use the term 'legitimacy' in the normative sense closely connected to legality. Sivakumaran, 'Courts of Armed Opposition Groups', above note 13, at 509–11. For a definition with empirical elements on the legitimacy of international law, an issue beyond this chapter, see T. Franck, *The Power of Legitimacy among Nations* (Oxford: Oxford University Press, 1990), at 24.

which are widely shared social goals,[119] often directly associated with legitimate institutions.[120] This is not only the case for the OECD countries but also in many traditional African and South American societies where so-called Chiefs apply the local customary law. In the Islamic world, Sharia courts are also a means to assert legitimacy. Thus, if armed groups operate courts and if, in the eyes of the local population, these courts contribute to more justice, this is likely to increase an armed group's empirical legitimacy.[121]

What are the implications if an armed group manages to increase its empirical legitimacy among its members and the local population, which in turn implies a higher degree of compliance with the armed group's rules?[122] The answer to this question depends on the actor, and it is therefore necessary to distinguish between the State on the territory of which the armed group is present, the international community and the local population.

For the State on the territory of which the armed group operates, such an increase in empirical legitimacy will be problematic. The State loses the loyalty of its population. Ultimately, empirical legitimacy is an important factor – among many others – that may lead to the recognition of secession,[123] but this is rare and only possible for well-consolidated

[119] Aside from the sharing of social goals between the governance actor and the governance addressee, Schmelzle identifies three more conditions under which the effective delivery of governance leads to higher empirical legitimacy: the governance addressee must hold an instrumental legitimacy belief (i.e., believe that effectiveness leads to legitimacy), associate the governance service with the governance actor and generalize the specific support for a policy into general support for the governance actor. Schmelzle, 'Evaluating Governance', above note 118, at 13–15. Schmelzle did not call the second to last condition 'association' but 'transparency'. However, in my view, it is sufficient that a governance actor is *somehow* associated with the governance service, rightly or wrongly, based on transparency or propaganda. It is fair to assume that these conditions under which effective governance leads to empirical legitimacy are often met in areas of limited statehood.

[120] J. Bakonyi and K. Stuvøy, 'Violence & Social Order beyond the State: Somalia & Angola' (2005) 32 *Review of African Political Economy* 359, at 374.

[121] Justice is also often said to be necessary for normative legitimacy. R. Keohane, Governance and Legitimacy, Keynote Speech Held at the Opening Conference of the Research Center (SFB) 700, SFB-Governance Lecture Series, No. 1, February 2007, at 6, www.sfb-governance.de/en/publikationen/lecture_series/ls1/SFB-Lecture-Series_1.pdf.

[122] Higher empirical legitimacy, which is defined as the perceived duty to follow an authority, leads almost by definition to higher compliance. M. Levi and A. Sacks, 'Legitimating Beliefs: Sources and Indicators' (2009) 3 *Regulation & Governance* 311, at 314.

[123] Consent by the local population to the secession, that is, high empirical legitimacy of the new State authority, is an essential criterion for the international community to accept

entities. Since the overall administration of justice vis-à-vis the civilian population is associated with legitimacy in many societies, States oppose courts by armed groups on their territory. On the other hand, States may more readily accept the judicial enforcement of the law of armed conflict vis-à-vis the *members* of the armed group. Any club in a peaceful society may sanction the violation of its norms, for example, by dismissing members. Although sanctions by armed groups go further than that, trials of their members have fewer implications for the legitimacy of the territorial State than cases where courts judge over civilians and seriously 'out-administer' the State.

The international community is interested in stability and (in particular OECD States) in the protection of their nationals as well as in not being associated with armed groups that systematically violate basic norms granting the protection of individuals. Therefore, the international community is opposed to legitimizing armed groups that cooperate with transnational terrorist networks or which systematically disregard basic rules designed to protect individuals. If an armed group does not fall under either of these categories, the international community may be willing to accept that it gains empirical legitimacy among the local population in order to prevent chaos.

An armed group's higher empirical legitimacy may also be to the advantage of the local population if the members of that armed group comply with their leadership and if the leadership is committed to international humanitarian law. If the population generally succumbs to the armed group's rule, this may mean stability and hence more security from ordinary criminals, too.[124] However, the price paid for such stability may be high. The Taliban and Al Shabab enforce *their* law and order. Their sanctions often abuse human rights (although they are more foreseeable than violence in more chaotic circumstances). It should not be overlooked, however, that it would be very difficult for an armed group to gain empirical legitimacy if its norms were diametrically opposed to those of the local population. Hence, in order to acquire empirical legitimacy, an armed group will have to show some degree of respect for the population's normative views unless it manages to fundamentally change them over time.

the creation of a new State. See, for example, Council of the European Union, '3029th Foreign Affairs Council Meeting: Conclusions on Sudan', 26 July 2010, para. 2, www.eu-un.europa.eu/articles/en/article_9977_en.htm.

124 Sivakumaran, 'Courts of Armed Opposition Groups', above note 13, at 509–10.

7. Conclusion: how should the international community react?

Summing up the discussion of whether courts of armed groups can be effective tools for inducing compliance with international humanitarian law, an essential condition is met: international humanitarian law and human rights law do not prohibit the operation of such courts. Moreover, the prohibition of double jeopardy does not impede subsequent accountability in case courts of armed groups conducted unfair or sham trials. Their courts increase the empirical legitimacy of the armed group, but this may – depending on the norms that the armed group enforces – have advantages for the local population, such as higher compliance with the law of armed conflict. If the leadership of an armed group is genuinely willing to enforce humanitarian law, courts of that armed group have a relatively high potential to be successful in inducing compliance. Although the armed group's courts discussed were mostly concerned with military discipline, they also enforced rules that protect individuals. The armed groups under scrutiny committed serious humanitarian law violations, including violations of due process guarantees, but they showed more respect for civilians than many armed groups without courts. Hence, it would seem that courts of armed groups can be a tool for inducing higher compliance with international humanitarian law, but one that is far from perfect.

What can be done to improve the situation? Opening up the dialogue with armed groups that possess courts would be an option. In case important humanitarian law or fair trial provisions are missing in the penal codes, it may, for example, be possible to persuade the armed group to insert them. Such dialogue could also improve the level of 'ownership' of the armed group over international law norms and hence improve the compliance record of the armed group.[125]

States fear that engaging with courts of armed groups would legitimize them.[126] However, the effect of international dialogue on empirical legitimacy depends largely on how the local society regards communication with external actors. Such views vary and armed groups may be able to influence the local population's belief about what is empirically legitimate. If so, armed groups would not necessarily present their relations with international actors as a source of their legitimacy as they

125 Sivakumaran, 'Courts of Armed Opposition Groups', above note 13, at 512–13.

126 This is probably the reason for which the DRC did not allow MONUC to fly in defence attorneys to take part in the MLC's trials. See above note 3 and corresponding text.

would make themselves dependent on actors beyond their control. In fact, armed groups are more likely to rely on charismatic or traditional forms of legitimacy or to gain legitimacy through effectiveness.[127]

It is also hard to see how international dialogue with an armed group could in itself increase its normative legitimacy. Contact with external actors is not inherently moral. However, the possible consequence of such interaction in the form of a higher standard of justice and security would enhance its normative and probably also its empirical legitimacy.

What is often meant by 'legitimacy' is the entitlement to govern as perceived by international actors ('international entitlement'). It is true that dialogue with armed groups can lead to international entitlement. However, this point should not be overstated, either. Is it realistic that an armed group is taken from a terrorist list because an impartial humanitarian organization involves it in a dialogue about certain issues? The reverse is more likely, that is that the State prohibits the activities of the humanitarian organization. States make their own judgments about the entitlement of an actor to govern and do not rely on whether non-governmental organizations or the UN engaged with them.[128] NGOs and the UN often engage with actors irrespective of the actor's deeds or normative views, and hence engagement does not imply any form of approval.

For these reasons, the international community should engage with armed groups about their courts. Indeed, Somalia is an extreme example which indicates that involving a State at the expense of a non-State actor is not always a viable option. It would be counterproductive to ignore Somaliland's courts only because it is not recognized as State. After all, the relatively well-consolidated de facto regime Somaliland is in a better position to install justice and security than the seriously threatened rump State of Somalia.

[127] For the example of UNITA, see Bakonyi and Stuvøy, 'Violence & Social Order', above note 120, at 370.

[128] See US Patriot Act (18 U.S.C. § 2339 B(a)(1)) (held constitutional by the US Supreme Court in *Holder v. Humanitarian Law Project*, 130 S. Ct. 2705 (2010)).

8

Comment – perspectives on courts established by armed opposition groups

DIETER FLECK

Let me first discuss the main proposition of Jan Willms' chapter that 'if the leadership of an armed group is genuinely willing to enforce humanitarian law, courts of that armed group have a relatively high potential to be a successful tool for inducing compliance'; second I will propose to further evaluate whether and under what conditions this potential could be convincingly used beyond the rather few armed conflicts in which such trials happened to take place; and third I will discuss other means for armed opposition groups to improve respect for international humanitarian law.

From 'rebel courts' to impartial judicial organs

Indeed, there are no insurmountable barriers in international humanitarian law for the establishment of criminal courts by non-State actors. As Jan Willms has scholarly deduced, any court offering the essential guarantees of independence and impartiality set out in Article 6(2) AP II may be considered today as being 'regularly constituted', as required under Article 3(1)(d), common to the Geneva Conventions (GC).[1] Impartiality and independence are thus essential parameters for a court to be regularly constituted. While this innovation was introduced in 1977 for non-international armed conflicts that meet a considerably high threshold,[2]

[1] K. Dörmann, *Elements of War Crimes under the Rome Statute of the International Criminal Court* (Cambridge: Cambridge University Press, 2003), at 412. His warning that 'special courts set up on an ad hoc basis by rebel groups' (as opposed to regularly constituted courts) are prohibited is debatable, as it appears to be based on a special understanding of the term 'ad hoc', a term that should, however, not exclude the establishment of a court for a situation which is limited in time and location, such as the ICTY, the ICTR, the Special Court for Sierra Leone or the Extraordinary Chambers in the Courts of Cambodia.

[2] See Art. 1(1) AP II: 'organized armed groups'; 'under responsible command'; 'control over a part of its territory'; 'carry out sustained and concerted military operations and to implement this Protocol'.

the 1998 ICC Statute with its Article 8(2)(c)(iv) and perhaps even customary law now confirm that this new reading is applicable in all internal armed conflicts as soon as the much lower threshold of Common Article 3 GC has been met.

Thus, courts established by armed opposition groups, which will be unconstitutional and illegal under the law of any State affected by an armed conflict, may well be legitimate and lawful under international humanitarian law. It may even be considered that – compared to more traditional forms to ensure compliance with existing obligations – such courts could have advantages for ensuring respect for international humanitarian law.[3]

There is, however, no international obligation for armed opposition groups to consider and implement the establishment of such courts. The Customary Law Study of the International Committee of Red Cross (ICRC) very convincingly confines the obligation to prosecute war crimes to States (Rule 158).[4] Non-State actors have no such obligation, but all military commanders including commanders of rebel forces must take all necessary and reasonable measures in their power to prevent the commission of war crimes and to punish the persons responsible (Rule 153). This obligation applies to any existing military chain of command. It calls for military leadership and disciplinary action, not necessarily for formal court procedures.

The question whether courts of armed opposition groups, once they have been established, are to be used systematically in the faithful exercise of command responsibility may well be in place, even if pertinent situations will appear to be too complex to allow for quick solutions. There will be too many different elements that must be considered in an armed conflict, yet the overall situation may gradually change when an armed opposition group exercises sustained political power on its territory: once such power is established, judicial control also will become necessary.

While it is reasonable to discuss whether such courts are meeting applicable legal standards in their procedures, it is not altogether easy to clearly define the pertinent rules to be applied during non-international armed conflicts. Conventional international humanitarian

[3] J. Somer 'Jungle Justice: Passing Sentence on the Equality of Belligerents in Non-international Armed Conflict' (2007) 89 *International Review of the Red Cross* 655; S. Sivakumaran, 'Courts of Armed Opposition Groups: Fair Trials or Summary Justice?' (2009) 7 *Journal of International Criminal Justice* 489.

[4] J.-M. Henckaerts and L. Doswald-Beck (eds.), *Customary International Humanitarian Law*, 2 vols. (Cambridge: Cambridge University Press, 2004), vol. I, at 607.

law hardly offers practical guidance in this respect. Custom is still rudimentary, thus leaving a great amount of discretion for national laws and practice.

A broader discussion under human rights perspectives should not be ruled out in this context. It may be recalled that fair trial guarantees which are essential for a proper application of international humanitarian law are in fact rooted in human rights law and general principles of criminal procedure. Neither the Hague law nor the Geneva Conventions have coined these guarantees which make the difference between justice and injustice as far as judicial procedures are concerned. The Geneva Conventions (I 49; II 50; III 129; IV 146) simply refer to 'effective penal sanctions' and to 'safeguards of proper trial and defence', thus presupposing a well-functioning judicial system rather than defining it. Article 75 AP I underlines fundamental human rights, including fair trial guarantees, but again the original sources for such principles and rules are to be found elsewhere. States have considerable freedom in regulating criminal justice. The more should this freedom apply to armed opposition groups establishing criminal courts during an armed conflict.

A first successful attempt to define common international standards for criminal justice has in fact been made under the auspices of the Human Rights Council, and although it was developed to apply in an armed conflict that is now generally considered as being international in nature, the main arguments may be relevant for courts established by insurgents in non-international armed conflicts as well: investigating the follow-up to the International Independent Fact Finding Mission by the Government of Israel and the Palestinian Side, the Human Rights Council had nominated a Committee to assess investigations for compliance with international standards of independence, impartiality, effectiveness, thoroughness and promptness. The Report of that Committee,[5] which identified 'expansive standards' under human rights law and 'less defined standards for investigations' under international humanitarian law, stated that '[s]everal criteria under human rights law can be met within the context of armed conflict'.[6] Yet it also underlined that 'there are constraints

[5] 'Report of the Committee of Independent Experts in International Humanitarian and Human Rights Law to Monitor and Assess any Domestic, Legal or Other Proceedings Undertaken by Both the Government of Israel and the Palestinian Side, in the Light of General Assembly Resolution 64/254, Including the Independence, Effectiveness, Genuineness of these Investigations and their Conformity with International Standards', UN-Doc A/HRC/15/50 (23 September 2010).

[6] Ibid. para. 30.

during armed conflict that do impede investigations'.[7] It will be simply impossible for the armed forces or even the police to formally investigate every death during an armed conflict. Security concerns will affect transparency of investigations. A standard of 'as effectively as possible' may thus apply to investigations in armed conflicts, and this is all the more true for insurgents in non-international armed conflicts.

Conditions for the use of impartial courts by armed opposition groups

The still rudimentary practice known so far has not provided a clear picture on the question whether armed opposition groups have effectively used criminal courts and tribunals to ensure compliance with international humanitarian law by their own forces. Where criminal procedures have been initiated, this may have generally been aimed at maintaining discipline rather than ensuring respect for humanitarian principles and rules. It may have served the purpose of deterring mass desertions rather than mass atrocities against civilians. It also appears that so far, there is no single case in which armed opposition groups have prosecuted war crimes committed by their adversaries.

It is hardly possible to generalize from the rather rudimentary information available so far. I would agree that written documents including the few penal codes which may have been used during armed conflicts are not the most relevant sources for what was happening in reality. Hence I suggest to empirically investigate the political goals pursued by courts of armed opposition groups. Even in the absence of written sentences, more light should be shed on their nature and purpose. What were the intentions of those initiating criminal proceedings, and what major results were achieved by the judgments? Were fair trial standards observed or neglected? It appears that the practice known so far, including that of courts established by the African National Congress (ANC) in South Africa (1961–1990), the Frente Farabundo Martí para la Liberación Nacional (FMLN) in El Salvador (1980–1992),[8] the National Resistance Army (NRA) led by Yoweri Museveni in Uganda since 1981, before he became president of his country in 1986, the Revolutionary United Front of Sierra Leone (1991–2002), the Mouvement de Libération

[7] Ibid. para. 32.

[8] See Americas Watch, 'Violations of Fair Trial Guarantees by the FMLN's Ad Hoc Courts' (New York, 1980).

du Congo (MLC) in the DRC and in the Central African Republic (1998–2002),[9] the Tigers of Tamil Eelam of Sri Lanka (1983–2009), the Sudanese People's Liberation Army (SPLA) in South Sudan (1983–2011) and the Maoist People's Courts in Nepal (reactivated in 2010),[10] was characterized by rather different conflict situations, different intentions and different intensities of court action. There is, indeed, a complex typology of non-international armed conflicts today with a set of rules much larger than Common Article 3 GC.[11] Even if no general conclusion could be reached, it should be possible (and, indeed, very worthwhile) to find out whether a particular rebel court was convincingly used to ensure compliance with fundamental rules of international humanitarian law.

Furthermore, the relevance of any such sentences for post-conflict peace building needs to be explored. Insurgents coming into power may either wish to make their own courts part of the new legal system of the State or neglect this episode altogether. In both cases, their attitudes and practices do inform the role of civilian governance post-conflict.[12] On the other hand, a government successfully defeating insurgents may still be obliged to consider the former rebel courts' practice in any decision on amnesties. In individual criminal procedures, sentences of such former courts may thus entail a factual observation of the *ne bis in idem* principle, even if it was never legally recognized.

The establishment of a functioning justice system is essential for post-conflict peace building. It may be indispensable to build on courts established by insurgents for this purpose, as shown by the situation in Somaliland, a country which did enjoy training support for judges under the UN Development Programme (UNDP), even if its self-proclaimed independence in 1991 remained unrecognized by any State or international organization.

9 A practice now under scrutiny of the ICC in the case of *Prosecutor v. Jean-Pierre Bemba Gombo.*

10 Somer, 'Jungle Justice', above note 3, at 690 (mentioning that these courts have been sought out by citizens due in part to 'lack of trust' in the State criminal justice system); OHCHR-Nepal, Human Rights Abuses by the CPN-M, Summary of Concerns (September 2006), at 4, nepal.ohchr.org/en/resources/Documents/English/reports/IR/Year2006/2006_09_21_Human%20Rights%20Abuses%20by%20the%20CPN-M.pdf.

11 See J. Pejic, 'The Protective Scope of Common Article 3: More Than Meets the Eye' (2011) 93 *International Review of the Red Cross* 189.

12 See Z. Mampilly, 'Insurgent Governance in the Democratic Republic of the Congo', Chapter 3 in this volume.

Other means for armed opposition groups to ensure respect for international humanitarian law

While it remains questionable whether the practice of armed groups' courts has contributed to effectively prosecute war crimes and protect victims of armed conflict, the role of other means to ensure compliance with international humanitarian law appears all the more relevant.

In this context, meta-legal considerations deserve to be mentioned first. I would think of the role of public opinion and its consideration by the parties to the conflict. The role of warring parties may be both reactive and proactive in that they will be interested in influencing the adversary by means of reciprocal behaviour and developing activities to win the hearts and minds of the civilian population. The free flow of information and international fact-finding activities may lead parties to the conflict to participate in a humanitarian dialogue which can be focused by the presence of the ICRC, by Security Council resolutions and by debates within the General Assembly and other UN bodies. Diplomatic steps taken by States and regional organizations and also activities of non-governmental organizations may exercise pressure to explain military operations and avoid atrocities which could lead to an increase of such pressure.

All parties to armed conflicts and their military commanders may realize that they are operating in a legal environment. They must consider their command responsibility and take necessary action for the maintenance of discipline and compliance with existing legal obligations. It is in this context that national implementing measures, dissemination of relevant rules and training will be essential for any professional conduct of military operations. Criminal courts are not in the centre of such activities, as they will become relevant only in extreme situations post factum. Neither political leadership nor military commanders can escape responsibility to prevent and halt criminal conduct by later punishing or referring the matter to a court.

In Nigeria, during the turmoil of its civil war in Biafra (1967–1970), a very effective one-page code of conduct for the government forces was issued in 1967.[13] It was made part of the military training for the regular armed forces and may have influenced their operations, even if many

[13] Operational Code of Conduct for Nigerian Forces, Directive to All Officers and Men of the Armed Forces of the Federal Republic of Nigeria on Conduct of Military Operations (July 1967).

atrocities were committed and little is known about implementation of humanitarian principles and rules by the insurgents who did not establish courts at that time.

In Uganda, a Code of Conduct for the Army was published as a State law in 1986,[14] that is, months after Yoweri Museveni was sworn in as president. However, the code was also binding on Museveni's guerrilla fighters and is therefore a result of battle experience.[15]

In neither of these two cases have convincing efforts been taken to investigate atrocities which were committed during the armed conflicts on both sides. At the end of other wars, in South Africa[16] and Guatemala,[17] such an investigation has widely been considered as a necessary part of post-conflict peace building.

In no such situations will a focus on international humanitarian law be sufficient. There now is a growing consensus that in non-international armed conflicts, both the government forces and armed opposition groups are bound not only by international humanitarian law but also by international human rights law. Non-State actors exercising control over a population over a certain time are enjoying not only human rights but also responsibilities under human rights law. They are certainly accountable for violations of peremptory norms.[18] However, the real test is not on the books, but in reality. It will depend on the international community as a whole, on governments and armed opposition groups, on civil society and on many individuals whether this promising development will continue and consolidate.

[14] Code of Conduct for the National Resistance Army, Legal Notice No. 1 (23 August 1986).

[15] See N. Kasfir, 'Guerrillas and Civilian Participation: The National Resistance Army in Uganda, 1981–86' (2005) 43 *Journal of Modern African Studies* 271, at 284.

[16] See L. Fernandez, 'Reparation for Human Rights Violations Committed by the Apartheid Regime in South Africa', in A. Randelzhofer and C. Tomuschat (eds.), *State Responsibility and the Individual: Reparation in Instances of Grave Violations of Human Rights* (The Hague: Martinus Nijhoff Publishers, 1999), 173–87.

[17] Comisión para el Esclarecimiento Histórico, 'Guatemala Memoria del Silencio' 1999, 12 volumes; C. Tomuschat, 'Clarification Commission in Guatemala' (2001) 23 *Human Rights Quarterly* 233.

[18] See, for example, C. Tomuschat, 'The Applicability of Human Rights Law to Insurgent Movements', in H. Fischer et al. (eds.), *Krisensicherung und humanitärer Schutz – Crisis Management and Humanitarian Protection* (Berlin: Berliner Wissenschaftsverlag, 2004), 573–91; A. Bellal, G. Giacca and S. Casey-Maslen, 'International Law and Armed Non-State Actors in Afghanistan' (2011) 93 *International Review of the Red Cross* 47.

9

The role of international criminal prosecutions in increasing compliance with international humanitarian law in contemporary African conflicts

ROBERT CRYER*

1. Introduction

In the recent past two decades, international criminal law has been tasked with many (indeed, too many) roles. In addition to retributivist aims, it has been asked to satisfy victims' demands for catharsis, write history and perhaps most prominently, deter international crimes.[1] It is questionable whether it can fulfil many of them at all.[2] For example, many international criminal lawyers are dubious of the ability of courts to write history.[3] Happily, the ability of international criminal law to fulfil many of these goals need not concern us for the purpose of this chapter. Here we are looking at two of the most relevant justifications given for international criminal processes for the question of the extent to which prosecutions can assist in increasing compliance with international humanitarian law. This piece will concentrate therefore on deterrence and denunciation/education. These two are linked but not identical, nor are they uncontroversial.

Prior to that, however, certain limitations of international criminal law in relation to ensuring compliance with international humanitarian

* Birmingham Law School. This piece builds, and expands upon, ideas contained in R. Cryer, 'The Role of International Criminal Prosecutions in Increasing Compliance with International Humanitarian Law' (2014) 44 *Israel Yearbook on Human Rights* 247.

1 See R. Cryer, H. Friman, D. Robinson and E. Wilmshurst, *An Introduction to International Criminal Law and Procedure*, 3d edn (Cambridge: Cambridge University Press, 2014), Chapter 2.

2 M. Damaška, 'What Is the Point of International Criminal Justice?' (2008) 83 *Chicago-Kent Law Review* 329, at 331.

3 See, for example, R. Wilson, *Writing History in International Criminal Trials* (Cambridge: Cambridge University Press, 2011).

law have to be identified. The most important of these is that only one of the four 'core' international crimes (aggression, genocide, crimes against humanity and war crimes) has a direct relationship with international humanitarian law. That is the law of war crimes. Although the term is often used in a loose sense to mean international crimes more generally, war crimes *stricto sensu* are a criminalized subset of violations of international humanitarian law.[4] Therefore, some of the norms contained in the law of war crimes are, in fact, somewhat narrower than those of humanitarian law,[5] and indeed some humanitarian law norms are not appropriate for criminalization, and therefore the two are not identical.[6] Therefore, prosecutions for war crimes can never be considered a means of ensuring compliance with all of international humanitarian law for the simple reason that such prosecutions cannot be for the full panoply of international humanitarian law rights and responsibilities.

Second, speaking specifically to the African context, Africa is (although it may be trite to say it) a large and diverse continent. Darfur province in Sudan alone, for example, is the size of France. North Africa, in particular the Arabic States (Libya, Egypt) are culturally, politically and economically far removed from many sub-Saharan States. East and West Africa are not, in and of themselves, readily analogizable. Indeed, even States that are reasonably close together, such as Uganda and Sudan, are very different places, and the reactions to international criminal law and its institutions are not the same.[7] Furthermore, the political systems in different African States include military dictatorships (Egypt), democracies (South Africa) and authoritarian regimes (Rwanda, Zimbabwe), all of which have different levels of stability. Libya, for example, is deeply unstable; Rwanda, on the other hand, is stable. Leading on from this, it is also the case that some countries are practically ungoverned by their central authorities (parts of the Democratic Republic of the Congo (DRC) spring to mind), while

[4] See generally R. Cryer, 'Individual Liability in International Law', in T. L. H. McCormack and R. Livoja (eds.), *Research Handbook on the Law of Armed Conflict* (London: Routledge, forthcoming).

[5] See, for example, R. Cryer, *Prosecuting International Crimes: Selectivity and the International Criminal Law Regime* (Cambridge: Cambridge University Press, 2005), at 262–84.

[6] See, for example, M. Bothe, 'The Protection of the Civilian Population and NATO Bombing on Yugoslavia: Comments on a Report to the Prosecutor of the ICTY' (2001) 12 *European Journal of International Law* 531.

[7] See on this S. M. H. Nouwen, *Complementarity in the Line of Fire: The Catalysing Effect of the International Criminal Court in Uganda and Sudan* (Cambridge: Cambridge University Press, 2013).

others are fully governed spaces.[8] Hence, it is important when speaking of Africa not to speak in an omnibus fashion that ignores these significant differences; therefore this contribution will at least attempt to contextualize its remarks.

Finally, as Olivier Bangerter has said elsewhere in this volume, 'better respect for international humanitarian law is primarily the result of inside action, and no one can respect international humanitarian law in the stead of parties to a conflict. Outsiders, such as political actors, humanitarian players, non-governmental organizations, the media or academics, can only have an indirect effect on respect for international humanitarian law'.[9] This is also the case for international criminal law, and it ought to be remembered that mechanisms other than international criminal law are also available to increase respect for international humanitarian law. The role of the International Committee of the Red Cross is one that immediately comes to mind.[10] These initial caveats noted, it is time to discuss the possibilities of prosecution in this regard.

2. Deterrence in international criminal law

Deterrence is one of the most well-known aims of criminal law; indeed, Gerhard Werle considers it to be probably the most important of the aims of international criminal justice, certainly more so than retribution.[11] Deterrence is usually said to have two parts, special and general deterrence. The former is individually focused in that the specific offender is intended to be dissuaded from undertaking the prohibited behaviour owing to their fear of being subject to the relevant punishment. As Dierdre Golash has put it, '[t]he threat of deterrent punishment seeks to operate on the will of the individual offender at the moment of temptation to commit the crime'.[12] We will return to this issue presently.

[8] See H. Krieger, 'Introduction', in this volume, at 6.

[9] O. Bangerter, 'Comment – Persuading Armed Groups to Better Respect International Humanitarian Law', Chapter 5 in this volume, at 113.

[10] S. Ratner, 'Law Promotion Beyond Law Talk: The Red Cross, Persuasion and the Laws of War' (2011) 22 *European Journal of International Law* 459; on human rights bodies, see D. Steiger 'Enforcing International Humanitarian Law through Human Rights Bodies', Chapter 12 in this volume, at 264–67.

[11] G. Werle, *Principles of International Criminal Law*, 2d edn (The Hague: T.M.C. Asser Press, 2010), at 34–35.

[12] D. Golash, 'The Justification of Punishment in the International Context', in L. May and Z. Hoskins (eds.), *International Criminal Law and Philosophy* (Cambridge: Cambridge University Press, 2010), 201–23, at 211.

General prevention, on the other hand, addresses the punishment of the individual offender to society more generally in that the punishment of the individual is *pour l'exemple des autres* – having seen that engaging in that conduct leads to punishment, they will come to the conclusion that they ought not engage in that conduct either, for fear of the same treatment or a more general sense that the law ought to be followed as that is the appropriate thing to do[13] (or, in Razian terms, create an idea that the rules themselves are second order reasons for action).[14] The latter is the more attractive idea from the point of view of a liberal criminal justice system in that the former raises the rather uncomfortable spectre of the treatment of the body of the condemned and the spectacle of the scaffold described by Michel Foucault in *Discipline and Punish.*[15] It is likely for this reason that the International Criminal Tribunal for the Former Yugoslavia (ICTY) has emphasized the rule of law rationale:

> During times of armed conflict, all persons must now be more aware of the obligations upon them in relation to fellow combatants and protected persons, particularly civilians. Thus, it is hoped that the Tribunal and other international courts are bringing about the development of a culture of *respect* for the rule of law and not simply the *fear* of the consequences of breaking the law, and thereby deterring the commission of crimes.[16]

Retributivists, on the other hand, do not think that this is ever acceptable, as it treats the punished person as a means to an end. This is particularly offensive to Kantians.[17] The ICTY's response that deterrence, as a result, ought not to be given undue prominence in a sentence[18] is not a complete response to such claims, because any additional sentence on this ground is unwarranted to such theorists.

These critiques aside, foundational documents of international criminal law enshrine deterrence. So, for example, the Genocide Convention is, in its full title, the Convention on the Prevention and Punishment of the Crime of Genocide, thereby clearly linking the role of prosecution and

[13] This is sometimes called positive general deterrence.

[14] J. Raz, *Practical Reason and Norms* (Princeton: Princeton University Press, 1990), at 39–40.

[15] M. Foucault, *Discipline and Punish and the Birth of the Prison*, translated by A. Sheridan, 2d edn (New York: Vintage Books, 1995), at 3–32.

[16] *Prosecutor v. Nikolić* (Sentencing Judgment) IT-02-60–1/S (2 December 2003), para. 89.

[17] See generally Cryer et al., *Introduction*, above note 1, at 32.

[18] *Prosecutor v. Nikolić*, above note 16, para. 90.

prevention. The same can be said about the 1984 UN Convention against Torture.[19]

Security Council Resolution 827, which set up the ICTY (and which Resolution 955, which set up the International Criminal Tribunal for Rwanda (ICTR), repeated, essentially verbatim), spoke clearly of the role of deterrence, saying that the Council was

> [d]etermined to put an end to such crimes and to take effective measures to bring to justice the persons who are responsible for them, . . . [c]onvinced that in the particular circumstances of the former Yugoslavia the establishment as an ad hoc measure by the Council of an international tribunal and the prosecution of persons responsible for serious violations of international humanitarian law would enable this aim to be achieved and would contribute to the restoration and maintenance of peace, . . . [and] [b]elieving that the establishment of an international tribunal and the prosecution of persons responsible for the above-mentioned violations of international humanitarian law will contribute to ensuring that such violations are halted and effectively redressed.[20]

The Rome Statute also foregrounds general and specific deterrence.[21] For example, paragraph 5 of the preamble states that the parties are '[d]etermined to put an end to impunity for the perpetrators of these crimes and thus to contribute to the prevention of such crimes'. Chambers of the International Criminal Court (ICC) have also relied on deterrence to reach various (not always consistent) conclusions about where the ICC should concentrate its energies.[22] Indeed, the Appeals Chamber went as far as to determine that deterrence is the 'cornerstone' of the ICC.[23] This goes too far. The ICC has set various goals by the Rome Statute, some deontological, some utilitarian, and the Statue does not set a hierarchy

[19] On both, see J. Méndez, 'Justice and Prevention', in C. Stahn and M. El-Zeidy (eds.), *The International Criminal Court and Complementarity* (Cambridge: Cambridge University Press, 2011), 33–51, at 34.

[20] UNSC Resolution 827 (25 May 1993), preamble.

[21] H. Olásolo, *The Role of the International Criminal Court in Preventing Atrocity Crimes through Timely Intervention* (The Hague: Eleven International Publishing, 2011), at 11. The negotiations for the Statute focused heavily on this rationale. See J. Klabbers, 'Just Revenge? The Deterrence Argument in International Criminal Law' (2001) 12 *Finnish Yearbook of International Law* 249, at 251.

[22] *Prosecutor v. Ntaganda* (Decision on The Prosecutor's Application for Warrants Of Arrest Article 58), Case No. ICC-01/04–01/07 (10 February 2006), para. 55; *Prosecutor v. Ntaganda* (Judgment on the Prosecutor's Appeal against the Decision of Pre-Trial Chamber I Entitled 'Decision on The Prosecutor's Application for Warrants Of Arrest Article 58'), Case No. ICC 01/04–01/07 (13 July 2006), paras. 73–75.

[23] Ibid.

between them.[24] There is no doubt that, rightly or wrongly, deterrence is an important goal that the drafters of the Rome Statute set for the ICC.

2.1. *Critiques of deterrence*

In addition to the philosophical difficulties mentioned above, there have been more practical critiques of the reliance of many international criminal lawyers on deterrence-based rationales. The two main ones are that deterrence-based rationales do not reflect the conditions under which international crimes are committed. The second, which is linked to a response to the first, is that the empirical basis for any deterrent function is missing or, indeed, points to a contrary conclusion.

2.1.1. Deterrence, rationality and international crimes/criminals

Turning first to the idea of rationality which, as mentioned above, is key to individual deterrence, one of the most sophisticated commentators on deterrence in international criminal law, Mark Drumbl, has expressed the difficulty as follows: 'because deterrence's assumption of a certain degree of perpetrator rationality, which is grounded in liberalism's treatment of the ordinary common criminal, seems particularly ill fitting for those who perpetrate atrocity'.[25]

It is true that there is little rationality to be expected of drugged child soldiers, for example. However, what needs to be remembered is that although war crimes will, sadly, almost inevitably be committed in armed conflicts, for the most part, they can be limited through proper command, which international criminal law encourages and also punishes in certain failures to exercise.[26] In this respect, it is important to note that although its norms are applicable to all, international criminal law, in particular international criminal prosecutions, tends to focus on those in leadership positions, and leaders tend to operate in a more autonomous fashion.[27] One of the reasons international criminal law has doctrines such as command responsibility, joint criminal enterprise and co-perpetration is to

[24] See, for example, M. Bergsmo and O. Triffterer, 'Preamble', in O. Triffterer (ed.), *Commentary on the Rome Statute*, 2d edn (Munich: C. H. Beck, 2008), 1–14, at 10–11.

[25] M. Drumbl, *Atrocity, Punishment, and International Law* (Cambridge: Cambridge University Press, 2007), at 171.

[26] P. Rowe, 'Military Misconduct during International Armed Operations: "Bad Apples" or Systemic Failure?' (2008) 12 *Journal of Conflict Security Law* 165.

[27] Ibid. 216.

ensure that those who lead, direct or permit such offences are responsible for them.[28] Leaders, in contrast to some of those in the lower ranks, are more likely to be rational actors, with a view to longer-term consequences. As Jakob von Holderstein Holtermann has said:

> Political and military leaders are generally placed in circumstances where their contribution plays a decisive role as events unfold. Even though they surely cannot perform mass atrocities single-handedly, their actions as leaders are undoubtedly necessary in order for them to take place . . . and there are several good reasons to suppose that, in contrast to foot soldiers, these leaders can, in the right circumstances, be deterred by the threat of punishment, i.e. that they are instrumentally rational in the sense desired.[29]

There are those, however, who disagree about political leaders. Jan Klabbers, for example, has argued that we just cannot apply the cost-benefit analysis that is assumed to be made by deterrence-based rationales. Such rationales simply do not apply to human rights violators who 'will act for political reasons, hoping, nay, expecting, that history will prove him or her right'.[30] This may apply to the ends sought, but that does not exclude the possibility of affecting the means adopted to achieve those ends.

Others argue that, particularly in the context of 'new wars' featuring 'militias, paramilitaries, gangs and loosely organized rebel groups instead of organized militias as the main actors, [that] economic motivations and mindless ethnic hatred had replaced national interests or ideological visions as the driving forces of these conflicts'.[31] This means, according to the proponents of such a view, that the rational calculation that forms the basis of theories of deterrence is missing in such contexts.[32] Others add that, with respect to non-State armed groups in particular, the absence of

[28] See R. Cryer, 'Prosecuting the Leaders: Promises, Politics and Pragmatics' (2009) 1 *Göttingen Journal of International Law* 45, at 55 et seq.

[29] J. von Holderstein Holtermann, '"A Slice of Cheese" – A Deterrence-Based Argument for the International Criminal Court' (2010) 11 *Human Rights Review* 289, at 306. This assertion is controverted by J. F. Alexander, 'The International Criminal Court and the Prevention of Atrocities: Predicting the Court's Impact' (2009) 54 *Villanova Law Review* 1, at 3, but he accepts that his skepticism is not based on a firm empirical base.

[30] Klabbers, 'Just Revenge? ', above note 21, at 253.

[31] N. Lamp, 'Conceptions of War and Paradigms of Compliance: The "New War" Challenge to International Humanitarian Law' (2011) 16 *Journal of Conflict and Security Law* 225, at 227, although he does not necessarily agree with such a view.

[32] F. Harhoff, 'Sense and Sensibility in Sentencing – Taking Stock of International Criminal Punishment', in O. Engdahl and P. Wrange (eds.), *Law at War: The Law as it Was and the Law as it Should Be: Liber Amoricum Ove Bring* (Leiden: Martinus Nijhoff Publishers, 2008), 121–40, at 127.

reciprocity (in the sense of belligerent privilege),[33] and a sense of ownership of international humanitarian law[34] provide further disincentives to comply, which further undermines any calculations such groups may make.

There are a number of responses that can be given to some such claims.[35] To begin, there is an empirical response, as Sandesh Sivakumaran has shown. In fact, rebel groups are not always as disorganized as they are often portrayed, and they frequently do have codes of conduct.[36] The image of armed groups as entirely unorganized is one that it not entirely borne out in practice. The second is to question about what these suggestions implicitly consider to be different about African conflicts and their protagonists. Nicolas Lamp asserts that in the context of mass international crimes, such as former Yugoslavia and Rwanda crimes, moral inversions may occur that lead to international crimes.[37] Similarly, Golash, looking at the sociological factors surrounding international crimes, avers that

> [m]ass atrocities often occur under a reign of terror by a despotic government or ruthless factions such as the LRA [Lord's Resistance Army] . . . Those who voluntarily participate in these crimes find themselves in situations in which the social pressure not to harm (some) others has suddenly been removed or, indeed, has been turned into its opposite pressure from either peers or authorities to target despised

[33] That is, immunity from criminal consequences for belligerent acts in accordance with international humanitarian law. On this, see M. Cherif Bassiouni, 'The New Wars and the Crisis of Compliance with the Law of Armed Conflict by Non-State Actors' (2008) 98 *Journal of Criminal Law and Criminology* 711, at 718; R. Provost, 'Asymmetrical Reciprocity and Compliance with the Laws of War', in B. Perrin (ed.), *Modern Wars: Armed Groups, Private Militaries, Humanitarian Organizations, and the Law* (Vancouver: University of British Columbia Press, 2012), 17–42; S. Rendeau, 'The Pragmatic Role of Reciprocity: Promoting Respect for International Humanitarian Law among Non-State Armed Groups', in B. Perrin (ed.), *Modern Wars*, 43–72.

[34] S. Sivakumaran, 'The Ownership of International Humanitarian Law: Non-State Armed Groups and the Formation and Enforcement of IHL Rules', in B. Perrin (ed.), *Modern Wars*, above note 33, 87–101; A. Petrov, 'Non-State Actors and Law of Armed Conflict Revisited: Enforcing International Law through Domestic Engagement' (2014) 19 *Journal of Conflict and Security Law* 279.

[35] The last two remain deeply problematic from the point of view of ensuring compliance with international humanitarian law.

[36] S. Sivakumaran, *The Law of Non-International Armed Conflict* (Oxford: Oxford University Press, 2012), at 170–80.

[37] Lamp, 'Conceptions of War', above note 31, at 255. To give him his due, Lamp does not claim that this is inevitable or limited to Africa; indeed, his examples are not drawn primarily from Africa.

> others... [Hence] [i]t is not realistic to think that the threat of punishment by an international body can counter the psychological, situational and social pressures that induce individuals to engage in atrocities.[38]

It is important in these situations, though, to take into account that in Africa, as in other conflicts, these moral inversions are not the outcome of immediate irrationality, but the culmination of processes of rational albeit deeply unpleasant calculations on the part of leaders.[39] As Susan Power, drawing upon the empirical research of Alison des Forges, has argued, 'people who play a role in mass killings and rapes are often doing so for the first time... individuals who have never killed before are deciding how far to go. Often as they make these decisions, they are looking left, and looking right, and gauging the consequences'.[40]

In the context of Africa in particular, the frequent invocation of this 'new war' paradigm often has a ring of very old-fashioned, colonial views of Africa and Africans as irrational, with all that this entails. To take one example,[41] Errol Mendes, a scholar who has undertaken work in the Office of the Prosecutor of the ICC, has taken a view that the ICC should have no truck with the Lord's Resistance Army, on the basis that

> Kony... claims that he is instructed in spiritual and military matters by holy spirits and is tasked with fighting evil by promoting the Ten Commandments of the Old Testament. He obviously has not learned that those Commandments include children honouring their parents and not committing murder. This mental incongruence must be kept in mind when one thinks about whether someone with the mental and psychological makeup of Kony can ever be a reliable peace partner to even begin to start a discussion on peace and justice.[42]

The question of whether the ICC should take anything said by Joseph Kony as reliable is a fair one, but the manner in which it is parlayed by Mendes, as one of mental capacity, is unhelpful. Often, even groups stigmatized as fanatical and driven by religious zeal rather than sober reflection act on rational grounds. The most prominent example of this

[38] Golash, 'The Justification of Punishment', above note 12, at 211–12, 215.

[39] P. Akhavan, 'Beyond Impunity: Can International Criminal Justice Prevent Future Atrocities?' (2001) 95 *American Journal of International Law* 7, at 7.

[40] S. Power, 'Stopping Genocide and Securing "Justice": Learning by Doing' (2002) 69 *Social Research* 1093, at 1101.

[41] It ought to be said that none of Drumbl, Golash, Lamp or Wipmann could be accused of making such simplistic assumptions.

[42] E. Mendes, *Peace and Justice at the International Criminal Court: A Court of Last Resort* (Cheltenham: Edward Elgar Publishing, 2010), at 97.

is the Lord's Resistance Army in Uganda. The LRA is often described in terms of religious fervour. However, when it came to issues of international criminal justice, its demands for amnesty and for the withdrawal of the indictments were clearly the outcome of rational calculation, as was the decision to engage in peace negotiations after the indictments came. Kony's actions, awful though they may be, ought not to simply be cast aside as pathological. The decisions of the senior members of the LRA may be, although deeply immoral, rational when the context is taken into account, as has been shown by Reed Wood in his contribution to this volume. Although his view is that short interests prevail with such groups, the point here is that the group makes rational calculations.[43]

This is not the only example. In relation to Sierra Leone, Foday Sankoh wanted money, Charles Taylor wanted money and power and Colonel Gaddafi wanted a West African fiefdom. These are not the aims of the blindly irrational or nihilistic. They may not be laudable goals, but they are understandable ones, and these leaders went about them in a manner which, at one level, was rational. Finally, the African Union's reaction to various aspects of the ICC's practice in indicting people, and that leaders will fight to the end rather than face prosecution, is a clear example of the acceptance of the rationality of the behaviour of the various actors, and therefore the criticism of the possibility of application of deterrence, on the basis that the protagonists are not rational, seems to be at least overstated. High-ranking leaders are rarely completely irrational.[44] Nor are they stupid. That sort of leader does not last long.

To take matters further on this, it is the case that even within the international criminal tribunals, an image of the African warlord who is the definitional 'Other', has been constructed. It is possible that the Special Court for Sierra Leone (SCSL), and perhaps other international (or internationalized) tribunals, have fallen victim to this simplistic stereotype. For example, Gerhard Anders has shown that in that court, the prosecution has frequently fallen into a narrative of Africa as being the 'dark continent' of nineteenth-century myth.[45] Similarly, M. Kamari Clarke has argued that representations of defendants before the international

[43] R. Wood, 'Understanding Strategic Motives for Violence against Civilians during Civil Conflict', in Chapter 2 of this volume, at 15–16, 26, 43.

[44] S. Roach, 'Justice of the Peace? Future Challenges and Prospects for a Cosmopolitan Court', in S. Roach (ed.), *Governance, Order and the International Criminal Court* (Oxford: Oxford University Press, 2009), 225–34, at 226–29.

[45] G. Anders, 'Testifying About "Uncivilized Events": Problematic Representations of Africa in the Trial Against Charles Taylor' (2011) 24 *Leiden Journal of International Law* 937.

tribunals involve constructions of 'African warlords' that are Western constructs rather than accurate representations of reality, and that such representations (in her terms 'spectacles') are examples of crass stereotypes that undermine to some extent international criminal law and fail to accurately reflect modern Africa.[46]

Such stereotypes ought not to be used by those discussing international criminal law. Indeed, to be fair, two of the most forthright critics of the deterrence rationale in international criminal law, Julian Ku and Jide Nzilibe, have made arguments in the specific context of African conflicts, precisely on the basis of rational calculation of the actors involved. Their argument is that the threat of ICC prosecution will not deter those who are engaged in possible international crimes to the extent that informal or extra-legal sanctions will.[47] In part, this is because – of the African leaders of coups that they evaluated – many were killed, exiled or arrested.

Their form of that argument is flawed for various reasons. The first is that although it is purportedly empirical, as with much law and economic scholarship, it relies on assumed interests rather than proof of them.[48] In their piece, the authors presume what the interests, motivations and intentions of the coupists were; there is no hint that any of the relevant actors were actually asked about what their motivations were. Second, as others have commented, their assumption is that evidence about coup plotters are probative of those who commit international crimes more generally and that the commission of atrocities are a necessary part of African conflicts, neither of which can be taken for granted.[49] Nonetheless, Ku and Nzilibe do at least seem to accept that there is rationality to the decisions made by such actors, a matter all too often overlooked by others. It is not the intention of this chapter to say that every decision in every conflict in Africa is characterized by rationality any more than it is in any area of the world. But what can be seen is that the groups engaged in such activities (or at least their leadership) often do so on the basis of rational calculations. And where rational calculations are entered into, there is at least room for the possibility for the fear of prosecution (hence deterrence) to enter the balance.

[46] M. Kamar Clarke, 'The Rule of Law Through Its Economics of Appearances: The Making of the African Warlord' (2011) 18 *Indiana Journal of Global Legal Studies* 7.

[47] J. Ku and J. Nzilibe, 'Do International Criminal Tribunals Deter or Exacerbate Humanitarian Atrocities?' (2006) 84 *Washington University Law Review* 777.

[48] See R. Cryer, 'The Limits of Objective Interests' (2006) 82 *International Affairs* 183.

[49] See Alexander, 'The International Criminal Court', above note 29, at 48–49. To be fair to Ku and Nzilibe, they are aware of the empirical limitations of their study.

Lastly in this regard, turning to governmental decision-making, in a detailed study of the actions of the governments of Uganda and Sudan with respect to the ICC and complementarity (on which, more later), Sarah Nouwen has found that those governments have engaged in a detailed cost-benefit analysis that interestingly comports with the rational decision-making capacity of governments, even those that are alleged to have committed international crimes (particularly in the case of Sudan).[50] Henceforth, the argument of an absence of rationality is not convincing or at least not universally valid.

2.1.2. The empirical base

This leads us to the empirical response to the critics of deterrence. Scholars and practitioners have frequently held that there has been a deterrent effect that can be traced back to the existence of the international criminal tribunals. So, for example, a number of scholars have asserted that the deterrent function of international criminal trials has been key to their importance.[51] It is, nonetheless, a frequently made criticism of deterrence-based justifications of punishment that empirically, it is difficult both at the domestic and particularly the international level to show that the threat of punishment has a deterrent effect. As Immi Tallgren put it: 'It is not easy to estimate how likely the preventive effect of the international system is. There are no grounds to exclude the possibility of such an effect. Neither is there evidence in its favor'.[52] Even though, as Samantha Power has said, showing deterrence involves proving a negative and is therefore difficult or perhaps impossible to do,[53] the difficulties in proving or disproving deterrence have not stopped critics of the deterrence rationale from adopting an empirical critique of deterrence in international criminal law.

In the past, the absence of enforcement of international criminal law – and the small number of offenders that international criminal tribunals have prosecuted – has been said, with no little justification, to have undermined the goal of deterrence, as people do not think that they are likely to be punished.[54] Indeed, even where there have been such tribunals, some

[50] Nouwen, *Complementarity*, above note 7, at 367 et seq.

[51] See Méndez, 'Justice and Prevention', above note 19, at 50.

[52] I. Tallgren, 'The Sense and Sensibility of International Criminal Law' (2002) 13 *European Journal of International Law* 561, at 569.

[53] Power, 'Stopping Genocide', above note 40, at 1100.

[54] See T. Farer, 'Restraining the Barbarians: Can International Law Help?' (2000) 22 *Human Rights Quarterly* 90, at 92–93.

have questioned whether there was any deterrent effect that is attributable to their existence. This critique has specifically been made with respect to the ICTY, in particular when the existence of that tribunal did not serve to prevent the Srebrenica massacre in 1995. This was, in the eyes of the heart and soul of the ICTY at the time, Antonio Cassese, among the darkest days in the Tribunal's history.[55] On the other hand, as David Wippman notes, there is some anecdotal evidence that there was some level of deterrence in that conflict that can be placed at the door of the ICTY.[56] Beyond this, as Power has explained, in spite of the difficulties, many critics may be looking in the wrong places for evidence:

> You cannot look for deterrence from institutions that only gained enforcement capacity *after* the atrocities had been carried out. If you were going to measure the impact of The Hague Tribunal – if social scientists were to figure out a formula for measuring prevention and deterrence – the place to apply that formula would not be Bosnia, but Kosovo.[57]

Such arguments are echoed, and amplified by James Alexander, who, adding the multi-factorial nature of decision-making in conflict situations, has said:

> Can policymakers, deliberating upon their countries' relationship with the ICC, come to firm conclusions about whether the ICC may be expected to serve as a net benefit or a net liability to the cause of preventing humanitarian atrocities? The answer is, in short, no . . . [T]he simple reality [is] that a rather large assortment of variables must be dealt with. Some of these variables, based as they are on historically novel characteristics of the ICC, are at present truly imponderable, having the potential to swamp the effects of the other variables in play.[58]

There has also been some more systematic work in this area now. In particular, Kathryn Sikkink has undertaken a large empirical study, based on trials around the world, and statistical analysis of human rights practices in countries that had what she describes as 'human rights' trials and the level of repression seen in later years there. On the basis of that study,

[55] J. Weiler, 'Editorial: Nino in His Own Words' (2011) 22 *European Journal of International Law* 931, at 943.

[56] D. Wippman, 'Atrocities, Deterrence and the Limits of International Justice' (1999) *Fordham International Law Journal* 473, at 475.

[57] S. Power, 'Stopping Genocide and Securing "Justice": Learning by Doing' (2002) 69 Social Research 1093, at 1100.

[58] Alexander, 'The International Criminal Court', above note 29, at 42.

she asserts that there is a deterrent function that accompanies criminal prosecutions of international crimes that can be statistically shown.[59]

Furthermore, anecdotal evidence from members of the UN Office of Political Affairs from on the ground is very much that the words 'The Hague' have a considerable chilling effect on actors in Africa, particularly given the focus of the ICC, to which we will return, on rebels and now also on government officials.[60] Furthermore, the reaction of many African leaders to the indictment of Omar al-Bashir and Muammar Gaddafi, which has been to call for the suspension of such indictments in the interests of international peace and security, certainly implies that the threat of prosecution is now being taken very seriously.[61] Leaders do not generally waste their time and political capital fulminating against trifling matters. Similarly, Fatou Bensouda, the (then) deputy Prosecutor of the ICC, has asserted that the ICC's activities have had 'an impact' in various countries in Africa.[62]

Probably the most detailed evaluation of the ICC's practice in this regard has come from Juan Méndez, who was the Secretary-General's Special Advisor on the Prevention of Genocide and remains one of the leading advocates for prosecutions as a means of prevention/deterrence. His first examples are the DRC, the Central African Republic, Kenya, Northern Uganda and Sudan. In all of these instances, Méndez asserts that threats of ICC action led to the exclusion of amnesties at the domestic level and that 'since the ICC became operational, conflict managers have learned that impunity and blanket amnesties are no longer in their toolkit'.[63]

This is interesting, and may be true (although the alleged offer made to Colonel Gaddafi to leave and go into exile may speak against this), but it has to be said that most of the examples do not prove the point that any deterrent effect can be placed at the door of the ICC. It may be, in the long run, that the continued delegitimation of amnesties and (which perhaps is not the same thing) ending impunity leads to deterrence and

[59] K. Sikkink, *The Justice Cascade: How Human Rights Prosecutions are Changing World Politics* (New York: W.W. Norton & Company, 2011), Chapter 6.

[60] Personal communication to the author, August 2011.

[61] R. Cryer, 'Selectivity in International Criminal Law', in F. Domb (ed.), *Building Peace in Post-Conflict Situations* (London: British Institute of International and Comparative Law, 2012), 153–91, at 183–89.

[62] B. Schiff, 'The ICC's Potential for Doing Bad When Pursuing Good' (2012) 26 *Ethics and International Affairs* 73, at 78.

[63] Méndez, 'Justice and Prevention', above note 19, at 40–46.

that the ICC has a role to play on point, but this is a thin thread to hold up international criminal justice. A more positive spin may be put on aspects of this, that is, that it does not seem that ICC activity had a negative effect on peace negotiations,[64] but that is not really the concern of this chapter.

One exception to the questionable relevance of these examples may be Kenya; there, considerable international engagement in relation to investigation and prosecution of those responsible for post-election violence in 2007 led the president and prime minister in 2009 to commit to preventing violence in the next election cycle.[65] The 2013 election was, by some distance, the most peaceful in Kenyan history, although ICC oversight is probably only one factor (but that itself is a significant development).

Looking to circumstances in which the ICC has not actually taken (judicial) action, Méndez may be similarly speaking to the wrong point when he notes that the ICC's oversight in the situation in Colombia arguably influenced the Colombian Constitutional Court in overturning an amnesty law[66] and that in Guinea it called for accountability in relation to crimes committed in Conakry in 2009, which led the government to cooperate with the Court and invite it to visit there.[67] Both may be heartening, but neither of these instances speak directly to deterrence per se.

Equally, at least in one situation, Méndez is probably on stronger ground. In relation to the Côte d'Ivoirean conflict in 2004, Méndez refers to a hugely tense situation, when over a weekend flashpoint, the media was filled with inflammatory rhetoric. Following his public intervention, noting the possibility of ICC investigations, calm returned. Méndez claims that 'the prospect of an ICC prosecution of those who used hate speech to instigate and incite the commission of international crimes was carefully analysed by persons in authority and their legal advisors . . . [T]he incident is [thus] sufficient anecdotal evidence that the threat of prosecution in some cases can stay the hand of the perpetrators of mass atrocities'.[68]

This is important, but, in addition to the fact that the other evidence he brings is far from perfect, there are two other factors that need to be dealt with before we can accept such assertions at face value. The first of these is that, as Méndez makes clear, his second set of pieces of evidence are related to the assumed catalytic effect of the regime of complementarity enshrined in the Rome Statute of the ICC.[69] The general assumption underlying that principle is that, given the idea that complementarity, which allows the ICC to take action if the relevant State (usually the *locus*

[64] Ibid. 45–46. [65] Ibid. 40–41. [66] Ibid. 47–48. [67] Ibid. 48–49. [68] Ibid. 47.
[69] The relevant section of his chapter is called 'Complementarity and Deterrence'.

delicti) is shown to be unwilling or unable to do so, will prompt such States into taking action leading to prosecutions themselves.[70]

However, such an assumption has recently been the subject of a significant empirical critique from Sarah Nouwen.[71] Nouwen questions the unproved causal pathway between the (implicit) assumptions behind the assertions that complementarity will cause domestic action (prosecutions) which should then pay into deterrence.[72] On the basis of detailed studies of Uganda and Sudan, Nouwen has found that '[n]otably, the one and only effect that is directly relevant for an invocation of complementarity before the Court, namely, the initiation of genuine domestic investigations and prosecutions of crimes within the ICC's jurisdiction, is for the most part yet to occur in Uganda and Sudan'.[73] As Nouwen notes, though, her study is of two States and does not claim to be a systematic study of all the effects of complementarity throughout all possible situations.[74] In both of the studies Nouwen undertakes, there is a relatively strong central government, which is more than capable of identifying, weighing and acting upon its interests. What remains to be done is to undertake a study of the calculations that complementarity does (or does not) inspire in other actors, particularly where there is limited governmental capacity. In those situations, absent action by non-State actors,[75] external governance mechanisms, such as the ICC, may be the only drivers for compliance with international humanitarian law.

The second issue that needs to be dealt with 'head-on' is the counterargument to the examples that have been given above, which is that, even if they are accurate, they are anecdotal and can therefore not make the case for deterrence. The most sustained critique of deterrence-based

[70] On the principle, generally see, among a huge literature, J. Kleffner, *Complementarity in the Rome Statute and National Jurisdictions* (Oxford: Oxford University Press, 2008); Stahn and El-Zeidy (eds.), *The International Criminal Court and and Complementarity*, above note 19.

[71] Nouwen, *Complementarity*, above note 7. [72] Ibid. 24–25.

[73] Ibid. 10. [74] Ibid. 31.

[75] On which, see, for example, Z. Mampilly, 'Insurgent Governance in the Democratic Republic of the Congo', Chapter 3 in this volume, at 53, 58–62; J. Willms, 'Courts of Armed Groups – A Tool for Inducing Compliance with International Humanitarian Law', Chapter 7 in this volume, at 149–80; D. Fleck, 'Comment – Perspectives on Courts Established by Armed Opposition Groups', in Chapter 8 of this volume, at 186–87; S. Sivakumaran, 'Implementing Humanitarian Norms through Non-State Armed Groups', Chapter 6 in this volume, at 125–46; and H. Krieger, 'Conclusion: Where States Fail, Non-State Actors Rise? Inducing Compliance with International Humanitarian Law in Areas of Limited Statehood', Chapter 21 in this volume, at 533–40, 546–53.

arguments has been made by Pádraig McAuliffe.[76] McAuliffe is deeply sceptical of what he sees as the messianic pretensions of international criminal lawyers, whom he sees as basing a naïve faith in international criminal law around human rights ideology and being invested in a project of developing international criminal law.[77] From this position, he argues that international criminal lawyers who support deterrence-based rationales are wedded to individual sentimental stories,[78] to say that

> [t]hese anecdotes may add something significant to our understanding of the restraining impact of international criminal law. Even if in-depth, small scale studies do not have universal applicability, they may impact beneficially on policy-making as 'plausibility probes' suggesting that a generated hypothesis should be tested in a wider selection of countries ... However, deterrence-based advocacy is less modest. It instead relies on these anecdotes to establish the overall credibility of deterrence. In doing so, it betrays the main shortcoming of single case analyses, namely that inferences drawn from them may not be applicable beyond the context in which the research takes place.[79]

This is a strongly made (and worded) argument, but there are considerable grounds for scepticism about the scepticism. The first is that it relies on a rather monolithic view of international criminal lawyers. It may be true that some international criminal lawyers may argue in the manner that McAuliffe suggests (or that they can be caricatured as such), but international criminal lawyers, including those with sympathy for deterrence as a rationale, belong to a broader proverbial church.[80] It is notable that McAuliffe, for example, does not provide a reference for his assertion and only later mentions one speech by the president of the ICC that supports it. This is therefore something of a straw-man argument, and indeed he also cites Theodor Meron as accepting that the evidence is 'anecdotal and uncertain'.[81] Most international criminal lawyers would not go further.

What perhaps can be said is that the number of pieces of anecdotal evidence are stacking up, and although they do not make a comprehensive

[76] P. McAuliffe, 'Suspended Belief? The Curious Endurance of the Deterrence Rationale in International Criminal Law' (2012) 10 *New Zealand Journal of Public International Law* 227.

[77] Ibid. 240–46. [78] Ibid. 255–56. [79] Ibid. 258–59.

[80] Although, on human rights influences, see also D. Robinson, 'The Identity Crisis of International Criminal Law' (2008) 21 *Leiden Journal of International Law* 925.

[81] McAuliffe, 'Suspended Belief?', above note 76, at 259 (citing T. Meron, 'War Crimes Law Comes of Age' (1998) 92 *American Journal of International Law* 462, at 463).

case, the more evidence there is, the stronger the case becomes that there can be a contribution to deterrence from international criminal prosecutions. It is true that there are huge epistemological problems with determining what causes (and therefore what may prevent) international crimes, as the decisions to undertake such conduct depends on many factors,[82] but this cuts both ways. Furthermore, it is almost certainly the case that a comprehensive study of all conflicts on this basis would simply be impossible; therefore, the best is the enemy of the good here.

A more philosophical response is given by von Holderstein Holtermann, who argues that whatever the problems of determining the extent to which punishment deters crime, such difficulties do not answer the question of whether criminal courts ought to be set up. This is because such difficulties do not make the case against deterrence arguments; they simply demonstrate the fact that we have to work on incomplete information, and therefore it becomes a question of what is more plausible. On different but related grounds, he asserts that the burden of proof is on those who deny the deterrent value of prosecution to show that this is the case.[83] His reason for doing so is that 'human beings are by and large instrumentally rational actors', and thus, intuitively, the fear of prosecution ought to have an effect on behaviour.[84] He has a point.

2.2. *Conditions for deterrence*

Whatever level of empirical evidence is required, few if any would argue that deterrence can be even contributed to without certain conditions being fulfilled. Méndez, for example, has argued that there are, in essence, two major criteria for deterrence. These are, first, certainty of application of the law, and second, that 'it has to follow its own rules, especially to allow the operation of the law without interference and not subject to political considerations . . . If courts and prosecutors are contemplated as levers to force the parties to negotiate, their independence and impartiality will be undermined because they will be turned on and off as political circumstances dictate'.[85] To this we ought to add the perceived legitimacy

[82] See, for example, S. Harrenhof, 'How Can Criminology Contribute to an Explanation of International Crimes?' (2014) 12 *Journal of International Criminal Justice* 231; J. G. Stewart, 'Overdetermined Atrocities' (NYU School of Law, Public Law Research Paper No. 12–53), papers.ssrn.com/sol3/papers.cfm?abstract_id=2152670.

[83] von Holderstein Holtermann, 'A Slice of Cheese', above note 29, at 294.

[84] Ibid. 295.

[85] Méndez, 'Justice and Prevention', above note 19, at 35–36.

of the process, which feeds into the perception of the political or other nature of the relevant court or tribunal.[86]

Any asserted deterrent function of prosecutions, of course, requires a credible threat of prosecution of such leaders. Turning to the context at hand (Africa), after decades of non-prosecution, many African leaders assumed that victory or exile would serve to ensure their freedom and their continued wealth and influence. However, for many, the indictment and eventual capture and prosecution of Charles Taylor was a considerable shock. An African leader who had negotiated and taken up exile in Nigeria and who had the support of well-known African figures such as Colonel Gaddafi and Omar al-Bashir found himself no longer welcome in his new home and was arrested and sent for trial.[87] In part, this was a political as much as a legal event, but the symbolic value of the arrest was huge.[88] Were al-Bashir to end up before the ICC, the message would become clearer, and given the horror with which most seem to view the possibility of being tried before an international criminal court, the possibility of specific deterrence ought not to be discounted. Hence, although prior to the 1990s there was little chance of anyone being prosecuted for international crimes, the tide is slowly turning against that position.

The real issue now is one that mixes the two criteria Méndez suggests. That is the prospect of selective enforcement. This is well-trodden ground, so it is not the intention of this piece to engage in detailed reflections on the selective aspects of international criminal law throughout its history. That has been done elsewhere.[89] What is important is the extent to which it characterizes modern practice, in particular in relations to Africa, and the extent to which it undermines the factors militating in favour of compliance.

Deterrence, insofar as it relies on the likelihood of prosecution, will, of necessity, be undermined if individuals think the law will not be enforced

[86] See, for example, A. Marston Danner, 'Enhancing the Legitimacy and Accountability of Prosecutorial Discretion at the International Criminal Court' (2003) 97 *American Journal of International Law* 510.

[87] See A. Tejan-Cole, 'A Big Man in a Small Cell: Charles Taylor and the Special Court for Sierra Leone', in E. L. Lutz and C. Reiger (eds.), *Prosecuting Heads of State* (Cambridge: Cambridge University Press, 2009), 205–27. On the links, see D. Crane, 'The Bright Red Thread: The Politics of International Criminal Law – Do We Want Peace or Justice? The West African Experience', in L. Sadat (ed.), *Forging a Convention on Crimes against Humanity* (Cambridge: Cambridge University Press, 2011), 59–77, at 59, 63.

[88] Tejan-Cole, 'A Big Man', above note 87, at 226–27.

[89] Cryer, *Prosecuting International Crimes*, above note 5.

against them. Therefore, the extent to which they may maintain leverage and ensure that international criminal law will only be applied to others is likely to be part of the rational calculation that may be entered into when deciding whether or not to commit international crimes. For example, Yoweri Museveni had little to fear when he referred the situation in Northern Uganda to the ICC to the extent to which he did not think the Prosecutor of the ICC would be interested in the Uganda People's Defence Force, as, in time, it proved he was not. The same applies for other 'self-referrals' to the ICC, where it has proved to be the case that the ICC Prosecutor has focused his work on the conduct of rebels rather than those who referred the situation (i.e., the government). There are limited exceptions to this, primarily in the context of the post-election violence in Kenya, where, after considerable African Union and other support for the possibility of ICC activity, the Prosecutor decided to proceed against all sides in the conflict on the basis of his *proprio motu* powers. The (for the most part) refusal of the Prosecutor to aggressively pursue either governmental figures in Africa (outside the context of Security Council referrals) or any actors outside of Africa may give rise to a feeling that such people are safe from the ICC, and this is something that a rational actor would take into account. Again, without a credible threat of prosecution, the deterrent effect is limited. Given the perception in Africa, justified or not, that the ICC is a political organ that is targeting certain African actors on political grounds,[90] rather than undertaking its processes on legal ones, responses and calculations with respect to it (including whether to commit international crimes) will be at the political level. This is a significant dilemma. The first Prosecutor of the ICC was fond of stating that he was above politics and would only follow the law in deciding what to do. For example, in Nuremberg in 2007, he said that '[a]s the Prosecutor of the ICC, I have been given a clear judicial mandate. I must apply the law without regard to political considerations'.[91] Few are convinced of this.[92] A more realistic view has been given by David Crane, the ex-Prosecutor of the Special Court for Sierra Leone:

[90] And this perception exists. See, for example, R. J. V. Cole, 'Africa's Relationship with the International Criminal Court: More Political than Legal' (2013) 14 *Melbourne Journal of International Law* 1.

[91] L. Moreno-Ocampo, 'Building a Future on Peace and Justice', Speech, Nuremberg, 24 June 2007.

[92] Although commentators disagree on whether or not the ICC's Prosecutors ought to admit that political factors are relevant to their work, see the Roundtable on 'The Political Ethics of the International Criminal Court' (2012) 26 *Ethics and International Affairs* 53.

> International criminal law is about politics. It is a naïve Chief prosecutor who plans for and executes his prosecution plans (if he or she has one) without keeping in mind the bright red thread of politics that permeates the entire existence of a tribunal or court. Conceived due to a political event and a creature of political compromise, politics is in the DNA of all of the justice mechanisms that make up the modern era of international criminal justice.[93]

The story he tells of how he had to guarantee the support, both logistical and military, to ensure the enforcement of the warrants of arrest from the United States and the UK and, at times, behind the back of the Special Representative of the Secretary-General is an interesting one.[94] But, in spite of its upbeat tone and image of practicality it adopts, it paints a picture of international criminal justice that is likely to remain heavily influenced by politics, and where politics enters, selective enforcement is soon to follow. Nor is his account unique in this regard.[95] As such, the role of international criminal prosecutions will remain, for the foreseeable future, a role which is circumscribed with politics.

Against this background, the way forward is to maximize the compliance effect of international criminal law as far as possible within the political boundaries in which it functions. Many of the assumptions about deterrence are binary. Either international criminal law deters international crimes or it does not. This is, to say the least, unnuanced. The better position to adopt is that prosecutions of violations of international criminal law are relevant to, and can contribute to, deterrence of international crimes. It is not necessary to assert that international criminal law, on its own, can deter international crimes. As many of the critics of deterrence in international criminal law have said, other aspects, such as sanctions, and military intervention may play a larger role in preventing international crimes than international criminal law.[96] But this is not the point. The more important question is whether the possibility of prosecution can contribute to the deterrence of international crimes rather than whether it can prevent violations of international humanitarian law on its own. This means that international criminal lawyers need to renounce the

93 Crane, 'The Bright Red Thread', above note 87, at 59. 94 Ibid. 70–71.

95 C. Del Ponte and C. Sudetic, *Madame Prosecutor: Confrontations with Humanity's Worst Criminals and the Culture of Impunity* (New York: Other Press, 2009); V. Peskin, *International Justice in Rwanda and the Balkans: Virtual Trials and the Struggle for State Cooperation* (Cambridge: Cambridge University Press, 2008).

96 K. A. Rodman, 'Why the ICC Should Operate within Peace Processes' (2012) 26 *Ethics and International Affairs* 59, at 60–63.

hubris of perfect deterrence. A realistic approach is required that accepts that international criminal justice is an example of the art of the possible, and therefore perfect deterrence, or a perfect separation between law and politics, simply cannot be achieved.

3. Denunciation/education

The other argument in favour of international criminal prosecutions contributing to compliance with international humanitarian law is that they can contribute to changing people's minds about what is acceptable and the creation of a culture of accountability and thus compliance. This role is strongly linked to the denunciatory/educative (or 'expressive') effect of international criminal prosecutions. Such justifications of punishment rely on the idea that one of the purposes of punishment is to denounce the behaviour and communicate to the offender and society at large that such conduct is wrongful, thus vindicating and publicizing the relevant norm.[97] As can be seen, this has specific and general aspects. As Lucia Zedner has explained, the communicative effect of prosecution is 'an opportunity for communicating with the offender, the victim and wider society the nature of the wrong done'.[98] The ICTY has asserted that international criminal law has this function,[99] and there is much to be said for the idea that international criminal law has, as a major function, if nothing else, the propagation of the norms that are encapsulated in its strictures. Kathryn Sikkink has also argued that much conduct which is law-compliant comes not simply from fear of punishment but from acculturation to the relevant norms.[100] This is similar to Payam Akhavan's view that

> [f]rom the criminal justice process emanates a flow of moral propaganda such that punishment of the individual offender is transformed into a means of expressing social disapproval. In addition to the fear and conscious moral influence of prosecution, it is also possible to create 'unconscious inhibitions against crime and perhaps establish a condition of habitual lawfulness' such that illegal actions will not present themselves consciously as real alternatives to conformity.[101]

[97] For an example of such theories being applied to international criminal law, see D. Amann, 'Group Mentality, Expressivism and Genocide' (2002) 2 *International Criminal Law Review* 93.

[98] L. Zedner, *Criminal Justice* (Oxford: Oxford University Press, 2007), at 109.

[99] *Prosecutor v. Kordić and Čerkez* (Judgment), Case No. IT-95-14/2 (17 December 2004), paras. 1080–1081.

[100] Sikkink, *The Justice Cascade*, above note 59, at 172–74.

[101] P. Akhavan, 'Justice in the Hague: Peace in Former Yugoslavia' (1999) 20 *Human Rights Quarterly* 737, at 746 (footnotes omitted).

It may be the case that the specific communicative role in international criminal law may be limited, owing to the fact that many of those prosecuted by international criminal tribunals denounce their legitimacy. In practice, it might be questioned whether specific communication will ever be a major aspect of international trials. Perhaps, therefore, general communication may be a better way to go.

In some ways, though, a more basic claim can be made. As Nicolas Lamp has observed, although ignorance of the law is no defence, it is clearly the case that the parties' compliance with the law can be helped by knowing what the relevant law is.[102] He argues that in the 'new wars' ensuring this is very difficult. Some, such as William Schabas, argue that the norms of international criminal law represent behaviour that is universally condemned as apodictically *mala in se*.[103] This, unfortunately, is not always the case, so it is useful to engage in a case study of a war crime that has only recently been clearly recognized as such and prosecuted at the international level. This is the war crime of child soldiering.

Although there were a number of universal and regional (African) treaties that dealt with the prohibition of recruitment and use of child soldiers, such conduct was a frequent and widespread characteristic of African conflicts and was seen by many as culturally appropriate, or at least not wrong on the basis that in Africa – or at least parts of it – it was a legitimate cultural practice and that the ability to act as a warrior was, for males, an indicium of the transition from childhood to adulthood.[104]

The first time child soldiering was subject to express criminalization, though, was in the Rome Statute in 1998. Article 8(2)(b)(xxvi) covers '[c]onscripting or enlisting children under the age of 15 years into the national armed forces or using them to participate actively in hostilities'. In international armed conflicts, and, more important for our purposes, owing to the fact that the majority of African conflicts are non-international, Article 8(2)(e)(vii) criminalizes analogous conduct in non-international armed conflicts (without the limitation 'into national armed forces').

102 Lamp, 'Conceptions of War', above note 31, at 241.

103 W. A. Schabas, 'Interpreting the Statutes of the ad hoc Tribunals', in L. C. Vohrah et al. (eds.), *Man's Inhumanity to Man: Essays in Honour of Antonio Cassese* (The Hague: Kluwer Law International, 2003), 847–88, at 887.

104 For a nuanced approach to the issue, see M. Drumbl, *Reimagining Child Soldiers in International Law and Policy* (Oxford: Oxford University Press, 2012). For express discussion on the question of child soldiers and whether it was or ought to be seen as inherently wrong and thus criminal, see B. Roth, *Sovereign Equality and Moral Disagreement: Premises of a Pluralist International Legal Order* (New York: Oxford University Press, 2011), at 267–68.

This was included in the Statute of the Special Court for Sierra Leone's Statute in Article 3(c). However, as that provision was initially drafted by the Secretary-General, it was more narrowly formulated than Article 8(2)(e)(vii) of the Rome Statute and limited to cases involving abduction and forced recruitment. Owing to his concern that the provision was not customary as far back as 1996 (the starting point of the jurisdiction of the Special Court), the Secretary-General sought to cast it as a specific application of Common Article 3. The Security Council disagreed strongly with the Secretary-General on this point and requested the Secretary-General to 'modify . . . [Article 4(c)] so as to conform it to the statement of the law existing in 1996 and as currently accepted by the international community'.[105] The Security Council's suggested modification was to language tracing that in the Rome Statute and appears to represent a claim that Article 8(2)(e)(vii) is not only customary now but was also customary law in 1996.

This question was bitterly contested in the Special Court for Sierra Leone in the *Norman* decision. In this case, the defence challenged the legality of the provision on the basis that customary international law did not recognize such an offence in 1996. The majority in that case determined on, it must be said, not a great deal of evidence that it did.[106] The controversial then President of the Tribunal, Geoffrey Robertson, disagreed, at least until the coming into being of the Rome Statute, and also raised a further point relating to the drafting of the Statute and the question of whether a defendant could have known whether or not international law criminalized the use of child soldiers.

> It might be thought odd that the state of international law in respect of child soldiers was doubtful to the UN Secretary-General in 2000 but was very clear to the President of the Security Council only two months later. If it was not clear to the Secretary-General and his legal advisers that international law had criminalised the enlistment of child soldiers, could it really have been clear to Chief Hinga Norman, or any other defendant at that time in embattled Sierra Leone?[107]

This is an interesting point. There are genuine questions about the extent to which the relevant actors were aware of the (existing or incipient) international prohibitions at this time. Although the enlistment and use

105 Letter from the Security Council to the Secretary-General (22 December 2000), UN Doc. S/2000/1234, at 2.

106 *Prosecutor v. Norman* (Decision on Preliminary Motion Based on Lack of Jurisdiction) SCSL-2004–14-AR72 (31 May 2004).

107 Ibid. Dissenting Opinion of Judge Robertson, para. 6.

of child soldiers is something of an NGO nostrum, genuine questions have begun to be raised about whether the focus on prosecution of the use of child soldiers represents a rather Western approach to matters, in particular the cultural specificity of the underlying notions relating to the prohibition.[108] In addition, some have questioned whether or not the large-scale crimes, such as the murders and rapes that have been alleged against the first ICC convict, Thomas Lubanga, who it is said did not know that the use of child soldiers was a crime,[109] ought to have been prosecuted for as well.

The prosecutions seem to have had a considerable effect on African actors, both in terms of the knowledge of the prohibition and their concern with living up to it for fear of appearing before the ICC. Again, some of the evidence here is anecdotal, in that those on the ground are not only being engaged, for example, by the UN officers in relation to child soldiers, but they are also raising the matter without prompting.[110] Also, there is some evidence that relevant African actors, upon hearing about the prosecution of Lubanga for using child soldiers, have brought children to international officials and have asked for them to be demobilized.[111] The importance of the ICC's focus on child soldiers was attested to by Radhika Coomaswarmy, the UN Special Representative on Child Soldiers, who testified before the ICC in the *Lubanga* case as follows:

> [L]et me state how important the work of the ICC is to every one of us who works in the field. The willingness on the part of the Court to prosecute these cases has sent many armed groups to us – the United Nations – willing to negotiate action plans for the release of children; most recently yesterday in Nepal where the release of 3000 children is about to begin today. We found your work to be so important . . . [112]

There is also some – admittedly ambiguous – evidence that the use of such soldiers is decreasing.[113] If nothing else, the fact that there are now a not insignificant number of children in Northern Uganda and South Sudan who are called 'Okambo' at least implies that the prosecution of

[108] Drumbl, *Reimagining Child Soldiers*, above note 104
[109] Méndez, 'Justice and Prevention', above note 19, at 49.
[110] Personal communication, above note 60. [111] Ibid.
[112] *Prosecutor v. Lubanga* (Transcript) Case No. ICC-01/04–01/06-T-223-ENG (7 January 2010), at 16. The comment is mentioned by William Schabas in humanrightsdoctorate .blogspot.co.uk/2010/01/deterrence-and-international-criminal.html.
[113] Child Soldiers International, 'Louder than Words' (2012), www.child-soldiers.org/ publications_archive.php.

the use of child soldiers has had a cultural impact.[114] Even so, perhaps the best evidence on point is in relation to the recent Libya conflict. The guidelines issued by the National Transitional Council (NTC) for their fighters included the demand that forces 'DO NOT allow persons who are less than 18 years of age to fight, even if they have volunteered to do so'. It is interesting to note that this did not come from the suggestion of an NGO from far away from the conflict but from the NTC itself. As Iain Scobbie, who helped draft the guidance, explains:

> When I discussed a draft of the guidelines at the Irish Centre for Human Rights in early May, it was pointed out that we had made no mention of child soldiers. To be honest, this was because we were working under pressure and were focused on our brief of explaining standards for detention and targeting. Shortly afterwards, however, the NTC itself asked for advice on child soldiers and we incorporated a few basic points in another revision.[115]

The difference between this and many conflicts in Africa even a decade ago is highly notable. It might be countered that there may have been other causative factors (such as the desire of the NTC to maintain support in the West), but, in spite of the perhaps mixed motives and the difficulties of establishing causative factors in international affairs more generally, this does give some hope for criminal prosecutions in the area of disseminating norms and providing for some level of inculcation of the norm. A sceptic might suggest that fighters on the ground do not read the statutes and judgments of international criminal tribunals. This is almost certainly true, but that is not the point. The real issue is ensuring that those who set out the codes of conduct are aware and think highly (for whatever reason) of the rules, and that they disseminate them in the relevant manner. It is of no practical import whether those on the ground are avid fans of the Geneva Conventions and other applicable rules of humanitarian law or simply have the clear guidance that the NTC provides. What matters is compliance and the extent to which prosecutions have led to it, and there are some grounds for cautious optimism here.

[114] I am grateful to Olympia Bekou for this point. See also S. Nouwen, 'Justifying Justice', in J. Crawford and M. Koskenniemi (eds.), *The Cambridge Companion to International Law* (Cambridge: Cambridge University Press, 2012), 327–51, at 327.

[115] I. Scobbie, 'Operationalising the Law of Armed Conflict for Dissident Forces in Libya' (31 August 2011), www.ejiltalk.org/operationalising-the-law-of-armed-conflict-for-dissident-forces-in-libya/#more-3711.

Like general and specific deterrence, the educative function is marred when selective enforcement becomes an issue. The denunciatory/educative function is intended, at both a micro and macro levels, to focus on the norm rather than the identity of the perpetrator. At the micro level, it is intended that the person is condemned and told that they have been condemned for what they did, not for who they are. The focus of the condemnation is the conduct, not the identity of the perpetrator. Selective enforcement starts to blur this message.

At the macro level, to prosecute some of those from one conflict or one side in a conflict and not another would confuse the message that prosecution is meant to have in this area. Again, it would imply that the identity of the perpetrator is relevant to whether the conduct is condemned. The point of generalized education is its emphasis on the importance of the norm itself. It is also the case that for there to be any sort of denunciatory/educative function, the relevant court must be seen as legitimate, to some extent, by the defendant (although this is, as mentioned above, not essential) and by society at large. Without this, the educative effect will be undermined. Unfortunately, there are clear pieces of evidence in the practice of the ICC – and international criminal law more generally – that it is far from perfect on point. If the ICC is perceived as being wrongly exclusively focused on Africa, and thus a tool of Western neo-colonialism, people will not be receptive to the message it seeks to inculcate about the unacceptability of the conduct prohibited by international criminal law.[116]

4. Conclusion

Much of what has gone before assumes that the case for international criminal law ought to be made on consequentialist grounds. Deterrence, as probably the strongest consequentialist argument for criminal prosecutions, has taken a front seat in those debates. This is unfortunate, as even if deterrence was out of the question, it would not mean that international criminal law was without justification. Nevertheless, it is hoped that this contribution has shown that, in spite of the considerable obstacles to international criminal prosecutions, such prosecutions may have some role to play in ensuring compliance with conflicts, including in Africa, and that Africa is no different to any other area of the world in this regard.[117] The evidence on point may be limited and anecdotal, but that does not

[116] See Cryer, 'Selectivity', above note 61.

[117] Sceptics may say that this is because the author is an international criminal lawyer who, although critical of some (perhaps many) of its aspects, is nonetheless a supporter of its ideals and of the regime in the main.

render it completely useless. If, for example, the Lubanga prosecution helped to lead to the demobilization of some child soldiers in sub-Saharan Africa and the NTC in Libya to prohibiting their use (even though that prohibition may not have been upheld in all circumstances), maybe this is an acceptable contribution to compliance with the norms against the use of child soldiers. As others have said, claiming deterrence '[i]s not a claim that everybody will be deterred all the time. It is a claim that some will be deterred some of the time [...] [and it is] a claim that it will deter a sufficient number of potential perpetrators to justify the costs of producing this effect'.[118]

Even if we take the above as given, though, what is most important in this regard for our purposes is that in many, although emphatically not all, conflicts in Africa, those conflicts occur against a backdrop of limited effective governance by official authorities. As such, the possibility of prosecution at the international level, either by international courts or by foreign domestic courts, is one of the few enforcement mechanisms that can exercise an inhibiting effect on the behaviour of the powerful. As Hannah Arendt put it: 'If genocide is an actual possibility in the future, then no people on earth... can feel reasonably sure of its continued existence without the help and protection of international law'.[119] In the absence of State-based incentive to comply with international humanitarian law it may fall to international law to provide the 'back stop' against the commission of crimes against international law. This function is not a new one. The point of including crimes against humanity in the Nuremberg Charter was that German criminal law did not fully protect (inter alia) the German (or stateless), Jewish, Roma and homosexual populations and hence the savings clause in Article 6(c) of the Charter, which applied crimes against humanity to conduct whether or not it was a violation of the criminal law in the *locus delicti*. The contribution that the threat of criminal prosecution can make to prevention of international crimes ought to be appraised in a manner that accepts that criminal justice has a role, but not necessarily a determinative one, in ensuring compliance with humanitarian law. In this regard, it is important to note that it ought not to be the case that anyone put all their eggs in the ICC's basket.[120] The Rome Statute itself does not claim that the ICC can, on its own, prevent

[118] von Holderstein Holtermann, 'A Slice of Cheese', above note 29, at 300.

[119] H. Arendt, *Eichmann in Jerusalem: A Report on the Banality of Evil* (Harmondsworth: Penguin Books, 1977), at 273.

[120] See, for example, K. A. Marshall, 'Prevention and Complementarity in the International Criminal Court: A Positive Approach' (2010) 17 *Human Rights Brief* 21, at 21.

international crimes; the optimistic preamble limits itself to the claim that the ICC can 'contribute' to the prevention of international crimes.[121]

As a result, we ought to approach the possible preventative role of international criminal law and the ICC with humility and an understanding of the limits of criminal justice.[122] Mark Osiel is correct in identifying the issue as 'aligning incentives' against the commission of such offences, rather than focusing on whether one mechanism does or does not prevent international crimes.[123] Just as there is more than one carrot available in responses to international crimes, there is more than one stick available, too – be they financial sanctions (targeted or otherwise), derecognition or non-recognition of various parties to conflicts (as happened in Libya in 2011), refusal to grant aid, loans or membership of international organizations.

In addition, it is important to remember the educative effect of international criminal law. The evidence we have, which is, again, anecdotal rather than systematic, is that the educative role of the ICC, in particular, has been quite strong and has had an impact on the ground. This needs to be kept in mind when the cost-benefit analysis is entered into (if we accept that it ought to be at all). It also has a bearing on aspects of institutional priority, in particular the extent to which outreach activities ought to be engaged with. The ICTY and ICTR have been criticized heavily in the past for their failings in this regard.[124] The ICC has been more proactive in this regard, and such an approach seems to have paid off, at least to a reasonable degree. Therefore, the possible role of prosecuting violations of international humanitarian law should not be written off. Prosecutions have a role to play, and some grounds upon which they may do so ought not to be ceded to the sceptics without something of a fight.

[121] Rome Statute Preamble, operative paragraph 5. This is implied by Tomer Broude in Comments to 'Invited Expert on Prevention Question, uclalawforum.com/prevention.

[122] Ibid. para. 4.

[123] M. Osiel, *Making Sense of Mass Atrocity* (Cambridge: Cambridge University Press, 2009).

[124] See, for example, D. Tolbert, 'The International Criminal Tribunal for the Former Yugoslavia: Unforeseen Successes and Foreseeable Shortcomings' (2002) 26 *Fletcher Forum of World Affairs* 7, at 13–14; G. K. McDonald, 'Problems, Obstacles and Achievements of the ICTY' (2004) 2 *Journal of International Criminal Justice* 558, at 567–69.

10

National courts

The situation in the Democratic Republic of the Congo

JEAN-MICHEL KUMBU

1. Introduction

The Democratic Republic of the Congo (DRC) was for more than twenty years the scene of a host of armed conflicts, which can be divided into three distinct periods. The first period, from 1993 to 1996, was marked by tensions and ethnic conflicts in the region of Kivu. It is 'the epicentre of the Congolese problem'.[1] The second is the one relative to the War of Liberation led by the Alliance of Democratic Forces for Liberation starting in October 1996 and which ended on 17 May 1997 with the overthrow of the regime of President Mobutu, who was replaced by Laurent Kabila with the support of its two main allies, Uganda and Rwanda. The final period began in August 1998 with the outbreak of the 'second Congo war',[2] subsequently to the 1996–1997 war, which involved many armed groups and in which at least eight African countries directly participated, so that it is called the 'first African world war'.[3]

These conflicts have resulted in the commission of the worst and most serious crimes of international law, massacres and sexual violence on

[1] T. Vircoulon, 'Réformer le peace making en République démocratique du Congo: Quand les processus de paix deviennent des systèmes d'action internationaux' (February 2009), www.ifri.org/?page=detail-contribution&id=5619&id_provenance=97.

[2] F. Reyntjens, 'La deuxième guerre du Congo: plus qu'une réédition' (1998–1999) *L'Afrique des grands lacs: Annuaire* 282.

[3] L. Sindjoun, *Les relations internationales africaines: entre Etats en crise et flux transnationaux*, (Dakar: Conseil pour le développement de la recherche en sciences sociales en Afrique (Codesria), 2002); C. Braeckman, *L'enjeu congolais: L'Afrique centrale après Mobutu*, (Paris: Fayard, 1999); B. Kabamba and O. Lanotte, 'Guerres au Congo-zaïre (1996–1999): Acteurs et scénarios', in P. Mathieu and J.-C. Willame (eds.), *Conflits et guerres au Kivu et dans la région des Grands Lacs: Entre tentions locales et escalade régionale* (Paris: L'Harmattan, 1999), 99–154.

a large scale, looting, destruction of private property without military necessity, a war without sparing anyone. Human Rights Watch estimated in a report published in July 2003, that 3.3 million civilians were killed in the DRC between 1998 and 2003 during that 'first African world war'. This is a record which makes this war the deadliest one for civilians since the Second World War.[4]

These barbaric acts have been condemned by several international authorities including the Security Council of the United Nations, the International Court of Justice and the African Court on Human and Peoples' Rights. However, the challenge of their national application continues to arise, all the more since few cases have so far been settled. In this regard, the role of the Congolese courts remains paramount, with two fundamental objectives. First, they must prevent oblivion: peace and national reconciliation are based on the victim's right to know the truth and obtain redress. This is the wish of the majority of the Congolese population.[5] In other words, peace, justice and reconciliation are indivisible goals, interconnected and mutually dependent, equally desired, and which cannot be achieved apart from each other. Second, the Congolese courts must avoid the feeling of impunity, because according to the remark made by the prosecutor Robert Jackson at the time of the first hearing of the Nuremberg trials in 1945 '[t]he crimes that we seek to condemn and punish have been so premeditated, perverse and devastating that civilization cannot tolerate [that] they could be ignored because we would not survive if they were repeated'.[6]

This leads to further investigation on three separate issues. First, how do the Congolese courts have jurisdiction for the repression of serious violations of international humanitarian law? Then, did they apply this law? And if so, in which cases, how and for what judicial efficiency? Finally, a comment needs to be made on the basis of seeking an alternative to the Congolese courts in order to make more efficient the struggle against impunity of perpetrators of serious crimes committed in the DRC.

[4] Human Rights Watch, 'Ituri: "Covered in Blood". Ethnically Targeted Violence in Northeastern DR Congo' (July 2003), at 1, www.hrw.org/sites/default/files/reports/DRC0703.pdf.

[5] P. Vinck et al., 'Living with Fear: A Population-based Survey on Attitudes about Peace, Justice and Social Reconstruction in Eastern Democratic Republic of the Congo', August 2008, at 2–3, escholarship.org/uc/item/9738b4pm#page-1.

[6] J.-P. Bazelaire and Th. Cretin, *La justice pénale internationale: Son évolution, son avenir, de Nuremberg à La Haye* (Paris: Presses Universitaires de France, 2000), at 42.

2. Jurisdiction

Under Congolese law, a great principle governs this matter and raises, in itself, the subsequent difficulties of applicability – the competence of military courts for serious international crimes: genocide, crimes against humanity and war crimes. In 2013, the Congolese courts of appeal acquired a limited competence to sue for the same crimes, but as they have not so far exercised this jurisdiction in any case, the study will focus on the competence of the military tribunals. For analysing some of the difficulties that the latter encounter, it is necessary to first give a brief overview of the judicial system of the DRC.

2.1. The judicial system of the DRC: an overview

The Congolese justice system has experienced three major changes. First, during colonization, there were two categories of courts: one specialized in the application of customary law and another in applying written law. Indeed, under the Decree of 15 April 1926, the Belgian colonial authorities for the first time recognized and organized the traditional courts. This legislation has been amended successively by two important decrees: the one dating from 22 February 1932 and the other dating from 14 December 1933. Subsequently, these three decrees were coordinated by a Royal Decree of 13 May 1938. The law thus constituted has, in turn, undergone some modifications. The latest was made by the Decree dating from 16 September 1959.

After independence, the newly independent State unified the judicial system. Indeed, the Ordinance-Law of 10 July 1968 bearing the Code of Organization and Jurisdiction provided, at the base of the court system, magistrates' courts to replace police courts and customary courts with greater competence. The Code of Organization and Jurisdiction established by the Ordinance-Law of 31 March 1982, as amended by the Ordinance-Law of 29 March 1983, upheld the magistrates' courts. However, temporarily, its 163rd section maintains the legal existence of customary courts where magistrates' courts are not yet installed.

Second, until the adoption of the Constitution of 18 February 2006, the Congolese justice system was governed by the principle of unity of jurisdiction. In reality though, the country had courts of a judicial[7] nature: the

[7] The judiciary encompasses two orders: (1) judicial order (civil and military courts), topped by the Cour de Cassation, and (2) administrative order (administrative courts) topped by the Conseil d'Etat (Articles 149, 153 and 154 of the Constitution).

civil courts and military courts, capped at the top by the Supreme Court of Justice.[8] There was therefore no legal specialty, except in terms of military courts, insofar as the same judges were deemed to hear all cases, whether civil, commercial, labour, criminal, administrative or constitutional.

Finally, this judicial system that the Constitution of 18 February 2006 just changed, at least on paper, installed the principle of duality of jurisdictions. Thereby three objectives shall be attained: the pursuit of efficiency, specialization and the rapid processing of cases.[9] By this principle, the Constitution has thus given a positive response to the doctrinal proposals for the devolution of Congolese legal disputes.[10] The principle of duality of jurisdictions establishes the coexistence of two separate judicial systems: the administrative courts, headed by the State Council, and the order of the judicial courts, topped by the Court of Cassation. These are called ordinary courts, which are supplemented by five other categories of specialized courts:

(a) The Constitutional Court;
(b) The military courts and tribunals, as organized by the Act of 18 November 2002 bearing the Code of Military Justice which is the counterpart of the Military Penal Code enacted on the same date. These two laws constitute the reform of the Ordinance-Law of 25 September 1972 on the Code of Military Justice;
(c) The commercial courts, as created and organized by the Act of 3 July 2001;
(d) The labour courts, as created and organized by the Act of 16 October 2002;
(e) The juvenile courts, established by the Act of 10 January 2009.

The criminal courts in Congolese law can be grouped into two categories: first, those which only partly are criminal courts, namely the Constitutional Court, all courts from the judicial branch (the Supreme Court, courts of appeal, high courts and district courts) as well as commercial

[8] Under Article 83(3) of the Code of Military Justice, 'the remedy for violation of constitutional provisions by the Supreme Military Court is heard by the Supreme Court of Justice sitting as the Constitutional Court'.

[9] Explanatory Memorandum to the Constitution of 18 February 2006, para. 3.

[10] BB Mboyo Empenge Ea Longila, 'La mégarde des modèles de constitutions euro-occidentales et l'élaboration d'une constitution zaïroise de développement véritablement intériste' (1996) 25 *Annales de la Faculté de Droit* 172; K. Ntabala, 'Quelle constitution pour la Troisième République face aux réalités zaïroises?' (1996) 25 *Annales de la Faculté de Droit* 98.

courts[11] and on the other hand those which completely are criminal courts, namely the military courts. Moreover, for the prevention of violations of international humanitarian law, the former were, in principle, exclusively competent, before Article 91 of the Law n°13/011-B of 11 April 2013 granted ordinary courts of appeal with parallel competence over international crimes. However, jurisdiction is limited *ratione personae*, excluding those who are otherwise subject to the competence of military tribunals (e.g., all civilians accused of having committed international crimes, together with soldiers or military commanders). This limitation indeed empties the substance of the new law and renders the new competence of the courts of appeal inoperative or even useless in practice.

Moreover, according to its Article 156, the new law definitely abolishes the transitory regime of customary courts and seals the unification of the Congolese judicial system. Before, these customary courts as transitory tribunals could only function where magistrates' courts were not yet installed, and dealt with minor problems of civil law, family issues in particular. In criminal matters, these courts could only prosecute infringements whose punishment did not exceed three months of principal penal constraint. The judges who sat there were not professionals, contrary to the magistrates of career who followed regular legal studies. Consequently, contrary to the situation in Rwanda, where the system of *Gacaca* tribunals have been installed in order to face the situation of numerous presumed minor perpetrators of the 1994 genocide, the international crimes which fell under the competence of the International Criminal Court (ICC) could not be brought before Congolese transitory customary courts.

2.2. *The punishment for violations of international humanitarian law in Congolese law: the competence of military courts*

The main principle is set forth in Article 161 of the Military Penal Code which provides: 'In the case of indivisibility or connection between certain offences and crimes of genocide, war crimes or crimes against humanity, military courts have exclusive jurisdiction'. At first glance, one might think that except in the case of indivisibility or connection, military tribunals are not competent to deal with international crimes under Congolese law.

[11] See J. M. Tasoki Manzele and D. Luaba Nkuna, 'L'institution du Tribunal de commerce dans le système judiciaire congolais: nature juridique, organisation, compétence et procédure' (2007) 36 *Annales de la Faculté de Droit* 355.

Yet, it is certain that they remain competent, considering the absence of a statute conferring, *expressis verbis*, jurisdiction to the ordinary courts, except in the case of those accused who fall under the competence of the courts of appeal as stated above. Moreover, the practice shows that no other civil court has heard a case relating to international crimes.

Within the military courts, such jurisdiction is distributed under the cardinal principle of *privilège de juridiction* [the privilege of jurisdiction]. Under Congolese law, this is a rule by which an authority (civil or military) is granted by the Constitution or by law to be tried before a higher court than that which normally would have been competent under the rules on jurisdiction, because of the duties he is exercising or has been exercising.[12] In military law, this is justified by the fact that the hierarchical principle requires that a military authority can be tried only by magistrates with a rank equal to or above his own.[13]

In addition, according to case law,[14] the rule of the privilege of jurisdiction does not protect the authority but instead protects its functioning. In no way does it contradict the principle of irrelevance of official capacity, firmly established both in law and international criminal law in the DRC. Moreover, the Supreme Court of Justice in its Ruling of 23 December 1986 saw the role of special jurisdiction as an essential guarantee for the proper administration of justice.[15] Indeed, if that authority was judged by a lower court than that which the Constitution or the law attributes to him, it could be feared that, because of his duties or his rank, this would influence the judges, regardless of all of the basic guarantees of a fair and due trial.

The military police courts are not competent under Congolese law for serious international crimes, considering the rate of the sentences. In any case, the exercise of jurisdiction of military courts over crimes raises two major legal problems. The first is its unconstitutionality. Indeed, one of the perverse effects of the Military Penal Code and the Military Judicial

[12] K. Balingene, 'Le statut judiciaire des autorités chargées de la gestion des entités territoriales de la RDC' (3 March 2010) *La Constitution en Afrique*, www.la-constitution-en-afrique.org/.

[13] M. Wetsh'okonda Koso Senga, 'La République démocratique du Congo: La justice militaire et le respect des droits de l'homme: l'urgence du parachèvement de la réforme' (June 2009), at 5, www.afrimap.org/english/images/report/AfriMAP-RDC-JusticeMilitaire-FR.pdf.

[14] R. Lukoo Musubao, *La jurisprudence congolaise en droit pénal* (Kinshasa: Éditions On s'en sortira, 2006), vol. I, at 225; see also K. Kaba Kashala, *Code judiciaire zaïrois annoté* (Kinshasa: Éditions Asyst, 1995), at 39.

[15] Supreme Court of Justice, RPA 121, 23 December 1986, *Bulletin des arrêts de la Cour suprême de Justice*, 1985–1989 (Kinshasa: 2002), 238.

Table 10.1 *Military Courts in the Democratic Republic of the Congo*[a]

N°	Jurisdictions	Competence	Ordinary seats	Composition of seats
01	Military High Court	All national territory (Article 6(2) Code of Military Justice)		
	(a) Kinshasa, capital of the DRC (Article 6 Code of Military Justice)			
(b) In exceptional circumstances, anywhere in the territory declared by the president of the Republic (Article 7(1) Code of Military Justice)				
c) In wartime, the president of the Republic may decide to organize mobile courts in the operational areas (Article 7(2) Code of Military Justice)	a) Five members, including 2 judges of career (Article 10(2))			

(cont.)

Table 10.1 *(cont.)*

N°	Jurisdictions	Competence	Ordinary seats	Composition of seats
b) On appeal, 5 members, 3 professional judges (Article 10(5) Code of Military Justice)				
02	Military Courts	The province or the town of Kinshasa (Article 12(1) Code of Military Justice)	County towns of the province, where the headquarters of the military region is based or at another location determined by the president of the Republic (Article 12(2) Code of Military Justice)	
In exceptional circumstances, the Minister of Defence can change the seat of the operational courts (Article 13(2) Code of Military Justice)	Five members: 2 judges of career (Article 16(1) Code of Military Justice)			

03	Operational Military Courts	Operational areas determined by the president of the Republic (Article 18(2) Code of Military Justice)	They support the troops in the operational areas (Article 18(1) Code of Military Justice)	Five members, including at least 1 career military officer
04	Garrison Military Courts	District, city, garrison or military base (Article 21(1) Code of Military Justice)	Head of the district, the city where the staff of the garrison is located or another place fixed by the president of the Republic (Article 21(2) Code of Military Justice)	
	Five members, including at least 1 professional judge (Article 22(2) Code of Military Justice)			
05	Military Police Tribunal	The jurisdiction of garrison (Article 23 Code of Military Justice)		Three members, including at least 1 career magistrate (Article 24(1) Code of Military Justice)

[a] Source: Defense Institute of International Legal Studies, quoted by Mr. Wetsh'okonda Koso Senga, 'La République démocratique du Congo', above note [13], at 35.

Table 10.2 *Personal jurisdiction of Congolese courts under the principle of the privilege of jurisdiction*

N°	Courts	Personal jurisdiction	Legal basis
01	Military High Court	(a) General officers of the armed forces of the DRC and members of the National Police and National Service of the same rank	
(b) People accountable before the Supreme Court of Justice for acts that fall under the jurisdiction of military courts			
(c) Magistrates of the High Military Court, the General Prosecutor, military courts, military courts operational, military hearings about these proceedings			
(d) Members of these military courts, prosecuted for acts committed in the course of or in connection with the performance of their duties as judges	Article 120 Code of Military Justice		
02	Military courts	(a) Senior officers of the armed forces of the DRC and members of the National Police and National Service Range	
(b) People answerable to the Court of Appeal for acts that fall under the jurisdiction of military courts			

Table 10.2 *(cont.)*

N°	Courts	Personal jurisdiction	Legal basis
(c) Officials of the Defence Department, the National Police, National Service and their auxiliary services (d) Military magistrates of garrison military courts, military public prosecutor's department and prosecutors of these military tribunals (e) Members of the military courts prosecuted for acts committed in the course of or in connection with the performance of their judicial functions			
	Article 121 Code of Military Justice		
03	Garrison military courts	The Congolese armed forces in a rank lower than major and members of the National Police and National Service of equal rank	
	Article 122 Code of Military Justice		
04	Military police courts	The Congolese armed forces, or similar, one below the rank of major, who commit acts punishable by law to a term of imprisonment of up to 1 year	Ibid.

Code of 2002 is that they expand the jurisdiction of military courts to civilians, particularly with regard to serious international crimes, while Article 156(1) of the Constitution of 18 February 2006 clearly imposes a fundamental restriction in these words: 'The military jurisdictions are competent for crimes committed by members of the armed forces and the National Police'. Strangely enough, the question was never raised and brought before the Congolese Constitutional Court for settlement.

The second problem is its contradiction with international human rights law.[16] Indeed, military justice has a hybrid nature. It is addressed to both the judiciary and the military chain of command. It therefore lacks independence, due to the control and interference of military commanders as well as politicians during the judicial proceedings.[17] Therefore, giving his opinion on the issue of the military justice, Nyabirungu Mwene Songa, currently one of the most famous criminal lawyers, said:

> The Military Criminal Code being a specific legislation cannot be the basis of the most fundamental values of the domestic and international public order, when we know that this role pertains to the ordinary penal code, where these values must be expressed in the most general, the most solemn and the most stable way for all citizens and people of the Republic.[18]

He adds: 'as a special law, military criminal law must return to the military barracks to deal only with what concerns it . . . '[19] General Likulia Bolongo said:

> The foundation of military criminal law is the need to maintain, permanently and constantly, a particular discipline in the armed forces and the implementation of the means to ensure state security and unity of the nation. Military criminal law is thus presented as an extension of the disciplinary action and a necessary complement to criminal law. Indeed, military criminal law imposes by force and restores order in the army when

[16] See Office of the High Commissioner for Human Rights, 'Report of the Mapping the Most Serious Violations of Human Rights and International Humanitarian Law Committed within the Territory of the Democratic Republic of Congo between March 1993 and June 2003' (2010), at 437–40, www.ohchr.org/Documents/Countries/ZR/DRC_MAPPING_REPORT_FINAL_EN.pdf.

[17] Wetsh'okonda Koso Senga, 'La République démocratique du Congo', above note 13, at 3.

[18] N. Mwene Songa, 'La réforme du droit pénal général congolais suite à la ratification du Statut de Rome', communication during the training seminar for lawyers on assistance to victims and those accused of international crimes, Avoctas sans Frontières, Permanent Mission in DRC: October 2007, at 36, quoted in the Mapping Project Report, above note 17, at 437.

[19] Ibid.

the disciplinary and criminal sanctions under the law are unable to ensure that order.[20]

Thus, if we cannot restrict the Congolese military justice to members of the armed forces and the national police, we will have to, at most – to quote another of Nyabirungu Mwene Songa's opinions – 'delete it'.[21]

3. The difficult exercise of Congolese military courts' jurisdiction regarding most serious international crimes

The international reputation of the DRC with regard to massive violations of human rights and international humanitarian law is opposite to the response that its judicial system has reserved to their authors. The overwhelming majority of them remain unpunished. Only certain cases were judged by few military tribunals. The prosecution has not been widespread, and it would be interesting to examine a few major causes, before lastly analysing, how courts have struggled to proceed legally.

3.1. The insufficiency of tried cases due to operational difficulties of the Congolese military justice

The non-governmental organization (NGO) Avocats sans Frontières observed that only thirteen cases were tried in 2009. Since then, few other cases have been tried. Taken together, they have been tried by the garrison military tribunals of Bunia, Goma, Bukavu, Mbandaka and Kisangani, and military courts of Katanga and Mbandaka, often at the appeal level, as well as the Operational Military Court of the North-Kivu Province. It is therefore appropriate to give a general idea in the shape of an array presenting fifteen different cases.

One can certainly be delighted by these judgments and that the condemned people indeed serve their sentences in the various prisons of the DRC. However, the compensation for the victims remains problematic in all of the cases where the State was condemned to pay damages.

[20] L. Bolongo, *Droit pénal militaire zaïrois* (Paris: Librairie Générale de Droit et de Jurisprudence, 1977), vol. I, at 2–3.

[21] M. Songa, 'L'infraction, la responsabilité, la sanction et la réparation dans la réforme du droit pénal congolais', in P. Akele Adau (ed.), *Réforme du Code pénal congolais: A la recherche des options fondamentales du Code pénal congolais* (Kinshasa: Éditions Centre d'Études pour l'Action sociale, 2008), at 305.

Table 10.3 *Overview of some cases of international crimes tried by Congolese military courts*[a]

N°	Cases	Summary of facts	Jurisdiction
01	*Mivova* Case	Between 20 and 22 November 2012, after the capture of the town of Goma by the M23 rebellion, several soldiers of the 41st and 393rd battalions of the armed forces of the DRC committed against civilians numerous crimes, including killings, acts of looting of private properties and rapes against women, in their zone of retreat in Minova.	
However, many of the accused (particularly senior military officers) were declared innocent by the judgment RP n°003/2013 of 4 May 2014, and some others were recognized responsible notably for war crimes.	Operational Military Court (North Kivu Province)		
02	*Ankoro*		
Case	Between 10 and 22 November 2002, soldiers of the 95th brigade of the armed forces of the DRC launched an attack against the civilian population of Ankoro, killing over 60 people, firing and destroying over 4,000 homes and looting more than 170 houses and public buildings.	Military Court of Katanga	

03	*Biyoyo*	
Case	Jean-Pierre Biyoyo Karhanga is the initiator of the insurgent movement called SFP (Social Front for Progress), actor of destabilization of the province of South Kivu. The 5 soldiers arrested were suspected of desertion from the lines of the national army, organization of an insurrectionary movement, recruitment of members and combatants in Uvira in 2 foreign countries (Rwanda and Burundi), kidnapping, arbitrary detentions of minors (in collaboration with the civilian defendant), recruitment of child soldiers and enrolment in foreign combat troops (all defendants). All of these events occurred between June 2004 and July 2005.	1st degree: Garrison Military Court of Bukavu.
Appeal: Military Court of South Kivu		
04	*Blaise Bongi*	
Case	Bongi Massaba, captain and commander of a company within the 4th integrated brigade of the armed forces of the DRC, is accused of having looted the property of the civilian population (motorcycle, motor pump, 2 solar panels, a radio and two baffles) from Tshekele village in Ituri on 20 October 2005 during clashes between the armed forces of the DRC and the Front for Patriotic Resistance of Ituri militia. Five people, all students, had been requisitioned to carry the pillage and were executed in the village of Bussing.	1st degree: Military Court of Bunia
Appeal: Military Court of the Eastern Province		

(cont.)

Table 10.3 *(cont.)*

N°	Cases	Summary of facts	Jurisdiction
05	*Gideon Between*		
Case	Between October 2003 and 12 May 2006, the day of his surrender, Gideon controlled a part of Katanga. During these years, he commanded a large group of Mai-Mai (about 2,000 fighters), who were unwilling to integrate into the national army, that destroyed a large area around Mitwaba, his hometown. Investigations by NGOs accuse Gideon and his troops of murdering the wife of the Park Director Upemba, having recruited and used children in its fighting troops, using firearms, creating insurrection, looting, cannibalism, destruction and mass rape in all areas in which its troops had control.	1st degree: Garrison Military Court of Kipushi	
06	*Gety/Bavi*		
Case	In October 2006, a mass grave containing more than 30 bodies of men, women and children was discovered in the hills of Gety and Bavi (60 km from Bunia). The killing was attributed to members of the 1st Integrated Brigade of the armed forces of the DRC. Some victims were reportedly tortured and raped before being killed and others were buried alive. The acts allegedly took place between August and September 2006.	1st degree: Garrison Military Court of Bunia Appeal: Military Court of the Eastern Province	

07	*Kahwa* Case	Kahwa was accused of having created in 2002 the insurrection of the 'Party for Unity and Safeguarding Integrity of Congo', having unlawfully detained war weapons with which he committed war crimes and crimes against humanity, particularly during the attack against the village of Zumbe. He was arrested on 9 April 2005 by the Congolese authorities and the peace support operation MONUC.	1st degree: Military Court of Bunia
Appeal: Military Court of the Eastern Province. Judgment issued on 13 August 2014 condemning the accused to 9 years in prison for war crimes and crimes against humanity.			
08 Case	*Kalonga Katamasi* In 2004, the defendants (Mai-Mai militiamen) abducted 10 women from the village of Kimanga Maniema and sexually abused them in the forest. One victim was forced to remain for 3 months as mistress of the main accused.	Garrison Military Court in Kindu	

(*cont.*)

Table 10.3 *(cont.)*

N°	Cases	Summary of facts	Jurisdiction
09	*Kilwa* Case	18 October 2004, more than 100 people were killed in the mining town of Kilwa in a counter-offensive led by the armed forces of the DRC against the rebel group MRLK who had taken the village a few days before (poorly equipped and poorly organized according to MONUC). It appears that many of the victims were executed arbitrarily and that the village was looted during the attack as well as after the flight of many people. The mining company Anvil Mining allegedly provided logistical support to the armed forces of the DRC during the attack: vehicles were reportedly used to transport corpses and looted property. Earth-work engines of the society were also used to bury the bodies.	1st degree: Military Court of Katanga
Appeal: Supreme Military Court			

10	*Military Observers*	
Case	Two MONUC military observers (a Malawian and a Jordanian) were murdered in May 2003 in Mungwalu (Bunia). According to the investigation, this double murder was committed due to suspicion of members of the Front for National Integration (FNI) towards MONUC, suspected of being on the side of the Union of Congolese Patriots (UPC).	First degree: Garrison Military Court
Appeal: Military Court of the Eastern province		
11	*Mitwaba*	
Case	As part of counter-attacks between the armed forces of the DRC and Mai-Mai in March–April 2005, soldiers from the 63rd brigade of the armed forces of the DRC imprisoned and tortured 95 alleged Mai-Mai civilians. Seventeen of them did not survive.	Military Court of Katanga
12	*Mutineers of Bunia*	
Case	During the night of 11 January 2007, dozens of members of the 1st Integrated Brigade mutinied, took automatic weapons and rocket launchers. They demanded payment of their bonus promised by the government for 2006 and valued at $50. During the uprising, 7 women were raped, a police officer was seriously injured and several shops and houses of Bankoko Quarter were looted.	1st degree: Garrison Military Court of Ituri

(*cont.*)

Table 10.3 (cont.)

N°	Cases	Summary of facts	Jurisdiction
Appeal: Military Court of the Eastern Province			
13	*Mutineers of Mbandaka*		
Case	On 30 June 2005, the end of the transition, the order was given to all members of the Equateur province to remain in barracks. One of them, a sub-lieutenant belonging to the *Mouvement de Libération du Congo* (MLC) contingent, had refused to obey this order, came out overnight and was found dead early in the morning. His death served as a pretext for his friends (between 3,000 and 4,000 men) to mutiny and steal within the city between 3 and 5 July. They broke the weapon shop and spilled into the streets, looting everything in their path, killing 6 people, raping 46 others, torturing, etc. within a radius of about 10 km, before being restrained by local loyalists and reinforcements sent from Kinshasa.	1st degree: Military Tribunal of Garrison of Mbandaka	
Appeal: Military Court of Equateur			

14 Case	*Pygmies from Walikale* As of 16 March 2009, the 85th Infantry Brigade of the armed forces of the DRC, then based in Walikale was ordered by the operational command of North Kivu to move towards the locality Hombo. This movement began on 18 March 2009. Armed forces of the DRC soldiers under the leadership of their commander Kalambay arrived in the village of Kissa, inhabited by pygmies who managed to settle there, where they committed systematic rape, looting, upset of houses, extortion and other acts of torture upon the civilians.	Garrison Court of Goma	
15	*The Songo Mboyo* Case	On 21 December 2003, soldiers of the armed forces of the DRC 9th Battalion, based in the localities of Songo Mboyo, demanded their pay diverted by their superiors according to them. They rebelled by targeting the local civilian population. Two series of mass rapes were committed on this occasion, including women of some senior army officers.	1st degree: Military Tribunal Garrison of Mbandaka
Appeal: Military Court of Equateur			

[a] Source: Avocats sans frontières, 'Étude de jurisprudence: L'application du Statut de Rome de la Cour pénale internationale par les juridictions de la République démocratique du Congo', Report published in March 2009, at 143. However, the addition of the Cases *of Minova and of the Pygmies from Walikale* is mine.

It is also symptomatic that, of all cases surveyed, only four involved senior officers of the armed forces of the DRC. In other words, the reduced number of tried cases adds to the fact that these generally concerned non-commissioned officers of the armed forces, militiamen or some former leaders of armed groups: in short, small fish, while the real culprits are largely outside the military justice system. When one becomes selective, one lacks independence. In addition, most of these cases occurred during itinerant hearings in which military courts were required to travel frequently over 200 km from their seats. Had it not been supported by donor funds, including the European Union and MONUC (renamed MONUSCO in July 2010), or pressure from the international community and Congolese civil society,[22] we must admit that these lawsuits would not have happened.

Indeed, the Congolese justice system is, in terms of budget and finance, suffocated by politics. First, the Superior Magistracy Council never received the authentic application of the Constitution by the government which provides that the judiciary has its own budget whose expenditures are approved by the First President of the Cour de Cassation. Furthermore, funds allocated never reach 1 percent of other budgets approved by parliament. For example, in 2007, its share stood at 0.87 percent of the general budget,[23] compared to only 0.5 percent of the budget for the fiscal year 2014,[24] which is obviously a rather remarkable setback. Thus, the operational resources are sorely lacking, and therefore the few inventoried cases seem to match the opportunistic approach of the military justice, apart from the lack of any coherent criminal prosecution policy.[25] Thus, a non-independent and financially suffocated justice is the obvious evil which prevents the greatest perpetrators of serious violations of international humanitarian law to be held accountable for their actions in the DRC.

[22] G. Kapiamba, 'Le rôle des organisations non-gouvernementales dans la lutte contre l'impunité', in Konrad Adenauer Foundation, *La justice nationale et internationale dans la lutte contre l'impunité en République démocratique du Congo* (Kinshasa: Konrad Adenauer Foundation, 2007), 101–04, at 103–04; L. Ngondji Ongombe, 'Les rôles des organisations non gouvernementales dans la lutte contre l'impunité' in Konrad Adenauer Foundation, *La justice nationale et internationale*, this note, 51–55, at 54.

[23] Law No. 07/002 of 07 July 2007 bearing the state budget for fiscal year 2007, document, vol. II, Ministry of Budget, Kinshasa, July 2007.

[24] Law No. 14/002 of 31 January 2014 concerning the state budget for fiscal year 2014, *Official Journal*, special volume, 55th Year, 3 February 2014.

[25] M. Wetsh'okonda Koso Senga, 'La République démocratique du Congo', above note 13, at 5.

3.2. *The legal matters settled by Congolese military courts*

Since January 2006, some Congolese military courts, facing litigation of international crimes, agreed to implement the provisions of the Rome Statute of the ICC in place of the National Military Criminal Code.[26] The Garrison Military Court of Mbandaka was the first jurisdiction to embark on that path in an interlocutory decision (*Mutineers of Mbandaka*).[27] This pioneer reasoning was confirmed at the first degree[28] and on appeal.[29] The direct applicability of the Statute was again ruled on by the same court in April 2006 (*Songo Mboyo*)[30] and confirmed on appeal by the Military Court of Equateur.[31] At the same time, the Garrison Military Court Ituri followed the same reasoning in the cases *Bongi*,[32] *Kahwa*[33] and *Bavi*[34] and saw its approach confirmed at the appeal level by the Military Court of the Eastern Province in the cases *Bavi*[35] and *Kahwa*.[36] The argument that establishes the direct application of the Rome Statute of the ICC instead of Congolese law varies somewhat from one judgment to another. The review of decisions reveals various reasons underlining the superiority of the Rome Statute over Congolese law. While some decisions have not analysed the matter of hierarchy of norms, such as in the *Kilwa* Case,[37] most of them have explicitly based their decision on the Constitution of 18 February 2006. In Article 153(4) it provides: 'The civil and military courts apply the ratified international treaties, laws and regulatory acts

[26] This part is largely inspired by Avocats sans frontières, 'Étude de jurisprudence', above note 23, at 21–23.

[27] The Garrison Military Tribunal of Mbandaka, *Mutineers of Mbandaka Case*, Interlocutory Order, 12 January 2006, PR 086/05.

[28] The Garrison Military Tribunal of Mbandaka, *Mutineers of Mbandaka Case*, 20 June 2006, PR 086/05 – RP 101/06.

[29] Military Court of Equateur Province, *Mutineers of Mandaka Case*, 15 June 2007, RPA 615/2006.

[30] The Garrison Military Tribunal of Mbandaka, *Songo Mboyo Case*, 12 April 2006, PR 084/05.

[31] Military Court of Equateur Province, *Songo Mboyo Case*, 7 June 2006, RPA 014/06.

[32] The Garrison Military Tribunal of Ituri, *Bongi* Case, 24 March 2006, RP 018/06.

[33] The Garrison Military Tribunal of Ituri, *Kahwa* Case, 2 August 2006, RP 039/06.

[34] The Garrison Military Tribunal of Ituri, *Bavi* Case, 19 February 2007, PR 101/06.

[35] Military Court of the Eastern Province, *Bavi* Case, 28 July 2007, PR 003/07 101/06-RPA. The ruling does not state reasons for the direct application of the Rome Statute of the ICC but relies on Article 8 of the Rome Statute on war crimes as the basis for its decision.

[36] Military Court of the Eastern Province, *Kahwa* Case, 28 July 2007, PR 039/06 023/07-RPA.

[37] Military Court of Katanga, *Kilwa* Case, 28 June 2007, RP 010/2006, at 30. The Military Court has merely referred to the Rome Statute without citing constitutional provisions or principles which justify its application.

so long as they are in conformity with the laws as well as customary law, unless the latter is contrary to public order or morality'. Furthermore, Article 215 gives priority to international treaties duly concluded and published vis-à-vis national laws: 'Lawfully concluded treaties and international agreements have, upon publication, an authority superior to that of the laws, upon the condition for each treaty or agreement to be implemented by the other party'. In the *Military Observers* Case, the Garrison Military Court Ituri concluded that 'Congolese positive law introduced in its arsenal the provisions of the Statute of the International Criminal Court, which from now on become a legal instrument constituting an integral part of Congolese penal law'.[38] The Garrison Military Court Mbandaka meanwhile referred to the Transitional Constitution of 4 April 2003 in the *Mutineers of Mbandaka*[39] Case.

Furthermore, some courts have held that it is the shortcoming of the Congolese legislation that justifies the application of the provisions of the Rome Statute of the ICC. Regarding incriminations, there are important differences between the Statute and Congolese military penal law regarding the definition of war crimes and crimes against humanity. Section 166 of the Congolese Military Criminal Code includes in the definition of crimes against humanity a great number of offences that constitute war crimes under the Rome Statute.[40] In the *Mutineers of Mbandaka* Case, the tribunal noted that the Military Criminal Code 'is confusing crimes against humanity with war crimes which is, moreover, clearly defined by the Rome Statute of the International Criminal Court'.[41] In its interlocutory decision in the Case *Songo Mboyo*,[42] the same court again found differences between the definition of crimes against humanity listed in the Statute and the Military Penal Code.[43] The definition of war crimes, as laid down by Article 173 of the Military Criminal Code, is so far removed from the one in the ICC Statute that it is unrelated to the one used in international humanitarian law. Both the Military Courts of Garrison of

[38] The Garrison Military Tribunal of Ituri, *Military Observers* Case, 19 February 2007, RP 103/2006, at 11.

[39] The Garrison Military Tribunal of Mbandaka, *Mutineers of Mbandaka*, above note 30, at 16.

[40] Article 166 of Law No. 024/2002 of 18 November 2002 on the Military Penal Code.

[41] The Garrison Military Tribunal of Mbandaka, *Mutineers of Mbandaka*, above note 30, at 16.

[42] The Garrison Military Tribunal of Mbandaka, *Songo Mboyo*, above note 32, at 12.

[43] Article 173 of the Military Penal Code: 'For war crime is defined as any violation of the laws of the Republic committed during the war and which are not justified by the laws and customs of war.'

Mbandaka[44] and Ituri noted the existence of this conflict of norms. In the *Bavi* Case, military judges in Ituri leant on the 2006 Constitution and previous decisions of military courts to set aside national penal provisions and to implement 'the essential provisions of the Rome Statute on crimes against humanity and war crimes'.[45] In addition, the Military Criminal Code omits certain acts penalized as crimes against humanity in the Statute, such as forced disappearances, or constituting war crimes, such as recruitment of child soldiers and wilful killing.

Concerning penalties, important problems of the hierarchy of norms also arise. The Military Penal Code provides no penalty for war crimes. To overcome this omission, pragmatic judges have chosen to implement the Rome Statute. Thus, in the *Bongi* Case,[46] the Military Court of Garrison in Ituri, concerned with acts constituting war crimes and noting the 'glaring gap' of the Military Penal Code, held that 'the Congolese legislature did not at all have the intention of letting this heinous crime go unpunished especially as it recognized the gravity of this crime by ratifying the ICC Statute'.[47] It therefore concluded that the lack of punishment was 'clearly a drafting error'[48] and that it was necessary to 'fill the gaps in domestic legislation by referring to the ICC Statute'.[49] Concerned about respect for the principle of legality,[50] which prohibits imposing a sentence that was not prescribed by law at the moment of the perpetration of the crime, the court held that 'the ratification [of the ICC Statute] by the DRC is part of the legislative arsenal due to legal monism paired with the principle of primacy of international law',[51] and therefore it was legitimate to directly apply not only the tangible elements of war crimes but also the sentences under the Rome Statute.[52] The Garrison Military Court Ituri assumed that the legislature did not intend to remove a fair sentence for war criminals

[44] The Garrison Military Tribunal of Mbandaka, *Mutineers of Mbandaka*, above note 29, at 6; The Garrison Military Tribunal of Mbandaka, *Mutineers of Mbandaka*, above note 30, at 16.

[45] The Garrison Military Tribunal of Ituri, *Bavi*, above note 36, at 36–37.

[46] The Garrison Military Tribunal of Ituri, *Bongi*, above note 34, at 10–11.

[47] Ibid. [48] Ibid. [49] Ibid.

[50] The fact that no level of punishment or technical penalty by reference exists for war crimes transforms the Congolese judge into a legislator and creates a distortion in the application of the principle *nulla poena sine lege*. This is a principle of international customary law recognized by the Constitution and national laws (notably Article 2 of the Military Penal Code). See on this L. Mutata Luaba, *Droit pénal militaire congolais. Des peines et des incriminations de la compétence des juridictions militaires en RDC* (Kinshasa: Publishing Service Documentation and Studies of the Ministry of Justice and Keeper of the Seals, 2005), at 572.

[51] The Garrison Military Tribunal of Ituri, *Bongi*, above note 34, at 11. [52] Ibid.

and that it was appropriate to apply the provisions of the Rome Statute in order to meet the objectives of the treaty ratification by the DRC.

Finally, the Military Penal Code provides that the death penalty may be pronounced under certain circumstances to punish crimes against humanity,[53] while the maximum penalty under the Rome Statute is life imprisonment. Some courts have therefore relied on this fact to avoid penalties under Congolese law. They invoked the general principle of the implementation of the least penalty in case of a conflict of laws in order to eliminate this provision of the Congolese Military Code. Yet, obviously, Article 77 of the Rome Statute does not prohibit States parties from applying the death penalty for crimes if this penalty is provided for in their national legislation. Furthermore, such a judicial reasoning is not legally convincing, because the principle of the least penalty only applies when a court has at its disposal several criminal rules equivalent in form. However, this is not the case in the DRC since the Rome Statute prevails over national laws according to Article 215 of the Constitution.

Thus, in the *Mutineers of Mbandaka* Case, the judges noted that 'the Rome Statute, less severe for the defendants, seems best suited by providing the protective mechanisms of victims' rights . . . In addition, in the presence of two conflicting laws, the most favourable to the accused will be applied'.[54] The same reasoning was the basis for the decision of this tribunal in *Songo Mboyo*.[55] In both judgments, the military court also based its decision on taking greater account of victims' rights under the ICC Statute. The Military Court of the Eastern Province, in the *Bongi* Case, considers that 'the provisions of the Rome Statute are, indeed, more humanizing, less severe in punishment, considering that the death penalty is ignored contrary to the Military Criminal Code . . . that it is for these reasons that the Military Court . . . decided to implement the Rome Statute'.[56]

In short, in all cases where the Congolese courts could impose the death penalty under the Military Penal Code, they have substituted this penalty for life imprisonment. It is regrettable that this step towards abolishing

[53] Article 167(2) of the Congolese Military Criminal Code.

[54] The Garrison Military Tribunal of Mbandaka, *Mutineers of Mbandaka*, above note 29, at 6.

[55] The Garrison Military Tribunal of Mbandaka, *Songo Mboyo*, above note 32, and Interlocutory Order, 20 January 2006, at 12. This reasoning was upheld on appeal 7 June 2006 by the Military Court of Equateur Province *Songo Mboyo*, above note 33, at 25.

[56] Military Court of the Eastern Province, *Bongi* Case, 4 November 2006, RPA 030/06, at 15–16.

the death penalty has not been endorsed by the Congolese parliament. During the regular session in September 2010, the National Assembly just declared the Bill abolishing the death penalty initiated by the member André Mbata, inadmissible. This raises the question whether this vote will have a negative influence on Congolese courts as they are led not to replace the death penalty with life imprisonment.

4. The search for an alternative to Congolese military justice for the punishment of serious international crimes: from the ICC to the creation of specialized chambers

This research is based on two objections, which already have been analysed, formulated against the Congolese military justice: its inability to try those most responsible for crimes committed in the DRC and its contradiction with the Constitution of 18 February 2006 and the norms of international humanitarian law. Formerly, it was believed that the International Criminal Court would serve as a sufficient judicial alternative, but in vain. Indeed, since the DRC referred the situation in eastern DRC to the ICC under Article 14 of the Rome Statute, only three Congolese subjects have been judged: Thomas Lubanga, Germain Katanga and Mathieu Ngudjolo Chui.[57] In all cases, the judicial machinery of the ICC is very cumbersome. For example, it took more than five years of litigation to finally find Thomas Lubanga guilty of having committed the war crimes of enlisting and conscripting children under the age of 15 years and using them to participate actively in hostilities. Worse, Bosco Ntaganda remained at large, and the government of the DRC was reluctant to submit him to the ICC until he surrendered himself in the aftermath of the outbreak of the M23 rebellion in 2013. Moreover, a problem persists: the principle of non-retroactivity of the ICC's jurisdiction means it cannot take into account crimes committed in the DRC before 1 July 2002.

In addition, the Congolese have a negative perception of the existence and working methods of the ICC. They have the impression that this Court is politicized and was created only to judge Africans. Its mechanisms are known and understood very little. Thus, in 2008, a population-based survey on attitudes about peace, justice and social reconstruction was carried out in eastern DRC which underlined: 'Among the means to achieve justice, the eastern Congolese population endorses the national court system

[57] See *Prosecutor v. Lubanga Dylo* (Arrest Warrant) ICC-01/04–01/06 (10 February 2006); *Prosecutor v. Bosco* (Arrest Warrant) ICC-01/04–02/06 (22 August 2006); *Prosecutor v. Katanga and Ngudjolo* (Arrest Warrant) ICC-01/04–01/07 (2 July 2007).

(51%), followed by the International Criminal Court (ICC) (26%), military courts (15%), and traditional/customary justice mechanisms (15%). Furthermore, there is strong desire for the international community to assist national prosecutions (82%)'.[58] Moreover, it is stated: 'Among the various trial options to hold war criminals accountable, there is a clear preference for national trials (45%), followed by internationalized trials in the DRC (40%). There is little support for no trials (8%) and international trials abroad (7%). In other words, 85 percent prefer that trials be held in the DRC, whether national or internationalized trials'.[59]

Therefore, in order to fight against impunity, the Congolese government, by force of circumstances, engaged itself in the process of creating specialized chambers within the appeal courts after the idea of setting up an ad hoc international criminal tribunal for the DRC received no positive response from the international community, since it is too expensive. In this regard, the government elaborated an important document in 2010 entitled 'Draft Law on Specialized Chambers for the Repression of Serious Violations of International Humanitarian Law: Organization, Functioning, Applicable Law, Jurisdiction and Procedure'.

The truth is that the draft law underscores that for economic reasons,[60] appellate courts have been grouped into four pools, each with a specialized chamber of first degree and three pools each with a specialized chamber of appeal. Indeed, a specialized chamber of first degree for the crime of genocide, war crimes and crimes against humanity will be created within the Courts of Appeal of Kinshasa/Matete, Lubumbashi, Bukavu and Kisangani. The jurisdiction of the special chamber of the first degree comprises the following:

(a) Court of Appeal of Kinshasa/Matete, including Kinshasa, the provinces of Bandundu, Bas-Congo and Equateur;
(b) Court of Appeal of Lubumbashi, including the provinces of Katanga, Kasai Occidental and Kasai Oriental;
(c) Court of Appeal of Bukavu comprising the provinces of South Kivu, North Kivu and Maniema;
(d) Court of Appeal of Kisangani, including the Eastern Province and the Province of Equateur.

[58] P. Vinck et al., 'Living with Fear', above note 5, 2. [59] Ibid.

[60] See Section B of the Explanatory Memorandum to the Draft Law on Specialized Chambers for the Repression of Serious Violations of International Humanitarian Law: Organization, Functioning, Applicable Law, Jurisdiction and Procedure.

Similarly, a specialized chamber of appeal for the crime of genocide, war crimes and crimes against humanity would have been created within the Courts of Appeal of Kinshasa/Gombe, Goma and Katanga. The jurisdiction of the specialized chamber of appeal is as follows:

(a) Court of Appeal of Kinshasa/Gombe: includes Kinshasa, the provinces of Bandundu, Bas-Congo and Equateur;
(b) Court of Appeal of Goma comprising the provinces of North Kivu, South Kivu, Maniema and Eastern Province;
(c) Court of Appeal of Kananga: includes the provinces of Kasai Occidental, Kasai Oriental and Katanga.

In any event, the creation of these specialized chambers requires three important points. First, it is in conformity with Article 149(6) of the Constitution of 18 February 2006 which provides that '[t]he law may establish special courts'. However, since many people responsible for crimes committed in the DRC are soldiers or members of the National Police, a crippling unconstitutionality therefore appears insofar as the same Constitution submits them to the criminal jurisdiction of military courts.[61] Therefore, from a legal perspective, the adoption of this special legislation requires a constitutional amendment.

Then one wonders why the title of the Draft Law appears to limit the jurisdiction of the specialized chambers to violations of international humanitarian law, even though certain international crimes, including genocide and crimes against humanity, may be committed in peacetime during which international humanitarian law is simply inapplicable.

Finally, as described and presented in 2010, these specialized chambers did not seem to be circumstantially conceived. They had the vocation to remain permanently in the Congolese judicial system and therefore would have been equipped with universal jurisdiction.[62]

5. Conclusion

While the victims are waiting for justice, the executive and legislative authorities do not hasten to find a solution to the structural and systemic

[61] Thus, since only military courts are competent to try offences committed by military personnel, a constitutional amendment is needed in order to allow these specialized non-military courts to try them.

[62] Articles 29–37 of the Draft Law on Specialized Chambers for the Repression of Serious Violations of International Humanitarian Law: Organization, Functioning, Applicable Law, Jurisdiction and Procedure.

weaknesses of the Congolese judicial power. The project of creation of the specialized chambers was finally commuted by the government in a bill of law establishing a mixed specialized court of human rights. The Senate rejected this bill in an extraordinary session on 22 August 2011, especially because it jeopardizes the sovereignty of the DRC insofar as the composition of the court to be created would include foreign personnel. Instead of setting up a new institution, it put forward the reinforcement of the current Congolese judicial apparatus to effectively fight against impunity. The result is a national cacophony and the recognition in 2013 of a still inoperative competence over international crimes for ordinary courts of appeal parallel to that of military tribunals. Then, in 2014, the government returned to the project of creating specialized criminal chambers, but the bill was again rejected by parliament. Such a political and legislative cacophony suffices to prove the unwillingness, doubled by the incapacity, of the country's political establishment to sue and judge all the suspects of international crimes committed in the DRC. Nevertheless, it is not too late to call both the government and the parliament to a sense of responsibility. The bill of Law organizing the Congolese specialized chambers should be reintroduced and adopted in parliament, despite not being a perfect solution. The law would reinforce the Congolese judicial system and has the advantage of addressing the emergency issue of justice for the victims.

11

Comment – the Congolese legal system and the fight against impunity for the most serious international crimes

BALINGENE KAHOMBO

Dans le contexte congolais, les magistrats ne peuvent pas être efficaces s'ils ne s'occupent que de vols d'œufs, de médisances, de voies de fait, etc., alors que les crimes de masse demeurent impunis et d'une impunité couronnée.

[In the Congolese context, magistrates cannot be effective as long as they are focused on egg thieves, slander, assault and battery, etc., while crimes in large numbers remain unpunished and of a dignified impunity.][1]

1. Introduction

The Democratic Republic of the Congo (DRC) has suffered an abundance of successive wars which have brought countless harmful consequences. Concerning the war that started on 2 August 1998, non-governmental organizations' reports,[2] echoed by a huge number of scholars,[3] describe it as the most substantive humanitarian disaster since the Second World War. In July 1999, even the Secretary-General of the United Nations declared:

> The United Nations is aware of harrowing accounts of famine and epidemics. Food security and economic conditions, in particular in urban centres, continue to deteriorate at an alarming rate. The conflict has

[1] M. S. Nyabirungu, 'Démocratisation et justice pénale internationale en Afrique', address presented during the scientific days of the faculty of law of the University of Kinshasa, on 25 and 26 May 2011, dedicated to the Africa Day on 25 May, with the topic: 'L'Union africaine et les défis de la démocratisation en Afrique: le paradoxe de l'inflation normative et de l'impuissance de l'action'.

[2] For example, Human Rights Watch, 'Ituri: "Covered in Blood". Ethnically Targeted Violence in Northeastern DR Congo', July 2003; Human Rights Watch, 'War Crimes in Kisangani: The Response of Rwandan-backed Rebels to the May 2002 Mutiny', August 2002.

[3] C. Hemedi Bayolo (ed.), *L'Eglise profanée: chronique des violations des droits du clergé pendant la guerre d'agression 1998–2000* (Kinshasa: Concordia, 2002).

> been characterized by appalling, widespread and systematic human rights violations, including mass killings, ethnic cleansing, rape and the destruction of property. The war's effects have spread beyond the subregion to afflict the continent of Africa as a whole.[4]

Globally, faced with the perpetration of those worst crimes of international law, the reaction of the Congolese legal system was disappointing. The numerous appeals of the United Nations Security Council concerning the DRC's obligation to stop impunity, 'by bringing to justice without delay perpetrators of grave violations of human rights and of international humanitarian law, with special attention to those responsible for . . . grave violations against women',[5] namely at the level of command, have been, at this point, in vain.

The term Congolese legal system encompasses Congolese positive law as well as the judicial institutions that are empowered, by administrating justice, to assure its application. It concerns namely courts and tribunals and the offices of public prosecutors adjoined to them. Those elements compose an entirety, organized and interacting and are influenced by internal and external factors.[6] The internal environment is composed of the internal dynamic of functioning competent judicial institutions. The external environment on the other hand is made up of all the components *alien* to the judicial aspect that can either negatively or positively produce influences upon rendering justice, starting precisely by politics.

Therefore, two pivotal questions arise. In fact, how can we explain this disappointing performance of the Congolese legal system? Is this due to the archaism of Congolese positive law or the inability of courts and tribunals and of public prosecutor's offices to render justice efficiently for all and then meet the unavoidable requirements of the fight against impunity?

This analysis is based upon the paradigm of the distinction, inside a legal system, between law – as a group of positive legal rules – and justice. In fact, the positive law includes a fundamentally peaceful, even pacifist, dimension whose purpose is the maintenance of public order and the protection of human rights. In contrast, justice has a conflicting nature, because it aims to establish the responsibilities, to deem who is wrong and who is right. From a political angle, the stakes are not the same. That

[4] 'Report of the Secretary-General on the United Nations Preliminary Deployment in the Democratic Republic of the Congo' (15 July 1999), UN Doc. S/1999/790, para. 13.

[5] UNSC Resolution 1794 (21 December 2007), para. 15.

[6] P. Braillard, *Théorie des systèmes et relations internationales* (Brussels: Bruylant, 1977), at 53.

is why it is normally easier to pass legal texts than to render justice by applying this law so laid.

This political and judicial dichotomy can help to understand the DRC's situation. In fact, the need for justice has led politicians to carry out important reforms within Congolese positive law, even though these reforms have not been achieved, yet (Section 2). Nonetheless, regardless of the existence of a political project to fight against impunity (Section 3), this legal regime has remained widely unapplied. The reasons are numerous. Therefore, we are faced with law without real justice (Section 4) concerning the international crimes committed, including serious violations of international humanitarian law.

2. The uncompleted reforms of the Congolese legal framework applicable to the most terrible international crimes: innovations and flaws to handle

One can trace back the origin of these reforms to 2002. Two special laws were passed: the law of 12 November 2002 laying down the Military Judicial Code (CJM), which is the counterpart of Law n° 024/2002, of the same date, bearing the Military Criminal Code. These two laws reform the Ordinance-Law of 25 September 1972 laying down the Military Justice Code. Following the adoption of a new Constitution through a referendum from 18 to 19 September 2005, enacted on 18 February 2006, three further new significant laws were put into force.

On 20 July 2006, the legislator passed two laws which introduced a specific legal regime applicable to sexual abuses. The first is Law n° 06/018 modifying and completing the decree of 30 January 1940 laying down the penal code. The second is Law n° 06/019 amending and completing the decree of 6 August 1959 laying down the penal procedure code. Both these laws aim mainly at the reinforcement of the repression of sexual abuses in compliance with Article 15 of the new Constitution. The third is Law n° 09/001 of 10 January 2009 laying down the special protection of the child. It enforces Article 41 of the Constitution.

This legal framework is the substratum of Congolese law regarding the most serious international crimes. Those laws have been passed for harmonizing the Congolese legislation with international obligations. Thus, in the preamble[7] of Law n° 06/018 of 20 July 2006, the lawmaker underscores as follows:

[7] Para. 4.

> Since now, Congolese penal law did not contain all the incriminations that international law has considered as infractions, as a protective barrier since 1946 against those who, powerful or powerless, infringe international law, namely humanitarian law, hence denying the civil population the quality and the values of humanity.

The legislator adds that this law 'amends and completes the Congolese penal Code through the incorporation of rules of international humanitarian law regarding infractions of sexual abuses'[8] and takes into consideration the protection of the most vulnerable people, especially women and children.

The innovations of this legal framework are on substantive and procedural law. Concerning the substance, the Military Criminal Code has a Title V called 'Crimes of genocide, crimes against humanity and crimes of war'.[9] Its Article 169(1)(7) incriminates, as does the Constitution,[10] any act of sexual abuse as a crime against humanity, as stipulated in Article 7(1)(g) of the Statute of the International Criminal Court (ICC). In fact, the offences of sexual abuse include a general concept which criminalizes numerous sorts of acts: rape, sexual slavery, forced prostitution, forced pregnancy, forced sterilization and all other forms of sexual abuse of a comparable gravity, for example, sexual mutilations and indecent assault.[11]

The Military Criminal Code does not contain, however, a definition of acts of sexual abuse. It is Law n° 06/018 of 20 July 2006 and the law laying down the protection of children where these acts are defined. The definition of rape that these laws have provided for is almost identical to the one stated in the text concerning the components of crimes regarding the substantial competence of the ICC.[12] But, the question is why the Congolese legislative body tries to restrict, tirelessly, the reach of sexual abuses to crimes against humanity, although the ICC Statute also incriminates them as war crimes and even though the International Criminal Tribunal for Rwanda (ICTR) held that sexual abuses 'constitute genocide in the same way as any other act as long as they were committed with the

[8] Para. 5.

[9] In Congolese law, the analysis of the crimes is provided by L. Mutala Luaba, *Traité de crimes internationaux* (Kinshasa: Editions Universitaires Africaines, 2008), at 433.

[10] Article 15.

[11] See also L. Banza Mbombo and C. Hemedi Bayolo, *Conflits armés en R.D. Congo: violences sexuelles contre les femmes, crimes sans châtiment, 2001–2004* (Kinshasa: Concordia, 2004), at 69.

[12] Article 7(1)(g)(1).

specific intent to destroy, in whole or in part, a particular group, targeted as such'.[13]

This limitation of Congolese positive law does not seem to be a deliberate one. The Military Criminal Code of 2002 has in general been badly drafted. The Code was adopted in a hurry by a non-elected legislative body[14] and under special circumstances of war dating back to 1998. It contains a lot of deficiencies: the confusion between war crimes and crimes against humanity, a lack of penalties for war crimes, the omission of certain acts that constitute crimes against humanity[15] and war crimes[16] under the ICC Statute. The Constitution of 2006 similarly lacks quality.[17] Its Article 15 is in essence merely the reiteration of Article 169(1)(7) of the Military Criminal Code. This limitation has been surpassed by the direct application of the ICC Statute by Congolese military courts in compliance with Article 215 of the Constitution, which gives priority to international treaties duly concluded and published through national legislation. In an alternative solution, scholars consider that sexual abuses may constitute war crimes or genocide under the Congolese Military Criminal Code if they are indirectly treated as attacks against the physical or mental integrity of individuals or a group.[18]

Concerning the requirements of prosecution, the Military Criminal Code stipulates, in Article 161, 'the competence of military jurisdictions to prosecute genocide, crimes against humanity and war crimes'. This Article stands in connection with the newly promulgated Law n°13/011-B of 11 April 2013 on the organization of civil judicial tribunals, which grants – by virtue of its Article 91(1) – the courts of appeal a parallel competence to try the same crimes.[19] Meanwhile, Article 163 of the Military Criminal

[13] *Prosecutor v. Akayesu* (Judgment) ICTR-96–4-T, T Ch I (2 September 1998), para. 731; see also *Prosecutor v. Kayishema and Ruzindana* (Judgment) ICTR-95–1-T (21 May 1999), para. 95.

[14] This body was called 'Assemblée constituante et legislative-Parlement de transition' and was created by President Laurent Désiré Kabila in 1999.

[15] For example, apartheid and forced disappearances.

[16] Such as the recruitment of children within the armed forces.

[17] See B. Mukadi, *Projet de Constitution de la République démocratique du Congo. Plaider pour une relecture* (Kinshasa: CRDS, 2005), at 83–85; A. Mampuya Kanunk'a Tshiabo, *Espoir et déception de la quête constitutionnelle congolaise: Clés pour comprendre le processus constitutionnel du Congo Kinshasa* (Nancy-Kinshasa: éditions Ama, 2005), at 99–120.

[18] Mutala Luaba, *Traité de crimes internationaux*, above note 9, at 211–13, 305–09; P. Akele Adau and A. Sita Muila Akele, *Les crimes contre l'humanité en droit congolais* (Kinshasa: éditions Centre Etude Pour L'Action Sociale, 1999), at 13.

[19] For details, see J.-M. Kumbu, 'National Courts: The Situation in the Democratic Republic of Congo', Chapter 10 in this volume, at 217.

Code prescribes 'the principle of the irrelevance of immunities or special procedural rules for official acts in case of prosecution for war crimes or crimes against humanity'. Once again, why has the lawmaker restricted the scope of this principle by excluding its application to the crime of genocide? This restriction does not have any particular explanation apart from the deficiency of the military criminal code related to its poor elaboration as stated above. It is rather more like an omission than a real restriction from the lawmaker and is circumvented by the direct application of the ICC Statute. In any case, Article 163 is an important mitigation to the regime of privileges and immunities in Congolese law.[20]

Concerning the acts of sexual abuses, Law n° 06/019 of 20 July namely adds the following innovations:

- During any step of the procedure, the victim is assisted by an attorney (see Article 1 of the amending law);
- The public prosecutor or the judge appoints a physician and a psychologist to deem the state of the victim of sexual abuses and to establish the appropriate cares and to estimate the depth of the undergone harms and its later deterioration;
- For purposes of discretion, the hearing of the case *in camera* should be declared by the judge whenever the public prosecutor or the victim demand so;
- The preliminary inquiry of a sexual abuse case is carried out within a month from the referral to the judicial authority, while the judgment must be delivered within three months after referral to the competent tribunal. But, at this point, the remaining concern lies on the accordance, in practice, of expeditious justice and complexity of inquiring in the matter of most serious international crimes.

Moreover, the Congolese law does not expressly grant the national jurisdictions universal competence in cases of the most serious international crimes. The rights of the defence are partially violated because solely a Congolese attorney is admitted to assist the defendant.[21] The lawmaker did not provide any reason why foreign advocates are excluded from military courts. But historically, this limitation comes from the regime of the former Code of Military Justice, enacted on 25 September 1972.[22] It seems

[20] G. Kilala Pene-Amuna, *Immunités et privilèges en droit positif congolais* (Kinshasa: Amuna, 2010); B. Kahombo, 'Le statut judiciaire des autorités chargées de la gestion des entités territoriales de la RDC' (3 March 2010), *La Constitution en Afrique*, www.la-constitution-en-afrique.org/.

[21] Article 61(2) of the Military Judicial Code.

[22] B. Likulia, *Droit pénal militaire zaïrois* (Paris: LGDJ, 1977), at 95–97.

to have been introduced for the protection of national security, insofar as cases related to military jurisdictions may convey State secrets. Likewise, except in cases of sexual abuse, Congolese law does not offer appropriate protection to victims and witnesses. For example, there is no compensation fund to relieve the victims. In almost all the cases judged by military tribunals, the Congolese State has been held liable for damages. However, it is not sure that all of the victims will receive their compensation. Not only does the government seem unwilling to apply relevant judicial decisions, but also the huge number of victims and the great amount of money to be released for compensation would challenge the financial capability of the State to honour its obligations. Besides, anonymity is not admitted during a Congolese judicial procedure. The right to deny the hearing of a witness is even guaranteed whenever the witness is not clearly identified.[23] This rule threatens the security of witnesses, a protection gap which the legislator needs to close. Yet, in order to partially fill this gap, the military tribunals have already decided to apply the ICC Statute, because among other reasons, it seems the most suitable because it has mechanisms for the protection of victims' rights.[24]

3. The political project to fight impunity: from simple goodwill to law without justice

The reform of the Congolese law is accompanied by two other important factors: political speeches and Congolese amnesties. These two factors show that a certain Congolese political project for fighting against impunity of most serious international crimes does exist.

The Congolese president, Joseph Kabila, during almost all of his political speeches, emphasized the question of justice and of fighting against impunity. He has declared it one of his priorities in his five-year programme, from 2006 to 2011, because he said justice is 'rightly . . . the guarantor for civilian peace and an essential factor for political stability and for social and economic development'[25] and that, as the preamble of the Constitution of 18 February 2006 states, 'the injustice and its corollaries . . . are the roots of the general inversion of values and of

[23] Article 242(3) of the Military Judicial Code.

[24] *Mutineers of Mbandaka* (Judgment on Preliminary Exception), Garrison Military Tribunal Mbandaka (12 January 2006), at 6; *Mutineers of Mbandaka* (Judgment), Garrison Military Tribunal Mbandaka (20 June 2006), at 16.

[25] J. Kabila Kabange, *Address to the Nation at the Celebration of the 49th Anniversary of National Independence* (Goma, 30 June 2009).

the ruin of the country'.[26] That is why, in his inauguration speech of 6 December 2006, he already declared 'the end of entertainment'[27] before announcing that the gates of Congolese jails would be opened to anyone who would infringe the law,[28] whoever he is, Congolese or stranger, young or old, city dweller or countryman, rich or poor, powerless or powerful.[29]

The government applied all of these good intentions by the policy of zero tolerance which aimed at three pivotal objectives.[30] First, fighting against impunity for serious crimes concerning sexual abuses is placed at a high level. Second, it aims at fighting against corruption and the embezzlement of public funds as an expression of a serious infringement of the social economic aspect of human rights, as the first cause of misery and national poverty that fuel armed conflicts. Third, reforming, reorganizing and reinforcing the capacities of justice to enable it to lead the fight for re-establishing the rule of law, which is the essential framework for the country's social and economic development and for the welfare of citizens.

The issue of Congolese amnesties should be seen in conjunction with these speeches. This concerns, on the one hand, the Decree-Law n° 03/001 of 15 April 2003 laying down an amnesty for acts of war, political offences and infractions of opinion perpetrated in the DRC during the period from 2 August 1998 to 4 April 2003. On the other hand, the Law n° 09/003 of 7 May 2009 sets forth an amnesty for war and insurrectional acts perpetrated in the regions of North and South Kivu during the period from June 2003 to 7 May 2009. Their political foundation is almost unique: aiming at 'accomplishing national reconciliation'[31] and 'to stop the war, the insecurity, and to seal the reconciliation between men and women from these two regions'.[32] Even so, Parliament was again able to

[26] J. Kabila Kabange, Speech Pronounced at the Closing Ceremony of the Session of Formation of 1000 New Magistrates (Kinshasa, 31 July 2010).

[27] J. Kabila Kabange, Inauguration Speech (Kinshasa, 6 December 2006). [28] Ibid.

[29] Kabila Kabange, *Speech Pronounced at the Closing Ceremony*, above note 26.

[30] L. Mbambi Lessa, *Speech Pronounced at the Conference upon the Implementation of Joint Specialized Chambers in the Democratic Republic of Congo*, organized by Human Rights Watch and the Congolese Coalition for Transitional Justice: *Mise en place des chambres spécialisées mixtes: éléments essentiels pour garantir leur indépendance, efficacité et crédibilité* (Goma, 6–7 April 2011), at 5.

[31] Accord global et inclusif sur la transition en République démocratique du Congo du 17 décembre 2002, Section III(8), *Official Journal of the DRC*, Special Number, vol. 44, 5 April 2003, at 51–61.

[32] See Preamble of the Law n° 09/003 of 7 May 2009, Laying down Amnesty for War and Insurrectional Acts Perpetrated in the Regions of North and South Kivu, *Official Journal of DRC*, Special Number, 50th year, 9 May 2009, at 11.

adopt a new amnesty through its Law n° 014/006 of 11 February 2014, which extends the covered period from 18 February 2006 to 20 December 2013. But, the Decree-Law of 2003 and both the legislative Acts of 2009 and of 2014 have imposed the non-applicability of amnesties to genocide, crimes against humanity and war crimes. It may therefore be argued that Congolese politicians agree by such a non-applicability that these crimes should not go unpunished, thus complying with the current state of international law.

Contrary to Jean-Paul Segihobe's opinion,[33] these amnesties have not led to impunity for international crimes because otherwise there would have been a trend not to prosecute core crimes. However, these amnesties arguably favour a climate of violence because those who create armed groups are not discouraged to re-take weapons and resume violence after being granted the first amnesty, since they are aware that they can be eligible to a new amnesty thanks to political reconciliation and peace process mechanisms. In that respect, the repeated Congolese amnesties appear somewhat counter-productive. They also raise the problem of interpreting some unclear expressions, such as 'war or insurrectional acts' and could therefore result into a big judicial controversy.

The Decree-Law of 2003 did not provide any definition for acts of war, political offences and infractions of opinion to which it is applicable. But, Article 2 of the Law of 2009 underlines that 'acts of war' are 'acts inherent to military operations authorized by the laws and customs of wars which, at the time of war, caused a prejudice to others'. However, it defines 'insurrectional acts' as 'acts of collective violence likely to put in danger the institutions of the Republic or to attack the integrity of the national territory'. These definitions have been confirmed in Article 3 of the Law of 2014. But they are so general that they fuel fears of their illegitimate application beyond their primary meaning. It is suggested that Congolese judges apply these texts very carefully whenever a difficulty arises. The judges are enlightened by scholars such as Nyabirungu Mwene Songa, who tries to specify the extent of the Congolese amnesty of 2003.[34]

[33] J.-P. Segihobe, 'Crimes, justice et amnisties en République démocratique du Congo: Quand recourir aux armes c'est fabriquer des droits', in S. Bucyalimwe Mararo (ed.), *Leadership et responsabilité: hommage à l'honorable Baltahazar Rugenera Mucyo Bwiru* (Uvira/Bukavu: Association Isoko-Kivu Association Isoko-Kivu, 2010), at 343.

[34] M. S. Nyabirungu, 'Le sens et la portée de l'amnistie présidentielle du 15 avril 2003' (2004) 1 *Revue pénale congolaise* 37–43.

Anyway, this political project of fighting against impunity, especially at the command and ruling level did not pass the step of simple good intentions. It has been so far a total fiasco. The politicians try, arbitrarily, to blame the magistrates for the lack of effectiveness instead of deepening their thoughts to seek the right cause. I am not personally convinced, contrary to President Kabila's statement, that it is possible to put 'the justice to the bench of the accused'.[35] Contrary indeed, Congolese politicians might be held responsible for this fiasco.

Likewise, all other earlier initiatives failed. The first example is the creation of the National Commission[36] in 1999 inquiring into the massacres and other atrocities and violations of international humanitarian law perpetrated in the DRC during the period from October 1996 to 30 May 1997, that is to say the period during which the so-called war of liberation initiated by the Alliance of the Democratic Forces for the Liberation of the Congo (AFDL) took place. In fact, up to the death of President Laurent Désiré Kabila, the Commission was unable to fulfil its mission before shelving indefinitely with the takeover of Joseph Kabila's regime. Then, all the *livres blancs* (white books, i.e., official reports) of the Ministry of Human Rights[37] never have been efficiently used at the national judicial level. Thus, Congolese positive law, even in its reformed version, remains, at this point, unapplied. It is a sort of law without justice.

[35] Kabila Kabange, *Address to the Nation*, above note 25.

[36] Interministerial Decree of 29 January 1999, The Larcier Codes, the Democratic Republic of the Congo, Tome VI, Administrative and Public Law, vol. I, Public Law, 2002, at 355.

[37] Ministry of Human Rights, 'Official Report on Massive Violations of Human Rights and Primary Rules of International Humanitarian Law by the Aggressors (Uganda, Rwanda, Burundi) at the East of the Democratic Republic of Congo, from 2 August 1998 to 5 November 1998', Kinshasa, December 1998; 'Official Report on Deliberated Violations of the Ceasefire Agreement of Lusaka of 10 July 1999, International Covenant on Civil and Political Rights, Primary Rules on International Humanitarian Law and Relevant Resolutions of the Security Council of the UN by the Aggressive Countries (Uganda, Rwanda, Burundi) and their Congolese Accomplices of RCD and of MLC in the held Territories of the Democratic Republic of Congo, from 11 July 1999 to 31 December 1999', Tome 3, Kinshasa, January 2000; 'Official Report on the Persistence of the Flagrant and Massive Violations of Human Rights and of International Humanitarian Law and the Specific Abuses Perpetrated to the Women by Rwandese, Ugandan and Burundian Troops and their Congolese Accomplices, from 1st January to 30 June 2001', Tome 4, Kinshasa, February 2002; 'Special Official Report on the Recurrent Violations of Human Rights and International Humanitarian Law in Kisangani', Kinshasa, June 2002; 'Special Official Report on the Latest Massacres, Cannibalistic Acts and Serious other Violations of Human Rights and International Humanitarian Law Perpetrated Mainly in Ituri, in North Kivu and South Kivu, from 1 September 2002 to 31 January 2003', Kinshasa, February 2003.

4. Law without Congolese justice: the paralyzing internal dynamics and the suffocating external influences

The first causes of the ineffectiveness, even the inertia, of the Congolese justice stem from inside. The judicial institutions are paralyzed by their own procedural rules. Even after the Courts of appeal have acquired parallel competence over serious international crimes, nothing changes as not a single proceeding in this regard has been carried out since 2013.

Military tribunals on their side cannot try a case on their own initiative. There is no direct referral to the military judge by the plaintiff. Processing via the military equivalent of the public prosecutor's office, which is called *auditorat*, is unavoidable. Consequently, the victim has no choice but to join the criminal case already in motion, by bringing a civil suit for damages. In other words, under Congolese law, the possibility of a victim referring to the military tribunal by private prosecution is excluded. Even if the military prosecutor arbitrarily decides to close the case, the victim has no way to appeal or challenge this decision. The access to justice, a pivotal human right, is restricted and infringed.[38] On the other hand, it is not forbidden for a 'civilian' office of public prosecutor to inquire into military issues. But at the end of the inquiry, the issue and all its relevant components must be transmitted to the competent military prosecutor.

To summarize, the office of public prosecutors carries out the preliminary inquiry, and then the tribunal shall render its decision. However, magistrates in the office of public prosecutors are almost judges in the DRC, because when they are inquiring, they can decide to stop the prosecution by closing the case. In other words, without the determination of the office of public prosecutor, the issue will never be transferred to the tribunal.

Things go amiss because the internal dynamics of the office of the public prosecutor are paralyzing, and the risk of impunity is obvious. In principle, both military and civilian public prosecutor's offices must work under this fundamental rule: the principle of hierarchy. It means that the magistrate examining the issue is subject to commands and injunctions in the scope of his responsibility. A case can be taken back by the prosecutor,

[38] B. Bibombe Muamba, 'Le droit à la justice et à un procès équitable, à travers la Déclaration universelle des droits de l'homme et le Pacte international relatif aux droits civils et politiques' (2007) *Annales de la Faculté de droit de l'Université de Kinshasa*, Special Edition, Human Rights, Commemoration of the 59th Anniversary of the Universal Declaration of Human Rights, 191–213.

either on his own initiative or theoretically under the injunctions of the judicial hierarchy and transferred to another magistrate. Likewise, the case can be recalled at any moment of the preliminary inquiry. In practice, injunctions, such as withdrawal and recall, do not always follow the administrative procedure and do not necessarily come from the judicial hierarchy. Even President Joseph Kabila acknowledged this situation in 2008 and stated: 'Very often, while the magistrates are acting according to their duty, and before they have concluded their preliminary inquiries, phone calls pour in from everywhere in order to paralyze the public prosecution. This is inadmissible, risking the establishment of a republic of untouchables'.[39]

The second cause of the inertia of the Congolese justice system is tied to suffocating external influences, in particular, political influence. At this point, two causes seem to be relevant. First, there is the financial suffocation of judicial institutions, which leads to a lack of basic financial supplies. Here lies a certain ambivalence in the attitude of the political powers, simulating to fight against impunity through speeches and positive law and meanwhile, in practice, impeding both the tribunals and the courts to render justice. It looks as if the reforms of Congolese positive law were elaborated for external diplomatic reasons when faced with urgent appeals from the international community aiming to compel the government to stop impunity. The lack of financial supplies becomes evident in the poor treatment of magistrates, whose livelihood eventually depends either on the 'charity of parties',[40] or at least on a bonus granted to them, leniently, by the political power.[41]

Second, the independence of the judges is severely undermined. The careers of magistrates are very instable. They suffer from inopportune permutations, which, without any necessity, are tied to administration and revocations disguised as retirements from office. Even the high magistrates of the Supreme Court of Justice do not escape it. For example, within less than five years (2007–2011), besides the general appointments, this highest Court was headed by four different first presidents. This instability, which is, one could say, chronic, pushes the magistrates to be trailed easily by the power of facts into the circle of political power if they want to keep

[39] J. Kabila Kabange, Speech on the State of the Nation (Kinshasa, 13 December 2008).

[40] The expression is a euphemism, because, fundamentally, it can take on a semi-legal form, such as corruption. It seems that at the Supreme Court of Justice, a day devoted to the 'charity of these parties' exists, which is named 'Good Friday'.

[41] B. Kahombo, 'La Cour suprême de Justice, Cour constitutionnelle transitoire' (2 February 2011) *La Constitution en Afrique*, www.la-constitution-en-afrique.org/.

their position for a long time. For this reason, the Supreme Court of Justice is characterized as a 'judicial chameleon that very often adapts to the political colours of the hour'[42] because of its 'enclosure in a logic of complaisance towards the political authorities'.[43]

It is plainly a matter of lack of independence of the judiciary, but not of competent magistrates, who actually do exist in the DRC. Furthermore, the politicians and their military commanders who have fought each other during the war and have perpetrated these crimes are actually in power. In such a destructive political atmosphere of 'the dictatorship of the political power over the judiciary',[44] miracles cannot be expected from the Congolese justice system. An alternative must be found – otherwise impunity will last a long time.

5. Conclusion

From the aforementioned, two pivotal conclusions must be drawn. First, the problems of the Congolese legal system are not due to incongruities of Congolese positive law with international standards. It is true that the latter still presents, in spite of all occurred reforms, numerous flaws, namely regarding defence rights and the protection of witnesses and victims. Proceedings do not meet the requirements of a fair trial for the repression of the most serious international crimes. Yet, the military tribunals have partially surpassed these flaws by applying the ICC Statute.

Second, the reformed law and the government-led project to fight against impunity are not reflected in the resources of the Congolese justice system. The latter suffers from two major problems. Internally, there are rules of procedure which impede the existence of an efficient justice rendered rightfully for all regardless of social rank. Externally, justice is suffocated by political power. The means of functioning are flawed and the career of magistrates is managed in such a manner that these magistrates are either led into opposition against the political authorities or to please the political regime in order to save their position. The judiciary is thus becoming an organism restricted to faithfulness not

[42] J. P. Kilenda Kakengi Basila, *L'Affaire des 315 magistrats de Kinshasa: une purge néo-mobutiste* (Paris: L'Harmattan, 2004) quoted by M. Wetsh'okonda Koso Senga, 'L'arrêt de la Cour suprême de Justice n° R.CONST.112/TSR du 5 février 2010 sur l'OHADA' (04 April 2010) *La Constitution en Afrique*, www.la-constitution-en-afrique.org/.

[43] Ibid. [44] Kahombo, 'La Cour suprême de Justice', above note 41.

to the State's purposes, for which the Congolese people yearn, but to the president and his regime. This is a matter of independence and credibility of the judiciary, which has simply become unable to render expected justice. An alternative is necessary. The matter is urgent, and the victims are waiting.

PART III

International organizations as actors for ensuring compliance

12

Enforcing international humanitarian law through human rights bodies

DOMINIK STEIGER

1. Introduction

The development of international humanitarian law in the twentieth century has led to a vast body of law. Whereas the law of international armed conflict evolved mainly up until the 1970s, the law of non-international armed conflict – aside from Common Article 3 to the Geneva Conventions (GC) and the Conventions' rudimentary Additional Protocol II (AP II) – experienced a boost about twenty years later with the International Criminal Tribunal for the Former Yugoslavia's (ICTY) famous dictum in the *Tadić* decision: 'What is inhumane, and consequently proscribed, in international wars, cannot but be inhumane and inadmissible in civil strife'.[1] Nevertheless, reality does not seem to keep pace with the evolvement of these rules. In the so-called asymmetrical wars, more and more 'fighters' resort to disregarding the rules of law.[2] Not only armies of African States but also highly advanced technological armies of Western States find it difficult to react effectively to these illegal tactics and often feel strangled by rules that they believe have not been accepted by them.[3] Additionally, human rights bodies have appeared on the scene since the late 1990s as new actors enforcing and interpreting international humanitarian law. Questions with regard to its application through human rights bodies and

[1] *Prosecutor v. Tadić* (Decision on the Defence Motion for Interlocutory Appeal on Jurisdiction) Case No. IT-94–1- AR72(2 October 1995), para. 119. See also J.-M. Henckaerts and L. Doswald-Beck (eds.), *Customary International Humanitarian Law*, 2 vols. (Cambridge: Cambridge University Press, 2004), vol. I.

[2] W. Heintschel von Heinegg, 'Asymmetric Warfare', in R. Wolfrum (ed.), *The Max Planck Encyclopedia of Public International Law* (Oxford: Oxford University Press, 2010, online edition, www.mpepil.com), para. 3.

[3] See, for example, J. Bellinger III and W. Haynes II, 'A U.S. Government Response to the International Committee of the Red Cross Study Customary International Humanitarian Law' (2007) 89 *International Review of the Red Cross* 443.

the relationship between the two bodies of law consequently arise. This development is of considerable importance for the war-ridden African continent because of the progress of the African human rights law system, most importantly the installation of the African Court for Human and Peoples' Rights in 2004, which issued its first judgment in 2009.[4]

Against this background, a closer look shall be taken at the enforcement of the rules of armed conflict through human rights bodies. This chapter will begin by shortly comparing the different human rights institutions enforcing the laws of war. It is suggested that human rights bodies as (quasi-)judicial bodies fill a gap left by the absence of an individual complaints procedure for violations of international humanitarian law.[5] Still, the other bodies vested with the power to enforce this body of law, such as the International Committee of the Red Cross (ICRC), also perform important and unique functions (Section 2). When taking a look at the merits, human rights bodies' findings on the laws of war at first sight tend to be rather cautious with regard to its application. Yet a closer look reveals that human rights bodies in some instances have transferred rules of international armed conflict to internal armed conflicts and introduced human rights standards, thereby furthering the notion of humanity in armed conflict situations. However, they have not yet solved all questions arising from the parallel application of the two bodies of law (Section 3).

2. Institutions enforcing international humanitarian law

A number of institutions were established to enforce international humanitarian law on the international level. The Geneva Conventions and Additional Protocol I (AP I) provide for enforcement mechanisms such as the ICRC and the Fact-Finding Commission foreseen in Additional Protocol I. Additionally, there are other institutions outside this system which contribute to the enforcement of the law of armed conflict as well. These institutions are mainly human rights bodies. Although they are first and foremost called upon to enforce human rights law, they perform an important task in the enforcement of international humanitarian law by judging State actions during armed conflicts, especially because

[4] See A. Zimmermann and J. Bäumler, 'Current Challenges facing the African Court on Human and Peoples' Rights' (7/2010) *KAS International Reports* 38.

[5] J. K. Kleffner and L. Zegveld, 'Establishing an Individual Complaints Procedure for Violations of International Humanitarian Law' (2000) 3 *Yearbook of International Humanitarian Law* 384.

they are the only institutions that allow for individual remedy. With all of their differences – and shortcomings – the respective institutions complement each other. They can be classified into judicial and non-judicial bodies.

2.1. Non-judicial bodies

One of the most important enforcement mechanisms is the ICRC.[6] Because it is a non-judicial, non-political, non-governmental and permanent body based on the principles of impartiality, confidentiality, neutrality and independence,[7] it has a high impact on the enforcement of international humanitarian law. The ICRC's chief concern can be characterized as halting breaches of humanitarian law while at the same time securing communication between all parties to the conflict.[8] It serves as an intermediary between conflicting States, has a right of initiative and, most important, has an explicit right to visit detainees in international armed conflicts.[9] While it is true that the mechanism of visiting detainees is of uttermost importance and was copied by human rights law mechanisms in several instances – for example, by the European Torture Convention[10] – it covers only a small part of the enforcement of humanitarian law, that is, the treatment of detainees. With regard to its other fields, the ICRC is also important since its statements, publications and studies help to interpret, develop and disseminate the law. Still, it does not have the right to interpret international humanitarian law authentically, although it possesses a persuasive authority. While it was argued in the context of detainees that the ICRC has given 'humanitarian law

[6] D. P. Forsythe and B. A. J. Rieffer-Flanagan, *International Committee of the Red Cross: A Neutral Humanitarian Actor* (London: Routledge, 2007).

[7] H.-P. Gasser, 'International Committee of the Red Cross (ICRC)', in R. Wolfrum (ed.), *The Max Planck Encyclopedia of Public International Law* (Oxford: Oxford University Press, 2013, online edition, www.mpepil.com), para. 6.

[8] Ibid. para. 19.

[9] Article 126 GC III, Articles 76 and 143 GC IV. This explicit right was extended in practice to non-international armed conflicts as well as situations of internal strife. See A. Aeschlimann, 'Protection of Detainees: ICRC Action Behind Bars' (2005) 87 *International Review of the Red Cross* 83, at 88, and Article 4 Statutes of the International Red Cross and Red Crescent Movement, www.icrc.org/eng/assets/files/other/statutes-en-a5.pdf.

[10] Articles 2, 7, 8 European Convention for the Prevention of Torture and Inhuman or Degrading Treatment or Punishment, Strasbourg, 26 November 1987, in force 1 February 1989, CETS No. 126.

the strength that is lacking in human rights law',[11] in general, the ICRC lacks means and methods that are conferred exclusively to human rights bodies.

Further, Article 90 AP I established the so called International Humanitarian Fact-Finding Commission. Similar to the ICRC, it is a permanent, non-political, non-governmental and non-judicial body and is based on the principles of impartiality, confidentiality, independence and neutrality.[12] It is competent to enquire into any facts alleged to constitute a grave breach or other serious violation of the Conventions or of Additional Protocol I and is thereby also empowered to give a legal assessment of the situation[13] and facilitate, through its good offices, the restoration of an attitude of respect for the Geneva Conventions and Additional Protocol I (Article 90(2)(c) AP I). Although it has the right of initiative,[14] States first have to accept its offer of inquiry or good services. Until now, the Commission was never put into action. Its first president called it a 'sleeping beauty'.[15] It seems unclear whether it will ever wake up.

In some ways, the Human Rights Council has replaced the ICRC since it has the power to establish fact-finding missions. The problem is, it is neither independent nor impartial, does not work on a confidential basis and is not only a governmental body but also a highly political organ. It is composed of the representatives of forty-seven States. Not all of them are known human rights defenders but rather human rights offenders. For example, in 2011, Libya and Cuba were members of the Human Rights Council. It thus lacks the authority of the other non-judicial institutions. Despite these disadvantages, its fact-finding missions contribute not only to the interpretation of law but also to the finding of facts – a gap in international humanitarian law due to the States' neglect to engage the International Humanitarian Fact-Finding Mission. For example, the Fact Finding Mission concerned with the Gaza conflict which issued the Goldstone Report was called upon to 'investigate all violations of international human rights law and international humanitarian law' by the Human

[11] J. Moreillon, 'What Is International Humanitarian law? The Role of the International Red Cross' (1982) 31 *American University Law Review* 819, at 827.

[12] H. Spieker, 'International (Humanitarian) Fact-Finding Mission', in R. Wolfrum (ed.), *The Max Planck Encyclopedia of Public International Law* (Oxford: Oxford University Press, 2013, online edition, www.mpepil.com), paras. 1, 27, 35.

[13] Ibid. para. 12. [14] Ibid. para. 16.

[15] Ibid. para. 37; see F. Kalshoven, 'The International Humanitarian Fact-Finding Commission: A Sleeping Beauty?' (2002) 17 *Journal of International Law of Peace and Armed Conflict* 213.

Rights Council.[16] Even though the mandate of the Human Rights Council does not address international humanitarian law explicitly, it refers to 'situations of violations of human rights, including gross and systematic violations'[17] and makes reference in the preamble 'to solving international problems of . . . humanitarian character'.[18] What distinguishes the Human Rights Council and its fact-finding missions from all other institutions is the ability of the General Assembly and even the Security Council to support its reports, thus providing its findings with a far greater weight and impact.

The Security Council of course may react independently from the Human Rights Council to breaches of the laws of war under Chapter VII of the UN Charter and has done so in the past, calling on parties to the conflict – State actors and non-State actors alike – to adhere to humanitarian law.[19]

2.2. *(Quasi-)judicial bodies*

Even though no genuine individual complaints procedure for violations of international humanitarian law exists, other institutions fill this gap. Next to human rights treaty bodies, the International Court of Justice (ICJ), the International Criminal Court (ICC), the International Criminal Tribunals for the former Yugoslavia and Rwanda and the hybrid tribunals are the only venues on the international level where binding decisions regarding breaches of international humanitarian law can be reached. The same holds true for national courts on the national level. The international judicial bodies are also non-political, impartial, neutral and independent, but they do not act confidentially.

The criminal tribunals and the ICC are of extraordinary importance for the enforcement of humanitarian law, but differ from human rights bodies. First, they do not judge acts of States but those of individuals. By this they might be missing the bigger picture since they solely have to

[16] UN Council on Human Rights, 'The Grave Violations of Human Rights in the Occupied Palestinian Territory Particularly Due to the Recent Israeli Military Attack against the Occupied Gaza Strip' (12 January 2009), UN Doc. A/HRC/S-9/L.17/Rev.2, para. 14.

[17] UNGA Resolution 60/251 (3 April 2006), para. 3.

[18] Ibid. preambular para. 1. Due to the lack of a special reference to international humanitarian law, it is questionable whether the Human Rights Council is acting ultra vires by conferring this power to the Fact Finding Mission.

[19] See, for example, UNSC Resolutions 1127 (28 August 1997); 1193 (28 August 1998); 1216 (21 December 1998); 1746 (23 March 2007); 2021 (29 November 2011).

establish personal responsibility. Second, only the respective prosecutors and States are able to initiate proceedings; therefore these institutions do not allow for furthering justice through an individual complaints procedure. Third, the ICC and the tribunals tend to focus only on few high-profile cases.[20] Fourth, the tribunals only have jurisdiction limited to the specific conflict they were set up for. Praiseworthy is the ICC Statute's ratification status of 114 States, which is about the same number of States that accepted the human rights individual complaints procedures and the competence of the ICC to award remedies.[21] Also, since the tribunals and the ICC are made up of Trial Chambers and an Appeals Chamber, errors of law can be corrected.

Furthermore, the ICJ and the national courts have contributed to the enforcement of international humanitarian law. The ICJ, however, can only be called upon by States or the General Assembly. Thus, only limited case law exists.[22] National courts are supposed to judge on grave breaches of international humanitarian law, as foreseen by Articles 49 GC I, 50 GC II, 129 GC III, 146 GC IV and 85 AP I. As important as this is, domestic courts often do not seem willing or able to prosecute these grave breaches.[23] Foreign national courts will in most cases find it difficult to overcome immunity. Finally, the grave breaches regime only applies to international armed conflicts, although States are of course free – within the boundaries of the rules of immunity and jurisdiction – to criminalize acts in non-international armed conflicts as well.

What makes human rights treaty bodies so valuable and unique in comparison to other institutions enforcing the law of armed conflicts is that they are the only available international fora for individuals and that they can award compensation.[24] The human rights courts are – next to the ICJ, which will often lack jurisdiction – the only institutions that

[20] J.-M. Henckaerts, 'Concurrent Application of International Humanitarian Law and Human Rights Law: A Victim Perspective', in R. Arnold and N. Quénivet (eds.) *International Humanitarian Law and Human Rights Law: Towards a New Merger in International Law* (Boston: Martinus Nijhoff Publishers, 2008), 237–67, at 248.

[21] Article 75 ICC-Statute.

[22] See V. Chetail, 'The Contribution of the International Court of Justice to International Humanitarian Law' (2003) 85 *International Review of the Red Cross* 235.

[23] As Y. Dinstein, 'Human Rights in Armed Conflict: International Humanitarian Law', in T. Meron (ed.), *Human Rights in International Law. Legal and Policy Issues*, 2 vols. (Oxford: Clarendon Press, 1984), vol. II, 345–68, at 359 (noting that national proceedings are often 'tainted with lack of objectivity').

[24] Article 41 ECHR, Article 63(2) Inter-American Commission on Human Rights, Articles 27 and 30 Protocol to the African Charter on Human and Peoples' Rights Establishing

can hand down judgments binding States instead of individuals. With regard to the human rights treaty bodies that are not courts, it can be said that they have a highly persuasive authority and thus in general further justice although their views are widely regarded as non-binding.[25] In addition, not only have human rights treaty bodies helped in attaining individual justice and compensations, but their judgments have also led to policy changes: in reaction to the judgments of the European Court of Human Rights concerning the armed conflict in Chechnya, Russia amended its legislation to comply with the Court's findings.[26] The same holds true for Israel, which changed its Rules of Engagement in response to the Goldstone Report.[27] All this helps in enforcing international humanitarian law and would not have happened without the human rights bodies, complementing other international and national courts.

Yet, it has to be kept in mind that the human rights treaty bodies might be overwhelmed by mass violations of human rights such as they occur in armed conflicts.[28] The human rights treaty bodies do not possess the legal and material means of investigating such violations, which might render a judgment on the merits impossible.[29] In this context, it is important to note that the European Court of Human Rights was flooded with cases from Chechnya, exhausting a huge amount of existing resources and thus affecting other cases as well. The first problem can be resolved by applying sensible standards of proof, taking into account that only States are in possession of decisive material. If the State fails to disclose

the African Court on Human and Peoples' Rights, Ouagadougou, 9 June 1998, in force 25 January 2004, Doc. OAU/LEG/EXP/AFCHPR/PROT (III).

25 C. Tomuschat, 'Making Individual Communications an Effective Tool for the Protection of Human Rights', in U. Beyerlin et al. (eds.), *Recht zwischen Umbruch und Bewahrung. Völkerrecht, Europarecht, Staatsrecht. Festschrift für Rudolf Bernhardt* (Berlin: Springer, 1995), 615–34, at 623.

26 Council of Europe, Committee of Ministers, Deputy Ministers, 'Violations of the ECHR in the Chechen Republic: Russia's Compliance with the European Court's Judgments' CM/Inf/DH(2006)32 revised 2 (12 June 2007), paras. 38, 85.

27 K. J. Heller, 'Israel's Changes in Response to the Goldstone Report', Opinio Juris (17 April 2011), opiniojuris.org/2011/04/17/israels-changes-in-response-to-the-goldstone-report.

28 See M. Bothe, 'Die Anwendung der Europäischen Menschenrechtskonvention in bewaffneten Konflikten, eine Überforderung?' (2005) 65 *Zeitschrift für ausländisches öffentliches Recht und Völkerrecht* 615, at 622.

29 See *Legal Consequences of the Construction of a Wall* (Advisory Opinion) [2004] ICJ Reports 240, Declaration Judge Buergenthal, who found that 'the absence in this case of the requisite information and evidence vitiates the Court's findings on the merits'.

such material, it allows the bodies to draw certain conclusions. A reversal of the burden of proof or drawing of adverse inference is nothing new to the human rights treaty bodies[30] and has been used by the European Court of Human Rights concerning cases of armed conflicts.[31] Of course, the security interests of the States must be taken into account. This is accepted by the European Court of Human Rights which has pointed out the possibility of *in camera* proceedings.[32] The second problem was tackled by the member States of the Council of Europe via Protocol No. 14, allowing, inter alia, for measures that make it possible for the Court to deal more efficiently with repetitive cases. It finally entered into force in 2010.

With regard to the different international judicial fora, one might be opposed to the possibility of diverging judgments, which could fragmentize humanitarian law by adding more opinions and interpretations. It must be kept in mind that it is crucial that States are convinced of a certain interpretation and have clear standards to adhere to, formulated in clear and precise terms. This is especially true for soldiers and commanders who have to know what they are allowed to do and what actions are prohibited.[33] But since the language of humanitarian law is not as clear as one might hope for – whether an attack is 'excessive' or not is open to interpretation as well as whether a precaution is 'feasible' or not – interpretation is needed to clarify the meaning of the law. This can best be achieved through the human rights bodies' views and binding judgments. In this context, two kinds of risks must be mentioned: first, overlapping jurisdictions might lead to diverging judgments. Second, the interpretation of humanitarian law by human rights bodies might lead to confusion by soldiers and commanders with regard to the exact content of the law and possibly even to their criminal conviction. The first danger is overrated: the example of the judicial dialogue between the European

[30] *Tomasi v. France* (Judgment) Series A No 241, European Court of Human Rights, 27 August 1992, paras. 110, 115; *Baldeón García v. Peru* (Judgment on Merits, Reparations and Costs) Inter-American Court of Human Rights, Series C No 147 (6 April 2006), para. 120; *Delgado Paez v. Colombia* (195/1985), Human Rights Committee, 12 July 1990, UN Doc. A/45/40 vol. II (1990) Annex IX, pp. 43–49, para. 5.6.

[31] *Isayeva v. Russia* (Judgment) Application No. 57950/00, European Court of Human Rights, 24 February 2005, para. 189.

[32] *Chahal v. United Kingdom* (Report 1996-V) Application No. 22414/93, European Commission of Human Rights, 15 November 1996, para. 131.

[33] Cf. C. Byron, 'A Blurring of the Boundaries: The Application of International Humanitarian Law by Human Rights Bodies' (2007) 47 *Virginia Journal of International Law* 839, at 892.

Court of Human Rights, the European Court of Justice and the national constitutional courts shows that harmony is possible and discussion is fruitful. Additionally, diverging judgments contribute to the evolution of international law[34] and can be perceived as a sign of the vitality of international law.[35] Such a 'laboratory of ideas [can lead to] efficiency and legitimacy through specialization, contestation and competition'.[36] With regard to new interpretations of humanitarian law, for example, the transferral of norms of international armed conflicts to internal armed conflicts,[37] the law as it is stipulated in the Geneva Conventions, the Additional Protocols and the ICC Statute would still remain the bottom line to be respected since international and national criminal courts alike need to adhere to the general principle of *nulla poena sine lege certa*. As long as no certainty is reached, criminal courts cannot convict due to ongoing discussions concerning the exact content of the law. Still, confusion may lead to a more cautious approach towards planning, ordering and executing attacks, which nonetheless is prescribed by international humanitarian law.

The decisions and statements of international judicial bodies and the Human Rights Council increase the pressure on States to comply with international humanitarian law. They help in publicizing it and thus raise the awareness of other enforcement mechanisms, that is, the public and the decision-makers, for the importance of the laws of war.[38] This judicial approach is unknown to the Fact-Finding Commission and the ICRC. In contrast, their unique strength lies in their diplomatic approach, as they generally rely on the principle of confidentiality. Thus, the human rights bodies complement the traditional enforcement mechanisms, all of them together helping to enforce international humanitarian law. The establishment of new fora is also good news for victims of violations of international humanitarian law, allowing them to take remedial action.

[34] This is highlighted by A. Reinisch, 'International Courts and Tribunals, Multiple Jurisdiction', in R. Wolfrum (ed.), *The Max Planck Encyclopedia of Public International Law* (Oxford: Oxford University Press, 2011, online edition, www.mpepil.com), para. 5.

[35] See J. Pauwelyn, 'Fragmentation of International Law', in R. Wolfrum (ed.), *The Max Planck Encyclopedia of Public International Law* (Oxford: Oxford University Press, 2006, online edition, www.mpepil.com), para. 17.

[36] Ibid. para. 24. [37] See below Section 3.4.

[38] L. Doswald-Beck and S. Vité, 'International Humanitarian Law and Human Rights Law' (1993) 293 *International Review of the Red Cross* 94, at 117.

3. The application of international humanitarian law through human rights bodies

Both kinds of institutions were criticized for upsetting the delicate balance between military necessity and humanity[39] by putting too heavy a burden on the armed forces by imposing human rights standards and by transferring norms of international armed conflict to internal armed conflicts. Still, their application of international humanitarian law by and large observed this balance while contributing to the enforcement of humanitarian law and to its interpretation. However, no coherent and sound dogmatic approach with regard to the relationship of both bodies of law has yet been found. The following analysis, encompassing all the quite different fields in which human rights bodies applied humanitarian law, will begin with jurisprudence concerning the threshold of its application (Section 3.1). In the following section, uncontroversial cases will be examined in which human rights bodies used international humanitarian law to reinforce their findings concerning human rights violations (Section 3.2). Then, situations of occupation and internment (Section 3.3), the principles of distinction (Section 3.4) and proportionality (Section 3.5), the duty to take precautions (Section 3.6) and the customary law character of international humanitarian law (Section 3.7) will be further scrutinized. Finally, omissions in its application will be briefly discussed (Section 3.8).

3.1. Threshold of applicability of international humanitarian law

The threshold of applicability of the law of armed conflict is sometimes difficult to ascertain. This is especially true with regard to internal armed conflicts.[40] In the first case ever decided by a human rights body in which norms of humanitarian law were applied,[41] the Inter-American Commission on Human Rights argued that an armed attack on a military barrack by forty-two armed men lasting about thirty hours and resulting

[39] See, for example, M. N. Schmitt, 'Military Necessity and Humanity in International Humanitarian Law: Preserving the Delicate Balance' (2010) 50 *Virginia Journal of International Law* 795, at 796.

[40] G. Abi-Saab, 'Non-International Armed Conflicts', in: UNESCO (ed.), *International Dimensions of Humanitarian Law* (Paris: Martinus Nijhoff Publishers, 1988), at 217–39.

[41] Leaving aside the Judgment *Engel et al. v. Netherlands* (Judgment) Application Nos. 5100/71, 5101/71, 5102/71, 5354/72, 5370/72, European Court of Human Rights, 8 June 1976, para. 72, where the Court mentioned Article 88 GC III, foreseeing different treatment of interned officers and soldiers.

in more than thirty deaths was governed by the standards of Common Article 3 GC.[42] Regarding the ICTY's Appeals Chamber *Tadić* decision,[43] which calls for 'protracted armed violence', it can be disputed whether the situation actually qualified as an armed conflict. Thus, it might be argued, that human rights bodies lack the necessary expertise to judge on humanitarian law and thus should refrain from doing so.

Although it is true that, in general, more expertise concerning humanitarian law is necessary for members of human rights bodies, to follow the advice that they should not judge on humanitarian law would only be possible if human rights bodies were not obligated to its application. It is true that at first glance one might wonder how it is possible for them to apply humanitarian law since, in principle, they are called upon to apply human rights law.[44] However, a second look shows that the application of the laws of war is not a matter of choice but instead is mandatory. This is due to four reasons: first, human rights conventions contain explicit references to 'international law', such as the human rights treaties' derogation clauses. They allow for the derogation of certain articles, 'provided that such measures are not inconsistent with its other obligations under international law', thereby requiring the adherence to humanitarian law norms if States derogate from their human rights obligations.[45] The African Charter on Human and Peoples' Rights (African Charter)[46] even contains the general duty to 'take into consideration . . . other . . . international conventions' (Article 61 African Charter). Also, some single norms refer to 'international law', for example, Article 7 European Convention on Human Rights (ECHR). Further, some of the newer human rights treaties such as the Maputo Protocol[47] explicitly obligate States parties to 'undertake to respect and ensure respect for the rules of international humanitarian law'. Second, human rights treaties

[42] *Juan Carlos Abella v. Argentina*, Case 11.137, Report No. 55/97, Inter-American Commission on Human Rights, OEA/Ser.L/V/II.95 Doc. 7 rev. at 271 (18 November 1997), paras. 154–156.

[43] *Prosecutor v. Tadić* (Decision), above note 1, para. 70.

[44] Article 19 ECHR; Article 63 ACHR; Article 45 African Charter.

[45] Article 15 ECHR; Article 4 ICCPR and Article 27 ACHR; see also Articles 60 and 61 African Charter.

[46] African Charter on Human and Peoples' Rights, Banjul, 26 June 1981, in force 21 October 1986, (1982) 21 ILM 58.

[47] Article 11 Protocol to the African Charter on Human and Peoples' Rights on the Rights of Women in Africa, Maputo, 11 July 2003, in force 25 November 2005, Doc. CAB/LEG/66.6; see also Article 38 of the Convention on the Rights of the Child, New York, 20 November 1989, in force 2 September 1990, 1577 U.N.T.S. 3.

contain broadly framed legal terms that call for further interpretation. For example, Article 6 International Covenant on Civil and Political Rights (ICCPR), guaranteeing the right to life, contains the term 'arbitrarily' which, in the context of an armed conflict, cannot reasonably be defined without recourse to humanitarian law which, for example, foresees the prohibition of certain weapons.[48] Third, in case a conflict exists between the two bodies of law, the human rights treaty bodies have to take a stance on the applicability of human rights law. According to the ICJ, humanitarian law constitutes *lex specialis* in relation to human rights law and thus might, in accordance with the rule of *lex specialis derogat legi generali*, render human rights norms, at least in parts, inapplicable.[49] Even if one does not follow the ICJ's approach,[50] a conflict of norms must be solved somehow, thus requiring human rights bodies to consider humanitarian law in order to establish whether a conflict of norms exists. Fourth, human rights bodies have to interpret the respective treaties by taking into account any relevant rules of international law applicable in the relations between the parties (Article 31(3) Vienna Convention on the Law of Treaties).[51] In times of armed conflict, this is, next to human rights law, humanitarian law. Since the human rights bodies have been criticized for their application of international humanitarian law, it should be emphasized that these aforementioned reasons show that they have been vested with this power by the States which have set up the respective mechanisms. Furthermore, as they almost never protested against the decisions of the human rights bodies, the States have acquiesced to the jurisprudence.[52] Especially the latter argument shows that the human

[48] *Legality of the Threat or Use of Nuclear Weapons* (Advisory Opinion) [1996] ICJ Reports para. 25.

[49] Ibid. para. 106; *Nuclear Weapons*, above note 48, para. 25.

[50] See below Section 3.3.

[51] See *Behrami and Behrami v. France, Saramati v. France, Germany and Norway* (Decision as to Admissibility) Application Nos. 71412/01, 78166/01, European Court of Human Rights, 2 May 2007, para. 122; *Al-Adsani v. United Kingdom* (Judgment) Application No. 35763/97 European Court of Human Rights, para. 55; *Banković et al. v. Belgium et al.* (Decision as to the Admissibility) Application No. 52207/99, European Court of Human Rights, para. 57; *Serrano-Cruz Sisters v. El Salvador* (Judgment on Preliminary Objections) Inter-American Court of Human Rights, Series C No 118 (23 November 2004), para. 119. It is disputed whether all parties to the first treaty must be a party to the second treaty as well. See Pauwelyn, 'Fragmentation', above note 35, para. 17.

[52] This might be understood as subsequent practice, Article 31(3) Vienna Convention on the Law of Treaties; cf. H. Krieger, 'Funktionen von Grund – und Menschenrechten', in O. Dörr, R. Grote and T. Marauhn (eds.), *EMRK/GG, Konkordanzkommentar zum europäischen und deutschen Grundrechtsschutz*, 2 vols., 2d edn (Tübingen: Mohr Siebeck, 2013), vol. I, at 287–365, para. 24.

rights bodies' approach of applying both bodies of law alike in situations of armed conflict as such has been accepted by the States. This power of human rights bodies to judge situations falling within the ambit of the laws of war is universally accepted today. The regional and universal human rights bodies,[53] the principal UN organs[54] and the International Law Commission (ILC)[55] all applied human rights in times of belligerent occupation and armed conflict.

By finding a duty to apply norms of humanitarian law, nothing has been said yet about how they have to be considered. The above-examined Inter-American Commission on Human Rights' decision was widely discussed, especially since its application of humanitarian law gave rise to objections.[56] The Inter-American Court of Human Rights clarified in a later case that human rights bodies are in principle allowed to apply international humanitarian law but that they must not conclude whether it was breached or not.[57] Rather, the Inter-American Court of Human Rights can only give 'an opinion in which the Court will say whether or not that [national] norm or that fact is compatible with the American Convention'[58] and not with international humanitarian law as such, which may only be considered, applied or interpreted within the

[53] General Comment on the Nature of the General Legal Obligation Imposed on States Parties to the Covenant (General Comment No. 31), Human Rights Committee, 26 May 2004, UN Doc. CCPR/C/21/Rev.1/Add.13, para. 11; UN Commission on Human Rights Resolution 1996/73 (23 April 1996); UN Council on Human Rights, 'Human Rights in Palestine and other Occupied Arab Territories: Report of the United Nations Fact Finding Mission on the Gaza Conflict ('Goldstone-Report')' (15 September 2009), UN Doc. A/HRC/12/48; *Isayeva, Yusupova and Bazayeva v. Russia* Application Nos. 57947/00, 57948/00 and 57949/00, European Court of Human Rights, 24 February 2005; *Isayeva v. Russia*, above note 31; *Juan Carlos Abella v. Argentina*, above note 42, paras. 157–171; *Las Palmeras Case* (Judgment on Preliminary Objections) Inter-American Court of Human Rights, Series C No 67 (4 February 2000); *Commission Nationale des Droits de l'Homme et des Libertés v. Chad* (Communication 74/92), Ninth Annual Activity Report 1995/1996 (ACHPR/AHG/207 (XXXII)).

[54] UNGA Resolution 2675 (XXV) (9 December 1970); UNSC Resolution 1265 (17 September 1999); *The Wall* (Advisory Opinion), above note 29, para. 106.

[55] ILC, 'Report of the International Law Commission on the Work of its 59th Session' (7 May–5 June and 9 July–10 August 2007), UN Doc. A/62/10, at 165 (Article 6 Draft Articles on the Effects of Armed Conflicts on Treaties).

[56] See, for example, L. Zegveld, 'The Inter-American Commission on Human Rights and International Humanitarian Kaw: A Comment on the Tablada Case' (1998) 324 *International Review of the Red Cross* 505.

[57] *Las Palmeras Case*, above note 53, para. 33.

[58] Ibid. See C. McCarthy, 'Human Rights and the Laws of War under the American Convention on Human Rights' (2006) 6 *European Human Rights Law Review* 762, at 763–70.

question of whether a human rights norm was violated. In fact, no human rights treaty body has yet stated whether a humanitarian law norm was breached. This is a sign of the human rights bodies' caution vis-à-vis humanitarian law, which they consider if necessary when arriving at the conclusion that human rights norms were violated by the State. By applying humanitarian law, as one observer stated with regard to the African Commission on Human and Peoples' Rights' 2005 decision in *Democratic Republic of Congo v. Burundi, Rwanda, Uganda*,[59] the human rights bodies 'confirmed the dwindling divide between international humanitarian law and human rights law'.[60]

3.2. *Humanitarian law as a means to reinforce human rights law*

Human rights bodies have used international humanitarian law to support their findings on breaches of human rights law. The most important case in this regard was decided by the African Commission on Human and Peoples' Rights in its aforementioned decision. Here, it relied heavily on the law of armed conflict. Killings, massacres, rapes, mutilations and other grave human rights abuses which 'constitute flagrant violations' of Articles 2 and 4 African Charter (respect for life; arbitrary deprivation of rights)[61] are also 'inconsistent with [the States'] obligations under Part III of the *Geneva Convention Relative to the Protection of Civilian Persons in Time of War* of 1949 and *Protocol 1 of the Geneva Convention*'.[62] With regard to judging on the raping of women and girls, it cited Article 76 AP I.[63] Further, the besieging of a hydroelectric dam 'taking Article 56 [AP I, protecting works or installations containing dangerous forces, and Article 23 Hague Regulations,[64] protecting the enemy's

[59] *Democratic Republic of Congo v. Burundi, Rwanda and Uganda* (Communication 227/99), Twentieth Activity Report of the African Commission of Human and People's Rights 2006 (EX.CL/279 (IX), at 112–31; cf. the contribution by F. Z. Ntoubandi, 'Comment - Enforcement of International Humanitarian Law through the Human Rights Organs of the African Union', in Chapter 13 of this volume.

[60] J. D. Mujuzi, 'Case Commentary: Interstate Communications under the African Charter on Human and Peoples' Rights: Confirming the Dwindling Divide between IHL and HRL? An Appraisal of the Democratic Republic of Congo v Burundi, Rwanda and Uganda (Communication 227/99)' 2007 *African Yearbook on International Humanitarian Law* 139, at 156.

[61] *Congo v. Burundi, Rwanda, Uganda*, above note 59, para. 80.

[62] Ibid. para. 79 (emphasis in original). [63] Ibid. para. 86.

[64] Convention (IV) Respecting the Laws and Customs of War on Land and its Annex: Regulations Concerning the Laws and Customs of War on Land, The Hague, 18 October 1907, in force 26 January 1910, 3 Martens Nouveau Recueil (ser. 3) 461.

property] into account . . . violated the Charter'.[65] The Inter-American Court of Human Rights used the same approach. For example, in the *Mapiripán Massacre* Case, it stated that Article 19 American Convention on Human Rights (ACHR), governing the protection of children, 'must be specified . . . taking into account . . . Protocol II'[66] and that in order 'to define the content and scope of Article 22 [ACHR (free movement)]', Protocol II is 'especially useful'.[67] Although the bodies enforced international humanitarian law by using it as a supplement, it should be kept in mind that – in accordance with the above mentioned jurisprudence of the Inter-American Court of Human Rights – human rights law alone was used as the basis for the human rights bodies' findings. This holds true as well for the African Commission on Human and Peoples' Rights, even if its language was not always entirely clear in this respect.[68] In the end, it listed only norms of the African Charter as being breached by the respondent States.[69]

3.3. *Occupation and internment*

With regard to the law of occupation and the rules of internment, the European Court of Human Rights in a landmark Judgment allowed Article 5 ECHR, the right to liberty and security, to supersede the right to intern civilians.[70] Also, the Fact Finding Mission on the Gaza Conflict has expressed itself on the matter.[71]

In Gaza, merely borders and airspace are controlled by Israel since it withdrew its troops in 2005. The application of occupation law is not self-evident. According to Article 42 Hague Regulations, a territory 'is considered occupied when it is actually placed under the authority of the hostile army. The occupation extends only to the territory where

[65] *Congo v. Burundi, Rwanda, Uganda*, above note 59, paras. 83, 84.

[66] *Mapiripán Massacre v. Colombia* (Judgment on Merits, Reparations and Costs) Inter-American Court of Human Rights Series C No 134 (15 September 2005), para. 153.

[67] Ibid. paras. 171–172. See also *Serrano-Cruz Sisters v. El Salvador* (Judgment on Merits, Reparations and Costs) Inter-American Court of Human Rights Series C No 120 (1 March 2005), para. 116; *Ituango Massacres v. Colombia* (Judgment on Preliminary Objections, Merits, Reparations and Costs) Inter-American Court of Human Rights Series C No 148 (1 July 2006), paras. 180, 209.

[68] *Congo v. Burundi, Rwanda, Uganda*, above note 59, paras. 79, 87, 98.

[69] Ibid. para. 98.

[70] *Al-Jedda v. United Kingdom* (Judgment) Application No. 27021/08, European Court of Human Rights, 7 July 2011, para. 110.

[71] 'Goldstone-Report', above note 53, paras. 275–279.

such authority has been established and can be exercised'. Although it has been argued that a position of potential control suffices,[72] the ICJ in its 2005 Judgment *Congo v. Uganda* only examined whether Uganda exercised actual control.[73] By applying occupation law to Gaza with the argument that Israel retains 'ultimate authority'[74] since it 'makes military incursions and from time to time hit[s] targets within the Gaza Strip',[75] the Fact Finding Mission supported the potential control requirement, adding to existing case law.

The European Court of Human Rights applied the European Convention on Human Rights to situations of occupation with regard to the internment of civilians and expressed itself on the relationship of the two bodies of law, allowing the right to liberty and security to trump the right to intern civilians absent a conflict of norms.[76] In order to examine whether the Court struck the right balance between humanity and military necessity and arrived at the right judgment in a situation in which two different norms applied, it is necessary to first discuss the question of extraterritorial jurisdiction of human rights bodies and then examine the relationship of the two different norms.

Since occupation will always be outside one's own territory, it is already questionable whether the European Court of Human Rights, and human rights bodies in general, may exercise their jurisdiction, which is of course a necessary prerequisite for the applicability of international humanitarian law. One could argue that States do not exercise jurisdiction outside their own territory, thus making a parallel application of human rights treaties in situations of occupation impossible. This notion is not supported by the human rights bodies' jurisprudence. Rather, in principle, human rights apply extraterritorially.[77] However, some exceptions exist within the European system, the European Court of Human Rights being the most reluctant of the human rights bodies to apply human rights on

[72] *Prosecutor v. Nletilic and Martinovic* (Judgment), Case No. IT-98-34-T (31 March 2003), para. 217; *A and B v. State of Israel*, Israel Supreme Court (11 June 2008) elyon1.court.gov.il/files_eng/06/590/066/n04/06066590.n04.pdf, para. 11.

[73] *Armed Activities on the Territory of the Congo (Democratic Republic of the Congo v. Uganda)* (Judgment) [2005] ICJ Reports 168, paras. 173, 177.

[74] 'Goldstone-Report', above note 53, para. 279. [75] Ibid. para. 278.

[76] *Al-Jedda v. United Kingdom*, above note 70, para. 109.

[77] General Comment No. 31, Human Rights Committee, above note 53, para. 10; *Armed Activities*, above note 73, para. 179; *Congo v. Burundi, Rwanda, Uganda*, above note 59; 'Report on Terrorism and Human Rights', Inter-American Commission on Human Rights, OEA/Ser.L/V/II.116 Doc. 5 rev. 1 corr. (22 October 2002), para. 44.

foreign territories.[78] It either requires the State to be in control of a person (personal notion)[79] or to exercise 'effective control of an area outside its national territory' (spatial notion).[80] The Inter-American Commission on Human Rights likewise requires the 'state's authority and control'.[81] These requirements very closely resemble the authority requirement of Article 42 Hague Regulations, leading to the assumption that jurisdiction will always be exercised within an occupation situation. Yet the European Court of Human Rights foresees an *espace juridique* clause calling for the application of the European Convention on Human Rights only within the member States (Article 56 ECHR).[82] Since this clause only applies to the spatial notion of jurisdiction, but not to its personal notion,[83] internment situations fall within the ambit of the human rights treaties. However, most other situations will also fall within the jurisdiction of the Court. Short of relinquishing the *espace juridique* requirement,[84] the European Court of Human Rights found a violation of the Convention by the United Kingdom after UK soldiers shot and killed five Iraqis in Iraq in 2003 while patrolling the streets. The Court did not argue that the occupation of Iraq alone was sufficient to establish the State's jurisdiction, but connected the personal with the spatial notion and found that the United Kingdom 'assumed authority and responsibility for the maintenance of security in South East Iraq. In these exceptional circumstances, the Court considers that the United Kingdom . . . exercised authority and control over individuals'.[85]

[78] See, for example, *Banković et al. v. Belgium et al.*, above note 51.

[79] *Öcalan v. Turkey* (Judgment) Application No. 46221/99, European Court of Human Rights, 12 March 2003, para. 93.

[80] *Banković et al. v. Belgium et al.*, above note 51, para. 70.

[81] 'Report on Terrorism', above note 77, para. 44; *Coard et al. v. United States*, Case 10.951, Report No. 109/99, Inter-American Commission on Human Rights, OEA/Ser.L/V/II.106 Doc. 3 rev. (29 September 1999), para. 37; *Armando Alejandro Jr. et al. v. Republic of Cuba*, Case 11.589, Report No. 86/99, Inter-American Commission on Human Rights, OEA/Ser.L/V/II.106 Doc. 3 rev. at 586 (29 September 1999).

[82] *Banković et al. v. Belgium et al.*, above note 51, para. 80; *Issa et al. v. Turkey* (Judgment) Application No. 31821/96, European Court of Human Rights, 16 November 2004, para. 74.

[83] *Öcalan v. Turkey*, above note 79, para. 93; *Issa et al. v. Turkey*, above note 82, para. 71.

[84] M. Milanovic, 'Al-Skeini and Al-Jedda in Strasbourg' (2012) 23 *European Journal of International Law* 121, at 129, even argues that the European Court of Human Rights has given up this requirement.

[85] *Al-Skeini et al. v. United Kingdom* (Judgment) Application No. 55721/07, European Court of Human Rights, 7 July 2011, para. 147.

After it has been established that the human rights bodies are in principle competent to judge actions which take place outside their territory, we shall return to the substantive law. The law of internment may serve as a paradigm for how the relationship between the two bodies of law has changed, particularly over the last years. In 1976, the European Commission of Human Rights declined to examine a breach of Article 5 ECHR, the right to liberty and security, with regard to prisoners of war.[86] This approach changed dramatically in 2011. In the *Al-Jedda* Case, the Court argued that with regard to Geneva Convention IV, 'under international humanitarian law internment is to be viewed not as an obligation on the Occupying Power but as a measure of last resort'.[87] Thus, the duty under Article 5 ECHR to ensure a person's liberty prevailed over the right to intern civilians according to Article 41 GC IV. This jurisprudence in principle can apply to the internment of civilians and prisoners of war alike since neither of them must be interned. Although one can certainly not argue that the internment of combatants can be regarded as a measure of last resort, nor can it be regarded as a duty since States only 'may subject prisoners of war to internment' and, so long as the prisoner agrees, may release or repatriate him before the end of hostilities (Article 21 GC III). This leaves room for both a narrow interpretation, restricting the European Court of Human Rights' finding only to civilians, and an extensive one, extending this jurisprudence to prisoners of war.

By allowing human rights law to trump humanitarian law as the European Court of Human Rights did in this instance, one could argue that the latter loses one of its most important instruments, that is, the power to remove civilians and – depending on one's interpretation of the Judgment – combatants from the scenery or battlefield and thus protecting the interning State against any possible threat the interned person would pose. Thus, this jurisprudence seems to be in opposition to the notion of military necessity and the ICJ's famous dictum declaring humanitarian law to be *lex specialis* to human rights law in case a situation is governed by both law regimes.[88] This *lex specialis* approach was expressly endorsed by

[86] *Cyprus v. Turkey* Application Nos. 6789/74 and 6950/75, European Court of Human Rights, Report, 10 July 1976, para. 313.

[87] *Al-Jedda v. UK*, above note 70, para. 107.

[88] *The Wall* (Advisory Opinion), above note 29, para. 106; *Nuclear Weapons*, above note 48, para. 25; cf. the contribution by Ntoubandi, 'Human Rights Organs of the African Union', above note 59.

the Inter-American Commission on Human Rights,[89] the Inter-American Court of Human Rights[90] and the Human Rights Committee[91] before the 2005 ICJ Judgment *Congo v. Uganda* concerning the application of both bodies of law in which the Court did not reiterate its approach.[92] Yet the ICJ and the other bodies have not clarified their understanding of *lex specialis.* Under the heading of 'Conflicts between Special Law and General Law', the International Law Commission's study on fragmentation discusses the concept of *lex specialis* at length[93] but finally comes to the conclusion that '[n]o general, context-independent answers can be given. [T]he lex specialis maxim cannot be meaningfully codified'.[94] In addition, the law of internal armed conflicts is not more specific than human rights. Rather the opposite is true.[95] Even if one were to accept the *lex specialis* thesis, two arguments speak in favour of the European Court of Human Rights' finding: first since it did not find an obligation but rather a right to intern civilians, it could not find a conflict between two rules, rendering the recourse to the conflict resolution mechanism unnecessary.[96] Also since Article 15 ECHR allows for the derogation of

[89] *Detainees in Guantánamo Bay, Cuba* Adoption of Precautionary Measures, Inter-American Commission on Human Rights (13 March 2002), (2002) 96 *American Journal of International Law* 730; *Juan Carlos Abella v. Argentina,* above note 42, para. 166.

[90] *Serrano-Cruz Sisters v. El Salvador,* above note 51, para. 111.

[91] General Comment No. 31, Human Rights Committee, above note 53, para. 11.

[92] *Armed Activities,* above note 73.

[93] ILC, 'Fragmentation of International Law: Difficulties Arising from the Diversification and Expansion of International Law: Report of the Study Group of the International Law Commission' (13 April 2006), UN Doc. A/CN.4/L.682, paras. 56–122. For a definition of conflict see ibid. para. 25.

[94] Ibid. para. 119. See the critique of the *lex specialis* rule by G. Gaggioli and R. Kolb, 'A Right to Life in Armed Conflicts? The Contribution of the European Court of Human Rights' (2007) 37 *Israel Yearbook on Human Rights* 115, at 118–19; A. Orakhelashvili, 'The Interaction between Human Rights and Humanitarian Law: Fragmentation, Conflict, Parallelism, or Convergence' (2008) 18 *European Journal of International Law* 161, at 181 ('not supported by efficient evidence'). See also M. Sassòli and L.M. Olson, 'The Relationship between International Humanitarian and Human Rights Law Where it Matters: Admissible Killing and Internment of Fighters in Non-International Armed Conflict' (2008) 90 *International Review of the Red Cross* 599.

[95] H. Krieger, 'A Conflict of Norms: The Relationship between Humanitarian Law and Human Rights Law in the ICRC Customary Law Study' (2006) 11 *Journal of Conflict and Security Law* 265, at 274; A. Paulus, 'The Protection of Human Rights in Internal Armed Conflict in Europe – Remarks on the Isayeva decisions of the European Court of Human Rights' (2007) *The Uppsala Yearbook of East European Law* 61, at 78.

[96] M. Kashgar, 'The ECtHR's Judgment in Al-Jedda and Its Implications for International Humanitarian Law' (2011) 24 *Journal of International Law of Peace and Armed Conflict* 229.

the guarantees enshrined in Article 5 ECHR, the States are able to avoid breaching the European Convention on Human Rights.[97] Thus, States are free to decide to which body of law they want to adhere to, offering them the possibility to resort to the different standard inherent in humanitarian law. Again, the States' acceptance of the Court's Judgment shows that they agree with it in principle.

3.4. *Principle of distinction*

Human rights bodies have applied the principle of distinction to non-international armed conflicts but have failed to elaborate further on it. The principle of distinction is the basic rule for targeting and requires all parties to the conflict to distinguish between civilians/civilian objects and combatants/military objectives at all times and not to directly attack said objects (Article 48 AP I). It clarifies that the only legitimate purpose of warfare is to weaken and destroy the enemy's military capacity. Accordingly, indiscriminate attacks, meaning attacks which strike military objectives and civilian objects without distinction, are prohibited (Article 51(4) AP I). For internal armed conflicts, Article 13 AP II foresees a rudimentary codification of the principle, only prohibiting direct attacks.

Regarding human rights law, it is settled case law that Article 2 ECHR does not only prohibit intentional killings but also unintended killings.[98] The European Court of Human Rights formulated this prohibition in its cases concerning internal armed conflicts (Chechnya and the Turkish conflict with the Kurds) with an explicit reference to civilians, stating that States are responsible for 'misdirected fire from agents of the State [that] has killed a *civilian*'.[99] This describes a situation in which the principle of distinction applies. But the Court neither mentioned nor elaborated on the principle of distinction even if it labelled the use of free-falling high-explosion aviation bombs with a damage radius exceeding 1,000 metres while civilians were fleeing the city through a supposedly 'safe

[97] H. Krieger, 'Notstand' in: O. Dörr, R. Grote and T. Marauhn (eds.), *EMRK/GG, Konkordanzkommentar zum europäischen und deutschen Grundrechtsschutz*, 2 vols., 2d edn (Tübingen: Mohr Siebeck, 2013), vol. I, at 417–43, para. 15–24.

[98] For example, *McCann et al. v. United Kingdom* (Judgment) Application No. 324, European Court of Human Rights, 27 September 1995, para. 148.

[99] *Ergi v. Turkey* (Judgment) Application No. 66/1997/850/1057, European Court of Human Rights, 28 July 1998, para. 79; *Isayeva v. Russia*, above note 31, para. 176 (emphasis added).

corridor'[100] as 'indiscriminate weapons',[101] a term well established in the context of international armed conflict but unknown to Additional Protocol II. The same holds true for the African Commission on Human and Peoples' Rights which used the term 'civilian' and 'civilian population'[102] but did not elaborate further on this categorization. By applying norms of the law of international armed conflict to a non-international armed conflict, the European Court of Human Rights transfers the higher degree of protection for civilians of Additional Protocol I to situations in which Additional Protocol II applies. Yet it is remarkable that the European Court of Human Rights did not explicitly apply the Geneva Conventions, the Additional Protocols nor even use the term 'armed conflict' in any of the cases concerning internal armed conflicts.[103] By this, the European Court of Human Rights on the one hand avoided the controversy whether all norms of Additional Protocols I are applicable to internal conflicts.[104] On the other hand, it missed an opportunity to clarify its stance on the relationship between both bodies of law and the application of international humanitarian law through human rights bodies. Still, the Court's jurisprudence was felt to provide 'a significant marker for the use of the Convention in the enforcement of international humanitarian law'.[105] This development is of considerable importance for African conflicts which are often of a non-international character since it leads to a merger of the norms of international armed conflicts with those of non-international armed conflicts, providing a higher degree of protection for civilians.

The Goldstone Report found a violation of the principle of distinction by the Palestinians as '[t]he launching of rockets and mortars which

100 *Isayeva v. Russia*, above note 31, para. 200. 101 Ibid. para. 191.

102 *Congo v. Burundi, Rwanda, Uganda*, above note 59, para. 88; *Human Rights Organisation and Centre on Housing Rights and Evictions (COHRE) v. Sudan* (Communications 279/03–296/05), 45th Ordinary Session of the African Commission of Human and People's Rights (13–27 May 2009), paras. 164, 166, 168, 176, 178, 223.

103 Though it did so in *Özkan et al. v. Turkey* (Judgment) Application No. 21689/93, European Court of Human Rights, 6 April 2004, para. 305 and – with an explicit reference to the *Isayeva* cases – in *Al-Skeini et al. v. United Kingdom*, above note 85, para. 164 and *Georgia v. Russia* (Decision) Application No. 38263/08, European Court of Human Rights, 13 December 2011, para. 72.

104 N. Lubell, 'Challenges in Applying Human Rights Law to Armed Conflict' (2005) 87 *International Review of the Red Cross* 737, at 744.

105 A. Reidy, 'The Approach of the European Commission and Court of Human Rights to International Humanitarian law' (1998) 324 *International Review of the Red Cross* 543, at 556 [French translation, the English original is to be found here: www.icrc.org/eng/resources/documents/misc/57jpgg.htm.

cannot be aimed with sufficient precisions at military targets breaches the fundamental principle of distinction'.[106] It was contended that 'the logic of the HRC [Human Rights Council's] Report's point is that a State lacking sophisticated, precision weapons loses its right of self-defense'.[107] This, of course, is not true: first, the question of self-defence is governed by the *ius ad bellum*, not the *ius in bello*. Second, *ius in bello* in fact outlaws certain weaponry (e.g., Article 51(4)(b) AP I). The Goldstone Report thus (re-)enforced the principle of distinction, emphasizing that certain means of warfare are illegal under certain circumstances.

To sum up, while both the European Court of Human Rights and the African Commission on Human and Peoples' Rights avoided elaborating explicitly on the principle of distinction but transferred the higher degree of protection of Additional Protocol I to situations of non-international armed conflict, the Fact Finding Mission has relied on it without adding much to its understanding. Here, some more expertise of humanitarian law is indeed necessary.

3.5. *Principle of proportionality*

The principles of proportionality in both bodies of law differ fundamentally. While the Gaza Fact Finding Mission relied on the excessiveness test (Article 51(5)(b) AP I),[108] the European Court of Human Rights in principle used the strict proportionality test of Article 2 ECHR but added notions of the excessiveness test (Section 3.5.1). Although it seems as if the European Court of Human Rights tried cautiously to incorporate the assessment of humanitarian law into its findings, it failed to arrive at a sound dogmatic way of doing so. In addition, more leeway than the Court offered needs to be given to States (Section 3.5.2).

3.5.1. The proportionality test in the human rights bodies' jurisprudence

The excessiveness test considers whether the collateral damage – and thus not the damage to the target – was excessive in comparison to the military advantage expected (Article 51(5)(b) AP I). It does not apply to combatants, who can be killed as long as they are not *hors de combat*, even if

[106] 'Goldstone Report', above note 53, para. 1747.

[107] N. Rostow, 'The Human Rights Council (Goldstone) Report and International Law' (2010) 40 *Israel Yearbook on Human Rights* 275, at 287.

[108] 'Goldstone Report', above note 53, para. 435.

their capture or wounding would pose no risk whatsoever to the opposing party. In contrast, the strict proportionality test examines whether means could have been employed that would have less violated human rights of either innocent bystanders or the target, while at the same time achieving the same aim. It also applies to fighters and combatants, leading to a duty to capture or wound fighters and combatants but only if the circumstances so permit.[109] This reflects a major difference to international humanitarian law, which does not support such an interpretation.[110] Thus, both tests aim at different objectives – the excessiveness test at prohibiting excessive use of force and the strict proportionality test at minimizing force as far as possible and protecting a different set of persons. However, they share a common nucleus, that is, in principle allowing for the death of a person under certain circumstances.

Article 2 ECHR stipulates that the deprivation of life does not contravene the European Convention on Human Rights if it results from the use of force which is no more than 'absolutely necessary (a) in defence of any person from unlawful violence, (b) to effect an arrest or prevent an escape . . . , or (c) in action lawfully taken for the purpose of quelling a riot or insurrection'. The European Court of Human Rights, in its cases concerning Turkey and Chechnya, only examined the question whether the State's military action was absolutely necessary without referring to the permissible aims. The decisive question for the Court was whether the State took 'all feasible precautions in the choice of means and methods . . . with a view to avoiding and, in any event, to minimising, incidental loss of civilian life'.[111] This phrasing is not the Court's own but

[109] See also W. Abresch, 'A Human Rights Law of Internal Armed Conflict: The European Court of Human Rights in Chechnya' (2005) 16 *European Journal of International Law* 741, at 764–67.

[110] But see J. Pictet, *Development and Principles of International Humanitarian Law* (Dordrecht: Martinus Nijhoff Publishers, 1985), at 75–76. See also the discussion evolving around Section IX of the ICRC Interpretative Guidance on the Notion of Direct Participation in Hostilities, W.H. Parks, 'Part IX of the ICRC "Direct Participation in Hostilities" Study: No Mandate, No Expertise, and Legally Incorrect' (2010) 42 *International Law and Politics* 769.

[111] *Isayeva v. Russia*, above note 31, para. 176; *Ergi v. Turkey*, above note 99, para. 79; *Özkan et al. v. Turkey*, above note 103, para. 297. Outside cases concerning armed conflict the Court used a slightly different wording, *McCann et al. v. United Kingdom*, above note 98, para. 194: '[T]he Court must carefully scrutinise . . . whether the anti-terrorist operation was planned and controlled by the authorities so as to minimise, to the greatest extent possible, recourse to lethal force.' See also F. Sperotto, 'Law in Times of War: The Case of Chechnya' (2008) 8 *Global Jurist*, Issue 2 (Topics), Article 5, www.degruyter.com/view/j/gj.2008.8.2/gj.2008.8.2.1250/gj.2008.8.2.1250.xml?format=INT.

derives from Article 57(2)(a)(ii) AP I. However, the Court used the norm in an inaccurate context: it argued that the action was not '*executed* with the requisite care for the lives of the civilian population',[112] although the duty to take precautions only applies to the planning of the action and not its execution.[113] Its execution is governed by the excessiveness test, which leaves more leeway for States than the duty to take precautions since it does not obligate States to 'minimize' losses. The Court's approach thus leads to a far higher standard than the law of armed conflict demands. Still, in using the language of Additional Protocol I the Court pretends to adhere to the standards of international humanitarian law. Thus, the Court did not find a sound dogmatic approach.[114]

The Goldstone Report, which in contrast to the European Court of Human Rights stayed silent on the issue of strict proportionality and only applied the excessiveness test, emphasized the *ex-ante* view a reasonable commander has to apply.[115] This differs from the usual human rights perspective which is in principle an *ex-post* perspective. However, although the Mission stresses this point, it nevertheless fails to observe it.[116] With regard to the killing of ninety-nine policemen in the Arafat City police headquarters, the Goldstone Report mentioned that the *anticipated* military advantage is of relevance but then did not address the issue of the expected number of civilian casualties.[117] This in part might be due to the non-participation of Israel in the Fact Finding Mission. Yet, whereas human rights treaty bodies can reverse the burden of proof, a fact-finding mission, supposed to find facts, cannot. On a factual basis the Mission displayed a troublesome one-sidedness since it only reversed the burden of proof with regard to Israeli actions.

3.5.2. Critique

While it is regrettable that the Goldstone Report did not once elaborate on the relationship of the two bodies of law, every addition to case law

[112] *Isayeva, Yusupova and Bazayeva v. Russia*, above note 53, para. 199; *Isayeva v. Russia*, above note 31, para. 200 (emphasis added). See also *Ergi v. Turkey*, above note 99, para. 80.

[113] Article 57(1) AP I requires in far more open terms that '[i]n the conduct of military operations, constant care shall be taken to spare the civilian population'.

[114] See also C. Byron, 'A Blurring of the Boundaries: The Application of International Humanitarian Law by Human Rights Bodies' (2007) 47 *Virginia Journal of International Law* 839.

[115] *Prosecutor v. Galić* (Judgment), Case No. IT-98-29-T (5 December 2003), para. 58.

[116] L. R. Blank, 'The Application of IHL in the Goldstone-Report: A Critical Commentary' (2009) 12 *Yearbook of International Humanitarian Law* 347, at 377.

[117] Ibid. 'Goldstone Report', above note 53, para. 437.

concerning the principle of proportionality is welcomed since it is open to interpretation in both bodies of law and even more so in international humanitarian law. The European Court of Human Rights, in turn, can be criticized for not considering the permissible aims as well as for its dogmatically incorrect approach regarding the duty to take precautions. However, the European Court of Human Rights was right in exercising some discretion with regard to the permissible aims regime. This is especially important when taking the notion of collateral damage and thus of military necessity into account. To allow for military necessity, it is also necessary to apply an *ex-post* perspective. Those two modifications of Article 2 ECHR need to be made in order to allow for military necessity. Thus, the Court's adherence to the strict proportionality test is dogmatically correct and in accordance with the principle of humanity.

First, the permissible aims regime of Article 2 ECHR does not in all cases allow for collateral damage, which in principle is legal according to Article 51(5)(b) AP I so long as the damage is not excessive. Still, the Court has applied the concept of collateral damage via the application of the duty to take precautions.[118] While the consideration of the concept of collateral damage is necessary if one does not want to render warfare impossible, the Court should have waived the recourse to the duty to take precautions, because it applied the norm in a wrong context and because the consideration of collateral damage could have been reached by simply not applying the permissible aims regime. Since the Court already misapplied the permissible aims regime, its recourse to the duty to take precautions was not only dogmatically wrong but also unnecessary. In the following, it will be shown that collateral damage is not allowed under the permissible aims regime which thus must be rendered inapplicable: as stipulated in lit. a), the first aim only allows for the killing of a person if the person is the attacker.[119] Thus, although the unintentional killing of a bystander might be justified,[120] collateral damage, which describes

[118] N. Quénivet, 'The Right to Life in International Humanitarian Law and Human Rights Law', in R. Arnold and N. Quénivet (eds.) *International Humanitarian Law and Human Rights Law: Towards a New Merger in International Law* (Boston: Martinus Nijhoff Publishers, 2008), 331–53, at 345–46.

[119] J. A. Frowein and W. Peukert, *Europäische Menschenrechtskonvention. EMRK-Kommentar*, 3d edn (Kehl: Engel, 2009), Article 2, para. 12. See also the German Constitutional Court which decided that shooting down an airplane taken over by terrorists would violate the right to life as long as civilians are on board, Judgment of the First Senate of 15 February 2006, 1 BvR 357/05, https://www.bundesverfassungsgericht.de/SharedDocs/Entscheidungen/EN/2006/02/rs20060215_1bvr035705en.html, para. 116.

[120] *McCann et al. v. United Kingdom*, above note 98, para. 148.

a killing of civilians that is intentional but incidental and might be legal according to humanitarian law, is not covered. Also, the second aim does not allow for collateral damage. The third aim might cover collateral damage but not in all situations. Since both an insurrection and a riot describe situations in which a crowd exerts some degree of violence,[121] the incidental but intentional death of a demonstrator – independent of the question covered by lit. a) whether he poses a threat – seems to be governed by lit. c). However, if one takes the strict proportionality principle into account, which in principle asks for the use of non-lethal force in law enforcement situations,[122] it seems difficult to imagine a situation in which Article 2 ECHR by itself allows for collateral damage. This might be the reason why in not one single case situated in an armed conflict the Court relied on this aim although certain events in occupation situations and internal armed conflicts might under specific circumstances be regarded as riots or insurrections. Still, even if lit. c) covered collateral damage to quell a riot or an insurrection, it cannot apply in an international armed conflict which cannot be classified as either of the two. Thus, even if lit. c) applied in internal armed conflicts, it would not apply in international armed conflicts. Here, the permissible aims regime clearly does not allow for collateral damage.

It might be argued that this result has no practical impact since in international armed conflicts human rights treaty bodies possess no jurisdiction. However, this argument might only be valid with regard to certain situations. Whereas the African Commission on Human and Peoples' Rights has applied human rights in an international armed conflict[123] and the Inter-American Commission on Human Rights applied the American Convention on Human Rights in a case in which a plane was shot down by another plane outside territorial waters,[124] the European Court of Human Rights is far more reluctant to assert its jurisdiction. In its *Banković* Case, in which the situation in question was outside the *espace juridique* and outside an occupation situation, it decided that it lacked jurisdiction.[125]

[121] C. Grabenwarter and K. Pabel, *Europäische Menschenrechtskonvention*, 5th edn (München: Beck, 2012), § 20, para. 15. An insurrection, being the stronger term, is defined as an uprising of parts of the population against the State.

[122] *Güleç v. Turkey* (Judgment) Application No. 21593/93, European Court of Human Rights, 27 July 1998, para. 71; *Simsek et al. Turkey* (Judgment) Application Nos. 35072/97, 37194/97, European Court of Human Rights, 26 July 2005.

[123] *Congo v. Burundi, Rwanda, Uganda*, above note 59.

[124] *Armando Alejandre Jr. et al. v. Republic of Cuba*, above note 81, para. 25.

[125] *Banković et al. v. Belgium et al.*, above note 51.

Still, as the development of the European Court of Human Rights' jurisdiction, especially in its *Al-Skeini* Judgment,[126] and the ample literature on this subject has shown, no clear-cut conclusion can be offered. States will certainly not exercise jurisdiction in every combat situation, which is obviously different from an occupation as far as the authority and control exercised by States are concerned. But it seems to be in line with the understanding of the Court to argue that in a special combat situation, for example, if a territory is not yet occupied but already controlled by an army and fighting recurs or in a situation in which lightly armed combatants are highly outnumbered by a heavily armed army and draw back instead of putting themselves *hors de combat*, a State exercises jurisdiction and is thus bound by human rights.

By allowing for some discretion with regard to the permissible aims and allowing for collateral damage, the Court opens up human rights law to international humanitarian law. This is the first important modification of the human rights standard. In addition, this modification precludes a confusion of the *ius in bello* and *ius ad bellum*: since the permissible aim of Article 2 ECHR speaks of the 'defence of a person from *unlawful* violence', it could be argued that any act of the party that has breached the *ius ad bellum* in principle leads to lawful violence by the adversary due to his right of self-defence. Then, the party that violated the *ius ad bellum* could never justify acts committed in the armed conflict. This would turn *ius in bello*'s rationale upside down which relies on the principle that it is applicable independently of a possible breach of the *ius ad bellum*. Consequently, the presumption that the lines between the *ius in bello* and the *ius ad bellum* might be blurred in the context of human rights law[127] is rebutted.

Second, the Court needs to draw upon an *ex-ante* view of a reasonable commander at the time of the action since an *ex-post* perspective would lead to disregarding the 'fog of war' and the special circumstances a soldier finds himself in since he or his comrades are always in danger of losing their lives.[128] Military necessity demands to take this into account. The

[126] See Milanovic, 'Al-Skeini and Al-Jedda in Strasbourg', above note 84, at 129, and also L. Doswald-Beck, 'The Right to Life in Armed Conflict: Does International Humanitarian Law Provide All the Answers?' (2006) 88 *International Review of the Red Cross* 881, at 893–94.

[127] See Abresch, 'Human Rights Law', above note 109, at 764–67.

[128] This is even true in today's high tech wars, as the death toll of the US and UK armies in Afghanistan and Iraq show. A war without victims on the side of the high-tech armies is only possible without soldiers on the ground.

Court failed to clarify this issue which would have been important since under human rights law in general an *ex-post* perspective applies: the State is responsible for everything it does, even if it acts in good faith. Even the margin of appreciation, which allows for some error of assessment and thus leads to a limited *ex-ante* perspective within its confines,[129] has to be regarded as an exemption from the general *ex-post* rule. In deviation from this rule, an *ex-ante* perspective applies in law enforcement situations. In the *McCann* Judgment, a case in which suspected terrorists were killed by UK soldiers in Gibraltar, the European Court of Human Rights for the first time deviated from the *ex-post* perspective and explained at length that an *ex-ante* perspective was necessary within a law enforcement situation.[130] Still, in these situations the *ex-post* perspective comes into play according to the Court's ruling via a duty to control and organize an operation.[131] Since Article 57 AP I's duty to plan and control refers to the *ex-ante* perspective as well and the *ex-post* perspective of human rights law is contrary to military necessity, it needs to be adjusted. This is the second modification.

Last – and most important – the question arises whether damage may not be 'excessive' or rather not 'absolutely necessary'. If one was to argue in favour of the excessiveness test, human rights law would play no role with regard to killings in combat situations. If one was to argue in favour of a strict proportionality test, a criterion foreign to international humanitarian law would be introduced. To render the discussion even more difficult, the strict proportionality test applies equally to combatants and fighters. Some States and military lawyers are heavily opposed to an interpretation and development of the law of armed conflict that would reduce their capability to wage war.[132] The discussion of

[129] See *Sunday Times* v. *United Kingdom* (Judgment) Series Application No. 6538/74, European Court of Human Rights (26 April 1979), para. 59: '[The margin of appreciation] does not mean that the Court's supervision is limited to ascertaining whether a respondent State exercised its discretion reasonably, carefully and in good faith. Even a Contracting State so acting remains subject to the Court's control as regards the compatibility of its conduct with the engagements it has undertaken under the Convention.'

[130] Ibid. para. 200.

[131] *McCann et al. v. United Kingdom*, above note 98, para. 213. In German law, it comes into play via a duty to compensate the victim of a police action under certain circumstances, § 70(2) Bayerisches Polizeiaufgabengesetz (Bavarian Police Law), Gesetz – und Verordnungsblätter der Länder 1990, at 397.

[132] See, for example, Parks, 'No Mandate, No Expertise, and Legally Incorrect', above note 110, at 786–87 and 796–812; A. Sofaer, 'The Position of the United States on Current Law of War Agreements: Remarks of Judge Abraham D. Sofaer, Legal Advisor, United

Chapter IX ('Restraints on the use of force in direct attack') of the 'Interpretative Guidance on the Notion of Direct Participation in Hostilities', which broke out because the ICRC argued that the concept of military necessity narrowed down the right to kill a soldier, shows how sensitive the issue of the principle of proportionality is. This discussion cannot be recounted here, but it should be emphasized that States ratified the human rights treaties, which apply in times of armed conflict, and promised to follow their rules. In case a conflict between norms exists, one could of course argue that the *lex specialis* rule applies. As has been shown, this is not a convincing road to follow, especially in internal armed conflicts where human rights law clearly is more precise and thus forms *lex specialis*.[133] Therefore, in the author's opinion, the human rights bodies should continue applying the strict proportionality test, even with regard to fighters. It is important to emphasize that in most cases no material differences emanate from the two different tests since unnecessary killings will mostly be excessive as well. With regard to fighters, the strict proportionality test asks of no soldier to endanger his or her life. But – to take an obvious example – soldiers in a heavily armoured vehicle following a single fighter who lost his gun and is running away on an open plain are not allowed to shoot to kill but must capture or wound the fighter. The application of the strict proportionality test is of course context-dependent.

It can been argued that because some armies might be better equipped to capture or wound than others, the resulting imbalance of duties might contribute to the disregard of international humanitarian law altogether since the reciprocity of duties constitutes one of the main factors of norm adherence.[134] But it has to be kept in mind that the duty depends on the abilities of the actors and the circumstances of the situation. Thus, every party to the conflict is able to follow the rules. This might be called a double standard, but the double standard with regard to an army's abilities is already firmly established in the law of armed conflict as can be seen by the frequent use of the word 'feasible' in Additional

States Department of State, January 22, 1987' (1987) 2 *American University Law Review* 460, at 468–69.

133 See above note 95.

134 Cf. M. N. Schmitt, 'Asymmetrical Warfare and International Humanitarian Law', in W. Heintschel von Heinegg and V. Epping (eds.), *International Humanitarian Law Facing New Challenges* (Berlin: Springer, 2007), 11–48, at 12 with regard to disadvantageous rules in general, and at 47 concerning reciprocity; Heintschel von Heinegg, 'Asymmetric Warfare', above note 2, paras. 3, 32.

Protocol I, which is understood as 'that which is practicable or practically possible, taking into account all circumstances at the time'.[135] In this context, it should also be recalled that international humanitarian law acknowledges the prohibition to cause unnecessary suffering,[136] which was labelled a 'cardinal principle' by the ICJ.[137] This prohibition mirrors the strict proportionality principle since unnecessary suffering is understood by the ICJ as 'a harm greater than unavoidable to achieve legitimate military objectives'.[138] Furthermore, applying the strict proportionality test fits into a development dating back to the nineteenth century. The law of armed conflict has always moved from narrowing down military necessity and increasing humanity while accepting that wars exist in this world.[139] Actions that were regarded as perfectly legal in earlier times have become illegal. *Kriegsräson* does not supersede *Kriegsmanier* anymore. For example, Additional Protocol I which had been rebuked especially by the UK and the United States has now widely developed into customary law; the UK has even, albeit with sixteen declarations, finally ratified it.[140] It can be noticed that the arguments of States and military lawyers seem to have remained the same over the course of time: from the nineteenth century until today the most important argument against the development of the principle of humanity was that too many restraints on the States would lead to even more victims.[141] This is as unconvincing today as it was back then.

[135] United Kingdom, Declaration of 12 December 1977, cited according to J. de Preux, 'Article 41', in Y. Sandoz, C. Swinarski and B. Zimmermann (eds.), *Commentary on the Additional Protocols of 8 June 1977 to the Geneva Conventions of 12 August 1949* (Geneva: Martinus Nijhoff Publishers, 1987), at 489.

[136] Article 23(e) Hague Regulations, which prohibits the employment of arms, projectiles, or material calculated to cause unnecessary suffering. Rule 70 of ICRC Customary Law Study; see Paulus, 'Internal Armed Conflict', above note 95, at 70.

[137] *Nuclear Weapons*, above note 48, para. 78.

[138] *Nuclear Weapons*, above note 48, para. 238.

[139] See Schmitt, 'Military Necessity', above note 39, at 796–816.

[140] Ibid. 813.

[141] In 1914, Kaiser Wilhelm II wrote to Emperor Franz Joseph I: 'My soul is torn asunder, but everything must be put to fire and blood. The throats of men and women, children and the aged must be cut and not a tree nor a house left standing. With such methods of terror . . . , the war will finish before two months, while if I use humanitarian methods it may be prolonged for years. Despite all my repugnance I have had to choose the first system.', cited according to C. Bingham, *Men and Affairs* (Sidney: Currawong, 1967), 334. Abraham Sofaer, the Legal Advisor of the United States Department of State stated with regard to the non-ratification of Additional Protocol I by the United States: 'In key respects, Protocol I would undermine humanitarian law and endanger civilians in war.' Sofaer, 'Position of the United States', above note 132, at 463.

By modifying the excessiveness test via the application of the strict proportionality test with regard to minimizing deaths of all persons, military necessity and the special situation of soldiers are being accounted for while enhancing respect for humanity. Thus, the States' mastery of international law is being honoured since they have opted for human rights law to be applicable in times of armed conflict. That they have not provided for context-independent solutions how to resolve a conflict cannot lead to a solution that simply denies human rights protection.

3.6. *Duty to take precautions in attack*

In order to guarantee that the principles of distinction and proportionality are adhered to in practice and to make sure that they become operational, Article 57 AP I prescribes certain precautionary measures that have to be taken during the targeting and decision-making process. In order to take constant care of civilians and civilian objects, those who plan or order an attack inter alia must do everything feasible to verify that no civilian object will be attacked, take all feasible precautions in the choice of means and methods of an attack in order to avoid or at least minimize damage to civilian objects, and give effective advance warning of attacks which might affect the civilian population, unless circumstances do not permit to do so.

The European Court of Human Rights in its discussion of the facts in the Chechen cases took a closer look at the planning and the conduct of the operation. Its method is rather simple: it gathered the various faults and shortcomings of the Russian forces – and summed up that 'the Court does not accept that [the operation] was planned and executed with the requisite care for the lives of the civilian population'.[142] In *Isayeva v. Russia*, the European Court of Human Rights found no evidence for the civilians being warned before the attack.[143] Further, the Court found a violation of the European Convention on Human Rights since 'there is no evidence that at the planning stage of the operation any serious calculations were made about the evacuation of civilians, such as ensuring that they were informed of the attack beforehand, how long such an evacuation would take, what routes evacuees were supposed to take, what kind of precautions were in place to ensure safety, what steps were to be

[142] *Isayeva, Yusupova and Bazayeva v. Russia*, above note 53, para. 199; *Isayeva v. Russia*, above note 31, para. 200.

[143] *Isayeva v. Russia*, above note 31, para. 187.

taken to assist the vulnerable and infirm etc'.[144] In *Isayeva, Yusupova and Bazayeva v. Russia*, the Court observed that a forward air controller was not present at the mission but sat at the control centre, unable to see the road and thus criticized that he was not able to deliver an independent evaluation of the targets.[145] By applying these rules which stem from the law of international armed conflict to non-international armed conflicts, the Court contributed in developing its character as customary law and its content. This is especially important since it is disputed whether the duty to give effective warning in advance forms part of customary law in non-international armed conflicts.[146] The Court thus adds to case law, which is scarce due to the absence of an individual complaints procedure for violations of international humanitarian law. Still, it could have been more precise by naming the norm.

In the Goldstone Report, the content of the duty to give an effective warning was misinterpreted by applying a standard nearly impossible to meet. The Report does not agree that Israel sufficiently fulfilled its obligation by dropping 2,500,000 leaflets, sending 165,000 pre-recorded telephone calls – all within a time period of three weeks – emitting radio broadcasts and so-called roof knocking,[147] that is, the shelling of rooftops of objects soon to be attacked with a non-exploding bomb that merely makes noise. The Goldstone Report did not find the warnings to be effective since they were not precise enough.[148] These legal findings overstretch the duty to give an effective warning, thereby negating military necessity during armed conflict by demanding specific warnings. Only general warnings are required, for example, a warning that certain types of objects will be attacked.[149] Since the aim of this duty is to give civilians

[144] Ibid. para. 189.

[145] *Isayeva, Yusupova and Bazayeva v. Russia*, above note 53, para. 188.

[146] M. Schmitt, C. Garraway and Y. Dinstein, 'The Manual on the Law of Non-International Armed Conflict' (San Remo: International Institute of Humanitarian Law, 2006), reprinted in (2006) 36 *Israel Yearbook on Human Rights* (Special Supplement), claiming to restate the law, names all duties of Article 57 AP I as being customary law in internal armed conflicts except the duty to give effective warning. But see J.-M. Henckaerts and L. Doswald-Beck (eds.), *Customary International Humanitarian Law*, above note 1, Rule 20, at 62–65.

[147] Blank, 'Application of IHL in the Goldstone-Report', above note 116, at 386.

[148] 'Goldstone Report', above note 53, paras. 539–541, 1920.

[149] C. Pilloud and J. de Preux, 'Article 57', in Y. Sandoz, C. Swinarski and B. Zimmermann (eds.), *Commentary on the Additional Protocols of 8 June 1977 to the Geneva Conventions of 12 August 1949* (Geneva: Martinus Nijhoff Publishers, 1987), at 687.

the possibility to protect themselves, rules of war, not being explicitly prohibited, cannot render the warning ineffective as long as they do not 'nullify the proper function of warnings'.[150] Still, even by over-interpreting the prerequisites, the Mission clarifies that certain standards have to be met and in fact – if not in law – every warring party in future will have to be measured against Israel's impressive efforts.

In emphasizing the duty to take precautions, both human rights bodies accentuated that the planning of an operation always has to take the individual into consideration and thus furthered the principle of humanity. But again, no clear line with regard to the relationship of both bodies of law is visible.

3.7. *International humanitarian law as customary law*

The European Court of Human Rights pronounced itself explicitly on the relationship of international humanitarian law and customary law in two cases. In *Kononov v. Latvia*, the European Court of Human Rights' Grand Chamber applied international humanitarian law to World War II on the basis of customary law, deciding that the differentiation between civilians and combatants already applied in 1944.[151] This decision has been greeted with applause,[152] especially since in the Chamber decision the Court denied the customary law character.[153] This shows the importance of a possibility to appeal and the ability of the human rights bodies to learn with regard to the application of the laws of war.

In another case, the European Court of Human Rights apodictically opined on today's customary law character of the Geneva Conventions as well as the Additional Protocols, holding that they constitute customary law.[154] This is a very progressive point of view since not all Geneva norms

[150] Ibid.

[151] *Kononov v. Latvia* (Judgment) Application No. 36376/04, European Court of Human Rights, 17 May 2010, paras. 204, 221. See G. Pinzauti, 'The European Court of Human Rights: Incidental Application of International Criminal Law and Humanitarian Law' (2008) 6 *Journal of International Criminal Justice* 1043.

[152] T. Kleinlein, 'Der EGMR und das Völkerstrafrecht im Rahmen von Artikel 7 EMRK' (2010) 37 *Europäische Grundrechtezeitschrift* 544, at 559.

[153] *Kononov v. Latvia* (Judgment) Application No. 36376/04, European Court of Human Rights, 24 July 2008.

[154] *Varnava et al. v. Turkey* (Judgment) Application Nos. 16064/90 et subsq., European Court of Human Rights, 10 January 2008, para. 130.

are usually considered to be customary law.[155] Thus, the Court overshot the mark. However, this statement, merely an *obiter dictum* not repeated by the Grand Chamber, should not be overestimated. Nevertheless, it shows that the human rights bodies should express themselves on matters of international humanitarian law with great caution.

3.8. *Human rights bodies' failure to apply international humanitarian law*

Human rights bodies have missed opportunities to apply and further the interpretation of the law of armed conflict. For example, Article 55 Hague Regulations foresees that the occupying State shall be regarded only as administrator and usufructuary of forests and agricultural estates. It must safeguard the capital of these properties and administer them in accordance with the rules of usufruct. It is disputed whether this norm applies to natural resources as well.[156] The African Commission on Human and Peoples' Rights in its aforementioned decision evaded this controversial issue, thereby missing a chance to contribute to the interpretation of international humanitarian law, although it found the exploitation of natural resources in the Democratic Republic of the Congo as violating Articles 21 and 22 African Charter (Right to Free Disposal of Wealth and Natural Resources; Right to Economic, Social and Cultural Development).[157] In its decision on the Darfur conflict, the Commission missed another chance to apply international humanitarian law.[158] Although it came to the conclusion that the situation in Darfur constituted an armed conflict[159] and used the terms 'civilians' and 'civilian population',[160] it neither mentioned the Geneva Conventions nor the Additional Protocols and, unlike the European Court of Human Rights, did not use its language except for the mentioned terms. Consequently, it failed to enforce international

155 See, for example, Schmitt, 'Military Necessity', above note 39, at 796, 812; Y. Dinstein, *The Law of Armed Conflict*, 2d edn (Cambridge: Cambridge University Press, 2010), at 10; Henckaerts and Doswald-Beck (eds.), *Customary International Humanitarian Law*, above note 1.

156 N. J. Schrijver, 'Natural Resources, Permanent Sovereignty over', in R. Wolfrum (ed.), *The Max Planck Encyclopedia of Public International Law* (Oxford: Oxford University Press, 2008, online edition, www.mpepil.com), para. 20.

157 *Congo v. Burundi, Rwanda, Uganda*, above note 59, para. 94.

158 *Human Rights Organisation and Centre on Housing Rights and Evictions (COHRE) v. Sudan*, above note 102.

159 Ibid. para. 201.

160 Ibid. paras. 164, 166, 168, 176, 178, 223.

humanitarian law. The absence of any discussion of international humanitarian law might be due to the fact that a non-international armed conflict took place in Darfur. Since it is still disputed which norms of the law of international armed conflict apply via customary law to non-international armed conflicts, the African Commission on Human and Peoples' Rights evaded dealing with this question by sticking to human rights law.

Last, it shall be mentioned that the human rights treaty bodies neither applied international humanitarian law nor human rights law to non-State actors. This is regrettable yet understandable since the bodies possess no jurisdiction with regard to non-State actors.[161] Thus, only remedies against States are possible. This is a major setback for the human rights regime, especially in the African context in which non-State actors are often party to an armed conflict.

The Goldstone Report also failed to apply international humanitarian law in particular with regard to Palestinian actions. To give just one example, the Report remained silent on the prohibition of perfidy (Article 23(b) Hague Regulations; Article 37(1) AP I). Because Palestinian armed groups generally wore civilian clothing and thus pretended to be civilians and have non-combatant status (Article 37(1)(c) AP I), the Report should have condemned them for doing so.[162] By these omissions the Mission undermines its authority, thus rendering its findings less convincing altogether. This has not contributed to the enforcement of the law of armed conflict.

4. Conclusion

Since human rights bodies are obliged to apply international humanitarian law and have done so in the past, its enforcement through these is a

[161] Whether non-State actors are bound by human rights law is disputed, cf. C. Tomuschat, 'The Applicability of Human Rights Law to Insurgent Movements', in H. Fischer et al. (eds.), *Krisensicherung und Humanitärer Schutz – Crisis Management and Humanitarian Protection: Festschrift für Dieter Fleck* (Berlin: Berliner Wissenschafts-Verlag, 2004), at 573–91.

[162] The Report only mentioned perfidy in one paragraph, but only condemned Israel for a breach of Article 37 AP I, 'Goldstone Report', above note 53, para. 1106. See the critique by Blank, 'Application of IHL in the Goldstone-Report', above note 116, at 362–64. See also 'Goldstone Report', above note 53, para. 494. Here, Article 58 AP I was omitted with regard to the use of human shields by the Palestinians.

development that cannot be turned back but will continue and intensify in the future. It serves justice and the protection of human beings and thus serves human rights. Since most authors agree that both bodies of law are applicable at the same time and yet the exact relation of the two bodies of law in case a real conflict emerges cannot be agreed upon, judgments are needed to further develop the law. Human rights treaty bodies play an invaluable role in this clarification process.

Human rights bodies have enriched the discussion, added to case law and by and large contributed to the enforcement of international humanitarian law and to its interpretation and have furthered the notion of humanity while at the same time observing the delicate balance between military necessity and humanity underlying humanitarian law in most cases. There is still room for improvement, for example, with regard to the aspect of applying the principle of proportionality or by giving up the reluctance to only implicitly apply the law of armed conflict without naming the rules in question. But, human rights bodies only started to apply this body of law and they have to find their way. It can already be called an achievement that they have not allowed human rights law to trump the laws of war as was probably hoped for by human rights activists on the other side of the spectrum trying to make war impossible by what is entitled 'lawfare'.[163] It is also important that they build case law concerning armed conflicts, which is scarce due to the absence of an individual complaints procedure for violations of international humanitarian law. To live up to this expectation, human rights bodies need yet more expertise.

By far the biggest achievement is that the principle of humanity is promoted on a substantive law level as well as on the institutional level. This has happened on the level of substantive law, for example, by calling for the military to minimize incidental loss of civilian life and by transferring rules applicable in international armed conflicts to non-international armed conflicts. On the institutional level, human rights bodies have furthered international humanitarian law since they subject international humanitarian law to judicial scrutiny and thus increase the pressure on States to comply with it. The human rights bodies' jurisprudence thus has the potential 'to drive military reform and improvement at an institutional level'.[164]

[163] See W. Schabas, 'Gaza, Goldstone, and Lawfare' (2010) 43 *Case Western Reserve Journal of International Law* 307.

[164] See Abresch, 'Human Rights Law', above note 109, at 764.

With regard to the relationship of the two bodies of law, the human rights treaty bodies have yet to find a coherent approach. The field of parallel application is still not fully explored. Due to the difficulties of reconciling two bodies of law, which have a different purpose, this will take some time and case law.

13

Comment – enforcement of international humanitarian law through the human rights organs of the African Union

FAUSTIN ZACHARIE NTOUBANDI

1. Introduction

One of the main propositions developed in the present chapter is that human rights bodies are capable of enforcing international humanitarian law.[1] The strongest argument usually raised in justification of such a claim is that international human rights law and international humanitarian law are two bodies of law that are closely connected. In effect, they 'share a "common nucleus of non-derogable rights and a common purpose of protecting human life and dignity"', which result in 'a substantial overlap in [their] application'.[2]

The question of the relationship between human rights law and international humanitarian law is more likely to arise in the context of armed conflict (and of belligerent occupation of foreign territory) to which the latter applies as *lex specialis*.[3] However, in carrying out their mandate, human rights bodies have developed a practice which consists in invoking international humanitarian law in the interpretation of human rights instruments.

In the paragraphs below, I will first consider whether the African Union's human rights bodies have followed the trend that consists in

[1] See contribution by D. Steiger, 'Enforcing International Humanitarian Law through Human Rights Bodies', Chapter 12 in this volume, at 263–99.

[2] D. Chindler, 'The International Committee of the Red Cross and Human Rights' (1979) 208 *International Review of the Red Cross* 3, at 9.

[3] In its jurisprudence, the International Court of Justice has clearly stated that in times of armed conflict, international humanitarian law is *lex specialis* vis-à-vis international human rights law; see in this respect *Legality of the Threat or Use of Nuclear Weapons* (Advisory Opinion) [1996] ICJ Reports 226, para. 25; also *Legal Consequences of the Construction of a Wall in the Palestinian Occupied Territories* (Advisory Opinion) [2004] ICJ Reports 136, para. 105.

incidentally enforcing international humanitarian law while discharging their human rights functions (Section 1). Then I will examine, briefly, a few difficulties inherent in the enforcement of international humanitarian law by the African Union's human rights organs (Section 2), before concluding with a short personal note on a more appropriate approach which the competent African Union organs may adopt in addressing issues that concern international humanitarian law.

2. International humanitarian law and the mandate of the African Union's human rights bodies

In the African Union's human rights architecture, two specific organs are envisaged to promote and enforce the rights and freedoms contained in the African Charter on Human and Peoples' Rights (African Charter);[4] these are the African Commission on Human and Peoples' Rights and the African Court of Justice and Human Rights.[5]

2.1. *The mission of the African Union human rights bodies*

2.1.1. The Commission

The Commission was initially established by Article 30 of the African Charter as the sole organ competent to enforce the rights and freedoms protected under the Charter. It has a threefold mandate, namely, a protective mandate, a promotional mandate and an interpretive mandate.[6]

Discharging a protective function requires the Commission to consider complaints and communications brought against States parties to the African Charter by individuals, non-governmental organizations or other States alleging violations of the Charter's rights. Under its promotional mandate, the Commission is called upon to disseminate the African Charter and sensitize the general public for human rights issues in an effort to enhance respect and recognition of the rights and freedoms protected by the Charter.[7] Dissemination may be done through the

[4] Banjul, 27 June 1981, in force 21 October 1986, OAU Doc. CAB/LEG/67/3 rev.5; (1982) 21 I.L.M. 58.

[5] For more details on the establishment of the Court, see, for example, Z. F. Ntoubandi, 'The African Court of Justice and Human Rights' (2009) 2 *Zeitschrift der Gesellschaft für afrikanisches Recht* 197.

[6] Article 45(1), (2) and (3) of the African Charter.

[7] M. du Plessis, 'A Court Not Found' (2007) 7 *African Human Rights Law Journal* 522, at 529–30.

organization of seminars, symposia and conferences in order to discuss human and peoples' rights issues; through the formulation of principles and rules aimed at solving legal problems related to human and peoples' rights and freedoms; and through cooperation with African and international institutions concerned with the promotion and protection of human rights.[8] Finally, the interpretive mandate of the Commission consists in giving sense, meaning and clarity to the provisions of the African Charter. In carrying out this latter mandate, the Commission may, in accordance with African Charter Articles 60 and 61, draw inspiration from or take into consideration other relevant areas of international law, including international humanitarian law.

An additional function is assigned to the Commission in a more general term and consists in performing 'any other tasks which may be entrusted to it by the Assembly of Heads of State and Government'.[9] The wording of this provision is broad enough to permit the Assembly of Heads of State and Government to empower the Commission to determine whether any conduct engaged in by an African State party to an armed conflict was in contradiction to the spirit of the African Charter.

2.1.2. The African Court of Justice and Human Rights

The African Court of Justice and Human Rights shall become the second organ of the African Union competent to enforce the African Charter. This organ will eventually result from a merger between the African Court of Justice and the African Court on Human and Peoples' Rights.[10] The Court will be the main judicial organ of the African Union.[11] It will be divided into two sections: the General Affairs Section and the Human Rights Section.[12] The latter shall hear cases of human rights violations, whereas the former shall have jurisdiction over all legal disputes not of a human rights character submitted to it under Article 28 of the Court's Statute.[13]

[8] Article 45(1)(a), (b) and (c) of the African Charter.

[9] Article 45(4) of the African Charter.

[10] See Article 2 of the Protocol on the Statute of the African Court of Justice and Human Rights, Addis Ababa, 1 July 2008 (not yet in force), www.au.int/en/treaties.

[11] Article 2(1) of the Statute of the Court as annexed to the Protocol on the Statute of the African Court of Justice and Human Rights.

[12] Article 16 of the Statute of the Court.

[13] Such disputes relate, inter alia, to the interpretation and application of the Constitutive Act of the African Union; the interpretation, application or validity of other Union Treaties and all subsidiary legal instruments adopted within the framework of the Union or the Organization of African Unity; any question of international law; all acts, decisions,

The Human Rights Section of the Court will have a contentious as well as an advisory jurisdiction. The contentious jurisdiction of the Court is established pursuant to Article 17(2) of the Statute of the Court, which provides that '[t]he Human Rights Section shall be competent to hear all cases relating to human and/or peoples' rights'. This provision is reinforced by Article 28, which specifies that:

> The Court shall have jurisdiction over all cases and all legal disputes submitted to it in accordance with the present Statute which relate [inter alia] to: . . . c) the interpretation and the application of the African Charter, the Charter on the Rights and Welfare of the Child, the Protocol to the African Charter on Human and Peoples' Rights on the Rights of Women in Africa, or any other legal instrument relating to human rights, ratified by the States Parties concerned; [and] d) any question of international law . . .

Moreover, Article 53 of the same document grants the Human Rights Section of the Court an advisory power. According to this Article, '[t]he Court may give an advisory opinion on any legal question at the request of the Assembly, the Parliament, the Executive Council, the Peace and Security Council, the Economic, Social and Cultural Council (ECOSOCC), the Financial Institutions or any other organ of the Union as may be authorized by the Assembly', providing that the subject matter of the advisory request is not being dealt with by the African Commission or the African Committee of Experts.[14]

It emerges from the foregoing account that the African Charter and the Protocol on the Statute of the Court establish the Commission and the Court as two human rights organs whose primary mandate is to enforce the provisions of the African Charter as well as other relevant human rights instruments adopted within the auspices of the African Union.[15] In principle, they will have no explicit mandate to determine the compatibility of the conduct of member States of the African Union with international humanitarian law instruments. However, certain provisions of the African Charter and of the Statute of the Court may be interpreted as implicitly permitting the Commission and the Court to make inroads into international humanitarian law in the fulfilment of their human rights mandate, at least in the context of non-international armed conflicts.

regulations and directives of the organs of the Union; all matters specifically provided for in any other agreements that States parties may conclude among themselves, or with the Union and which confer jurisdiction on the Court; etc.

[14] Paras. (1) and (3). [15] As well as the Organization of African Unity, its predecessor.

As will be demonstrated below, the Commission and the African Court on Human and Peoples' Rights[16] have not hesitated, in their practice, to make pronouncements concerning violations by States parties to the African Charter of the applicable rules and principles of international humanitarian law in situations of armed conflict.

2.2. *Enforcing international humanitarian law through the practice of the African Union human rights organs*

2.2.1. Practice of the Commission

As indicated in the previous subsection, the Commission may perform, in addition to its human rights functions, 'any other tasks which may be entrusted to it by the Assembly of Heads of State and Government'.[17] Such tasks may include investigating allegations of gross violations of human rights committed in the course of armed conflicts, which would ordinarily fall within the purview of international humanitarian law.[18] In addition, according to Articles 60 and 61 of the African Charter, the Commission may draw inspiration from, or consider, other areas of international law in carrying out its mandate. In two of its communications and in at least one of its resolutions, the Commission has relied on these two provisions to reaffirm its authority to address issues of human rights violations committed in the context of armed conflict.

The first communication[19] in this regard was brought by the *Commission nationale des droits de l'homme et des libertés* against Chad for serious violations of human rights committed in Chad by the agents of that State. Such alleged violations included the harassment of journalists, arbitrary arrests and detention of persons, killings, disappearances, inhuman treatment of prisoners and torture. In making its findings against Chad, the Commission stated that '[t]he African Charter, unlike other human rights instruments, does not allow for States Parties to derogate from their treaty obligations during emergency situations. Thus, even a civil war . . . cannot be used as an excuse by the State for violating or permitting violations of rights in the African Charter'.[20]

[16] It shall be noted that this Court will remain competent to hear human rights petitions until the African Court of Justice and Human Rights becomes operational.

[17] Article 45(4) African Charter.

[18] At least insofar as the maxim *lex specialis derogat legi generali* is applied strictly.

[19] *Commission Nationale des Droits de l'Homme et des Libertés v. Chad* (Communication 74/92, Judgment), 18th Ordinary Session, October 1995.

[20] Ibid. para. 21.

This communication actually reiterates the continued application of the African Charter in armed conflict situations, due to the non-existence of a derogatory clause in the text of the Charter.

The second communication is an inter-State communication,[21] which raised issues of human rights violations committed in the territory of the Democratic Republic of the Congo (DRC) by foreign armed forces. In this communication, the DRC accused Burundi, Rwanda and Uganda of grave and massive violations of human and peoples' rights committed in its eastern provinces by their respective armed forces and by rebel forces under their respective control. Such violations included the mass killing of the civilian population, including women and children, sexual crimes, forced disappearances, deportations, looting and pillage of the riches of the DRC.

The Commission recognized that the criminal activities of the rebels and armed forces of Burundi, Rwanda and Uganda carried out within the territories of the DRC did not only fall 'within the province of humanitarian law, but also within the mandate of the Commission' pursuant to the combined effect of Articles 60 and 61 of the African Charter.[22] The Commission explicitly indicated that these two provisions enable it to draw inspiration from international human rights law and other general or special international conventions laying down general principles, as well as legal precedents and doctrine recognized by African States. It went on to argue that by virtue of Articles 60 and 61, the four Geneva Conventions of 1949 and their two Additional Protocols of 1977 constitute part of the general principles of law recognized by African States, which may be taken into consideration in determining cases before it.[23] However, the Commission did not go so far as to interpret the relevant provisions of the Geneva Conventions and their Additional Protocols and to 'indicate the appropriate measures to punish the authors of the war crimes or crimes against humanity, as the case may be, and the creation of an ad hoc tribunal to try the crimes committed against the Democratic Republic of Congo . . . in collaboration with the United Nations',[24] as the DRC had requested.

It is remarkable that the Commission did not elaborate further on the relation between international humanitarian law, which constitutes *lex specialis* in the present case and human rights law as incorporated

[21] *DRC v. Burundi, Rwanda and Uganda* (Communication 227/99, Judgment), 33rd Ordinary Session, May 2003.

[22] Ibid. para. 64. [23] Ibid. paras. 70 and 78. [24] Ibid. para. 11(f).

in the African Charter. Noting that both branches of law apply in the context of armed conflict, it would perhaps have been appropriate for the Commission to delimit the scope of the application of the Charter's rights and freedoms within such a context. This was rightly done, for instance, by the International Court of Justice in its Advisory Opinion in the *Nuclear Weapons* Case,[25] where it examined the protection of the right to life under the International Covenant on Civil and Political Rights and under international humanitarian law and noted that:

> [T]he protection of the International Covenant on Civil and Political Rights does not cease in times of war, . . . whereby certain provisions may be derogated from in a time of national emergency. Respect for the right to life is not, however, such a provision. In principle, the right not arbitrarily to be deprived of one's life applies also in hostilities. The test of what is an arbitrary deprivation of life, however, then falls to be determined by the applicable *lex specialis*, namely, the law applicable in armed conflict which is designed to regulate the conduct of hostilities. Thus, whether a particular loss of life, through the use of a certain weapon in warfare, is to be considered an arbitrary deprivation of life contrary to Article 6 of the Covenant, can only be decided by reference to the law applicable in armed conflict and not deduced from the terms of the Covenant itself.[26]

In a subsequent opinion,[27] the International Court of Justice stated that '[a]s regards the relationship between international humanitarian law and human rights law, there are . . . three possible situations: some rights may be exclusively matters of international humanitarian law, others may be exclusively matters of human rights law; yet others may be matters of both these branches of law'.[28]

Nonetheless, the interpretative position adopted above by the Commission seems to indicate that in the African human rights context, all rights and freedoms are matters of both international humanitarian law and human rights law.

Likewise, in its Resolution on the Situation of Human Rights in the Darfur Region in Sudan, the Commission expressed its deep concern about the

> continuing grave *violations of human rights and international humanitarian law* in Darfur committed by the parties to the conflict, in particular the continued depopulation of vast areas in the region of their indigenous owners, threats of violence, intimidation and assault against UN agencies

[25] See above note 3. [26] *Nuclear Weapons*, above note 3, para. 25.

[27] *Legal Consequences of the Construction of a Wall*, above note 3. [28] Ibid. para. 106.

> and humanitarian organizations, the targeting and killing of [African Union] troops in Darfur, and the killing and abduction of staff members of national and international humanitarian organizations.[29]

The Commission finally concluded by calling upon the government of Sudan to immediately cease violations of human and peoples' rights.

In the foregoing cases, the Commission seems to have adopted the view that in the context of armed conflicts every act committed in violation of international humanitarian law would also constitute a violation of the African Charter. Such an approach tends to ignore international humanitarian law as the applicable *lex specialis* in situations of armed conflict. Its consequence is to blur the line between human rights law and international humanitarian law. This position is in sharp contradiction with what prevails in the Inter-American system, where the Inter-American Court and Commission must 'deduce the applicable human rights standard by reference to international humanitarian law as the applicable *lex specialis* and take the relevant provisions of the Geneva Conventions into consideration as elements for the interpretation of the American Convention'.[30] It also departs from the line of interpretation adopted by the International Court of Justice in the *Nuclear Weapons* and the *Wall* Advisory Opinions.

Nevertheless, what is clear is that the combination of Articles 60 and 61 of the African Charter gives a broad indication of the status of international humanitarian law in the African human rights architecture. International humanitarian law serves as an interpretive tool for determining violations of specific provisions of the African Charter. In addition, Article 45(4) of the Charter opens up an avenue to the Assembly of Heads of State and Government to entrust the Commission with an international humanitarian law task. Such a task may consist, as the Darfur case above reveals, in ordering a State party to the African Charter to cease violations of human rights law and international humanitarian law. However, the Commission tends to ignore the guidelines set by Articles 60 and 61 of the Charter by imprudently qualifying any human rights violation occurring in the context of armed conflict as a violation of both the African Charter and international humanitarian law without further ado. What may perhaps explain such a stance is the absence of a derogatory clause in the African Charter, as the Commission has clearly indicated in Communication 74/92.

[29] See Annex III of its 19th Activity Report at 33 (emphasis added).

[30] *Bámaca Velásquez v. Guatemala*, Inter-American Court of Human Rights Series C No 70 (25 November 2000), at 321.

2.2.2. The Court's practice

As stated earlier on, the Human Rights Section of the African Court of Justice and Human Rights shall have contentious jurisdiction over all cases and legal disputes which relate, inter alia, to human rights issues and to any question of international law. In addition, its advisory jurisdiction covers any legal question which it might be requested to address.

To date, the only case brought before the African Court on Human and Peoples' Rights[31] which also raises questions of international humanitarian law relates to the violent repression of peaceful demonstrations in Libya on 16 February 2011. In this case,[32] the Commission accused the Libyan authorities of engaging in conduct which amounts to serious and massive violations of human rights guaranteed under the African Charter, notably serious violations of the right to life and to the integrity of the person, freedom of expression, demonstration and assembly.[33] The Court found that the alleged violations occurred and were still taking place. Consequently, it ordered provisional measures requesting the Libyan authorities to refrain from any further action in conflict with the African Charter.

Although no doubt existed concerning the international humanitarian law character of a number of violations identified by the Court,[34] it nevertheless preferred to only apply the African Charter, thus missing a good opportunity to elaborate further on the status of international humanitarian law in the African human rights architecture. The Court's only reference to international humanitarian law was noting that organizations such as the Peace and Security Council of the African Union and the UN Security Council have considered that the attacks perpetrated by the Libyan forces against the civilian population were committed 'in violation of human rights and International Humanitarian Law' and 'may amount to crimes against humanity'.[35] It did not find it necessary to distinguish further between the acts constituting violations of the African Charter and those amounting to violations of international humanitarian

[31] As mentioned previously, this Court will address cases of human rights violations until the Protocol that established the African Court of Justice and Human Rights enters into force and the Court becomes operational.

[32] *African Commission on Human and Peoples' Rights v. Great Socialist People's Libyan Arab Jamahiriya* (Application No. 004/2011, Order for Provisional Measures), 25 March 2011.

[33] Ibid. para. 2.

[34] See in this respect the wording of UNSC Resolutions 1970 (26 February 2011) and 1973 (17 March 2011).

[35] See *African Commission on Human and Peoples' Rights v. Libya*, above note 32, para. 21.

law. What the Court actually did is simply to follow in the Commission's footsteps in invoking human rights law and international humanitarian law in situations of armed conflict without further ado.

In sum, Articles 60, 61 and 45(4) of the African Charter as well as Articles 53 and 28(d) of the Statute of the African Court of Justice and Human Rights provide the Commission and the Court, respectively, with a legal basis to have recourse to international humanitarian law in cases of human rights violations committed in the context of internal conflicts in Africa. However, the power of these human rights organs to actually enforce international humanitarian law still needs to be clearly elaborated and delimited.

3. Difficulties inherent in the enforcement of international humanitarian law by the human rights organs of the African Union

3.1. Rejection of the practice of the International Criminal Court

Today, there is a growing reluctance in Africa to see Africa's most notorious criminals being transferred to the headquarters of the International Criminal Court (ICC) in The Hague to be prosecuted for violations of international humanitarian law committed in the context of internal conflicts. Most Africans have the feeling that, among the most notorious criminals roaming our planet, the ICC only targets Africans, thus making this institution an instrument used by Western nations to dominate weaker African countries.[36]

In reaction to the ICC's practice concentrating only on notorious African criminals, various institutions of the African Union have started to adopt measures intended to progressively reduce the influence of the ICC on the continent. Thus, in October 2008, the Commission issued a report recommending, inter alia, the creation of a special tribunal for Kenya to investigate, prosecute and try those bearing the greatest responsibility for crimes committed during the 2007 general elections in Kenya; such crimes include crimes against humanity.[37] It may be worthwhile to

[36] Up to now, all alleged criminals indicted by the ICC are Africans; the most recent case is the speedy and secret indictment and transfer to The Hague on 29 November 2011 of the former president of Ivory Coast, Mr. Laurent Gbagbo, on charges of crimes against humanity; many aspects of his indictment and transfer are arguably in contradiction with the applicable procedural rules of the ICC.

[37] See 'Report of the Commission of Inquiry into Post-Election Violence', 15 October 2008, kenyastockholm.files.wordpress.com/2008/10/the-waki-report.pdf.

note that the rationale behind establishing a special tribunal for Kenya was to prevent the ICC from considering the case.

One of the most unambiguous condemnations of the ICC's attitude towards African criminals came from Jean Ping, President of the African Union Commission, after the ICC indicted Muammar Kadhafi for alleged crimes against humanity in connection with the most recent Libyan revolution. He stated in this regard that '[nous] sommes contre la manière dont la CPI fonctionne' [We are against the way the ICC works]. Luis Moreno Ocampo, Prosecutor at the ICC 'ne condamne que des Africains, il ne juge que des Africains. En Afghanistan, au Pakistan, à Gaza, en Tchétchénie, au Sri Lanka . . . il n'y a qu'en Afrique qu'il y a des problèmes ? C'est la question qu'on se pose' [only condemns Africans, he only tries Africans. In Afghanistan, Pakistan, Gaza, Chechnya, Sri Lanka . . . is it only in Africa that problems exist? That is the question!]. He went on to declare that 'Nous sommes en train de créer une cour criminelle en Afrique. Il ne reste plus que la ratification des chefs d'Etat et la Cour criminelle sera opérationnelle' [We are establishing a criminal court in Africa. All that fails for the criminal court to be operational is ratification by the Heads of State].[38]

This apprehension towards the practice of the ICC may lead either to a total mistrust of international humanitarian law as implemented by The Hague criminal forums, or to its appropriation and enforcement by the African Union organs in order to avoid sending more Africans to The Hague. In the latter case, and in line with the suggestion Jean Ping made above, the jurisdiction of the African Court of Justice and Human Rights may well be extended by the creation of a section with jurisdiction over matters of international humanitarian law. Such a section could well coexist with the General Affairs and the Human Rights Sections of the African Court of Justice and Human Rights.

3.2. *Insufficient qualification of judges*

The lack of adequate qualification in international humanitarian law questions may also constitute an impediment to an efficient enforcement of international humanitarian law by the African Union's human rights organs. In effect, most of the commissioners and judges elected for the Commission or the Human Rights Section of the African Court of Justice

[38] A. Hart, 'Cour pénale internationale: l'Afrique entre en résistance', www.camerounlink.net/fr/news.php.

and Human Rights are not required to have competence in international humanitarian law. Thus, Article 31 of the African Charter requires members of the Commission to have 'competence in matters of human and peoples' rights', while Article 4 of the Statute of the African Court of Justice and Human Rights provides for the qualification of judges in the following manner:

> The Court shall be composed of impartial and independent judges elected from among persons of high moral character, who possess the qualifications required in their respective countries for appointment to the highest judicial offices, or are juris-consults of recognized competence and experience in international law and/or, human rights law.

Moreover, each candidate for election to the Human Rights Section of the Court will be required to prove his/her 'recognized competence and experience in Human Rights law'.[39]

It is therefore clear from the letter of the African Charter and the Statute of the African Court of Justice and Human Rights that the officials elected for the position of commissioner or judge will likely be more qualified in matters of human rights law and general international law than in international humanitarian law matters. To remedy this situation, it is perhaps time that the African Union takes adequate measures to ensure that a certain number of its commissioners and judges possess the necessary knowledge and expertise in the specific field of international humanitarian law. Such measures would constitute the only guarantee for an efficient incorporation and implementation of international humanitarian law within the African Union system of human rights protection. They may also serve as a prelude to the creation of a 'Humanitarian Law Section' of the African Court of Justice and Human Rights.

4. Conclusion

What one can gather from the foregoing analysis is that the enforcement of international humanitarian law is not expressly envisaged in the African Charter and in the Statute of the African Court of Justice and Human Rights. Therefore, the Commission and the African Court on Human and Peoples' Rights have avoided any direct interpretation of the specific provisions of the Geneva Conventions and their Additional Protocols. It is also true that the African Charter and the Statute of the

[39] Article 6(1)(ii) of the Statute of the African Court of Justice and Human Rights.

African Court of Justice and Human Rights do not expressly prohibit the Commission and the Court from invoking international humanitarian law in the interpretation of the relevant human rights instruments of the African Union. This possibility is even prescribed by a number of provisions which clearly require an interpretation that takes into consideration other areas of international law. International humanitarian law is part of such law. The African human rights bodies are therefore permitted to resort to international humanitarian law in order to fill in gaps existing in the African Charter and in other African Union human rights instruments, as the Commission's decision in the DRC case reveals.

The few cases in which the Commission and the African Court on Human and Peoples' Rights have hitherto invoked international humanitarian law relate to situations of non-international armed conflicts to which international humanitarian law ordinarily applies as *lex specialis*, and to which human rights law applies only partially. Since such conflicts are not adequately regulated under current international law, the Commission and the Court tend to use international humanitarian law in such a context either as an interpretive tool for the relevant Charter's rights and freedoms or as a source of normative human rights standards for the protection of persons. The absence of a derogation clause in the African Charter clearly strengthens this contention. In this way, one may argue that in the context of non-international armed conflicts, the African Union's human rights bodies have transformed the maxim *lex specialis derogat legi generali* into *legi generali* (in this case human rights law) *completat lex specialis* (the part of international humanitarian law applicable to non-international armed conflicts). This approach contributes to filling in the gaps inherent in both the African human rights law system and the part of international humanitarian law applicable to non-international armed conflicts.

14

The UN Security Council's special compliance systems – the regime of children and armed conflict

REGINA KLOSTERMANN

1. The regime of children and armed conflict

Different rules of international humanitarian law seek to protect children during armed conflict. International human rights treaties such as the Convention on the Rights of the Child and its Optional Protocols also entail many provisions on children affected by war. Nevertheless, many parties to armed conflicts around the world violate children's rights, especially during war. Children are the most vulnerable group of society affected by armed conflict. A considerable number are directly integrated into States' armed forces or non-State armed groups, and even without direct integration, their rights are affected. More than ever, during an armed conflict, children are exposed to risks of death, injury, permanent disability, trauma and other forms of serious human rights violations, such as ill-treatment and torture, rape and other forms of sexual violence.[1] This chapter discusses the involvement of the Security Council in securing compliance with those international norms dealing with children and armed conflict.

The UN started directly dealing with the issue of children affected by armed conflict in the mid-1990s due to the increasing involvement and recruiting of children in non-international armed conflicts around the world. Since 1999, the Security Council's resolutions, statements and debates on children and armed conflict have generated significant incentives and pressure to hold parties accountable for violations of child rights, to induce work by diverse entities to protect and assist children in

[1] L. Withers, 'Child-Soldiers: How to Engage in Dialogue with Non State Armed Groups', in C. Bellamy and J. Zermatten (eds.), *Realizing the Rights of the Child* (Zurich: rüffer & rub, 2007), 227–333, at 228–29.

conflict, and to begin to redress impunity.[2] Recognizing the special protection children need, the Security Council tried to enhance compliance with the relevant norms and standards deriving from both international humanitarian law and human rights law by installing a detailed system of action and tools to respond to infringements of international obligations. It has identified six grave violations, which affect children most in armed conflict: killing and maiming of children, recruitment or use of child soldiers, rape and other forms of sexual violence, abduction of children, attacks against schools and hospitals and denials of humanitarian access. These build the foundation of the Security Council's interference and are the relevant standards the Security Council seeks compliance with. The international attention paid to this subject led to considerable results – at least regarding the recruitment of child soldiers. Many armed forces and armed groups have entered into action plans in collaboration with the UN and released children from their ranks. In those cases, the involvement of the Security Council surely enhanced compliance with international norms and standards. On the other hand, there are still parties to armed conflicts which have not been convinced or impressed by the action taken by the Security Council. Thus, questions remain whether the installed mechanism is apt to enhance compliance by those actors as well.

This chapter attempts to analyse whether the Security Council is generally competent to install a mechanism for enhancing compliance with existing norms and standards and whether the system established by the Security Council is effective. The term 'effective' means to produce the intended or expected result. In other words, the system established by the Security Council can be regarded as effective if it achieves its stated aim of protecting children. One way to measure effectiveness is whether it is generally capable of enhancing compliance. Parties concerned comply for various reasons with norms and standards. In this regard, political theorists traditionally isolate three ideal-type motivations, namely coercion, self-interest and legitimacy.[3] This chapter will demonstrate that the system established by the Security Council is generally capable of enhancing compliance with the relevant norms from a theoretical point of view as it meets those three criteria identified. However, as the established system

[2] UNICEF, 'Machel Study, 10-Year Strategic Review: Children and Conflict in a Changing World' (April 2009), at 46, www.unicef.org/publications/files/Machel_Study_10_Year_Strategic_Review_EN_030909.pdf.

[3] I. Hurd, 'Legitimacy and Authority in International Politics' (1999) 53 *International Organizations* 379.

also generates some legitimacy restraints, it does not reach its full potential and does not adduce the capacities it could to enhance compliance.

2. The involvement of the Security Council on children and armed conflict

In the beginning of the 1990s, the international community became aware of an increasing number of child recruitment during non-international armed conflicts around the world. As of 1993, the subject of children affected by armed conflict has been brought to the attention of the UN. First, the UN's involvement led to the appointment of a Special Representative of the Secretary-General who was and still is mainly responsible for raising awareness. Since 1998, the Security Council became involved. It had realized that the impact of armed conflict on children was a significant issue for peace and security. Many non-international armed conflicts had led to high civilian casualties, especially among women and children, and children were being used as an instrument of war both by national armies and by rebel groups.[4] It realized that child soldiers, displaced families and communities as well as refugee flows across boarders hindered long-term regional and international stability.[5] Since 1999, the Security Council has been actively seized with this issue and adopted eight resolutions concerning children and armed conflict.[6] Significant progress has been achieved as the resolutions have changed from addressing children's needs for protection to urging member States and civil society to actively involve themselves in protecting children.[7] Although the early resolutions contained mainly generic statements, the Security Council by now has established a whole system concerning children and armed conflict and is still broadening its involvement. The first key development was the installation of a 'list of shame', generated by the Secretary-General, naming the parties violating child rights. In a second step, the Security

[4] Security Council Report, 'Cross-Cutting Report: Children and Armed Conflict' (4 February 2008), para. 3, www.securitycouncilreport.org/ cross-cutting-report/lookup-c-glKWLeMTIsG-b-3877213.php.

[5] Security Council Report, 'Profile: Children and Armed Conflict' (12 July 2006), www.iilj.org/courses/documents/ChildrenandArmedConflict12July2006-SecurityCouncilReport.pdf.

[6] UNSC Resolution 1261 (25 August 1999); UNSC Resolution 1314 (11 August 2000); UNSC Resolution 1379 (20 November 2001); UNSC Resolution 1460 (30 January 2003); UNSC Resolution 1539 (22 April 2004); UNSC Resolution 1612 (26 July 2005); UNSC Resolution 1882 (4 August 2009); UNSC Resolution 1998 (12 July 2011).

[7] C. True-Frost, 'The Security Council and Norm Consumption' (2007) 40 *New York University Journal of International Law and Politics* 115, at 168.

Council installed a Working Group on Children and Armed Conflict and a monitoring and reporting mechanism. In the following, the development of the whole system will be demonstrated.

In 1993, pursuant to a recommendation of the Committee on the Rights of the Child, the General Assembly adopted Resolution 48/157[8] requesting the Secretary-General to appoint an expert to undertake a comprehensive study on the impact of armed conflict on children. This can be seen as the starting point of the UN's involvement and especially of the Security Council's aim to improve the protection of war-affected children. Following the General Assembly's resolution, Graca Machel was appointed and submitted a report entitled 'Impact of Armed Conflict on Children'[9] in 1996. In her study, she demonstrated the centrality of the issue of children affected by armed conflict to international human rights, peace and security.[10] In the aftermath of this study, the General Assembly adopted a resolution recommending the Secretary-General to appoint a Special Representative of the Secretary-General on Children and Armed Conflict. Olara Otunnu was appointed as the first Special Representative in 1997; the issue of children and armed conflict had finally arrived on the regular agenda of the Secretariat. The Special Representative of the Secretary-General on Children and Armed Conflict and her office work in close collaboration with the Secretary-General. The Special Representative of the Secretary-General on Children and Armed Conflict is an important actor in the implementation process and her office plays a central role in smoothing the flow of information between UN bodies on the ground and the headquarters.[11]

The issue of children affected by armed conflict has been formally placed on the agenda of the Security Council since 1998. Resolution 1261 of 25 August 1999[12] was the first thematic resolution dealing with children and armed conflict, clearly identifying children and armed conflict as a global priority to be addressed by the Security Council rather than by regional or national entities only.[13] In its Resolution 1314 of 11 August

[8] UNGA Resolution 48/157 (20 December 1993).

[9] UNGA Resolution A/51/306 (26 August 1996) and Add. 1.

[10] Statement of the Secretary-General on 'Promotion and Protection of Rights of Children' (9 September 1996), UN Doc. A/51/150, para. 2.

[11] Security Council Report, 'Children and Armed Conflict' (4 February 2008), above note 4, para. 5.3.

[12] UNSC Resolution 1261, above note 6.

[13] Security Council Report, 'Profile: Children and Armed Conflict' (12 July 2006), above note 5.

2000,[14] the Security Council reaffirmed its strong condemnation and requested parties to armed conflict to include, where appropriate, provisions for the protection of children, including the disarmament, demobilization and reintegration of child combatants in peace processes. It paid special attention to the protection of refugees and introduced provisions for protecting children in UN peacekeeping missions.

Significant progress was achieved in Resolution 1379 of 20 November 2001[15] as the Security Council asked the Secretary-General to attach a list to his report naming parties to armed conflicts that use or recruit children in violation of their international obligations. Therefore, the Secretary-General annexed, in accordance with Article 99 UN Charter, the requested list, which became known as the 'list of shame', to all of his subsequent reports. Introducing this list was groundbreaking because it was the first time the Security Council showed its aim to hold violators accountable.[16] In comparison to Resolutions 1261 and 1314, Resolution 1379 signifies a huge step forward to a new role of the UN institution in protecting children affected by armed conflict. Starting as an admonishing institution calling on the parties responsible to 'undertake all feasible measures' or 'to act where appropriate', the Security Council then became an institution demanding clear action by requesting the list of 'naming and shaming' and therefore producing visible results itself.

Still, the list is the core of the whole system. In order to do the listing, the Secretary-General relies on information gained through the monitoring and reporting mechanism via country task forces. Those collect information on the ground and transmit them to the Office of the Special Representative of the Secretary-General on Children and Armed Conflict. They also monitor the progress of parties which already have been listed in preceding reports. The list of the Secretary-General is therefore – by now – on the one hand, already a result of the monitoring and reporting mechanism, while on the other hand, it functions as a starting point since the country reports contain documentation about the progress being made by the listed parties.

Following the first report with an annexed list, the Security Council in its Resolution 1460[17] of 30 January 2003 expressed its concern about the large number of parties listed but at the same time voiced its

[14] UNSC Resolution 1314, above note 6. [15] UNSC Resolution 1379, above note 6.

[16] Security Council Report, 'Profile: Children and Armed Conflict' (12 July 2006), above note 5.

[17] UNSC Resolution 1460, above note 6.

willingness to enter into dialogue with those parties. It supported the Secretary-General's call for an 'era of application' after years of awareness raising and norm strengthening. This resolution was again characterized by a stronger and more direct wording, when the Security Council called on the parties to 'immediately halt'[18] the recruitment of child soldiers. It requested the Secretary-General to report further on the progress of the parties listed, to assess the violations of rights and abuses of children in armed conflict, and to make special proposals on ways to ensure monitoring and reporting in a more efficient way within the existing UN system.[19] Resolution 1539[20] was adopted on 22 April 2004. Concerned about the slow progress, the Security Council urged the Secretary-General to devise an action plan for a systematic and comprehensive monitoring and reporting mechanism. Furthermore, Resolution 1539 is the first resolution where the Security Council directly addressed the parties listed and called upon these parties to prepare within three months concrete, time-bound action plans to halt recruitment.[21] But more important, along with earlier attempts to achieve an impact on the armed groups recruiting children, it expressed its 'intention to consider imposing targeted and graduated measures through country specific resolutions such as the ban on the export or supply of small arms . . . against these parties if they refuse to enter into dialogue'.[22]

Two innovative steps to enhance compliance with international norms on children and armed conflict, namely a monitoring and reporting mechanism and a Working Group on Children and Armed Conflict were introduced by Resolution 1612[23] of 25 July 2005. The systematic and comprehensive monitoring and reporting mechanism was meant to be a 'mechanism to collect and provide timely, objective, accurate and reliable information on the recruitment and use of child soldiers'.[24] The Secretary-General was asked to implement this mechanism without delay, starting with countries on the agenda, and continuing with countries not on the agenda of the Security Council. With this comprehensive and structured mechanism for collecting and transmitting information, the Council started to be better positioned to take more concrete action against violations of international norms and standards relating to children and armed conflict.[25] On the institutional side, Resolution 1612 was

[18] Ibid. para. 3. [19] Ibid. para. 16. [20] UNSC Resolution 1539, above note 6.

[21] Ibid. para. 5. [22] Ibid.

[23] UNSC Resolution 1612, above note 6. [24] Ibid. para. 2.

[25] Security Council Report, 'Profile: Children and Armed Conflict' (12 July 2006), above note 5.

groundbreaking as well since the Security Council decided to 'establish a working group consisting of all members of the Council to review the reports of the [monitoring and reporting] mechanism . . . , to review the action plans . . . and to consider other relevant information presented to it'.[26] After considering the information necessary, the Working Group makes recommendations to the Security Council on possible measures to promote the protection of children and armed conflict, which by now has become the key mechanism through which the Security Council remains engaged.[27] As Resolution 1612 was not specific about how the Working Group should work, the members of the Working Group developed their own working methods, and by 2006, the Working Group had prepared a toolkit including twenty-six possible actions[28] and responses against perpetrators of grave violations. These actions differ between assistance, démarches, enhanced monitoring, the improvement of mandates and other measures. One can observe that, while not all tools have been used,[29] the most commonly used ones are letters or appeals to parties concerned, open and closed meetings with those parties and requests to UN bodies and agencies or donors.[30] Usually, the Working Group concentrates on different tools to address a particular situation. Over time, it became more creative in using the possible tools in the toolkit, also using press statements.[31] This has been an innovative way of handling situations which are not on the Security Council's agenda, such as Sri Lanka. Through these press statements, the chair of the Working Group was able to reach and address non-State actors, informing them and maybe referring to the possibility of stronger action in future.[32] Another practice which came up over the years was the writing of letters by the chair of the Working Group which were forwarded by the President of the Security Council. The Security Council Cross-Cutting report reviews this action as a result of some members who wanted to draw

[26] UNSC Resolution 1612, above note 6, para. 8.

[27] B. Nylund and I. Hyllested, 'Protecting Children Affected by Armed Conflict: Accountability for Monitoring, Reporting, and Response' (2010) 2 *Journal of Human Rights Practice* 71, at 78.

[28] 'Options for Possible Action by the Children Affected by Armed Conflict Working Group of the Security Council "Toolkit"', Addendum to UN Doc. 2006/724 (11 September 2006).

[29] A detailed analysis of the tools used and not used can be found at Watchlist, 'UN Security Council Resolution 1612 and Beyond: Strengthening Protection for Children in Armed Conflict' (May 2009), www.watchlist.org/reports/pdf/PolicyPaper_09.pdf.

[30] Ibid. 14.

[31] Security Council Report, 'Children and Armed Conflict' (4 February 2008), above note 4, para. 4.2.

[32] Ibid. para. 8.2.

a distinction between situations on the agenda and situations not on the agenda of the Security Council.[33] In 2010, the Working Group renewed its working methods, and, for the first time, members of the Working Group did a site visit. Furthermore, it recommended for the first time a regional strategy for monitoring and reporting on the Lord's Resistance Army[34] trying to respond to its cross-border activities.

Additionally, the Security Council again expressed in Resolution 1612 its intention to consider targeted sanctions and graduated measures through country-specific resolutions.[35] Since 2009, there has been a stronger interaction between the Working Group, the Special Representative of the Secretary-General on Children and Armed Conflict (as information provider) and Sanctions Committees. Twice, targeted sanctions were established because of the violation of child rights in 2008. And in August 2010, the Sanctions Committee on the Democratic Republic of the Congo (DRC) added the practice of recruitment and use of children as criteria against nine individuals already under sanctions.[36]

All in all, the monitoring and reporting system has been established relatively easily, and also the Working Group, after a year of consolidation, started working, reporting and recommending to the Security Council. Despite some improvements, it was criticized that only one of the six grave violations was reported and monitored. Therefore, the Security Council enlarged the scope of its involvement and requested in its Resolution 1882[37] of 4 August 2009 that the Secretary-General also include in his reports those parties that engage in patterns of killing and maiming of children and/or rape and other forms of sexual violence against children.[38] In 2011, it also requested in its Resolution 1998[39] of 12 July 2011 the inclusion of attacks on schools and hospitals in the annexes. It therefore further strengthened and expanded the monitoring and reporting mechanism. By now, the Council has a Working Group on Children

[33] Security Council Report, 'Cross-Cutting Report No. 1: Children and Armed Conflict' (15 April 2009), para. 5.3, www.securitycouncilreport.org/site/c.glKWLeMTIsG/b.5099181/k.A91/CrossCutting_Report_No_1brChildren_and_Armed_Conflictbr15_April_2009.htm.

[34] See Security Council Report, 'Cross Cutting Report: Children and Armed Conflict', (6 July 2011), at 3, www.securitycouncilreport.org/cross-cutting-report/lookup-c-glKWLeMTIsG-b 7539609.php.

[35] UNSC Resolution 1612, above note 6, para. 8.

[36] Security Council Report, 'Children and Armed Conflict' (6 July 2011), above note 34, para. 3.2.

[37] UNSC Resolution 1882, above note 6.

[38] Ibid. para. 3.

[39] UNSC Resolution 1998, above note 6.

and Armed Conflict, a monitoring and reporting mechanism supported from a taskforce made up of UN agencies – including the United Nations International Children's Emergency Fund (UNICEF), the UN Development Fund and the Department of Peacekeeping Operations – focusing on gathering information on violations against children in armed conflict and regular Secretary-Generals' reports containing two annexes of parties listed. The Secretary-General is supported by his Special Representative for Children and Armed Conflict. This all may lead to action plans by the parties concerned or sanctions against them in order to improve their compliance with international norms and standards.

3. Competence of the Security Council to take action regarding children and armed conflict

The Security Council installed a system based upon six grave violations deriving from standards and norms from international humanitarian law and international human rights law trying to enforce existing treaty and customary law. First and foremost, the Security Council acts therefore as an enforcement body. Therefore, it will be shortly analysed whether it is generally competent to act as an enforcement body with regard to children and armed conflict. On the other hand, the Security Council sometime also broadens the scope of the law applicable and acts as a standard setter as it accesses rules from different regimes of law. In a second part, it will be discussed whether the Security Council is competent to set standards with regard to children's rights.

3.1. Competence to act in regard to children and armed conflict

Subject to Article 24(1) UN Charter, the Security Council has the primary responsibility for the maintenance of international peace. Following Article 39 UN Charter, the Security Council 'shall determine the existence of any threat to peace, breach of peace, or act of aggression and shall make recommendations, or decide what measures shall be taken in accordance with Articles 41 and 42, to maintain or restore international peace and security'. Even Kelsen already mentioned that the role of the Security Council was not to maintain or restore the law, but to remain or restore peace, which is not necessarily identical with the law.[40]

[40] H. Kelsen, *The Law of the United Nations* (London: London Institute of World Affairs, 1950), at 294.

Nevertheless, it is accepted practice today that a breach of international humanitarian law can constitute or be considered a 'threat to the peace'.[41] For many years, the Security Council did not deal with armed conflict at all,[42] and it was not before 1967 until it urged parties to a conflict to respect the Geneva Conventions (GC). Since then, the Security Council has increased its involvement and has taken several decisions on the implementation of international humanitarian law.[43] Nevertheless, the Charter of the United Nations has no express provision empowering the Security Council to uphold international humanitarian law.[44] However, it may act through legal means when a certain situation, namely a threat to peace, exists.[45] In 1993, the Security Council expressly considered violations of international humanitarian law as a threat to peace for the first time.[46] In practice, even though the Charter does not vest the Council with the ability of enforcing additional Charter law, the Council's members have done so on numerous occasions.[47] There has been a significant overlap when the Council has qualified diverse breaches of international law as constituting threats to peace.[48] From a legal standpoint, the deviation from the Charter can be rationalized on the grounds that the Charter has been used by UN organs as a flexible document rather than one that must be confined strictly to its wording.[49] It is possible, by way of interpretation, to attribute to an institution rights which it does not possess according to the provisions by which it was created, provided that these rights are in harmony with the nature and objectives of the said institution.[50] This

[41] See for an analysis of the argumentation M. Roscini, 'The United Nations Security Council and the Enforcement of International Humanitarian Law' (2010) 43 *Israel Law Review* 330, at 333.

[42] See T. van Baarda, 'The Involvement of the Security Council in Maintaining International Humanitarian Law' (1994) 12 *Netherlands Quarterly of Human Rights* 137, at 138.

[43] C. Bourloyannis, 'The Security Council of the United Nations and the Implementation of International Humanitarian Law' (1991–1992) 20 *Denver Journal of International Law and Policy* 335, at 340.

[44] Van Baarda, 'Maintaining International Humanitarian Law, above note 42, at 143.

[45] R. Higgins, 'The Place of International Law in the Settlement of Disputes by the Security Council' (1970) 64 *American Journal of International Law* 1, at 16.

[46] See Roscini, 'Enforcement of International Humanitarian Law', above note 41, at 334.

[47] S. Ratner, 'The Security Council and International Law', in D. Malone (ed.), *The UN Security Council – From the Cold War to the 21st Century* (The Hague: International Peace Academy, 2004), 591–607, at 601.

[48] Roscini, 'Enforcement of International Humanitarian Law', above note 41, at 334.

[49] J. Quigley, 'The 'Privatization' of Security Council Enforcement Action: A Threat to Multilateralism' (1995–1996) 17 *Michigan Journal of International Law* 249, at 259.

[50] Ibid. 260; *Competence of the General Assembly* (Advisory Opinion) [1950] ICJ Reports 1, Dissenting Opinion Judge Alvarez, at 12.

is, in fact, the only way the Security Council may serve its tasks, because it has 'grown well beyond its initial function as a political forum and [by now] serves important legal functions . . . Today it embraces establishing complex regimes to enforce its decisions and passing resolutions of general rather than specific application'.[51] Generally, as Rosalyn Higgins puts it, 'it is for the Council, and the Council alone, to determine the existence of such a threat'.[52] So mainly it is not only a matter of effectiveness to leave the Security Council with the entire decision concerning what constitutes a threat to peace, a breach of peace or an act of aggression.[53] Therefore, a breach of international humanitarian law in general can be regarded as a threat to peace.

Nevertheless, as Roscini asks correctly, 'the question is, . . . whether any violation of international humanitarian law can qualify as a threat to the peace in the sense of Article 39 UN Charter. [And, even] though the Security Council enjoys a broad discretion in determine the existence of such a threat, [its power] is not unlimited'.[54] Roscini sees the limit where a threat to peace is artificially created as a pretext for the realization of ulterior purposes.[55] Like every authority acting upon the rule of law, the limits of its competence generally emanate from the statute creating it. Therefore, the International Criminal Tribunal for the former Yugoslavia (ICTY) as well already stated that the powers of the Security Council especially with regard to Article 39 UN Charter are not unlimited: 'While the "act of aggression" is more amenable to a legal determination, the "threat to the peace" is more of a political concept. But the determination that there exists such a threat is not a totally unfettered discretion, as it has to remain, at the very least, within the limits of the Purposes and Principles of the Charter'.[56] In practice, it has been accepted that the Security Council shall act only when the violation has reached a certain intensity which can most clearly be seen by the acceptance of severe human rights violations as a threat to the peace. Therefore, as Herdegen analysed and which is

[51] S. Chesterman, 'The UN Security Council and the Rule of Law' (2008) *New York University School of Law, Public Law and Legal Theory Research Paper Series*, Working Paper No. 08–57, p. i.

[52] Higgins, 'The Place of International Law', above note 45, at 16.

[53] United Nations Conference on International Organizations, XII 505 cited in P. Neusüß, *Legislative Maßnahmen des UN-Sicherheitsrates im Kampf gegen den internationalen Terrorismus* (Utz Verlag: München, 2008), at 180; see also Roscini, 'Enforcement of International Humanitarian Law', above note 41, at 334.

[54] Roscini, 'Enforcement of International Law', above note 41, at 340. [55] Ibid. 335.

[56] *Prosecutor v. Tadic* (Decision on the Defence Motion for Interlocutory Appeal on Jurisdiction), Case No. IT-94-1-AR72 (2 October 1995), para. 29.

also valid for international humanitarian law violations, 'the rank of the breached norm or value, the severity of the violation and its effects need to be taken into consideration in order to establish a threat to the peace'.[57]

The requested intensity is met with regard to the situation of children and armed conflict. In Resolution 1261, the Security Council first identified children and armed conflict as an issue affecting international peace and security, therefore falling under the aegis of the Security Council.[58] Already in its Resolution 1314, the Security Council referred to 'committing of systematic, flagrant and widespread violations of international humanitarian and human rights law, including that relating to children, in situations of armed conflict may constitute a threat to international peace and security, and in this regard [it] reaffirms its readiness to consider such situations and, where necessary to adopt appropriate steps'.[59] Also, the Security Council accepts that a certain intensity is needed as a precondition for its involvement. By now, the Security Council seeks to enhance compliance with and is reporting and monitoring the so-called six grave violations. The norms protecting children affected by armed conflict come either from treaty law or international customary law. In its Resolution 1539 (2004) the Security Council 'strongly condemns the recruitment and use of child soldiers[60] by parties to armed

[57] Roscini, 'Enforcement of International Humanitarian Law', above note 41, at 336 (citing M. Herdegen, *Die Befugnisse des UN-Sicherheitsrates: Aufgeklärter Absolutismus im Völkerrecht* (Heidelberg; C. F. Müller, 1998), at 16).

[58] UNSC Resolution 1261, above note 6; T. Webster, 'Babes with Arms: International Law and Child Soldiers' (2007) 39 *George Washington International Law Review* 251.

[59] UNSC Resolution 1314, above note 6, para. 9.

[60] Incontestably, recruiting or using children under the age of 15 is prohibited under international humanitarian law as is stipulated in Article 77(2) Additional Protocol I to the Geneva Conventions (AP I) and Article 4(3)(c) Additional Protocol II to the Geneva Conventions (AP II). The statutes of the UN-endorsed international tribunals all include provisions classifying the recruitment and use of children under the age of 15 years in armed conflict as a war crime; the Rome Statute of the International Criminal Court (ICC) stipulates this in Articles 8(2)(b) and 8(2)(e). Furthermore, the Special Court for Sierra Leone in the *Hinga Norman* Case ruled that the recruitment and use of children in armed conflict is also a war crime under customary law (see *Prosecutor v. Norman* (Decision on the Preliminary Motion) SCSL-04–14-AR72E (31 May 2004) paras. 17–24.

Human rights treaties contain the prohibition of child recruitment as well. While Article 38 of the Convention on the Rights of the Child (CRC) depicts the provisions generally known from international humanitarian law, in recent years, human rights treaty law has raised the acceptable minimum age for direct participation in hostilities to 18. Article 1 of the Optional Protocol to the Convention on the Rights of the Child on the Involvement of Children in Armed Conflict stipulates that States parties shall take all feasible measures to ensure that members of their armed forces who have not attained

conflict in violation of international obligations applicable to them, killing and maiming of children[61], rape and other sexual violence mostly committed against girls[62], abduction and forced displacement[63], denial of

the age of 18 years do not take a direct part in hostilities, and subject to Article 2, the States parties shall ensure that persons who have not attained the age of 18 years are not compulsorily recruited into their armed forces. Equally, the African Charter on the Rights and Welfare of Children, which defines a child as every human being below the age of 18, obliges States parties to take all necessary measures to ensure that no child takes directly part in hostilities and that States refrain, in particular, from recruiting any child.

61 The principles of distinction and proportionality of international humanitarian law already require fighters to distinguish between combatants and civilians and prohibit damage beyond military necessity. Also, Common Article 3(1)(a) GC prohibits violence to life and person, in particular, murder of all kinds, mutilation, cruel treatment and torture. Additionally, torture and cruel, inhumane or degrading treatment are prohibited in international and non-international conflicts for all parties by Article 32 GC IV, Article 75(2) AP I and Article 4(2) AP II. Human rights treaties declare the importance of the right to life, liberty and security of a person as well. Article 6 CRC states that States parties recognize that every child has the inherent right to life and no child shall – according to Article 37(a) CRC – be subjected to torture or other cruel, inhuman or degrading treatment or punishment. Killing and maiming of children violates the prohibition of torture and cruel, inhumane or degrading treatment (see Article 5 of the Universal Declaration of Human Rights; Article 6 International Covenant on Civil and Political Rights (ICCPR)), provisions which cannot be derogated – not even in times of war. The Convention on the Rights of the Child does not contain any rules concerning derogation at all.

Murder under the ICC Statute is categorized as a crime against humanity if it is committed as part of a widespread or systematic attack directed against a civilian population, with knowledge of the attack. Articles 6, 7 and 8 of the Rome Statute. Mentionable is also the fact that the ICTY has recognized in *Kunarac, Kovac und Vucoviv* (*Prosecutor v. Kunarac, Kovac and Vucovic* (Judgment), Case No. IT-96-23-T (22 February 2001), para. 864) that when children are the victims of murder, torture or injury it amounts to 'aggravating circumstances' of such crimes. See also Office of the Special Representative of the Secretary-General for Children and Armed Conflict, Working Paper No. 1, 'The Six Grave Violations Against Children During Armed Conflict: The Legal Foundation', October 2009, at 6.

62 Forbidden under international humanitarian law as inhumane treatment under Common Article 3 GC, especially by Article 27(2) GC IV, Articles 75(2), 76(1) and 77(1) AP I; Article 4(2)(e) AP II and by international customary law as stated by Rule 93 of the ICRC Customary Law Study. J.-M. Henckaerts and L. Doswald-Beck, *Customary International Law*, 2 vols. (Cambridge: Cambridge University Press, 2005), vol. I, at 327. The Rome Statute of the International Criminal Court states that rape, sexual slavery, enforced prostitution, forced pregnancy, enforced sterilization or 'other forms of sexual violence of comparable gravity' may constitute war crimes and crimes against humanity, Articles 7(1)(g), 8(2)(c), 8(2)(e). Relevant human rights provisions are included in the Convention Against Torture, the Convention for the Suppression of the Traffic in Persons and of the Exploitation of the Prostitution and Others, in the International Covenant on Cultural and Political Rights and the Convention for the Elimination of all Forms of Discrimination Against Women.

63 Common Article 3 GC requires humane treatment and it goes without saying that abducting children against their will for using them in armed conflicts falls out of the scope of

humanitarian access to children[64] [as well as] attacks against schools and hospitals[65] . . .'[66]

The member States agreed upon those violations to be the most severe for children affected by armed conflict, and the violations were defined as such since 'they constitute especially egregious violations against children'.[67] Therefore, the Security Council also accepts practical and legal limits before engaging in regard to children and armed conflict. Since it

this obligation. Abduction is also prohibited under customary law. Moreover, the forced displacement or deportation of a civilian population is prohibited under Article 49 GC IV and the arbitrary deprivation of liberty is prohibited by Articles 34 GC IV, 147 GC IV, 75(2) AP I and Article 4(2) AP II. Forced disappearance is also seen as a war crime under the ICC Statute. The prohibition of enforced disappearances and abduction is also reflected in human rights treaties. Article 9 ICCPR and the International Convention Against the Taking of Hostages prohibit this in general, Articles 2 and 25 of the International Convention for the Protection of All Persons from Enforced Disappearance explicitly outlaw the abduction of children.

[64] Denial of this access to children as well as attacks against humanitarian workers is prohibited under international humanitarian treaty and customary law. For example, subject to Article 15(4) AP I, medical personnel shall have access to any place where their services are essential. Moreover, the protection of humanitarian relief personnel is one of the oldest maxims of the laws of armed conflict as Article 15 Hague Convention of 1907 on Respecting the Laws and Customs of War on Land already shows. The attack on humanitarian assistance personnel and vehicles is defined as a war crime subject to Article 8(2)(b) and Article 8(2)(e) of the ICC Statute. Likewise, a child in need shall receive humanitarian assistance under human rights treaty law. Article 22 CRC and, with an identical wording, Article 23 of the African Charter of the Rights and Welfare of the Child state that States parties shall take appropriate measures to ensure that a child who is seeking refugee status or who is considered a refugee in accordance with applicable international or domestic law and procedures shall, whether unaccompanied or accompanied by his or her parents or by any other person, receive appropriate protection and humanitarian assistance in the enjoyment of applicable rights.

[65] Schools and hospitals are civilian objects often providing shelter to children during conflict. Attacks against schools are prohibited under international humanitarian treaty (see Articles 11 and 18 GC IV) and customary law (see J.-M. Henckaerts and L. Doswald-Beck, *Customary International Humanitarian Law*, above note 62, at 34–71, Rules 10–22 ICRC Customary Law Study). Targeting such objects in the absence of military necessity is already prohibited under the general principle of distinction (see also Articles 48 and 52 AP I; *The Legality of the Threat or Use of Nuclear Weapons* (Advisory Opinion) [1996] ICJ Reports 226, para. 78). Intentionally targeting schools or hospitals during war-time constitute a war crime in international and non-international armed conflicts, according to Article 8(2)(b) and Article 8(2)(e) of the ICC Statute.

While inducing the monitoring and reporting mechanism also for this grave violation in 2011, the Security Council mainly recurred to Article 28 CRC, the right to education. According to Article 24 CRC, children also have the right to access to healthcare services.

[66] UNSC Resolution 1539, above note 6, para. 1.

[67] 'Report of the Secretary-General on Children and Armed Conflict' (9 February 2005), UN Doc. A/59/695-S/2005/72, para. 68.

only deals with grave violations reflecting flagrant and widespread violations of international humanitarian and human rights law, a certain intensity of the violations of the law are assumed, and therefore the Security Council still acts within its boundaries. The severity of violations and intensity is a good reason to justify the violations of child rights as a threat to the peace.[68]

Over the years, the Security Council has 'increasingly developed new mechanisms and techniques to stress and implement the responsibility of individuals and states'.[69] As seen, the Council is competent to install a regime concerned with children and armed conflict in order to reduce the violations of obligations of international humanitarian law and international human rights law.

3.2. Competence to set standards

While the Security Council is competent to act as an enforcement body of international child rights, its concentration on the six grave violations might reveal further problems. This concentration on some fundamental principles deriving from different regimes of international law may be seen as setting standards by the Security Council itself.

The six grave violations all derive from international humanitarian law and international human rights law which are two different regimes of international law. So far, no consistent approach exits on how those two regimes relate to each other. The Security Council does not differentiate in concrete terms between the system of international humanitarian law and human rights law and one could argue that its engagement thus might lead to confusion between those two regimes of law. Since the

[68] Moreover, the Secretary-General based the involvement on the practical possibility to monitor the six grave violations. See ibid. It is at least questionable if the Security Council is allowed to choose certain violations over others surpassing a certain degree of intensity out of practical reasons because they can be monitored more easily. But generally the choice of its activities is left to the body acting. Since the Security Council is competent to deal with the problem of children affected by armed conflict constituting a threat to peace and security, it generally has the competence to choose the degree of its involvement based on various reasons, and therefore as well out of practical reasons. The decision by the UN Security Council to focus on these six violations grows out of its determination to fight impunity by delineating specific, targeted crimes committed by persistent violators of child rights. See UNICEF, 'Machel Study', above note 2, at 21.

[69] G. Nolte, 'The Different Functions of the Security Council with Respect to Humanitarian Law', in V. Lowe, A. Roberts, J. Welsh, and D. Zaum (eds.), *The United Nations Security Council and War, The Evolution of Thought and Practice since 1945* (New York: Oxford University Press, 2008), 519–35, at 534.

Security Council combines international human rights and international humanitarian law standards in one system, it is at least questionable if this leads to an unwanted influence on international treaty or customary law. Therefore, one may pose the question whether the Security Council has the power to change current systems by entangling two regimes of law which are not (yet) unquestionably seen as being applicable at the same time. But from a practical point of view, this entanglement could also improve the acceptance of the system of the Security Council. As it is based upon the most fundamental norms deriving from both systems, it outlines the importance of those standards to the parties.

Nevertheless, it could lead, in consequence, to the result that standards deriving from one system of law are suddenly applied to the other. This possible entanglement might lead to – by some State actors – an unwanted influence on the formation of international humanitarian law by the Security Council and a possible role of the Security Council to set standards.

Generally speaking, the Security Council seems to be aware of the danger that its actions may lead to an unwanted entanglement. The Security Council for these reasons avoids any legal classification. This can also be seen in the reports of the Secretary-General stating that the listing does not state anything about the legal quality of the conflict concerned: 'Pursuant to resolution 1612 the report[s are] guided by criteria for determining the existence of an armed conflict found in international humanitarian law and international jurisprudence; reference to a situation of concern is not a legal determination, and reference to a non-State party does not affect its legal status'.[70]

Moreover, two examples will demonstrate that its influence by setting standards in this area is still low at the moment. First, it will be analysed if its approach to consider children as children under the age of 18 (straight 18 approach) may influence other opinions. Generally, the question until what age children shall be regarded as children is still under discussion. Especially in international humanitarian law and the Geneva Conventions, the relevant age is 15. Nevertheless, the Security Council applies the age limit of 18 and tries to convince parties to accept the age of 18 as a common standard. However, its application of a straight 18 approach concerning the relevant age for children has not influenced standards of international humanitarian law so far. The

[70] 'Report of the Secretary-General on Children and Armed Conflict' (26 March 2009), UN Doc. A/63/785-S/2009/158, fn. 11.

second example is the listed violation of attacks on schools and hospitals. Under international humanitarian law, they can be regarded – under certain circumstances – as dual-use objects, which is not reflected by the understanding of the Security Council. Nevertheless, up until now, one cannot say if its involvement concerning schools and hospitals also has an impact on basic principles of international humanitarian law considering that the principle of military necessity might be affected.

3.2.1. Straight 18 approach

One of the six grave violations listed is the recruitment or use of child soldiers. Even Graca Machel already identified the recruitment and use of child soldiers as one of the most alarming trends in armed conflict.[71] Child soldiers are recruited in many different ways: some are conscripted, some are abducted and others are forced to join armed groups to defend their families.[72] In addition to being forcibly recruited, children join armed groups 'voluntarily' for various reasons of which poverty and economic reasons are the root causes.[73] Other driving factors are that children seek protection, and some join in for ideological reasons.[74] Recruitment is therefore defined as the compulsory forced or voluntary conscription or enlistment of children into any kind of armed forces or organized armed groups.[75] Once recruited, children do not necessarily carry arms; they are also used in any other capacity, including but not limited to cooks, porters and messengers, and often girls are recruited for sexual purposes and for forced marriage.[76]

Despite wide condemnation and response over the last decade, the recruitment of boys and girls into armed groups and armed forces continues. Incontestably, recruiting or using children under the age of 15 is prohibited under international humanitarian law,[77] and human rights treaties contain the prohibition of child recruitment as well.[78] In recent years, human rights treaty law, such as Article 1 of the Optional Protocol to the Convention on the Rights of the Child on the Involvement

[71] Graca Machel Report, 'Impact of Armed Conflict on Children' (26 August 1996), UN Doc. A/51/306, para. 34.

[72] See ibid. para. 36. [73] Ibid. para. 39. [74] Ibid. paras. 40–43.

[75] UNICEF, 'Machel Study', above note 2, p. 21.

[76] See also UNICEF, 'Definition of Child Soldier in the Cape Town Principles and Best Practices' (30 April 1997).

[77] Ibid.

[78] This is also defined as the worst form of child labour in Article 3(a) of the International Labor Organization Convention 182.

of Children in Armed Conflict, has raised the acceptable minimum age for direct participation in hostilities to 18.

Human rights and, in the meanwhile, also humanitarian organizations have adopted the 'straight 18' approach, setting the universal definition of childhood to every person below the age of 18. By now, the Office of the Special Representative of the Secretary-General on Children and Armed Conflict has, in cooperation with UNICEF and the Office of the High Commissioner for Human Rights, launched a two-year global campaign called 'Zero under 18'. This campaign focuses on encouraging States to sign and ratify the Optional Protocol and therefore to establish 18 years as a minimum age for voluntary recruitment. Moreover, States that are already member States are urged to amend their binding declaration raising the minimum age for recruitment in the armed forces to 18.[79] This may, even slowly, change the general perception in international humanitarian law and may lead to an equalization of the two systems of law. For this reason, States have already stressed the importance of local and national definitions in accordance with their own traditions.[80]

In fact, by applying human rights standards, the Security Council influences the perception of the relevant rules. The campaign of the Office of the Special Representative clearly advocates towards establishing human rights standards without taking into account deviating humanitarian law standards. And even though the Security Council does not change the law itself by advocating, it puts pressure on States towards the application of a certain law.[81] However, by now the Secretary-General still applies standards in accordance with the role of the relevant party, despite the fact that he is promoting the straight 18 approach:

> The minimum international standard to which all Member States on the list are held is the Convention on the Rights of the Child. When appropriate, the conduct of States was also assessed in accordance with the Optional Protocol to the Convention on the Rights of the Child on the involvement of children in armed conflict, Additional Protocol II to the Geneva Conventions, International Labour Organization (ILO) Convention No. 182 concerning the elimination of the worst forms of child labour, and the African Charter on the Rights and Welfare of the Child.

79 R. Coomaraswany, 'The Optional Protocol to the Convention on the Rights of the Child on the Involvement of Children in Armed Conflict – Towards Universal Ratification' (2010) 18 *International Journal of Children's Rights* 535, at 548–49.

80 D. Rosen, 'Who Is a Child? The Legal Conundrum of Child Soldiers' (2009–2010) 25 *Connecticut Journal of International Law* 81, at 96.

81 N. Jamal, *Der Einfluss der Resolutionen des Sicherheitsrats der Vereinten Nationen auf das humanitäre Völkerrecht* (Berlin: Weißensee Verlag, 2009), at 332.

> The conduct of non-State armed groups was assessed in accordance with the widely accepted minimum international standard that children under age 15 shall not be conscripted or enlisted into armed forces or groups or used by them to participate actively in hostilities in either international or internal armed conflicts. This standard echoes the Convention on the Rights of the Child, Additional Protocol II to the Geneva Conventions, the Rome Statute of the International Criminal Court and the statute of the Special Court for Sierra Leone. In States that have ratified the Optional Protocol to the Convention on the Rights of the Child on the involvement of children in armed conflict, non-State armed groups are held to that higher standard, prohibiting all recruitment and use of children under 18. Commitments made in peace agreements or to my Special Representative were also taken into account.[82]

3.2.2. Dual use of schools

Another problem which may arise is that the standards set by the Security Council undermine some principles of international humanitarian law by mainly referring to or taking into account human rights standards. One example is the grave violation of human rights through attacks on schools and hospitals. This includes targeting educational or medical facilities resulting in their total or partial destruction. Schools and hospitals are civilian objects often providing shelter to children during conflict.[83] In Afghanistan, for example, 133 incidents of school attacks were documented between August 2006 and July 2007 alone.[84] Attacks on schools endanger education during war, especially in helping to pave the way to post-conflict recovery.[85] Attacks against schools are prohibited under international humanitarian treaty[86] and customary law[87]. Nevertheless, under the principle of military necessity, schools and also hospitals are not absolutely protected under international humanitarian law. And, when they are used as military objects, they can – as objects of dual use – be attacked legally. So far, it is not clear whether the approach of the Security Council shares this differentiation. In its Resolution 1998 (2011), the Security Council requests the Secretary-General 'to also include in the annexes to his report on children and armed conflict those parties to

[82] 'Report of the Secretary-General on Children and Armed Conflict' (26 November 2002), UN Doc. S/2002/1299, paras. 30–31.

[83] Special Representative of the Secretary-General for Children and Armed Conflict, 'Six Grave Violations', above note 61, at 13.

[84] UNICEF, 'Machel Study', above note 2, at 22.

[85] See ibid. 22.

[86] See Articles 11 and 18 GC IV.

[87] Henckaerts and Doswald-Beck, *Customary International Humanitarian Law*, above note 62, vol. I, at 34–71, Rules 10–22.

armed conflict that engage, in contravention of applicable international law, in recurrent attacks on schools and/or hospitals . . . [and/or] in recurrent attacks or threats of attacks against protected persons in relation to schools and/or hospitals in situations of armed conflict'.[88] So far, no more detailed information about the listing process and the relevant criteria for being listed is available. Generally, it is up to the Secretary-General to define more clearly what is understood by the terms and under which conditions a party will be listed. Nevertheless, the Security Council seems to be aware of the problematic differentiation of the international human rights and the international humanitarian law approach when it urges the parties 'to armed conflict to refrain from actions that impede children's access to education and to health services and requests the Secretary-General to continue to monitor and report on, inter alia, the military use of schools and hospitals in contravention of international humanitarian law, as well as on attacks against, and/or kidnapping of teachers and medical personnel'.[89] On the other hand, this broad definition leaves space for interpretation, which may also be in the interest of some member States that use schools for military purposes. By now, a clearer picture can only be drawn once the Secretary-General has started setting up the criteria and the listing process on that violation.

Clearly, the engagement of the Security Council in this regard influences the perception of the law protecting children in armed conflict. Nevertheless, as those examples show, it respects the different approaches taken by the States in treaty and customary law, even though it tries to move them towards a better protection of children. One has to keep in mind that the Security Council only refers to norms and standards which are created out of State consent. Compared to other fields of action, it does not build its involvement upon new rules and does not act as a legislator itself.

4. Compliance with child rights and the Security Council's mechanism

As seen, the Security Council is competent to engage with the issue of children and armed conflict by installing a mechanism that seeks to help compliance with relevant norms. Nevertheless, the question remains whether the system installed by the Security Council is effective. It is effective when it reaches its goal of enhancing compliance. From a practical point of view this attempt can generally be seen as successful insofar as the

[88] UNSC Resolution 1998, above note 6, para. 3. [89] Ibid. para. 4.

Security Council's installed regime meets and at the same time adds various incentives to comply with the law and already has led to considerable results. One can observe that many parties were willing to enter into dialogue and action plans with the UN in order to reduce their violations of child rights. On the other hand, there are still many parties which continue to violate child rights. Therefore, it may be helpful to understand why actors comply with norms at all and if the Security Council's system adds incentives to increase the actor's motivation to comply with the norms.

Reasons to comply with norms and standards of international law are manifold, and the attempts of explanations vary in international relation theory and international law. Legal theories explain compliance by a range of different interpretations, from a managerial model to reasons of legitimacy.[90] As legal theories generally fail to identify different motivations why actors obey international law, this chapter draws on theories of international relations to analyse whether the Security Council's regime on children and armed conflict uses the right incentives. Especially political theorists traditionally isolate three ideal-type motivations by which the reasons of compliance with norms may be explained.[91] The party in question complies with a rule (1) because the actor fears the punishment of rule enforcers, (2) because the actor sees the rule as in its own self-interest and (3) because the actor feels the rule is legitimate and ought to be obeyed.[92] Hurd calls those three criteria coercion, self-interest and legitimacy.[93] He describes them as the Weberian ideal types for modes of social control, by which each generates compliance with society's rules by a different mechanism.[94] Even though most of the studies deal with State actors, these observations are also valid for non-State actors, as other works also identify similar reasons for non-State actors.[95] Where rules or norms exist, compliance with them may be achieved by one or a combination of these motivations.[96] Analysing the mechanism concerning

[90] A general analysis of different legal theories can be found at A. Guzman, 'A Compliance-Based Theory of International Law' (2002) 90 *California Law Review* 1826, at 1888.

[91] See a general analysis by K. Raustiala and A.-M. Slaughter, 'International Law, International Relations and Compliance', in W. Carlsnaes, T. Risse and B. Simmons (eds.), *Handbook of International Relations* (Los Angeles: Sage, 2002), 538–59.

[92] Hurd, 'Legitimacy and Authority in International Politics', above note 3, at 379.

[93] Ibid. 380. [94] Ibid. 383.

[95] A. Bellal and S. Casey-Maslen, 'Enhancing Compliance with International Law by Armed Non-State Actors' (2011) 3 *Goettingen Journal of International Law* 175, at 191 et seq.

[96] Hurd, 'Legitimacy and Authority in International Politics', above note 3, at 380.

children and armed conflict installed by the Security Council will show that it meets some of those criteria, but nevertheless fails to fully support all the motivations identified.

4.1. Coercion and self-interest

Two obvious reasons for compliance are coercion and self-interest. Actors obey the law because they are forced to do so by a higher authority or because it is in their own interest. Hurd describes coercion as a relation of asymmetrical physical power among agents, where this asymmetry is applied to change the behaviour of the weaker agent. The rule itself is irrelevant except as a signal for what kind of behaviour will and will not incur the penalty.[97]

The belief that compliance in fact promotes self-interest is another possible motivation for compliance with rules. Some scholars argue that the notion of mutual benefit is a reasonable concept of compliance.[98] Generally, it is taken for granted that international law is most viably defined as the process of decisions by which the members of the larger community of mankind clarify and secure their common interest. This may explain why most norms of international law are obeyed.[99] But it does not explain why actors do not comply with norms of international law and how compliance with those norms can be enhanced. In those cases, the positive incentives for the actors must be strengthened. At the same time, as Hurd rightly acknowledges, self-interest needs to be carefully defined if it is supposed to be a useful concept of social science. The boundaries of a self-interest explanation need to be clearly drawn so as not to subsume all other categories. He describes the situation in which the actor is motivated by coercion and in which the actor is motivated by self-interest both as situations of choice in which the actor compares the benefits of its acting to the risks.[100] The difference between the two is that in the case of coercion, the actor is threatened with a negative impact which he needs to avert, while in the case of acting out of self-interest, the outcome is seen as positive by the actor himself.

97 Ibid. 383–84.

98 This is called managerial theory by A. Chayes and A. Handler Chayes, *The New Sovereignty: Compliance with International Regulatory Agreements* (Cambridge: Harvard University Press, 1998).

99 'Almost all nations observe almost all principles of international law and almost all their obligations almost all the time', L. Henkin, *How Nations Behave* (New York: Praeger, 1968), at 47.

100 Hurd, 'Legitimacy and Authority in International Politics', above note 3, at 386.

The 'list of shame', which entails the threat with targeted sanctions as a consequence of being listed and finally the application of sanctions by the Sanctions Committees, enables the Security Council to work with the motivations of coercion and self-interest. One can assume that parties comply with rules in their self-interest in order to get de-listed from the Secretary-General's list of shame. Having the annexed list, which is compiled by the Secretary-General and acknowledged by the Security Council, is generally seen as a significant step forward towards putting pressure on those concerned to stop abusing children.[101] The parties on the list are determined by the Secretary-General. The decisive factor is the groups' non-compliance with relevant obligations among the grave violations the Secretary-General is authorized to report on. The Secretary-General decides which parties to list based on information gathered by a wide range of sources, including entities of the UN system, such as peace operations and country teams. While it was criticized that in the first years the recruitment of children was the only trigger for placing a group on the Secretary-General's annexes,[102] the Security Council enlarged the system in 2009, and now the killing and maiming of children, rape and other forms of sexual violence and attacks against schools and hospitals are relevant triggers as well.

Many concerned parties seem to take the situation of being listed on the Secretary-General's annexes seriously. This is already evidenced by public statements of the Karennis National Progressive Party aiming at being removed from the list.[103] The mere existence of the annexed list and the fact that parties are mentioned there helped to convince parties to enter into action plans and to comply with international standards of child rights. The Special Representative to the Secretary-General on Children and Armed Conflict reports that citing the consequences of the monitoring and reporting mechanism, including targeted sanctions, could be a highly effective tool to obtain commitments.[104] For example, in 2008, she visited the Central African Republic and met with Commander Lauren

101 Security Council Report, 'Children and Armed Conflict' (4 February 2008), above note 4, para. 3.

102 UNSC Resolution 1379, above note 6.

103 Karenni National Progressive Party, 'Appeal for the Karenni Army's Name to be Removed from the List of Non-State Armed Groups Making Use of Child Soldiers in Armed Conflict', Press Release No. 02/09, 18 April 2009, theirwords.org/media/transfer/doc/1_mm_knpp_ka_2009_14-9ad6c2a28ce5f6d514aa4291d586c9c2.pdf.

104 Security Council Report, 'Children and Armed Conflict' (15 April 2009), above note 33, para. 5.4.

Djim We of the Armée Populaire pour la Restauration de la République et la Démocratie. She reports that the Commander had been unaware that he was listed in the Secretary-General's annexes but upon understanding the consequences he agreed to hand over children.[105]

Still, on first sight, being on the list does not have any direct impact since possible sanctions still need to be set by the Sanctions Committee. Therefore, the motivation for compliance might be more of self-interest than of coercion. But what the list does is officially name the parties concerned. Public shaming does influence parties' behaviour as the public opinion counts a lot in a more and more globalized world. States parties as well as non-State actors lose a lot of support when violating children's rights since there is a common global sense that children need to be protected. This can already be seen by the wide acceptance of the Convention on Child Rights and the large support UNICEF and other children's organizations are experiencing. Being listed also means being exposed to the threat of targeted sanctions which might have a convincing effect on the parties listed. Therefore, it is still an external trigger that leads parties to comply with the norms and standards after being listed by the Secretary-General. The list fulfils the criteria of influencing parties by coercion rather than triggering their self-interest.

Another tool used by the Security Council which is clearly supposed to work through coercion is the threat with and finally the use of targeted sanctions by the Security Council. While there are quite a few parties who – after being listed – engaged in action plans in order to halt the violations of children's rights, there are still a number of persistent perpetrators – groups that have been listed in every subsequent report. In those cases, sanctions imposed by the Security Council work as a means of coercion and should therefore improve compliance. After having already considered targeted measures in its Resolution 1539, it took several years until the Security Council imposed them in two cases, namely, with regard to Côte d'Ivoire and the DRC. In both cases, sanctions had already been imposed on those parties, but the recruitment and use of child soldiers was added to the pre-existing sanctions as additional criteria. Resolution 1698 (2006) extended the scope of possible sanctions in the DRC to include the designation of political and military leaders recruiting or using children in armed conflict in violation of applicable international law and individuals committing serious violations of international law involving the targeting of children in situations of armed

[105] Ibid. para. 5.4.

conflict, including killing and maiming, sexual violence, abduction and forced displacement.[106] As the conflict deteriorated, the Council adopted two resolutions enhancing the sanction regime regarding the DRC.[107] Resolution 1807 (2008) extended travel bans and financial measures to perpetrators of serious human rights abuses, including the targeting of children and killing and maiming of children, sexual violence, abduction and forced displacement. Another Resolution from 2008, Resolution 1857, extended the sanctions' regime to those obstructing access to or distribution of humanitarian assistance in the eastern part of the DRC.[108]

In the DRC, there has been a situation of instability and armed conflict for years. The situation of children is still very difficult, and today, as many as 30,000 Congolese children are still fighting and living with armed forces and militia groups.[109] Despite all efforts of the international community, the situation for children is not improving a lot. That is why serious action against persistent perpetrators is needed. UNICEF and others organizations are proposing the establishment of a Sanctions Committee exclusively for grave violations against children in situations of armed conflict.[110] Meanwhile, following the authority given in Resolution 1857, more individuals have become objects of targeted measures: in 2009, the Sanctions Committee on the DRC subjected three individual commanders of the armed group Forces Démocratiques de Libération du Rwanda to asset freezes and travel bans citing the abduction and sexual abuse of girls and recruitment of boys.[111] Furthermore, the communication between the different bodies in the UN system improved. As the Secretary-General reports, the Security Council Committee invited the Special Representative for Children and Armed Conflict to brief the Sanctions Committee in May 2010 for the first time. As a result, several individuals were included on the Committee's list of individuals and

[106] UNSC Resolution 1698 (31 July 2006), para. 13.

[107] Security Council Report, 'Children and Armed Conflict' (6 July 2011), above note 34, at 23.

[108] See also ibid. [109] Ibid.

[110] UNICEF, 'Machel Study', above note 2, at 48–49; this proposition raises different questions which cannot be discussed in this chapter. The impact is questionable since the means are not different than the sanctions applied by the Sanctions Committee on the DRC. It would only be relevant for other situations. Furthermore, it will be necessary to discuss how this Sanctions Committee should deal with situations not on the agenda of the Security Council.

[111] Department of Public Information, 'Press Release' (3 March 2009), UN Doc. SC/9608; 'Report of the Secretary-General on Children and Armed Conflict' (23 April 2011), UN Doc. A/65/820-S/2011/250, paras. 205–206.

entities against which targeted measures will be imposed on the basis of verified information regarding, inter alia, their recruitment and use of children.[112] As of this writing, the list was last updated in 2014.

Generally, targeted sanctions are seen as an effective tool to remind actors of their legal obligations[113] since these enormously raise the political costs for their actions. Moreover, especially banning the export of light weapons into regions where children are involved in fighting can have a real effect as one of the main reasons for their direct participation in hostilities is the proliferation of these weapons.[114] Anyhow, so far, no short- or long-term impact of the imposed sanctions has been observed. Taking into account the explanations of Hurd that coercion is a matter of a relation of asymmetrical physical power among agents, where this asymmetry is applied to changing the behaviour of the weaker agent, it is still questionable if those targeted sanctions work with persistent perpetrators. Influencing the weaker agent is only possible if the so-called weaker agent accepts its weakness in regard to the more powerful agent. Therefore, it is at least questionable whether the sanctions chosen (such as travel bans or asset freezing) can really have an impact on people acting somewhere beyond any control and across borders of different countries without any political ideology or the demand of being internationally accepted. Nevertheless, it is a useful tool for other actors who can be influenced by the pressure the Security Council exercises on them. So far, it seems that the threat of sanctions is more effective than the impact of the real sanctions imposed on parties. Those parties who are threatened by possible targeted sanctions act before the sanctions are imposed and enter into action plans with the United Nations. However, in order to keep its credibility, in cases where the mere threat of sanctions is not working, the Security Council must act and must apply those sanctions on a regular basis.

Another question in this regard is whether the threat or the coercion measure itself must be lawful. Do questions and doubts about the UN Security Council's system reduce its impact? In the case of an impact of sanctions on State and non-State actors as a means of coercion, there

[112] The updated list can be found at www.un.org/sc/committees/1533/pdf/1533_list.pdf.

[113] S. von Schorlemer, *Kindersoldaten und bewaffneter Konflikt, Nukleus eines umfassenden Schutzregimes der Vereinten Nationen* (Frankfurt/Main: Peter Lang, 2009), at 273.

[114] S. Liebig, 'Das Fakultativprotoll zum Übereinkommen über die Rechte des Kindes betreffend die Beteiligung von Kindern an bewaffneten Konflikten', in S. von Schorlemer (ed.), *Die Vereinten Nationen und die Entwicklung der Rechte des Kindes* (Aachen: Shacker, 2004), 159–87, at 184.

should be no negative influence. As Hurd describes it, in the case of coercion, the actor who obeys a rule because of coercion is motivated by the fear of punishment from a stronger power.[115] In the case of sanctions, the threat to its economic and personal freedom is used in order to reach obedience to the law. As long as the motivation of compliance is based upon coercion, the illegality of the tool applied does not change this fear of punishment.[116] Nevertheless, although the different motivations can be analytically separated from the others, in practice they are rarely found in pure isolation.[117] Therefore, the answer must be adapted if the illegality of a tool reduces other motivations, which will be discussed as a matter of legitimacy.

With its 'list of shame' and possible sanctions, the Security Council mainly uses coercion. It tries to influence the perpetrators by raising their political and economic costs when they violate children's rights. So far, only the Special Representative of the Secretary-General on Children and Armed Conflict has worked directly with the parties in order to enhance their motivation to respect child rights out of self-interest. Especially for non-State actors, it may not be clear at first sight that respecting children's rights during an armed conflict is in their self-interest. The Security Council should further concentrate on informing parties by strengthening the position of the Special Representative, in order to motivate the perpetrators out of coercion and out of self-interest.

4.2. *Legitimacy*

Another possible motivation for compliance is legitimacy or, as Thomas Franck noted once: 'Legitimacy has the power to pull toward compliance those who cannot be compelled'.[118]

A definition of this term is given by Mark Suchman, an organizational sociologist. He defines legitimacy as 'a generalized perception or assumption, that the actions of an entity are desirable, proper, or appropriate within some socially constructed system of norms, values, beliefs and definitions'.[119] This definition encompasses on the one hand the sense

[115] Hurd, 'Legitimacy and Authority in International Politics', above note 3, at 383.

[116] But certainly it will have an impact on the motivation to adhere to a rule due to its legitimacy. See Section 2.2.4 of this chapter.

[117] Hurd, 'Legitimacy and Authority in International Politics', above note 3, at 383.

[118] T. Franck, *The Power of Legitimacy among Nations* (New York: Oxford University Press, 1990), at 24.

[119] M. Suchman, 'Managing Legitimacy: Strategies and Institutional Approaches' (1995) 20 *Academy of Management Review* 571, at 574.

within the individual of the appropriateness of a body and, on the other hand, the contextual cultural origin of the standards of appropriateness.[120] Legitimacy, as Hurd uses it, refers to the normative belief by an actor that a rule or institution ought to be obeyed.[121]

Also, legal theories of compliance refer to legitimacy as a possible reason for compliance.[122] Franck defines legitimacy as a 'property of a rule or rule-making institution which itself exerts a pull toward compliance on those addressed normatively because those addressed believe that the rule or institution has come into being and operates in accordance with generally accepted principles of right process'.[123] His definition shares the subjective approach of the sociologists but tries to objectivise it at the same time as it is based upon the underlying assumption that a rule or institution is perceived as legitimate if it follows a certain structure and foreseen process. The fundamental premise underlying its legitimacy theory is therefore that States obey rules perceived to have 'come into being in accordance with the right process'.[124] Franck argues that four factors determine whether a State complies with international obligations: determinacy, symbolic validation, coherence and adherence.[125] Where these four factors are present, legitimacy theory would predict strong pressure towards compliance, and where they are absent, it would predict a very limited impetus in that direction.[126] In this chapter, it is assumed that the subjective approach is necessarily underpinned by an objective structure. Nevertheless, the four criteria identified by Franck are not sufficient, as there are generally accepted standards which go further. Those common standards derive from four regimes of the international legal system: international human rights law, international humanitarian law, international criminal law and international refugee law, and include international criminal justice standards and represent universally applicable standards and must therefore serve as a normative basis for all United Nations' activities in support of justice and the rule of law:[127]

[120] Hurd, 'Legitimacy and Authority in International Politics', above note 3, at 388.

[121] Ibid. 381.

[122] T. Franck, 'Legitimacy in the International System' (1988) 82 *American Journal of International Law* 705; Franck, *The Power of Legitimacy among Nations*, above note 118.

[123] T. Franck, *Fairness in International Law and Institutions* (Oxford: Clarendon Press, 1995), at 24.

[124] Franck, 'Legitimacy in the International System', above note 122, at 706.

[125] Ibid. 713–25.

[126] Guzman, 'A Compliance-Based Theory of International Law', above note 91, at 1834 (citing Franck, 'Legitimacy in the International System', above note 122, at 713).

[127] 'Report of the Secretary-General on the Rule of Law and Transitional Justice in Conflict and Post-Conflict Societies' (23 August 2004), UN Doc. S/2004/616, para. 9.

> [Those] norms and standards have been developed and adopted by countries across the globe and have been accommodated by the full range of legal systems of [UN] Member States, whether based in common law, civil law, Islamic law, or other legal traditions. As such, these norms and standards bring a legitimacy that cannot be said to attach to exported national models which, all too often, reflect more the individual interests or experience of donors and assistance providers than they do the best interests or legal development needs of host countries.[128]

The UN itself claims that these norms and standards also set the normative boundaries of its actions, such that, for example, United Nations tribunals can never allow for capital punishment, United Nations-endorsed peace agreements can never promise amnesties for genocide, war crimes, crimes against humanity or gross violations of human rights, and, where the United Nations are mandated to undertake executive or judicial functions, they must comply with international standards for human rights in the administration of justice.[129]

An act or institution enacted within those boundaries can therefore be seen as legitimate only if it follows the rule of law. Following the United Nations understanding of the rule of law,

> it refers to a principle of governance in which all persons, institutions and entities, public and private, including the State itself, are accountable to laws that are publicly promulgated, equally enforced and independently adjudicated, and which are consistent with international human rights norms and standards. It requires, as well, measures to ensure adherence to the principles of supremacy of law, equality before the law, accountability to the law, fairness in the application of the law, separation of powers, participation in decision-making, legal certainty, avoidance of arbitrariness and procedural and legal transparency.[130]

When the UN itself declares the rule of law as a normative basis for their activities, the Security Council's regime on children and armed conflict must meet those standards.

Concerning an existing system, there are two relevant factors. On the one hand, the underlying norms and their application must be legitimate, and on the other hand, the body trying to enforce these norms must act legitimately. Even Max Weber already emphasized that rules tend to achieve compliance when the actor perceives both the rule and the ruler as legitimate.[131] And in regard to the acting of the Security Council, Bruno Simma already concluded in 1994, 'that – in the last resort – the

[128] Ibid. para. 10. [129] Ibid. paras. 9–10. [130] Ibid. para. 6.

[131] Cited in Franck, 'Legitimacy in the International System', above note 123, at 709.

effectiveness of the council will depend on the legitimacy of its decision. If Council decisions appear to be strained, far-fetched or even unjust, States may increasingly hesitate to implement them'.[132]

The UN Security Council's system on children and armed conflict is based upon the six grave violations, which are based on fundamental principles taken from international humanitarian law and human rights law, and those actions concerned are prohibited under both regimes of law. Generally, norms and standards of international human rights law and international humanitarian law are seen as legitimate since they derive from international treaty law and international customary law. Both systems generate norms based on the principle of consensus and by accepting the point of view of the parties concerned, they are widely accepted, and their legitimacy is not questioned. Therefore, the question is not if the international norms of protecting children affected by war upon which the system of the UN is built are legitimate themselves, but whether the application of the norms[133] by the Security Council can be considered legitimate.

In the following, different criteria of the rule of law will be analysed. It will be shown that the mechanism on children and armed conflict meets some legitimacy objections which might have the capacity to weaken the authority and credibility of the UN Security Council and its sanction tools. As a consequence, it is at least possible that parties are less likely to fulfil their obligations. Four basic principles of the rule of law that seek to prevent the misuse or abuse of power and those, identified by Farrall, such as due processes, transparency, consistency and equality[134] shall guide the way of the analysis.

4.2.1. Due process

'The principle of due process requires that a party against which it is proposed to exercise coercive power should be given a fair hearing and be granted the opportunity to express their point of view regarding the

[132] B. Simma, 'From Bilateralism to Community Interest in International Law' (1994) *Recueil des Cours* 250, at 281–82.

[133] Sabine von Schorlemer calls it 'praxisrelevante Konkretisierung des Regelwerkes[practice relevant concretization of the rules]', in Schorlemer, *Kindersoldaten und bewaffneter Konflikt*, above note 113, at 290.

[134] Farrall also identifies proportionality as a basic principle, but since exact information about the respective targeted sanctions is not available, it is not possible to judge their proportionality in detail.

potential decision'.[135] The principle of due process, as a part of the rule of law, is applicable to every step of this listing process in which personal rights are possibly infringed since it aims to prevent the misuse and abuse of political power. 'In the context of UN sanctions, the principle of due process requires that States, non-state actors and individuals against which coercive measures are to be applied should be afforded the possibility to present their version of events and, in the case of individuals, to be presumed innocent until proven guilty'.[136]

The listing process of groups or State forces violating child rights takes place without any participation of the group concerned. It is rather the Secretary-General who, based on information gathered by the Office of the Special Representative of Children and Armed Conflict and different country teams, decides whether a group is listed or not. There is no right of the perpetrator to be heard in advance; some of the parties listed did not even know such a list existed.[137] This procedure clearly violates the principle of due process, even though, on first sight, being listed has no direct impact on the parties other than publicly shaming them. But the Secretary-General also encourages the Security Council[138] as well as other institutions to consider the information provided in the lists in its deliberations and actions concerning country-specific situations. This enlarges the possible impact the listing itself may have.

A second point of concern is the de-listing process. In its 2007 report, the Secretary-General described de-listing for the first time:

> Parties who fully comply with terms set forth in action plans and undertake verified measures to address all other grave violations for which they have been cited, to the satisfaction of the country-level task forces on monitoring and reporting or United Nations country teams and the Task Force on Children and Armed Conflict, will be considered for de-listing from the annexes. De-listing does not in any way negate the requirement for continued monitoring of formerly listed parties by the country team. Should it be determined that the de-listed parties recruit and use children at a later point in time or fail to allow continuous and unhindered access to the United Nations for verification, they will be re-listed onto the annexes and the Security Council alerted to non-compliance.[139]

[135] J. Farrall, *United Nations Sanctions and the Rule of Law* (Cambridge: Cambridge University Press, 2007), at 423.

[136] Ibid. 423. [137] See text to above note 106.

[138] For instance, 'Children and Armed Conflict' (26 November 2002), above note 82, para. 28.

[139] 'Report of the Secretary-General on Children and Armed Conflict' (21 December 2007), UN Doc. A/62/609-S/2007/757, para. 17.

The first official document where more detailed information about the procedures of listing and de-listing are described in is the Secretary-General's report about children and armed conflict from 13 April 2010, as requested by the Security Council in its Resolution 1882 (2009). As far as the listing is concerned, the Secretary-General explains what is understood by the different violations. Once listed, 'a party will be de-listed on the condition that there is United Nations-verified information that it has ceased commission of all the said grave violations[[140]] against children for which the party is listed in the Secretary-General's report on children and armed conflict, for a period of at least one reporting cycle'.[141] 'As part of the de-listing process, a party to the conflict, whether a State or non-state actor, is required to enter into dialogue with the United Nations to prepare and implement a concrete, time-bound action plan to cease and prevent grave violations committed against children for which the party has been listed in the Secretary-General's report on children and armed conflict, in accordance with Security Council resolutions 1539 (2004), 1612 (2005) and 1882 (2009)'.[142] When an actor is de-listed, he is still under special observation. That actor will be monitored as long as the Secretary-General remains concerned that such violations may reoccur.[143] 'The de-listed party must ensure continuous and unhindered access to the United Nations for monitoring and verification of compliance with commitments for a minimum period of one reporting cycle following de-listing, failing which it may be re-listed in the annexes, and the Security Council alerted to the non-compliance'.[144]

In this whole process, there is no procedure foreseen by which the party listed may defend itself or object to being listed. No legal procedures of control of the decision of the listing or de-listing are foreseen. Since there are no other means available, two non-State armed groups listed tried to get removed from the list through public statements.[145] The only possible interaction with the perpetrator takes place on the level of the Working Group, which may use invitations and hearings of the parties

[140] See 'Report of the Secretary-General on Children and Armed Conflict' (9 February 2005), above note 67.

[141] 'Report of the Secretary-General on Children and Armed Conflict' (13 April 2010), UN Doc. A/64/742-S/2010/181, para. 178.

[142] Ibid. para. 179. [143] Ibid. para. 180. [144] Ibid. para. 180.

[145] Karenni National Progressive Party, 'Press Release No 02/09', above note 103 ('Appeal for the Karenni Army's name to be removed from the list of non-state armed groups making use of child soldiers in armed conflict').

before commenting on a situation. Nevertheless, this is just one tool out of many, and the Working group is also not obliged to enter into dialogue. Therefore, no right to participate or even to be heard is guaranteed.

In fact, imposed sanctions have an even more severe impact. These are applied by the Sanctions Committees and follow the general procedures of UN-targeted sanctions. And therefore they meet the same legitimacy constraints that have been discussed since the instalment of the Security Council's sanctions regime under Resolution 1267.[146] UN member States, listed individuals and entities, domestic and international courts and tribunals, human rights non-governmental organizations and other UN organs claim that the sanctions regime established by Resolution 1267 does not secure targeted individuals procedural due process rights, especially the right to an effective remedy.[147]

Some of these concerns were met by different resolutions dealing with the Sanctions Committees and their procedure. In 2008, for example, the Security Council sought to strengthen its review procedures and adopted Resolution 1822 which instructed the Sanctions Committees to review the listed names and to keep the lists as accurate as possible. In terms of transparency, Resolution 1822 foresees that the list and a short reasoning for the listing need to be made public. Subsequently, the Security Council requested the Secretary-General in its Resolution 1730 (2006)[148] to establish within the Secretariat, a focal point to receive de-listing requests as part of its commitment to ensure that fair and clear procedures exist for placing individuals and entities on sanctions lists and for removing them. With regard to the Al-Qaida Sanctions List, the Security Council took another significant step in this direction by establishing, by its Resolution 1904 (2009), the Office of the Ombudsperson.[149]

[146] See, for example, N. Birkhäuser, *Sanktionen des Sicherheitsrats der Vereinten Nationen gegen Individuen* (Frankfurt/Main: Peter Lang, 2007); T. Biersteker and S. Eckert, 'Strengthening Targeted Sanctions Through Fair and Clear Procedures: White Paper Prepared by the Watson Institute Targeted Sanctions Project Brown University' (30 March 2006); J. Genser and K. Barth, 'When Due Process Concerns Become Dangerous: The Security Council's 1267 Regime and the Need for Reform' (2010) 33 *Boston College International and Comparative Law Review* 1.

[147] G. Willis, 'Security Council Targeted Sanctions, Due Processes and the 1267 Ombudsperson' (2011) 42 *Georgetown Journal of International Law* 673.

[148] UNSC Resolution 1730 (19 December 2006).

[149] A detailed analysis of the role of the Ombudsperson can be found in Willis, 'Security Council Targeted Sanctions', above note 147.

However, as Willis rightly acknowledges, the new procedures do not satisfy international legal standards of due process.[150] Neither the focal point for de-listing nor the Ombudsperson is an independent review mechanism since neither has the authority to de-list individuals autonomously, and they do not have the power to grant an effective remedy. Moreover, specific rules for de-listing are lacking, and the Sanctions Committee, which already takes the initial decision, remains the decision-maker in the review process. Therefore, the sanctions regime remains weak and attackable and consequently, the possibility remains for the sanctions regime to be undermined by its defects. As mentioned before, it may be in the parties' self-interest to get de-listed, but this interest will be reduced if no working procedure is foreseen to realize this de-listing. Furthermore, concerning the regime of children and armed conflict, this lack of participation may lead to a lower willingness to enter into dialogue with the UN since no influence on the initial listing process and the sanction regime is possible.

4.2.2. Transparency

'The principle of transparency requires that in the exercise of political power, decision-making should be as open and transparent as possible. The reasoning of a particular decision should therefore be apparent to those affected by the ultimate decision. Moreover, it should be clear that power is exercised in accordance with legitimate authority'.[151] The question of transparency can be tackled on different levels. Generally, the principle of transparency requires that decision-making concerning political power should be as clear and transparent as possible. Thus, the reasoning leading to a particular decision should be clear to those affected by the ultimate decision, as well as the broader public.[152]

It goes without saying that full transparency is hindered when most of the meetings of the Working Group are not official or public or even announced. Moreover, the annual working plan of the Working Group is not announced. The parties concerned may not have an insight when their matter is discussed and decided upon. Another problem is that decisions of the Working Group or subsequent decisions of the Sanctions Committees are not taken timely. Parties concerned, therefore, cannot foresee

[150] Ibid. 737; J. Genser and K. Barth, 'When Due Process Concerns Become Dangerous', above note 146, at 38.

[151] Farrall, *United Nations Sanctions and the Rule of Law*, above note 135, at 186.

[152] Ibid. 185–86.

the consequences of their own behaviour with regard to the mechanism installed.

In the context of the UN sanctions, transparency requires that the Security Council's decision-making process should be as open as possible, with the reasons for applying and modifying sanctions clearly expressed by the Security Council and its Sanctions Committees.[153] These standards are not met by the mechanism on children and armed conflict. There are various examples for missing transparency. Evidently, problems deriving from the lack of due process rights lead to missing transparency. Even though the Secretary-General published[154] some criteria concerning how a group may be listed or de-listed, the whole process remains unclear. The same is valid for the imposed sanctions. The choice of the groups is, on the one hand, a political one, and on the other, a practical one. However, as already seen, the criteria are unclear. For State forces and non-State armed groups violating child rights an improvement of transparency may also help increase the acceptance of enforcement measures of the Working Group and the Security Council.

4.2.3. Equality and consistency

'The principle of equality requires that all parties over whom political power is wielded should be considered equal before that power... In the context of the UN sanctions equality requires that sanctions should not be imposed selectively'.[155] Consistency is another relevant principle and it requires 'that political power should be exercised in a consistent manner... In the context of UN sanctions it [means] that the Council should seek to ensure... that its practice is consistent from one sanction regime to another'.[156]

So far, only a few sanctions have been applied. It appears that there is reluctance or difficulty to find a consensus on enforcing serious responses. Suggestions of applying targeted sanctions or referring to the ICC have been met with resistance.[157] The Security Council's constitution as a political organ sometimes hinders the process of decision-taking, which may lead to a delay of the whole process. This means that persistent

[153] Ibid. 40. [154] See text accompanying note 144 above.

[155] Farrall, *United Nations Sanctions and the Rule of Law*, above note 135, at 41.

[156] Ibid. 41.

[157] Security Council Report, 'Children and Armed Conflict' (4 February 2008), above note 4, para. 8.2.

perpetrators have been targeted by UN sanctions while others, constantly violating the same rights, remain unsanctioned.

Furthermore, the practice of the Security Council or its Sanctions Committees is not foreseeable. In 2010, there was a time gap of seven to thirteen months between the review of the Secretary-General's reports and the conclusions of the Working Group.[158] During this time, information gathered may become outdated. Due to the heavy workload, timely follow-ups are missing as well, which could have an impact on the willingness of the parties to comply with their obligations.

The concerns mentioned in regard to transparency and equality are all based upon the lack of due process. The Security Council urgently needs to work on the process rights in order to respond to the legitimacy constraints, as those examples clearly show. This may even improve compliance by actors already listed and in general improve its credibility as an enforcement body of child rights.

5. Conclusion

As seen, the Security Council developed a complex system to enhance compliance with international standards of protecting children affected by armed conflict. With the established system, the Security Council created a unique model to respond to infringements of children's rights, which has shown reasonable success in convincing parties concerned to enter into action plans and release children from their ranks.

On the other hand, various parties do not comply at all with their international obligations concerning children's rights, and this has not changed at all – even since the involvement of the Security Council. In those cases, as the example of the DRC shows, even years after the implementation, the Monitoring and Reporting mechanism shows little impact. The reasons are manifold. As has already been stated, the Council may need to consider ways of speeding up the process between suggesting sanctions and actually holding individuals accountable in order to maintain its credibility.[159] Furthermore, the limited application of sanctions in practice raises questions about the effectiveness of this tool,[160] and a

[158] Security Council Report, 'Cross-Cutting Report – Children and Armed Conflict' (2 June 2010), para. 4.1, www.securitycouncilreport.org/site/c.glKWLeMTIsG/b.6071139/k.E2D6/CrossCutting_Report_No_1brChildren_and_Armed_Conflictbr2_June_2010.htm.

[159] Security Council Report, 'Children and Armed Conflict' (6 July 2011), above note 34, at 25.

[160] Ibid. 26.

lack of a unified and strong political will among Council members on this issue has also been a problem.[161] Many issues still lie ahead, and measures are needed to improve the effectiveness of the system. The challenge of political will and means for targeted measures must be resolved by member States if the progress that has been registered over the past several years in addressing impunity is to be sustained and extended. Its work and actions are based on the political will of the members of the Security Council and their partners implementing these at the national level. With regard to the political system, there are still many fundamental questions remaining, such as the readiness of the member States, political discussions and especially fair procedures or legal certainty. Moreover, there are still various aspects such as a lack of transparency or timely responses or follow-ups[162] which may reduce the willingness of the parties to comply with their obligations. Legitimacy constraints also reduce the credibility of the Security Council as an enforcement body in general.

Hurd concludes his analysis of motivations for compliance that all of his three models (coercion, self-interest and legitimacy) assume that actors are 'interested' in the sense of pursuing their interests, and thus self-interest must add something more. This may be another reason the Security Council cannot be fully successful if success is defined as all actors obeying the relevant rules on children and armed conflict. Because, as the example of the Lord's Resistance Army shows, all incentives given and all different approaches taken do not change much since they simply do not want to comply. All in all, it must be stressed that an effective monitoring, reporting and compliance regime depends largely on the collaboration of a number of critical stakeholders, particularly member States, UN system partners, non-governmental organizations and local civil society. When one of those actors falls apart, the enforcement of the law in question becomes less probable.

Nevertheless, despite all of these unsolved issues, the Security Council has established a worthy system for enhancing compliance with international norms protecting children affected by armed conflict. It has the power to enhance compliance by using coercion, and if the Security Council improves its willingness to guarantee a fair process and work more transparently, it thereby could even increase the impact of its system. The regime on children and armed conflict already enjoys general

[161] This is due to the high cost of the peacekeeping operation in the DRC and concerns about the feasibility of changing the role of the peacekeeping mission. See ibid. 26.

[162] See text accompanying note 159 above.

acceptance by the UN as well as several States and non-State actors. Still, the number of persistent perpetrators is high, and some groups, such as the Lord's Resistance Army, will not be ready to comply with those standards for many years, but there is a considerable number of parties ready to follow those norms. Having a Working Group, a monitoring and reporting mechanism and an active Special Representative has given this issue a high profile which has proven useful in persuading groups to release children[163] and at least has the potential to show equal results regarding the other grave violations.

[163] Security Council Report, 'Children and Armed Conflict' (2 June 2010), above note 158, at 2.

15

Ensuring peacekeepers' respect for international humanitarian law

SIOBHÁN WILLS

1. Introduction

This chapter sets out to analyse the effectiveness of the mechanisms available for ensuring the accountability of peacekeepers for violations of international humanitarian law, with particular focus on forces deployed to Africa. It has been well known ever since the peacekeeping missions to Somalia in the early 1990s that some peacekeepers do engage in abusive behaviour of vulnerable persons and that the problem is sufficiently widespread to be of serious concern. Problems have arisen to some degree in most missions but notably in Chad, the Côte d'Ivoire, the Democratic Republic of the Congo (DRC), Haiti, Liberia, Sierra Leone and Somalia, as well as in Bosnia, Kosovo and East Timor. Sexual exploitation and abuse is especially problematic[1] but also other forms of exploitation such as profiting from forced labour and plundering resources. Such abuses have given rise to numerous reports by the Secretary-General and a commitment by the UN to a 'zero tolerance' policy, particularly of sexual exploitation and abuse; to improvements in training and appointment of specialized personnel by the UN Department of Peacekeeping Operations; and to the inclusion of conduct undertakings into the model Memorandum of Understanding used for drafting terms of agreement

[1] C. Csaky, 'No One to Turn to: The Under-Reporting of Child Sexual Exploitation and Abuse by Aid Workers and Peacekeepers' (2008); S. Martin, 'Must Boys be Boys: Ending Sexual Exploitation and Abuse in Peacekeeping Missions' (2005); N. Dahrendorf for UN Department of Peacekeeping Operations, 'Sexual Exploitation and Abuse: Lessons Learned Study, Addressing Sexual Exploitation and Abuse in MONUC' (March 2006); Wilton Park, 'Report on Wilton Park Conference WP914 – Women Targeted or Affected by Armed Conflict: What Role for Military Peacekeepers?' (June 2008), www.wiltonpark.org.uk/wp-content/uploads/wp914-report.pdf; M. O'Brien, 'Overcoming Boys-Will-Be-Boys Syndrome: Is Prosecution of Peacekeepers in the International Criminal Court for Trafficking, Sexual Slavery and Related Crimes against Women a Possibility?' (Master's Thesis, University of Lund, 2004).

with troop-contributing States.[2] However, the fact remains that despite efforts by the UN, abuse by peacekeepers continues to be a pervasive problem.

Not all abuses committed by peacekeepers amount to violations of international humanitarian law, but many of the more serious ones would come within the terms of the Geneva Conventions (GC), in particular Geneva Convention IV, were it applicable. Many abuses violate applicable international human rights law, which in some respects may provide a better avenue for accountability than international humanitarian law, but that discussion is beyond the scope of this chapter. The guidelines on the applicability of international humanitarian law to UN personnel set out in the Secretary-General's Bulletin ST/SGB/1999/13 of 6 August 1999 assume that international humanitarian law is binding on peacekeepers in its entirety or not at all and that it only applies to personnel while they are 'actively engaged as combatants'.[3] This chapter argues that this approach to whether peacekeepers are bound by international humanitarian law is no longer tenable (and was in any case never very clear) because peacekeeping has evolved to become far more interventionist than was ever envisaged when it was first created in the 1950s.[4] Moreover, since Security

[2] Comprehensive review of the whole question of peacekeeping operations in all their aspects: UN General Assembly (UNGA), 'Letter dated 24 March 2005 from the Secretary-General to the President of the General Assembly' (24 March 2005), UN Doc. A/59/710; Secretary-General's Bulletin 'Special Measures for Protection from Sexual Exploitation and Sexual Abuse' (9 October 2003), UN Doc. ST/SGB/2003/13; Special Committee on Peacekeeping Operations, 'Annex to Report of the Special Committee on Peacekeeping Operations and its Working Group' (12 June 2007) A/61/19 (part III); UNGA, 'General Assembly Adopts Recommendations on Peacekeeping Operations, Including United Nations Standards of Conduct' (24 July 2007), UN Doc. GA/10605.

[3] Comprehensive review of the whole question of peacekeeping operations in all their aspects: UN General Assembly (UNGA), 'Letter dated 24 March 2005 from the Secretary-General to the President of the General Assembly' (24 March 2005), UN Doc. A/59/710; Secretary-General's Bulletin 'Special Measures for Protection from Sexual Exploitation and Sexual Abuse' (9 October 2003), UN Doc. ST/SGB/2003/13; Special Committee on Peacekeeping Operations, 'Annex to Report of the Special Committee on Peacekeeping Operations and its Working Group' (12 June 2007) A/61/19 (part III); UNGA, 'General Assembly Adopts Recommendations on Peacekeeping Operations, Including United Nations Standards of Conduct' (24 July 2007), UN Doc. GA/10605. Secretary-General's Bulletin 'Observance by United Nations Forces of International Humanitarian Law', New York, 6 August 1999, in force 12 August 1999, UN Doc. ST/ SGB/1999/13. The Bulletin is an internal document of the UN. It is binding on UN troops but does not in itself create direct legal obligations for States. ICRC, 'Report of Experts Meeting on Multi-National Operations' (11–12 December 2003), at 2.

[4] UN peacekeeping evolved during the Cold War as an alternative means of managing relations between member States because superpower opposition prevented the Security

Council members often need to make significant compromises to secure agreement between them on the drafting of resolutions (at least enough to avoid a veto), peacekeeping mandates are often worded in opaque terms that are open to a range of interpretations. This has contributed to the increased blurring of the distinction between peacekeeping and enforcement action.

While the dichotomy between civilian and 'member of the armed forces of a party to the conflict' remains the primary basis for the application of targeting rules (supplemented by the rule allowing targeting of civilians 'for such time as they are directly participating in hostilities'), it is no longer the case that it is only persons 'engaged as combatants' who have obligations under international humanitarian law. Civilians may also have obligations under international humanitarian law if their acts or omissions have a direct nexus to the armed conflict,[5] even if that nexus is not so close as to deprive them of protection from attack under Article 51(3) of Additional Protocol I to the Geneva Conventions (AP I).[6] Moreover, although peacekeepers may be protected persons for the purposes of targeting, they wield considerably more power locally, by virtue of belonging

Council from reaching the consensus needed to authorize enforcement action. Military units were deployed to mitigate the effects of local violence and to assist the parties in maintaining peace, but only with the consent of the parties to the conflict. They were normally commanded and controlled by the Secretary-General: S. Wills, *The Responsibility to Protect: The Obligations of Peacekeepers* (Oxford: Oxford University Press, 2009), at 3; M. Bothe, 'Peacekeeping', in B. Simma (ed.), *The Charter of the United Nations: A Commentary*, 2d ed. (Oxford: Oxford University Press, 2002), 648–700, at 662, para. 7; M. Berdal, 'The UN Security Council and Peacekeeping', in V. Lowe, A. Roberts, J. Welsh and D. Zaum (eds.), *The UN Security Council and War: The Evolution of Thought and Practice since 1945* (Oxford: Oxford University Press, 2008), 175–205, at 176; UN Department of Peacekeeping Operations, 'General Guidelines for Peacekeeping Operations' UN Doc. UN/210/TC/GG95 (1995), at 2–3.

5 J.-M. Henckaerts and L. Doswald-Beck (eds.), *Customary International Humanitarian Law*, 2 vols. (Cambridge: Cambridge University Press, 2005), vol. I, Rule 158, at 607–11; 'Special Issue on Private Military Companies' (2006) 88 *International Review of the Red Cross; Prosecutor v. Tesch and two Others* (Zyklon B Case), British Military Court Hamburg, 1946, I Law Reports of Trials of War Criminals, 103; *Prosecutor v. Akayesu* (Judgment) ICTR-96-4-T (2 September 1998), para. 630.

6 The ICRC's Interpretive Guidance on the Notion of Direct Participation in Hostilities notes that 'while collective punishment, hostage-taking, and the ill-treatment and summary execution of persons in physical custody are invariably prohibited by IHL [international humanitarian law], they are not part of the conduct of hostilities. Such conduct may constitute a domestic or international crime and permit the lawful use of armed force against the perpetrators as a matter of law enforcement or defence of self or others'. N. Melzer, Legal Adviser ICRC, 'Interpretive Guidance on the Notion of Direct Participation in Hostilities under International Humanitarian Law' (2009), at 62.

to an 'army' (and a foreign one at that), than an ordinary civilian resident of the host State; and they should be held to a higher standard of conduct and accountability.

2. Changes in the nature of peacekeeping

The UN Department of Peacekeeping Operations believes that 'UN peacekeeping is at a crossroads. The scale and complexity of peacekeeping today are straining its personnel, administrative and support machinery. New political, military and financial challenges threaten to erode the unity of vision and purposes of the global peacekeeping partnership'.[7] This is undoubtedly true and has implications for the status and accountability of troops. The last decade has seen the number of peacekeepers deployed increase fivefold. The aims and objectives of peacekeeping have also changed radically. This is due in part to the response to the UN's failure to prevent widespread commission of international crimes (including genocide, crimes against humanity, war crimes and ethnic cleansing) notably in Somalia, Rwanda and the former Yugoslavia in the 1990s and in the DRC more recently and also in part due to the response to the increased complexity of missions, which has been building inexorably since the end of the Cold War. UN peacekeeping mission objectives are now manifold and various. They frequently include civilian protection, decommissioning, State-building, facilitating democratic processes (e.g., elections), supporting the host State government and establishing a government or some sort of administration in areas of limited statehood. Indeed, Kofi Annan in his 2002 report, 'No Exit Without Strategy', suggested three key objectives that contribute to successful peace building: 'consolidating internal and external security, strengthening political institutions and good governance, and promoting economic and social rehabilitation and transformation'.[8] None of these objectives would have been relevant to traditional peacekeeping missions as Hammarskjöld had envisaged them.[9] Some of the more recent mission objectives, such

7 Department of Peacekeeping Operations and Department of Field Support, 'A New Partnership Agenda: Charting a New Horizon for United Nations Peacekeeping' (July 2009), at ii.

8 'Report of the Secretary-General on No Exit Without Strategy: Security Council Decision-Making and the Closure or Transition of United Nations Peacekeeping Operations' (20 April. 2001), 4 UN Doc. S/2001/394 para. 44; R. Gowan, 'The Strategic Context: Peacekeeping in Crisis, 2006–08' (2008) 15 *International Peacekeeping* 453, at 463.

9 Hammarskjöld drafted the guiding principles for peacekeeping operations in 1958, which still form the bedrock of peacekeeping doctrine. 'Report of the Secretary-General: Summary Study of the Experience Derived from the Establishment and Operation of the Force' (9 October 1958), UN Doc. A/3943.

as civilian protection, are routinely mandated under Chapter VII of the UN Charter.

The liberal vision of the transformative power of peace operations reflected in Kofi Annan's 'No Exit Without Strategy' report, draws on and is supported by policy documents such as 'Recovering from Conflict: Strategy for an International Response', produced by the New York Center on International Cooperation in 2000, which states that: '[a]lthough each post-conflict situation (like each conflict) possesses unique attributes, recovery typically involves a "triple transition": from war to peace; from a controlled to a market economy; and from authoritarianism (or totalitarianism) to democracy'.[10] To some critics, the liberal agenda that is now at the heart of UN peace operations and explicitly stated to be so (which would not have been possible during the Cold War), renders peacekeeping missions, especially the more complex ones, less an impartial means of assisting neighbouring States to maintain peace between themselves, but more a form of imperialism.[11] Nizami, writing in 1993 on the *Emergence of Africa in International Politics*, argued that 'there is not a single instance of peacekeeping that one could cite which has helped the struggle of the peoples of the third world against oppression and imperialism'.[12] Pugh, writing critically in 2005 on the 'political economy of peace building', comments that '[s]ilence surrounds the role of interventionary core capitalism in perpetuating poverty through discriminatory policies that structure the global economy'.[13] He argues that 'the discursive trope of imperial peacebuilding pathologises populations in war-torn societies as if suffering from congenital incapacities that need treatment through forms of therapeutic governance... Archived as congenitally incapable of governance and statehood, these societies require forms of trusteeship that inevitably reflect the priorities of the trustees'.[14] More controversially, Mamdani has challenged the widely

[10] S. Forman, S. Patrick and D. Salomons, 'Recovering from Conflict: Strategy for an International Response' (2000), at 6; Gowan, Peacekeeping in Crisis, above note 8.

[11] C. Schellhaas and A. Seegers, 'Peacebuilding: Imperialism's New Disguise?' (2009) 18 *African Security Review* 2; S. Razak, *Dark Threats and White Knights: The Somalia Affair, Peacekeeping, and the New Imperialism* (Toronto: University of Toronto Press, 2004); M. Ottaway and B. Lacina, 'International Interventions and Imperialism: Lessons from the 1990s' (2003) 23 *SAIS Review of International Affairs* 2; P. Bennis, *Calling the Shots: How Washington Dominates Today's U.N.* (New York: Olive Branch Press, 1996).

[12] T. A. Nizami, *Emergence of Africa in International Politics* (New Delhi: Mittal Publications, 1993), at 78.

[13] M. Pugh, 'The Political Economy of Peacebuilding: A Critical Theory Perspective' (2005) 10 *International Journal of Peace Studies* 23, at 33.

[14] Ibid. 34.

held view that the Sudanese government's attacks on civilians in Darfur amount to crimes against humanity (a view that is supported by the results of a UN enquiry and numerous NGO reports),[15] claiming that equally large numbers of civilians have been killed in Iraq, but that these have been described differently to serve a different political agenda.[16]

The primary purpose for which the UN was founded was not to protect civilians, or to impartially arbitrate on inter-State and intra-State disputes, or to bring about a fairer distribution of the earth's resources, but instead, it was to reduce (ideally eliminate entirely) the risk of inter-State war, especially between the major powers. Hence, it is not surprising that peacekeeping (created in response to the inability of Security Council members to agree on policy responses to threats to international peace and security during the Cold War) serves not only as a means of curtailing and stabilizing conflict but also as a means of advancing the interests or mitigating threats to the interests, of international, regional and local powers. The problem is exacerbated by the fact that the ambitious mandates of current missions tend to be drawn up by the more powerful States on the Security Council (who generally also provide the funding); but it is generally the less developed States that provide the troops who take the risks, giving rise to the criticism that the West 'shouldn't be allowed to make the rules if it won't play the game'.[17]

In the African context, France is praised for its willingness to undertake peacekeeping missions in its former colonies (in contrast to most other major powers, at least until recently),[18] but it is also criticized because

[15] International Commission of Inquiry on Darfur (ICID), 'Report of the International Commission of Inquiry on Darfur to the United Nations Secretary-General, Pursuant to Security Council Resolution 1564 of 18 September 2004' (25 January 2005); US Agency for International Development (USAID), The Humanitarian Situation in Sudan; P. Kagwanja and P. Mutahi for the Institute for Security Studies, 'Protection of Civilians in African Peace Missions: The Case of the African Union Mission in Sudan, Darfur' (2007), at 2; S. Chin and J. Morgenstein for Refugees International, 'No Power to Protect: The African Union Mission in Sudan' (11 September 2005), at 1.

[16] Mamdani writes that 'the violence in [Iraq and Darfur] is named differently. In Iraq, it is said to be a cycle of insurgency and counter-insurgency; in Darfur, it is called genocide. Why the difference? Who does the naming? Who is being named? What difference does it make?' M. Mamdani, 'The Politics of Naming; Genocide, Civil War, Insurgency' (2007) 29 *London Review of Books* 5.

[17] E. Paddon, 'Partnering for Peace: Implications and Dilemmas' (2011) 18 *International Peacekeeping* 516, at 520.

[18] US Africa Command was created by Presidential order in 2007 and became active in 2008. Its Mission Statement declares that 'United States Africa Command, in concert with interagency and international partners, builds defense capabilities, responds to crisis, and

its desire to support a strong Francophone presence in the continent ensures that missions in which it is involved are deployed in such a way as to ensure that Francophone interests are protected. Operation Turquoise (a French-led mission to Rwanda undertaken from June to August 1994, immediately after the genocide) is a notable example of this problem. The protected area established by the French forces also gave safe haven to escaped members of the Rwandan Armed Forces and leaders of the *interhamwe* (many of them participants in the genocide). France had supported the Rwandan government militarily right up until the genocide began.[19] More recently, France has been criticized for seeking to manipulate the deployment of UN and EU missions to Chad and the Central African Republic in 2009 in order to keep the regime of Idriss Déby in power.[20]

At a regional level, Nigeria, the dominant power in West Africa, has drawn criticism that it views the Economic Community of West African States (ECOWAS), of which it is the lead player, as 'an expression of that country's foreign policy rather than an impartial agent of West African peacemaking',[21] especially in relation to the Economic Community of West African States Monitoring Group (ECOMOG) missions in the 1990s to Sierra Leone and Liberia. Part of the problem is the rivalry between some of the ECOWAS States (divided partly but not exclusively on whether they were traditionally French or English speaking),[22] which led to a lack of political consensus on the ECOMOG mandate with some ECOWAS member States opposed to the ECOMOG mission and a few even actively supporting the rebels against it.[23] Arguably, '[a]s experiences in West Africa demonstrate, regional organisations have greater interest in responding to conflicts since they are directly affected. But being closer to the conflicting parties also means that members of a regional body often

deters and defeats transnational threats in order to advance U.S. national interests and promote regional security, stability, and prosperity.' AFRICOM Mission Statement, http://www.africom.mil/what-we-do.

[19] A. Adebajo, *Liberia's Civil War: Nigeria, ECOMOG and Regional Security in West Africa* (Boulder, Colorado: Lynne Rienner, 2002), at 245–47; Paddon, 'Partnering for Peace', above note 17, at 526.

[20] A. Adebajo, 'UN Peacekeeping in Africa', International Peace Institute (2011), at 230.

[21] Paddon, 'Partnering for Peace', above note 17, at 526.

[22] Benin, Niger and Togo have traditionally been close to Nigeria, and Senegal has traditionally been supported by the Economic Community of West African States (ECOWAS). Adebajo, *Liberia's Civil War*, above note 19, at 11.

[23] J. Kabia, *Humanitarian Intervention and Conflict Resolution in West Africa* (Ashgate: Farnham Publishing Company, 2009), at 192.

have vested interests and may find it difficult to remain neutral'.[24] ECOMOG's efforts to provide humanitarian assistance in the face of extreme levels of human suffering in Sierra Leone and Liberia (to which ECOMOG responded robustly despite not having a Security Council mandate, albeit with limited success owing to lack of resources) led directly to the establishment of the Organization of African Unity's Mechanism for Conflict Prevention, Management and Resolution and subsequently to the inclusion in the Constitutive Act of the African Union (the successor to the Organization of African Unity) of a right to intervene in member State's 'in respect of grave circumstances, namely war crimes, genocide and crimes against humanity'.[25]

2.1. *Use of force*

The circumstances in which peacekeepers can use force have been gradually expanding since the UN Mission in the Congo (ONUC) in the early 1960s. Within the expanded concept of self-defence normally permitted to peacekeepers today,[26] use of force is usually authorized in response to 'hostile intent' as well as hostile attack. The Rules of Engagement for Operation Restore Hope, the 1992 US-led humanitarian intervention in Somalia, interpreted 'hostile intent' to include merely being armed:

> Within those areas under the control of U.S. forces, armed individuals may be considered a threat to U.S. forces and the relief effort whether or not the individual demonstrates hostile intent. Commanders are authorized to use all necessary force to disarm and demilitarize groups or individuals in those areas under their control.[27]

In Somalia, it is traditional for men to carry arms. The Rules of Engagement for the UN peacekeeping mission that replaced Operation Restore Hope, UNOSOM II, took an even more robust approach that 'left the impression that the response to unarmed harassment could be the same

[24] Ibid.

[25] Constitutive Act of the African Union, Lomé, 11 July 2000, in force 26 May 2001, 2158 U.N.T.S. 3, Article 4(h); Kabia, *Humanitarian Intervention*, above note 23, at 187.

[26] 'Report of the Secretary-General on the Implementation of Security Council Resolution 340' (27 October 1973), UN Doc. S/11052/Rev.1; T. Findlay, *The Use of Force in Peace Operations* (Oxford: Oxford, University Press, 2002), at 100.

[27] Rules of Engagement for Operation Restore Hope, para. 3(11), www.globalsecurity.org/military/library/policy/army/fm/100-23/fm100_10.htm.

as that envisaged for armed threat, namely deadly force'.[28] In the absence of any means of enforcing law and order, people, including teenagers, were shot for minor crimes, such as theft.[29]

Patrice Sartre, a retired French General who served in the Central African Republic, the DRC and Rwanda, as well as in the former Yugoslavia, has argued that while the peacekeeping doctrine is still based on the idea of the consent of the parties, the concept has lost 'some of its weight', particularly when the local population, or the force itself, are at risk of attack:

> [P]eacekeeping is impelled to go beyond an exclusively defensive posture, and allow itself limited and local offensive actions, with the proviso that they are not diverted toward coercive ends that remain beyond its remit. This more robust attitude cannot be legitimated by the concept of self-defence alone, on which the (purely defensive) use of force was previously based. It now seems necessary to base it on a duty to protect, a task that the international community gives to peacekeeping missions.[30]

The suggestion that the duty to protect provides a legal basis for peacekeepers to take offensive action is a radical development when compared with the original conception of peacekeeping as it was first posited in the 1950s, but that concept separated from a full alignment with practice fairly early on. For example, in 1962, the UN Mission in the Congo (ONUC) took decisive action (including the use of air attacks) to end the secession of the province of Katanga. However, acting Secretary-General U Thant insisted that the measures taken came within the remit of self-defence and that '[t]he purpose of the present military operations is to regain and assure our freedom of movement, restore law and order, and to ensure that for the future UN officials in Katanga are not subject to attacks; and meanwhile to react vigorously in self-defence to every assault on our present positions, by all the means available to us'.[31] But at the

[28] R. Murphy, *UN Peacekeeping in Lebanon, Somalia and Kosovo: Operational and Legal Issues in Practice* (Cambridge: Cambridge University Press, 2007), at 161.

[29] Ibid. The torture and killing of a young boy for breaching the perimeter of the Canadian mission's camp was only one of a number of such incidents of excessive use of force to control minor criminality in areas of limited statehood. M. J. Kelly, *Restoring and Maintaining Order in Complex Peace Operations* (The Hague: Kluwer, 1999), at 28.

[30] P. Sartre, 'Making Peace Keeping More Robust: Protecting the Mission, Persuading the Actors' (New York: International Peace Academy, August 2011), at 2.

[31] Quoted in G. Draper, 'The Legal Limitations Upon the Employment of Weapons by the United Nations Force in the Congo' (1963) 12 *International and Comparative Law Quarterly* 387, at 406.

time, the issues that arose in the DRC were thought unlikely to arise again an assumption that has shown to be mistaken. A number of key troop-contributing States are uneasy at the extensive scope of the changes in the conceptual basis of peacekeepers' authority to use force, in part because of operational consequences, including the higher risks to troops and also because of 'the fact that it is seen by some member states as a Western-driven agenda'.[32] Controversy is particularly acute in relation to the Intervention Brigade authorized to operate within the MONUSCO peacekeeping mission but authorized as a peace enforcement brigade to 'carry out targeted offensive operations in a robust, highly mobile and versatile manner' to 'neutralize [armed] groups' in the DRC.[33] A 2010 report based on a number of debates organized by the Center on International Cooperation at New York University on 'Building More Effective Peace Operations' noted that there is a 'need to achieve strategic agreement among peacekeeping stakeholders on key issues that have recently proven divisive. In particular, reaching consensus on issues like the protection of civilian [sic] and the implications of robust peacekeeping would be useful in providing clearer mandates and potentially illustrate the limitations of UN peacekeeping in relation to both capabilities and ultimate objective'.[34]

2.2. *Protection of civilians*

The commitment to protection has increased steadily since the Security Council adopted the first of a series of resolutions on the protection of civilians in 1999.[35] Since 1999, most UN peacekeeping mandates have included an undertaking to protect civilians. Usually, the mandate authorizes (often under Chapter VII) the protection of civilians under threat of imminent attack in the immediate vicinity of the force, insofar as protection is within its capabilities; but this expectation is not always consistent with the limited resources available to many peacekeeping missions. Thus, Resolution 1291 of February 2000 authorized the UN Mission in the Congo (MONUC) to protect civilians 'under imminent threat of violence' insofar as it deems protecting them to be 'within

[32] Paddon, 'Partnering for Peace', above note 17, at 524–25.

[33] UNSC Resolution 2098 (28 March 2013).

[34] Center on International Cooperation, 'Towards More Inclusive Mandate-Making, More Effective Mandate Implementation', at 3, cic.es.its.nyu.edu/sites/default/files/mandate_bkgrnden.pdf.

[35] United Nations Security Council (UNSC) Resolution 1265 (17 September 1999).

its capabilities'.[36] However, the Secretary-General in his February 2001 report, after expressing concern over credible reports of massacres of civilians and terrible cruelties perpetrated against them, said that 'it is important to stress' that protection of local population was outside the capabilities of the mission.[37]

Today, protection of civilians has become the top priority for the current UN mission in the DRC[38] and a core activity for peacekeeping missions in general. It is increasingly a central topic in the political debates surrounding mission mandates. The language of civilian protection, developed essentially in the context of peacekeeping, has now dovetailed with the separate but related concept of the responsibility to protect.[39] The blurring of the two concepts has developed to such an extent that the intervention in Libya in 2011 (which included direct assistance to the rebels in the form of intelligence and air support) was premised on a commitment 'to protect civilians and civilian populated areas under threat of attack' (language that bears close parallels with civilian protection provisions routinely included in most peacekeeping mandates adopted since 1999) rather than on the prevention of genocide, crimes against humanity, war crimes and ethnic cleansing, the criteria set out in the General Assembly World Summit resolution of 2005 and endorsed by the Security Council in 2006.[40] The relevant provisions of the latter resolutions drew on the 'responsibility to protect' concept developed in 2001 by the International Commission on Intervention and State Sovereignty, in response to calls from Kofi Annan to find some means of resolving the potential conflict between respect for State sovereignty and the protection of human rights, in the wake of strong criticism of the Kosovo bombing campaign of 1999, particularly from African States.

In a similar vein to the Libya intervention of 2011, the civilian protection provisions of the mandate for the UN peacekeeping mission in Côte d'Ivoire (which was assisted by the French mission Licorne operating

[36] UNSC Resolution 1291 (24 February 2000) para. 8.

[37] 'Sixth Report of the Secretary-General on MONUC' (12 February 2001), UN Doc. S/2001/128 paras. 54–64, 77.

[38] In UNSC Resolution 1925 (28 May 2010): the Council '[e]mphasizes that the protection of civilians must be given priority in decisions about the use of available capacity and resources and authorizes MONUSCO to use all necessary means, within the limits of its capacity and in the areas where its units are deployed, to carry out its protection mandate'.

[39] International Commission on Intervention and State Sovereignty (ICISS), *The Responsibility to Protect* (Ottawa: International Development Research Centre, 2001).

[40] UNGA Resolution A/RES/6/1 (24 October 2005) para. 139; UNSC Resolution 1674 (28 April 2006) para. 4.

under the same mandate) also formed the basis for Secretary-General Ban Ki-moon's request to Licorne to assist Alassane Outarra's forces in forcing former President Laurent Gbagbo to relinquish power. Gbagbo had refused to recognize the legitimacy of elections in Outarra's favour and was attacking civilians in order to hold onto power. Resolution 1975 condemned 'the decision of Mr. Laurent Gbagbo not to accept the overall political solution proposed by the High-Level panel put in place by the African Union' and urged him 'to immediately step aside'. It also authorized the United Nations Mission in Côte d'Ivoire (UNOCI) and Licorne under Chapter VII to protect civilians 'under imminent threat of physical violence, within its capabilities and its areas of deployment, including to prevent the use of heavy weapons against the civilian population'.[41] Arguably, Licorne's support to the rebels against Gbagbo in their ten-day battle for Abidjan went beyond the strict provisions of Resolution 1975; but the Secretary-General was clearly of the view that, unless Gbagbo was forced to leave, the situation would rapidly deteriorate into civil war. Gbagbo's appalling human rights record is not in doubt; but there has been criticism that the international community's approach has not been impartial. Gbagbo was sent to The Hague in 2011, but in that same year, 'former rebels loyal to Ouattara' were 'still committing abuses such as executions and torture'.[42] In May 2011, Amnesty International reported that 'UNOCI has a mandate to protect the civilian population yet in some cases it clearly failed to do this'. When challenged on this, UNOCI officials said that 'it is the duty of the state to protect civilians'.[43] In its 2012 World report on Côte d'Ivoire, Amnesty International concluded that '[i]nternational actors that had rightfully taken a hardline stance against the Gbagbo camp's abuses during the conflict – including the United Nations, the European Union, France, and the United States – appeared less willing to publicly pressure Ouattara's government on the same issues and on the importance of impartial accountability'.[44]

[41] UNSC Resolution 1975 (30 March 2011).

[42] A Gray-Block, 'Gbagbo, Ouattara Forces Engaged in War Crimes: ICC', Reuters, 23 June 2011, www.reuters.com/article/2011/06/23/us-ivorycoast-icc-idUSTRE75M76620110623.

[43] Amnesty International, 'Côte d'Ivoire: Both Sides Responsible for War Crimes and Crimes against Humanity', 25 May 2011, www.amnesty.dk/english/node/3311.

[44] Human Rights Watch, 'World Report 2012: Côte d'Ivoire', www.hrw.org/world-report-2012/c-te-d-ivoire.

The Licorne intervention in Côte d'Ivoire was undertaken at the same time as the intervention against Quadaffi was underway in Libya. In fact the Secretary-General in his address to the extraordinary session of the Security Council on Human Rights in Africa, convened in February 2011 primarily in response to the crisis in Libya, spoke first on the situation in Côte d'Ivoire, stressing the link between human rights and democracy:

> Before we discuss the deeply disturbing situation in Libya, allow me to quickly update the Council on developments elsewhere in Africa . . .
>
> As I have said before, Côte d'Ivoire is an important test for democracy throughout Africa. More than 20 elections are scheduled to be held throughout the continent this year. As elsewhere, the region's leaders must listen to their people. They must respect fundamental human rights. When it comes to democracy and free elections, the will of the people must prevail.
>
> We meet at a critical moment – potentially a defining moment – for the Arab world. Fundamental issues of peace and stability are at stake, most immediately at this moment in Libya.[45]

Civilian protection and the right to democratic governance are being treated as linked concepts quite explicitly, something that would have been difficult in the Hammarskjöld era. Nevertheless, despite the robust use of force by peacekeepers to provide protection in some situations, it is still the case that whether or not UN peacekeeping missions undertake civilian protection depends to a large extent on the resources of the mission, its other objectives, its relationship with the host State and with other local powerful agencies and the intentions of the States contributing to the mission.

2.3. *Stabilization as a mission objective*

'Stabilization' is a relatively recent form of mission objective, initially developed by Western countries to address weak governance, endemic instability and violent conflict in Afghanistan and Iraq. In recent years, 'stabilization' has also become a core objective of UN peacekeeping missions, notably in Sudan, Haiti and the DRC.[46] The UN has not yet produced a separate stabilization doctrine; but the UK's 'Joint Doctrine Publication 3.40', published in November 2009, bluntly states that

[45] UNSC Meeting Record (25 February 2011), UN Doc. S/PV.6490.

[46] E. Paddon and G. Lacaille, 'Stabilising the Congo' (December 2011), at 2; S. Bailey, 'Humanitarian Action, Early Recovery and Stabilisation in the Democratic Republic of Congo' *HPG Working Paper* (2011).

stabilization 'is undertaken in pursuit of the national interest'.[47] The 'ultimate purpose' of a stabilization operation is to 'strengthen an existing political order, or to reshape it, to become more acceptable to that nation's population and more consistent with the UK's strategic interests. However, stabilization is rarely a goal in its own right'.[48] The US doctrine on Stability Operations makes similar points.[49] The UN would no doubt take a more nuanced approach since it does not have strategic interests of its own other than those of its most powerful members, but support for one side (normally the 'legitimate' government) is inherent in the concept of stabilization support. This can pose problems where the government itself poses serious threats to the population, as is the case in the DRC. The UN missions to the DRC are some of the largest and most complex the UN has ever deployed.

2.4. Peacekeepers' relationships with host State governments: the DRC

The UN Mission in the Congo (MONUC) began as a peace support mission in 2000 but was replaced by the UN Organization Stabilization Mission in the Democratic Republic of the Congo (MONUSCO) in 2010 (largely under pressure from Joseph Kabila, president of the DRC, who insisted on the change). Kabila has made it clear that if the UN is not willing to 'uncritically support the state and specifically the FARDC [Forces Armées de la République Démocratique du Congo], it ha[s] no business in the country'.[50] The DRC is a 'failed State', and its weakness 'is most visible in the security sector, where the Congolese national army, the Forces Armées de la République Démocratique du Congo (FARDC), is largely unpaid and poorly trained'.[51] The armed forces of the DRC are also 'often the single greatest threat to the Congolese and routinely terrorises civilians, extorting protection money, looting villages, raping and killing civilians'.[52]

The UN Mission came under particularly severe criticism in 2009 when Kabila, in accordance with a secret pact made with Kagame of Rwanda,

[47] UK Ministry of Defence, 'Joint Doctrine Publication 3.40: Security and Stabilisation: The Military Contribution' (2009), at 203.

[48] Ibid. xv.

[49] US Army, 'Manual FM 3–07 Stability Operations' (October 2008).

[50] Paddon and Lacaille, 'Stabilising the Congo', above note 46, at 22.

[51] Ibid. 6.

[52] Ibid. 6; Human Rights Watch, 'Renewed Crisis in North Kivu' (October 2007); Unreported World, The UN's Dirty War, Channel 4, 23 June 2006, 7.35 pm; A. Hartley, 'UN Accused over Congo Village Massacre', *The Observer*, 18 June 2006, www.guardian.co.uk/world/2006/jun/18/congo.theobserver.

integrated former rebels into the armed forces of the DRC, including some known war criminals. Thus MONUC found itself supporting forces with war criminals, including some that have been indicted by the International Criminal Court.[53] In the wake of these criticisms, UN forces in the DRC have striven to make their support for FARDC forces conditional on monitoring their conduct. But carrying out this policy has proved difficult in practice, partly because of limited UN resources, but primarily because the mission was designed to support a government committed to building peace throughout the country, whereas the government is more interested in augmenting its own power.[54] According to a 2011 Force Migration Policy Briefing by Oxford's Refugee Studies Centre, stabilization in the DRC 'must be understood as a policy geared towards stabilising a particular kind of state that many Congolese see as counter-productive to the long-term goals of peace and stability'.[55] As one local official asserted, 'how can the UN have a mandate both to protect civilians and stabilise the state – when it is agents of that state that need stabilising in order to bring about protection'.[56]

In response to the problems facing MONUC, the UN adopted a Human Rights Due Diligence Policy[57] that applies to all United Nations entities

[53] Former general of the Congrès National pour la Défense du Peuple (CNDP), Bosco Ntaganda, became a commander of the armed forces of the DRC, despite his indictment by the International Criminal Court for war crimes. He also has suspected ties to the mineral trade in the east of the country and may be linked to an ongoing investigation regarding the seizure of 400kg of gold and US$ 1.8 million at the Goma airport in February 2011. 'Quagmire in East Set to Blight DRC Elections', Integrated Regional Information Networks (IRIN), 22 July 2011, www.unhcr.org/refworld/docid/4e301a0a2.html.

[54] Paddon and Lacaille, 'Stabilising the Congo', above note 46, at 19.

[55] Ibid. 20.

[56] Ibid. 12; Adebajo, 'UN Peacekeeping in Africa', above note 20, at 242; 'Congo Supreme Court Upholds Joseph Kabila's Election Victory', *The Guardian*, 16 December 2011, www.guardian.co.uk/world/2011/dec/17/congo-joseph-kabila-election-victory. US observers from the Atlanta-based Carter Center – founded by former President Jimmy Carter – issued a statement saying the vote lacked credibility. David Pottie, one of the senior observers with the Carter Center, said it was impossible to have 100 percent voter turnout in a region where less than 2 percent of the roads are paved, and equally improbable for all the votes to go to Kabila when there were eleven candidates on the ballot. The election took place amid significant unrest in Congo's east, where dozens of militia groups and rebels are active. Government soldiers and rebels have raped women, men and children and burned down villages. Hundreds of thousands of people have been forced to flee their homes because of violence. The fighting is fuelled by the competition to control mines, many operated by soldiers, rebels and militiamen who use the minerals to fund their armed groups.'

[57] See annex to 'Identical Letters Dated 25 February 2013 from the Secretary-General Addressed to the President of the General Assembly and to the President of the Security Council' (5 March 2013), UN Doc. A/67/775–S/2013/110.

providing support to non-UN security forces. The mandate for the UN Mission to Mali (MINUSMA) is one of the first to specifically reference the policy. Resolution 2164 of June 2014 authorizes:

> MINUSMA to take fully into account the need to protect civilians and mitigate risk to civilians, including, in particular, women, children and displaced persons and civilian objects in the performance of its mandate as defined in paragraphs 13 and 14 above, where undertaken jointly with the Malian Defence and Security Forces, in strict compliance with the Human Rights Due Diligence Policy on United Nations Support to non-United Nations Security Forces (S/2013/110);[58]

The Due Diligence Policy states that before support is given an assessment of 'the risk of the recipient entity committing grave violations of international humanitarian law, human rights law or refugee law' must be made and 'procedures for monitoring the recipient entity's compliance with international humanitarian, human rights and refugee law' must be established as part of an effective implementation framework.[59] Grave violations for the purposes of the policy include a 'pattern of repeated violations of international humanitarian, human rights or refugee law committed by a significant number of members of the unit' and the 'presence in a senior command position of the unit of one or more officers about whom there are substantial grounds to suspect', inter alia, '[f]ailure to take effective measures to prevent, repress, investigate or prosecute other violations of international humanitarian, human rights or refugee law committed on a significant scale by those under their command'.[60] The policy requires that if the record of the recipient entity is good enough to allow the UN to provide support but nevertheless subsequently the recipient entity does commit grave violations and

> despite intercession by the United Nations entity concerned, the United Nations receives reliable information that provides substantial grounds to suspect that the recipient entity is continuing to engage in grave violations of international humanitarian, human rights or refugee law, then the United Nations entity must suspend or withdraw support from the recipient.[61]

Missions may be reluctant to withdraw support from a recipient after a mission has been deployed because the mission might then run a high risk of being targeted by the former recipient; so withdrawing support

[58] UNSC Resolution 2164 (25 June 2014).
[59] Due Diligence Policy, above note 57, para. 2.
[60] Ibid. para. 12.
[61] Ibid. para 27.

might mean withdrawing entirely, leaving the local population with no UN presence at all.

The DRC is not the only State to seek to manipulate the role and scope of peacekeeping missions either by forum shopping or by curtailing operational consent and thus limiting the effectiveness of any mission. It took 'arm-twisting' by China to eventually persuade the Sudanese government to permit a UN mission to Darfur in 2007. The Bashir government had long resisted a UN mission preferring 'an ineffectual AU [African Union] force that was clearly unable to keep the peace', alleging that the UN mission was simply a means of the West extending its neocolonial influence in the region.[62] However, the UN mission has been severely hampered in its effectiveness ever since it deployed by numerous operational constraints imposed by the Sudanese government.[63] The governments in Côte d'Ivoire, Burundi and Chad 'have all sought to assert their sovereignty by reducing the role of the UN in their countries'.[64] The UN Mission in Ethiopia and Eritrea was eventually terminated in 2008 because the restrictions on operational consent were crippling the mission.[65]

3. Peacekeepers' unwitting complicity in abuse: Liberia

The problems faced by UN peacekeepers in the DRC in supporting a government whose forces attack and abuse the local population has garnered a high level of attention, particularly in 2009 shortly after the Kabila's decision to give known war criminals positions in the armed forces of the DRC. Unfortunately, these kinds of tensions also operate at a more localized level in many operations, but they rarely get the kind of publicity the DRC abuses attract, because the overall benefits of the operation are perceived to outweigh the suffering caused by human rights abuses committed by local forces and officials.

The UN Mission in Liberia (UNMIL) is a good example. UNMIL, which was established by Security Council resolution 1509 on 19 September 2003, has been viewed very positively for its success in supporting the restructuring of the country's security apparatus; disarmament and demobilization of armed groups; their rehabilitation and reintegration;

62 Adebajo, 'UN Peacekeeping in Africa', above note 20, at 209.

63 B. Jones, 'Peacekeeping in Crisis? Confronting the Challenges Ahead' (2009) 154 *Royal United Service Institute Journal* 5, at 80.

64 Ibid. 242.

65 The restrictions continued despite the Security Council's reiterated 'demand' that Eritrea cooperate with the mission: UNSC Resolution 1798 (30 January 2008) para. 2.

and law reform. The Rules of Engagement for UNMIL allowed for the use of force 'up to and including deadly force . . . to protect civilians, including humanitarian workers, under imminent threat of physical violence, when competent local authorities are not in a position to render immediate assistance'.[66] While the security situation in Liberia remains fragile and violence against women in particular remains a serious problem, a public opinion survey conducted in 2006 indicated that 94 percent of respondents believed that the security situation had improved during UNMIL's deployment, and 91 percent believed that the force conducted itself professionally. Eighty-eight percent believed that UNMIL had helped to improve human rights conditions in Liberia 'by bringing peace to Liberia through increased security, disarmament, and enabling people to have freedom of movement' and also by raising awareness of human rights, holding human rights seminars and intervening on behalf of victims.[67]

However, this is not the full picture: corruption remains rife within Liberian society and continues to present one of the biggest challenges to the UN and other international agencies currently operating there. The former president of the Transitional Government, Gyude Bryant, was charged with corrupt practices while in office but was eventually acquitted. Independent international reports continue to highlight successive administrative and political failure to deal with what has become an endemic societal problem. One Washington-based commentator recently observed that 'among the many failures of the political administration in Liberia, there is one clear and undisputable failure – a failure so clear that both supporters and critics of the government are undivided in their acknowledgment that corruption once declared by President Sirleaf as Public Enemy Number One has become Public Friend Number One'.[68] These problems are not new. The signs were obvious to the senior leaders of UNMIL as far back as 2005, yet little was done to address it. In one particular instance, the UNMIL military was employed to actually propagate corruption, and, in spite of several subsequent reports up the chain of

[66] United Nations Mission in Liberia (UNMIL), Rules of Engagement – Soldiers Pocket Card. A starred postscript adds 'when and where possible, permission to use force should be sought from the immediate superior commander'.

[67] J. Krasno, 'Public Opinion Survey of UNAMSIL's Work in Sierra Leone', External Study undertaken for the UN Department of Peacekeeping Operations, conducted January–February 2005 by City College of New York and Yale University (July 2005), at 5–6, 11–17.

[68] J. A. Toe for National Endowment for Democracy, 'Liberia: Elections, Justice, Corruption and the Role of the International Community' (24 February 2011).

command to UN headquarters, the matter was never satisfactorily dealt with.

In March 2005, the Swedish & Irish Quick Reaction Force received an order (pursuant to a request from local officials) to move into the rubber plantation of the Liberia Agriculture Company, near Buchanan, in order to arrest a group of armed terrorists who were about to destabilize the region. The Quick Reaction Force despatched its strongest military unit and arrived with armoured vehicles and heavy weapons. However, when they got there, they discovered that the 'terrorists' were in fact the leaders of the plantation workers who were lobbying for an increase in their \$2.60 weekly wage. The plantation management had offered an increase of 0.16 cents per person per week, but the workers had rejected this and were holding out for something better. While he was taking in the situation, the commander of the Quick Reaction Force observed that a peacekeeping force from another troop-contributing State was also present and, by its presence, lending its authority to the actions that were taking place. Under cover of the show of force displayed by the two UN units present with their tanks and heavy weapons, the managers of the plantation rounded up the strike leaders and had them beaten and taken away by their henchmen. The eventual outcome for the strikers was a return to work with no increase at all in their wages.

These events were reported fully to the UNMIL civilian and military leadership, who were made aware of what had transpired. However, there is no record of any corrective action having been taken, of any investigation having been initiated nor of any official at any level in Liberian society being personally called to account.[69] Goal Number 5 of UNMIL's Integrated Mandate Implementation Plan was the establishment of safeguards for human rights. This goal demanded, among other things: ratification of international human rights conventions; monitoring human rights violations; strengthening national human rights capacity; establishing an independent national human rights commission; establishing a truth and reconciliation commission; and promoting the rule of law.

4. Applicability of international humanitarian law to peacekeepers

The International Committee of the Red Cross' (ICRC) Study on Customary International Humanitarian Law notes that 'all States have an obligation to investigate war crimes allegedly committed by their nationals

[69] Author's interview with Swedish/Irish Quick Reaction Force.

or armed forces, or on their territory', whether committed in international or non-international armed conflicts and, 'if appropriate to prosecute the suspects'; and that 'all States have the right to vest universal jurisdiction in their national courts over war crimes'.[70] One of the key problems with regard to ensuring the accountability of peacekeepers is to determine whether peacekeeping forces have obligations under the Geneva Conventions despite the fact that the Conventions are formally applicable only to parties to the conflict and, if so, whether peacekeepers may be subject to the international humanitarian law rules providing for universal jurisdiction for acts that would be crimes if committed by a party to the conflict.

Although the UN has never claimed outright exemption from the laws of armed conflict, for a long time, the UN was reluctant to recognize that international humanitarian law applied to its peacekeeping forces. For example, in relation to the Congo conflict of the 1960s, a dispute, which was never resolved, arose between the ICRC and the UN as to whether Common Article 3 GC applied to ONUC forces engaged in combat in Katanga. G.I. Draper, discussing this in 1965, suggested that it 'is not an impossible solution that [Common] Article 3 [GC] applies as between the Government and rebel forces, but not as between the UN Force and either of the other contending elements'.[71] Daphna Shraga, Senior Legal Officer at the Office of the Legal Counsel of the UN writing in her personal capacity, observed that for 'nearly half a century, the UN was disinclined to recognize the applicability of international humanitarian law or to abide by its provisions'.[72] The ICRC, in a statement to the General Assembly on 16 November 1995, observed that '[t]he ICRC has always taken the view that all the provisions of international humanitarian law are applicable when UN contingents resort to the use of force, whereas the UN has held the view that it is bound only by the "principles and spirit" of the humanitarian law treaties. These respective positions have been restated many times'.[73]

[70] Henckaerts and Doswald-Beck, *Customary International Humanitarian Law*, vol. I, above note 5, Rules 157 and 158.

[71] G. Draper, 'The Geneva Conventions of 1949' (1926) 14 *Receuil des cours de L'Académie de Droit International* 1, at 59, 95.

[72] D. Shraga, 'UN Peacekeeping Operations: Applicability of International Humanitarian Law and Responsibility for Operations-Related Damage' (2000) 94 *American Journal of International Law* 406.

[73] UNGA, 'Statement by the International Committee of the Red Cross', Fourth Committee, Agenda item 86, 16 November 1995.

However, early in the 1990s, public outcry at abuses committed by peacekeepers, notably in Somalia and in Bosnia-Herzegovina, led to demands for clearer guidelines on the obligations of peacekeepers under international humanitarian law; but it took until 1999 before the Secretary-General's Bulletin on Observance by UN Forces of International Humanitarian Law was ready for promulgation.

One reason for the delay was the fact that international humanitarian law, especially the law of international armed conflict, was (and to a large extent still is) perceived as a unitary regime granting privileges as well as obligations to the belligerent parties, in particular the 'combatant's privilege' which permits soldiers to kill enemy armed forces without fear of prosecution for the crime of murder (provided that they comply with the rules on distinction and proportionality). However, the combatant's privilege, since it extends to all parties to the conflict, also renders all combatants liable to be killed. States are likely to be reluctant to contribute to peacekeeping missions if there was a high probability that their soldiers would not be returning home. Therefore, States were concerned to ensure that any assertion of peacekeepers' obligations under international humanitarian law did not extend to rendering them liable to be shot at. There was also concern that if applicability of the international humanitarian law regime could be split into components, then it might be possible to benefit from the privileges of international humanitarian law without being subject to the risks, which could have the effect of undermining respect for international humanitarian law more generally.[74] The Secretary-General's Bulletin on Observance by UN Forces of International Humanitarian Law, which only applies to forces that are UN commanded and controlled, states that '[t]he fundamental principles and rules of international humanitarian law are applicable to UN forces when in situations of armed conflict they are actively engaged therein as combatants, to the extent and for the duration of their engagement. They are accordingly applicable in enforcement actions or in peacekeeping operations when the use of force is permitted in self-defence'.[75] The Bulletin does not make clear the obligations of non-combatant troops.[76]

A major difficulty with applying the Bulletin in practice is the absence of any definition of what it means to be 'actively engaged' in an armed conflict

[74] A. Roberts and R. Guelff, *Documents on the Laws of War*, 3d ed. (Oxford: Oxford University Press, 2002), at 625; C. Greenwood, 'Protection of Peacekeepers: The Legal Regime' (1997) 7 *Duke Journal of Comparative & International Law* 185, at 186.

[75] Secretary-General's Bulletin, above note 3, Section 1.1. [76] Ibid. Section 1.2.

'as combatants, to the extent and for the duration of their engagement'. Is there a distinction between being engaged in combat and being engaged as a combatant? If there is a distinction, what are the criteria for determining when a peacekeeper is engaged as a combatant?

The wording of the Bulletin suggests parallels with the provisions of Additional Protocol I to the Geneva Conventions (AP I) dealing with a civilian's temporary loss of protected status. Article 51 AP I provides, inter alia, that a civilian shall not be made the object of attack 'unless and for such time as they take a direct part in hostilities'. An over-simplistic parallel with the situation of peacekeepers would be to hold that peacekeepers remain entitled to the protections due to civilians 'unless and for such time as they take a direct part in hostilities' in the same way as all other civilians. But unlike civilians, through the provisions of the Secretary-General's Bulletin on Observance by UN Forces of International Humanitarian Law, they would not only temporarily lose protected civilian status 'for such time as they take a direct part in hostilities', but, being members of the contributing State's armed forces, they would also gain combatant status (and thus the protections and obligations of international humanitarian law) 'to the extent and for the duration of their engagement' as combatants, in the same way as all other combatants. Thus, peacekeepers would be civilians when they are not actively in engaged in fighting, and combatants when they are. However, such an approach is simply unworkable.

Quite apart from the difficulties in determining when use of force in self-defence crosses the threshold of participation in an armed conflict, there is the difficulty of assessing when they cease to be combatants and regain protection from attack. What is meant by 'to the extent' of their engagement as combatants? Suppose a peacekeeping force finds itself engaged in fierce combat against rebel armed forces on Monday (for example, to protect civilians from a potential massacre), but by Tuesday the situation is calm. Does international humanitarian law become applicable to them on Monday? Do they then regain protected status on Tuesday? Suppose then that on Thursday there are some incidents that entail some use of force but, if viewed as an isolated incident, would be regarded as within self-defence norms on the use of force and therefore might not be regarded as sufficient to render the peacekeepers combatants. Does the fact that the peacekeeping force was engaged in combat on Monday affect the analysis? Suppose all is calm for another fortnight after which there is another confrontation, but this time against State armed forces rather than rebel armed groups. How is the mission's legal advisor to work out whether and when international humanitarian law applies? And if international humanitarian law does apply, is it the law of international armed conflict or the law of non-international armed conflict? Does it vary depending on what forces the peacekeepers are fighting: armed groups one day, State armed forces another?

If the law of international armed conflict applies on Monday, persons falling into the hands of peacekeepers are protected by the Geneva Conventions (provided they fall into one of the categories of protected persons). Attacks against the peacekeepers will not necessarily be a crime, but peacekeepers falling into the hands of hostile forces will presumably be protected (though by what provisions may be debatable; if captured are they prisoners of war?).[77] By Tuesday, when all is calm, if the mission's legal advisor, relying on the Bulletin, determines that the troops are no longer 'actively engaged as combatants', do the Geneva Conventions cease to apply? What will the position be by Thursday, by Monday in a fortnight, in three weeks' time? Local warring armed groups may be equally confused: as the American Bar Association has observed 'it is asking too much for a Somali clan warrior or Bosnian militiaman' to understand these types of distinctions in levels of conflict.[78]

A more practical approach might be to regard peacekeepers as bound to comply with international humanitarian law rules all the time, regardless of whether international humanitarian law is formally applicable, an approach that many peacekeeping missions have tended to adopt anyway. The problems that have arisen have occurred in the areas of accountability, training and commitment, rather than in any disagreement as to expected standards of troop behaviour. Troop-contributing States do not claim that abuse of civilians is acceptable. The Bulletin was intended to remedy the problem of a lack of accountability for conduct that would breach international humanitarian law if committed by a party to the conflict. But whether it achieves this purpose is highly debatable. The

[77] Prisoner-of-war status might mean that peacekeepers could be held until the close of hostilities. What criteria should be used to determine the close of hostilities in the case of peacekeepers who temporarily become engaged as combatants in an ongoing war?

[78] American Bar Association, Section of International Law and Practice Standing Committee on World Order under Law, Report to the House of Delegates, 'Safety of UN and Associated Personnel: Recommendation' (1997) 31 *International Lawyer* 195, at 200.

Bulletin itself, even if it were flawless, would still only be of limited value without a strong commitment on the part of the UN, as well as contributing States, to ensure that the standards it set out are enforced. The UN can undertake administrative investigations into misconduct by UN forces, but it is not equipped to undertake criminal prosecutions. These remain the responsibility of the troop-contributing State. The UN can put pressure on troop-contributing States to investigate violations of international humanitarian law by their forces. It could refuse to accept troop contributions from States with a poor record of peacekeeper's conduct or a poor record of investigating (and, if necessary, of prosecuting) violations of international humanitarian law and other unethical conduct inappropriate for a peacekeeping mission; but politically, this may be difficult where there is a need for troop contributions and a shortage of States willing to contribute.

The UN often has difficulty in securing contributions to peacekeeping missions, particularly where there appears to be little direct advantage to the contributing State; and, as a result, it has traditionally been reluctant to pursue allegations against its forces. In 2000, London-based lawyer Geoffrey Robertson and former South Australian State Prosecutor Michael Hourigan planned to sue the UN for alleged complicity in the Rwandan genocide, acting for two Rwandan women whose families were among the victims. The women said that the UN soldiers who were assigned to protect them either ran away or handed their families over to the Hutu militia to be killed. One of the women said that the UN soldiers who were supposed to protect her and her family were drinking and socializing with the Hutus while she and her children were being tortured.[79] Kofi Annan argued that not only did the UN have nothing to answer for, but also, 'if we allowed our peacekeepers to be brought to courts and tried over matters like this, that would be the end of peacekeeping'.[80] Unfortunately, such a protective attitude towards the sensibilities of troop-contributing States can undermine the legitimacy of a peacekeeping mission (even one that is broadly successful in carrying out its objectives), particularly given that traditional peacekeeping is now the exception. As noted above, current missions are frequently highly interventionist, and, in some instances, peacekeeping missions have even aspired to 'social transformation' of the host State.[81]

[79] M. Riley, 'UN to Seek Immunity on Rwanda', Sydney Herald, 14 January 2000, www.globalpolicy.org/security/issues/rwanda/suit.htm.

[80] Ibid. [81] Paddon, 'Partnering for Peace', above note 17, at 517.

5. Possible mechanisms for enhancing accountability of peacekeepers

Arguably, the Geneva Conventions impose certain obligations on the contracting parties even when they are not actively engaged in a conflict, for example, to ensure that their troops are trained in international humanitarian law should war arise. Under Common Article 1 GC, contracting parties undertake to 'to ensure respect for' the Conventions. As the ICRC Commentary to Geneva Convention IV states, the motive of the Convention is 'a lofty one . . . universally recognized as an imperative call of civilization'.[82] Moreover, '[t]he proper working system of protection provided by the Convention demands in fact that that the contracting Parties should not be content merely to apply its provisions themselves, but should do everything in their power to ensure that the humanitarian principles underlying the Conventions are applied universally'.[83] A number of commentators, including the former president of the ICRC,[84] argue that whether or not it was originally intended to do so, the meaning of Common Article 1 GC now encompasses obligations on parties not involved in a conflict to ensure that the four Conventions are respected by all parties that are engaged in conflict.[85] Common Article 1 GC is referred to in Resolution XXIII, adopted at the Tehran Conference on Human Rights in 1968, which urges States to take steps to ensure that other States respect humanitarian law. The preamble states that 'States parties to the Red Cross Geneva Conventions sometimes fail to appreciate their responsibility to take steps to ensure respect of these humanitarian rules in all circumstances by other States, even if they are not themselves directly involved in the conflict'.[86]

[82] Ibid. [83] Ibid.

[84] J. Kellenberger, 'The Two Additional Protocols to the Geneva Conventions: 25 Years Later – Challenges and Prospects', 26th Round Table in San Remo on current problems of international humanitarian law (2002), www.icrc.org/eng/resources/documents/misc/5e2c8v.htm.

[85] L. Boisson de Chazournes and L. Condorelli, 'Common Article 1 of the Geneva Conventions Revisited: Protecting Collective Interests' (2000) 82 *International Review of the Red Cross* 67, at 70; H. P. Gasser, 'Ensuring Respect for the Geneva Conventions and Protocols: The Role of Third States and the United Nations', in H. Fox and M. A. Meyer (eds.), *Armed Conflict and the New Law: Effecting Compliance* (London: British Institute of International and Comparative Law, 1993) vol. II, 15–53, at 16, 24–25; U. Palwankar, 'Measures Available to States for Fulfilling their Obligation to Ensure Respect for International Humanitarian Law' (1994) 298 *International Review of the Red Cross* 9, at 9 et seq.; K. Sachariev, 'States' Entitlement to Take Action to Enforce Humanitarian Law' (1989) 270 *International Review of the Red Cross* 177, at 186.

[86] UNGA Resolution 32/41 (XXIII) (12 May 1968) para. 9.

In 1990, the Security Council adopted Resolution 681 calling upon the High Contracting Parties to Geneva Convention IV to ensure respect by Israel, for its obligations under that Convention.[87] On 5 December 2001, a Conference of the High Contracting Parties to Geneva Convention IV published a declaration in a similar vein.[88] Likewise, in 2004, the International Court of Justice stated that it follows from Common Article 1 GC 'that every State party to that Convention, whether or not it is a party to a specific conflict, is under an obligation to ensure that the requirements of the instruments in question are complied with'.[89] If States are obliged to ensure respect for the Geneva Conventions by third parties (even when they themselves are not engaged in the conflict), then it is arguable that they are also obliged to ensure that their own forces respect the Conventions (even though they themselves are not engaged in the conflict), at least in situations that closely parallel armed conflict. Common Article 1 GC is now considered to constitute customary international law.[90]

The ICRC's Study on Customary International Humanitarian Law states that grave breaches of the Geneva Conventions can only be committed 'in an international armed conflict . . . against persons or property protected under the provisions of the relevant Geneva Convention'.[91] If this statement were to be construed literally, it would exclude the possibility of grave breaches being committed by anyone that is not a party to the conflict: a person only becomes a protected person under the Geneva Conventions once he or she falls into the hands of a party to the conflict. For example, captured soldiers only become entitled to prisoner-of-war status if they are captured by a State party to the conflict. Similarly, a civilian only becomes a protected person under Geneva Convention IV if he falls into the hands of a State party to the conflict other than their own State or one that has normal diplomatic relations with their own State (although some fundamental provisions are applicable to everyone in occupied territory). However, the ICRC's Study on Customary International Humanitarian Law is very clear that a war crime can be committed

87 UNSC Resolution 681 (20 December 1990) paras. 5–6.

88 Conference of the High Contracting Parties to the Geneva Convention: Declaration (5 December 2001).

89 *Legal Consequences of the Construction of a Wall in the Occupied Palestinian Territory*, (Advisory Opinion) [2004] ICJ Reports 136, para. 157.

90 *Military and Paramilitary Activities in and against Nicaragua* (Nicaragua v. USA) (Judgment) [1986] ICJ Reports 14, para. 220.

91 Henckaerts and Doswald-Beck, *Customary International Humanitarian Law*, vol. I, above note 5, Rule 156.

by anyone, including civilians: 'Practice in the form of legislation, military manuals and case-law shows that war crimes are violations committed either by members of the armed forces or civilians against members of the armed forces, civilians or protected objects of the adverse party'.[92] The Trial Chamber of the International Criminal Tribunal for Rwanda in the *Akayesu* case noted that it 'is, in fact, well-established, at least since the Tokyo trials, that civilians may be held responsible for violations of international humanitarian law'[93] and pointed to a number of World War II trials where civilians were held liable if they had had a link or connection with a party to the conflict, in particular the Zyklon B case.[94] The ICRC now takes the view that '[e]veryone in situations of armed conflict: states, organized armed groups, multi-national forces, civilians and the staff of private military/security companies' is bound by international humanitarian law.[95]

Since civilians, by definition, are not parties to the conflict, determining whether an act or omission of a civilian is a war crime must surely depend on whether and to what extent there is a nexus to a *situation* of armed conflict involving the armed forces of one or more States. The rape of a protected person by a soldier belonging to the armed forces of a party to the conflict would be a war crime. The rape of one civilian by another would not necessarily be so, although it might if there was a sufficient nexus with the conflict. What about rape by soldiers belonging to a foreign army that is not party to the conflict but is present in the locality in which the armed conflict is taking place? Would it be necessary to prove some nexus with the armed conflict for it to be a war crime? Arguably, in the case of a peacekeeping mission, this issue could be resolved by adopting the view that the very need for a peacekeeping mission creates a sufficient nexus with the conflict to render peacekeepers potentially accountable for war crimes, and by adopting this view as legally enforceable policy within the troop-contributing State's domestic military law and in the Memorandum of Understandings with troop-contributing States. Such an approach would not necessarily render international humanitarian law 'applicable' in the sense of rendering the force a party to the conflict subject to the full range of obligations and privileges of international

[92] Ibid. Rule 156. [93] *Prosecutor v. Akayesu*, above note 5, para. 630.

[94] *Prosecutor v. Tesch*, above note 5, 103.

[95] ICRC, 'FAQ: International Humanitarian Law and Private Military/Security Companies' (9 October 2007) www.icrc.org/Web/eng/siteeng0.nsf/html/pmc-fac-230506; Special Issue on Private Military Companies, above note 5.

humanitarian law. According to the International Tribunals for the former Yugoslavia and Rwanda, the nexus to an armed conflict required to render a crime a war crime requires only that it is significantly 'shaped' by the armed conflict. The Appeals Chamber of the ICTY in *Kunarac* stated that:

> What ultimately distinguishes a war crime from a purely domestic offence is that a war crime is shaped by or dependent upon the environment – the armed conflict – in which it is committed. It need not have been planned or supported by some form of policy. The armed conflict need not have been causal to the commission of the crime, but the existence of an armed conflict must, at a minimum, have played a substantial part in the perpetrator's ability to commit it, his decision to commit it, the manner in which it was committed or the purpose for which it was committed.[96]

However, this does not mean that every act facilitated by an armed conflict situation constitutes a war crime. The ICTR, which cited *Kunarac* with approval, added that

> if a non-combatant takes advantage of the lessened effectiveness of the police in conditions of disorder created by an armed conflict to murder a neighbour he has hated for years, that would not, without more, constitute a war crime[97]

Crimes committed by peacekeepers against the local population, even rape and assault in situations where the motivation is largely opportunistic, would have a greater nexus to the armed conflict (if there is an armed conflict) than the example of a civilian murdering his long-hated neighbour since peacekeepers' relationship with the local population, and their power over individuals within it, is not the result an incidental consequence of the chaos of war but of purposeful deployment by the Security Council in response to the conflict. Thus, in most cases, the existence of the armed conflict would 'have played a substantial part' in the peacekeeper's ability to commit the crime, his decision to commit it and the manner in which it was committed, in a way that is different in nature to that of a civilian merely exploiting the breakdown of order.

6. Conclusion

The development of the 'responsibility to protect' principle and its acceptance (in qualified form) by both the Security Council and General

[96] *Prosecutor v. Kunarac et al.* (Judgment), Case No. IT-96-23/1-A (12 June 2002), para. 58.
[97] *Prosecutor v. Rutaganda* (Judgment), Case No. ICTR-96-3 (26 May 2003), para. 570.

Assembly has injected a new element into the already existing protection duties of peacekeepers and, in doing so, has strengthened and expanded these to a much higher and more explicit level of priority than existed before the genocides and massacres in Rwanda and Bosnia-Herzegovina in the 1990s. In addition, mandates of peacekeepers have become highly complex and cover a wide range of undertakings that frequently entail significant transformation of the political, social and economic order of the locality in which the mission is deployed. Peacekeepers now frequently also take on a stabilization role, supporting the host government. Unfortunately, host governments and officials with power in the region in which the mission is deployed may be more interested in advancing their own power and wealth than the well-being of the local population.

The Secretary-General's Bulletin on Observance by UN Forces of International Humanitarian Law raises almost as many questions as it answers. These questions need to be resolved either by clarification of the Bulletin's terms or by revising the approach to peacekeepers' obligations under international humanitarian law.

Common Article 1 GC requires the High Contracting Parties 'to respect and ensure respect' for the Geneva Conventions, which can be construed as entailing an obligation not only to behave in accordance with the Conventions but also to ensure respect by others insofar as it is possible to do so. Peacekeepers would normally have a greater capacity to provide protection than ordinary civilians; and peacekeeping mandates today generally authorize the force to provide protection 'within its capacity'. Under this approach, peacekeepers would have prima facie legal obligations under Common Article 1 GC to respond to violations of the Conventions by others if they are able to do so. This would entail elevating the protection obligations of peacekeepers to a core function of all operations and therefore subordinate to other objectives (such as facilitating elections).[98]

Another approach would be to focus on peacekeepers' nexus to the conflict (in conjunction with their military role) rather than focusing on their status as combatants. Since the ICRC now takes the view that '[e]veryone in situations of armed conflict: States, organised armed groups, multi-national forces, civilians and the staff of private military/

[98] UNTAC was criticized for prioritizing the successful holding of elections in Cambodia above human rights protection. S. R. Ratner, *The New UN Peacekeeping: Building Peace in Lands of Conflict after the Cold War* (New York: St. Martin's Press, 1996), at 181; UN, *The Blue Helmets: A Review of United Nations Peacekeeping*, 3d edn (New York: United Nations, 1996), at 467.

security companies' is bound by international humanitarian law,[99] it would be possible to take the approach that peacekeepers are legally bound to comply with international humanitarian law in all circumstances in which their operations form a nexus with the armed conflict even when they are not formally parties to it. Since mitigating the harmful effects of an armed conflict is usually a core function of all peacekeeping missions, a nexus with an armed conflict could be taken as presumed and asserted in the Memorandums of Understanding with troop-contributing States.

However, adopting these approaches would not be sufficient on their own to ensure that peacekeepers behave in ways that command respect; it requires the political will to prioritise the human rights and protection obligations of UN missions over and above everything else. The legitimacy of peacekeeping will be greatly undermined if peacekeepers mandated to protect civilians and support human rights commit abuses themselves or ignore abuses committed by the host State or by local officials, especially if the host State relies on the power and authority of the UN mission to maintain control. Arguably, peacekeeping is now at a critical stage in which, if not well managed, participation in a mission may turn out to be as damaging as not taking action at all. Peacekeepers cannot stand by in the face of serious human rights abuses; they therefore need a robust mandate to respond to atrocities. The more robust a mission's mandate, the more important it is that the obligation to apply it impartially is stringently adhered to. However, unless the mission is deployed under an enforcement mandate (and given the resources to fulfil it), they may find it impossible to undertake protection obligations without the support of the host government. The host government (or other legitimate authority with which the UN mission is mandated to work) may itself be prone to human rights abuses; or it may find that the need to entrench its own power (to maintain stability as well to serve the personal interests of its leaders) results in a tendency to use excessive force or rely on corruption and favouritism to control local communities. Difficulties arose quite dramatically in the DRC, but it is also a problem at a less dramatic level for other missions, including ones that are generally perceived to be successful, as the example of UNMIL's unwilling participation in the corrupt practices of local officials illustrates.

Unless serious consideration is given to finding a solution to these problems, it is possible that peacekeeping may overreach itself, intervening in

[99] ICRC, Private Military/Security Companies, above note 95; 'Special Issue on Private Military Companies' above note 5.

domestic situations with comprehensive mandates but heavily supportive of one party (turning a blind eye to some of its activities), giving further fuel to the allegations made by some critics that peacekeeping has become a tool of UN 'imperialism'. Counter-arguments to the effect that such allegations are exaggerated or opportunistic will not be enough to maintain the reputation of the UN if evidence of partiality, especially complicity in war crimes and human rights abuses, continues to surface and is not effectively dealt with. In response to allegations that some peacekeepers' conduct during the genocide in Rwanda in 1994 rendered them directly complicit in some of the killings, Kofi Annan argued that, not only did the UN have nothing to answer for, but also, 'if we allowed our peacekeepers to be brought to courts and tried over matters like this, that would be the end of peacekeeping'.[100] Arguably, failure to hold peacekeepers to account for the commission of war crimes, or for effectively condoning the commission of war crimes by local forces through failure to act, may also mean the end of peacekeeping.

[100] Riley, 'UN to Seek Immunity', above note 79.

16

Comment – obligations of States contributing to UN peacekeeping missions under Common Article 1 of the Geneva Conventions

MATTHEW HAPPOLD

Am I my brother's keeper?[1]

1. Introduction

In Resolution 1674 on the protection of civilians in armed conflict,[2] the Security Council affirmed its commitment to the doctrine of the responsibility to protect. To that end, the Council went on to state that it would continue to ensure that the mandates of UN peacekeeping missions included, 'where appropriate and on a case-by-case basis', provisions on the protection of civilians. The form of wording indicates that the responsibility to protect was not considered by the Security Council to exist as a self-executing legal rule, but as a political doctrine requiring implementation to acquire legal force in any particular instance.[3] In recent years, most UN peacekeeping forces have been given mandates entitling them to use force to protect civilians from deliberate attack.[4]

[1] Genesis 4.9 (King James Version). [2] UNSC Resolution 1674 (20 April 2006).

[3] See also the 2005 UN Global Summit Outcome Document, UNGA Resolution 60/1 (20 October 2005) para. 139. For discussion of the meaning and implications of the responsibility to protect, see A. J. Bellamy, 'Whither the Responsibility to Protect? Humanitarian Intervention and the 2005 World Summit' (2006) 20 *Ethics and International Affairs* 143; C. Stahn, 'Responsibility to Protect: Political Rhetoric or Emerging Legal Norm?' (2007) 101 *American Journal of International Law* 99; E. Massingham, 'Military Intervention for Humanitarian Purposes: Does the Responsibility to Protect Doctrine Advance the Legality of the Use of Force for Humanitarian Ends?' (2009) 91 *International Review of the Red Cross* 803.

[4] Indeed, as Resolution 1674 indicates, such language predates it. See S. Wills, *Protecting Civilians: The Obligations of Peacekeepers* (New York: Oxford University Press, 2009), at 51–71.

What the responsibility to protect is sometimes said to be with regard to the *jus ad bellum*, Common Article 1 of the 1949 Geneva Conventions – which provides that '[t]he High Contracting Parties undertake to respect and to ensure respect for the present Convention in all circumstances' – has been claimed to be with regard to the *jus in bello*; imposing a legal obligation on third States to intervene when parties to armed conflicts commit, or fail to prevent, atrocities.[5] Insofar as such a view encompasses forcible intervention, it is erroneous, not least because it mischaracterizes the responsibility to protect as the concept has developed within the United Nations.[6]

What the comparison highlights, however, is that Common Article 1 GC (whatever its scope) is a rule embedded within international humanitarian law. It would, of course, be quite possible to include a rule governing when States can use force within a treaty of a humanitarian nature, but one might consider that the rule's *jus ad bellum* character would have to be made unambiguously evident.[7] This cannot be said to have been done as regards Common Article 1 GC. Neither the text, nor its context, nor the *travaux préparatoires* lend support to such an interpretation. The first thing, therefore, that can be said about Common Article 1 GC is that it does not permit the use of force when it would not otherwise be permitted under the *jus ad bellum*. In the peacekeeping context, this means that Common Article 1 GC cannot serve as a ground additional to those in a mission's mandate permitting peacekeepers to use force other than in self-defence and defence of the mandate.[8]

This view, of course, implies that Common Article 1 GC applies to UN peacekeepers. This is not a matter beyond doubt. The first difficulty is the question of attribution: who is responsible for the conduct of UN peacekeepers? If it is the United Nations itself, rather than the troop-contributing States, then another issue arises: how is the UN bound by the obligations codified in Common Article 1 GC? Both issues will be

[5] This is something Siobhán Wills comes quite close to arguing in her contribution to this book. S. Wills, 'Ensuring Peacekeepers' Respect for International Humanitarian Law', Chapter 15 in this volume, at 378–9.

[6] 2005 UN Global Summit Outcome Document, above note 3.

[7] This is true in particular because, when construing a treaty provision, it must be considered in the context of the treaty in which it is embedded. See Article 31(1) Vienna Convention on the Law of Treaties.

[8] See 'Report of the Secretary-General on the Implementation of Security Council Resolution 340' (27 October 1973), UN Doc. S/11052/Rev. 1, para. 5; UN Department of Peacekeeping Operations, 'United Nations Peacekeeping Operations: Principles and Guidelines' (2008), at 35.

addressed before considering the principal topic of this chapter: what obligations does Common Article 1 GC require of States contributing troops to UN peacekeeping missions? It will be argued that Common Article 1 GC does impose duties upon troop-contributing States but that they are qualified by the control that the UN exercises over national contingents during peacekeeping operations. In particular, whatever the general scope of Common Article 1 GC, it does not impose any positive obligation on troop-contributing States to ensure respect for international humanitarian law by parties to conflicts which peacekeeping missions seek to police.[9] Such a duty (if it exists) lies solely with the UN.

2. The attribution of acts by peacekeeping operations

To begin with, it might be argued that because peacekeepers are under the command of an international organization, they are only bound to comply with the obligations which the organization has assumed.[10] The International Law Commission's Draft Articles on the Responsibility of International Organizations (DARIO) provide that:

> The conduct of an organ of a State or an organ . . . that is placed at the disposal of [an] international organization shall be considered under international law an act of the . . . organization if the organization exercises effective control over that conduct.[11]

Draft Article 7 DARIO is the counterpart to Article 6 of the International Law Commission's (ILC) Articles on State Responsibility (ASR), which states that:

> The conduct of an organ placed at the disposal of a State by another State shall be considered an act of the former State under international law if the organ is acting in the exercise of elements of the governmental authority of the State at whose disposal it is placed.[12]

[9] Or, at least, it imposes no duties additional to those which all States parties to the Geneva Conventions have as regards such situations.

[10] Or which bind them directly as individuals. It is assumed, for present purposes, however, that Common Article 1 GC does not directly bind individuals. This would seem to follow from the provision's wording. Certainly, discussion of its content has always been premised on the assumption that it binds States.

[11] ILC, 'Report on the Work of Its Sixty-Third Session, Article 7 Draft Articles on the Responsibility of International Organizations (Conduct of Organs of a State or Organs or Agents of an International Organization Placed at the Disposal of Another International Organization)' (26 April–3 June and 4 July–12 August 2011) Supp. No. 10 (A/66/10) para. 87.

[12] ILC, 'Draft Articles on the Responsibility of States for Internationally Wrongful Acts', Annex, UNGA Resolution 56/83 (12 December 2001).

Article 6 ASR, in particular, seems to suggest it that responsibility is single, not joint, depending on whose behalf the organ is acting. It is an 'either/or' situation.

In its comments on the Draft Articles on the Responsibility of International Organizations,[13] the United Nations argued that the proper distinction for the purpose of attribution of responsibility was between UN operations under UN command and control, and UN-authorized operations under national or regional command and control.[14] National contingents placed at the disposal of the UN by troop-contributing States are 'transformed' into organs of the United Nations and their conduct is attributable to the United Nations.[15] As the 1990 model status-of-forces agreement for peacekeeping operations states: '[A] United Nations peacekeeping operation [is] a subsidiary organ of the United Nations'.[16] It is not necessary, according to the UN, to demonstrate that the control exercised by the organization over all aspects of the operation was 'effective'.[17] Indeed, it might be thought that the test is not one of 'effective control' at all, given that it contradicts Article 5 DARIO's insistence that the control be over the impugned conduct.[18] Rather, the relevant distinction for determining whether effective control exists is the 'horizontal' one between UN operations and UN-authorized operations.

The United Nations' approach might be thought to have the virtue of avoiding a factual inquiry into whether effective control is exercised over particular conduct on a case-by-case basis. It also seems to reflect the practice of the Organization and the views of troop-contributing States.[19]

[13] ILC, 'Responsibility of International Organizations: Comments and Observations Received from International Organizations' (17 February 2011), UN Doc. A7CN.4/637/Add.1.

[14] This is, of course, also an argument against the decision of the European Court of Human Rights in *Behrami and Behrami v. France* and *Saramati v. France, Germany and Norway* (Decision) Applications No. 71412/01 and 78166/01, 2 May 2007, as KFOR (unlike UNMIK) was not a subsidiary organ of the Security Council.

[15] ILC, 'Responsibility of International Organizations: Comments', above note 13, at 10–12.

[16] 'Report of the Secretary-General on Article 5, Model Agreement between the United Nations and Member States Contributing Personnel and Equipment to United Nations Peace-keeping Operations, Annex, Comprehensive Review of the Whole Question of Peace-Keeping Operations in All Their Aspects' (23 May 1991), UN Doc. A/46/185.

[17] ILC, 'Responsibility of International Organizations: Comments', above note 13, at 13.

[18] T. Dannenbaum, 'Translating the Standard of Effective Control into a System of Effective Accountability: How Liability Should be Apportioned for Violations of Human Rights by Member State Troop Contingents Serving as United Nations Peacekeepers' (2010) 51 *Harvard Journal of International Law* 113, at 153.

[19] Some seven other States made third-party interventions supportive of the respondents in *Behrami and Saramati*, above note 14, paras. 96–117, while Spain advanced similar

However, insofar as national and international courts have addressed the issue, they have tended to apply (or, at least purport to apply) an effective control standard.[20] The exception is the European Court of Human Rights in *Behrami and Saramati*, where the Court held that the relevant test was 'whether the [United Nations Security Council] retained ultimate authority and control' over Kosovo Force (KFOR).[21] However, that decision has been the subject of extensive and cogent criticism,[22] and in *Al-Jedda*, the Court determined that the impugned conduct was attributable to the United Kingdom on the ground that 'the United Nations Security Council had neither effective control nor ultimate authority and control over the acts and omission of troops within the Multi-National Force',[23] which seems to mark a retreat from its previous conclusions. The recent decision of the Hague Court of Appeal in litigation concerning the conduct of Dutchbat during the fall of Srebrenica also applied what is now Article 7 DARIO.[24]

Nor, even on its own terms, does the UN's approach exclude the possibility that some conduct by peacekeepers might be attributed to the troop-contributing State, or that responsibility might, in some circumstances, be shared between the UN and the troop-contributing State. National contingents remain discrete units within UN peacekeeping operations, with their own internal command structures, so that commands can only be given by the UN Force Commander through the National Contingent

arguments in *Kurbogaj and Kurbogaj v. Spain* (1374/2005), Human Rights Committee, 11 August 2006. See also the arguments of the British Government in *Al-Jedda v. United Kingdom* (Judgment) Application No. 27021/08, European Court of Human Rights, 7 July 2011, paras. 64–68.

[20] For early examples, see *Attorney-General v. Nissan* [1970] AC 179 (House of Lords) and *N.K. v. Austria*, 77 International Law Reports 470 (1979) (Oberlandesgericht Wien). Both cases, however, were decided through the application of national, rather than international, law rules of attribution.

[21] *Behrami and Saramati v. UK*, above note 14, para. 133.

[22] A. Sari, 'Jurisdiction and International Responsibility in Peace Support Operations: The Behrami and Saramati Cases' (2008) 8 *Human Rights Law Review* 151; M. Milanović and T. Papić, 'As Bad as It Gets: The European Court of Human Rights' Behrami and Saramati Decision and General International Law' (2009) 58 *International and Comparative Law Quarterly* 267; F. Messineo, 'The House of Lords in Al-Jedda and Public International Law: Attribution of Conduct to UN-Authorized Forces and the Power of the Security Council to Displace Human Rights' (2009) 56 *Netherlands International Law Review* 35.

[23] *Al-Jedda v. UK*, above note 19, para. 84.

[24] See T. Dannenbaum, 'The Hague Court of Appeal on Dutchbat at Srebrenica Part 2: Attribution, Effective Control and the Power to Prevent', EJIL: Talk!, 10 November 2011, www.ejiltalk.org/the-hague-court-of-appeal-on-dutchbat-at-srebrenica-part-2-attribution-effective-control-and-the-power-to-prevent-2/.

Commander. Although the Force Commander exercises operational command and control over the contingent, the contributing State retains administrative authority and disciplinary and criminal jurisdiction over its troops.

The United Nations has not taken the view that peacekeepers' conduct can never be attributed to troop-contributing States. In particular, it does not consider itself responsible for 'off-duty' acts of members of peacekeeping forces, a term it interprets widely. In 1986, the UN Office of Legal Affairs stated that:

> We believe that a soldier may be considered off-duty not only when he is 'on leave' but also when he is not acting in an official or operational capacity while either inside or outside the area of operations... We consider the primary factor in determining an 'off-duty' situation to be whether the member of a peace-keeping mission was acting in a non-official/non-operational capacity when the incident occurred...[25]

A corollary to this approach would seem to be that in such circumstances the conduct of peacekeepers can be attributed to troop-contributing States, providing, of course, that the general conditions for attribution are satisfied. The United Nations also takes the view that, although it remains responsible to third parties for the conduct of peacekeepers, if the loss, damage, death or injury suffered is a result of the gross negligence or wilful misconduct of the personnel of a contributing State, that State will be liable to the UN for such claims.[26] The reason the UN seeks to maintain sole responsibility in such situations has been characterized by the Organization itself as 'political'.[27] Given this policy basis for the UN's position, it might be thought that the underlying legal reality is that there exists concurrent responsibility.

Moreover, whereas it is implicit in the European Court of Human Rights' decision in *Behrami and Saramati* that the activities of KFOR and the United Nations Mission in Kosovo (UNMIK) in Kosovo were solely

[25] 'Memorandum to the Director, Office for Field Operational and External Support Activities: Liability of the United Nations for Claims Involving Off-Duty Acts of Members of Peace-Keeping Forces – Determination of "Off-Duty" Versus "On-Duty" Status' (1986) *United Nations Juridical Yearbook* 300.

[26] See Article 9 Memorandum of Understanding between UN and [participating State] contributing resources to [the United Nations Peacekeeping Operation], Chapter 9, Manual on Policies and Procedures Concerning the Reimbursement and Control of Contingent-Owned Equipment of Troop/Police Contributors Participating in Peacekeeping Missions (29 January 2009), UN Doc. A/C.5/63/18.

[27] ILC, 'Responsibility of International Organizations: Comments', above note 13, at 14.

attributable to the United Nations, the Court appears to have taken a different view in *Al-Jedda*, stating that:

> The Court does not consider that, as a result of the authorisation contained in Resolution 1511, the acts of soldiers within the Multi-National Force became attributable to the United Nations or – *more importantly, for the purposes of this case – ceased to be attributable to the troop-contributing nations.*[28]

The last part of the sentence seems clearly to envisage that responsibility can be dual as well as sole. The Hague Court of Appeal in the *Dutchbat* Case was more explicit in its analysis, stating that:

> [T]he Court adopts as a starting point that the possibility that more than one party has 'effective control' is generally accepted, which means that it cannot be ruled out that the application of this criterion results in the possibility of attribution to more than one party.[29]

The Court based its conclusions on what is now Article 7 DARIO, the text of which cannot be said to prohibit such a result.[30] Indeed, the commentary to Article 3 DARIO, which sets out the general principle that every internationally wrongful act of an international organization entails the international responsibility of that organization, specifically states that:

> The fact that an international organization is responsible for an internationally wrongful act does not exclude the existence of parallel responsibility of other subjects of international law in the same set of circumstances.[31]

Consequently, the (rather unsatisfactory) conclusion is that the conduct of peacekeepers may be attributed either to the United Nations or to the relevant troop-contributing State and, indeed, in some situations, to both. The real debate is where the lines are to be drawn. Certainly, when conduct is attributable to the troop-contributing State, Common Article 1 GC would appear to be applicable. Whether it is when conduct is attributable to the United Nations remains to be seen.

3. Does Common Article 1 GC bind the United Nations?

It is obvious that the United Nations is not bound by the 1949 Geneva Conventions, to which only States can adhere. However, this does not

[28] *Al-Jedda v. UK*, above note 19, para. 80.

[29] LJN: BR5388, Gerechtshof's-Gravenhage, 200.020.174/01 (English translation), para. 5.9, uitspraken.rechtspraak.nl/inziendocument?id=ECLI:NL:GHSGR:2011:BR5388.

[30] ILC, 'Report on the Work of its Sixty-Third Session', above note 11. [31] Ibid. para. 6.

necessarily mean that the UN is not bound to comply with any distinct but identical non-treaty-based norm.[32] In the *Nicaragua* Case, the International Court of Justice (ICJ) addressed the content of Common Article 1 GC and concluded that the provision reflected general principles of humanitarian law. The Court considered

> that there is an obligation on the United States Government, in the terms of Common Article 1 GC, to 'respect' the Conventions and even 'to ensure respect' for them 'in all circumstances', since such an obligation does not derive from the Conventions themselves, but from the general principles of humanitarian law to which the Conventions merely give specific expression.[33]

The reference to 'general principles of humanitarian law' seems to refer to the 'general principles of law recognized by civilized nations' referred to as a source of international law in Article 38(1)(c) of the Court's Statute. The phrase also contains echoes of the ICJ's earlier Judgment in the *Corfu Channel* Case, when it spoke of 'elementary considerations of humanity, even more exacting in peace than in war'[34] and, indeed, of the Martens clause, which refers to 'the principles of the law of nations, as they result from the usages established among civilized peoples, from the laws of humanity, and the dictates of the public conscience'.[35]

The UN Secretary-General's 1999 Bulletin on the Observance of UN Forces of International Humanitarian Law states that:

> The fundamental principles and rules of international humanitarian law are applicable to UN forces in situations of armed conflict they are actively engaged therein as combatants, to the extent and for the duration of their engagement. They are accordingly applicable in enforcement actions, or in peacekeeping operations when the use of force is permitted in self-defence.[36]

Given the ICJ's characterization of Common Article 1 GC as embodying 'general principles of humanitarian law', it might be thought its provisions fall squarely within the body of 'fundamental principles and rules'

[32] See *Case concerning Military and Paramilitary Activities in and against Nicaragua (Nicaragua v. USA)* (Merits) (Judgment) [1986] ICJ Reports 14; T. Meron, 'The Geneva Conventions as Customary Law' (1987) 81 *American Journal of International Law* 348.

[33] *Nicaragua Case*, above note 32, para. 104.

[34] *Corfu Channel Case (UK v. Albania)* (Judgment) [1949] ICJ Reports 4, at 22.

[35] Preamble, 1907 Hague Convention (IV) respecting the Laws and Customs of War on Land (1908) 2 *American Journal of International Law Supplement* 9.

[36] Secretary-General's 'Bulletin on Observance by UN Forces of International Humanitarian Law' (6 August 1999), UN Doc. ST/SGB/1999/13.

to which the Bulletin refers. The only difficulty would seem to be the Bulletin's limited scope, intended to avoid peacekeepers being seen as parties to conflicts save to the extent that they are actually engaged as combatants,[37] which might be thought to create difficulties as regards the applicability of Common Article 1 GC.[38] However, as an international organization enjoying international legal personality – one, indeed, specifically tasked in its constituent instrument to seek solutions to 'international problems of [a] humanitarian character' and to promote and encourage 'respect for human rights and for fundamental freedoms for all'[39] – it might be thought that the United Nations should in any case be bound by the obligations enunciated in Common Article 1 GC, whether they are customary norms, general principles of law or something else.[40]

4. The extent of obligations under Common Article 1 GC

All this discussion, it might be said, is simply persiflage obscuring the real issue: the extent of troop-contributing States' obligations under Common Article 1 GC. The wide scope of Common Article 1 GC, however, provides the key to its application as regards States contributing troops to UN peacekeeping operations, insofar as it applies not only during conflicts to which those States are parties but also at all times. UN member States are under no duty to contribute troops to UN peacekeeping operations. A decision to do so is a voluntary act of the State which results in an agreement between that State and the United Nations setting out the terms of the troops' participation in the mission. Contributing States remain able to withdraw their troops from an operation at any time.[41]

[37] So as to maintain their privileges under the Convention on the Safety of United Nations and Associated Personnel, New York, 9 December 1994, in force 15 January 1999, 2051 U.N.T.S. 391, which makes it a crime under international law to attack peacekeepers not so engaged.

[38] On an expansive reading, this applies largely to States which are not parties to particular conflicts. See text accompanying notes 44–55 below.

[39] Article 1(3) UN Charter.

[40] F. Mégret and F. Hoffmann, 'The UN as a Human Rights Violator? Some Reflections on the United Nations' Changing Human Rights Responsibilities' (2003) 25 *Human Rights Quarterly* 314. See also Wills, 'Ensuring Peacekeepers' Respect', above Chapter 15, note 5, at 369–74.

[41] See C. Lynch, 'India Threatens to Pull Plug on Peacekeeping', Foreign Policy Turtle Bay Blog, 14 June 2011, turtlebay.foreignpolicy.com/posts/2011/06/14/india_threatens_to_pull_plug_on_peacekeeping.

All of this supports the conclusion that Common Article 1 GC applies to troop-contributing States both as regards their conduct in general and, additionally, in situations where a Force Commander issues orders which would entail violations of international humanitarian law. In the first place, a contributing State continues to be responsible for training and promotions, and retains disciplinary and criminal jurisdiction over its troops throughout the operation. Even on its narrowest reading, Common Article 1 GC is said to require a Contracting Party to 'ensure respect' for international humanitarian law among persons within its jurisdiction because it has the ability vis-à-vis such persons to disseminate the tenets of international humanitarian law and to sanction violations of it.[42] In 1996, the UN Secretary-General, in a report addressing the scope of UN liability for activities of UN forces, referred to troop-contributing States' 'obligation to ensure respect for international humanitarian law by members' of their forces specifically on the basis that contributing States retain an exclusive right to exercise criminal jurisdiction over contingent members.[43] In addition, although operational command and control rests in the hands of the UN Force Commander, the majority of national contingents reserve the right to consult their own capital directly. In particular, if soldiers of a contingent are required to act in a manner that would clash with the normal principles under which they are expected to operate in their own national armed forces, their contingent commander has the right to refer the matter to his Minister of Defence, thus permitting a decision to be made at the highest level whether to obey a legally dubious order.

Neither of these conclusions would seem controversial. What is less clear is the extent of contributing States' obligations as regards the conduct of persons other than their own troops. Again, there are two facets to the issue: to what extent does Common Article 1 GC impose obligations to seek to ensure respect for international humanitarian law as regards other elements of a UN peacekeeping mission, and to what extent does it apply as regards parties to conflicts which the operation seeks to police?

42 F. Kalshoven, 'The Undertaking to Respect and Ensure Respect in All Circumstances: From Tiny Seed to Ripening Fruit' (1999) 2 *Yearbook of International Humanitarian Law* 3.

43 'Report of the Secretary-General on Financing of the United Nations Protection Force, the United Nations Confidence Restoration Operation in Croatia, the United Nations Preventive Deployment Force and the United Nations Peace Forces Headquarters – Administrative and Budgetary Aspects of the Financing of the United Nations Peacekeeping Operations: Financing of the United Nations Peacekeeping Operations' (20 September 1996), UN Doc. A/51/389.

The debate centres on the breath of the obligation in Common Article 1 GC 'to ensure respect . . . in all circumstances'.[44] As early as the 1950s, it has been argued, an expansive interpretation was recognized, with Pictet's Commentary stating that:

> The use of the words 'and to ensure respect' was . . . deliberate: they were intended to emphasise and strengthen the responsibility of the Contracting Parties . . . It follows, therefore, that in the event of a Power failing to fulfil its obligations, the other Contracting Parties (neutral, allied or enemy) may, and should, endeavour to bring it back to an attitude of respect for the Convention.[45]

The word 'should' in the passage is ambiguous, as it does not necessarily denote the existence of any legal obligation (particular when used in conjunction with, rather than in juxtaposition to, 'may'); and Adam Roberts and Frits Kalshoven have shown that such an interpretation has no basis in the negotiating history of the Geneva Conventions.[46] Nonetheless, the view that Common Article 1 GC requires that Contracting States not party to a conflict between other Contracting States to attempt to ensure those latter States' compliance with the Geneva Conventions through

[44] Articles on the subject include P. Benvenuti, 'Ensuring Observance of International Humanitarian Law: Function, Extent and Limits of the Obligations of Third States to Ensure respect of IHL' (1989–1990) *Yearbook of the International Institute of Humanitarian Law* 27; L. Condorelli and L. Boisson de Chazournes, 'Quelques remarques à propos de l'obligation des états de "respecter et faire respecter" le droit international humanitaire "en toutes circonstances"', in C. Swinarski (ed.), *Studies and Essays on International Humanitarian Law and Red Cross Principles in Honour of Jean Pictet* (The Hague: Martinus Nijhoff Publishers/ICRC, 1984), at 17–35; N. Levrat, 'Les conséquences de l'engagement prise par les Hautes parties contractantes de "faire respecter" les Conventions humanitaires', in F. Kalshoven and Y. Sandoz (eds.), *Implementation of International Humanitarian Law* (The Hague: Martinus Nijhoff Publishers/ICRC, 1989), at 263–96; H. Gasser, 'Ensuring Respect for the Geneva Conventions and Protocols: The Role of Third States and the United Nations', in H. Fox and M. Meyer (eds.), *Armed Conflict and the New Law: Ensuring Compliance* (London: British Institute of International and Comparative Law, 1993), at 15–49; B. Kessler, 'The Duty to "Ensure Respect" under Common Article 1 of the Geneva Conventions: Its Implications on International and Non-International Armed Conflicts' (2001) 44 *German Yearbook of International Law* 498; U. Palwankar, 'Measures Available to States for Fulfilling Their Obligation to Ensure Respect for International Humanitarian Law' (1994) 298 *International Review of the Red Cross* 9; L. Boisson de Chazournes and L. Condorelli, 'Common Article 1 of the Geneva Conventions Revisited: Protecting Collective Interests' (2000) 837 *International Review of the Red Cross* 67.

[45] J. Pictet (ed.), *Commentary on the Geneva Conventions of 12 August 1949*, 4 vols (Geneva: International Committee of the Red Cross, 1952), vol. I, at 226.

[46] A. Roberts, 'The Laws of War: Problems of Implementation in Contemporary Conflicts', in European Commission, *Law in Humanitarian Crisis* (1995), at 31–32; Kalshoven, 'The Undertaking to Respect', above note 42, at 11–28.

diplomatic means, retorsion and even reprisals, is one that has been advanced by a number of commentators and is the favoured interpretation of the provision by the International Red Cross/Red Crescent Movement.[47]

Such an interpretation has also been supported by the International Court of Justice. The Court's conclusion in the *Nicaragua* Case, referred to above,[48] were rather more nuanced, read in context, than often described, being made in relation to the publication and dissemination of a Central Intelligence Agency (CIA) manual on psychological guerrilla warfare which recommended use by insurgents of a variety of acts contrary to Common Article 3 GC. It was the distribution of this manual to the Contras at a time when, at the least, the United States was aware of allegations that they were violating international humanitarian law that was the basis for the Court's ruling that the US had breached its international obligations. In the circumstances, therefore, the Court's comments can only be read as providing that Common Article 1 GC requires that a State does not encourage or incite other persons to breach international humanitarian law, rather than necessarily including any positive obligation to ensure that such persons do not do so.

In its advisory opinion on the *Legality of the Wall*, however, the International Court of Justice went further. Having held that Israel was in breach of certain obligations under international humanitarian law of an *erga omnes* nature,[49] the Court stated that:

> Article 1 of the Fourth Geneva Convention, a provision common to the four Geneva Conventions, provides that 'The High Contracting Parties undertake to respect and to ensure respect for the present Convention in all circumstances.' It follows from that provision that every State party to that Convention, whether or not it is a party to a specific conflict, is under an obligation to ensure that the requirements of the instruments in question are complied with.[50]

The Court did not, however, expand on what this obligation might require beyond stating that the States parties to Geneva Convention IV

[47] See address by J. Kellenberger, President of the ICRC, *Ensuring Respect for International Humanitarian Law in a Changing Environment and the Role of the United Nations*, 60th Anniversary of the Geneva Conventions – ministerial working session, 26 September 2009, www.icrc.org/eng/resources/documents/statement/geneva-conventions-statement-260909.htm.

[48] *Nicaragua Case*, above note 32.

[49] *Legal Consequences of the Construction of a Wall in the Occupied Palestinian Territory* (Advisory Opinion) [2004] ICJ Reports 136, at 199.

[50] Ibid. 199–200.

were 'under an obligation, while respecting the United Nations Charter and international law, to ensure compliance by Israel with international humanitarian law as embodied in that Convention'.[51] This would seem to say little more than that States parties are not permitted to breach the UN Charter (which, of course, prohibits the use of force save in self-defence or pursuant to a valid Chapter VII Security Council resolution) in seeking to ensure compliance with Geneva Convention IV. What was left open was whether States are permitted (or even obliged) to take countermeasures to ensure compliance; countermeasures being measures which are only lawful *qua* countermeasures, but otherwise unlawful.[52]

Nor did the International Court of Justice provide any authority for its interpretation of Common Article 1 GC. The Court simply pronounced *ex cathedra.* It cannot be said that there is no authority for such a view. In particular, the conference of High Contracting Parties of Geneva Convention IV concerning the application of international humanitarian law to the occupied Palestinian territories was convened on the basis of Common Article 1 GC.

When recommending the convening of the conference, the UN General Assembly (UNGA) did so on the basis that the conference would discuss 'measures . . . to ensure respect [for Geneva Convention IV] in accordance with common Article 1'.[53] Ambassador Maurer of the Swiss Federal Department of Foreign Affairs (which convened the conference) said in his statement opening the conference's 2011 session that:

> The legal basis of this Conference is provided by the first article of the Geneva Conventions: Common Article 1 states that all High Contracting Parties must not only undertake to *respect* their obligations but must also

[51] Ibid 200.

[52] ILC Articles on State Responsibility studiously avoid taking a position on whether countermeasures taken by non-injured States in response to breaches of *erga omnes* obligations are lawful. Article 54 ASR simply states that the Articles' provisions on countermeasures do 'not prejudice the right of any State, entitled under article 48, paragraph 1, to invoke the responsibility of another State, to take lawful measures against that State to ensure cessation of the breach and reparation in the interest of the injured State or of the beneficiaries of the obligation breached'. The term 'lawful measures' is, of course, entirely question-begging. But see C. Tams, *Enforcing Obligations Erga Omnes in International Law* (Cambridge: Cambridge University Press, 2005); L.-A. Sicilianos, 'Countermeasures in Response to Grave Violations of Obligations Owed to the International Community as a Whole', in J. Crawford, A. Pellet and S. Olleson (eds.), *The Law of International Responsibility* (Oxford: Oxford University Press, 2010), at 1137–48.

[53] UNGA Resolution ES-10/6 (9 February 1999).

> *ensure respect* for them *in all circumstances*. This is the reason why... we are here today.[54]

And the conference declaration itself stated that:

> The participating High Contracting Parties call upon all parties, directly involved in the conflict or not, to respect and to ensure respect for the Geneva Conventions in all circumstances, to disseminate and take measures necessary for the prevention and suppression of breaches of the Conventions.[55]

Ultimately, however, all in substance the declaration did was reiterate the already generally-held view that Geneva Convention IV applied to the Occupied Palestinian territories.[56] An elephant produced a mouse.

Conversely, articles by Frits Kalshoven and Carlo Focarelli have strongly argued against an expansive reading of Common Article 1 GC.[57] Their research shows that such an interpretation was not envisaged by the provision's drafters, nor by those of the analogous Article 1(1) of Additional Protocol I to the Geneva Conventions. Only from the late 1970s did it find any real support in doctrine and in the resolutions of international organizations. When acting individually, however, States have been loath to give it any content. At best, subsequent concordant practice is patchy. And given the wide variety of violations of international humanitarian law that occur continuously, coupled with the near-global ratification of the Geneva Conventions, one might expect that action to ensure compliance would be the norm, unless one were to assume that most States are in breach of their obligations under Common Article 1 GC most of the time, which seems unlikely. One might conclude that Common Article 1 GC empowers rather than obliges States to intervene when parties to conflicts breach their obligations under the Geneva Conventions, but this would seem contrary to the plain meaning of Common Article 1 GC. It might also be argued that it imposes an obligation but leaves to States to determine the means by which to comply with it. But, again, this seems wrong

[54] Conference of High Contracting Parties to the Fourth Geneva Convention, Geneva, 5 December 2001, Opening Statement by the Chair Read by Ambassador Peter Maurer (emphasis in original).

[55] Conference of High Contracting Parties to the Fourth Geneva Convention, Geneva, 5 December 2001, Declaration, para. 4.

[56] For further details, see M. Happold, 'The Conference of High Contracting Parties to the Fourth Geneva Convention' (2001) 4 *Yearbook of International Humanitarian Law* 389.

[57] Kalshoven, 'The Undertaking to Respect', above note 42; C. Focarelli, 'Common Article 1 of the 1949 Geneva Conventions: A Soap Bubble?' (2010) 21 *European Journal of International Law* 125.

since such an obligation is, in reality, no obligation, given that States can define for themselves what compliance entails. The International Court of Justice's conclusions in the *Legality of the Wall* Advisory Opinion, in consequence, appear unsubstantiated.

Even taking an expansive view of Common Article 1 GC, however, it might be thought that it has no specific implications for States contributing troops to UN peacekeeping operations – for two reasons. In the first place, such States would already have positive obligations under Common Article 1 GC to ensure that the parties to the conflict which the operation seeks to police respect international humanitarian law; that is, the State would be obligated not as a troop contributor to the peacekeeping mission but simply as a party to the Geneva Conventions. And second, and more important, operational control over national contingents participating in UN peacekeeping operations lies with the UN Force Commander. In other words, a contingent's relations to parties to the conflict are determined by the Force Commander. When so acting, the Force Commander exercises effective control over the contingent, which, in turn, acts as an organ of the United Nations, whose agent the Force Commander is. The contingent's conduct is attributable to the UN and engages its international responsibility. The key question, in this context, therefore is the extent of the UN's obligations under the norms of customary international law mirroring Common Article 1 GC.

A more complex issue is whether troop-contributing States are obliged under Common Article 1 GC to ensure respect for international humanitarian law by other members of the peacekeeping mission or persons collaborating with the mission. In 1961, in a memorandum by the International Committee of the Red Cross (ICRC) on the application of the 1949 Geneva Conventions to armed forces put at the disposal of the United Nations,[58] the ICRC implied that Common Article 1 GC required troop-contributing States to ensure that peacekeeping operations respected international humanitarian law. The ICRC's 1961 interpretation of Common Article 1 GC thus argues for a duty to take steps to ensure that the peacekeeping operation as a whole respects international humanitarian law. On the one hand, it might be argued that the mutual relations of the various elements within a peacekeeping mission are determined by the Force Commander in the exercise of his powers of operational command

[58] International Committee of the Red Cross, 'L'Application des Conventions de Genève par les Forces Armées Mises a la Disposition des Nations Unies' (1961) 43 *Revue Internationale de la Croix Rouge* 592.

and control. This seems correct, so far as it goes. On the other hand, however, as we have already seen, Common Article 1 GC should be seen as encompassing an obligation to refuse orders given by a Force Commander which would entail breaching international humanitarian law.[59] If this is the case, then it is difficult to see any real difference between being obliged to refuse to obey an illegal order (that is, one that would result in a breach of international humanitarian law), and being obliged to refuse cooperation with another person when doing so would facilitate a breach of international humanitarian law by that other person. Such an obligation would seem to fit snugly within the International Court of Justice's view of the scope of Common Article 1 GC (or, to be more precise, its customary analogue) in the *Nicaragua* Case as requiring States to avoid encouraging or inciting others to breach international humanitarian law. It would also seem in conformity with the ILC Articles on State Responsibility provisions on aid and assistance in the commission of an internationally wrongful act.[60] Indeed, in both contexts, we seem to be discussing areas where both the UN and the troop-contributing State's international responsibility are engaged, something which seems to have been recognized, on the UN's side, in the Security Council's decisions regarding MONUC and its successor MONUSCO's relations with the armed forces of the Democratic Republic of the Congo.[61]

5. Conclusion

To conclude, Common Article 1 GC does impose obligations on States contributing troops to UN peacekeeping missions, but those obligations are qualified by the control that the UN exercises over national contingents and are negative rather than positive. Troop-contributing States continue to be obliged to ensure that their troops do not violate international humanitarian law. They are also required to prevent their troops from facilitating violations of humanitarian law by others, whether those other

[59] See text accompanying notes 42–43 below.

[60] ILC, 'Articles on the Responsibility of States', above note 12, Article 16. For further analysis, see H. Aust, *Complicity and State Responsibility* (Cambridge: Cambridge University Press, 2011).

[61] UNSC Resolutions 1856 (22 December 200), 1906 (23 December 2009), 1925 (28 May 2010) and 1991 (28 June 2011). See also UN Department of Public Information, 'United Nations Peacekeeping Force Commanders Discuss Strategies for Overcoming Operational Challenges in Meeting with Security Council Membership' (27 July 2011), UN Doc. SC/10343.

persons be other members of the mission or persons (e.g., the national forces of the host State) cooperating with it. In extreme cases, both obligations might require them to refuse to comply with orders given by the Force Commander and even to withdraw from the mission. However, Common Article 1 GC (and its analogue in customary international law) does not impose any positive obligations on troop-contributing States additional to those that it requires of any States not party to conflicts where international humanitarian law is being violated. To the extent that such obligations exist in the peacekeeping context, they are incumbent on the United Nations, given its effective control over the operations of its peacekeeping missions, with the contemporary practice of the Security Council indicating a recognition of a duty to protect civilians.

17

Comment – UN peacekeeping in the Democratic Republic of the Congo

The travails of civilian protection

DENIS M. TULL

1. Introduction

State institutions in war-torn countries are ineffective, and all parties to a conflict are prone to commit human rights abuses. In this context, the task to protect civilians from harm often falls, if at all, under the remit of a United Nations peace operation. In 1999, the UN Security Council held its first debate on the protection of civilians, noting that civilians formed the vast majority of casualties in violent conflicts and recognizing large-scale human suffering as a contributing factor to instability and conflict. The following decade brought 'ten years of normative progress' (Ban Ki-moon) as human suffering was placed in the spotlight, including in the context of peacekeeping.[1] As a result, the protection of civilians has become a primary function of UN peace operations, as reflected by UN Security Council mandates. Based on Chapter VII of the UN Charter, the first explicit protection mandate was the UN Mission in Sierra Leone. Subsequently, most UN peace operations have been authorized by the UN Security Council to use 'all means necessary' to protect civilians under imminent threat of physical violence, including missions in Burundi, Liberia, Côte d'Ivoire, Sudan and the Democratic Republic of the Congo (DRC).[2] Thus, alongside other typical peacekeeping tasks such as monitoring ceasefires, disarming combatants and organizing elections, civilian protection has become a mainstream activity of Chapter VII-based UN peace operations. Taking protection issues even further,

[1] 'Report of the Secretary-General on the Protection of Civilians in Armed Conflict' (19 May 2009), UN Doc. A/2009/277, at 2.

[2] A. J. Bellamy and P. D. Williams, 'The New Politics of Protection? Côte d'Ivoire, Libya and the Responsibility to Protect' (2011) 87 *International Affairs* 828.

in 2008, the Security Council ordered a UN operation (United Nations Mission in the Democratic Republic of the Congo, MONUC) for the first time to consider civilian protection as its highest priority. This explicit protection mandate and the sheer size of the mission created immense expectations about the effective protection of civilians by this particular mission.

Although the conflict in the DRC has its particularities and can rightly be considered as an extremely demanding environment for peacekeepers, the challenges of civilian protection are not unlike those in other countries where complex peace operations have recently been deployed. The case of the UN mission in the DRC, MONUC/MONUSCO, is illustrative of the many conceptual, operational and practical problems peacekeepers are facing.[3] The case also illuminates the extent to which protection issues have produced important lessons. It also resulted in processes of organizational learning which are likely to leave an imprint on the international practice of civilian protection, within and outside the UN system.

2. The trajectory of the mission

For a number of years, MONUSCO has been the world's largest UN peacekeeping force. Starting as a small observer mission to monitor a ceasefire agreement in the DRC in 1999, it was progressively expanded in terms both of its mandate and its size. In 2003, its troop levels reached 8,700 armed personnel, following a comprehensive peace agreement signed by the DRC's warring factions. However, it quickly turned out that the formation of a government of national unity did not bring the DRC any closer to peace. In the eastern parts of the country, particularly the provinces of North Kivu and South Kivu, a host of Congolese and foreign militia groups continued to wreak havoc. The absence of effective State institutions, fluid and shifting alliances, the entanglement of neighbouring countries, local conflicts over land and identity and the exploitation of mineral resources continued to feed a vicious cycle of violence. Internal displacements continued unabated while massacres of

[3] As of 1 July 2010, the mission was renamed 'UN Organization Stabilization Mission in the Democratic Republic of the Congo' (MONUSCO). The new name, which suggested that the DRC had entered a post-conflict phase, was a concession by the UN Security Council (UNSC) to the government of the DRC. For the sake of clarity, I will refer to the mission as MONUSCO throughout the text.

civilians occurred frequently, sometimes even when UN peacekeepers were present as in Bunia (2003) and Bukavu (2004). As a result, the UN Security Council boosted MONUSCO's troop levels, which surmounted 15,000 in 2004 and over 18,000 in 2006. As of mid 2015, no less than thirteen years after the DRC's peace agreement, 21,067 uniformed personnel continued to serve in the mission. An estimated 2.8 million people remained displaced in the DRC, including 1 million in North and South Kivu.[4] This reflected little progress in comparison to the peak year of 2003, when internal displacement had reached 3.2 million, but it compared unfavourably to the year 2006 when the DRC's internal displacement had fallen to 1.1 million, its lowest level since 1999. In other words, the rise of internal displacement indicated an unrelenting protection crisis.

The search for peace and security in the DRC thus followed a seemingly paradoxical trajectory: on the one hand, the national peace process made slow but steady progress, while on the other hand, violence showed few signs of abating, despite the incremental build-up of the UN peacekeeping mission. The 2002 peace agreement among the major belligerent parties ushered in a transitional government of national unity, which somehow decreased the level of insecurity in the country, leading to the 2006 ('post-conflict') elections. However, the seeming political progress of the peace process was neither linear, nor did it lead to reduced levels of violence. After 2002, violence shifted on two levels. Geographically, it moved from the centre of the country to the eastern DRC, which became the theatre of violence as the ceasefire among the major belligerent factions was respected along the official demarcation line at the centre of the country after 2002. Second, violence also shifted from relatively organized fighting to a form of violence which was underwritten by increasingly blurred motivations. Conquering and holding territory was rarely its main function as warring factions fragmented into an ever growing number of smaller armed groups. Violence against civilians, often directed against women in particular, became one of the most pervasive forms of insecurity, prompting a former MONUSCO commander to argue that it had become 'more dangerous to be a woman than a soldier in an armed conflict'.[5]

[4] 'Report of the Secretary-General on the UN Organization Stabilization Mission in the Democratic Republic of the Congo' (10 March 2015), UN Doc. S/2015/172, at 16.

[5] P. Worsnip, 'UN Council Urges Action on Sexual Violence in War', Reuters, 16 June 2008.

3. The evolution of the mandate

When MONUSCO was created in 1999, protecting civilians was not on the mind of its planners. A year later, when the observer mission was transformed into a peacekeeping force, its mandate explicitly stated that the mission was to protect civilians under imminent threat.[6] However, protection was neither considered as a prominent task, nor was the mission, as the Secretary-General warned, capable of carrying out protecting activities.[7] The failure of peacekeepers to prevent massacres of civilians in Bunia in 2003 prompted the UN Security Council to provide MONUSCO with a more robust position that authorized the entire mandate under Chapter VII. Barely one year later, however, MONUSCO failed again – this time to prevent insurgents from taking the provincial capital of Bukavu in South Kivu, where numerous human rights abuses were committed. The Bukavu crisis was another blow to the mission and its credibility in the DRC. Across the country, civilians attacked MONUSCO personnel and installations, venting their anger against the mission. Again, the UN Security Council reacted by strengthening the operation and its mandate, calling upon the mission to act more robustly in defence of its mandate, especially to disrupt armed groups and to prevent violence against civilians.

An important impetus for robust action came in early 2005 when nine peacekeepers were killed in an ambush by a militia group. At the same time, security threats to the upcoming elections, in which the international community put great stock to move the peace process forward, drove the UN Security Council to urge MONUSCO to fully exploit its mandate, that is, to implement and defend it more aggressively. More specifically, Resolution 1592 (2005) encouraged MONUSCO to use forceful cordon and search tactics against violent groups. A second important innovation was the call on the government of the DRC to develop with MONUSCO a concept of operations for the disarmament of the numerous foreign combatants by its army and 'with the assistance of MONUSCO, within its mandate and capabilities'. Direct support for and even cooperation with the army of the DRC were to become major strategic elements of the mission in the pursuit of its mandate, including civilian protection.

[6] UNSC Resolution 1291 (24 February 2000), para. 8.

[7] V. Holt, G. Tyler and M. Kelly, Protecting Civilians in the Context of UN Peacekeeping Operations. Successes, Setbacks, and Remaining Challenges (New York: UN Department for Peacekeeping Operations, 2009), at 245.

The mission increased its support for the Congolese State, seeking to assist it in establishing a State monopoly over coercion, ultimately in the hope – failed, so far – to hand over its security functions and make itself redundant.

The strategic shift was in tune with the result of the relatively successful 2006 post-conflict elections, which finally provided the country with a democratically legitimated government. For the UN and the international community at large, the elections were therefore a milestone in the transition from war to peace to a democratic and stable country.[8] Accordingly the international community considered the post-election period as a new dawn. It pledged to closely cooperate with the government to consolidate peace and democracy in the country, even airing (premature) ideas about an eventual drawdown and withdrawal of MONUSCO.[9]

As a result of MONUSCO's revised mandate, the mission focused on a wide array of post-conflict challenges, including support for the consolidation of State authority and the protection of civilians.[10] However, a renewed insurgency in North Kivu quickly shattered optimistic expectations about a more secure post-election environment. This and the mushrooming of other militias in the two Kivu provinces sparked a pervasive humanitarian and protection crisis which continued at the time of writing. In response, the UN Security Council stressed the importance of protecting civilians by placing the highest priority on the crisis in the Kivus. MONUSCO belatedly started to transfer the bulk of its military resources to the east, a move that was only completed in early 2008 when the mission had shifted 90 percent of its troops to the area. However, the situation continued to deteriorate. MONUSCO was caught in the middle of fighting that involved the ineffective army of the DRC and countless Congolese national and foreign militia groups. In November 2008, a highly publicized massacre of more than 150 civilians in North Kivu occurred close to a UN base, prompting the UN Security Council to once more revise MONUSCO's mandate. One month after the killings, it made

[8] 'Special Report of the Secretary-General on the Elections in the Democratic Republic of the Congo' (26 May 2005), UN Doc. S/2005/320, at 1.

[9] 'Twenty-Third Report of the Secretary-General on the United Nations Organization Mission in the Democratic Republic of Congo' (20 March 2007), UN Doc. S/2007/156, at 13. In 2007, the UN Secretary-General had sketched the benchmarks for the progressive drawdown of the mission. These included not only the disarmament and demobilization of Congolese and foreign armed groups but also the sufficient capacity of the DRC's army and police to maintain a stable security environment after MONUSCO's withdrawal.

[10] UNSC Resolution 1756 (15 May 2007).

the unprecedented decision to unambiguously declare the protection of civilians as the key priority of the mission.[11]

4. Assessing protection performance

In light of the sustained humanitarian crisis in the eastern DRC, persistent internal displacements and continued massacres of civilians, there is little doubt that MONUSCO has failed to meet the expectations raised by its protection mandate. Some would even argue that the mission has been a high profile protection failure, due to the yawning gap between its performance on the one hand and its mandate on the other, arguably 'the most assertive mandate yet regarding the protection of civilians', especially after 2008.[12] However, the reasons behind MONUSCO's inability to live up to the ambitions of its political masters in the UN Security Council were not dissimilar to the challenges facing other UN operations and peacekeeping in general.[13]

To begin with, the eastern DRC has been a particularly hostile and difficult environment for peacekeepers. Notwithstanding the complexity of rapidly changing dynamics of the conflict, violence and insecurity have been pervasive across the region. In North Kivu alone, MONUSCO estimated in 2011 that several dozen security-related 'incidents' occurred each day. The fact that even blue helmets and humanitarian organizations were targeted (the latter on an almost daily basis) attested to the lawlessness of the region and the pervasive insecurity to which ordinary civilians were exposed.[14]

Second, MONUSCO, as many other UN missions before it, had to cope with a wide discrepancy between mandated tasks and available resources. In quantitative terms, the absolute number of peacekeepers in the DRC was high. But relative to the size of its theatre of operations or the population it was meant to protect, MONUSCO was one of the smallest missions in recent years. In 2011, for example, it had deployed roughly

[11] UNSC Resolution 1856 (22 December 2008).

[12] V. K. Holt and T. C. Berkman, 'The Impossible Mandate? Military Preparedness, the Responsibility to Protect, and Modern Peace Operations', Henry L. Stimson Center, September 2006, at 91.

[13] For a more general assessment of MONUSCO's mandate implementation, see D. M. Tull, 'Peacekeeping in the DR Congo: Waging Peace and Fighting War' (2009) 16 *International Peacekeeping* 215.

[14] 'Report of the Secretary-General on the UN Organization Stabilization Mission in the Democratic Republic of the Congo' (12 May 2011), UN Doc. S/2011/298, at 6.

a third of its uniformed personnel (5,100 peacekeepers) in North Kivu, one of the DRC's most violent provinces. Yet this seemingly high number did not amount to much when compared to the size of the province. Had MONUSCO sought a presence throughout the entire province, it would have been able to deploy only two peacekeepers per village.

Third, MONUSCO was constrained by a shortage of critical support, notably force multipliers. Given that the relatively small size of the mission prevented it from establishing a ubiquitous presence, its ability to protect civilians depended on highly mobile troops. In this regard, the eastern DRC's mountainous terrain and the near total absence of infrastructure, roads in particular, worked heavily against the mission. In addition, it was not infrequent that the mission faced a shortfall of military utility helicopters and attack helicopters. In July 2011, for example, the mission's North Kivu Brigade had neither an attack nor a utility helicopter at its disposal. The UN Secretary-General described the consequences for the protection mandate: 'Joint operations with the Congolese Armed Forces have had to be postponed, investigations of allegations of mass human rights violations have had to be delayed, and some deployments to protection hot-spots have had to be deferred'.[15] He warned that 'the Mission is no longer able to carry out critical parts of its priority mandated tasks, including in relation to the protection of civilians', putting the mission 'at risk of failure'.[16]

5. Strategic directions

Notwithstanding its resource constraints, the mission's efforts to implement its protection mandate have also been hampered by doubtful strategic directions. Lacking an executive mandate, MONUSCO did not establish a transitional administration in the DRC, substituting State authority. Rather, the strategic objective was to end the fighting, organize elections and then provide assistance to the new government in its effort to expand State authority throughout the country. This intervention policy, implemented in many other countries, created serious difficulties for the mission's protection mandate.

First, the State-building paradigm led MONUSCO to consider all armed non-State groups as obstacles to peace in the DRC. Since a political

[15] 'Letter dated 20 September 2011 from the Secretary-General Addressed to the President of the Security Council' (20 September 2011), UN Doc. S/2011/589.

[16] Ibid.

solution to the presence of these armed groups (foreign and national) was not available, MONUSCO began military campaigns against these groups in 2009, seeking to put pressure on them to disarm, usually in cooperation with the armed forces of the DRC. This created three kinds of problems.

First, military operations against militias were almost by necessity accompanied by human rights violations as civilians were either displaced by the fighting or were caught in the crossfire. In the eastern DRC, this problem was exacerbated by the tactics of armed groups, which often attacked local communities as an act of revenge for military operations. One group, the Rwandan Forces Démocratiques pour la Libération du Rwanda (FDLR), even sought to provoke a humanitarian catastrophe, hoping this would lead to an international outcry which in turn would force MONUSCO and the armed forces of the DRC to stop their offensive. This reasoning was not entirely baseless. Military efforts to weaken armed groups had devastating civilian costs, causing scores of civilian deaths as well as a 30 percent increase in internal displacement to 2 million people by late 2009.

To make matters worse, the army of the DRC was an unreliable, ineffective partner of the UN operation, prone to commit abuses of civilians wherever it was deployed. Thus, the civilian cost of what may otherwise have been considered a worthy attempt to establish a secure environment raised a host of questions, political and legal. As the Forces Démocratiques pour la Libération du Rwanda had envisioned correctly, it caused a storm of protests by non-governmental organizations, which called on MONUSCO to stop military operations, describing the humanitarian toll as 'unacceptable and disproportionate to the results' the military action had achieved.[17] Even worse, one human rights group argued that the cooperation with the reckless army of the DRC 'implicated' UN peacekeepers in human rights violations.[18] The head of the mission, Alan Doss, conceded the 'moral and practical dilemmas', but implicitly suggested that the long-term gains justified the 'unpalatable choice'.[19] This was a controversial line to take, both within the mission and the wider UN system. For example, a senior UN human rights official observed that once MONUSCO had begun joint military operations with the armed forces of the DRC, its ability to fulfil its protection mandate 'was certainly

[17] X. Rice, 'UN-Backed Congo Military Offensive a "Humanitarian Disaster"', *The Guardian*, 13 October 2009.

[18] Human Rights Watch, 'Eastern DRC: Surge in Army Atrocities', 2 November 2009.

[19] M. Tran, 'UN Denies Complicity in War Crimes', *The Guardian*, 11 November 2009.

compromised by its failure to design and implement from the outset a comprehensive civilian protection strategy'.[20] This echoed the advice of the UN Office of Legal Affairs, which argued that MONUSCO should not participate in operations when there were credible grounds to believe that the better units involved of the Congolese army might violate international humanitarian law.[21] It is beyond doubt that human rights violations took place during or as a result of military operations against armed groups. Moreover, they had been predictable given the long history of human rights abuses by the armed forces of the DRC, its inability or unwillingness to properly plan operations with MONUSCO, the history of vicious tactics by the armed group Forces Démocratiques pour la Libération du Rwanda and finally the resource constraints of MONUSCO. Furthermore, persistent rumours (denied by the government) suggested that Bosco Ntaganda, a war criminal indicted by the International Criminal Court, played a prominent (if informal) role in the military operation, raising the spectre that the UN mission was supporting army units under the control of a person indicted by the International Criminal Court.

Therefore, MONUSCO's strategy put it in an uncomfortable place. Renouncing military operations meant that armed groups continued to exist and hence to commit human rights abuses. But waging war against armed groups was neither the mandate of the mission, nor was the peace operation equipped to do this. But withholding support for the armed forces of the DRC was likewise a thorny option. As MONUSCO officials argued, they had reason to believe that cooperating with the armed forces of the DRC limited the abuses by the army. By extension, however, it also meant that those abuses that were committed by the Congolese army indirectly implicated the mission, courtesy of its cooperation with the armed forces of the DRC.

Peacekeeping operations face a general dilemma when engaging in ambitious peace-building and State-building exercises. Absent an executive mandate for a quasi-trusteeship (as in Kosovo or Timor Leste), peacekeepers are neither meant to substitute State institutions, nor are they able to do so. Consequently, they need to cooperate with and support local State authorities that are almost by definition ineffective and in need

[20] Human Rights Council, 'Report of the Special Rapporteur on Extrajudicial, Summary or Arbitrary Killings, Philip Alston' (1 June 2010), UN Doc. A/HRC/14/24/Add.3.

[21] The leaked correspondence between the Department for Peacekeeping Operations and the Office of Legal Affairs is available at documents.nytimes.com/united-nations-correspondence-on-peacekeeping-in-the-democratic-republic-of-the-congo#p=1.

of 'reconstruction'. However, it has been shown time and again that local authorities do not necessarily share the objectives set out by the foreign promoters of reconstruction policies. This has direct implications for the protection mandate of peacekeepers. In the DRC, for example, the regime of President Joseph Kabila showed very little interest in the reform of the security sector, that is, the formation of an effective national army, which donors considered to be the key reconstruction priority and a benchmark for MONUSCO's eventual drawdown.[22] The reason was that the regime was not so much interested in abstract notions of public security as a collective good. It is first and foremost concerned with its own security and survival, which was protected by a praetorian guard that served for all intents and purposes as the president's militia. In this system of privatized security, rebuilding an effective national army was not only redundant for the government but even dangerous as potential challengers and coup plotters could have risen in its midst. Thus, the government did not share donor enthusiasm for security sector reform, accounting to a large extent for the fact that the DRC still had no effective army nearly a decade after the peace agreement. As a result, the UN Security Council was forced to maintain the large UN mission in the DRC, where it had to protect civilians not only against a host of militias but also against its alleged 'partner', that is, the ill-disciplined army.

6. Peacekeeping innovations

For all the criticism that MONUSCO has received, there is little doubt that the mission engaged in institutional learning over time, particularly as regards its protection mandate.

Some innovations were forced upon the mission. Most notably, this concerned its conditionality policy vis-à-vis the army of the DRC. Entering into effect in late 2009, the policy was a reaction to international protests against MONUSCO's support for the abusive army of the DRC and the civilian cost of their joint military operations against recalcitrant militias. To pre-empt further allegations of complicity in human rights abuses, the policy set out conditions under which MONUSCO was to participate in or support operations with the armed forces of the DRC. Under its terms, the mission pledged not to assist the armed forces of the DRC if there were substantial grounds for believing that there was

[22] H. Boshoff et al., *Supporting SSR in the DRC: Between a Rock and a Hard Place* (The Hague: Netherlands Institute of International Relations Clingendael, 2010).

a risk that such units would violate international humanitarian, human rights or refugee law in the course of a military operation. One year on, however, the mission 'found that it was not possible . . . to demonstrate whether the conditionality policy was having an impact on FARDC [armed forces of the DRC] behavior, which is a central objective'.[23] In truth, this was not surprising. After all, the conditionality policy served more as a devise to protect the mission from accusations of complicity with human rights abuses committed by the armed forces of the DRC than influencing their behaviour as such. The latter idea rested on the assumption that the government of the DRC was desperate for MONUSCO's support of the armed forces of the DRC. As explained before, this was a shaky assumption when considering that the government of President Kabila had little interest in strengthening its army as long as the militias roaming in the far-flung eastern DRC did not constitute a direct threat to the regime in Kinshasa. The political logic behind this reasoning created another dilemma for MONUSCO. Criticizing the government would have further strained an already tenuous relationship, with the possible result that the government would have withdrawn its consent to the mission.[24]

A further obstacle to an effective conditionality policy was its limited degree of implementation. In practice, the policy meant that MONUSCO screened battalion commanders of the armed forces of the DRC for human rights violations prior to providing support for their units, not the entire military unit. But the mere fact that an officer was not a human rights abuser was insufficient to guarantee that the unit in question (and, more precisely, its soldiers) would abstain from committing human rights abuses. In addition, MONUSCO had to continuously monitor the behaviour of these units and to intercede with authorities of the DRC in cases of violations of human rights by the armed forces of the DRC. The tendency of the government to frequently change battalion commanders on short notice and without informing MONUSCO posed yet another challenge to the mission.

It should also be noted that the conditionality approach developed in the DRC became the basis for a UN-wide policy, that is, the 'Human

[23] 'Report of the Secretary-General on the UN Organization Stabilization Mission in the DR Congo' (8 October 2010), UN Doc. S/2010/512, at 11.

[24] D. M. Tull, 'When They Overstay Their Welcome: UN Peacekeepers in Africa', (2013) 17 *Journal of International Peacekeeping* 179.

Rights Due Diligence Policy on UN Support to Non-UN Security Forces' (HRDDP), unveiled in early 2013.[25]

In addition to the conditionality policy, other innovations were more actively designed to improve the mission's protection performance within existing constraints and in light of the recognition that the mission would never be able to respond to, let alone pre-empt, all possible threats all the time. Underlying tactical innovations was the recognition that the mission had entertained somewhat detached relations to the population it was mandated to protect.[26] A generally passive attitude, a static posture, gaps in logistics and manpower and language barriers converged in a culture of incomprehension and mutual distrust between peacekeepers and the local population.[27] Driven by the priority of the protection mandate, the new tactics placed great emphasis on vastly increased engagement with local communities in an effort to gather more information about security-related developments and to broaden protection efforts by expanding the areas MONUSCO could reasonably cover within the limits of its capacities.

Through the development of an area grid forward deployment, the mission widened and intensified its presence in insecure areas. Chief among the new tactics was the creation of Joint Protection Teams (JPT). Composed of military and civilian mission personnel (political affairs, civil affairs, human rights, etc.), Joint Protection Teams were small ad hoc missions, deployed to remote or high-risk locales to gather information about protection-relevant developments. Thus, they were also to intensify communication between local communities on the one hand and civilians and military personnel on the other in an effort to strengthen the capacity of MONUSCO's military personnel to anticipate and prevent attacks against civilians. To staff the Joint Protection Teams, personnel from the substantive sections of the mission were reassigned temporarily, creating shortages elsewhere.

[25] See annex to 'Identical Letters Dated 25 February 2013 from the Secretary-General Addressed to the President of the General Assembly and to the President of the Security Council' (5 March 2013), UN Doc. A/67/775–S/2013/110.

[26] Refugees International, 'DR Congo: Support Community-Based Tools for MONUSCO', 3 May 2001.

[27] A series of well-known failures and scandals had further tarnished MONUSCO's credibility. In addition to protection failures in places like Bunia, Bukavu and Kiwanja, the sexual exploitation of girls and woman as well as the bartering of weapons and mineral resources (by a few peacekeepers) contributed to MONUSCO's poor reputation among the local population.

Another essential tactic of the mission was to widen as much as possible its grid of military bases through the establishment of Company Operating Bases (COB) and Temporary Operating Bases (TOB), respectively semi-permanent or temporary military bases of 50 up to 100 blue helmets that were deployed to often remote high-risk localities. Critical to the effectiveness of forward military bases as well as information gathering was the introduction of Community Liaison Assistants (CLA). These were locally recruited staff with the requisite local language skills and knowledge of local politics to collect and relay relevant information from local communities to the peacekeepers and, if necessary, vice versa. Where a direct presence was not possible, the mission distributed mobile phones and high frequency radios among vulnerable communities to improve emergency communication and to reduce delays in timely responses. However, the implementation of these Community Alert Networks (CAN) was hampered by the fact that large areas of the eastern DRC were not covered by cell phone networks. The mission also increased community and information exchange across the various sections of the mission, the entire UN country team and other partners (i.e., humanitarian organizations). The vastly improved information flow was fed into various coordination and decision-making bodies that were responsible for incorporating protection issues into military plans and most critically evaluating and shifting protection priorities to 'must protect' locations.

7. Conclusion

The fast growing relevance of the concept of civilian protection in the realm of UN peacekeeping marks an important step forward. But the experience of MONUSCO in the DRC suggests that the protection of civilians, as a practice and a strategy, is still in its infancy compared to its development as a concept and normative aspiration. There has also been a drawback. The growing prominence of civilian protection and its imprint on peacekeeping mandates has contributed to a crisis of expectations; that is, the widespread belief that UN peacekeepers should and indeed are able to protect civilian populations in war-torn countries against all potential threats, all the time. Inevitable disappointments have ushered in allegations of serial peacekeeping failures, undermining the political credibility of UN peacekeeping and even the UN at large.

Perhaps inevitably, the practice of civilian protection by peace operations has struggled to keep pace with the normative discourse. As is widely acknowledged, implementing protection mandates has been constrained by the absence of an operational definition of the concept.[28] More than ten years after the issue of civilian protection first appeared on the agenda of the UN Security Council and dozens of protection mandates later, the concept remains ill-defined. A consensus is only slowly emerging that civilian protection is not a military task alone, requiring integrated political, civilian and humanitarian cooperation to be effective. The translation of the concept into a strategy remains arguably the most daunting test. As the case of MONUSCO indicates, taking protection seriously has ramifications for many other mandate tasks and concepts and vice versa. In the DRC, the most obvious tension emerged between the 'priority' to protect civilians and the task to support the government in its effort to expand State authority, which led to intense UN support for the State, including for military operations of the national army against a variety of militias. The assumptions behind this approach highlighted the extent to which the discourse on armed non-State actors and so-called peace spoilers and warlords had an unfortunate consequence. External efforts to build a *State*-sponsored order have tended to overlook that the State and its agencies were as much a part of the problem as they may be part of the solution. Cruelly enough, this was only recognized by the UN mission and decision-makers in New York once human rights organizations had accused MONUSCO of possible complicity in war crimes.

The State-building task points to another problem that has limited the effectiveness of civilian protection in the DRC. For the better part of MONUSCO's existence, civilian protection, though mentioned in its mandate, was not very high on its agenda. Although the UN Security Council incrementally moved it up the list of priorities, it was only in 2008 that civilian protection unequivocally became the main concern. Given the long list of mandated tasks it was asked to fulfil, MONUSCO was not able to prioritize civilian protection, nor was it encouraged to do so by the UN Security Council, which failed to provide it with political guidance in the allocation of its scarce resources. By expanding the mandate of MONUSCO (and other peace operations) through the additional and exceedingly challenging task of protection, long-standing debates once more surfaced about the prerequisites of effective peacekeeping, namely clear, credible and achievable mandates, well-crafted strategies and, finally, resources that match the mandates. It can be plausibly argued that these conditions were never met in the case of MONUSCO, although

[28] Holt, Tyler and Kelly, *Protecting Civilians in UN Peacekeeping Operations*, above note 7, at 11.

not all of its failures should be attributed to factors that were outside of its control.

Despite adverse circumstances and a persistently grim humanitarian situation in the eastern DRC, the UN mission made a virtue out of necessity by improvising and developing civilian protection tools. These innovations were signs of institutional learning inside of the mission. It is to be hoped that they will benefit learning processes in other missions and across the UN system. But this kind of learning will be insufficient in its own right. To meet the highly complex challenge of civilian protection, the UN will have to develop doctrines and strategies of protection, providing UN missions in the field with clear operational and political guidance. Once protection is connected to a mission's overall objectives and strategies, more effective approaches will certainly be possible, provided that missions receive adequate resources. But no amount of resources will be sufficient as long as mission objectives and strategies are not coherent. This will require a clearer understanding both of intervention priorities and the political interests of local actors.

PART IV

The role of third States

18

Common Article 1 of the Geneva Conventions

Scope and content of the obligation to 'ensure respect' – 'narrow but deep' or 'wide and shallow'?

ROBIN GEIß

1. Introduction

More than ten years after 9/11, calls for an urgent reform of the ostensibly obsolete humanitarian legal framework have faded. Yet a central and seemingly eternal dilemma of humanitarian law remains: how to ensure better compliance with international humanitarian law? Official statements of the International Committee of the Red Cross (ICRC) over the past decade(s) have consistently identified the lack of respect for existing rules as the main challenge to the humanitarian legal order.[1] In the armed conflicts in Syria, the Democratic Republic of the Congo (DRC) and (South) Sudan, this lack of respect, albeit a seemingly endemic feature of non-international armed conflicts worldwide, has been particularly obvious. Of course, as is well known, over the past two decades, the laws of war have become increasingly prominent on the Security Council's agenda; its reactions to violations of international humanitarian law ranging from denunciations and focused demands for implementation to the creation of ad hoc institutional mechanisms. But even if the Security Council has developed into the 'major intergovernmental institution' acting in the field of international humanitarian law,[2] its reactions to violations of international humanitarian law are still rather sporadic. Against this

[1] See J. Kellenberger, President of the ICRC, 'Sixty Years of the Geneva Conventions: Learning from the Past to Better Face the Future', 2009, www.icrc.org/eng/resources/documents/statement/geneva-conventions-statement-president-120809.htm.

[2] G. Nolte, 'The 'Different Functions of the Security Council with Respect to Humanitarian Law', in V. Lowe (ed.), *The United Nations Security Council and War* (Oxford: Oxford University Press, 2008), 519–35, at 534.

background, the ICRC has recently been invited by the 31st International Conference of the Red Cross and Red Crescent 'to pursue further research' with regard to possible models for an enhanced compliance mechanism in the field of humanitarian law.[3] Judging, however, by the history of the International Fact-Finding Commission (Article 90 of Additional Protocol I to the Geneva Conventions (AP I)) and more recently, tentative attempts to turn the United Nations Human Rights Council into a central international humanitarian law monitoring body,[4] which have met with strong resistance from various member States,[5] it seems that prospects for a functioning central international humanitarian law monitoring body are as remote as ever. Against this background, much hope has traditionally been vested in Common Article 1 of the four Geneva Conventions (Common Article 1 GC).[6] Common Article 1 GC, in the relevant part, provides that '[t]he High Contracting parties undertake . . . to *ensure respect* for the present Convention *in all circumstances*'.[7] It is on this legal basis that the International Court of Justice (ICJ) in its *Wall* Advisory Opinion held that 'all the States parties to the [Fourth] Geneva Convention . . . are under an *obligation*, while respecting the United Nations Charter and international law, to ensure compliance by Israel [i.e. another State] with international humanitarian law . . . '[8] But already Judges Kooijmans[9] and

[3] Resolution 1 of the 31st International Conference of the Red Cross and Red Crescent, Geneva, Switzerland, 28 November–1 December 2011, para. 6: 'invites the ICRC to pursue further research, consultation and discussion in cooperation with States, . . . to enhance and ensure the effectiveness of mechanisms of compliance with international humanitarian law'.

[4] P. Alston, J. Morgan-Foster and W. Abresch, 'The Competence of the UN Human Rights Council and its Special Procedures in Relation to Armed Conflicts: Extrajudicial Executions in the War on Terror' (2008) 19 *European Journal of International Law* 183.

[5] See Letter dated 4 May 2006 from the United States to the Special Rapporteur on Extrajudicial, Summary, or Arbitrary Executions, UN Doc. A/HRC/4/20/Add.1, 12 March 2007, at 344.

[6] Repeated (verbatim) in Article 1(1) Additional Protocol I to the Geneva Conventions and Article 1(1) Protocol III to the Geneva Conventions of 12 August 1949, and relating to the Adoption of an Additional Distinctive Emblem, Article 38(1) of the Convention on the Rights of the Child provides that 'States Parties undertake to respect and to ensure respect for rules of international humanitarian law applicable to them in armed conflicts which are relevant to the child'.

[7] The French version of Common Article 1 GC provides: '[l]es Hautes Parties contractantes s'engagent à respecter et à faire respecter la présente Convention en toutes circonstances'.

[8] *Legal Consequences of the Construction of a Wall on the Occupied Palestinian Territory* (Advisory Opinion) [2004] ICJ Reports 136, para. 159 (emphasis added).

[9] Ibid. Separate Opinion of Judge Kooijmans, para. 50.

Higgins[10] in their Separate Opinions – not to mention the literature[11] – were rather critical about the Court's assertions concerning Common Article 1 GC. Notably, Judge Kooijmans concluded that while he was certainly not in favour of a restricted interpretation of Common Article 1 GC, he simply did 'not know whether the scope given by the Court to this Article ... [was] correct as a statement of positive law'.[12] Indeed, despite its more than sixty years of history, the debate over Common Article 1 GC has not abated. For some, Common Article 1 GC is nothing more than a 'soap bubble',[13] that is, an 'innocuous opening phrase' serving merely as a recommendatory reminder of obligations and entitlements that exist regardless of Common Article 1 GC.[14] For others, and it seems safe to say that this is by far the prevailing view, Common Article 1 GC is a provision of 'quasi-constitutional nature'[15] that obliges States to take all measures in their power, including non-forcible countermeasures,[16] in order to induce other (contracting) States as well as organized armed groups operating in another State's territory to comply with the rules of international humanitarian law.[17] Before taking a closer look at this

[10] Ibid. Separate Opinion of Judge Higgins, para. 39.

[11] Cf. I. Scobbie, 'Smoke, Mirrors and Killer Whales: the International Court's Opinion on the Israeli Barrier Wall' (2004) 5 *German Law Journal* 1107, 1116 et seq.

[12] *Legal Consequences of the Construction of a Wall*, above note 8, Separate Opinion of Judge Kooijmans.

[13] C. Focarelli, 'Common Article 1 of the 1949 Geneva Conventions: A Soap Bubble?' (2010) 21 *European Journal of International Law* 125.

[14] 'No such legal liability attaches to their *moral duty* to endeavor to ensure respect by their peers', F. Kalshoven, 'The Undertaking to Respect and Ensure Respect in All Circumstances: From Tiny Seed to Ripening Fruit' (1999) 2 *Yearbook of International Humanitarian Law* 3, at 60 (emphasis added).

[15] L. Boisson de Chazournes and L. Condorelli, 'Common Article 1 of the Geneva Conventions Revisited: Protecting Collective Interests' (2000) 82 *International Review of the Red Cross* 67, at 68.

[16] B. Kessler, 'The Duty to 'Ensure Respect' Under Common Article 1 of the Geneva Conventions: Its Implications on International and Non-International Armed Conflicts' (2001) 44 *German Yearbook of International Law* 498, at 506.

[17] Ibid. 516; Boisson de Chazournes and Condorelli, 'Protecting Collective Interests', above note 15, at 76 et seq.; P. Benvenuti, 'Ensuring Observance of International Humanitarian Law Functions, Extent and Limits of the Obligations of Third States to Ensure Respect of International Humanitarian Law' (1992) *International Institute of Humanitarian Law, Yearbook 1989/90* 27, at 33; H.-P. Gasser, 'Ensuring Respect for the Geneva Conventions and Protocols: The Role of Third States and the United Nations', in H. Fox and M. Meyer (eds.), *Effecting Compliance, Armed Conflict and the New Law* (London: British Institute for International & Comparative Law, 1993), at 15–21; U. Palwankar, 'Measures Available to States for Fulfilling their Obligation to Ensure Respect for International Humanitarian Law' (1994) 43 *International Review of the Red Cross* 9, at 10; F. Azzam, 'The Duty of Third

controversy, it seems worthwhile to first point out the issues which seem to be agreed upon in relation to Common Article 1 GC. It is widely accepted and has repeatedly been confirmed by the ICJ that Common Article 1 GC is reflective of customary international law.[18] Moreover, there is also agreement that Common Article 1 GC applies to both international as well as non-international armed conflicts.[19] Most important, it is undisputed that by virtue of Common Article 1 GC, all States parties to the Geneva Conventions are under a hard and fast legal obligation to respect the Geneva Conventions and to ensure respect by their organs and private individuals under their jurisdiction. But beyond these areas of clarity, the precise nature, scope and content of Common Article 1 GC remain debated. Obviously, it is of little avail to know that Common Article 1 GC is customary and applies to non-international armed conflicts as long as the scope and content of the provision remain unclear. There are three areas of ambiguity and controversy; they will be the focus of this analysis.

First of all, it remains debated whether Common Article 1 GC goes beyond the agreed internal-compliance dimension[20] and whether States – including States that are not even involved in an armed conflict[21] – by virtue of undertaking 'to ensure respect', are also obliged to ensure respect vis-à-vis external transgressors, namely other States and possibly extraterritorially operative organized armed groups. The ICJ has emphasized that the wording 'to undertake' means 'to accept an obligation . . . It is not merely hortatory or purposive'.[22] Thus, whatever it is that Common Article 1 GC entails, States are obliged to do it. Therefore, the issue is not whether Common Article 1 GC is only recommendatory or obligatory – for it is clearly obligatory. Rather, the controversy turns on the meaning of the wording 'to ensure respect . . . in all circumstances'. There are

States to Implement and Enforce International Humanitarian Law' (1997) 66 *Nordic Journal of International Law* 55, at 68.

[18] *Military and Paramilitary Activities in and against Nicaragua* (*Nicaragua v. USA*) (Merits) [1986] ICJ Reports 14, para. 220; *Legality of the threat or use of Nuclear Weapons* (Advisory Opinion) [1996] ICJ Reports 226, para. 79; *Legal Consequences of the Construction of a Wall*, above note 8, para. 158.

[19] *Nicaragua*, ibid. paras. 219–220; Kessler, 'Article 1 of the Geneva Conventions', above note 16, at 507 et seq.

[20] Focarelli distinguishes between a State-compliance meaning and an individual-compliance meaning. Focarelli, 'Common Article 1: A Soap Bubble?', above note 13, at 125.

[21] *Legal Consequences of the Construction of a Wall*, above note 8, para. 158.

[22] *Application of the Convention on the Prevention and Punishment of the Crime of Genocide* (*Bosnia and Herzegovina v. Serbia and Montenegro*) (Judgment on the Merits) [2007] ICJ Reports 43, para. 162.

mainly three ways this can be interpreted. First, it could have an internal-compliance dimension only, hence merely emphasizing that States must respect the Conventions at all times. According to that interpretation, Common Article 1 GC could arguably not even be construed as a recommendation to enforce the provisions of the Geneva Conventions vis-à-vis external transgressors. Second, this terminology can be accorded an external-State-compliance dimension, meaning that States parties to the Geneva Conventions are obliged to ensure respect by other States. Third, it could point to a general-external-compliance dimension, in which case Common Article 1 GC entails an obligation to ensure respect vis-à-vis all external transgressors (i.e., other States and in the case of common Article 3 GC extraterritorial armed groups).

Second, provided Common Article 1 GC has such an external-compliance dimension – and I will argue that it does – the actual content of the obligation needs to be clarified. What does 'ensuring respect' actually entail? In this regard, it is unclear whether the obligation to ensure respect requires States to react to each and every or only to certain (serious) breaches of the Geneva Conventions and whether the obligation is limited to breaches in times of armed conflict or also extends to all peacetime breaches, for example, a failure to disseminate or to implement required legislation.[23] Absent any detailed analysis of this issue, the general assumption seems to be that the obligation to ensure respect entails reactions to each and every breach of each and every provision of the Geneva Conventions or its Additional Protocols.[24] Moreover, it is questionable whether the obligation to ensure respect merely requires reactions to recent or ongoing violations or whether it has to be construed as a continuous obligation requiring States not only to react but also to proactively prevent future violations and generally to help other States to better comply with their various obligations under the Geneva Conventions.

Third, it remains unclear what measures – again, provided Common Article 1 GC indeed has an external-compliance dimension – States are obliged and/or entitled to take in order to induce compliance by other

[23] Clear expressions on the matter in the literature are rare. However, there seems to be a widespread and arguably prevailing assumption that the obligation to ensure respect relates to all (i.e., minor and major) breaches of all provisions of the Geneva Conventions and their Protocols. Kessler argues in favour of an even more general obligation to 'assist' and 'help' other States to comply, Kessler, 'Article 1 of the Geneva Conventions', above note 16, at 506.

[24] Ibid. 504 et seq.

States. Is it conceivable that States should be obliged to adopt all measures that are objectively in their power – as is often argued – despite the fact that States have only rarely exploited the full panoply of diplomatic means in reaction to breaches of international humanitarian law? And are States limited in their reactions to the adoption of lawful measures, or does Common Article 1 GC entitle (and/or oblige) them also to employ (non-forcible) counter-measures? Finally, what is the relationship between Common Article 1 GC and the various provisions of the Geneva Conventions and its Additional Protocol I that provide for specific mechanisms to be resorted to in order to react to violations of the Geneva Conventions by other States?

2. Does Common Article 1 GC have an external-compliance dimension?

2.1. Does Common Article 1 GC have an external-State-compliance dimension?

Does Common Article 1 GC have an external-State-compliance dimension?[25] The wording of Common Article 1 GC is inconclusive on the matter. Certainly, ensuring respect means making someone respect the conventions – but whether this includes only individuals or also other States remains open. The 'in all circumstances' formula is not helpful in this respect. Although it is still debated what precisely is meant by the term 'in all circumstances',[26] it is clear that it does not mean 'by all actors'. Nevertheless, it should also be pointed out that there is certainly no indication in the wording of Common Article 1 GC that would militate against an external-State-compliance dimension. In this respect, it is telling that in 1993, Judge Lauterpacht already argued with respect to Article I of the 1948 Genocide Convention that 'the undertaking . . . to prevent genocide is not limited by reference to person or place so that, on its face, it could be said to require every party positively to prevent genocide wherever it occurs'.[27] Indeed, the same holds true with regard to Common

[25] For a recent in-depth analysis of this question see Focarelli, 'Common Article 1: A Soap Bubble?', above note 13.

[26] Ibid. 157 et seq.

[27] *Application of the Convention on the Prevention and Punishment of the Crime of Genocide* (*Bosnia and Herzegovina v. Serbia and Montenegro*) (Provisional Measures) (Order of 13 September 1993) [1993] ICJ Reports 325, Individual Opinion of Judge Lauterpacht, para. 115.

Article 1 GC. Therefore, it may be concluded that the wording of Common Article 1 GC is at least sufficiently open to accord an external-State-compliance dimension to the obligation to ensure respect.

However, it has been argued that a comparison of Common Article 1 GC with similar provisions in human rights treaties militates against such an external-State-compliance meaning of the 'ensure respect' clause.[28] The argument is that no human rights treaty containing a phrase similar to the 'ensure respect' terminology of Common Article 1 GC has ever been understood to imply that contracting States are obliged to react to human rights violations of other contracting States.[29] Rather, 'prevent' or 'ensure respect' terminology in a human rights treaty is exclusively accorded an internal-compliance meaning.[30] This statement may be contested already on the grounds of the judgment of the ICJ in the *Bosnian Genocide* Case and arguably also – albeit less convincingly – on the basis of the admittedly rather unique *Ilascu* Case of the European Court of Human Rights.[31] What is more, it seems doubtful whether international humanitarian law and human rights treaty regimes would indeed require a similar interpretation of the 'ensure respect' formula. Humanitarian law treaties – unlike human rights treaties – are per se applicable extraterritorially, whereas human rights treaties apply extraterritorially only under certain circumstances.[32] It is telling in this regard that the ICJ acknowledged an

[28] Focarelli, 'Common Article 1: A Soap Bubble?', above note 13, at 138 et seq.

[29] Ibid. 139, 142.

[30] The respect and ensure respect dichotomy in human rights treaties is simply reflective of the distinction of negative and positive obligations requiring States (negatively) to abstain from infringing upon human rights and positively to ensure protection from private encroachment. Focarelli, 'Common Article 1: A Soap Bubble?', above note 13, at 139.

[31] In the *Ilascu* Case, the European Court of Human Rights condemned Moldova for not having taken adequate steps aimed at inducing the Russian Federation to stop breaches of the Convention against Moldovan nationals in the Transnistrian territory. In this context, the Strasbourg court affirmed a positive obligation of Moldova under Article 1 of the European Convention on Human Rights (ECHR) (which speaks of 'shall secure to everyone within their jurisdiction') 'to take diplomatic, economic, judicial or other measures in its power' to this end; *Case of Ilascu and others v. Moldova and Russia* (Judgment) Application No. 48787/99, European Court of Human Rights, 8 July 2004, paras. 331, 339. Nevertheless, it is indeed highly doubtful whether the *Ilascu* case confirmed a full-fledged external-State-compliance dimension of Article 1 ECHR or whether the Court relied on an extended internal-compliance dimension by (over-)stretching the concept of jurisdiction. See the partly Dissenting Opinion of Judge Loucaides, according to whom the Court stretched the concept of jurisdiction 'to an unrealistic and absurd extent'. Ibid.

[32] R. Wilde, 'Trigger State Obligations Extraterritorially: The Spatial Test in Certain Human Rights Treaties' (2007) 40 *Israel Law Review* 503.

external-compliance dimension only with respect to the Genocide Convention and only on the basis of the argument that 'the obligation each State thus has to prevent and to punish the crime of genocide is *not territorially limited* by the Convention'.[33] Thus, turning to the drafting history of Common Article 1 GC, it must be conceded that the travaux préparatoires do not support an(y) intention of the drafters to give this provision an external-compliance dimension.[34] In view of the far-reaching and at least in 1949 (i.e., some twenty years before the *Barcelona Traction* Case) revolutionary implications of a treaty obligation to ensure respect vis-à-vis other States, one would certainly have expected at least some discussion of the issue, but in fact there is none.[35] As Kalshoven has shown in his seminal study of the drafting history of Common Article 1 GC, at the time, discussions focused on internal conflicts and States' domestic spheres.[36] Thus, the rationale for the inclusion of the 'ensure respect' clause was to confirm an undertaking by the High Contracting Parties that they would guarantee respect for the Conventions not only by their organs but also by their populations as a whole. Against this historic background, it cannot but be concluded that originally the words 'ensure respect' were only meant to emphasize the internal-compliance dimension of Common Article 1 GC.[37] All of this, however, does not forestall a dynamic interpretation of Common Article 1 GC and the possibility to accord a different meaning to the 'ensure respect' formula today.[38] Indeed, there is an abundance of practice from States and international organizations spanning a period of over thirty years supporting an

[33] *Application of the Convention on the Prevention and Punishment of the Crime of Genocide (Bosnia and Herzegovina v. Serbia and Montenegro)* (Preliminary Objections) [1996] ICJ Reports 595, para. 31. It must be conceded that the ICJ in the *Bosnian Genocide Case* did not (and had no reason to) explicitly refer to other States. Rather, the Court is referring to other 'actors', a term, however, which comprises other non-State actors as well as other States. See *Bosnian Genocide Case*, above note 22, para. 430.

[34] *Legal Consequences of the Construction of a Wall*, above note 8, Separate Opinion of Judge Higgins, para. 39; ibid. Separate Opinion of Judge Kooijmans, para. 50.

[35] 'I have not found in the records of the Diplomatic Conference even the slightest awareness on the part of government delegates that one might ever wish to read into the phrase "to ensure respect" any undertaking by a contracting State other than an obligation to ensure respect for the Conventions by its people "in all circumstances". *Kalshoven*, 'The Undertaking to Respect and Ensure Respect', above note 14, at 28.

[36] Ibid. [37] Ibid. 60.

[38] *Legal Consequences for States of the Continued Presence of South Africa in Namibia (South West Africa)* (Advisory Opinion) [1971] ICJ Reports 31, para. 53.

external-State-compliance dimension of Common Article 1 GC.[39] There is no need to rehash all of this once again; practice in this regard has been meticulously analysed elsewhere.[40] A few observations will suffice. First of all, the voice of idealism is strong in the debate over whether Common Article 1 GC has an external-State-compliance dimension or not. As mentioned at the outset, much hope has been vested in Common Article 1 GC for lack of other effective compliance mechanisms. As a consequence, it seems that an external-State-compliance dimension of Common Article 1 GC has at times been asserted rather than reasoned.[41] Apart from the *Wall* Advisory Opinion, another prominent example in this context is the seemingly widespread assertion that the re-inclusion of Common Article 1 GC in Additional Protocols I (1977) and III (2005) amounts to a 'subsequent agreement between the parties' (Article 31(3)(b) of the 1969 Vienna Convention on the Law of Treaties), from which an external-State-compliance dimension of the 'ensure respect' clause could be deduced. While it is true that the diplomatic conferences of 1974–1977 and 2004–2005 unconditionally reaffirmed Common Article 1 GC, there was once again hardly any debate about the actual meaning of this provision.[42] As far as an external-State-compliance dimension is concerned, the drafting history of the protocols is simply as inconclusive as the travaux préparatoires of the 1949 conventions.[43] Second, at times, it seems more emphasis has been laid on the interpretation of the ICRC Commentaries on Common Article 1 than on the interpretation of the actual provision. The ICRC Commentaries have strongly influenced the debate over Common Article 1 GC.[44] However, it must be conceded that the

39 Boisson de Chazournes and Condorelli, 'Common Article 1 Revisited' above note 15, at 69 et seq.: 'the last half century the practice of States and international organizations, buttressed by jurisprudential findings and doctrinal opinions, clearly supports the interpretation of Common Article 1 GC as a rule that compels all States, whether or not parties to a conflict, not only to take active part in ensuring compliance with rules of international humanitarian law by all concerned but also to react against violations of that law'.

40 Ibid. 85; Kessler, 'Article 1 of the Geneva Convention', above note 16, at 504; Focarelli, 'Common Article 1: A Soap Bubble?', above note 13, at 128; See also J.-M. Henckaerts and L. Doswald-Beck, *Customary International Humanitarian Law*, 2 vols. (Cambridge: Cambridge University Press, 2009), vol. I, Rule 144.

41 Judge Kooijmans concerns voiced in view of the ICJ's assertions about Common Article 1 GC thus apply to the debate at large.

42 Kalshoven, 'The Undertaking to Respect and Ensure Respect', above note 14, at 47–48.

43 Focarelli, 'Common Article 1: A Soap Bubble?', above note 13, at 135.

44 Ibid. 133 et seq.; Kalshoven, 'The Undertaking to Respect and Ensure Respect' above note 14, at 28 et seq.

Commentaries – albeit they unequivocally support an external-compliance dimension of Common Article 1 GC – entail some ambiguity regarding the question whether there is indeed an obligation for States to induce other States into compliance. Notably, the Commentaries provide in the relevant part that 'in the event of a Power failing to fulfil its obligations, the other Contracting Powers (neutral, allied, or enemy) *may, and should*, endeavour to bring it back to an attitude of respect for the Conventions'.[45] Finally, there is no denying that in many relevant instances States have been highly selective in their reactions to breaches – including egregious breaches – of international humanitarian law.[46] In this regard, it may be recalled that in his Individual Opinion of 1993 Judge Lauterpacht, while expressing sympathy for the idea of an 'individual and collective responsibility of States for the prevention of genocide wherever it may occur' contemplated whether '[t]he limited reaction of the parties to the Genocide Convention in relation to these episodes may represent a practice suggesting the *permissibility of inactivity*'.[47] Nevertheless, meanwhile, of course, the ICJ has confirmed an external-compliance dimension of the obligation 'to prevent'.[48] It has done the same (and even more explicitly) with regard to Common Article 1 GC,[49] and while it is undeniable that State practice has

[45] See J. S. Pictet (ed.), *Commentary on the Geneva Conventions of 12 August 1949*, vol. I: Geneva Convention for the Amelioration of the Condition of the Wounded and Sick in Armed Forces in the Field (Geneva: ICRC, 1952); id., *Commentary on the Geneva Conventions of 12 August 1949*, vol. II: Geneva Convention for the Amelioration of the Condition of Wounded, Sick and Shipwrecked Members of the Armed Forces at Sea (Geneva: ICRC, 1960); id., *Commentary on the Geneva Conventions of 12 August 1949*, vol. III: Geneva Convention Relative to the Treatment of Prisoners of War (Geneva, ICRC: 1960); id., *Commentary on the Geneva Conventions of 12 August 1949*, vol. IV: Geneva Convention Relative to the Protection of Civilian Persons in Time of War (Geneva, ICRC: 1958), Also available at www.icrc.org/ihl.nsf/CONVPRES?OpenView. For a meticulous analysis, see Focarelli, 'Common Article 1: A Soap Bubble?', above note 13, at 134, who also points to another inconsistency, namely the fact that the commentary regarding the Third Convention only speaks of 'should' whereas the commentaries to the first, second and fourth Geneva Convention speak of 'may and should'.

[46] And even where States have not reacted to all breaches of the Geneva Conventions, they have hardly ever been accompanied by allegations of breaches of Article 1 GC I-IV committed by inactive States.

[47] *Bosnian Genocide Case*, Individual Opinion of Judge Lauterpacht, above note 27, para. 115 (emphasis added).

[48] *Bosnian Genocide Case*, above note 22, p. para. 430.

[49] *Legal Consequences of the Construction of a Wall*, above note 8, p. para. 158.

been selective, the decisive question is whether it has been too selective.[50] In this regard, the answer is no. Time and again, States that were not individually injured have reacted to violations of international humanitarian law. Armed conflicts – especially in the last two decades – have impelled numerous unilateral calls by States that the Geneva Conventions should be abided by.[51] Moreover, there are no records of any State ever objecting to the ICRC's consistent affirmation that States are under a legal obligation to ensure respect for the Geneva Conventions vis-à-vis other States, nor have ICRC appeals to the international community met critique.[52] And while the ICRC's Customary Law Study has elicited strong objections by some States – as far as can be seen – no State has ever voiced critique with regard to Customary Law Rule 144, which provides that '[t]hey [States] *must* exert their influence, to the degree possible, to stop violations of international humanitarian law'.[53] What is more, the United Nations General Assembly[54], the Security Council[55] and more recently the Human Rights Council[56] all have accepted an obligatory external-compliance dimension of Common Article 1 GC.[57] Repeatedly, these bodies have adopted resolutions explicitly referring to Common Article 1 GC and calling upon States to exert all efforts to ensure

[50] C. Tams, *Enforcing Obligations Erga Omnes in International Law* (Cambridge: Cambridge University Press, 2005), at 234.

[51] Henckaerts and Doswald-Beck, *Customary International Humanitarian Law*, vol. I, above note 40, at 512.

[52] Appeal of 20 March 1979, reprinted in 'Conflict in Southern Africa: ICRC Appeal' (1979) 19 *International Review of the Red Cross* 85; Appeal of 9 May 1983; see 'Africa – Latin America – Asia – Middle East' (1983) 23 *International Review of the Red Cross* 209, at 220.

[53] The corresponding commentary emphasizes that the rule has an external-State-compliance dimension. See Henckaerts and Doswald-Beck, *Customary International Humanitarian Law*, vol. I, above note 40, at 509 et seq. (emphasis added).

[54] UNGA Resolution 58/97 (17 December 2003), para. 3; UNGA Resolution 59/122 (10 December 2004), para. 3.

[55] UNSC Resolution 681 (20 December 1990), para. 5.

[56] Human Rights Council Resolution S-9/1 (12 January 2009), UN Doc. A/HRC/RES/S-9/1, preambular para. 9. According to the Goldstone Report: 'This provision [Common Article 1 GC] entails obligations not only in relation to actors and conduct within the jurisdiction of each State but also in relation to the *international enforcement* of the Conventions.' Human Rights Council, 'Human Rights in Palestine and other Occupied Arab Territories, Report of the United Nations Fact-Finding Mission on the Gaza Conflict', UN Doc. A/HRC/12/48, 25 September 2009 (emphasis added).

[57] For a comprehensive collection of relevant practice regarding Common Article 1 GC, see Henckaerts and Doswald-Beck, *Customary International Humanitarian Law*, vol. II, above note 40, practice relating to Rule 144.

respect for the Geneva Conventions by other contracting States.[58] Thus, notwithstanding certain ambiguities in the ICRC Commentaries and the selectivity in States' reactions, and, while admitting that it may be an exaggeration to state that practice over the last half century supports an external-State-compliance dimension of Common Article 1 GC,[59] practice over the last twenty years certainly does.

2.2. *Does Common Article 1 GC have a non-State-actor-compliance dimension?*

As mentioned above, it is widely agreed that the obligation to ensure respect as it is laid out in Common Article 1 GC also extends to non-international armed conflicts.[60] The wording of Common Article 1 GC requires that respect be ensured for the Geneva Conventions in their entirety, thereby including non-international armed conflicts in the sense of Common Article 3 GC. Given that Common Article 3 GC can be violated by States as well as by organized armed groups, it would seem to follow that the obligation to ensure respect, in the context of a non-international armed conflict, relates not only to violations by other States but also to violations by organized armed groups. Notably, the ICJ in the *Bosnian Genocide* Case referred to other 'actors', thereby comprising both other non-State actors as well as other States.[61] Thus, rather than speaking merely of an external-State-compliance dimension, it seems suitable to speak of a general-external-compliance dimension in order to construe the obligation to ensure respect in line with the widely shared position that the obligation applies to international and non-international armed conflicts alike.

[58] In Resolution S-9/1 of 12 January 2009, above note 56, the UN Human Rights Council reaffirmed that each State party to the Fourth Geneva Convention 'is under the obligation to respect and ensure the respect for the obligations arising from that Convention'. In view of the explicit reference to Common Article 1 GC in many of the resolutions, it would seem somewhat far-fetched to accord merely a recommendatory character to these various resolutions. But see Focarelli, 'Common Article 1: A Soap Bubble?' above note 13, at 157.

[59] Boisson de Chazournes and Condorelli, 'Protecting Collective Interests', above note 15, at 69 et seq.

[60] See Kessler, 'Article 1 of the Geneva Conventions', above note 16, at 508.

[61] *Bosnian Genocide Case,* above note 22, paras. 430, 434.

3. The content of the obligation to ensure respect

Thus, Common Article 1 GC has an external-compliance dimension, and, by virtue of the obligation to ensure respect, States are obliged to ensure respect for the Geneva Conventions also vis-à-vis other (contracting) States as well as organized armed groups involved in non-international armed conflicts. This raises the follow-up question about the actual content of the obligation to 'ensure respect'. Clearly, it is an obligation of conduct and not one of result.[62] States are required to exercise due diligence to fulfil this obligation, that is, they are required to do what may reasonably be expected of them under the given circumstances of each particular instance. Thus, as with any due diligence obligation, it would be impossible to prescribe the precise conduct required in all possible future scenarios in the abstract.[63] Ultimately, the notion of due diligence always calls for an assessment *in concreto* since due diligence may require different actions under different circumstances.[64] Yet notwithstanding the necessity of a case-by-case assessment, there are also certain (general) points of reference that can be – and must be – determined in the abstract. After all, one needs to know what exactly it is that has to be done with due diligence – before being able to assess whether due diligence was indeed exercised in a specific situation. In this regard, the first thing one needs to know is when and under which circumstances the obligation to ensure respect is triggered. Is it a continuous obligation that persists regardless of any prior violation of the Conventions and that is generally aimed at helping other States to better conform with all of their obligations under the Geneva Conventions?[65] Or is the obligation to ensure respect designed

[62] In this regard, Common Article 1 GC in its external-State-compliance dimension is no different from the obligation to ensure respect in its internal-compliance dimension as it is to be found in human rights treaties. See *Velásquez-Rodríguez v. Honduras* (Judgment on the Merits) Inter-American Court of Human Rights Series C No 4 (29 July 1988), para. 172, finding the State of Honduras responsible for the involuntary disappearance of Angel Manfredo Velásquez Rodríguez because it failed to take appropriate steps to prevent or punish private individuals who caused Mr. Rodríguez to disappear.

[63] Judge Kooijmans in his Separate Opinion to the *Wall* Advisory Opinion seemed to suggest that States by virtue of Common Article 1 GC are entitled to nothing else than the issuing of political demarches; see *Legal Consequences of the Construction of a Wall*, above note 8, Separate Opinion of Judge Kooijmans, paras. 47 et seq. As Scobbie has already remarked, there is no justification for such a narrow approach. See Scobbie, 'Smoke, Mirrors and Killer Whales', above note 11, at 1119.

[64] *Bosnian Genocide Case*, above note 22, para. 430.

[65] Kessler, 'Article 1 of the Geneva Conventions', above note 16, at 502–07; Gasser, 'Ensuring Respect for the Geneva Conventions', above note 17, at 31–32. In fact, it has even been

as a reaction to specific violations and therefore only activated by acute breaches of the Geneva Conventions? And, if so, are States obliged to react to each and every violation of any given provision of the Geneva Conventions, including minor breaches or failures to abide by such provisions that apply in times of peace? Only if these abstract questions are settled can it be determined what behaviour the exercise of due diligence in the fulfilment of the obligation to ensure respect would require in a particular situation.

3.1. What activates the obligation to ensure respect?

The obligation to ensure respect in Common Article 1 GC is phrased as a continuous obligation. On the face of its wording it is not conditioned in any manner nor dependent on any (prior) event or violation, albeit it is often depicted in such a way.[66] Rather, by the wording of Common Article 1 GC, States are obliged to ensure respect in all circumstances. Thus, it would follow that all States are constantly required to react to all breaches of the Geneva Conventions. Such a broad interpretation is immediately convincing and in line with the original intention of the drafters of Common Article 1 GC, insofar as the internal-compliance dimension of the obligation to ensure respect is concerned. However, it is less clear whether such a comprehensive scope can also be ascribed to the external-compliance dimension of this obligation.

In an external context it could be argued that such a sweeping interpretation of the obligation to ensure respect would simply lead to unrealistic results. If indeed all States were constantly required to react to all breaches by external transgressors, including peacetime breaches, of each and every GC provision, arguably almost all States would constantly be violating their obligation to ensure respect.[67] The following example may serve as an illustration. The grave breaches regime of the Geneva Conventions requires States to enact legislation necessary to provide

argued that 'whenever the humanitarian crisis reaches such a degree that it amounts to a serious violation of the conventions – Common Article 1 obliges the High Contracting Parties to enforce the Conventions through humanitarian measures'. Kessler, 'Article 1 of the Geneva Conventions', above note 16, at 507.

[66] The ICRC Customary Law Rule 144, second sentence, provides: 'They must exert their influence, to the degree possible, to stop violations of international humanitarian law'. See Henckaerts and Doswald-Beck, *Customary International Humanitarian Law*, vol. I, above note 40, at 509.

[67] Focarelli, 'Common Article 1: A Soap Bubble?', above note 13, at 156 et seq.

effective penal sanctions for persons committing grave breaches. As is well known, a number of States have failed to (adequately) implement the grave breaches regime domestically.[68] Does that mean in each case that the 193 other States that are not doing anything about those States' failure to enact the required legislation domestically are constantly in breach of their obligation to ensure respect for the Conventions?[69] And does this in turn mean that all States that remain inactive with respect to the 193 States violating their obligation to ensure respect under Common Article 1 GC are also violating their obligation to ensure respect? In other words, does Common Article 1 GC also relate to breaches of Common Article 1 GC, with the potential result of endless chains of breaches?

Many of the often-lamented inconsistencies in the interpretation of Common Article 1 GC result from this dilemma. While the great majority of authors accepts that Common Article 1 GC entails an obligation to ensure respect by other States, most authors feel uneasy about imposing such an onerous obligation on States to react to all violations of all provisions of the Geneva Conventions at all times. An easy way out of this dilemma is to argue that Common Article 1 GC simply has no external-compliance dimension in the first place. This argument however, while it may still have been valid thirty years ago, no longer holds up today. Indeed, most authors try to evade the dilemma not by denying the obligatory external-compliance dimension of Common Article 1 GC but by focusing on the content of the obligation, trying to make the 'obligation as discretionary' as possible. Some authors are trying to identify the minimal obligatory content that could possibly be given to this obligation, short of denying an obligatory character altogether. Thus, it has been argued that States, albeit obliged to ensure respect, are entirely free not only in their choice of measures but also with regard to the decision whether to act at all.[70] Evidently, however, if Common Article 1 GC entails an obligation to ensure respect vis-à-vis third States, and in view of the wording 'undertake' and the international practice described above it clearly does, then States cannot be entirely free to

[68] K. Doermann and R. Geiß, 'The Implementation of Grave Breaches into Domestic Legal Orders' (2009) 8 *Journal of International Criminal Justice* 703.

[69] The obligation to ensure respect is a primary obligation. Although triggered by a violation of international humanitarian law, the obligation to ensure respect is incumbent on States which did not themselves commit the illegal act. Of course, as a primary obligation, failure to ensure respect in and of itself is also an illegal act which entails State responsibility.

[70] Kessler, 'Article 1 of the Geneva Conventions', above note 16, at 506 et seq.

decide whether to act or not to act, nor can there be unfettered discretion as to the measures that may be employed. While the due diligence standard grants States a margin of flexibility, it does not permit inaction nor does it leave room for unfettered discretion. After all, States are only free to choose among those measures that fulfil the due diligence requirement.

Moreover, it could potentially also be argued that the obligation to ensure respect in its external-compliance dimension is limited to 'serious breaches' of the Geneva Conventions. The practice commonly referred to in order to support an external-compliance dimension of the obligation to ensure respect, as far as can be seen, typically deals with instances of a certain gravity, and violations that occur in times of armed conflict rather than in peacetime.[71] Kessler therefore speaks of a duty that arises in 'exceptional cases'.[72] Indeed, given that by virtue of Articles 40 and 41 of the ILC Articles on State Responsibility only serious breaches of the narrow category of *ius cogens* norms trigger an obligation to 'cooperate',[73] it would *prima facie* seem logical to require at least a similar 'threshold of gravity' with regard to the far wider circle of norms to which the obligation to ensure respect in Common Article 1 GC applies, namely violations of all the provisions contained in the Geneva Conventions.

There are, however, strong arguments in favour of a broader conception of the obligation to ensure respect in its external-compliance dimension. First, concerns that a broad conception of this obligation would be unrealistically burdensome for States are attenuated by the fact that the obligation to ensure respect is a due diligence obligation, that is, States are in any case only obliged to do what can reasonably be expected under the circumstances of each particular instance, for example, to exert their influence. Second, the 'seriousness' of a violation is not a precise threshold for triggering a positive duty to act and may be criticized as creating considerable legal uncertainty.[74] Rather than affecting the application of

[71] See references above, notes 54–57.

[72] Kessler, 'Article 1 of the Geneva Conventions', above note 16, at 505.

[73] ILC, 'Report of the International Law Commission' (23 April–1 June and 2 July–10 August 2001), 53rd Session, UN Doc Supplement No. 10 (A/Res/56/10), at 43.

[74] Nevertheless, the threshold of *serious violations* is not alien to the Geneva Conventions (Articles 89, 90(2)(c)(i) AP I nor to the ILC Articles on the responsibility of States for internationally wrongful acts (Article 40(2)). As has been concluded elsewhere, on the whole it appears to be an acceptable standard to States; Tams, 'Enforcing Obligations Erga Omnes', above note 50, at 248.

the obligation to ensure respect, the seriousness of a breach is to be taken into consideration when determining the actual content of the obligation to ensure respect in a given case. In this regard, the due diligence nature of the obligation allows for graduated responses proportionate to the seriousness of the breach in question. As a general rule, the more serious and imminent a breach, the more will be required of States. And while States cannot reasonably be expected to immediately and directly react to each and every (minor, peace-time) breach of the Geneva Conventions when and wherever it occurs, if such (minor) breaches occur continuously and over an extended period of time, States could reasonably be expected to exert their influence to stop such breaches even if they do not qualify as 'serious breaches'. Common Article 1 GC makes it clear that the provisions contained in the Geneva Conventions are binding *erga omnes partes*[75] and that all States parties to the Geneva Conventions share a common interest in upholding these provisions.[76] Against this backdrop, and given that in times of armed conflict even 'minor' violations of the Geneva Conventions by one party can quickly lead to an escalatory spiral of more and ever graver violations, the obligation to ensure respect in both its internal- and external-compliance dimensions should be construed broadly to require positive steps whenever provisions of the Geneva Conventions are breached.

It follows that any breach of the Geneva Conventions by another State, irrespective of where and when it occurs, activates the obligation to ensure respect. The same holds true with regard to breaches by other external (non-State) transgressors insofar as they are bound to respect the Geneva Conventions.[77] With respect to the precise point in time at which the duty to take positive steps arises, guidance may be derived from the ICJ's judgment in the *Bosnian Genocide* Case. There, the Court held, with regard to the obligation 'to prevent' genocide, that 'a State's obligation to prevent, and the corresponding duty to act, *arise at the instant* that the State learns of, or should normally have learned of, the existence of a

[75] See J. Crawford, *State Responsibility: The General Part* (New York: Cambridge University Press, 2013), at 370.

[76] Generally on the concept of obligations *erga omnes partes*, see *Questions Relating to the Obligation to Prosecute or Extradite (Belgium v. Senegal)* (Judgment on the Merits) [2012] ICJ Reports 33, para. 69.

[77] Notably, the ICJ in the *Bosnian Genocide Case*, with regard to the obligation 'to prevent' genocide, also referred to violations by other 'actors'. *Bosnian Genocide Case*, above note 22, paras. 430, 434.

serious risk that genocide will be committed'.[78] The wording of Common Article 1 GC certainly allows for such a broad conception of the obligation to ensure respect and the object and purpose of this provision would seem to require it. Therefore, the ICJ's reasoning regarding the obligation to prevent genocide should also be applied to the obligation to ensure respect for the Geneva Conventions.

Situated in the context of general public international law, the obligation to ensure respect in Common Article 1 GC can therefore best be described to contain a specification of the general concept expressed in Articles 48 and 54 of the ILC Articles on State Responsibility. According to Article 48, '[a]ny State other than an injured State *is entitled to invoke* the responsibility of another State . . . if the obligation breached is owed to a group of states [or the international community as a whole]'.[79] Similarly, the saving clause contained in Article 54 of the ILC Articles does 'not prejudice the *right* of [non-injured] States . . . to take lawful measures'.[80] Common Article 1 GC goes further in that it entails not only an *entitlement* to 'invoke' (Article 48) or a *right* to 'take lawful measures' (Article 54) but also an *obligation* to act if the Geneva Conventions are breached. In doing so, it follows the structure of Articles 40 and 41 of the ILC Articles. However, unlike these provisions, it is not limited only to *serious* breaches of obligations arising from *peremptory norms* (*ius cogens*),[81] but also comprises all breaches of the wider circle of norms contained in the Geneva Conventions, such as obligations owed to all of the States parties of the Geneva Conventions (*erga omnes partes*).[82]

4. What measures are to be employed to ensure respect?

By virtue of the due diligence nature of the obligation to ensure respect, States are obliged to do what can reasonably be expected of them. Regarding the undertaking to prevent genocide, the ICJ explained that 'the

[78] *Bosnian Genocide Case*, supra note 22, para. 431 (emphasis added). However, as far as a State's responsibility for the breach of said obligation to prevent is concerned, the ICJ was more cautious and, in accordance with Article 14(3) of the ILC Articles on State Responsibility, held that 'a State can be held responsible for breaching the obligation to prevent genocide only if genocide was actually committed. It is at the time when commission of the prohibited act . . . begins that the breach of an obligation of prevention occurs'.

[79] Emphasis added. [80] Emphasis added. [81] Emphasis added.

[82] Crawford, *State Responsibility: The General Part*, above note 75, at 370.

obligation of States parties is . . . to employ *all means reasonably available to them*, so as to prevent genocide so far as possible'.[83] Naturally, States cannot reasonably be expected to actively monitor all other States in the world at all times. However, wherever armed conflict breaks out, the obligation to monitor intensifies; due diligence in times of armed conflict requires closer monitoring than in times of peace. Thus, with regard to countries that are involved in an armed conflict – international as well as non-international – States can reasonably be expected to follow the events in that country more closely and with a specific awareness for possible violations of international humanitarian law. Should they detect breaches, they will be under an obligation to take positive steps to end those violations.[84] What exactly is owed by States in terms of positive measures in such a situation will depend on a variety of parameters ranging from the kind and extent of harm occurring, their relationship with the transgressor and their capacity to influence the situation, which in turn hinges on factors such as geographical proximity and the strength of the political links.[85] Moreover, the ICJ has reiterated, both with respect to the obligation to prevent genocide as well as with regard to the obligation to ensure respect under Common Article 1 GC, that 'every State may only act within the limits of international law'.[86] While it seems undisputed today that, by virtue of Common Article 1 GC I, States are not entitled to take unilateral military action to discharge their obligation, there is ongoing controversy over whether the obligation to ensure respect also entails an entitlement to adopt countermeasures in response to humanitarian law violations of other States.

[83] *Bosnian Genocide Case*, above note 22, para. 430. The Court also held that 'responsibility is . . . incurred if the State *manifestly failed to take all measures to prevent* genocide which were within its power, and which might have contributed to preventing the genocide'. (emphasis added).

[84] The ICJ held that '*if* the State has available to it means *likely* to have a deterrent effect . . . , it is under a duty to make *such use* of these means as the circumstances permit'. Ibid. para. 431. In *Ilascu v. Moldova and Russia*, above note 31/, para. 331, the European Court of Human Rights held that 'the State in question must endeavor, with *all legal and diplomatic* means available to it vis-à-vis third actors, to continue to guarantee the enjoyment of the rights and freedoms defined in the Convention'.

[85] *Bosnian Genocide Case*, above note 22, para. 430; Kessler, 'Article 1 of the Geneva Conventions', above note 16, at 506.

[86] *Legal Consequences of the Construction of a Wall*, above note 8, para. 158; *Bosnian Genocide Case*, above note 22, para. 431.

4.1. Does Common Article 1 GC provide an entitlement to take non-forcible countermeasures?

The question therefore is whether States, in order to fulfil their obligation to ensure respect, may (and depending on the circumstances must) resort to non-forcible countermeasures as defined in Chapter II of the International Law Commission's Draft Articles on State Responsibility. Theoretically, a right or obligation to resort to countermeasures could be construed in two ways: either third States are rendered specially affected by virtue of Common Article 1 GC and are therefore injured States in accordance with Article 42(b)(i) ASR,[87] or Common Article 1 GC, by virtue of subsequent State practice, has developed beyond the state of the law as it is described in the International Law Commission's Commentary to Article 54 ASR, by entitling non-injured States to resort to countermeasures so as to enforce unremedied breaches of humanitarian obligations in the collective interest.

It is submitted that Common Article 1 GC (at this stage) serves neither of these functions. There is simply no indication — neither in its wording nor in State practice – that Common Article 1 GC provides a treaty-specific *lex specialis* rule that would either qualify all States faced with a breach of international humanitarian law as injured States – the 'specially affected' clause has a factual, not a legal dimension. That is, States are specially affected because of factual circumstances, not because of legal prescription[88] – nor is there sufficient (or rather any) proof that Common Article 1 GC has developed beyond the content of the International Law Commission's saving clause in Article 54 ASR. While Article 48 ASR provides that any State other than the injured State is entitled to *invoke* the responsibility of another State, provided the obligation breached is owed to the international community as a whole (i.e., it is an obligation *erga omnes*),[89] it is less clear whether and to what extent such (non-injured) third States may assert a right to react to unremedied breaches by taking countermeasures.[90] Under Article 54 ASR, any such

[87] M. Sassòli, 'State Responsibility for Violations of International Humanitarian Law' (2002) 84 *International Review of the Red Cross* 401, at 423.

[88] J. Crawford, *The International Law Commission's Articles on State Responsibility: Introduction, Text and Commentaries* (Cambridge: Cambridge University Press, 2002), Article 42.

[89] According to Article 48 (2) ASR, such a State may demand (a) cessation and (b) performance in the interest of the beneficiaries of the obligation breached.

[90] B. Simma, 'From Bilateralism to Community Interest in International Law' (1994-VI) 250 *Recueil des cours* 217; Tams, *Enforcing Obligations Erga Omnes*, above note 50, at 249 et seq.

State may only 'take *lawful measures* against that State to ensure cessation of the breach and reparation in the interests of the injured State or of the beneficiaries of the obligation breached'. The International Law Commission thus deliberately left it open whether there indeed exists a right of third parties to take countermeasures in the collective interest. As the International Law Commission put it, the current state of international law on countermeasures taken in the general or collective interest is uncertain;[91] State practice is sparse and only involves a limited number of States.[92] At present, there appears to be no clearly recognized entitlement of States (other than the injured State) to take countermeasures in the collective interest.[93] While the law may be developing in this area in the direction of a right to take countermeasures in the collective interest,[94] there is at present no indication that Common Article 1 GC has developed further than general public international law. As far as can be seen, there are no instances in which States have responded to breaches of the Geneva Conventions by unilateral (non-forcible) countermeasures on the basis of Common Article 1 GC. Indeed, it is telling that the International Law Commission's Commentary on Article 54 ASR, while listing relevant instances where non-injured States have reacted against breaches by adopting economic sanctions and similar measures, does not even mention Common Article 1 GC.[95] Moreover, in the *Wall* Advisory Opinion, the ICJ reminded States that, in carrying out their obligation to ensure respect under Common Article 1, they should respect 'the UN Charter and international law'.[96] This militates in favour of an interpretation that excludes (unlawful) countermeasures. While the statement in and of itself is not fully conclusive in this respect – after all, if Common Article 1 GC allowed countermeasures, they would not violate international law – in view of the uncertain status of the law regarding countermeasures in the collective interest, one may safely assume that the ICJ would have provided an explanation rather than an unqualified reminder to abide by international law, had it wished to indicate that Common Article 1 GC entitles to employ (unlawful) countermeasures in the collective interest.

[91] Crawford, *Articles on State Responsibility*, above note 88, Article 54, marginal no. 6.

[92] Ibid. [93] Ibid. [94] Tams, *Enforcing Obligations Erga Omnes*, above note 50, at 248.

[95] Crawford, *Articles on State Responsibility*, above note 88, Article 54, marginal nos. 3 and 4.

[96] *Legal Consequences of the Construction of a Wall*, above note 8, para. 158.

4.2. *Relationship of Common Article 1 GC to other specific provisions in the Conventions and Protocols*

Thus, the due diligence obligation to ensure respect under Common Article 1 GC is to be fulfilled exclusively by resort to lawful measures. This raises the question about the relationship between Common Article 1 GC and the various provisions of the Conventions and Protocols that foresee specific lawful measures vis-à-vis transgressor States. In this respect, it has been argued that measures available against transgressor States already flow from these other – more specific – provisions, that these provisions operate in their own right and that therefore Common Article 1 GC is void of any autonomous legal meaning and largely redundant.[97] Indeed, States parties to the Geneva Conventions and to its Additional Protocol I may convene meetings of the High Contracting Parties (Article 7 AP I), they may resort to the Protecting Powers institution or its substitutes and they may call upon the International Fact-Finding Commission (Article 90 AP I); in addition, formal enquiries may be instigated upon request of a party to the conflict (Articles 52 GC I, 53 GC II, 132 GC III, 149 GC IV). In addition to these discretionary measures, States are under an obligation to enforce the system of repression of grave breaches, and, according to Article 89 AP I: '[i]n situations of *serious violations* of the Conventions or of this Protocol, the High Contracting Parties undertake to act, jointly or individually, in cooperation with the United Nations and in conformity with the United Nations Charter'. Nevertheless, whereas most of the above-mentioned provisions foresee discretionary powers,[98] Common Article 1 GC is obligatory. And, while the undertaking to ensure respect – depending on the circumstances – may be fulfilled by having resorted to these specific (institutionalized) mechanisms, States also have various other options to exercise due diligence in the fulfilment of their obligation to ensure respect. In any case, given that the procedural requirements for some of these mechanisms are rather high, convening a meeting of the High Contracting Parties requires approval by a majority of the States parties to Additional Protocol I to the Geneva Conventions, it may well be that, under Common Article 1 GC, States parties to the Geneva Conventions are required to resort to additional measures. Additionally, Common Article 1 GC prescribes a minimum duty to monitor compliance with the Geneva Conventions, specifically in situations of armed conflict. Such an obligation is not entailed in any of the above-cited specific

[97] Focarelli, 'Common Article 1: A Soap Bubble?', above note 13, at 151. [98] Ibid. 150.

provisions. The grave breaches regime belongs to the internal-compliance sphere and for this reason already cannot be invoked as having absorbed Common Article 1 GC in its external-compliance dimension. Finally, whereas the obligation to react to breaches of the Geneva Conventions resides in Common Article 1 GC as well as in Additional Protocols I and III, Article 89 AP I, a provision which remarkably already its sponsors called confusing,[99] reiterates that, in cases of serious breaches, the obligation under Common Article 1 GC must be carried out in conformity with the United Nations Charter and in cooperation with the United Nations. It would seem that the two provisions work hand in hand. However, given that the main objective of both Common Article 1 GC as well as Article 89 AP I is to ensure respect with international humanitarian law, it seems plausible to argue that cooperation with the United Nations in the sense of Article 89 AP I does not automatically relieve States of their obligations under Common Article 1 GC. In this respect, it is telling that the ICJ in the *Bosnian Genocide* Case, in spite of the fact that the Genocide Convention in Article VIII specifically provides for the activation of the United Nations collective security system, pointed out that the unqualified undertaking to ensure respect in Article I of the Genocide Convention has a 'separate legal existence of its own', that the duty to prevent is both 'normative and compelling' and that it 'is not to be read merely as an introduction to later express references to legislation, prosecution and extradition' but that 'in particular . . . [the] undertaking to prevent, creates obligations distinct from those which appear in the subsequent Articles'.[100] In particular, with regard to the activation of the collective security system, the Court held that '[e]ven if and when these organs [i.e., organs of the United Nations] have been called upon, this does not mean that the States parties to the Convention are relieved of the obligation to take such action as they can to prevent genocide from occurring, while respecting the United Nations Charter and any decisions that may have been taken by its competent organs'.[101] Nothing would seem to bar transposing these findings to Common Article 1 GC.

Thus, it is submitted that Common Article 1 GC is not rendered redundant by virtue of the specific mechanisms foreseen in the Geneva Conventions and its Additional Protocols. Nevertheless, it has rightly been pointed out that '[a]ny effective attempt by a State to ensure respect for

[99] Sassòli, 'State Responsibility for Violations', above note 87, at 428.
[100] *Bosnian Genocide Case*, above note 22, para. 427. [101] Ibid.

international humanitarian law, especially in the event of massive violations, would be difficult, if not impossible, without the political support of the community of States'.[102] Therefore, collective action through the United Nations, namely the Security Council, may often be the most effective way to ensure respect in case of grave breaches.[103] Given that all individual members of the Security Council are subject to the obligation to ensure respect under Common Article 1 GC, it may be asked which impact this obligation has on the exercise of membership rights, namely voting rights, by individual members of the Security Council.[104] Contrary to the reasoning of the European Court of Human Rights in the *Behrami* and *Saramati* Cases,[105] it seems more plausible to argue that members of the Security Council remain under their individual obligation to ensure respect even when voting in the Council.[106] Of course, this cannot mean that member States are bound to vote positively for whatever resolution is contemplated in the Security Council as a response to serious violations of international humanitarian law. But as a minimum it may be possible to deduce an obligation to justify a veto or to explain a negative vote.[107]

5. Conclusion

Common Article 1 GC I-IV is neither a soap bubble nor the panacea for international humanitarian law's eternal dilemma of ensuring compliance for its provisions. It is a central component in the toolbox of mechanisms necessary to ensure better compliance, but one should be cautious not to overstretch or overestimate the possibilities of this provision. It is noteworthy that some time ago, the United Nations Secretary-General described the concept of the Responsibility to Protect, whose scope has gradually been narrowed down to comprise only core crimes (i.e., the crimes laid out in Articles 6, 7 and 8 of the Statute of the International

[102] Palwankar, 'Measures Available to States', above note 17, at 18. [103] Ibid.

[104] A. Zimmermann, 'The Obligation to Prevent Genocide: Towards a General Responsibility to Protect', in U. Fastenrath et al. (eds.) *From Bilateralism to Community Interest: Essays in Honour of Judge Bruno Simma* (Oxford: Oxford University Press 2011), 629–48, at 643.

[105] *Behrami and Behrami v. France and Saramati v. France, Germany and Norway* (Decision) Application Nos. 71412/01 and 78166/01, European Court of Human Rights, 2 May 2007, para. 149.

[106] Zimmermann, 'The Obligation to Prevent Genocide', above note 104, at 644.

[107] A. Peters, 'The Responsibility to Protect: Spelling out the Hard Legal Consequences for the UN Security Council and its Members', in Fastenrath et al. (eds.) *From Bilateralism to Community Interest*, above note 104, 297–325, at 323 et seq.

Criminal Court), as 'narrow but deep'.[108] With Common Article 1 GC and in view of the great hopes that are often vested in this provision, there is a risk that it could be perceived or gradually turned into something that is 'wide but shallow' and ultimately meaningless. Descriptions of Common Article 1 GC as a 'soap bubble' certainly hint in that direction.[109] Indeed, the scope of application of this obligation is wide. It applies to any breach of the Geneva Conventions wherever it occurs. But States are neither required to achieve the impossible, that is, to stop and prevent each and every violation wherever it occurs, nor are they entirely free in their discretion whether and how to react if breaches occur. Rather, States are obliged to react to breaches of the Geneva Conventions and to do what can reasonably be expected of them in order to put a stop to, or, in the case of an imminent threat, prevent violations of the provisions of the Geneva Conventions. It follows from the due diligence character of this obligation that the graver the violation in question, the more will be expected of States to bring it to an end. Thus, although the obligation to ensure respect in Common Article 1 comprises a broad spectrum of violations and corresponding reactions prima facie justifying a designation of Common Article 1 as 'wide but shallow', in cases of graver violations, the content of the obligation to ensure respect is narrowed down, and more decisive responses are required. Moreover, the wording of Common Article 1 is sufficiently open to accommodate future developments that would further 'deepen' the obligation to ensure respect, namely, the development of a right (and thereby in some instances an obligation) to take countermeasures in the collective interest and in response to violations of the Geneva Conventions.

[108] 'Report of the Secretary-General on Implementing the Responsibility to Protect' (12 January 2009), UN Doc. A/63/677, para. 11(c).

[109] Focarelli, 'Common Article 1: A Soap Bubble?', above note 13.

19

Complicity in violations of international humanitarian law

HELMUT PHILIPP AUST

1. Introduction

In 2010, the UN High Commissioner for Human Rights presented the results of a so-called 'Mapping Exercise' on violations of international humanitarian law in the long and entrenched conflict in the Democratic Republic of the Congo (DRC).[1] One of the conclusions of this report is that there have been massive violations of international humanitarian law on all sides to the conflict. The participation of a number of States in these violations raises the question of the responsibility of States which did not directly commit these violations themselves, but rather furnished support for these wrongful acts. Different forms of complicity in violations of international humanitarian law are conceivable. Complicity can consist in logistical or military support for conduct which violates international humanitarian law. This support can be closely related to actual violations of humanitarian law on the ground. It could conceivably also be more remote in terms of advice given by military advisors or in the granting of rights of passage for troops which later commit violations of international humanitarian law.

In the last few years, the issue of complicity in violations of international law has received a growing amount of attention. For international law, it is to a certain extent a new phenomenon to focus not only on the responsibility of the main actor which is responsible for a given wrongful act, but also to consider the role of actors which have aided or assisted in

[1] Office of the UN High Commissioner for Human Rights, 'Report of the Mapping Exercise Documenting the Most Serious Violations of Human Rights and International Humanitarian Law Committed within the Territory of the Democratic Republic of the Congo between March 1993 and June 2003, August 2010, www.ohchr.org/en/Countries/AfricaRegion/Pages/RDCProjetMapping.aspx.

the commission of wrongful acts.[2] This chapter will focus on complicity of what is here called 'public' actors in international law with violations of international humanitarian law committed by other 'public' actors. The 'publicness'[3] of the actors refers to their quality as States and international organizations. Accordingly, this chapter is not concerned with the responsibility of States for the conduct of individuals, although – as we will see – the boundaries between the 'public' and the 'private' sphere may sometimes be hard to identify in contemporary African conflicts such as the one in the Great Lakes Region. In the following, I will first briefly outline the importance of complicity understood in this sense for such conflicts (Section 2). Subsequently, I will present the applicable international legal rules concerning complicity (Section 3). This will lead to a discussion of some particularly challenging factors for this framework which may arise from conflicts such as the one in the DRC (Section 4).

2. The importance of complicity in contemporary African conflicts

It is not within the ambit of this chapter to present an inventory of violations of international humanitarian law to which aid or assistance has been furnished by other actors. Nonetheless, some brief remarks on the role of 'public' forms of complicity in the conflicts in the Great Lakes Region are in order, especially with respect to the conflict in the DRC since 1994.[4] It is not intended to present historical truths or to side with a particular party to the conflict. It is, however, important to show that 'public' complicity as defined above had a role to play in this context. When

[2] In 1939, Roberto Ago found the idea of State responsibility for complicity to be 'inconceivable', R. Ago, 'Le délit international' (1939) 68 *Recueil des Cours de l'Académie de Droit International* 415, at 523. Forty years later, Ago was the Special Rapporteur of the ILC who introduced a draft provision in this regard. See 'Seventh Report on State Responsibility' (8 May–28 July 1978), UN Doc. A/CN.4/307 and Add. 1–2, YBILC 1978, vol. II, part one, 31, at 60. On the growing attention for complicity and other forms of multi-actor responsibility, see A. Nollkaemper and D. Jacobs, 'Shared Responsibility in International Law: A Concept Paper' (2013) 34 *Michigan Journal of International Law* 359, as well as the contributions in A. Nollkaemper and I. Plakokefalos (eds.), *Principles of Shared Responsibility in International Law – An Appraisal of the State of the Art* (Cambridge: Cambridge University Press, 2014).

[3] This expression is borrowed from A. von Bogdandy, P. Dann and M. Goldmann, 'Developing the Publicness of Public International Law: Towards a Legal Framework for Global Governance Activities' (2008) 9 *German Law Journal* 1375, where it was used in a different context.

[4] This is the period covered by the 'Mapping Exercise'. It should be noted that the conflict continues, especially in the Kivus. See J. K. Stearns, *Dancing in the Glory of Monsters – The Collapse of the Congo and the Great War of Africa* (New York: Public Affairs, 2011), at 8.

the enforcement of international humanitarian law in African conflicts is discussed, one sometimes can have the impression that 'the State' has no role to play in these conflicts. Accordingly, the focus of the discussion is concerned with the binding character of international humanitarian law for non-State actors and how they could be enticed to comply with these rules.[5] While it is certainly true that non-State actors were central to the conflict in the DRC and also contributed to some of its worst excesses, it would be a mistake to completely disregard the inter-State or 'public' level. At some point, at least seven foreign States were directly involved with their armed forces in the DRC conflict and had troops on the ground (Angola, Burundi, Chad, Namibia, Rwanda, Uganda, Zimbabwe). Sudan also took part in the fighting with its air force. And other States, such as the Central African Republic, Libya, South Africa and Zambia were indirectly involved in the conflict and rendered support in various forms to the parties of the conflict. Due to this widespread involvement of African States, the conflict in the DRC has also been called 'Africa's World War'.[6] For the period of 1998–1999, Gérard Prunier categorized the States involved into four different groups, distinguishing between core participants of the conflicts and more remote forms of involvement. This classification alone suggests that different degrees of involvement in violations of international humanitarian law will be identifiable as well.[7]

At the same time, it is, of course, true that the conflict in the DRC cannot be analysed solely in terms of an inter-State conflict.[8] This would neglect not only the role of both the various involved rebel groups and militias but also the fact that even the involved States made use of – alongside their armed forces – proxy groups and elements of rebels. This makes it at times difficult to establish the boundaries between conduct which can be attributed to a State and conduct which emanates from non-State actors.[9] Nonetheless, States were involved. From the perspective of international law, this calls for an analysis of the question under what conditions aiding and assisting States incur responsibility in conflicts such as the Congolese one.[10] The States involved also take these claims

[5] See, for example, A. Bellal and S. Casey-Maslen, 'Enhancing Compliance with International Law by Armed Non-State Actors' (2011) 3 *Goettingen Journal of International Law* 175.

[6] G. Prunier, *Africa's World War* (Oxford: Oxford University Press, 2009).

[7] Ibid. 201–02. [8] Ibid. xxxiv. [9] Cf. ibid. 336–37.

[10] See also, for a plea not to leave State responsibility out of consideration, P. Okowa, 'State and Individual Responsibility in Internal Conflicts: Contours of an Evolving Relationship' (2009) 20 *Finnish Yearbook of International Law* 143, at 145.

seriously. This is confirmed by the reaction of a number of States to the UN Mapping Exercise in 2010.[11] Burundi, for example, issued a formal diplomatic note to the UN in order to protest the accusation that it had collaborated with any armed forces present on the territory of the DRC.[12]

The issue of complicity also played a role in 2009 when the UN presence in the DRC, MONUC[13] was accused of complicity in violations of international humanitarian law committed by the armed forces of the DRC.[14] These accusations were levelled against the UN by Human Rights Watch. According to this NGO, the UN provided military firepower, transport, rations and fuel for government forces committed to an operation directed against Rwandese Hutu militias. As a note from the UN Office of Legal Affairs to the International Law Commission (ILC) of the UN stated:

> In the course of MONUC-assisted operations it became apparent that elements of Government-led forces, notably the Armed Forces of the Democratic Republic of the Congo (FARDC) who were the beneficiaries of UN assistance, committed violations of human rights and international humanitarian law of the kind they were supposed to prevent with United Nations aid.[15]

This insight subsequently prompted a modification of MONUC's mandate. Previously, Security Council Resolution 1856 included a number of references to the necessary respect for international humanitarian law, without however directing these calls specifically to MONUC.[16] Following the allegations in 2009, first a policy of conditionality was developed by the UN Secretary-General. Later, this policy was inscribed into the text of Security Council Resolution 1906 in which it is provided that the support of MONUC to FARDC-led military operations against

[11] On the generally heated discussion about the report, see, for instance, H. French, 'U.N. Congo Report Offers New View on Genocide', *New York Times*, 28 August 2010, at A1.

[12] Burundi, 'Diplomatic Note', 21 September 2009, www.ohchr.org/Documents/Countries/CD/DRC_Report_Commetnts_Burundi.pdf.

[13] Established by UNSC Resolution 1279 (30 November 1999).

[14] M. Tran, 'UN Denies Complicity in Congo War Crimes', *The Guardian*, 11 November 2009, www.guardian.co.uk/world/2009/nov/11/congo-un-rebels-rwanda-kimia; and J. Gettleman, 'U.N. Told Not to Join Congo Army in Operation', New *York Times*, 10 December 2009, at A8, www.nytimes.com/2009/12/10/world/africa/10congo.html.

[15] International Law Commission Responsibility of International Organizations: Comments and Observations Received from International Organizations (17 February 2011), UN Doc. A/CN.4/637/Add. 1, at 18.

[16] UNSC Resolution 1856 (23 December 2008), preamble and operative paras. 3(g), at 22–23.

foreign and Congolese armed groups is strictly conditioned on FARDC's compliance with international humanitarian, human rights and refugee law.[17] In the same resolution, the UN Security Council also decided that the cooperation between MONUC and the FARDC should be carried out on the basis of joint planning and that MONUC should intercede with the FARDC command 'if elements of a FARDC unit receiving MONUC's support are suspected of having committed grave violation of such laws'.[18] Most recently, in early 2013, the Secretary-General has formulated a 'UN Human Rights Due Diligence Policy' (HRDDP).[19] This policy aspires to define in a broader way the limitations for UN cooperation with actors who are deemed to be engaged in grave violations of international humanitarian law, human rights law and refugee law. Whereas this policy is not limited to the situation in the DRC, its genesis was very much linked to the above-noted concerns about UN complicity with human rights violations in the DRC. If anything, this goes to show that the conflict in the DRC has acutely raised the awareness of the impact that support by third actors – be they States or international organizations – can have upon the commission of violations of international law.[20]

The UN example also shows that the topic under consideration concerns not only regional actors. In fact, recent African history is replete with examples of the unfortunate influence of non-African States. Among the most controversial examples, one may refer to the role of France in the 1994 genocide in Rwanda.[21]

3. International responsibility for complicity

In light of these considerations, it is now time to turn to the applicable international legal framework. In the context of international humanitarian law, it is opportune to examine the preliminary question which

[17] UNSC Resolution 1906 (23 December 2009), operative para. 22. [18] Ibid.

[19] See annex to 'Identical Letters Dated 25 February 2013 from the Secretary-General Addressed to the President of the General Assembly and to the President of the Security Council' (5 March 2013), UN Doc. A/67/775–S/2013/110. The HRDDP has already been 'implemented' by the Security Council in Resolution 2098 (28 March 2013), para. 12(b).

[20] For more details on the HRDDP, see H. P. Aust, 'The UN Human Rights Due Diligence Policy: An Effective Mechanism against Complicity of Peacekeeping Forces?' (2015) 20 *Journal of Conflict and Security Law* 61.

[21] See further R. Dallaire, K. Manocha and N. Degnarain, 'The Major Powers on Trial' (2005) 3 *Journal of International Criminal Justice* 861; F. Grünfeld and A. Huijboom, *The Failure to Prevent Genocide in Rwanda: The Role of Bystanders* (Leiden: Martinus Nijhoff Publishers, 2007).

set of rules covers questions of State responsibility for complicity. A first impulse could be to regard the relevant standards to follow from Article 3 of the 1907 Hague Convention IV[22] and Article 91 of Additional Protocol I to the Geneva Conventions which provide for a special rule covering the responsibility of States for the conduct of their armed forces during armed conflicts. However, these rules only apply insofar as they concern independent and direct violations of international humanitarian law which can be attributed to States parties to a conflict. States may, however, also contribute to the violation of the rules of international humanitarian law committed by other parties without themselves violating international humanitarian law directly.

Due to these situations, we need to think about the impact of the international rules on complicity. These rules are important when we have to consider the role of outside actors (States and international organizations) which are not themselves parties to a conflict, yet which furnish support to one of the warring factions. In this scenario, the law of neutrality may also be applicable. Contrary to what is sometimes asserted,[23] this body of law has not become obsolete.[24] It continues to regulate the position of third States which wish to remain impartial in a given conflict. Yet the law of neutrality is not exhaustive with respect to the legal consequences of interference of those States in armed conflicts. When a State which consistently aspires to be neutral violates its obligations under the law of neutrality, it will eventually lose its status as a neutral power. Consequently, it may turn into a lawful target for measures of self-defence given that all other conditions for the exercise of this right are met.[25] It is a different question whether third States contribute to violations of international humanitarian law and could therefore incur responsibility for their aid or assistance. For an analysis of the problem of complicity in violations of international humanitarian law, we thus need to analyse both the rules of the law of international responsibility and possible modifications which may be owed to the influence of international humanitarian law.

[22] IV Hague Convention, The Hague, 18 October 1907, in force 26 January 1910, Martens, *Nouveau Recueil Général de Traités*, Series III, vol. 3, at 461.

[23] See, for example, H. Kelsen, 'Théorie du droit international public' (1953) 84 *Recueil des Cours de l'Académie de Droit International* 1, at 60; L. Henkin, 'Force, Intervention, and Neutrality in Contemporary International Law' (1963) 57 *American Society of International Law Proceedings* 147, at 159.

[24] See *Legality of the Threat or Use of Nuclear Weapons* (Advisory Opinion) [1996] ICJ Reports 226, para. 89.

[25] H. P. Aust, *Complicity and the Law of State Responsibility* (Cambridge: Cambridge University Press, 2011), at 382–83.

A brief remark on terminology is in order. The law of international responsibility consists of secondary rules of international law as opposed to primary, or substantive, rules. Whereas the primary rules lay down specific substantive obligations which require a certain form of conduct or the achievement of certain results by States, the law of international responsibility comes into effect once there has been a violation of a primary rule of international law. These secondary rules of international law then govern issues as diverse as the attribution of conduct to a State or international organization, circumstances precluding wrongfulness, the content of responsibility as well as its implementation.[26]

3.1. General international law

The relevant starting point for the analysis of general international law is the work of the ILC. Both the Articles on State Responsibility[27] (ASR) and the Draft Articles on the Responsibility of International Organizations[28] (DARIO) include provisions which stipulate that a State (or an international organization, respectively) is responsible for the aid or assistance it gives to another State/international organization, if it does so with knowledge of the circumstances of the internationally wrongful act and if the act would also be internationally wrongful if committed by that State/international organization (Articles 16 ASR, 14 and 58 DARIO).

3.1.1. Legal status of the provisions on complicity

As such, the outcome of the work of the ILC has no binding force. However, as the work of the ILC aspires not only to progressively develop the law but also to codify it, large parts of the ILC's Articles on State Responsibility and the Draft Articles on the Responsibility of International Organizations may be taken to represent customary international law. With respect to Article 16 ASR, it was for some time debated whether this provision actually had a basis in customary international law.[29] In 2007, the

[26] J. Crawford, 'Introduction', in J. Crawford (ed.), *The International Law Commission's Articles on State Responsibility. Introduction, Text and Commentaries* (Cambridge: Cambridge University Press, 2002), 1–60, at 14–16.

[27] 'Articles on the Responsibility of Stats for internationally wrongful acts', annexed to UNGA Resolution 56/83 (12 December 2001).

[28] ILC, 'Draft Articles on the Responsibility of International Organizations' (30 May 2011), UN Doc. A/CN.4/L.778.

[29] Sceptical in this regard: W. Heintschel von Heinegg, 'Wider die Mär vom Tod des Neutralitätsrechts', in H. Fischer et al. (eds.), *Krisensicherung und Humanitärer Schutz/Crisis Management and Humanitarian Protection, Festschrift für Dieter Fleck* (Berlin: Berliner

International Court of Justice (ICJ) affirmed in its *Genocide Convention* Case that Article 16 ASR indeed represented customary international law.[30] Although this finding of the Court was not supported by any particular analysis of practice and *opinio juris*, it is ultimately convincing.[31] What is also important is that this provision met very little resistance from States when the work of the ILC was discussed in the Sixth Committee of the General Assembly. A large majority of the more than forty States that commented directly on the issue of complicity favoured its inclusion in the ILC's Articles on State Responsibility. In fact, only Germany and Switzerland for some time upheld their opposition to the existence of such a rule in customary international law.[32] There has been practically no objection to the inclusion of parallel provisions into the ILC's Draft Articles on the Responsibility of International Organizations.[33]

The framework of general international law includes an additional and more specific obligation of non-assistance for situations in which a 'serious breach of a peremptory norm under general international law' has occurred. For these cases, Articles 41(2) ASR and 42(2) DARIO set forth that States/organizations shall not render aid or assistance to the maintenance of the situation brought about by this breach.

3.1.2. Material standards for responsibility for complicity

Despite the general acceptance of the principle embodied in Article 16 ASR and the other provisions on complicity in the law of international responsibility, uncertainties remain with respect to particular issues. For instance, it is disputed whether the aid or assistance given should cross a minimum threshold. Is even the most remote form of support sufficient

Wissenschafts-Verlag, 2004), 221–41, at 222, fn. 4; for early criticism of the work of the ILC on complicity, see E. Klein, 'Beihilfe zum Völkerrechtsdelikt', in I. von Münch (ed.), *Staatsrecht – Völkerrecht – Europarecht: Festschrift für Hans-Jürgen Schlochauer* (Berlin: de Gruyter, 1981), at 425–38.

30 *Application of the Convention on the Prevention and Punishment of the Crime of Genocide (Bosnia and Herzegovina v. Serbia and Montenegro)* (Judgment) [2007] ICJ Reports 43, para. 419.

31 For a detailed analysis of the customary law status of Article 16 ASR, see Aust, *Complicity and State Responsibility*, above note 25, at 97–191. Among prior analyses of international practice, mention should be made of J. Quigley, 'Complicity in International Law – A New Direction in the Law of State Responsibility' (1986) 57 *British Yearbook of International Law* 77; A. Felder, *Die Beihilfe im Recht der völkerrechtlichen Staatenverantwortlichkeit* (Zurich: Schulthess, 2007).

32 Aust, *Complicity and State Responsibility*, above note 25, at 169–74.

33 Cf. ILC, 'Comments and Observations received from Governments' (14 February 2011), UN Doc. A/CN.4/636.

to trigger the responsibility of the helping State? The ILC has not given many indications in this respect. In the commentary, it made contradictory indications, stipulating at the same time that the support given must actually facilitate the commission of the act and that sometimes the support given may only have been an incidental factor.[34] If Article 16 ASR is viewed in the light of the general principles governing which form of conduct can lead to the responsibility of States and international organizations, it makes sense to require some form of causality between the support given and the actual wrongful act which has been committed. If such a requirement would not be needed, responsibility for complicity would degenerate into a basis of responsibility for attempted contribution to wrongful acts – a concept which is clearly alien to international law. At the same time, the requirement of causality cannot be too demanding. If it were understood as a *conditio sine qua non* requirement, the 'helping' State would have to be treated as a main actor and would incur joint responsibility with the State to which it has rendered the support.[35] On the other side of the spectrum, it emerges from international practice that States are not willing to accept responsibility for very minor forms of participation.[36] Furthermore, it is accepted in the jurisprudence of international courts that the 'mere association' with a State in a given operation does not alone lead to responsibility.[37]

3.1.3. Subjective standards for responsibility for complicity

Another controversial issue pertains to the subjective threshold for the responsibility of a complicit State/international organization. There is near consensus that Article 16 ASR requires some form of subjective element on the part of the helping State.[38] Otherwise, the ubiquitous

[34] ILC Commentary, Article 16 ASR, paras. 1 and 5, reprinted in Crawford, *ILC's Articles on State Responsibility Commentary*, above note 26.

[35] Cf. I. Brownlie, *State Responsibility* (Oxford: Oxford University Press, 1983), at 191.

[36] See Aust, *Complicity and State Responsibility*, above note 25, at 203–07 for a discussion of the position of States in the context of the adoption of the Cluster Munitions Convention in Dublin, May 2008.

[37] *Saddam Hussein v. Albania, Bulgaria, Croatia, Czech Republic, Denmark, Estonia, Hungary, Iceland, Ireland, Italy, Latvia, Lithuania, the Netherlands, Poland, Portugal, Romania, Slovakia, Slovenia, Turkey, Ukraine and the United Kingdom* (Decision) Application no. 23276/04 European Court of Human Rights, (14 March 2006).

[38] For the various views in literature, see Felder, *Beihilfe und Staatenverantwortlichkeit*, above note 31, at 256 et seq.; Quigley, 'Complicity in International Law', above note 31, at 109 et seq.; Klein, 'Beihilfe zum Völkerrechtsdelikt', above note 29, at 431–32, 435–36; G. Nolte and H. P. Aust, 'Equivocal Helpers – Complicit States, Mixed Messages and International Law' (2009) 58 *International and Comparative Law Quarterly* 1, at 13 et seq.

presence of cooperation and mutual support in today's international legal system would make all States potentially responsible for complicity all of the time. A purely objective rule on complicity would effectively mean that international cooperation would turn into a particularly hazardous and risky affair. Beyond this general level of consensus, there is a debate about the level of subjective relation which the aiding or assisting State needs to have vis-à-vis the wrongful act committed by the main actor.

In this respect, it can first of all be noted that a previous ILC draft article on complicity, which was adopted on first reading in 1996, required that the aid or assistance given to another State must be 'rendered *for* the commission of an internationally wrongful act'.[39] This requirement is no longer included in Article 16 ASR. Instead, Article 16 ASR only refers to the 'knowledge of the circumstances of the internationally wrongful act'. According to the commentary, this is supposed to mean that 'the aid or assistance must be given *with a view to* facilitate the commission of the act and must actually do so'.[40]

The Commentary thus narrows the textual meaning of Article 16 and goes against the main principle of the ILC Articles which, *in general*, presuppose no distinct or separate requirement of fault or wrongful intent for an internationally wrongful act.[41] It, thus, appears that the ILC wants Article 16 to be interpreted narrowly so that the 'knowledge' element turns into something more akin to a requirement of wrongful intent.[42] Likewise, the International Court of Justice has, *mutatis mutandis*, adopted this approach in its *Genocide Convention* Case. Here, the Court was faced with the special intent requirement from the Genocide Convention, namely *dolus specialis* which is directed towards the elimination of a group under Article II of the Convention. Applying Article 16 ASR by means of analogy, the Court held that

> [t]here is no doubt that the conduct of an organ or a person furnishing aid or assistance to a perpetrator of the crime of genocide cannot be treated as complicity in genocide unless *at the least* that organ or person acted

[39] The draft article as adopted on first reading in 1996 was first formulated in 1978. See Yearbook of the International Law Commission, vol. I (1978), at 269, para. 2 (emphasis added).

[40] ILC Commentary, Art. 16, margin number 3, reprinted in Crawford, *ILC's Articles on State Responsibility Commentary*, above note 26.

[41] J. Crawford, *State Responsibility – The General Part* (Cambridge: Cambridge University Press, 2013), at 60–62.

[42] See similarly A. Boivin, 'Complicity and Beyond: International Law and the Transfer of Small Arms and Light Weapons' (2005) 87 *International Review of the Red Cross* 467, at 471.

> knowingly, that is to say, in particular, was aware of the specific intent (*dolus specialis*) of the principal perpetrator.[43]

If the analogy to Article 16 ASR is supposed to be meaningful, this entails that knowledge of the circumstances of the wrongful act is required *at the least* (as the Court has put it) also with respect to Article 16. Moreover, the words 'at the least' suggest that, as a general rule, more than mere knowledge is required.[44] Most authors who have expressed views on the issue of complicity have, however, been sceptical towards the intent and knowledge requirements provided for by the ILC.[45] A variety of authors criticize the intent requirement for making 'the whole construction of complicity unworkable'.[46] It would be especially difficult to prove the intent of the assisting State of actually wishing to further the commission of the wrongful act.[47] Some authors would thus require only the possibility of knowledge,[48] either in terms of due diligence[49] or foreseeability.[50] In addition, it is also debated whether the assisting State must actually share the purpose of the primary lawbreaker or whether it is sufficient to wish to further the concrete conduct to which assistance is furnished.[51] Some

[43] *Application of the Genocide Convention* (Judgment), above note 30, para. 421 (emphasis added).

[44] Nolte and Aust, 'Equivocal Helpers', above note 38, at 14; Crawford, *State Responsibility*, above note 41, at 407–08.

[45] See, for example, Felder, *Beihilfe und Staatenverantwortlichkeit*, above note 31, at 261 et seq.; Klein, 'Beihilfe zum Völkerrechtsdelikt', above note 29, at 435–36.

[46] B. Graefrath, 'Complicity in the Law of International Responsibility' (1996) 29 *Revue Belge de Droit International* 370, at 375; Quigley, 'Complicity in International Law', above note 31, at 111, who suggests to substitute the intent of the State by the culpa of its agents. Ibid. 109.

[47] Boivin, 'Complicity and Beyond', above note 42, at 471; Felder, *Beihilfe und Staatenverantwortlichkeit*, above note 31, at 261; B. Simma, 'Grundfragen der Staatenverantwortlichkeit in der Arbeit der International Law Commission' (1985) 24 *Archiv des Völkerrechts* 357, at 380.

[48] O. Corten, 'Quels droits et quels devoirs pour les États tiers? Les effets juridiques d'une assistance à un acte d'aggression', in K. Bannelier et al. (eds.), *L'intervention en Irak et le droit international* (Paris: Pedone, 2004), 105–28, at 113.

[49] For a due diligence requirement *de lege ferenda*, see S. Talmon, 'A Plurality of Responsible Actors: International Responsibility for Acts of the Coalition Provisional Authority in Iraq', in P. Shiner and A. Williams (eds.), *The Iraq War and International Law* (Oxford: Hart, 2008), 185–230, at 219.

[50] V. Lowe, 'Responsibility for the Conduct of Other States' (2002) 101 *Kokusaiho Gaiko Zassi/The Japanese Journal of International Law and Diplomacy* 1, at 8; B. D. Smith, *State Responsibility and the Marine Environment – The Rules of Decision* (Oxford: Oxford University Press, 1988), at 12.

[51] R. S. Clark, 'Obligations of Third States in the Face of Illegality – Ruminations Inspired by the Weeramantry Dissent in the Case Concerning East Timor', in A. Anghie (ed.),

authors, however, have expressed support for the intent requirement as conceived by the ILC.[52]

In the view of the present author, it is indeed intent which is required for responsibility under Article 16 ASR and its corresponding provisions in the ILC's Draft Articles on the Responsibility of International Organizations. A number of considerations speak in favour of this view. First, among the States which have commented on the provision which became Article 16 ASR, more States were of the opinion that the intent element should be strengthened than that the provision should be interpreted in a more objective fashion.[53] As Article 16 ASR is a provision indicative of customary international law, the views of States should be taken into consideration as evidence of their *opinio juris*. Second, to interpret Article 16 ASR objectively means to reverse the burden of proof in the situation of court proceedings. Whenever support would be derailed for unlawful purposes, it would then fall upon the supporting State to exonerate itself. This would stand in contrast to the procedural maxim that the State which wishes to bring a claim has to furnish the necessary evidence for its claim.[54] Third, the systematic relationship between the general rule of Article 16 ASR and special, more demanding rules against complicity should be taken into consideration. Not only in the field of international humanitarian law, as we shall see below, can we find rules which may not technically address situations of complicity but which nevertheless apply in scenarios comparable to those in which issues of complicity arise. Examples in this regard are obligations of prevention,

Legal Visions of the 21st Century – Essays in Honour of Judge Christopher Weeramantry (The Hague: Kluwer, 1998), 631–51, at 648, fn. 60; Lowe, 'Responsibility for Other States', above note 50, at 8–9.

52 See M. Brehm, 'The Arms Trade and States' Duty to Ensure Respect for Humanitarian and Human Rights Law' (2008) 12 *Journal of Conflict and Security Law* 359, at 385; J. Künzli, *Vom Umgang des Rechtsstaats mit Unrechtsregimes – Völker- und landesrechtliche Grenzen des Verhaltensspielraums der schweizerischen Außenpolitik gegenüber Völkerrecht missachtenden Staaten* (Bern: Stämpfli, 2008), at 408; Nolte and Aust, 'Equivocal Helpers', above note 38, at 13 et seq.; M. L. Padelletti, *Pluralità di Stati Nel Fatto Illecito Internazionale* (Milano: Giuffrè, 1990), at 76 (but see also ibid. 97 for some critical remarks); T. Stein, 'International Measures against Terrorism and Sanctions by and against Third States' (1992) 30 *Archiv des Völkerrechts* 38, at 49.

53 See, for example, the statement of the United Kingdom in ILC, 'State Responsibility: Comments and Observations Received from Governments' (25 March 1998), UN Doc. A/CN.4/488, at 75–76; on the importance not to overstretch State approval in this regard, see also Crawford, *State Responsibility*, above note 41, at 408.

54 C. F. Amerasinghe, *Evidence in International Litigation* (Leiden: Martinus Nijhoff Publishers, 2005), at 61–62; S. Rosenne, *The Law and Practice of the International Court of Justice 1920–2005*, vol. III, 4th edn (Leiden: Martinus Nijhoff Publishers, 2006), at 1040.

such as Article I of the 1948 Genocide Convention[55] or the obligation of *non-refoulement* in human rights law.[56] Although the structure of the obligation against *refoulement* is different from the complicity situation covered by Article 16 ASR, the actual handing over of persons is subject to international law limits deriving both from the general framework of international responsibility and from the more specific obligation of *non-refoulement*.[57] Technically, the obligation of *non-refoulement* does not prove for responsibility on the basis of support for the maltreatment of a given person. However, if understood in a functional sense, it prevents the coming into existence of responsibility for complicity. For the prohibition of *non-refoulement* to be violated we need not establish the intent of the State handing over the person. All that is needed is a serious risk that maltreatment will occur. This considerably lowers the standards under which a State handing over a person may incur responsibility compared to Article 16 ASR. Accordingly, we are faced here with an example of how international law provides for more protection against complicity in a context where there are important and overwhelming policy objectives for stricter standards of conduct.

3.2. International humanitarian law

The rules provided for in the ILC's Articles on State Responsibility and Draft Articles on the Responsibility of International Organizations only provide the bottom line of what international law requires of complicit States and international organizations. With respect to States, more demanding standards can be derived from the special rules of international humanitarian law. In this respect, Common Article 1 of the Geneva Conventions (GC) is the key provision. It holds that '[t]he High Contracting Parties undertake to respect and to ensure respect for the present Convention in all circumstances'.

[55] Convention on the Prevention and Punishment of the Crime of Genocide, Paris, 9 December 1948, in force 12 January 1951, 78 U.N.T.S. 277.

[56] See, for example, *Soering* v. *United Kingdom* Application no. 14038/88 (ECHR, 7 July 1989).

[57] See also C. J. Tams, 'The Abuse of Executive Powers: What Remedies?', in A. Bianchi and A. Keller (eds.), *Counterterrorism: Democracy's Challenge* (Oxford: Hart, 2008), 313–34, at 318; UK House of Lords/House of Commons, Joint Committee on Human Rights, 'Allegations of UK Complicity in Torture', Twenty-Third Report of Session 2008–2009, HL Paper 152, HC 230, published on 4 August 2009, para. 23. For a different view – insisting on the structural differences between complicity and refoulement, see Felder, *Beihilfe und Staatenverantwortlichkeit*, above note 31, at 133; M. Hakimi, 'State Bystander Responsibility' (2010) 21 *European Journal of International Law* 341, at 366.

3.2.1. Binding obligation or hortatory rule?

While the exact scope and meaning of this provision is dealt with in another part of this book[58], we cannot entirely disregard this provision in our context. Highly contested, and for our purposes the relevant issue, is the question whether the wording 'to ensure respect' is supposed to establish an obligation of States. Widely diverging views are held whether this provision entails a binding obligation to take measures and whether the provision applies not only with respect to the compliance of non-State actors with the Geneva Conventions but also vis-à-vis other States.[59] Some authors have held the view that it merely provides for a possibility of States to insist upon the application of the relevant rules of the Geneva Conventions in armed conflicts to which they are not a direct party.[60] However, several arguments point into the direction that binding obligations arise from Common Article 1 GC. In the 'semi-official' commentary to the Conventions, edited by Jean Pictet, it is held that:

> The proper working of the system of protection provided by the Convention demands in fact that the Contracting Parties should not be content merely to apply its provisions themselves, but should do everything in their power to ensure that the humanitarian principles underlying the Conventions are applied universally.[61]

In addition, the view that Common Article 1 GC comprises an obligation 'to ensure respect' was also held at the Tehran Conference on Human Rights in 1968 which adopted, without opposition, a resolution in which it was recognized that

> States parties to the Red Cross Geneva Conventions sometimes fail to appreciate their responsibility to take steps to ensure the respect of these humanitarian rules in all circumstances by other States, even if they are not themselves directly involved in an armed conflict.[62]

[58] See the contribution of R. Geiß, 'Common Article 1 of the Geneva Conventions: Scope and Content of the Obligation to "Ensure Respect" – "Narrow but Deep" or "Wide and Shallow"?', Chapter 18 in this volume.

[59] See, for an overview of the relevant arguments, C. Focarelli, 'Common Article 1 of the 1949 Geneva Conventions: A Soap Bubble?' (2010) 21 *European Journal of International Law* 125.

[60] F. Kalshoven, 'The Undertaking to Respect and Ensure Respect in All Circumstances: From Tiny Seed to Ripening Fruit' (1999) 2 *Yearbook of International Humanitarian Law* 3, at 60.

[61] J. Pictet (ed.), *Convention (IV) relative to the Protection of Civilian Persons in Time of War: Commentary* (Geneva: International Committee of the Red Cross, 1958), at 16.

[62] International Conference on Human Rights, Tehran, 1968, Resolution XXIII of 12 May 1968, preambular paragraph 9, www.icrc.org/ihl.nsf/WebPrint/430-FULL?OpenDocument.

The International Court of Justice also interpreted the obligation 'to ensure respect' as having its roots in customary international law and as requiring States not to encourage violations of international humanitarian law by others.[63] The Court was even more explicit in its *Wall* Opinion, where it held that Common Article 1 GC provides that 'every State party to that Convention, whether or not it is a party to the specific conflict, is under an obligation to ensure that the requirements of the instruments in question are complied with'.[64] Finally, reference can be made to the study on customary international humanitarian law conducted by the ICRC.[65] Rule 144 provides that States may not 'encourage violations of international humanitarian law by parties to an armed conflict. They must exert their influence, to the degree possible to stop violations of international humanitarian law'.

An obvious paradox of a too strict reading of Common Article 1 GC is that if it really imposes binding obligations on States to take measures in order to induce other States to comply with international humanitarian law, the rather sparse practice of enforcement measures would indicate that during most armed conflicts most States parties to the Geneva Conventions would be in breach of their obligation under Common Article 1 GC.[66] While a certain tension between reality and normative order is inherent in law, the relationship between the two should not be overstretched. Accordingly, we need to ask ourselves what a reasonable interpretation of Common Article 1 GC can be. When this provision is at the same time a binding obligation but does not entail that States must take positive action in order to enforce international humanitarian law if violated by other States, could not at least an obligation of non-assistance in violations of international humanitarian law be a sensible form of middle ground between the different positions?

3.2.2. Non-assistance as 'ensuring respect'?

The ICRC Commentary to Rule 144 expressly points to Article 16 ASR in order to support the customary status of the rule.[67] In this respect,

[63] *Case Concerning Military and Paramilitary Activities in and against Nicaragua (Nicaragua v. United States of America)* (Judgment) (Merits) [1986] ICJ Reports 14, paras. 220, 255. For criticism in this regard, see ibid., Separate Opinion of Judge Ago, para. 6.

[64] *Legal Consequences of the Construction of a Wall in the Occupied Palestinian Territory* (Advisory Opinion) [2004] ICJ Reports 136, para. 158.

[65] J.-M. Henckaerts and L. Doswald-Beck, *Customary International Humanitarian Law*, 2 vols. (Cambridge: Cambridge University Press, 2005), vol. I, at 509 et seq.

[66] See Focarelli, 'Common Article 1', above note 59, at 151.

[67] Henckaerts and Doswald-Beck, *Customary International Humanitarian Law*, above note 65, at 511; see also D. Turns, 'Implementation and Compliance', in E. Wilmshurst and

the study finds itself in line with those voices in literature which affirm that Common Article 1 GC does indeed impose an obligation 'to ensure respect' for the Convention,[68] but would not require States to take countermeasures or even forcible measures in order to live up to this obligation. Rather, the concrete content of Common Article 1 GC could, in this respect, be understood as at least requiring States not to render aid or assistance to violations of the Geneva Conventions.[69] In this respect, there is some debate whether Article 16 ASR could be said to imply the general principle which underlies this interpretation of Common Article 1 GC.[70] A problematic issue of this debate is the conflation of encouragement with complicity, which occurs frequently. In the general law of State responsibility, incitement or encouragement do not render a State responsible.[71] In the context of international humanitarian law, the ICJ has, however,

S. Breau (eds.), *Perspectives on the ICRC Study on Customary International Humanitarian Law* (Cambridge: Cambridge University Press, 2007), 354–76, at 364–65.

[68] See, first and foremost, L. Condorelli and L. Boisson de Chazournes, 'Quelques remarques à propos de l'obligation des Etats de 'respecter et faire respecter' le droit international humanitaire 'en toutes circonstances'', in C. Swinarski (ed.), *Etudes et essais sur le droit international humanitaire et sur les principes de la Croix-Rouge en l'honneur de Jean Pictet* (Leiden: Martinus Nijhoff Publishers, 1984), 17–35, at 24, 26; see also T. Meron, *Human Rights and Humanitarian Norms as Customary Law* (Oxford: Clarendon Press, 1989), at 30–31; Brehm, 'Arms Trade and States' Duty', above note 52, at 385–86; B. Kessler, *Die Durchsetzung der Genfer Abkommen von 1949 in nicht-internationalen bewaffneten Konflikten auf Grundlage ihres gemeinsamen Art. 1* (Berlin: Duncker & Humblot, 2001), at 109; D. Fleck, 'International Accountability for Violations of the Ius in Bello: The Impact of the ICRC Study on Customary International Humanitarian Law' (2006) 11 *Journal of Conflict and Security Law* 179, at 182; F. Azzam, 'The Duty of Third States to Implement and Enforce International Humanitarian Law' (1997) 66 *Nordic Journal of International Law* 55, at 58–59; M. Sassòli, 'State Responsibility for Violations of International Humanitarian Law' (2002) 84 *International Review of the Red Cross* 401, at 421; T. Rensmann, 'Die Humanisierung des Völkerrechts durch das ius in bello – Von der Marten'schen Klausel zur Responsibility to Protect' (2008) 68 *Zeitschrift für ausländisches öffentliches Recht und Völkerrecht* 111, at 120.

[69] D. Schindler, 'Die erga omnes-Wirkung des humanitären Völkerrechts', in U. Beyerlin et al. (eds.), *Recht zwischen Umbruch und Bewährung – Festschrift für Rudolf Bernhardt* (Berlin: Springer, 1995), 199–211, at 204; Azzam, 'Duty of Third States', above note 68, at 70; A. Imseis, 'Critical Reflections on the International Humanitarian Law Aspects of the ICJ Wall Advisory Opinion' (2005) 99 *American Journal of International Law* 102, at 115; Felder, *Beihilfe und Staatenverantwortlichkeit*, above note 31, p. 149; Künzli, *Umgang des Rechtsstaats mit Unrechtsregimes*, above note 52, at 329–30.

[70] See, for instance, Kessler, *Durchsetzung der Genfer Abkommen*, above note 68, at 106 et seq.

[71] Ago, 'Seventh Report on State Responsibility', above note 2, para. 63; *Nicaragua Case*, above note 63, Dissenting Opinion of Judge Schwebel, at 388–89; Graefrath, 'Complicity and International Responsibility', above note 46, at 373; Künzli, *Umgang des Rechtsstaats mit Unrechtsregimes*, above note 52, at 407; Nolte and Aust, 'Equivocal Helpers', above note 38, at 13.

deduced the prohibition to encourage violations of the law from Common Article 1 GC.[72] Accordingly, responsibility of third parties under Common Article 1 GC could be said to commence at a lower threshold than it is the case for Article 16 ASR.[73] For those cases in which assistance to violations of international humanitarian law is at stake, it is very well possible to construe Article 16 ASR as the *lex generalis* and Common Article 1 GC as *lex specialis*.[74] The strict criteria embodied in Article 16 ASR, especially with respect to the requisite degree of intent, may then be attenuated once complicity enters the scope of applicability of Common Article 1 GC.[75]

The obligation to ensure respect for the observance of international humanitarian law thus impacts on the required vigilance of the potentially complicit State. Marco Sassòli described this process with respect to the transfer of weapons in a situation in which systematic violations of international humanitarian law occur in the State to which the weapons are transferred. Under the strict rules of Article 16 ASR, it would need to be established with certainty that the weapons were used for the concrete violations and the transferring State could possibly maintain that it did not render the support for the violation of international humanitarian law. However, such a narrow understanding of the obligations incumbent upon the assisting State would no longer be possible under the heightened standard imposed by Common Article 1 GC: ensuring respect for international humanitarian law would thus demand more from the complicit State than the general rule which is enshrined in Article 16 ASR.[76]

3.2.3. Practical consequences

However, one should also note scepticism with respect to the practical impact of Common Article 1 GC, a provision which would only be rarely used.[77] At least in theory, Common Article 1 GC is, however, a valuable addition to the rules on complicity. It may thus contribute to further

[72] *Nicaragua Case*, above note 63, paras. 220, 255.

[73] Turns, 'Implementation and Compliance', above note 67, at 365.

[74] Brehm, 'Arms Trade and States' Duty', above note 52, at 385–86; Sassòli, 'State Responsibility', above note 68, at 413; see also Condorelli and Boisson de Chazournes, 'respecter et faire respecter', above note 68, at 22.

[75] Brehm, 'Arms Trade and States' Duty', above note 52, at 386.

[76] Sassòli, 'State Responsibility', above note 68, at 413; Brehm, 'Arms Trade and States' Duty', above note 52, at 386; Kessler, *Durchsetzung der Genfer Abkommen*, above note 68, at 110.

[77] Cf. R. Kolb, *Ius in bello: Le droit international des conflits armés* (Basle: Helbing, 2003), at 243; see also Condorelli and Boisson de Chazournes, 'respecter et faire respecter', above note 68, at 27.

'limit' complicit State action with normative barriers. At first sight, this may sound rather vague. However, the recent case law of the ICJ shows the potential of positive obligations to hold complicit States responsible. Article I of the Genocide Convention provides: '[t]he Contracting Parties confirm that genocide, whether committed in time of peace or in time of war, is a crime under international law which they undertake to prevent and to punish'.

In its *Genocide Convention* Case, the ICJ found responsibility of Serbia and Montenegro under this provision for not having done all that was in their powers to prevent the genocide in Srebrenica from occurring. This is particularly interesting for our purposes as the Court had previously denied that there was responsibility for complicity under Article III(e) of the Genocide Convention.[78] This provision which, according to the Court, is structurally similar to Article 16 ASR, possessed a subjective threshold that was not possible to establish in the case at hand. However, when the Court considered responsibility under Article I of the Convention, among other things, it referred to the constant level of support by the Federal Republic of Yugoslavia to the Bosnian Serbs.[79] This support was crucial for the establishment of the violation of the obligation to prevent genocide under Article I. Although the reasoning of the Court was heavily criticized in literature,[80] it shows a willingness and flexibility of the ICJ to hold complicit actors accountable, even if the fairly demanding requirements of the rules on complicity are not met.

When we analyse the approach of the ICJ in this case, we can hold that it is evidence of a strong teleological interpretation of the Genocide Convention.[81] In a somewhat deductive reasoning, the Court established that Article I of the Convention was not a mere *chapeau*, repeating symbolically the pledge of the States parties to the Convention. For a long time, it was disputed whether the obligation to prevent emanating from Article I would actually constitute an obligation for States.[82] This question

[78] *Application of the Genocide Convention* (Judgment), above note 30, paras. 419 et seq.

[79] Ibid. para. 434. For criticism on this point, see ibid. Dissenting Opinion of Judge ad hoc Mahiou, para. 127; ibid. Declaration of Judge Keith.

[80] A. Cassese, 'On the Use of Criminal Law Notions in Determining State Responsibility for Genocide' (2007) 5 *Journal of International Criminal Justice* 875, at 887.

[81] See also O. Ben-Naftali, 'The Obligations to Prevent and Punish Genocide', in P. Gaeta (ed.), *The UN Genocide Convention – A Commentary* (Oxford: Oxford University Press, 2009), 27–57, at 33.

[82] See N. Jørgensen, 'State Responsibility and the 1948 Genocide Convention', in G. S. Goodwin-Gill and S. Talmon (eds.), *The Reality of International Law – Essays in Honour of Ian Brownlie* (Oxford: Oxford University Press, 1999), 273–91, at 275 et seq.

has been put to rest by the Court in its decision. For the interpretation of Common Article 1 of the Geneva Conventions, this case may have some spill over effects. Common Article 1 GC can be the object of the same kind of teleological interpretation which the Court established in its *Genocide Convention* Case. In fact, with respect to Common Article 1 GC, there are – despite some criticism[83] – more solid grounds of practice upon which such a teleological interpretation can build than was the case in the *Genocide Convention* Case. The ICJ itself has also provided the ground for such an interpretation with its repeated references to Common Article 1 GC.[84]

4. Challenges for the international rules on complicity in contemporary African conflicts

It is now time to analyze the particular challenges contemporary African conflicts, such as the one in the DRC, pose for this normative framework. It is not intended here to analyze whether particular parties to the conflict complied with these rules, were responsible for certain violations or provided reparation for violations afterwards.

4.1. The complexity of conflicts: distinguishing between the State and non-State actors

The complexity of the conflict in the DRC is a first and massive challenge to the application of the rules of international responsibility. As it has been noted in literature:

> The presence of several foreign armies, internal Congolese rebels, as well as foreign insurgents has resulted in a conflict which has aspects of a civil war, a rebellion and an interstate conflict at the same time. This raises two distinct problems. First, the complexity of the conflict makes it difficult to identify relevant actors, evaluate the evidence and attribute responsibility in line with the accepted legal categories . . . A second problem is that of identifying the applicable substantive law.[85]

Of these two problems, the second one is of lesser importance for our topic. Both with respect to the general rules of international responsibility

[83] See Focarelli, 'Common Article 1', who relegates the ICJ decision to a footnote in his otherwise detailed treatment (above note 59, at 140, fn. 96).

[84] See above notes 63 and 64.

[85] P. Okowa, 'Congo's War: The Legal Dimension of a Protracted Conflict' (2006) 77 *British Yearbook of International Law* 203, at 209–10.

and Common Article 1 of the Geneva Conventions, it can be observed that they apply indiscriminately whether a given conflict is international in character or not.[86] The scope of wrongful acts to which aid or assistance may be rendered and which then triggers responsibility depends of course on the qualification of the conflict. In non-international armed conflicts, there will be the additional problem of seeing which State can actually invoke violations of international humanitarian law as an injured State in the sense of Articles 42 and 48 ASR. But these are distinct questions which are not related specifically to the question of complicity.

The first problem – the identification of relevant actors – is more significant, however, as the boundaries between the side representing a 'State' and insurgents and rebels who claim to represent the State may at times be difficult to establish. It has been noted that over the entire period of the DRC conflict, at least three rebel groups have claimed with some plausibility to represent governmental authority.[87]

4.1.1. Victorious rebel movements

That the distinction between States and non-State actors may shift over the course of a conflict also found some resonance in the ILC's Articles on State Responsibility. Article 10 ASR provides that, under certain circumstances, the conduct of an insurrectional movement may be considered acts of that State if this movement later turns into the government of a State.[88] For the problem of complicity, this is a particularly interesting situation: does this retroactive establishment of State responsibility also extend to Article 16 ASR? There is no apparent reason why this should not be the case. In this respect, the transitional stage becomes important. In the very moment when the new government is established, previous support for the rebels changes its character. It is no longer support for a private actor,

[86] See *Nicaragua Case*, above note 63, paras. 219–220; *Armed Activities on the Territory of the Congo* (*Democratic Republic of the Congo v. Uganda*) [2005] ICJ Reports 168, Separate Opinion of Judge Simma, para. 33; R. Wolfrum and D. Fleck, 'Enforcement of International Humanitarian Law', in D. Fleck (ed.), *The Handbook of International Humanitarian Law*, 2d edn (Oxford: Oxford University Press, 2008), 675–722, at 708; A. Zimmermann, 'The Obligation to Prevent Genocide: Toward a General Responsibility to Protect?', in U. Fastenrath et al. (eds.), *From Bilateralism to Community Interest: Essays in Honour of Judge Bruno Simma* (Oxford: Oxford University Press, 2011), 629–45, at 636; but see Focarelli, 'Common Article 1', above note 59, at 159–60.

[87] Okowa, 'Congo's War', above note 85, at 212.

[88] See on this provision J. d'Aspremont, 'Rebellion and State Responsibility: Wrongdoing by Democratically Elected Insurgents' (2009) 58 *International and Comparative Law Quarterly* 427.

but suddenly moves into the scope of application of Article 16 ASR. This is an important factor for 'helping' States to take into account that when they intervene with support in a given conflict which pits a government against a rebel force, they need to be aware that the legal standards against which their support is rendered may change *a posteriori*.

4.1.2. Unsuccessful rebel movements

Another problem, however, is raised if a rebel movement is eventually not successful in becoming the new government. In this case, we are in the scope of application of the general rules pertaining to the attribution of the conduct of non-State actors to a State.[89] However, how should we conceive the situation in which a rebel movement, first, successfully establishes its authority as the new government of a State and then, later on, is overthrown by another rebel movement or the previous government? Does the character of its acts as attributable to the State then change again? Here, general principles of international law speak in favour of the assumption that another change in government leaves all responsibility of the State which had previously been established untouched. It is a general rule of international law that the obligations of a State are unaffected by a change of government.[90] In other words, responsibility which has been established on the basis of Article 10 ASR is not subject to the condition that this rebel movement stays in power. A difficult question is then, however, how much time needs to elapse before attribution on the basis of Article 10 ASR can be affirmed. It is probably not possible to establish clear-cut and abstract standards in this respect.

4.1.3. Power-sharing agreements

Another difficult scenario is the conclusion of a 'power-sharing agreement' between a government and a rebel group.[91] Here, the question can also be posed how such an agreement impacts on the determination of issues of responsibility. For example, the government of national unity that was established in the DRC in 2002 consisted of the previous government forces as well as of previous rebel groups. The agreement

[89] See also P. Dumberry, 'New State Responsibility for Internationally Wrongful Acts of an Insurrectional Movement' (2006) 17 *European Journal of International Law* 605, at 606; G. Cahin, 'Attribution of Conduct to the State: Insurrectional Movements', in J. Crawford, A. Pellet and S. Olleson (eds.), *The Law of International Responsibility* (Oxford: Oxford University Press, 2010), 247–56, at 252–53.

[90] P. Daillier, M. Forteau and A. Pellet, *Droit international public*, 8th edn (Paris: L.G.D.J., 2009), at 601; Dumberry, 'New State Responsibility', above note 89, at 609.

[91] See also d'Aspremont, 'Rebellion and State Responsibility', above note 88, at 434.

did not clarify, however, who should bear responsibility for the conduct of the previous rebel forces.[92] At first glance, the general rules of attribution laid down in the ILC's Articles on State Responsibility provide no basis for attributing previous acts of the rebel group automatically to the State by virtue of the movement's participation in the governmental machinery.[93] A different assessment could, however, flow from the rule which is laid down in Article 11 ASR. According to this provision, conduct can be attributed to the State 'if and to the extent that the State acknowledges and adopts the conduct in question as its own'. Generally, it is required that such acknowledgement or adoption must be 'clear and unequivocal'.[94] Accordingly, the mere participation of a rebel group in a government of national unity would not automatically lead to the attribution of previous conduct of this group to a State.[95]

4.1.4. Exercise of public authority in the absence of State governance

Another provision which could have an impact on situations such as the one in the DRC is Article 9 ASR. According to this provision, conduct which is carried out in the absence or default of the official authorities may under, some circumstances, be considered as an act of a State. The conditions for the applicability of Article 9 are threefold: the conduct must relate to the exercise of elements of governmental authority, it must have been carried out in the absence of governmental authority and the circumstances in which it was carried out must have called for the exercise of those elements of authority.[96] The ILC Commentary itself notes that this provision only applies in exceptional cases among which it counts 'revolution, armed conflict or foreign occupation'.[97] However, one can very well ask the question whether these situations are indeed so exceptional in contemporary African conflicts. Article 9 ASR raises particular questions when applied in the context of areas of limited statehood. Apparently, the ILC departed from the assumption that a governmental authority which has lost control over parts of its territory is still in place. It is also

[92] Okowa, 'Congo's War', above note 85, at 227.
[93] A previous ILC draft also considered attribution in such a case. See also d'Aspremont, 'Rebellion and State Responsibility', above note 88, at 434.
[94] ILC Commentary, Article 11 ASR, para. 9, reprinted in Crawford, *ILC's Articles on State Responsibility Commentary*, above note 26.
[95] Crawford, State Responsibility, above note 41, at 176.
[96] ILC Commentary, Article 9 ASR, para. 3, reprinted in Crawford, *ILC's Articles on State Responsibility Commentary*, above note 26.
[97] Ibid. Article 9 ASR, para. 1.

not modelled on the situation in which a rebel group benefits from large portions of support by foreign states. At some point, such support could actually turn into direction and control and would then fall under the principle of attribution which is laid down in Article 8 ASR.[98] But when the threshold of 'effective control' is not met – yet massive support is given to a rebel movement – should the conduct then really be attributed to the forum State? The underlying consideration of Article 9 ASR is the self-organization of citizens who take up some governmental responsibilities in the absence of a State distributing proper forms of governance. This may especially be the case in the scenario of a *levée en masse* against an intervening foreign State.[99] In some circumstances, it may actually be the case that self-government by rebel groups falls into this category.[100] But in many situations, it would stretch the *telos* of Article 9 ASR to apply it to situations in which a rebel group purports to exercise governmental authority.

4.1.5. Interim conclusion: problems in identifying 'the State'

All of these considerations, which are partially taken from international practice and are partially hypothetical yet inspired by the conflict in the Great Lakes Region, may show that for the issue of complicity, very difficult issues of delimitation arise. These relate to a fundamental criterion for the applicability of the rules on complicity: the identification of the actors responsible for internationally wrongful acts as constituting the State. For the operation of the rules of international responsibility, this is of primordial importance. The whole regime of international responsibility rests on the assumption that 'public' and 'private' conduct can be distinguished.[101] Different rules apply depending on whether States and international organizations interact with other States or with non-State actors. The conduct of private individuals can only be attributed to the State under very restrictive conditions. Beyond these rather restrictive rules, there so far is no consensus on how support for wrongful acts by non-State actors shall be dealt with. This is partly owed to the fact that it remains unclear under what conditions and to what extent rebel forces

[98] On the various tests, see A. Cassese, 'The Nicaragua and Tadic Tests Revisited in Light of the ICJ Judgment on Genocide in Bosnia' (2007) 18 *European Journal of International Law* 649.

[99] G. Cahin, 'The Responsibility of Other Entities: Armed Bands and Criminal Groups', in Crawford, Pellet and Olleson (eds.), *Law of International Responsibility*, above note 89, 331–41, at 335.

[100] Ibid.

[101] For a critical view on this, see C. Chinkin, 'A Critique of the Public/Private Dimension', (1999) 10 *European Journal of International Law* 387.

can be held responsible under international law.[102] One of the reasons complicity with wrongful acts committed by non-State actors is not an accepted category in international law is that States and non-State actors have traditionally been seen to be situated on different levels. Complicity seems to imply a relationship between legal subjects on the same level.[103] This state of affairs has indirectly led to one of the most heated discussions of the last ten years on how support for or acquiescence in terrorist activities or the mere fact of harbouring terrorist actors shall be dealt with in the regime of international responsibility. Various States and other actors as well as voices in literature have called for a broadening of the bases of attribution so as to also include complicity with non-State actors as a ground for responsibility.[104]

Also in the type of situation which interests us here, we could find arguments for a change in the rules pertaining to the attribution of conduct of non-State actors. Especially in light of our considerations on Articles 9 and 10 ASR and the shifting boundaries between what constitutes State conduct and non-State conduct, would it not make sense to establish new rules of attribution and/or complicity which would allow us to hold States and international organizations responsible under the same conditions regardless of whether they support 'public' or 'private' wrongdoing?

4.2. Common standards by virtue of Common Article 1 GC?

Yet, this may be a discussion which is eventually unnecessary and may even be potentially counterproductive for the development of international law.

[102] See the cryptic remark of the ILC in its commentary on Art. 58 ASR, para. 2 (reprinted in Crawford, *ILC's Articles on State Responsibility Commentary*, above note 26): 'it is not excluded that developments may occur in the field of individual civil responsibility'. Specifically on direct responsibility of rebel groups, see Cahin, 'Responsibility of Other Entities', above note 99, at 337–41; Okowa, 'State and Individual Responsibility', above note 10, at 180–87.

[103] See D. Anzilotti, 'La responsabilité internationale des Etats à raison des dommages soufferts par des étrangers' (1906) 13 *Revue générale de droit international public* 5, at 14–15; P. Schoen, *Die völkerrechtliche Haftung der Staaten aus unerlaubten Handlungen* (Breslau: Kern, 1917), at 35 et seq. For a contemporary assessment, see T. Becker, *Terrorism and the State – Rethinking the Rules of State Responsibility* (Oxford: Hart, 2006), at 19 et seq; O. de Frouville, 'Attribution of Conduct to the State: Private Individuals', in Crawford, Pellet and Olleson (eds.), *Law of International Responsibility*, above note 89, 257–80, at 275–77.

[104] For two very detailed studies on this issue, see Becker, *Terrorism and the State*, above note 103; K. N. Trapp, *State Responsibility and International Terrorism* (Oxford: Oxford University Press, 2011); see also the recent contribution of M. Jackson, *Complicity in International Law* (Oxford: Oxford University Press, 2015), at 176 et seq.

4.2.1. The gap-filling function of Common Article 1 GC

The reason this discussion is unnecessary may be seen in the existence of Common Article 1 GC. In the interpretation we have presented above, this provision requires States to refrain from supporting violations of international humanitarian law. This prohibition applies regardless of whether the violations have been committed by States or non-State actors.[105] Accordingly, we are here in the presence of a normative framework which – in the special situation of armed conflicts – already requires States not to support wrongful conduct irrespective of the authorship of these violations. Additionally, Common Article 1 GC even remedies some of the deficiencies of Article 16 ASR (and the corresponding provisions in the ILC's Draft Articles on the Responsibility of International Organizations) which would render it very difficult to operate in the situation of conflicts such as the one in the DRC. For example, Common Article 1 GC does not set forth such a high threshold in terms of intent as Article 16 ASR does. This may be partially explained by the logic of the law of international humanitarian law. In the course of an armed conflict, typically a large number of violations of the law occur. In order not to hamper the attribution of responsibility, the Hague Convention of 1907 already rested on the assumption of 'objective responsibility' as set forth in its Article 3.[106]

A definition of a broader basis of responsibility in the law of international responsibility would potentially also be counterproductive. We need to keep in mind that this field of law includes general rules which apply across the whole spectrum of international law. Accordingly, we should be cautious with respect to developments which try to accommodate these rules to specific problems and factual situations. This is one lesson of the debate on the 'war against terrorism', in which a host of calls for broader bases of attribution arose, but – for good reasons – ultimately remained unsuccessful.[107]

4.2.2. The remaining importance of the general rules

At the same time, the general rules of international responsibility retain a distinct field of application. It is uncertain whether Common Article 1 of the Geneva Conventions also imposes obligations on the UN. The question of whether the UN itself is bound by international

[105] Zimmermann, 'Obligation to Prevent Genocide', above note 86, at 636.

[106] Sassòli, 'State Responsibility', above note 68, at 406.

[107] On the related issue of self-defence against non-State actors, cf. T. Ruys, *'Armed Attack' and Article 51 of the UN Charter – Evolutions in Customary Law and Practice* (Cambridge: Cambridge University Press, 2010), 485–89.

humanitarian law has been the subject of much debate.[108] Depending on the type of authorization and mandate, troops will still be bound by international humanitarian law by virtue of the international obligations of the troop-contributing States. However, in situations of UN peacekeeping where 'command and control' is vested in the UN,[109] it needs to be carefully established on what basis the requirement to respect international humanitarian law actually rests.[110] Quite frequently, the UN Security Council itself stipulates in its resolutions that all actions of peacekeeping troops need to respect international humanitarian law.[111] The HRDDP, formulated by the UN Secretary-General and mentioned at the outset, is another attempt to fill possible gaps with respect to the obligations of the UN in this field.[112]

Another reason the general rules retain significance is not limited to the situation in which international organizations operate. There is a growing discussion in academia, among NGOs and in international organizations whether individuals can directly claim reparation for violations of international humanitarian law,[113] a possibility that is at least not ruled out by the ILC's Articles on State Responsibility, as Article 33(2) makes clear.[114] The traditional view in this regard is that reparation for such violations is owed to the State whose citizens were the victims of such events.[115]

[108] See generally on this question G. Nolte, 'The Different Functions of the Security Council with Respect to Humanitarian Law', in V. Lowe et al. (eds.), *The United Nations Security Council and War* (Oxford: Oxford University Press, 2008), 519–35; J. Drohla, 'Die Bindung der Vereinten Nationen an das humanitäre Völkerrecht', in J. Bäumler et al. (eds.), *Akteure in Krieg und Frieden* (Tübingen: Mohr Siebeck, 2010), 93–113. See also the contribution of M. Happold, 'Comment – Obligations of States Contributing to UN Peacekeeping Missions under Common Article 1 of the Geneva Conventions', Chapter 16 in this volume.

[109] On this notion, see K. Schmalenbach, *Die Haftung Internationaler Organisationen im Rahmen von Militäreinsätzen und Territorialverwaltungen* (Frankfurt/Main: Peter Lang, 2004), 107–11.

[110] See the Secretary-General's 'Bulletin on the Observance of International Humanitarian Law' (6 August 1999), UN Doc. ST/SGB/1999/13.

[111] For an overview of practice see Nolte, 'Functions of the Security Council', above note 108.

[112] 'Identical letters', above note 19.

[113] See A. Fischer-Lescano, 'Subjektivierung völkerrechtlicher Sekundärregeln – die Individualrechte auf Entschädigung und effektiven Rechtsschutz bei Verletzungen des Völkerrechts', (2007) 45 *Archiv des Völkerrechts* 299.

[114] ILC Commentary, above note 26, Article 33 ASR, para. 4.

[115] R. Wolfrum and D. Fleck, above note 86, at 708; C. Tomuschat, 'Individuals', in Crawford, Pellet and Olleson (eds.), *Law of International Responsibility*, above note 89, 985–91, at 988–89; W. Heintschel von Heinegg, 'Entschädigung für Verletzungen des humanitären Völkerrechts' (2003) 40 *Berichte der Deutschen Gesellschaft für Völkerrecht* 1, at 25.

As we can see in a number of international documents[116] and in the arguments plaintiffs make before domestic courts, this view is nowadays challenged.[117] It is not the subject of this chapter to take a view on this matter.

The question may be asked, however, whether a violation of Common Article 1 GC and responsibility on the basis of the complicity provisions in the ILC's Articles on State Responsibility and Draft Articles on the Responsibility of International Organizations entail different consequences. Violations of Common Article 1 GC establish responsibility on a macro-level. The State in question has generally breached its obligation to ensure respect for international humanitarian law. It is questionable whether an individual could bring a claim against a foreign State for such a violation (regardless of the problems to find a suitable avenue for such a claim). The damage accruing to this individual would need to be linked to some precise violation of the obligation to 'ensure respect'. In comparison, this is somewhat easier in the case of support for specific violations of international humanitarian law which renders the supporting State or international organization responsible under the general rules of international responsibility. Here, as well, difficult issues of establishing the intent to further the commission of the wrongful act will arise. But it is at least conceivable that the precise impact of support on a given wrongful act can be more clearly established than is the case with a violation of Common Article 1 GC. Here again, responsibility for a violation of Common Article 1 GC can be compared to responsibility under Article I of the Genocide Convention. In its *Genocide Convention* Case, the Court decided not to grant compensation to Bosnia-Herzegovina. Instead, it opted for satisfaction as the appropriate form of reparation.[118] While it

[116] See UNGA, 'Basic Principles and Guidelines on the Right to a Remedy and Reparation for Victims of Gross Violations of International Human Rights Law and Serious Violations of International Humanitarian Law' (16 December 2005) UNGA Resolution 60/147.

[117] By way of example, one can refer here to the current proceedings initiated by the families of victims of the attack on the bridge of Varvarin. See decision of the German Federal Court of Justice, Case No. III ZR 190/05, Decision of 2 November 2006, reprinted in *Juristenzeitung* 2007, at 532–36, available with an English translation and introduction by this author as ILDC 887 (DE 2006) at opil.ouplaw.com/view/10.1093/law:ildc/887de06.case.1/law-ildc-887de06?rskey=TIYLIS&result=2&prd=ORIL. See also German Federal Constitutional Court, Case No. 2 BvR 2660/06, Decision of 13 August 2013.

[118] *Application of the Genocide Convention* (Judgment), above note 30, para. 463; for criticism of the Court's approach in this regard see A. Gattini, 'Breach of the Obligation to Prevent and Reparation thereof in the ICJ's Genocide Convention Judgment' (2007) 18 *European Journal of International Law* 695.

can be wondered whether this was due to the special character of the prohibition of genocide in international law, it was also owed to the fact that the Court had difficulties to establish the 'causal nexus between the Respondent's violation of its obligation of prevention and the damage resulting from the genocide at Srebrenica'.[119]

5. Concluding observations

What lessons can we draw from these considerations for the book's overarching theme of compliance with international humanitarian law? A number of general considerations can be formulated: it is today firmly accepted that aiding or assisting another State in the commission of internationally wrongful acts entails the responsibility of the helping State/international organization if certain conditions are met. This rule is supplemented by the obligation to ensure respect for international humanitarian law under Common Article 1 of the Geneva Conventions. The general rules on complicity and this special rule need to be viewed together in order to derive the standards under which complicit States/international organizations become responsible for violations of international humanitarian law. Taken together, the rules on complicity present an additional layer for the upholding of the international rule of law. They make it clear that also indirect violations of the law can trigger responsibility. They thus widen the circle of responsible actors which may have a positive influence on compliance with international humanitarian law. This effect should not, however, be taken for granted. Considerable problems remain with respect to the implementation of this framework of responsibility. The problems for contemporary African conflicts lie not so much in doctrinal uncertainty but rather in the often extremely complex situations on the ground under which the identification of responsible authors will often be difficult. Nonetheless, both the general rules and Common Article 1 GC are flexible enough to accommodate these complex situations.

[119] *Application of the Genocide Convention* (Judgment), above note 30, para. 462.

20

International responsibility for humanitarian law violations by armed groups

KIRSTEN SCHMALENBACH

1. Introduction: armed group violence in the Great Lakes Region

For decades, Africa's Great Lakes Region has been a theatre of armed conflicts with diverse causes and levels of intensity. The causes of the armed conflicts in the Great Lakes Region are manifold: ethnic, religious and racial tension, poverty, disputes over land access and natural resources, weak governmental structures and militarized societies are just a few of the concurrent contributing factors.[1] The ongoing devastating conflict in the Democratic Republic of the Congo (DRC), to name but one example, is a disastrous blend of civil war and regional conflict involving several adjacent States and approximately twenty-five armed groups; the atrocities and the aftereffects of the war have claimed the lives of more than 3 million men, women and children so far, making it Africa's most lethal conflict in history.[2]

Without minimizing the infamous role of national armies in the rampant conduct of war, non-State armed groups have played a central role in the deathly dynamic of the Great Lake Region conflicts. They range from well-organized rebel groups and militia, at times with political objectives, to loosely formed gangs of bandits. Many of these armed groups are, to a greater or lesser degree, allied with each other, hegemonic rivalry or enmity notwithstanding. A few are attached to a local base; others engage in cross-border activities; most of them are backed and supported by

[1] For a detailed analysis, see Swedish International Development Agency, 'A Strategic Conflict Analysis for the Great Lakes Region' (March 2004), at 24, www.globalstudies.gu.se/digitalAssets/808/808119_conflict.pdf.

[2] The exact death toll is disputed. See Human Security Report Project, *Human Security Report 2009/2010: The Causes of Peace and the Shrinking Costs of War* (New York: Oxford University Press, 2011), http://www.hsrgroup.org/human-security-reports/20092010/text.aspx.

different governments;[3] and all of them have a poor record of compliance with international humanitarian law. The atrocities of the Lord's Resistance Army against civilians, to take a single example, are regularly the focus of the United Nations,[4] non-governmental human rights organizations[5] and even the United States government.[6] Between January and August 2011, the United Nations Office for the Coordination of Humanitarian Affairs received reports of 254 attacks by the highly mobile rebel group on civilians in the DRC, South Sudan and the Central African Republic, resulting in 126 deaths and the abduction of 368 persons.[7] The UN Secretary-General confirmed that attacks of the Lord's Resistance Army, comprising some 500 combatants, typically include killings of civilians, abductions especially of children and women, the recruitment and use of both boys and girls as combatants and in other roles, serious sexual violence, including rape and sexual slavery, forced marriage, mutilations, looting and the destruction of property.[8]

Taking the armed conflicts in the Great Lakes Region as the backdrop, this chapter examines two areas: first, the responsibility of non-State armed groups and their supporting States for the widespread violations of humanitarian law, and second, the responsibility of the invested States for their support of the armed groups and their failure to prevent the latter's atrocities. With a view to Robert Cryer's article 'International Criminal Prosecution' in this volume, the following study does not address the individual responsibility for atrocities under international criminal law but focuses on the collective responsibility of armed groups and States.

2. Contextualizing the system of international responsibility

The collective responsibility of armed groups and States under international law is triggered by the infringement of a specific legal obligation of the respective actor under international law (so-called 'primary rules'). With reference to the armed conflicts in the Great Lakes Region,

[3] Swedish International Development Agency, 'A Strategic Conflict Analysis', above note 1, at 142 et seq.

[4] 'Report of the Secretary-General on the Lord's Resistance Army – Affected Areas Pursuant to Security Council Press Statement of 21 July 2011' (4 November 2011), UN Doc. S/2011/693.

[5] Human Rights Watch Report, 'Trail for Death, LRA Atrocities in Northeastern Congo' (27 March 2010), www.hrw.org/sites/default/files/reports/drc0310webwcover_0.pdf.

[6] Lord's Resistance Army Disarmament and Northern Uganda Recovery Act of 2009, 111th Congress, 2nd Session, at 1067, United States Public Law 111–172.

[7] 'Report of the Secretary-General on the Lord's Resistance Army', above note 4, para. 11.

[8] Ibid. para. 12.

the relevant primary rules whose breach can in principle be a source of international responsibility fall within three categories: first, the prohibition to use armed force and to intervene in the internal affairs of another State; second, obligations under legally binding Security Council resolutions; and third, substantive rules of international humanitarian law and other legal obligations applicable during armed conflicts such as human rights law.

The most fundamental obligations of non-intervention and non-use of armed force first and foremost concern inter-State relations. Considering the transnational dimension of the Congo wars, it comes as no surprise that the DRC approached the International Court of Justice (ICJ) three times in order to claim that Uganda,[9] Rwanda[10] and Burundi[11] committed acts of aggression against the DRC. In the proceedings brought against Uganda, the only application that resulted in a judgment on the merits, the respondent acknowledged that it had given training and military support to the rebel group Mouvement de Libération du Congo.[12] Even though the ICJ could not establish that Uganda exercised effective control over the armed group,[13] it concluded in reference to its *Nicaragua* Judgment that Uganda had violated its obligations arising from the principles of non-use of force and non-intervention[14] not only by sending its own regular forces but also by supporting irregular forces on the territory of the DRC.[15] With regard to the anti-Ugandan armed groups operating without hindrance from DRC soil, the ICJ considered whether the DRC had breached its 'duty of vigilance' – that is, the State's due diligence obligation under the principle of non-intervention – by tolerating the armed group based within its territory.[16] The lack of effective governmental

[9] *Armed Activities on the Territory of the Congo (Democratic Republic of the Congo v. Uganda)* (Judgment) [2005] ICJ Reports 168, para. 163.

[10] *Armed Activities on the Territory of the Congo (New Application: 2002) (Democratic Republic of the Congo v. Rwanda)* (Jurisdiction and Admissibility) [2006] ICJ Reports 6, para. 11.

[11] *Armed Activities on the Territory of the Congo (Democratic Republic of the Congo v. Burundi)* (Application Instituting Proceedings) 23 June 1999, www.icj-cij.org/docket/files/116/7151.pdf.

[12] *Armed Activities*, above note 9, para. 160.

[13] For details on the rules on attribution, see Chapter 3.3 of this contribution.

[14] See United Nations General Assembly (UNGA) 'Friendly Relations Declaration' (24 October 1970) Resolution 2625 (XXV) Principle 1, para. 9, reflecting customary international law; *Armed Activities*, above note 9, paras. 162, 300.

[15] *Armed Activities*, above note 9, para. 163.

[16] Ibid.; see also *Corfu Channel Case (UK v. Albania)* (Judgment) [1949] ICJ Reports 4, at 22; H. Tonkin, 'Common Article 1: A Minimum Yardstick for Regulating Private Military and Security Companies' (2009) 22 *Leiden Journal of International Law* 779, at 789–90.

authority in the relevant region, however, cleared the DRC of this reproach.[17]

In its judgment, the ICJ for reasons of fact finding relied on a series of Security Council Resolutions addressing the war in the Great Lakes Region. The international responsibility of Uganda for non-compliance with these resolutions (Article 25 UN Charter),[18] however, was not a subject of the DRC's application. According to the International Peace Institute Security Council Database, the Security Council Resolutions spelled out 295 specific demands between 1989 and 2006 to the parties of the conflict in the DRC, more than in any other civil war.[19] In most cases, the Security Council called upon parties to cease breaches of international law.[20] The resolutions' demands, however, may transcend general and contractual international obligations by measuring all addressed parties by the same yardstick. In its Resolution 1291 (2000) on the situation in the DRC, for example, the Security Council called upon all parties to the conflict to refrain from or cease any support of those suspected of involvement in war crimes.[21] Such mandatory measures are addressed not only to States involved in the conflict but also to the various rebel groups[22] without necessarily implying the latter's responsibility as separate international persons in the case of non-compliance with the Security Council demands.[23]

The international responsibility of actors triggered by the violation of the non-use of force and non-intervention principles and by their non-compliance with mandatory Security Council Resolutions raises several questions regarding the status of armed groups under these international obligations. These aspects, however, fall outside the scope of the present study given its focus on the violation of international humanitarian law obligations by armed groups and the resulting responsibilities.

17 *Armed Activities*, above note 9, para. 301.

18 V. Gowlland-Debbas, 'Responsibility and the United Nations Charter', in C. Crawford, A. Pellet and S. Olleson (eds.), *The Law of International Responsibility* (Oxford: Oxford University Press, 2010), 115–38, at 123.

19 J. Cockayne, C. Mikulaschek and C. Purry, 'UN Security Council and Civil War: Insights from New IPI Study', International Peace Institute (7 September 2010), at 19, www.ipinst.org/media/pdf/publications/ipi_rpt_unsc_and_civil_war_epub.pdf.

20 Cf. United Nations Security Council (UNSC) Resolution 1234 (9 April 1999), para. 6.

21 UNSC Resolution 1291 (24 February 2000), para. 15.

22 Cf. UNSC Resolution 1258 (6 August 1999), para. 4.

23 Cf. J. Crawford, 'The System of International Responsibility', in Crawford, Pellet and Olleson (eds.), *International Responsibility*, above note 18, 17–33, at 19.

3. State responsibility for the conduct of armed groups

3.1. *Facts and data on State support for armed groups*

The attribution of acts of private actors to a State is among the most sensitive and controversially discussed issues in international law. This comes as no surprise since the relevant rules of international law draw the dividing line between the public and private sphere by determining when an armed group's conduct is regarded as State conduct due to the strength of the ties between the latter and the armed group.[24] Based on customary law, the pertinent rules of attribution illustrate the often-lamented international law dilemma. The dilemma is that States, which are not only the international lawmakers but also self-serving parties, are called upon to legally assess what many of them consider an effective tool in international relations: empowering and sponsoring domestic armed groups in the territory of another State. Cunningham, Gleditsch and Salehyan compiled a set of data on rebel groups that included information on their foreign support.[25] Of the altogether 285 rebel groups that have been active between 1945 and 2008 on a worldwide scale, 134 had explicit or widely accepted links to foreign States, and a further thirty groups had allegedly been supported by foreign States. Among those States that frequently sponsor rebel groups are Russia, China and the United States, but also African States such as Libya, Sudan and Tanzania.[26] This has especially been the case with the civil wars around the Great Lakes Region in Africa where numerous rebel groups have been heavily and often openly supported by various foreign States. The analysis shows that the vast majority of governmental support for rebels has involved direct military assistance, particularly arms transfers,[27] and territorial access to grant both safe haven and operational bases within the supporting State. According to the narratives of this

[24] J. Crawford (Special Rapporteur of the International Law Commission), Yearbook of the International Law Commission, vol. II, part 1 (1998), at 33, para. 154.

[25] D. Cunningham, K. Gleditsch and I. Salehyan, 'Non-State Actor Data' (7 March 2012), privatewww.essex.ac.uk/~ksg/eacd.html; see also D. Cunningham, K. Gleditsch and I. Salehyan, 'It Takes Two: A Dyadic Analysis of Civil War Duration and Outcome' (2009) 53 *Journal of Conflict Resolution* 570.

[26] I. Salehyan, 'The Delegation of War to Rebel Organizations' (2010) 3 *Journal of Conflict Resolution* 493, at 497 et seq.

[27] See D. Fruchart, 'United Nations Arms Embargoes, Their Impact on Arms Flows and Target Behaviour: Case Study: Democratic Republic of the Congo 2003–2006', Stockholm International Peace Research Institute (2007), at 7, books.sipri.org/files/misc/UNAE/SIPRI07UNAEDRC.pdf.

database,[28] the Burundi rebel group Conseil National pour la Défense de la Démocratie, taken as an example, was supported by Zaire/DRC in 1993 by allowing the group to operate from Zairian soil; in the Second Congo War (1998–2003), a splinter group of the Conseil National pour la Défense de la Démocratie was allowed by the Congolese government to operate from and maintain military bases in the DRC. Likewise, it has been established that in the same conflict, the Congolese rebel group Rassemblement Congolais pour la Démocratie was supported by Rwanda, Uganda and Burundi with military supplies, bases and even troops. Until the Sudanese government officially withdrew its support in 2001, the Ugandan rebel group Lord's Resistance Army was able to maintain bases in Southern Sudan and received military support from the Sudanese government in their fight against both Uganda and the DRC.[29] Far less frequently, States sent in their own regular forces in direct support of the rebel groups. One example of direct military support is the 1996 insurgence of the Alliance of Democratic Forces for the Liberation of Congo-Zaire (AFDL) against the Zairian president Mobutu Sese Seke which was extensively backed by Rwandese and Angolan troops. The difficulties in obtaining reliable information about the degree and the nature of State support is evidenced by the Final Report of the Group of Experts set up by the UN Secretary-General to investigate the violence by armed groups in Kivu Provjnce of the DRC including the allegation that the government of Rwanda provided support for the Congolese rebel group Congrès National pour la Défense du Peuple during the Second Congo War.[30] The inquiry committee found evidence – mostly through eyewitnesses – that Rwandan authorities had been complicit in the recruitment of (child) soldiers by the rebel group, facilitated the supply of military equipment and sent officers and units from its regular forces to the DRC in support of the rebel group.[31] Yet, the degree of Rwanda's influence on the rebel group's actions in the DRC and the manner in which the latter put the assistance to use remain opaque.

[28] The following information is obtained from D. Cunningham and K. Gleditsch, 'Non-State Actor Data, Case Description Note' (7 March 2007), privatewww.essex.ac.uk/~ksg/eacd.html.

[29] There is suspicion that the Sudanese military still provides the Lord's Resistance Army with material and intelligence assistance even though the Republic of Sudan has officially ceased its support, see M. Wilkerson, 'Why Can't Anyone Stop the LRA?', Foreign Policy, 19 April 2010, foreignpolicy.com/2010/04/15/why-cant-anyone-stop-the-lra/.

[30] Group of Experts, 'Final Report of the Group of Experts in the Democratic Republic of the Congo' (12 December 2008), UN Doc. S/2008/773.

[31] Ibid. para. 61.

3.2. *The impact of legal attribution on State behaviour*

Given that combat conducted by a State's regular armed forces in the territory of another State is costly with regard to resources and lives, not to mention that this could easily damage the State's international reputation, it is easy to imagine why, from a rationalist's perspective, States prefer to leave ground combat to domestic rebel groups which have local knowledge and enjoy some extent of local support.[32] Arguably, restrictive normative rules of attribution in conjunction with a high standard of proof which purges the State from any responsibility for the rebel group's atrocities may add to the advantages of delegation within the State's cost-benefit analysis. To reverse the argument, the development of more far-reaching rules of attribution under international law that expand the sphere of public responsibility may add to the cost of delegation, for example, due to reputational concerns or fear of retaliation,[33] and thus might contribute to a more robust level of compliance.[34] Admittedly, these assumptions lack empirical support. It cannot be denied however, that the non-attribution of war crimes committed by armed groups to the supporting State smacks of tacit acquittal even if the supporting State has been found internationally responsible for not preventing the war crimes committed by the armed group. With this in mind, ICJ Judge Al-Khasawneh warned in his Dissenting Opinion to the 2007 *Bosnia Genocide* Judgment:

> [When] the shared objective is the commission of international crimes, to require both control over the non-state actors and the specific operations in the context of which international crimes were committed is too high a threshold. The inherent danger in such an approach is that it gives States the opportunity to carry out criminal policies through non-state surrogates without incurring direct responsibility therefore.[35]

The harsh reactions to the ICJ Judgment did not prove him wrong.[36]

32 Salehyan, 'Delegation', above note 26, at 503–05.

33 R. Brewster, 'Unpacking the State's Reputation' (2009) 50 *Harvard Journal of International Law* 231, at 231.

34 Cf. C. Chinkin, 'A Critique of the Public/Private Division' (1999) 19 *European Journal of International Law* 387, at 395.

35 *Application of the Convention on the Prevention and Punishment of the Crime of Genocide (Bosnia and Herzegovina v. Serbia and Montenegro)* (Judgment) [2007] ICJ Reports 43, Dissenting Opinion of Vice-President Al-Khasawneh, para. 39.

36 C. Tosh, 'Genocide Acquittal Provokes Legal Debate', Institute for War and Peace Reporting, iwpr.net/report-news/genocide-acquittal-provokes-legal-debate; A. Cassese, 'A Judicial Massacre', *The Guardian*, 27 February 2007, www.guardian.co.uk/commentisfree/

3.3. *Reconciling the ILC's Articles on State Responsibility and ICJ jurisprudence*

It seems reasonable that having the task to visualize and apply the normative rules of attribution as developed in time-honoured State practice, the ICJ does not take into account compliance-based theories. Over time, the Court has developed a set of rather restrictive rules of attribution that divides the private from the public sphere of responsibility, with the famous 1986 *Nicaragua* Judgment[37] and the 1980 *Iran Hostage* Judgment[38] leading the way. When the International Law Commission presented the Articles on State Responsibility (ASR) in 2001, its provisions on attribution (Articles 4 to 11 ASR) can be rightly described as an accurate legislative conclusion to State practice and international jurisprudence without chiselling the ICJ's restrictive prerequisites for attribution in stone. With regard to armed groups' atrocities and their attribution to the supporting State, only two articles are of immediate relevance: Article 4 ASR, dealing with the attribution of acts of State organs, and Article 8 ASR, dealing with the attribution of acts of private persons or entities. With a view to Article 9 ASR, it is noteworthy that some States in the Great Lakes Region do not exercise effective governmental control throughout the entire country, which is especially true for the DRC. However, under Article 9 ASR, measures of armed groups relating to the public security sector in areas devoid of governmental control would be attributable to the territorial State, if at all, and not to the foreign sponsoring State. In addition, attribution would fail anyway given that rebel activity is the major cause for the lack of governmental control in certain areas. This makes the exercise of governmental functions by rebel groups not legitimate in the eyes of Article 9 ASR.[39]

3.3.1. Article 4: the total dependence test

Even though many details surrounding the support for armed group are shrouded in uncertainty, one fact is clear: armed groups of the Great Lakes Region such as the Lord's Resistance Army, the Congrès National

2007/feb/27/thejudicialmassacreofsrebr; J. Kranz, 'Die völkerrechtliche Verantwortlichkeit für die Anwendung militärischer Gewalt' (2010) 48 *Archiv des Völkerrechts* 281, at 301.

37 *Case concerning Military and Paramilitary Activities in and against Nicaragua (Nicaragua v. United States of America)* (Merits) (Judgment) [1986] ICJ Reports 14.

38 *Case concerning United States Diplomatic and Consular Staff in Tehran (United States of America v. Iran)* (Judgment) [1980] ICJ Reports 3.

39 O. de Frouville, 'Attribution of Conduct to the State: Private Individuals', in Crawford, Pellet and Olleson (eds.), *International Responsibility*, above note 18, 257–80, at 272.

pour la Défense du Peuple or the Conseil National pour la Défense de la Démocratie are not part of the organization of the sponsoring State, that is, they do not have the status of organs under the latter's internal laws (*de iure* organs). This does not exclude, however, the applicability of Article 4 ASR to the armed groups mentioned. In the 2007 *Bosnia Genocide* Case, the ICJ seized upon the opportunity to clarify what was already pointed out in the 1986 *Nicaragua* Judgment: armed groups acting in fact on behalf of a State (de facto organs) fall within the scope of Article 4 ASR[40] because they must be, for legal purposes, equated with *de iure* State organs even if that status does not follow from internal law.[41] The status as de facto organs, in contrast to *de iure* organs, emanates from a particularly high degree of State control over the armed group in all fields of their activities, which amounts – according to the ICJ – to a relationship of complete dependence (*Nicaragua* test I).[42] Even the slightest margin of real independence from the State's power of command, as evidenced by disagreement over strategic options, for example, destroys the required nexus between the State and the armed group.[43] In light of the high threshold of dependence, it goes without saying that political, military and logistical relations between the sponsoring State and the armed group does not suffice to fall within the scope of Article 4 ASR.[44] The ICJ is often criticized for requiring total dependency of a de facto organ, because it makes the legal concept virtually insignificant.[45] In light of the available data on State support for armed groups in the Great Lakes Region, there is some merit to that critique. On top of this, Article 8 ASR is not suitable to serve as a 'catch-all provision' for the attribution of armed groups' atrocities to the supporting States, at least if the ICJ's effective control requirement (*Nicaragua* test II) is applied to the available facts.

[40] *Application of the Convention on the Prevention and Punishment of the Crime of Genocide (Bosnia and Herzegovina v. Serbia and Montenegro)* (Judgment) [2007] ICJ Reports 43, paras. 385–395.

[41] Ibid. para. 392; *Nicaragua Case*, above note 37, para. 109.

[42] *Bosnian Genocide Case*, above note 40, para. 393.

[43] Ibid. para. 394; cf. T. Becker, *Terrorism and the State, Rethinking the Rules of State Responsibly* (Oxford and Portland: Hart Publisher, 2006), at 69: 'the bond . . . must be shown to be so substantial and persuasive that it is virtually indistinguishable from the legal relationship between a State and its own officials'.

[44] *Bosnian Genocide Case*, above note 40, para. 394.

[45] See J. Griebel and M. Plücken, 'New Developments Regarding the Rules of Attribution?, The International Court of Justice's Decision on Bosnia v. Serbia' (2008) 21 *Leiden Journal of International Law* 601, at 612–14.

3.3.2. Article 8: the overall and effective control test

When the International Law Commission's Special Rapporteur Crawford drafted Article 8 ASR in 2001, he took into account the open resistance of the International Criminal Tribunal for the former Yugoslavia (ICTY) to the ICJ's effective control rule,[46] which demands effective State control over armed groups' actions contrary to humanitarian law for the purpose of attribution.[47] In its 1999 *Tadić* Judgment, the ICTY Appeals Chamber diminished the basis of attribution to overall State control over hierarchically organized armed groups: in contrast to effective control, overall control requires no proof of the direct involvement of the State in the specific unlawful operation.[48] It is sufficient if the State controls the armed group at a general level that goes beyond financing, training and equipping, but also involves organizing, coordinating and helping in the general planning of military actions conducted by the armed group.[49] According to the ICTY, effective State control in the sense of the *Nicaragua* test is only required in cases of single individuals or unorganized groups.[50] At the time when Crawford drafted Article 8 ASR, the ICTY *Tadić* Judgment had the potential to initiate a development in international law that might have prompted the ICJ to reconsider its Nicaragua test, even though Crawford already indicated that the rebellious ICTY was not directly concerned with questions of State responsibility.[51] In the 2007 *Bosnia Genocide* Case, the ICJ elaborated on Crawford's reservations by rebuking: 'Insofar as the "overall control" test is employed to determine whether or not an armed conflict is *international*, which was the sole question which the Appeals Chamber was called upon to decided, it may well be that the test is applicable and suitable . . .'[52] However, the Court continued that logic does not require the same test to be adopted in resolving two issues which are very different in nature: first, rules of attribution that are decisive for the State's involvement in an international armed conflict, and second, rules of attribution that trigger the State's responsibility for specific acts committed in the

[46] International Law Commission, Commentary on the Draft Articles on State Responsibility, Yearbook of the International Law Commission, vol. II, part 2 (2001), at Article 8, para. 5.

[47] *Nicaragua Case*, above note 37, para. 115.

[48] *Prosecutor v. Tadic* (Judgment), Case No. IT-94-1-A (15 July 1999), para. 145.

[49] Ibid. paras. 131, 145. [50] Ibid. para, 124.

[51] International Law Commission, Commentary on State Responsibility, above note 46, Article 8, para. 5.

[52] *Bosnian Genocide Case*, above note 40, para. 404 (emphasis added).

course of this conflict.[53] Admittedly, the ICJ's rebuke has its merits. There can be no question that State practice may develop different rules of attribution in different areas of international law. Some of them happen to be identical in content, for example, with regard to the attribution of acts of *de iure* State organs, while others vary, for instance, when *ultra vires* acts or acts of private persons must be assessed. Nonetheless, that does not render the *Tadić* Judgment meaningless in other areas of international law. If the attribution of armed groups' conduct to the State results in the internationality of the armed conflict under international humanitarian law, the applied rules of attribution – the *Tadić* test – may indeed trigger the State's international responsibility at least with regard to a possible violation of the prohibition to use force in international relations (Article 2(4) UN Charter). However, the ICJ in its 1986 *Nicaragua* Judgment interpreted the non-use of force principle very broadly, accepting that the training and arming of rebel groups already constituted a violation of Article 2(4) UN Charter. Consequently, the attribution of rebel groups' conduct to the State for the purpose of Article 2 para. 4 UN Charter does not substantially add to the State's responsibility in this respect.[54]

In its 2007 *Bosnia Genocide* Judgment, the ICJ did not call into question that the State's overall control over armed groups (*Tadić* test) may result in the attribution of the armed groups' military operations to the controlling State. However, the attribution of the armed group's military operation to the controlling State does not necessarily imply that every single act of war is thus attributable. Some acts, especially those contrary to international humanitarian law, can still be considered non-attributable if the State did not exercise effective control over these specific acts (*Nicaragua* test II). Following this logic, violations of humanitarian law by members of armed groups are '*ultra vires*' in relation to the overall-controlling State but do not fall within the scope of Article 7 ASR. According to Article 7 ASR, *ultra vires* acts are only attributable to a State if the actor is either *de iure* or de facto an organ of the State (Article 4 ASR).[55] In contrast, within

[53] Ibid. para. 405.

[54] It is worth noting, though, that in its 2005 *Armed Activities* Judgment, the ICJ not even mentioned the ICTY's overall-control test in order to assess whether Uganda, who had acknowledged the training and military support of the Mouvement de Libération du Congo, violated Article 2(4) of the UN Charter. Even here, the Court stuck to the 'Nicaragua test' and consequently denied the attribution of the armed group's acts to Uganda for the purpose of Article 2(4) UN Charter. *Armed Activities Case*, above note 9, para. 160.

[55] L. Condorelli and C. Kreß, 'The Rules of Attribution: General Considerations', in Crawford, Pellet and Olleson, *International Responsibility* (eds.), above note 18, 221–36, at 229–30.

the scope of Article 8 ASR *ultra vires* acts are in principle not attributable to the State; the contextual interpretation of Article 7 ASR as well as its explicit references to the conduct of organs and persons empowered to exercise elements of governmental authority confirm this understanding of Article 8 ASR.[56] The *Nicaragua* test II harmoniously blends in with this interpretation of Article 8 ASR given that the required effective control of the State over a specific action of the armed group excludes the armed group exceeding the mandate or instructions from attribution,[57] which is a separate issue from isolated instances of disobeying orders that do not challenge the State's effective control over the specific action.[58] Based on these considerations, the ICJ was right to say that the ICTY's overall control test may have its authority within the realm of international criminal law without calling into question the effective control test within the scope of Article 8 ASR.

3.3.3. Rehousing the overall control test

The above interim result concerning the effective control test does not mean that the ICJ's understanding of the rules of attribution is set in stone. It is rather a question of whether the ICJ in its 2007 *Bosnia Genocide* Judgment ignored relevant changes in State practice and international jurisprudence when adhering to its 25-year-old *Nicaragua* jurisprudence. The analysis of State practice and case law is, however, hampered by the judicial and academic confusion about where to draw the line distinguishing de facto organs of a State and the State's control over acts of non-organs. Traditionally, the term 'de facto organ' was used to denominate persons who are not *de iure* organs (Article 4 ASR) but whose conduct is nonetheless attributable to the State on various grounds (Articles 5, 8 and 9 ASR).[59] Since the 2007 *Bosnia Genocide* Judgment,

56 M. Milanović, 'State Responsibility for Acts of Non-State Actors' (2009) 22 *Leiden Journal of International Law* 307, at 317.

57 C. Kreß, 'L'organe de facto en droit international public, Réflexions sur l'imputation a l'État de l'acte d'un particulier a la lumière des développements récents' (2001) 105 *Revue Générale de Droit International Public* 93, at 135–36.

58 International Law Commission, Commentary on State Responsibility, above note 46, Article 8 ASR, para. 8.

59 See, for example, Griebel and Plücken, 'New Developments', above note 45, at 614: de facto organs fall under the scope of Article 8 ASR; Kreß, L' organe de facto, above note 57, at 95 ; A. Epiney, 'Zur Rechtsfigur des de facto-Organs im Recht der Staatenverantwortlichkeit', in A. Fischer-Lescano et al. (eds.), *Peace and Liberty, Festschrift Michael Bothe* (Berlin: Nomos Verlag, 2008), 883–96, at 883 et seq.

one has to accept that the term 'de facto organ' moved once and for all under the legal umbrella of Article 4 ASR. Building on the clear wording of Article 4 ASR, the ICJ rightly concluded that a State must control its de facto organ (the actor), but need not control the specific conduct (the action). In contrast, Article 8 requires nothing other than the State's control over a specific conduct; the provision's wording 'under the direction or control of that State in carrying out the conduct', its relation to Article 7, as well as the ICJ's jurisprudence[60] confirm this specific focus of Article 8 ASR. Proceeding from this, international case law falls into place despite the ubiquitous confusion about the term 'de facto organ'. In the 2001 case of the *Riofrío Massacre*, the Inter-American Commission on Human Rights decided that, for the purpose of determining the international responsibility of Colombia under the American Convention on Human Rights, it sufficed to prove that members of paramilitary groups and Colombian regularforces had carried out joint operations with the knowledge of superior officers.[61] Indeed, there was evidence that *de iure* organs of the State helped the paramilitary group to coordinate and carry out the massacre in Riofrío as well as to then cover it up.[62] Under these circumstances, the Commission decided that the members of the paramilitary groups acted as 'agents' of the State and as a result of which the Commission was exempted from deciding who exactly had performed the massacre. The use of the term 'agent' requires some clarifications. Evidently, the Commission did not demand the armed group's organ-like hierarchical connection with the State, that is, the latter's control over the armed group, but a close collaboration of the regular forces with the armed group's conduct, which brings the case under the scope of Article 8 ASR. The ICJ also considers the presence of regular State forces in the armed groups' military operations to be strong evidence for the State's effective control over the armed groups' atrocities.[63] The International Commission of Inquiry in Darfur noted in its final report

[60] See *Bosnian Genocide Case*, above note 40, para. 400: 'It must however be shown that this "effective control" was exercised, or that the State's instructions were given, in respect of each operation in which the alleged violations occurred, not generally in respect of the overall actions taken by the persons or groups of persons having committed the violations.'

[61] *Corporación Colectivo de Abogados 'José Alvear Restrepo' v. Republic of Colombia*, Case 11.645, Report No. 62/01, Inter-American Commission on Human Rights, OEA/Ser.L/V/II.111 Doc. 20 rev. at 758 (6 April 2001), para. 51; see also *Case Monsignor Oscar Arnulfo Romero Y Galdámez v. El Salvador*, Case 11.481, Inter-American Commission on Human Rights, OEA/Ser.L/V/II.106 Doc. 3 rev. at 671 (13 April 2000), para. 64.

[62] *Riofrío Massacre*, above note 61, para. 52.

[63] See *Bosnian Genocide Case*, above note 40, paras. 411–412.

of January 2005: 'When militias attack jointly with the armed forces, it can be held that they act under the effective control of the Government'.[64] From all this follows that the effective control criterion presupposes the presence of a significant number of regular State forces when the armed group commits atrocities in violation of international humanitarian law. Without this presence, the effective control of the State over specific humanitarian law violations of the armed groups is almost impossible to prove.

These findings do not sideline the overall control test applied by the ICTY in its *Tadić* Judgment. Given that the ICTY required overall control of the State (Yugoslavia) over the armed group (Bosnian Serbs) and not over the latter's specific acts, the overall control test does not substantiate Article 8 ASR but Article 4 ASR. Consequently, the *Tadić* test does not challenge the *Nicaragua* test II (Article 8 ASR) but the *Nicaragua* test I (Article 4 ASR: de facto organs).[65] At this point, the question arises whether international practice and jurisprudence supports the view that – in line with the *Nicaragua* test I – the complete dependence of de facto organs on the State is required in order to attribute all acts including those which are *ultra vires* (Article 7 ASR), or whether overall control suffices (*Tadić* test). The requirement of total dependency appears justifiable if logically linked with the *de iure* organ's status directly addressed in Article 4 ASR. Regular State forces are organs according to the State's internal law and operate under the direct authority of the State; military de facto organs – even though lacking the legal status – must be equally under the military authority of the State which includes the real authority to impose and enforce instructions regarding operational conduct. This interpretation is in line with Article 6 ASR, which deals with *de iure* organs placed at the disposal of another State: in order to be 'placed at the disposal' pursuant to Article 6 ASR, the regular forces of the sending State must operate under the military authority of the receiving State.[66] Translated into military language, the ICJ's understanding of

[64] International Commission of Inquiry in Darfur, 'Report to the UN Secretary-General of 25 January 2005' (25 January 2005), UN Doc. S/2005/60, para. 123. The explicit (not cited) reference to the ICTY *Tadić* Judgment is explained by the fact that Antonio Cassese was not only chairing judge of the ICTY and as such responsible for the *Tadić* Judgment but also chairman of the International Commission of Inquiry in Darfur.

[65] S. Talmon, 'The Responsibility of Outside Powers for Acts if Secessionist Entities' (2009) 58 *International and Comparative Law Quarterly* 493, at 507.

[66] International Law Commission, Commentary on State Responsibility, above note 46, Article 6 para. 3.

absolute dependency of de facto organs is the State's power of operational and tactical command and control over the armed group.[67] It is the State that issues operational directives, assigns tasks and deploys the armed group in order to achieve the operational goals. The State's military authority over the armed group derives from the integration of the latter into the State's chain of command. The European Court of Human Rights in its 1996 *Loizidou* Judgment on the merits of the case – referred to by the ICTY in order to support the overall control test – took a different path when qualifying the local authorities of Northern Cyprus as an administration 'subordinated' to Turkey.[68] Based on the fact that the Turkish forces were engaged in active long-term duties all over Northern Cyprus, the Court concluded that Turkey exercised 'effective overall control' throughout the territory. This may put Turkey in the position of having decisive influence over local politics and actions but does not necessarily deprive the local authority of a certain degree of real autonomy.[69] It was the effective overall territorial control that entailed, according to the European Court of Human Rights, Turkey's responsibility for all activities of the local Northern Cyprian authorities regardless of whether Turkish authorities had knowledge of specific acts.[70] Considering the details of the case, it is safe to say that the local authorities were regarded as de facto organs of Turkey and therefore fall within the extended scope of Article 4 ASR (see above).[71]

Irrespective of whether the *Loizidou* Judgment is convincing in all of its details, it is obvious that the European Court of Human Rights dealt with the very specific situation of an occupying power in relation to its domestic puppet regime. Armed groups' atrocities in a territory effectively governed

[67] For comparison, see the operational and tactical command and control of the United Nations over national UN Peacekeeping contingents, *de iure* organs of the sending States. United Nations Department for Peacekeeping Operations, 'Authority, Command and Control in United Nations Peace Operations' (February 2008), www.peacekeepingbestpractices.unlb.org/PBPS/Library/Authority, Command and Control in UN PKOs FINAL SIGNED 15 Feb 08.pdf.

[68] *Loizidou v. Turkey* (Judgment) Application No. 15318/89, European Court of Human Rights, 18 December 1996, para. 52.

[69] Talmon, 'Responsibility of Outside Powers', above note 65, at 511.

[70] *Loizidou Case,* above note 68, para. 62.

[71] Talmon, 'Responsibility of Outside Powers', above note 65, at 510; S. Talmon, *Kollektive Nichtanerkennung illegaler Staaten* (Tübingen: Mohr Siebeck Verlag, 2006), at 522; A. de Hoogh, 'Articles 4 and 8 of the 2001 International Law Commission Articles on State Responsibility, the Tadić Case and Attribution of Acts of Bosnian Serb Authorities to the Federal Republic of Yugoslavia' (2001) 72 *British Yearbook of International Law* 255, at 273.

or controlled by the sponsoring State may lower the control standard for de facto organs as advocated by the European Court,[72] if only for reasons of judicial pragmatism. In the *Tadić* Judgment, however, the ICTY dealt with State support of an armed group operating in the adjacent State. As for the remaining case law referred to by the ICTY in order to substantiate its overall control test, they are equally ill-matched. Especially the extensively cited *Yeager* Case of the Iran-United States Claims Tribunal concerns a situation that falls within the scope of Article 9 ASR,[73] given that the newly established post-revolutionary government of Iran tolerated the government-like authority exercised by the irregular Revolutionary Guards within Iranian territory.[74] All of this reflects badly on a possible development in law with regard to the degree of control over de facto organs (Article 4 ASR) if the potential de facto organ operates outside of the territory of the sponsoring State. As if this were not enough, the *Tadić* Case of the ICTY and all subsequent criminal judgments[75] confirm that the overall control test does not reflect proper international judicial practice to demonstrate the legal development within the scope of Article 4 ASR. The ICTY, as already pointed out, was neither concerned with the legal attribution of unlawful acts in order to determine the State's responsibility for this act, nor was the ICTY case law prejudicial for the determination of de facto organs. Therefore, it remains to be seen if human rights bodies or judicial organs concerned with State responsibility will build on *Tadić* and will utilize the overall control test within the extended scope of Article 4 ASR. This is not unlikely given that the *Nicaragua* test I, requiring complete dependency of de facto organs, would lead to unsatisfactory results, especially in human rights contexts. Besides, lowering the degree of control for de facto organs to overall control does not expose the law of State responsibility to inconsistencies. Provided that this mode of reasoning has any relevance in international law, there is no demand from logical necessity that the qualification as a de facto organ (Article 4 ASR) requires

72 De Hoogh, 'Articles 4 and 8', above note 71, at 287.

73 Cf. International Law Commission, Commentary, above note 46, Article 9, para. 2.

74 *Kenneth P. Yeager v. Islamic Republic of Iran* (1987) 17 Iran-United States Claims Tribunal Reports vol. IV 92, para. 45.

75 The overall-control test of the Appeals Chamber in the *Tadić* Case is now settled jurisprudence at the ICTY. See *Prosecutor v. Aleksovski* (Judgment), Case No. IT-95-14/1-A (24 March 2000), paras. 131–134; *Prosecutor v. Delalić* et al. *(Ĉelebici Case)* (Judgment), Case No. IT-96-21-A (20 February 2001), para. 26; *Prosecutor v. Naletilić and Martinović* (Judgment), Case No. IT-98-34-T (18 March 2003), para. 183; *Prosecutor v. Brđanin* (Judgment), Case No. IT-99-36-T (1 September 2004), para. 124.

a higher degree of State control than the attribution of specific non-State acts (Article 8 ASR).

3.4. *A new rule of attribution? The harbouring test*

Returning to the armed conflicts in the Great Lakes Region, it is worth noting that in light of the facts at hand, most cases of armed group support in the region do not meet the requirements of the overall control test (*Tadić* test). Even the ICTY does not consider the mere financing and equipping of armed groups as sufficient to consider them de facto organs and justify the attribution of their conduct.[76] The same is valid under the ICJ's absolute dependency understanding of Article 4 ASR (*Nicaragua* test I) and its effective control approach under Article 8 ASR (*Nicaragua* test II).

The discussed rules of legal attribution relating to acts of de facto organs (Article 4 ASR) and non-organs (Article 8 ASR) are not necessarily conclusive since new rules of attribution may emanate from recent State practice, for example, in answer to 'private' military bases on the territory of the sponsoring State. As pointed out, many States in the Great Lakes Region support armed groups by providing safe havens within their territories. It is, however, difficult to evidence that international practice is moving towards a 'harbouring test' as the basis of attribution.

Harbouring as a possible new rule of attribution has been extensively discussed[77] in the course of the 2001 Afghanistan war when the international community accepted the argument of the United States that the use of armed force against Afghanistan was an act of self-defence.[78] Article 51 UN Charter, according to the traditional understanding, requires that the use of force in self-defence must be a response to an armed attack

[76] *Tadić* Case, above note 48, para. 145.

[77] From the wide range of literature see, for example, T. Becker, *Terrorism and the State*, above note 43, at 231 et seq.; G. Travalio and J. Altenburg, 'State Responsibility for Sponsorship of Terrorist and Insurgent Groups: Terrorism: State Responsibility and the Use of Military Force' (2003) 4 *Chicago Journal of International Law* 97, at 102 et seq.; R. Grote, 'Between Crime Prevention or Prosecution and the Laws of War: Are the Traditional Categories of International Law Adequate for Assessing the Use of Force against International Terrorists?', in C. Walter et al. (eds.), *Terrorism as a Challenge for National and International Law: Security v. Liberty* (Heidelberg: Springer Verlag, 2004), 951–87, at 974.

[78] See the Letter from the United States Representative to the United Nations to the President of the Security Council (7 October 2001), UN Doc. S/2001/946; for further references, see notes 82–84 below.

attributable to a State.[79] This, in Judge Kooijmans' words, 'has been the generally accepted interpretation for more than 50 years'.[80] However, the armed attack against the United States, the terrorist attacks of September 11th, were the deeds of Al-Qaida, a terrorist group allegedly harboured but not controlled by the government of Afghanistan. Indeed, the United States did not even accuse the Afghan government of having exercised any kind of control over Al-Qaida.[81] Neither has the United States given serious consideration to Al-Qaida's possible status as a de facto organ of Afghanistan. It was the harbouring of the terrorist group in Afghanistan that made the State of Afghanistan a legitimate target for acts of self-defence in the eyes of NATO,[82] the Organisation of American States,[83] the UN[84] and the vast majority of UN member States. Security Council Resolutions 1368 (2001) and 1373 (2001), both of them drafted by the United States but unanimously adopted by the Council, especially provoked Judge Kooijmans to observe in his Separate Opinion in the *Armed Activities* Case that the traditional understanding of Article 51 UN Charter appears no longer to be shared by the Security Council.[85]

Indeed, it cannot be denied that the attacks of September 11th and the empathetic reactions of the international community have left their marks on the interpretation of Article 51 UN Charter. However, this period of empathy from the international community was not necessarily the hour of birth of a new rule of attribution linked to the harbouring of terrorists. The wording of Article 51 UN Charter is broad enough to absorb, as a result of the newly emerged State practice, the right to self-defence against an act of non-State violence under the condition that the State gives the private authors of the armed attack refuge on its territory. Even though the harbouring State's territorial integrity is impinged by the act of self-defence, the harbouring State is barred from claiming a violation of the prohibition to use force (Article 2(4) UN Charter) since it allows

[79] F. Mégret, 'War? Legal Semantics and the Move to Violence' (2002) 13 *European Journal of International Law* 361, at 379.

[80] *Legal Consequences of the Construction of a Wall in the Occupied Palestinian Territory* (Advisory Opinion) [2004] ICJ Reports 136, Separate Opinion of Judge Kooijmans, para. 35.

[81] E. Nielsen, 'State Responsibility for Terrorist Groups' (2010/11) 17 *UC Davis Journal of International Law and Policy* 151, at 173.

[82] Statement by the North Atlantic Council (2001) 40 ILM 1267.

[83] Organization of American States, 'On Terrorist Threats to the Americans' (2001) 40 ILM 1273.

[84] UNSC Resolution 1368 (12 September 2001); UNSC Resolution 1373 (28 September 2001).

[85] *Armed Activities Case*, above note 9, Separate Opinion of Judge Kooijmans, para. 28.

the terrorist groups to launch armed attacks against other States. The legal problems associated with such 'extraterritorial law enforcement'[86] under the legal umbrella of Article 51 UN Charter are manifold and do not concern this contribution. This is evident from that fact that an instant customary rule attributing an armed attack launched by a non-State actor to the harbouring State would constitute *lex specialis* for the purpose of self-defence. In other words, it would be a legal element of a primary rule of international law which defines the prerequisites of the right to self-defence. To argue that harbouring constitutes a new rule of attribution that triggers the responsibility of the harbouring State in all fields of international law, including international humanitarian law, overstretches the significance of the Afghanistan war for the development of general international law.

4. State responsibility for the support of armed groups

Given that a broad spectrum of State support for armed groups – especially the harbouring, financing, logistical help and transfer of arms – does not trigger the direct responsibility of these States for the atrocities committed by the benefiting armed groups, the support itself must be put to a legality test. The international responsibility for the State's complicity in private wrongdoing is another field of legal uncertainties. Article 16 ASR addresses responsibility for acts of aid and assistance, but only in inter-State relations.[87] It is interesting to note that in the *Bosnian Genocide* Case, the ICJ showed a certain generosity when utilizing Article 16 ASR in the context of Article III(e) of the Genocide Convention[88] in order to determine whether Serbia-Montenegro was responsible for the genocidal acts commissioned by the army of Republika Srpska.[89] However, the ICJ was far from suggesting that by way of analogy Article 16 ASR could be simply extended to all cases of State aid and assistance granted to private actors. There are compelling reasons for restraint: Article 16 ASR requires that the benefiting State has committed an internationally wrongful act (for which it is internationally responsible) with the help and the

[86] Y. Dinstein, *War, Aggression and Self-Defence* (Cambridge: Cambridge University Press, 2005), at 244.

[87] See the contribution of H. P. Aust, 'Complicity in Violations of International Humanitarian Law', Chapter 19 in this volume, at 460 et seq.

[88] Convention on the Prevention and Punishment of the Crime of Genocide, New York, 9 December 1948, in force 12 January 1951, 78 U.N.T.S. 277.

[89] *Bosnian Genocide Case*, above note 40, para. 420.

knowledge of the supporting State. However, clear-cut legal obligations under international law whose violation triggers the international responsibility of the benefiting private armed group are exceedingly rare.[90] In addition, Article 16 ASR establishes the international wrongfulness of complicity on the level of secondary rules of State responsibility.[91] Consequently, the provision is subsidiary to primary rules imposing an international obligation not to aid or assist armed groups under the conditions set out in this rule.[92] Article 1 of the American Convention on Human Rights is such a primary rule, which has been extensively used by the Inter-American Court of Human Rights when confronted with the policy of some Latin American States to aid and to shield paramilitary groups engaged in civilian massacres. In the 2005 *Mapiripán Massacre* Case, the Court observed that 'international responsibility may arise also from the acts of individuals, which, in principle, are not attributable to the State. The State Parties to the Convention have *erga omnes* obligations to respect protective provisions and to ensure the effectiveness of the rights set forth therein under any circumstances and regarding all persons'.[93]

Proceeding from this general observation on the State's primary obligation under Article 1(1) of the Convention, the Court noted that, while the acts that took place in Mapiripán were committed exclusively by members of paramilitary groups, the massacre could not have been conceived and carried out without State support. The collaboration, acquiescence and tolerance by the armed forces of the State, including a number of high officials whose action or lack thereof, was vital in making the massacre possible.[94] Hence, Colombia was found to be responsible for the acts committed by the paramilitary group due to the non-fulfilment of its *erga omnes* treaty obligations to ensure the effective exercise of human rights

[90] D. Amoroso, 'Moving towards Complicity as a Criterion of Attribution of Private Conduct: Imputation of States of Corporate Abuses in the United States Case Law' (2011) 24 *Leiden Journal of International Law* 989, at 994.

[91] H. P. Aust, *Complicity and the Law of State Responsibility* (Cambridge: Cambridge University Press, 2011), at 273.

[92] On the relation between the primary/secondary norm distinction and its relation to the *lex specialis* principle, see A. Gourgourinis, 'General/Particular International Law and Primary/Secondary Rules: Unitary Terminology of a Fragmented System' (2011) 22 *European Journal of International Law* 993, at 1025 et seq; for a *lex specialis* relation between the American Convention on Human Rights and the law of State responsibility, see *Case of the Mapiripán Massacre* (Judgment) Inter-American Court of Human Rights Series C No. 134 (15 September 2005), para. 107.

[93] Ibid. para. 111. [94] Ibid. para. 120.

in relations among individuals.[95] Even though the case law is far from conclusive, the Court seems to differentiate between the 'attribution of responsibility'[96] – that is, the responsibility of a State for a wrongful act irrespective of who committed the act – and the 'attribution of conduct' addressed in Articles 4 through 11 ASR.[97] The latter category comprises not only atrocities committed by armed groups under the effective control of State organs[98] but also the unlawful support and shielding of armed groups' acts by public authorities ('complicity'). The former category ('the attribution of responsibility') comprises all cases where the State failed to respect protective human rights ('due diligence').[99] In this case, the Court considered the State responsible for the consequences of private misconduct. Irrespective of whether the Inter-American Court of Human Rights overstretches the responsibility scheme under the Convention, it is safe to say that primary rules may blur or even remove the traditional divide between the public and the private sphere.

Article 1(1) of the American Convention on Human Rights, the linchpin of the Court's rulings, obliges States parties 'to ensure to all persons subject to their jurisdiction the free and full exercise of those rights and freedoms'. This wording is not too removed from Article 1 Common to all four Geneva Conventions, which stipulates: 'The High Contracting Parties undertake to respect and to ensure respect for the present Convention in all circumstances'. Given that no (judicial) treaty organ has been entrusted by States parties with the authoritative interpretation of the Geneva Conventions, the exact scope of Common Article 1 to the Geneva Conventions (GC) remains subject to controversies and legal uncertainties.[100] ICJ case law does not encourage an overly broad and idealism-driven application of the provision. In the 1986 *Nicaragua* Judgment, the Court found that the United States supported the Contras

95 Ibid. para. 123.

96 *Case of the Pueblo Bello Massacre* (Judgment) Inter American Court of Human Rights Series C No. 140 (31 January 2006), paras. 113, 133.

97 For this distinction, see Amoroso, 'Moving Towards Complicity', above note 90, at 993; International Law Commission, Commentary on the Draft Articles on the Responsibility of International Organizations, Yearbook of the International Law Commission vol. II, part 2 (2011), at 55, para. 3.

98 See Section 3.3 of this chapter.

99 *Velásquez-Rodríguez v. Honduraz* (Judgment) Inter-American Court of Human Rights Series C No. 4 (28 July 1988), para. 172.

100 See the contribution of R. Geiß, 'Common Article 1 of the Geneva Conventions: Scope and Content of the Obligation to 'Ensure Respect' – 'Narrow but Deep' or 'Wide and Shallow'?', Chapter 18 in this volume, at 422 et seq.

extensively by recruiting, training, arming, equipping, financing and supplying them with arms;[101] in light of these findings, it is noteworthy that the Court was content with pointing out that the distribution of the United States warfare manual on psychological operations[102] was contrary to Common Article 1 GC because it encouraged the Contras to act in violation of Common Article 3 of the four 1949 Geneva Conventions.[103] The limited application of Common Article 1 GC by the ICJ must not be regarded as an insignificant detail in a complex Judgment. The Court instead exhibited a very specific notion of the scope of Common Article 1 GC: first, Common Article 1 GC applies not only to international but also to internal conflicts, at least to the extent that the latter are covered by Common Article 3 GC.[104] Second, States parties are obliged to ensure respect for the Convention by armed groups, even if the latter are not subject to the jurisdiction of that State, which provides Common Article 1 GC with an extraterritorial reach.[105] And third, the support provided by the State must encourage[106] armed

[101] *Nicaragua Case*, above note 37, para. 228.

[102] *Nicaragua Case*, above note 37, para. 255.

[103] *Nicaragua Case*, above note 37, paras. 220, 256.

[104] This is also the dominating view in academic writing. L. Boisson de Chazournes and L. Condorelli, 'Common Article 1 of the Geneva Conventions Revisited: Protecting Collective Interests' (2000) 82 *International Review of the Red Cross* 67; H. Tonkin, *State Control over Private Military and Security Companies in Armed Conflict* (Cambridge: Cambridge University Press, 2011), at 128; D. Fleck, 'International Accountability for Violations of the Ius in Bello: Impact of the ICRC Study on Customary International Humanitarian Law' (2006) 11 *Journal of Conflict and Security Law* 179, at 182.

[105] For acceptance of this understanding, see also the Montreux Document on Pertinent International Legal Obligations and Good Practice for States Relating to Operations of Private Military and Security Companies during Armed Conflict of 17 September 2008, which states in No. 3 that Contracting States have an obligation, within their power, to ensure respect for international humanitarian law by private military and security companies they contract, in particular to: (b) not encourage or assist in, and take appropriate measures to prevent, any violations of international humanitarian law by personnel of private military and security companies. UN Doc. A/63/467. See also Tonkin, *State Control*, above note 104, at 130; Tonkin, 'Common Article 1', note above 16, at 787.

[106] Cf. B. Kessler, 'The Duty to 'Ensure Respect' under Common Article 1 of the Geneva Conventions: Its Implications on International and Non-International Armed Conflicts' (2001) 44 *German Yearbook of International Law* 498, at 503. Judge Schwebel, in his Dissenting Opinion to the *Nicaragua* Judgment, rejected the Court's finding that under customary international humanitarian law, the encouragement of the commission of war crimes was an internationally wrongful act. *Nicaragua Case*, above note 37, Dissenting Opinion of Judge Schwebel, para. 259. For support of his opinion, Schwebel cited International Law Commission Special Rapporteur R. Ago, *Yearbook of the International Law*

groups' behaviour contrary to their obligations under humanitarian law and this 'encouragement was offered to persons in circumstances where the commission of such acts was likely or foreseeable'.[107] This excerpt of the *Nicaragua* Judgment deserves closer scrutiny. Whether the supportive measures must be regarded as an encouragement to commit acts in violation of Common Article 3 GC must be assessed on the basis of objective criteria. In the *Nicaragua* Case, the United States manual openly advised to 'neutralize' certain 'carefully selected and planned targets' such as judges.[108] However, not every act of encouragement or incitement is, according to the ICJ, unlawful under Common Article 1 GC.[109] Without finding support in the compact wording of Common Article 1 GC, the ICJ introduced a second element commonly associated with the causality link between wrongdoing and injury (Article 31 ASR) as well as due diligence obligations:[110] the commission of acts contrary to humanitarian law by the armed groups must be 'likely and foreseeable' for the State organs at the time their act of encouragement is performed. This is the case when the armed groups have already been engaged in humanitarian law violations and the encouraging State organs are fully aware of the fact.

It is interesting to note that in contrast to Article 1 GC, the foreseeability of war crimes does not suffice within the normative framework of Article 16 ASR, the general rule on complicity.[111] According to its prevailing interpretation, Article 16 ASR requires not only the State's intent

Commission vol. II, part 1 (1978), at 54, paras. 62–63 (Commentary to Draft Article 25 on complicity of a State in the internationally wrongful act of another State).

107 *Nicaragua Case*, above note 37, para. 256. 108 Ibid. para. 255.

109 But see the much broader customary law rule elaborated on by J.-M. Henckaerts and L. Doswald-Beck (eds.), *Customary International Humanitarian Law*, 2 vols. (Cambridge: Cambridge University Press, 2009), vol. I, at 509, Rule 144 ('States may not encourage violations of international humanitarian law by parties to armed conflict. They must exert their influence, to the degree possible, to stop violations of international humanitarian law').

110 This is the so-called proximate causation. For details, see L. Castellanos-Jankiewicz, 'Causation and International State Responsibility', Amsterdam Center for International Law, Research Paper No 2012–07 (SHARES Series), at 57–58, www.sharesproject.nl/wp-content/uploads/2012/01/Castellanos-Causation-and-International-State-Responsibility1.pdf. In the context of the duty to prevent harm, the International Law Commission regards the 'forseeability' of a possible harm as a 'general principle'. See International Law Commission Commentary on Article 3 of the Draft Articles on Prevention of Transboundary Harm for Hazardous Activities, Yearbook of the International Law Commission, vol. II, part 2 (2001), at 153, para. 5.

111 For a different opinion see V. Lowe, 'Responsibility for the Conduct of Other States' (2002) 101 *Japanese Journal of International Law and Diplomacy* 1, at 8.

to collaborate in the commission of the unlawful act but also the State's knowledge how the benefiting State – or armed group – intends to utilize the support.[112] Along this line is the ICJ's interpretation of Article III(e) of the Genocide Convention which prohibits complicity in genocide: '[A]n accomplice must have given support in perpetrating the genocide with full knowledge of the facts'.[113] In contrast, the *Nicaragua* Judgment neither requires the intent of State organs to facilitate the commission of specific war crimes nor the positive knowledge of State organs that the benefiting group actually plans to employ the support in such a manner. If the past behaviour of the armed group is meaningful enough and details are known to the sponsoring State, the commission of future war crimes is likely and foreseeable. Nonetheless, it would be wrong to conclude that – on the basis of the ICJ jurisprudence – Common Article 1 GC covers all kinds of support for armed group provided that the armed group's infamous reputation is well known.[114] Given that the ICJ focused on the United States manual on psychological operations and set aside all other forms of United States support such as arming, training and financing of the Contras the relevant acts under Common Article 1 GC must qualify as an encouragement or incitement to commit war crimes. Harbouring and financing as well as logistic support for armed groups do not per se meet this requirement; they may incite armed activities but not necessarily violations of Common Article 3 GC. The same is valid for the transfer of arms and the training of combatants if assessed in isolation. If, however, the specific type of arms or the characteristics of the training or logistic support display a clear encouragement to continuously disregard the obligation under Common Article 3 GC, the responsibility of the aiding State under Article 1 GC is established. Yet, the linkage between the support of warfare and the encouragement to commit war crimes is difficult to prove. It therefore comes as no surprise that the ICJ did not even mention Common Article 1 GC in the 2005 *Armed Activities* Case, despite the fact that Uganda had admitted to the military support of rebel groups in the DRC.

112 R. Ago, Seventh Report on State Responsibility, Yearbook of the International Law Commission vol. II, part 1 (1978), at 58, para. 72; International Law Commission, Commentary on State Responsibility, above note 46, Article 16, paras. 4–5; for details see the contribution of Aust, 'Complicity', above note 87, at 451.

113 *Bosnian Genocide Case*, above note 40, para. 432.

114 That does not mean that instigating armed groups' activities in another State's internal conflicts is not prohibited under customary international law. See 'Friendly Relations Declaration', above note 14, Principle 1, para. 9.

5. State responsibility for the failure to prevent armed groups' atrocities

On the basis of the foregoing considerations, the question remains whether the State is responsible for not having done everything in its power to prevent the commission of war crimes by the armed groups it sponsors. Apparently, the ICJ gives no consideration to the idea of merging the obligation of States not to assist armed groups in the commission of war crimes under the ambit of Common Article 1 GC with the obligation under the due diligence principles to prevent armed groups from committing war crimes in foreign territory. Neither the 1986 *Nicaragua* Judgment nor the 2005 *Armed Activities* Judgment addresses the latter aspect. At first glance, the Court's reluctance appears reasonable given that the due diligence principle usually operates under the condition that a State has territorial jurisdiction which enables its public authorities to prevent private wrongdoing.[115] In the *Armed Activities* Case, for example, the ICJ held that Uganda, as an occupying power, bore the duty to take appropriate measures to prevent the acts of violence perpetrated by private parties in the Congolese region under its military control (Article 43 Hague Regulations of 1907[116]).[117] It is undeniable, however, that the wording of Common Article 1 GC – especially the phrase 'to ensure respect for the present Convention in all circumstances' – implies an extraterritorial scope of the due diligence obligation with regard to private wrongdoing.[118] This understanding is in line with the ICJ's notion of Common Article 1 GC regarding acts of encouragement as displayed in the 1986 *Nicaragua* Judgment.[119] The 2007 *Bosnia Genocide* Judgment also indirectly supports the extraterritorial application of the due diligence obligation under Common Article 1 GC, even though the Court was eager to discourage any general implications of its interpretation of Article I of the Genocide Convention regarding other international due

[115] See *Trail Smelter* Arbitral Tribunal (Decision) (March 1941) 35 *American Journal of International Law* 674, at 716; *Corfu Channel Case*, above note 16, at 18; see also Tonkin, 'Common Article 1', above note 16, at 790.

[116] Convention (IV) Respecting the Laws and Customs of War on Land and its Annex: Regulations Concerning the Laws and Customs of War on Land, The Hague, 18 October 1907, in force 26 January 1910, 3 Martens Nouveau Recueil (ser. 3) 461.

[117] *Armed Activities Case*, above note 9, para. 178.

[118] This applies to those obligations within the restraints of international law. Kessler, 'Article 1 of the Geneva Conventions', above note 106, at 507–09, 511–16.

[119] *Nicaragua Case*, above note 37.

diligence obligations.[120] First of all, the Court held that Yugoslavia (or Serbia-Montenegro) violated its obligation to prevent the genocide in Srebrenica committed by the Bosnian Serbs even though Yugoslavia had no effective control over this area. In addition, the Court made it clear that the crucial determining factor of the due diligence obligation is the State's capacity to effectively influence the acts of armed groups.[121] This capacity may suffer – as the Court noted – from the geographical distance between the State and the armed group's scene of activities.[122]

With regard to States that support armed groups with weaponry, logistics, safe haven and money, it is important to emphasize that the obligation to prevent war crimes does not per se outlaw support for armed groups.[123] The violation of the obligation to prevent does not result from positive action but from the failure to act – sins of omission as opposed to sins of commission.[124] It is rather a question of whether the sponsoring State has effective influence over the armed group's behaviour due to the financial or military support provided by the State and whether the State could have reasonably been aware, due to the specific circumstances such as past behaviour of the armed group, of the serious risks of war crimes ('foreseeablity').[125] If first, the supporting State's effective influence has been established, for example, owing to the strength of the political, military and financial links between the State and the armed group,[126] and second, the State has an awareness concerning the armed group's behaviour which should voice serious concerns within the State,[127] then the failure to cut off the support amounts to a violation of Common Article 1 GC.

6. International responsibility of armed groups

All that has been said so far reveals that the traditional State-centred rules of responsibility bring about a 'responsibility gap', the effects of

[120] *Bosnian Genocide Case*, above note 40, para. 429.

[121] Ibid. para. 430. [122] Ibid. para. 430.

[123] For its unlawfulness under the UN Charter, see Section 3 of this chapter.

[124] *Bosnian Genocide Case*, above note 40, para. 432.

[125] Ibid. para. 436. For the foreseeability criterion, see also *Keenan v. United Kingdom* (Judgment) Application No. 27229/95, European Court of Human Rights, 30 April 2001, para. 90: 'knew or ought to have known'.

[126] Cf. *Bosnian Genocide Case*, above note 40, para. 434.

[127] Cf. *Bosnian Genocide Case*, above note 40, para. 438.

which can be seen in the Great Lakes Region.[128] As a rule, the State targeted by the armed group's military operations is not responsible for the latter's humanitarian law violations. The State's due diligence obligation to protect civilians from atrocities committed by armed groups operating on its territory (Common Article 1 GC[129]) may still exist although it is made practicably impossible by the State's lack of law enforcement capabilities in combat zones that are characteristic of internal armed conflicts of high-level intensity.[130] One can even argue that Additional Protocol II to the Geneva Conventions shifts the responsibility to prevent war crimes to the armed group provided that they have effective control over a part of the State's territory (Article 1 Additional Protocol II).[131] States which support the armed group in their civil strife escape responsibility for the latter's atrocities thanks to rigid rules of attribution. A State's responsibility for having assisted armed groups in their humanitarian law violations and for not having done everything in its power to prevent humanitarian law violations complements the protection of civilians under the Geneva Convention but does not bring about the State's obligation to take responsibility for the atrocities themselves. All of this calls for the international responsibility of the armed group, the actual perpetrator of the humanitarian law violations.

6.1. *Group responsibility for the violation of humanitarian law*

If an armed group participates in an internal armed conflict addressed in Common Article 3 GC or Additional Protocol II and fulfils the group-specific requirements set out in these provisions, the armed group's obligations under international humanitarian law are relatively well defined. Thus, its responsibility under international law for the failure to comply with its own legal obligations appears to be a self-evident result of logical deduction: where there is an international legal obligation, there is – in the case of a breach – international responsibility (*ubi responsabilitas,*

[128] Or 'accountability gap'. Cf. L. Zegveld, *Accountability of Armed Opposition Groups in International Law* (Cambridge: Cambridge University Press, 2001), part 2.

[129] For the responsibility of every State to protect its own population from war crimes, see UNGA, 'World Summit Outcome of 15 September 2005' (15 September 2005) Resolution 60/1, para. 138; cf. also *Case of Ergi v. Turkey* (Judgment) Application No. 66/1997/850/1057, European Court of Human Rights, 28 July 1998, para. 79.

[130] Kessler, 'Article 1 of the Geneva Conventions', above note 106, at 508.

[131] Zegveld, *Accountability of Armed Opposition Groups*, above note 128, at 218.

ibi ius).[132] Providing the collective responsibility of armed groups with a sound legal basis, however, is not as simple as that.[133] International practice has not specified the 'new legal relationship'[134] arising from the armed group's violation of Common Article 3 GC or other international humanitarian law obligations. Clear-cut rules pertaining to attribution, wrongfulness and legal consequences are still remote. It even seems that States are reluctant to explicitly hold armed groups responsible so as not to emphasize the legal personality of non-State actors under international law.[135] This was probably not the ulterior motive of the ICJ when addressing the devastating role of armed groups in the Congolese conflict.[136] Nonetheless, the ICJ's cautious language speaks volumes:

> [The Court] observes that the actions of the various parties in the complex conflict in the DRC have contributed to the immense suffering faced by the Congolese population. The Court is painfully aware that many atrocities have been committed in the course of the conflict. It is incumbent on all those involved in the conflict to support the peace process in the DRC and other peace processes in the Great Lakes area, in order to ensure respect for human rights in the region.[137]

The Security Council does not leave it at that but directly approaches the responsibility of armed groups in the DRC. The sources of their numerous legal obligations, however, remain vague. The Security Council

> *[d]emands* that all armed groups, in particular Forces Démocratiques de Libération du Rwanda (FDLR) and the Lord's Resistance Army (LRA), immediately cease all forms of violence and human rights abuses against the civilian population in the DRC, in particular against women and children, including rape and other forms of sexual abuse, and demobilize.[138]

[132] A. Pellet, 'The Definition of Responsibility in International Law', in Crawford, Pellet and Olleson (eds.), *International Responsibility*, above note 18, 3–16, at 4.

[133] For an excellent survey on the topic see Zegveld, *Accountability of Armed Opposition Groups*, above note 128, at 133 et seq.

[134] International Law Commission, Commentary on State Responsibility, above note 46, Article 1, para. 3.

[135] Most ceasefire or peace agreements concluded with insurrectional groups that contain mutual commitments to respect human rights and humanitarian law are not explicitly labeled as international agreements creating rights and duties under international law. For details, see K. Schmalenbach, 'Article 3', in Dörr/Schmalenbach (eds.), *Vienna Convention on the Law of Treaties, A Commentary* (Heidelberg: Springer Verlag, 2012), 49–81, at paras. 52–56.

[136] *Armed Activities Case*, above note 9, para. 221.

[137] *Armed Activities Case*, above note 9, para. 221.

[138] UNSC Res 1991 (29 June 2011), operative para. 13. Declaring demands like, addressed to 'all parties' to the conflict, this is the constant practice of the Security Council.

By contrast, the Inter-American Commission on Human Rights provided a refreshingly precise legal assessment of the responsibility of armed groups in the 1997 *Tablada* Case:

> Unlike human rights law which generally restrains only the abusive practice of State agents, Common Article 3's mandatory provisions expressly bind and apply equally to both parties to internal conflicts, i.e. government and dissident forces: Moreover, the obligation to apply Common Articles 3 is absolute for both parties and independent of the obligations to the other. Therefore, both the MTP [Movimiento Todos por la Patria] attackers and the Argentines armed forces had the same duties under humanitarian law, and neither party could be held responsible for the acts of the other.[139]

The Inter-American Commission on Human Rights, which in 1999 declared its competence to monitor within the framework of State reports compliance of armed groups with international humanitarian law,[140] did not dwell on the prerequisites of the armed group's responsibility for violations of Common Article 3 GC. The Commission in the *Tablada* Case, however, took the opportunity to emphasise that Common Article 3 GC applies to low-intensity and open-armed confrontations between relatively well organized armed forces or groups.[141] The Security Council, in contrast, does not pay particular attention to the elements of Common Article 3 GC when pointing at armed groups' obligations in internal conflicts. In light of the ambiguous international practice, the question arises whether Common Article 3 GC and Additional Protocol II to the Geneva Conventions – that is, the primary law obligations – require a minimum level of military organization, a minimum intensity and duration of the conflict as well as the exercise of territorial control by the group, an issue

See C. Tomuschat, 'The Applicability of Human Rights Law to Insurgent Movements', in H. Fischer (ed.) *Krisensicherung und Humanitärer Schutz, Festschrift Fleck* (Berlin: Berliner Wissenschafts-Verlag 2004), 573–91, at 573.

139 *Joan Carlos Abella v. Argentina (Tablada* Case*)*, Case 11.137, Report No. 55/57, Inter-American Commission on Human Rights, OEA/Ser.L/V/II.95 Doc. 7 rev. (18 November 1997), para. 174. In the *Las Palmeras* Case, the Inter-American Court of Human Rights rejected the Commission's jurisdiction to decide a case on the basis of humanitarian law. *Case of Las Palmeras v. Colombia* (Judgment on Preliminary Objections), Inter-American Court of Human Rights Series No. 67 (4 February 2000), para. 34. For the diverging views as to whether armed groups are bound by human rights obligations, see A. Clapham, 'Human Rights Obligations of Non-State Actors in Conflict Situations' (2006) 88 *International Review of the Red Cross* 491, at 501–08.

140 Inter-American Commission on Human Rights, Third Report on the Situation of Human Rights in Colombia, OEA/Ser.L/V/II.202 Doc 2 (26 February 1999).

141 *Tablada Case*, above note 139, para. 152.

that has been extensively discussed elsewhere.[142] Within the confines of this chapter, it suffices to say that the groups' responsibility requires an entity which is – de facto or *de iure* – distinguishable from its individual members. The naming of the group by its members as well as a perceptible degree of organization, especially hierarchical structures indicates the separate legal existence of the armed group for the purpose of the law of international responsibility.

6.2. *Rules of attribution*

Armed groups are rarely established under domestic law or formally recognized as associations or political parties by national legal systems. Nonetheless, they are political and military entities which act through their agents. This means that the rules of attribution are just as vital in this context as in the context of States and international organizations – even though they are much less discussed.[143] Generally speaking, international practice is not very instructive on that score; most international bodies which are concerned with armed groups' violence do not linger over the nexus between the combatants and the armed group.[144] However, their reports suggest the obvious: that above all else, the rules of attribution pertaining to military activities focus on the military command and control structure. In his 2011 report on the Lord's Resistance Army, for example, the UN Secretary-General observed:

> Currently, it is estimated that LRA [Lord's Resistance Army] comprises less than 500 combatants operating under the command of Joseph Kony . . . In September, there were unconfirmed reports that following orders by Joseph Kony, groups of LRA combatants moved from the Democratic Republic of the Congo into eastern Central African Republic and Western Bahr el-Ghazal State in South Sudan. While Joseph Kony and Okot Odhiambo have reportedly remained in the Central African Republic, other LRA senior commanders remain highly mobile.[145]

The attempt to prove the existence of an institutional link between individual combatants and the armed group may run into practical difficulties,

[142] Zegveld, *Accountability of Armed Opposition Groups*, above note 131, at 134 et seq.

[143] But see ibid. 152–55.

[144] See, for example, 'Report of the Secretary-General on Children and Armed Conflict in Chad' (9 February 2011), UN Doc. S/2011/64; 'Report of the Secretary-General on the Lord's Resistance Army', above note 4.

[145] 'Report of the Secretary-General on the Lord's Resistance Army', above note 4, at 2, para. 8.

even though formal membership registrations may exist, these are hard to find for outsiders. Not quite so rare are traces of uniforms or badges that shed some light on the formal affiliation with and standing within the armed group. At best, the group's chain of command, tied in with the disciplinary power over individuals exercised on behalf of the group, indicates de facto membership of the group. This relationship can be compared to the position of a de facto organ within a State (Article 4 ASR).[146] With all due caution, such an analogy is straightforward if the organizational structure of the armed groups resembles that of regular State forces.[147] In all remaining cases where the position of the acting combatants within the hierarchical order of the armed group remains dubious, the effective military command becomes the focus for the rules of attribution. If a military commander can be identified and organizationally linked to the armed group, the conduct of all individual combatants acting under the commander's military command and control are attributable to the group. This does not mean, however, that the high and rigid control standards of Article 8 ASR[148] are to be simply translated lock, stock and barrel to the nascent law of group responsibility. At least the UN, as was illustrated above, takes a rather practical view on the matter of attribution when blaming armed groups for committing atrocities.

6.3. *Legal consequences of the armed group's responsibility*

The notion of a 'new legal relationship' that emerges between the injured party and the wrongdoer the very moment the internationally wrongful act occurs can be traced back to Anzilotti.[149] Since the International Law Commission breathed life into his theory, the concept is generally accepted as a suitable analytical frame for the law of international responsibility.[150] But who is the injured party that enters into the 'new legal relationship' with the infringing armed group? Would it be only the territorial State that considers the members of the armed group ordinary criminals under its domestic criminal jurisdiction? At this point, it is worth noting that the rules under the umbrella of Common Article 3

[146] See Section 3.3 of this chapter.

[147] Zegveld, *Accountability of Armed Opposition Groups*, above note 131, at 155.

[148] See Section 3.3 of this chapter.

[149] D. Anzilotti, *Corso di Diritto Internazionale*, 4th edn (Padua: CEDAM, 1955), vol. 1, at 385.

[150] International Law Commission, Commentary on State Responsibility, above note 46, Article 1, para. 3.

GC are commonly regarded as 'obligations which are essentially of an *erga omnes* character'.[151] Consequently, each State is entitled to invoke the responsibility of the armed group for the breach of Common Article 3 GC, as a member of the international community as a whole and for that reason as a right-holder in the new legal relationship (Article 48 ASR applied analogously).[152] That is all the more important given that armed groups do not enjoy jurisdictional immunity before 'foreign' national courts. However, as is often the case with *erga omnes* obligations, the absence of corresponding State practice is significant in itself.[153] With regard to the legal consequences resulting from the breach of Common Article 3 GC, many Security Council resolutions express what is reflected in Article 48(2)(a) ASR: the armed group must immediately cease the violations of humanitarian law.[154] The call to desist, however, does not address the question of reparation, which deserves greater attention. To begin with, the UN General Assembly's Resolution on Basic Principles and Guidelines on the Right to Remedy and Reparations of 2006, even though it is legally non-binding, rests on the assumption that serious violations of humanitarian law by non-State actors trigger an obligation to make reparations:

> States shall, with respect to claims by victims, enforce domestic judgments for reparation against individuals or entities liable for the harm suffered and endeavour to enforce valid foreign legal judgements for reparation in accordance with domestic law and international legal obligations. To that end, States should provide under their domestic laws effective mechanisms for the enforcement of reparation judgements.[155]

151 *Legal Consequences of the Construction of a Wall in the Occupied Palestinian Territory* (Advisory Opinion) [2004] ICJ Reports 136, para. 157; see also Kessler, 'Article 1 of the Geneva Conventions', above note 106, at 508.

152 International Law Commission, Commentary on State Responsibility, above note 46, Article 48, para. 10.

153 But see the Basic Principles and Guidelines on the Right to Remedy and Reparation for Victims of Gross Violations of International Human Rights Law and Serious Violations of International Humanitarian Law, adopted by the UNGA on 21 March 2006, UN Doc. A/RES/60/147: (c) Provide those who claim to be victims of a human rights or humanitarian law violation with equal and effective access to justice, as described below, irrespective of who may ultimately be the bearer of responsibility for the violation'.

154 To name but one example, UNSC Resolution 771 (13 August 1992) concerning the situation in Bosnia and Herzegovina, para. 3 '[d]emands that all parties and others concerned in the former Yugoslavia, and all military forces in Bosnia and Herzegovina, immediately cease and desist from all breaches of international humanitarian law'.

155 UNGA Resolution 60/147, above note 153, Chapter IX, para. 17; for an analysis see R. Dudai, 'Closing the Gap: Symbolic Reparation and Armed Groups' (2011) 93 *International Review of the Red Cross* 1, at 7–8.

Few peace agreements substantiate the armed group's obligation under international law to make reparation as a consequence of humanitarian law violations.[156] One example is the Agreement on Accountability and Reconciliation between the Government of Uganda and the Lord's Resistance Army of 29 June 2007. Clause 9.2 of the Agreement stipulates: 'The Parties agree that collective as well as individual reparations should be made to victims through mechanisms to be adopted by the Parties upon further consultation'. No information is available regarding the execution of the far-reaching reparations clause. Another example of a reparations clause that embraces armed group violence is the Darfur Peace Agreement between the Government of Sudan, the Sudan Liberation Movement and the Justice and Equality Movement, signed on 5 May 2006. According to paragraph 199 of the Agreement, 'war-affected persons in Darfur have an inalienable right to have their grievances addressed in a comprehensive manner and to receive compensation. Restitution and compensation for damages and losses shall necessitate massive mobilization of resources'. In October 2006, Sudan forwarded to the UN Security Council a Presidential decree establishing the Darfur Compensation Commission for war-affected Persons.[157]

These bits and pieces of international practice cannot hide the fact that the international obligations of armed groups to compensate their victims still lacks a solid foundation even though one could easily argue that the responsibility to make reparation is the natural consequence of the wrongdoing.[158] The ICRC Study on Customary International Humanitarian Law was not able to identify beyond doubt a rule under general international law that obliges armed groups to make full reparations.[159] On the other hand, the existing agreements on reparations cannot be treated as irrelevant; they contribute to the emerging foundations of international obligation of armed groups to make reparation in cases of humanitarian law violations.[160]

[156] See, for example, the Comprehensive Agreement on Respect for Human Rights and International Humanitarian Law in the Philippines, signed 16 March 1998 between the Government of Philippines and the National Democratic Front of the Philippines.

[157] Yearbook of the United Nations, 2006, vol. 60, at 287.

[158] E.-C. Gillard, 'Reparation for Violations of International Humanitarian Law' (2003) 85 *International Review of the Red Cross* 529, at 535.

[159] Henckaerts and Doswald-Beck, *Customary International Humanitarian Law*, above note 109, vol. I, Rule 150, at 549–50.

[160] F. Francioni and N. Ronzitti, *War by Conduct: Human Rights, Humanitarian Law and Private Contractor* (Oxford: Oxford University Press, 2011), at 260.

7. Conclusion

The Articles on the Law of State Responsibility rest on the assumption that a State is only responsible for its own conduct. State practice and jurisprudence is far from modifying or questioning this basic principle that is accompanied by traditionally rigid rules of attribution. States which have supported armed opposition groups causing civil strife and operating on foreign soil, as typified by the Great Lakes conflicts, have benefited enormously from the current state of play. Obviously, a State's responsibility for having aided in the commission of humanitarian law violations or for not having prevented them has little deterrent effect on either the sponsoring State or the supported armed group. In addition, the tangible 'responsibility gap' created by the traditional rules of attribution will continue to exist until closed by well-defined rules setting up the international responsibility of armed groups for their infringements of humanitarian law standards. Even though tentative developments in the law are perceivable, the current legal uncertainties are far too numerous to adequately address the armed groups' unabated violence in the Great Lakes Region. Therefore, it is valid to say that the inactivity of the international community of States in its function as the international law maker is one decisive factor for the palpable 'responsibility gap' for armed group violence. Bearing the numerous war victims in the Great Lakes Region in mind, this observation then raises the question of the international community's political and moral responsibility for the failure to act.

21

Conclusion

Where States fail, non-State actors rise? Inducing compliance with international humanitarian law in areas of limited statehood

HEIKE KRIEGER

1. Introduction

Many of the perpetuated armed conflicts in the Great Lakes Region in Africa take place in war-torn areas of limited statehood. Fragmented armed groups fight each other or the armed forces of a government, which represents only the remainder of collapsed State structures. These conflicts are characterized by a high number of civilian victims, often resulting from utter disregard for international humanitarian law. While the government is unable to implement and enforce rules and decisions because the State has lost its monopoly over the means of force,[1] the rise of armed, violent non-State actors collides with the State-centric traditional nature of public international law. Thus, (classical) compliance structures in international humanitarian law seem to lose their significance, as they predominantly rely on the State for law enforcement and therefore mainly accommodate States' interests when inducing compliance.[2]

However, if the State is no longer able to enforce the law or comply with it, the question arises as to who may replace the State.[3] Beginning

[1] T. Risse and T. Börzel, 'Human Rights – The New Agenda', Transworld – The Transatlantic Relationship and the Future Global Governance, Working Paper 07, December 2012, at 10; on failing States, see R. Geiß, *Failed States* (Berlin: Duncker&Humblot, 2005); D. Thürer, 'Failing States', in R. Wolfrum (ed.), *The Max Planck Encyclopedia of Public International Law* (Oxford: Oxford University Press, 2009, online edition, www.mpepil.com).

[2] In the general discussion, the terms 'compliance' and 'enforcement' are used. While 'enforcement' refers to coercive measures, 'compliance' is a broader concept which includes both hierarchical and non-hierarchical instruments. See M. Bothe, 'Compliance', in R. Wolfrum (ed.), *The Max Planck Encyclopedia of Public International Law* (Oxford: Oxford University Press, 2010, online edition, www.mpepil.com).

[3] Risse and Börzel, 'Human Rights – The New Agenda', above note 1, at 9, 11.

with an analysis of the State's restricted capabilities to induce compliance in areas of limited statehood (Section 2), this chapter submits that, to some extent, non-State actors[4] may compensate for the State's inabilities. Taking into account empirical political science studies on compliance, the chapter argues that such non-State actors have a twofold role to play: as addressees of compliance efforts as well as norm entrepreneurs and norm inducers. The chapter contends that there is no real alternative other than to engage with armed groups (Section 3). Here, despite of the conflicts' changing character, traditional incentives (reciprocity, self-interest, reputation) still matter for inducing the willingness to comply with the law. Yet a severe dilemma arises: the necessity to engage with armed groups contradicts basic interests of States in general, and of the governments concerned in particular. Since efforts to improve compliance with international humanitarian law must take into account the position and the interests of armed groups, non-State actors, NGOs in particular, have become an essential part in the overall pattern of inducing compliance, since they can act more independently of State interests (Section 4). However, even though their perceived neutrality increases their role in inducing compliance, only a mix of instruments will improve the mechanisms' effectiveness.

2. Restricted capabilities of States to induce compliance

National enforcement mechanisms seldom work appropriately in areas of limited statehood. Armies often lack a strict and stable military hierarchy; hence, military discipline is barely maintained, and the risk of mutiny is high. For instance, the armed group M23, which was responsible for a rebellion in the eastern Democratic Republic of the Congo (DRC) in 2012, consisted of soldiers who had mutinied against the Congolese State Army.[5] Moreover, it is at the very least doubtful that training and

[4] The term is used here in a broad sense, encompassing all actors which are not directly related to the State; for such a use see M. Wagner, 'Non-State Actors', in R. Wolfrum (ed.), *The Max Planck Encyclopedia of Public International Law* (Oxford: Oxford University Press, 2013, online edition, www.mpepil.com), para. 1. From a juridical perspective, the differentiation is often drawn between public actors such as the State or State-empowered international organizations, and private actors, such as transnational enterprises and non-governmental organizations. See Wagner, ibid. para. 3.

[5] N. Wilén, 'Identifying the Spoilers in the Security Sector Reform – Disarmament Demobilisation and Reintegration Process in the Congo' (2013) 29 *Defense & Security Analysis* 117, at 122.

instruction of soldiers includes an adequate introduction to international humanitarian law as envisaged in Article 83 AP I. Since the criminal justice system is often affected by the breakdown of State structures, military justice may not work as a means of enforcement either.[6] This is acknowledged by Article 17 of the Statute of the International Criminal Court (ICC Statute), which lays down the principle of complementarity. According to Article 17(1)(a), a case before the ICC is inadmissible if it is being investigated by a State that has jurisdiction, unless the State is genuinely unable to carry out the investigation. Article 17(3) of the ICC Statute defines inability as follows: 'In order to determine inability in a particular case, the Court shall consider whether, due to a total or substantial collapse or unavailability of its national judicial system, the State is unable to obtain the accused or the necessary evidence and testimony or otherwise unable to carry out its proceedings'.

Based on an interpretation of Article 17(3) of the ICC Statute, some criteria can be identified that illustrate when and why a judicial system is incapable of enforcing international humanitarian law. The Trial Chambers, the reports of the Office of the Prosecutor, as well as international human rights standards, help to shape the meaning of a substantial collapse[7] as the lack of a viable legal infrastructure, in particular with a view to protection of fair trial standards and rights of the accused; inaccessibility of the courts; insufficient material resources and experienced and independent judicial personnel; the lack of adequate operative law and of a sufficient infrastructure for investigations, in particular with a view to police capability; as well as an adequate system for the protection of victims.[8] In addition to criteria concerning the quality of the judicial system, the general situation, especially with regard to the security situation, has to be taken into account.[9] The latter criterion is particularly decisive

[6] N. Lamp, 'Conceptions of War and Paradigms of Compliance: the "New War" Challenge to International Humanitarian Law' (2011) 16 *Journal of Conflict and Security Law* 225, at 233.

[7] S. Williams and W. Schabas, 'Article 17 – Issues of Admissibility', in O. Triffterer (ed.), *Commentary on the Rome Statute of the International Criminal Court*, 2d edn (München: Beck, 2008), 605–27, at 624.

[8] UNSC, 5459th meeting (14 June 2006), UN Doc. S/PV.5459, at 3; Human Rights Watch, 'Democratic Republic of the Congo: Confronting Impunity' (January 2004), at 6, www.hrw.org/sites/default/files/reports/drc0104.pdf; W. Burke-White, 'Complementarity in Practice: The International Criminal Court as Part of a System of Multilevel Global Governance in the Democratic Republic of Congo' (2005) 18 *Leiden Journal of International Law* 557, at 576.

[9] UNSC, 5459th meeting, above note 8, at 3.

because the *travaux préparatoires* reveal that many African States did not want Article 17 to apply to situations where human rights standards are not fully met.[10]

The situation in the DRC is a case in point. Although President Kabila had admitted Congo's inability to try Thomas Lubanga Dyilo in its national judicial system, upon referring the situation in the DRC to the ICC in 2004,[11] Trial Chamber I decided in 2006 that the judicial system had already improved.[12] In response to the ICC's activities with regard to the DRC, parts of the government had pushed for judicial reforms in order to claim that there was no need for complementary ICC proceedings.[13] However, observers from the DRC suggest that the military justice system still faces severe handicaps when dealing with war crimes. As of 2014, only about fifteen major cases had been tried before military tribunals in the DRC. Only four cases dealt with senior officers.[14] The reasons for these shortcomings are diverse and reflect the challenges with which law compliance is confronted in areas of limited statehood. While the UN Security Council has repeatedly called on the DRC to stop impunity,[15] national efforts on this topic have faced numerous legal, political and social challenges. It is doubtful that there is an adequately operative legal system in place to deal with serious human rights violations.[16] Criminal legislation enacted in the wake of the 'Second Congo War' lacked

[10] P. Kastner, 'Africa – A Fertile Soil for the International Criminal Court' (2010) 85 *Die Friedens-Warte* 131, at 136.

[11] ICC-01/04–01/06–32-US-Exp-AnxA1, 21 March 2004: 'En raison de la situation particulière que connaît mon pays, les autorités compétentes non sont malheureusement pas en mesure de mener des enquêtes sur les crimes mentionnés ci-dessus ni d'engager les poursuites nécessaires sans la participation de la Cour Pénale Internationale.'

[12] *Prosecutor v. Lubanga* (Decision on the Prosecutor's Application for a Warrant of Arrest) ICC-01/04–01/06–8 (10 February 2006), para. 36.

[13] Burke-White, 'Complementarity in Practice', above note 8, at 570.

[14] B. Kahombo, 'Comment – The Congolese Legal System and the Fight Against Impunity for the Most Serious International Crimes', Chapter 11 in this volume, at 257; J.-M. Kumbu, 'National Courts: The Situation in the Democratic Republic of the Congo', Chapter 10 in this volume, at 238; 'Report of the Secretary-General on the Protection of Civilians in Armed Conflict' (22 May 2012), UN Doc. S/2012/376, para. 7; Human Rights Watch, 'DR Congo: Arrest Bosco Ntaganda for ICC Trial' (13 April 2012), www.hrw.org/news/2012/04/13/dr-congo-arrest-bosco-ntaganda-icc-trial.

[15] UNSC Resolution 1565 (1 October 2004), para. 5(g); UNSC Resolution 1925 (28 May 2010), preamble; UNSC Resolution 2147 (28 March 2014), preamble.

[16] Kumbu, 'National Courts', above note 14, at 229, 245–46; 'Special Report of the Secretary-General on the Democratic Republic of the Congo and the Great Lakes Region' (27 February 2013), UN Doc. S/2013/119, para. 5: 'The weakness of the judiciary and penitentiary systems has also contributed to the state of general instability.'

consistency and deviated significantly from the ICC Statute, for instance, by omitting certain crimes such as forced disappearances and recruiting children in the armed forces, or entirely excluding penalties for the commission of war crimes.[17] Only in 2013, Congolese civilian courts of appeal received a restricted competence to prosecute serious human rights violations; accordingly, military courts will decide on most cases.[18] It is widely believed that the judiciary is devoid of political independence.[19] A lack of material resources also hinders the judiciary from efficient investigations and domestic prosecutions.[20] It is unlikely that victims will receive any monetary compensation.[21] These shortcomings within the legal system are aggravated by a politically biased incoherent prosecution policy.[22]

Thus, Human Rights Watch stated in 2014:

> While there has been some progress with national and international trials, the vast majority of the perpetrators of these crimes remain unpunished. The trials that have taken place in Congo's military courts have faced numerous challenges, including with regard to the quality of investigations, protection of victims and witnesses, respect of the rights of the accused, and ability to prosecute senior level commanders most responsible for the crimes.[23]

Moreover, there is a certain risk that the fragile peace process will be undermined by serious criminal prosecutions.[24] Thus, it was reported that the M23 armed group justified its rebellion with the government's alleged failure to carry out the peace agreement of 23 May 2009. The agreement was concluded between the DRC government and the Congrès

[17] Kahombo, 'Comment – The Congolese Legal System', above note 14, at 251. Since late 2013, a legal reform is underway to implement the ICC Statute into Congolese law. Human Rights Watch, 'Democratic Republic of Congo: No More Delays for Justice' (1 April 2014), www.hrw.org/news/2014/04/01/democratic-republic-congo-no-more-delays-justice.

[18] Kumbu, 'National Courts', above note 14, at 219; Burke-White, 'Complementarity in Practice', above note 8, at 583.

[19] Human Rights Council, 'Report of the Special Rapporteur on the Independence of Judges and Lawyers' (11 April 2008), UN Doc. A/HRC/8/4/Add.2; Burke-White, 'Complementarity in Practice', above note 8, at 577 et seq; Kumbu, 'National Courts', above note 14, at 238.

[20] Burke-White, 'Complementarity in Practice', above note 8, at 566.

[21] Kahombo, 'Comment – The Congolese Legal System', above note 14, at 253; Kumbu, 'National Courts', above note 14, at 229.

[22] Kahombo, 'Comment – The Congolese Legal System', above note 14, at 257–58; Human Rights Watch, 'Arrest Bosco Ntaganda for ICC Trial', above note 14.

[23] Human Rights Watch, 'No More Delays for Justice', above note 17.

[24] Burke-White, 'Complementarity in Practice', above note 8, at 566; Human Rights Watch, 'Arrest Bosco Ntaganda for ICC Trial', above note 14.

National pour la Défense du Peuple (CNDP) on the basis of which the CNDP was recognized as an official political party. Its military wing was also integrated into the State's armed forces.[25] The rebellion was seen by some observers as a reaction against the government's efforts to destabilize the position of the CNDP's military chief of staff Bosco Ntaganda inter alia by pushing calls for his arrest and transfer to the ICC.[26]

3. Engaging armed groups

Where the State has lost control over territory and people, international humanitarian law presupposes, as stated in Common Article 3 GC and Additional Protocol II, that within their area of control, armed groups assume responsibility. Thus, efforts to induce compliance must engage armed groups as much as they engage States.

3.1. Restricted capabilities of armed groups to induce compliance

However, a restricted capacity to comply is not only characteristic of State actors in areas of limited statehood. Violent non-State actors will often have not (yet) established stable and effective structures with strong leadership required to guarantee effective compliance. The capacity of armed groups to train and instruct members and to take disciplinary, as well as punitive, sanctions differs considerably.[27] Likewise, the ability to act at the international level on the basis of central command and control structure also varies. However, empirical research strongly suggests that compliance with international humanitarian law requires an authority

[25] African History, M23, africanhistory.about.com/od/glossarym/g/def-M23.htm; Wilén, 'Identifying the Spoilers', above note 5, at 121. See also 'Special Report of the Secretary-General on the Democratic Republic of Congo and the Great Lakes Region' (27 February 2013), UN Doc. S/2013/119, paras. 12 et seq.

[26] Wilén, 'Identifying the Spoilers', above note 5, at 122; Human Rights Watch, 'DR Congo: M23 Rebels Committing War Crimes' (11 September 2012) www.hrw.org/news/2012/09/11/dr-congo-m23-rebels-committing-war-crimes. In March 2013, Ntaganda himself requested his transfer to the ICC where charges against him were confirmed in June 2014. ICC, *Prosecutor v. Ntaganda* (Decision Pursuant to Article 61(7)(a) and (b) of the Rome Statute on the Charges of the Prosecutor Against Bosco Ntaganda) ICC-01/04–02/06–309 (9 June 2014).

[27] Official Working Document of the 31st International Conference of the Red Cross and Red Crescent, 'International Humanitarian Law and the Challenges of Contemporary Armed Conflicts', Geneva October 2007, at 47; M. Mack and J. Pejic, 'Increasing Respect for International Humanitarian Law in Non-International Armed Conflicts', February 2008, at 11, www.icrc.org/eng/assets/files/other/icrc_002_0923.pdf.

with competence for decision-making and negotiating with public and private international actors. Thus, accountability can be allocated to a central command with the minimum clarity legally required.[28]

One way to address these challenges is for the law to try to adapt its normative preconditions to the facts on the ground by attempting to adequately address the factual situation. International humanitarian law has established a two-tiered system for the applicable law: only armed groups which fulfil the demanding threshold of Article 1(1) of Additional Protocol II to the Geneva Conventions (AP II, Additional Protocol II) are bound by Additional Protocol II. In all other cases of non-international armed conflict, the minimum standard of Common Article 3 GC applies.[29] Such an approach is, inter alia, justified because compliance with some of the obligations under the AP II, such as Article 4 and 5 AP II, requires sufficiently stable (infra-)structures.[30] This linkage between obligation and compliance is explicitly laid down in Article 1(1) AP II, which requires 'dissident armed forces or other organized armed groups which, under responsible command, exercise such control over a part of its territory as to enable them to carry out sustained and concerted military operations and to implement this Protocol'.[31] The high threshold of Additional Protocol II can be seen as a realistic approach since the prerequisites – 'being under responsible command and in control of a part of the territory concerned' – reflect those circumstances on the ground that will allow an armed group to comply with the Protocol.[32] Thus, according to the Commentary of the International Committee of the Red Cross (ICRC), while

[28] H. Jo and K. Bryant, 'Taming of the Warlords: Commitment and Compliance by Armed Opposition Groups in Civil Wars', in T. Risse, S. Ropp and K. Sikkink (eds.), *The Persistent Power of Human Rights: From Commitment to Compliance* (Cambridge: Cambridge University Press, 2013), 239–58, at 243; for a legal discussion of the required degree of centralization and organization, see A. M. La Rosa and C. Wuerzner, 'Armed Groups, Sanctions and the Implementation of International Humanitarian Law' (2008) 90 *International Review of the Red Cross* 327, at 329; S. Sivakumaran, *The Law of Non-International Armed Conflict* (Oxford: Oxford University Press, 2012), at 175.

[29] International Committee of the Red Cross, *Commentary on the Additional Protocols of 8 June 1977 to the Geneva Conventions of 12 August 1949* (Geneva, 1987), Article 1, at 1348, no. 4447.

[30] Ibid. Article 1, at 1352, no. 4466.

[31] For indicia when the required degree of organization is fulfilled, see Sivakumaran, *The Law of Non-International Armed Conflict*, above note 28, at 170 et seq.

[32] ICRC Commentary, above note 29, Article 1, at 1353, no. 4470; M. Sassòli and Y. Shany, 'Should the Obligations of States and Armed Groups under International Humanitarian Law Really Be Equal?' (2011) 882 *International Review of the Red Cross* 425, at 430 et seq.

it is not necessary that armed groups be organized as efficiently as regular armed forces, an organization is required that is inter alia 'capable . . . of imposing discipline in the name of a de facto authority'.[33] Likewise, in cases of Common Article 3 GC, a lower degree of organization and control is required, which nonetheless enables the armed group to comply with the obligations under that Article.[34] Consequently, international humanitarian law has long acknowledged the rise of violent non-State actors and created obligations whose applicability depends primarily on the armed groups' capacity to comply.[35]

3.2. *Flaws in the willingness to comply*

However, even if there is at least a rudimentary capability to comply, this is not sufficient to motivate any actor to actually do so. In some conflicts, at least half of the number of dead civilians can be attributed to the actions of armed groups.[36] Thus, the question remains as to whether adequate safeguards to guarantee an armed group's willingness to comply have been built into the international (legal) system.

3.2.1. Identifying an actor's reasons for compliance

'Compliance with an international obligation means a behaviour or a situation which is in conformity with the international obligations of a subject of international law'.[37] In order to induce such behaviour, it is necessary to identify reasons why actors comply with the law. International Relations and International Legal Theory alike have identified manifold reasons for compliance. Most of the conclusions are based on theoretical considerations, though some do stem from empirical analysis. Some approaches are concerned with international law in general;

[33] ICRC, *Commentary*, above note 29, Article 1, at 1352, no. 4463.

[34] L. Moir, *The Law of Internal Armed Conflict* (Cambridge: Cambridge University Press, 2002), at 36. See also on the linkage between status and ability to comply. *Prosecutor v. Boskoski and Tarculovski* (Judgment), Case No. IT-04-82-T (10 July 2008), para. 196; L. Zegveld, *The Accountability of Armed Opposition Groups in International Law* (Cambridge: Cambridge University Press, 2002), at 135, 140.

[35] International criminal tribunals, however, apparently do not put much emphasis on this prerequisite, see Sivakumaran, *The Law of Non-International Armed Conflict*, above note 28, at 177 et seq.

[36] O. Bangerter, 'Measures Armed Groups Can Take' (2011) 882 *International Review of the Red Cross* 353, at 356.

[37] Bothe, 'Compliance', above note 2, para. 1; from the perspective of social sciences, see Jo and Bryant, 'Taming of the Warlords', above note 28, at 241.

others focus on the laws of war in particular. In both fields, there are vivid discussions about which theory is most appropriate to explain the reasons for compliance with international law. It is not the aim of the present analysis to discuss flaws in the various compliance theories, but rather to deduce reasons for compliance from the diverging theories, as well as from those few empirical studies of compliance with international humanitarian law. Such an eclectic approach might be criticized as lacking theoretical consistency. However, while coherence is an important advantage of an explanation based on one particular theory, at the same time, it creates the risk of either an actor-driven or structure-driven bias.[38] Since the different theories advance, at least partly, motives that derive from different levels of analysis, they work complementarily. Given the circumstances of its applicability in a 'situation of disorder',[39] compliance with the laws of war is a particularly complex issue, which requires taking into account these different perspectives and levels of analysis. This multi-level approach is reflected in the mix of instruments which international law has developed for ensuring actors' compliance with it.[40]

The present analysis assumes that actors only partly – if at all – comply with a rule just because it is the law. Therefore, it does not focus on the structure of the norm, its coherence or its determinacy as a prerequisite for compliance.[41] Instead, it inquires as to the relation between the law and an actor's social behaviour.[42] On this basis an actor's willingness to comply with a norm of international law can be conceptualized in two ways: by a so-called logic of appropriateness and by the logic of consequences.[43] Compliance because of self-interest and reciprocal behaviour, fear of sanctions and reputation follows the logic of consequences, while the logic of appropriateness furthers legitimacy, substantial moral agreement, as

[38] M. Finnemore and K. Sikkink, 'International Norm Dynamics and Political Change' (1998) 52 *International Organizations Law Review* 887, at 913.

[39] Bothe, 'Compliance', above note 2, para. 66.

[40] M. Bothe, 'Neue und alte Konzepte der Durchsetzung des humanitären Völkerrechts', in V. Epping (ed.), *Brücken bauen und begehen – Festschrift für Knut Ipsen* (München: Beck, 2000), 23–40, at 23; S. Ratner, 'Law Promotion beyond Talk: The Red Cross Persuasion and the Laws of War' (2011) 22 *European Journal of International Law* 459, at 485.

[41] See, on these prerequisites, T. Franck, *Fairness in International Law and Institutions* (Oxford: Clarendon Press, 1995), at 30.

[42] M. Burgstaller, *Theories of Compliance with International Law* (Leiden: Martinus Nijhoff Publishers, 2005), at 85.

[43] J. March and J. Olsen, 'The Institutional Dynamics of International Political Orders' (1998) 52 *International Organizations Law Review* 943, at 949.

well as habit and a sense of duty, as compliance motives.[44] Accordingly, it is necessary to identify the relevant norm addressees, since motives for compliance may vary according to the position the actors hold in the international system. Traditionally, compliance theory focuses on the question of why States comply with international law.[45] Although these theories take into account that non-State actors play a decisive role, they ultimately focus on the State 'as the engine and target of compliance'.[46] However, this approach is flawed. It is the rise of non-State actors in war-torn areas of limited statehood that challenges the traditional compliance structure of international humanitarian law and requires a broader perspective. Especially in international humanitarian law and international criminal law, there are other actors with international legal personality that must comply with the norms. Armed groups are bound by the rules applicable in non-international armed conflicts according to Common Article 3 GC, as well as Additional Protocol II and customary international law. In addition, unlike other fields of international law, humanitarian law is concerned not only with policy decisions and their implementation by State organs but also with acts of the individual, that is, combatants or civilians, during wartime. Responsibility is not only incurred by the State itself; the individual is also responsible for violations of the laws of war. Thus, reasons for compliance must also be explained from the perspective of individuals (Section 3.2.2) and armed groups (Section 3.2.3).

3.2.2. The danger of socializing individuals into violence

Efforts to induce compliance with individuals are confronted with the danger that individuals might be more prone to be socialized into violence in perpetuated armed conflicts under the conditions of precarious statehood.

Under the premise of the logic of appropriateness, it is somewhat astonishing that substantial moral agreement is not sufficient to induce a high rate of compliance with international humanitarian law if actors actually comply with norms because 'they understand the behaviour to be good, desirable, and appropriate'.[47] Many of the obligations, in particular

[44] C. Schmelzle, 'Evaluating Governance: Effectiveness and Legitimacy in Areas of Limited Statehood', *SFB-Governance Working Paper Series*, No. 26, November 2011, at 9, www.sfb-governance.de/publikationen/working papers/wp26/SFB-Governance-Working-Paper-26.pdf.

[45] Bothe, 'Compliance', above note 2, para. 4.

[46] Ratner, 'Law Promotion beyond Talk', above note 40, at 485.

[47] Finnemore and Sikkink, 'International Norm Dynamics and Political Change', above note 38, at 912.

those concerning protected persons, are so fundamental and concern such basic human needs that most of them can be seen as a manifestation of general moral agreement.[48] In principle, many rules of international humanitarian law are intuitive, and their content reflects efforts to confine the effects of war on civilians and prevent escalation. Accordingly, the fundamental rules of international humanitarian law, such as the principle of distinction and non-combatant immunity, are considered to be *ius cogens*.[49]

Yet such substantial moral agreement alone is apparently insufficient to instil compliance under the particular circumstances of armed conflict. A study conducted by the ICRC on 'the Roots of Behaviour in War' explains that group pressure is a major reason an individual soldier may not conform to substantial rules by which he or she would abide as a single individual:

> The individual may not normally be a killer but the group certainly is . . . The combatant is no longer a totally autonomous individual . . . This is a situation that favours the dilution of the individual responsibility of the combatant . . . The individual within a group has a 'natural' tendency to assign a higher value to his own group and a lesser one to other groups . . . It has to be emphasized that when another group is declared to be an enemy, these tendencies become all the more acute. Thus, it is quite easy for the group to slide into criminal behaviour and perhaps even to end up promoting and encouraging it.[50]

One consequence of group conformity is the tendency to depersonalize, which in turn promotes the loss of a sense of individual

[48] This is particularly true for the rules concerning protected persons. See H. Krieger, 'Protected Persons', in R. Wolfrum (ed.), *The Max Planck Encyclopedia of Public International Law* (Oxford: Oxford University Press, 2011, online edition, www.mpepil.com); see, however, for an increasing uneasiness with the concept of collateral damage G. Hankel, *Das Tötungsverbot im Krieg: Ein Interventionsversuch* (Hamburg: Hamburger Edition, 2011); R. Merkel, 'Die kollaterale Tötung von Zivilisten im Krieg: Rechtsethische Grundlagen und Grenzen einer prekären Erlaubnis des humanitären Völkerrechts' (2012) 67 *Juristenzeitung* 1137; B. Cronin, 'Reckless Endangerment Warfare: Civilian Casualties and the Collateral Damage Exception in International Humanitarian Law' (2013) 50 *Journal of Peace Research* 175.

[49] M. E. O'Connell, 'Historical Development and Legal Basis', in D. Fleck (ed.), *The Handbook of International Humanitarian Law*, 3d edn (Oxford: Oxford University Press, 2013), Sections 101–150, at 136; S. Oeter, 'Methods and Means of Combat', in Fleck (ed.), *Handbook of International Humanitarian Law*, this note, Sections 401–479, at 448.

[50] D. Muñoz-Rojas and J.-J. Frésard, 'The Roots of Behaviour in War – Understanding and Preventing IHL Violations', 2004, at 6 et seq., www.icrc.org/eng/assets/files/other/icrc_002_0853.pdf.

responsibility. These tendencies are aggravated by the inclination of combatants to perceive their superiors in the chain of command as those responsible.[51] Moreover, a spiral of violence can be observed. If soldiers are victimized, humiliated and traumatized during an armed conflict, there is a higher likelihood that they themselves will perpetrate violations of the laws of war. A moral disengagement of combatants can also result from certain mechanisms to justify violations that they themselves have perpetrated. For instance, illegal acts may be considered as legitimate means for certain ends, such as a group's or a State's survival. Effects might be euphemistically minimized or denied, and such behaviour might be coupled with a tendency to dehumanize the enemy.[52]

Conflicts in war-torn areas of limited statehood are characterized by many of the preconditions for entering into a spiral of violence. In the context of normalization of war, fighters and soldiers are victimized, humiliated and traumatized, often by their own superiors, and socialized into war. This development is particularly apparent in the cases of child soldiers.[53] The first UN Report on the Impact of Armed Conflict on Children stated:

> The progressive involvement of youth in acts of extreme violence desensitizes them to suffering. In a number of cases, young people have been deliberately exposed to horrific scenes. Such experience makes children more likely to commit violent acts themselves and may contribute to a break with society. In many countries . . . children have even been forced to commit atrocities against their own families or communities.[54]

Yet it is important to keep in mind that forms of socializing individuals into violence equally apply to international armed conflicts, such as World War II.[55] What are required, in any event, are efforts on the side of the responsible – commanders of armed groups and States' armed forces alike – to prevent or break the spiral of violence. If group pressure and a shift of individual responsibility to the command level are typical

[51] Ibid. [52] Ibid. 8 et seq.

[53] Despite modern discourses on child agency and child soldiers joining armed groups voluntarily, the effects of victimization, humiliation and traumatization, which also apply to adults, should not be overlooked. For a particularly sceptical view of the dominant perception of child soldiers as victims, see M. Drumbl, *Reimagining Child Soldiers in International Law and Policy* (Oxford: Oxford University Press, 2012), at 12 et seq.

[54] Report of the expert of the Secretary-General, 'Impact of Armed Conflict on Children' (26 August 1996), UN Doc. A/51/306, para. 48.

[55] e.g. C. Browning, *Ordinary Men: Reserve Police Battalion 101 and the Final Solution in Poland* (New York: Harper Collins, 1998).

preconditions for committing war crimes, it is evident that egregious violations of the laws of war are in general systematic crimes and only occasionally individual ones.[56] Consequently, efforts to induce compliance with the individual must be initiated by the military and political command level and must aim to create a habit and sense of duty within the individual.

In order to overcome an individual's tendency to enter into a spiral of violence, international humanitarian law has traditionally been enforced through a professionalized process of norm internalization. The laws of war were traditionally seen as a code of honour for the military profession laying down 'how an honourable soldier would behave in a certain situation'.[57] This approach corresponds to findings in social science that 'professional training does more than simply transfer technical knowledge; it actively socializes people to value certain things above others'.[58] Adequate military training, integrating rules of international humanitarian law, is considered to be essential for creating respect for the law because iterated behaviour and habit consolidate norms among the members of a profession.[59] Accordingly, Article 83(1) AP I stipulates an obligation of the States parties 'to include the study of [international humanitarian law] in their programmes of military instruction'. The importance of adequate dissemination of international humanitarian law and training of soldiers has been confirmed by UNSC Resolution 1894 of 11 November 2009.[60]

[56] M. Bussmann and G. Schneider, 'Strategie, Anarchie oder fehlendes internationales Engagement? Zur Logik von Einseitiger Gewalt in Bürgerkriegen' (2012) 33 *Deutsche Stiftung Friedensforschung* 1, at 4.

[57] S. Oeter, 'Civil War, Humanitarian Law and the United Nations' (1997) 1 *Max Planck Yearbook of United Nations Law* 195, at 214.

[58] Finnemore and Sikkink, 'International Norm Dynamics and Political Change', above note 38, at 905.

[59] Finnemore and Sikkink, 'International Norm Dynamics and Political Change', above note 38, at 904 et seq.; Muñoz-Rojas and Frésard, 'The Roots of Behaviour in War', above note 50, at 15; Mack and Pejic, 'Increasing Respect for International Humanitarian Law', above note 27, at 15; J. Morrow, 'When Do States Follow the Laws of War' (2007) 101 *The American Political Science Review* 559, at 571.

[60] The UN Security Council 'calls upon all parties concerned, (a) to ensure the widest possible dissemination of information about international humanitarian . . . law [, and] (b) to provide training for public officials, members of armed forces and armed groups, personnel associated to armed forces, civilian police and law enforcement personnel, and members of the judicial and legal professions; and to raise awareness among civil society and the civilian population on relevant international humanitarian . . . law, as well as on the protection, special needs and human rights of women and children in conflict situations, to achieve full and effective compliance'; for a corresponding obligation under

While there are certain attempts among armed groups to rely on norm internalization – such as in the case of the Mouvement des Nigériens pour la Justice (MNJ), which made its members swear an oath on the Quran including the pledge to refrain from harming civilians[61] – empirical findings show that only a minority of individuals living in areas of armed conflict know about the rules of international humanitarian law.[62] If there is no room for professional training in order to create a habit of norm-compliance, the logic of consequences, particularly the fear of sanctions, may induce individual soldiers and fighters to comply.

Based on its experience, seen in practice as well as in empirical research, the ICRC emphasizes the importance of the fear of sanctions as an instrument for inducing compliance of the individual soldier. The ICRC starts from the assumption that

> the behaviour of combatants is determined mainly by three parameters: (1) their position within a group, which leads them to behave in conformity with what the group expects of them, (2) their position in a hierarchical structure, which leads them to obey authority (because they perceive it as legitimate or it acts on them as a coercive force, or a mixture of the two), (3) the process of moral disengagement favoured by the war situation, which authorizes recourse to violence against those defined as being the enemy.[63]

Under these conditions, a spiral of violence can only be interrupted if group behaviour is controlled by superiors through strict orders accompanied by a realistic threat of swift and immediate sanctions. Only such swift and immediate sanctions can stop a constant increase in violence because otherwise, violations become continuously more severe and more acceptable.[64] In order to instigate a fear of sanctions, these instruments need to be imposed coherently. Individual combatants would otherwise not be stopped from committing violations of international humanitarian law as they would assume that they are highly unlikely to be punished. The threat of punishment must be a realistic one.[65] Since war crimes are,

customary international law, see Rule 142 of the Customary International Humanitarian Law (CIHL).

61 O. Bangerter, 'Comment – Persuading Armed Groups to Better Respect International Humanitarian Law', Chapter 5 in this volume, at 121.

62 Sivakumaran, *The Law of Non-International Armed Conflict*, above note 28, at 434.

63 Muñoz-Rojas and Frésard, 'The Roots of Behaviour in War', above note 50, at 15.

64 Ibid. 16.

65 Official Working Document of the 31st International Conference of the Red Cross and Red Crescent, 'International Humanitarian Law', above note 27, at 32.

in general, systematic crimes in that the command level fails to prevent or even incites soldiers to customize to violence,[66] there appears to be a stronger pull for leaders at the command level to socialize individuals into violence than into norm compliance in war-torn areas of limited statehood.

3.2.3. No more compliance-pull for warlords?

Some authors explain this pull not to comply on the basis of the 'new wars' theory.[67] They hold that international humanitarian law can no longer direct actors' behaviour in conflicts in war-torn areas of limited statehood. They argue that the parties' interest is, per se, incompatible with the law because they pursue a policy of ethnic cleansing and economic exploitation. It is held that actors would neither care for considerations of reciprocity, nor reputation or fear of sanctions.[68] Under such conditions, it would indeed be hard to conceive how the logic of consequence could be applied, at all. However, such an approach partly works on the underlying assumption that violent non-State actors, such as warlords, would not be rational actors whose behaviour could not be affected by strategic considerations.

This interpretation neglects to acknowledge that the use and non-use of force may still be instrumental, and that armed groups pursue coherent strategies and demands which are at least partly based on political motivations.[69] Violence against civilians is rarely an aim in itself, but rather regularly an instrument for attaining a different goal.[70] Voices from practice argue that random violence hardly ever occurs, but that even the most shocking atrocities are politically motivated, sometimes with the aim of gaining the attention of the international community.[71] There is

[66] Muñoz-Rojas and Frésard, 'The Roots of Behaviour in War', above note 50, at 8.

[67] Proponents of this theory include: M. Kaldor, *New and old Wars: Organized Violence in a Global Era*, 3d edn (Cambridge: Polity Press, 2012); H. Münkler, *The New Wars* (Cambridge, Polity Press, 2005).

[68] N. Lamp, 'Conceptions of War', above note 6, at 242 et seq.; R. Geiß, 'Asymmetric Conflict Structures' (2006) 88 *International Review of the Red Cross* 757, at 770, 773; C. Bassouni, 'The New Wars and the Crisis of Compliance with the Law of Armed Conflict by Non-State Actors' (2008) 98 *The Journal of Criminal Law and Criminology* 711, at 765 et seq.; M. Sassòli, 'The Implementation of International Humanitarian Law: Current and Inherent Challenges' (2007) 10 *Yearbook of International Humanitarian Law* 45, at 49.

[69] The genuinely political approach of armed groups is emphasized by Bassouni, 'The New Wars and the Crisis of Compliance', above note 68, at 767.

[70] Bussmann and Schneider, 'Strategie, Anarchie oder fehlendes internationales Engagement?', above note 56, at 15.

[71] Bangerter, 'Comment – Persuading Armed Groups', above note 61, at 119.

strong empirical evidence to suggest that political aspirations and strategic considerations are decisive, even if observers tend to classify conflicts as mere irrational 'warlordism'.[72] The ICRC emphasized in its empirical report, 'The Roots of Behaviour in War', that 'violations of international humanitarian law are not generally the work of sick, sadistic or irrational individuals'.[73] Accordingly, Reed Wood criticizes assumptions based on the 'new wars' theory from the perspective of political science; empirically, it is difficult to prove that genocide has replaced military victory as a political aim since there appears to be no clear relation between ethnic conflicts and the number of civilian victims of any type of conflict.[74] The 'new wars' theory cannot explain variations in violence across conflicts and over time. Thus, it does not sufficiently take into account the dynamics of conflict and overemphasizes its static elements.[75] Reed Wood illustrates that even the Uganda Lord's Resistance Army (LRA), which is known for its particularly heinous violence towards civilians, changed its strategy over time. He proves that incentives for increasing violence against civilians are a lack of resources, military capabilities and civilian support. Armed groups turn to violence in order to compensate for a loss of resources. In war-torn areas of limited statehood, rebels and warlords aim to affect civilian activities and use violence against civilians in order to avoid military defeat.[76]

Moreover, empirical research on governance insurgency and compliance with international law demonstrates that armed groups tend to provide governance structures, including security, if they have established effective and centralized control of a territory with unified command structures.[77] Thus, armed groups, such as the Rassemblement Congolais pour la Démocratie (RCD) in the DRC, the United Somali

[72] On the danger that international criminal courts and western perceptions of armed conflicts on the African continent construct stereotypes, see Cryer, 'The Role of International Criminal Prosecutions in Increasing Compliance with International Humanitarian Law in Contemporary African Conflicts', Chapter 9 in this volume, at 198.

[73] Muñoz-Rojas and Frésard, 'The Roots of Behaviour in War', above note 50, at 8.

[74] R. Wood, 'Understanding Strategic Motives for Violence against Civilians during Civil Conflict', Chapter 2 in this volume, at 17; R. Wood, 'Rebel Capability and Strategic Violence against Civilians' (2010) 47 *Journal of Peace Research* 601.

[75] Wood, 'Understanding Strategic Motives for Violence', above note 74, at 17–18, 21.

[76] Ibid.; Bussmann and Schneider, 'Strategie, Anarchie oder fehlendes internationales Engagement?', above note 56, at 18 et seq.

[77] Z. Mampilly, *Rebel Rulers: Insurgent Governance and Civilian Life during War* (Ithaca, New York: Cornell University Press, 2011); Wood, 'Understanding Strategic Motives for Violence', above note 74, at 21–24.

Congress (UCS)-faction in Somalia or the Sudan People's Liberation Movement/Army (SPLM/A) in South Sudan, have granted the ICRC access.[78] Correspondingly, Mampilly illustrates that, among the forty warring factions in the DRC, many of the organizations have attempted to establish governance structures. Their failure to do so is not based on a disinterest in civilian protection, but rather stems from organizational reasons, among others. Even the RCD, which is generally regarded as a typical example of warlordism, attempted to provide for civilian welfare.[79] Thus, there is a presumption that traditional incentives for compliance still matter but need to be adjusted to the particular situations of conflicts in war-torn areas of limited statehood.

3.3. *The remainders of traditional incentives: self-interest and expectations of reciprocal behaviour*

In social science, realism and the rational choice theory have drawn attention to the interests of the relevant actors as a major reason for compliance. Realism[80] basically disputes the idea that the legal nature of an international obligation is of any significance for compliance. Its most rigorous proponents suggest that international law does not, in and of itself, influence an actor's behaviour at all, if vital (national) interests are concerned.[81] Traditional realists focusing on the State hold that the anarchic character of the international system prompts States to protect their vital interests and to strive for power and security.[82] From this point of view, compliance

[78] Jo and Bryant, 'Taming of the Warlords', above note 28, at 244. However, granting access can have reverse effects insofar as reports of human rights violations can be unfavorable to their international reputation. The RCD, for instance, tried to restrict access to certain areas or used violence in rural areas which were not under local or international observation. See Mampilly, 'Insurgent Governance in the Democratic Republic of the Congo', Chapter 3 in this volume, at 76.

[79] Mampilly, 'Insurgent Governance', above note 78, at 67.

[80] The most prominent works include H. Morgenthau, *Politics among Nations: The Struggle for Power and Peace*, 2d edn(New York: Knopf, 1948); H. Morgenthau, 'Positivism, Functionalism, and International Law' (1940) 34 *American Journal of International Law* 260; G. Kennan, *American Diplomacy 1900–1950* (Chicago: University of Chicago Press, 1951); E. H. Carr, *The Twenty Years' Crisis, 1919–1939: An Introduction to the Study of International Relations* (London: Harper Torchbooks, 1964).

[81] J. Mearsheimer, 'The False Promise of International Institutions' (1995) 19 *International Security* 5, at 9 et seq.; F. A. Boyle, 'The Irrelevance of International Law' (1980) 10 *California Western International Law Journal* 193, at 198.

[82] J. Grieco, 'Anarchy and the Limits of Cooperation: A Realistic Critique of the Newest Liberal Institutionalism' (1988) 42 *International Organizations Law Review* 485, at 488.

with international law will only take place if it reflects a State's self-interest, not because of its character as a normative commitment.[83] Since interests are uncertain in the realm of high politics, for instance, in national security, 'the validity of the rules depends upon a balance of power' which will be subject to constant changes.[84] A more recent variant of realism is reflected in the instrumentalist and the rational choice strand,[85] which also start from a concept of interests and submits that international law will only be relevant if it has an effect on an actor's calculation of interests. Accordingly, non-compliance is an option, if it appears to be more rational to further short-term self-interest, while others obey the law.[86]

International law has long acknowledged that self-interest is a major compliance-pull in a decentralized legal system by building international treaties on reciprocity.[87] As long as international law lacks centralized enforcement mechanisms, reciprocity, as a particular form of self-interest, is a major instrument to stabilize international relations.[88] However, as a legal concept, reciprocity must not be confused with social aspects of reciprocity where motivations to comply are based on an expectation of in-kind responses. As a principle of international law, reciprocity refers to 'the maxim that a State basing a claim on a particular norm of international law must accept that rule as also binding upon itself [so that] a certain conduct by one party is . . . judicially dependent upon that of the other party'.[89] While this understanding holds true for general international law,[90] international humanitarian law builds on the aspect of social

[83] Morgenthau, 'Positivism, Functionalism, and International Law', above note 80, at 277.

[84] Ibid. 278 et seq.

[85] Major works include E. Posner and A. Sykes, *Economic Foundations of International Law* (Cambridge, Mass.: Harvard University Press, 2013); J. Goldsmith and E. Posner, *The Limits of International Law* (Oxford: Oxford University Press, 2005); E. Posner, 'Do States Have a Moral Obligation to Obey International Law?' (2003) 55 *Stanford Law Review* 1901, at 1917.

[86] R. Keohane, *Power and Governance in a Partially Globalized World* (London: Routledge, 2002), at 119.

[87] B. Simma, *Das Reziprozitätselement im Zustandekommen völkerrechtlicher Verträge: Gedanken zu einem Bauprinzip der internationalen Rechtsbeziehungen* (Berlin: Duncker & Humblot, 1972); F. Parisi and N. Ghei, 'The Role of Reciprocity in International Law' (2003) 36 *Cornell International Law Journal* 93.

[88] B. Simma, 'Reciprocity', in R. Wolfrum (ed.), *The Max Planck Encyclopedia of Public International Law* (Oxford: Oxford University Press, 2008, online edition, www.mpepil.com), para. 1.

[89] Ibid. para. 2.

[90] Reciprocity as a legal concept is particularly important in relation to *ius ad bellum*, law of diplomatic privileges and immunities, international economic relations and the treatment of aliens. See Simma, 'Reciprocity', above note 88, paras. 8 et seq.

expectations in terms of expectations of reciprocated behaviour, since 'the obligation to respect and ensure respect for the Geneva Conventions does not depend on [legal] reciprocity'.[91] Therefore, international humanitarian law relies on the actor's motives insofar as its enforcement presupposes that no party to a conflict can expect the adversary to respect the legal limitations of warfare if the party itself violates those rules.[92]

Empirical research in social science suggests that, in international armed conflicts, reciprocal expectations are the major reason for compliance for the State as well as for the individual soldier.[93] Accordingly, the German Military Manual states: 'Soldiers must treat their opponents in the same manner that they themselves wish to be treated'.[94] Reciprocal expectations are particularly significant because they can instil compliance in the combat theatre itself.[95] Unlike other instruments of compliance, fear of retaliation does not work ex post, but in the heat of an ongoing armed conflict.[96] In the words of Dinstein:

> Many norms . . . (usually accepted in peacetime, when the exigencies of war do not loom on the horizon) may prove too onerous once put to test . . . If belligerent Parties refrain from contravening them, notwithstanding a perception that these norms tie their hands too strenuously, it is largely due to the knowledge that any deviation is likely to entail painful retaliation.[97]

[91] Rule 140 CIHL: Netherlands, Special Court of Cassation, *In re Rauter*, Judgment of 12 January 1949 (1955) Annual Digest 16, 526 § 202; United States, Military Tribunal at Nuremberg, *United States of America v. Wilhelm von Leeb et al. (Case No. 12 – the High Command Trial)*, Judgment of 27 October 1948, 9 *Trials of War Criminals Before the Nuremberg Military Tribunals* 1, 481; see, however, Art. 2 Hague Convention IV Respecting the Laws and Customs of War on Land (1907); see in general J. de Preux, 'The Geneva Conventions and Reciprocity' (1985) 25 *International Review of the Red Cross* 25; R. Provost, *International Human Rights and Humanitarian Law* (Cambridge: Cambridge University Press, 2002), at 136 et seq.

[92] S. Vöneky, 'Implementation and Enforcement of International Humanitarian Law', in Fleck (ed.), *Handbook of International Humanitarian Law*, above note 49, Sections 1401–1436, at 1404, 1406; Oeter, 'Civil War, Humanitarian Law and the United Nations', above note 57, at 214; S. Sivakumaran, *The Law of Non-International Armed Conflict*, above note 28, at 245.

[93] Morrow, 'When Do States Follow the Laws of War', above note 59, at 561 et seq.

[94] Bundesministerium der Verteidigung, *Humanitäres Völkerrecht in bewaffneten Konflikten – Handbuch*, ZDv 15/2 (1992), no. 1204.

[95] Geiß, 'Asymmetric Conflict Structures', above note 68, at 760.

[96] Y. Dinstein, *The Conduct of Hostilities under the Law of International Armed Conflict*, 2d edn (Cambridge: Cambridge University Press, 2010), at 254.

[97] Ibid. 254.

Consequently, belligerent reprisals are considered to be a very important means of enforcing international humanitarian law, at least in international armed conflicts.[98]

The empirical argument that expectations of reciprocal behaviour are decisive for compliance by the individual soldier is based on the observation that compliance is worst where treatment of civilians is concerned; the record of compliance improves where there is a direct threat of retaliation for soldiers, for instance, in cases of treatment of prisoners of war. While every soldier is, in principle, capable of committing atrocities against civilians, civilians will, in most cases, not be able to attack soldiers.[99] This demonstrates that reciprocal expectations have a 'Janus-face'[100] since fear of individual retaliations will only direct the soldier's behaviour if there is a certain prospect that the enemy soldier will actually fight back and violate the laws of war in response to an infringement. Since individual soldiers are not entitled to undertake belligerent reprisals,[101] reciprocal expectations on the level of the individual only appear to induce compliance if individuals are prepared to infringe the laws of war regardless of their legal obligations.

The 'Janus-face' character of reciprocal expectations as a means for inducing compliance is also present at the State level. While fear of retaliation is the major argument for the permissibility of belligerent reprisals as an instrument for enforcing international humanitarian law, the danger of abuse and escalation inherent in the concept of unilateral counter-measures has triggered a wide-ranging prohibition of reprisals against specific categories of protected persons and objects.[102] While expectations of reciprocal behaviour may thus further compliance, they may simultaneously endanger the stability of the international order.[103]

[98] US, *The Commander's Handbook on the Law of Naval Operations*, Edition July 2007, 6.2.4.: belligerent reprisals constitute 'an act that would otherwise be unlawful but which is justified as a response to the previous unlawful acts of an enemy'. Arguing for the non-applicability in non-international armed conflicts, see V. Bilkova, 'Belligerent Reprisals in Non-International Armed Conflict' (2014) 63 *International and Comparative Law Quarterly* 31, at 63 et seq.

[99] Morrow, 'When Do States Follow the Laws of War', above note 59, at 567 et seq.

[100] Simma, 'Reciprocity', above note 88, para. 16.

[101] The decision to use reprisals must be authorized by the highest political level. Oeter, 'Methods and Means of Combat', above note 49, Section 486.

[102] Bothe, 'Compliance', above note 2, para. 67.

[103] Geiß, 'Asymmetric Conflict Structures', above note 68, at 771; Simma, 'Reciprocity', above note 88, para. 16.

When considering armed groups in war-torn areas of limited statehood, some authors have doubted that reciprocal expectations and self-interest have any role to play in inducing compliance with international humanitarian law.[104] International humanitarian law (no longer) appears to be, in and of itself, entirely beneficial for all relevant actors, due to a lack of strict legal reciprocity and asymmetries in regard to reciprocal expectations.[105] Such expectations presuppose parallel interest of the conflicting parties. Research in social sciences has stressed that self-interest as a content-dependent compliance motive requires that the rules are more or less in every actor's self-interest.[106] Such a common ground seems to be unlikely in non-international armed conflicts.[107] Moreover, according to this argument, international humanitarian law no longer corresponds to other self-interests of the conflicting parties because military victory no longer appears to be the parties' primary interest in war-torn areas of limited statehood.[108] Since international humanitarian law is built on the compromise between military necessity and humanitarian considerations, the balance will dissolve if overcoming the enemy is no longer the parties' main goal.[109]

However, a closer look at practical experience and empirical research demonstrates that reciprocal expectations and self-interest still matter as a motive for compliance in war-torn areas of limited statehood. Although economic exploitation and ethnic motivations play a considerable role in such conflicts, one must bear in mind that self-interest in particular is context-dependent as a motive for compliance. Accordingly, in its 2007 report on international humanitarian law and the 'Challenges of Contemporary Armed Conflicts', the ICRC stressed that any attempt to induce compliance must start from a strategic approach and must consider 'the unique characteristics of a specific situation [and] understand a party's motivations and interests in order to explain why it is in the party's interest to comply with the law'.[110] In war-torn areas of limited statehood,

[104] Lamp, 'Conceptions of War', above note 6, at 248 et seq.; T. Pfanner, 'Asymmetrical Warfare from the Perspective of Humanitarian Law and Humanitarian Action' (2005) 87 *International Review of the Red Cross* 149, at 161.

[105] Geiß, 'Asymmetric Conflict Structures', above note 68, at 776.

[106] Schmelzle, 'Evaluating Governance', above note 44, at 11.

[107] Geiß, 'Asymmetric Conflict Structures', above note 68, at 760, 773; Pfanner, 'Asymmetrical Warfare', above note 104, at 161.

[108] Lamp, 'Conceptions of War', above note 6, at 234, 243. [109] Ibid. 243.

[110] Official Working Document of the 31st International Conference of the Red Cross and Red Crescent, 'International Humanitarian Law', above note 27, at 49.

there is a great diversity of parties. Consequently, conflict structures vary considerably, as do motives.[111] There are examples from the conflict in Chad where expectation of reciprocal behaviour also affected the decisions of armed groups. Fighters were given orders not to harm civilians because rebels feared retaliation by families and clans.[112] This example reflects that many of the conflicts in war-torn areas of limited statehood are in fact symmetrically fought between various armed groups; hence, expectations of de facto reciprocity still matter. Accordingly, in his 2009 report on the protection of civilians in armed conflict, the UN Secretary-General argued that 'the incentives for armed groups to comply with the law should be emphasized, including increased likelihood of reciprocal respect for the law by opposing parties'.[113]

From a normative perspective, the law of non-international armed conflict was created with the awareness that reciprocal expectations are more limited in this field.[114] Accordingly, the high threshold of applicability in Additional Protocol II also tries to guarantee some conditions for reciprocal expectations.[115] Only armed groups which are similar to a State are bound by the Protocol's obligations. Thereby the Protocol creates a certain symmetry within the regime of non-international armed conflict. Moreover, it is conceivable that armed groups have certain interests in common with States' armed forces. Rules on prisoners and wounded and sick soldiers spring to mind.[116] Although the law of non-international armed conflict does not provide for an adequate prisoner of war regime, in the past, armed groups have issued commitments to apply the Geneva Convention III.[117] Efforts to ban landmines are another area where States and armed groups have common interests. Both actors are affected by their indiscriminate effects, and, therefore, both have an interest in their removal or non-use.[118]

[111] Ibid. 46 et seq.

[112] Bangerter, 'Comment – Persuading Armed Groups', above note 61, at 118–19.

[113] 'Report of the Secretary-General on the Protection of Civilians in Armed Conflict', above note 14, para. 41.

[114] Geiß, 'Asymmetric Conflict Structures', above note 68, at 776. [115] Ibid. 777.

[116] O. Bangerter, 'Reasons Why Armed Groups Choose to Respect International Humanitarian Law or Not' (2011) 93 *International Review of the Red Cross* 353, 366; Geiß, 'Asymmetric Conflict Structures', above note 68, at 776.

[117] S. Sivakumaran, 'Lessons for the Law of Armed Conflict from Commitments of Armed Groups: Identification of Legitimate Targets and Prisoners of War' (2011) 93 *International Review of the Red Cross* 463, at 479.

[118] U. Schneckener and C. Hofmann, 'The Power of Persuasion: The Role of International Non-Governmental Organizations in Engaging Armed Groups', Chapter 4 in this volume, at 99–101.

In some cases, accession of armed groups to the Geneva Call Deed of Commitment for Adherence to a Total Ban on Anti-Personnel Mines and for Cooperation in Mine Action[119] prompted the territorial State to accede to the 1997 Ottawa Treaty.[120]

Moreover, other forms of self-interest might also have a bearing on compliance by armed groups and States' armed forces alike. Certain norms foster a greater interest in international cooperation than others. In the present volume, Schneckener and Hofmann have shown that norms with a technical dimension, such as a ban of landmines, evoke several aspects of self-interest from armed groups. Since removal of landmines requires a certain technical know-how, the willingness to cooperate internationally increases.[121] Military efficiency as a self-interest is also involved when norm entrepreneurs can raise the argument that compliant behaviour will have a positive impact on the efficiency, discipline and internal functioning of an armed group.[122] Economic interests are, in general, a major self-interest that influences the behaviour of non-State actors. The ICRC is reported to use economic arguments underpinning the prospect that compliant behaviour might result in (additional) foreign economic support for the armed group or for a State.[123] Thus, it would be premature and hasty to negate that self-interest and reciprocity do not have a role to play in inducing compliance in war-torn areas of limited statehood.

3.4. *Fostering an armed group's interest in international reputation as an enduring dilemma*

Interest in international and national reputation represents a particular form of self-interest. Rational choice theory and constructivism alike have drawn attention to rewards as another motive for compliance. Guzman has based his State-centred rational choice approach to international law on reputation as the major factor for a compliance pull of international law. He submits that self-interest is decisive for a State's compliance decision, but international law influences this decision, on the one hand because of fear of sanctions, and on the other hand because

[119] For a text of the Deed, see www.genevacall.org/wp-content/uploads/dlm_uploads/2013/12/DoC-Banning-anti-personnel-mines.pdf.

[120] Schneckener and Hofmann, 'The Power of Persuasion', above note 118, at 102.

[121] Ibid. [122] Ratner, 'Law Promotion beyond Talk', above note 40, at 478.

[123] Ibid.; Jo and Bryant, 'Taming of the Warlords', above note 28, at 242.

non-compliance may result in a loss of reputation.[124] He holds that this impact will not always be strong enough to change the State's behaviour. According to Guzman, the impact depends, inter alia, on the identities of the States involved.[125] Also, from the perspective of constructivism, reputation plays a major role as a reason for compliance. Finnemore and Sikkink have argued that it is the State's identity in relation to the international community that renders reputation a decisive incentive for compliance: 'state leaders conform to norms in order to avoid the disapproval aroused by norm violation and thus to enhance national esteem (and, as a result, their own self- esteem)'.[126] Not only do the costs incurred by being labelled a 'rogue state' trigger States' compliance, but also the fact that international reputation 'has become an essential contributor to perceptions of domestic legitimacy held by a state's own citizens . . . international legitimation is important insofar as it reflects back on a government's domestic basis of legitimation and consent and thus ultimately on its ability to stay in power'.[127]

Accordingly, considerations for public opinion are considered to be essential motives for a State's compliance with international humanitarian law, especially in view of the prominent role of mass media in armed conflicts. Public knowledge of gross violations may spoil the fighting morale, as well as the consent of the State's population.[128] However, this argument relies very much on the constructivist explanation that domestic legitimacy might depend on a State's international reputation and the States' perspective that international reputation is an asset at all. It is closely related to liberalism and democratic States.[129] Consequently, Lamp has submitted that public opinion and reputation have no role to play in the 'new wars'. Since the killing of civilians appears to become acceptable where ethnic conflicts are conducted, armed groups in such circumstances

[124] A. Guzman, 'A Compliance-based Theory of International Law' (2002) 90 *California Law Review* 1823, at 1825; Guzman, 'Reputation and International Law' (2006) 34 *Georgia Journal of International and Comparative Law* 379, at 386 et seq.

[125] Guzman, 'A Compliance-based Theory of International Law', above note 124, at 1828 et seq.; B. Delcourt, 'Compliance, Theory of', in R. Wolfrum (ed.), *The Max Planck Encyclopedia of Public International Law* (Oxford: Oxford University Press, 2011, online edition, www.mpepil.com), para. 11.

[126] Finnemore and Sikkink, 'International Norm Dynamics and Political Change', above note 38, at 903 et seq.

[127] Ibid. 902 et seq.

[128] Vöneky, 'Implementation and Enforcement of International Humanitarian Law', above note 92, at Section 1405.

[129] Delcourt, 'Compliance, Theory of', above note 125, para. 14.

'usually do not have to fear that publicity for their actions would lose them support in their own populations. In some endemic conflicts in which perpetual warfare constitutes a form of life for the participants – the Hutu militias in Eastern Congo and the Lord's Resistance Army (LRA) in Northern Uganda are examples – it is hard to imagine how public opinion could have any effect on the warring parties' actions'.[130]

Nonetheless, one must also be aware that, in terms of reputation as a motive for compliance, armed groups vary considerably. While some groups operate as political actors pursuing long-term political goals, others may lack such goals, as well as any coherent and stable structure.[131] Reputation will work as a motive for compliance only if an armed group cares about civilian support and relies on core constituents. Interest in reputation also depends on its military capability; the stronger the group, the more it will be interested in political aims since it will appear to be a realistic scenario that the group might replace the government. In such a case, national and international reputation becomes important for political survival. The groups' awareness of these mechanisms might depend on the existence of a political wing.[132] Irrespective of the variations in armed groups, all of these groups have to address the question of how to relate to the civilian population. Controlling and winning over the local population is a way to demonstrate the strength of an armed group, while a failure to do so might cause their control to be challenged. 'In order to ensure their viability, insurgencies cannot rely solely on coercive means, but must also gain a degree of consent from the civilian population'.[133] Moreover, armed groups can promote their legitimacy in the eyes of the civilian population in their territory by improving the populations' living conditions, which in turn will affect the political stability of the group's control.[134] In addition, the practice of the ICRC is partly built on the assumption that the 'target's domestic or international reputation' still matters.[135] Thus, the ICRC has experienced that only very exceptionally armed groups are unwilling to engage with humanitarian

[130] Lamp, 'Conceptions of War', above note 6, at 246 et seq.

[131] Jo and Bryant, 'Taming of the Warlords', above note 28, at 242; Mampilly, 'Insurgent Governance', above note 78, at 45–46, 49.

[132] Jo and Bryant, 'Taming of the Warlords', above note 28, at 245; Mampilly, 'Insurgent Governance', above note 78, at 46.

[133] Mampilly, 'Insurgent Governance', above note 78, at 46. [134] Ibid.

[135] Ratner, 'Law Promotion beyond Talk', above note 40, at 478; Schneckener and Hofmann, 'The Power of Persuasion', above note 118, at 97.

organizations at all.[136] Some of the measures of the UN Security Council, such as the so-called 'List of Shame', also rely on the assumption that reputation matters for armed groups.[137] The UN Secretary-General has repeatedly stated that factors inducing compliance 'include the need for popular support and the group's self-image and self-interest'.[138] Thus, there is evidence that reputation at the local level, as well as on the international level, remains a powerful motive for compliance.

Consequently, empirical research unfolds a severe dilemma: the likelihood that armed groups will comply with norms of international humanitarian law increases as these groups grow stronger. By contrast, if a group is weakened, it will most likely increase its levels of violence against civilians. As a hypothetical consequence, one option might be to stabilize rebel groups. The more stable and effective an armed group becomes, and the more it complies with international law and negotiates with international public and private actors, the more it gains in terms of legitimacy.

Of course, it is highly unlikely that States or international organizations would directly pursue such an approach. The States' unwillingness to engage with armed groups is a matter not only of vested interests, but also of law. It is primarily the prohibition of intervention into the internal affairs of a State that restricts corresponding efforts. Some forms of material assistance might amount to subversive intervention, thereby violating the principle of non-intervention.[139] Since training, for instance, is in principle forbidden,[140] supporting armed groups in teaching international humanitarian law during training might, under certain circumstances, be considered illegal too. In a given situation, the classification will also depend on the evaluation of whether or not a particular form of promoting international humanitarian law compliance amounts to humanitarian help, which is, in principle, permissible.[141] Moreover, while

[136] Bangerter, 'Comment – Persuading Armed Groups', above note 61, at 117–18.

[137] R. Klostermann, 'The UN Security Council's special compliance systems – the regime of chidren and armed conflict', Chapter 14 in this volume, at 315–17, 335.

[138] 'Report of the Secretary-General on the Protection of Civilians in Armed Conflict', above note 14, para. 42.

[139] P. Kunig, 'Intervention, Prohibition of', in R. Wolfrum (ed.), *The Max Planck Encyclopedia of Public International Law* (Oxford: Oxford University Press, 2008, online edition, www.mpepil.com), para. 24.

[140] *Military and Paramilitary Activities in an against Nicaragua (Nicaragua v. United States of America)* (Judgment) [1986] ICJ Reports 14, paras. 228, 242; *Armed Activities on the Territory of the Congo (Democratic Republic of the Congo v. Uganda)* (Judgment) [2005] ICJ Reports 168, paras. 161 et seq.

[141] Kunig, 'Intervention, Prohibition of', above note 139, para. 35.

support of a people exercising their right to self-determination would be privileged,[142] contemporary conflicts in general do not fall under this category since the decolonization process has come to an end. Many of the present-day conflicts are therefore categorized as terrorism and thus criminalized. Armed groups such as the Liberation Tigers of Tamil Eelam (LTTE) were or are still included on lists of terrorists. Accordingly, the restrictive traditional interpretation of self-determination and secession also draws legal limits for States who wish to promote a rebel group's stability for the sake of compliance with international humanitarian law.

Nonetheless, some States acknowledge more and more a need for directly engaging with armed groups, as long as 'engagement does not constitute political recognition of these groups'.[143] Similarly, the UN Secretary-General has emphasized repeatedly the 'continuing importance of enhancing compliance with international humanitarian law by non-State armed groups and the corresponding need for humanitarian actors to engage with such groups to that end and to gain safe access to people in need of assistance'.[144] Even the UN Security Council in a presidential statement 'recognizes the need for consistent engagement by humanitarian agencies with all parties to armed conflict for humanitarian purposes, including activities aimed at ensuring respect for international humanitarian law'.[145] However, there are still reasons to assume that such a development contradicts basic interests, especially of those States which are engaged in a military conflict with armed groups.[146] The scepticism about engaging armed groups is repeatedly revealed by the UN Security Council's discussion on Protection of Civilians in Armed Conflicts. For instance, in 2012, Colombia – a State fighting armed groups in its territory – fiercely rejected the suggestion of the UN Secretary-General to engage more actively with armed groups:

> Nevertheless, the existence or absence of engagement on the part of the United Nations with these groups is not a decisive factor in the application of the rules governing armed conflicts. Focusing on the possibility of engagements of certain actors with illegal armed groups simply diverts

[142] UNGA Resolution 3314 (XXIX) (14 December 1974).

[143] UNSC, 6790th Meeting (25 June 2012), UN Doc. S/PV 6790, Statement of the Representative of Germany, at 23.

[144] 'Report of the Secretary-General on the Protection of Civilians in Armed Conflict' (22 November 2013), UN Doc. S/2013/689, para. 38.

[145] Statement by the President of the Security Council (12 February 2013), UN Doc. S/PRST/2013/2, at 4.

[146] 'Report of the Secretary-General on the Protection of Civilians in Armed Conflict', above note 14, paras. 44 et seq.

> attention from the truly fundamental issue – the lack of political will to comply with international humanitarian law. An effective guarantee of the rights of civilians during hostilities does not require engagement with non-State groups, but rather the decision on the part of those parties, either to abandon altogether the use of violence and pursue their goals through democratic debate, or, if they decide to persist in their armed struggle, to comply with international humanitarian law.[147]

Moreover, Colombia has criticized the idea that 'there should be ongoing and direct engagement between non-State armed groups and the relevant United Nations bodies'.[148] The dilemma was explicitly named by the UN Secretary-General when he stated that 'focus on recognition and legitimacy is problematic in that it detracts from the more serious issue of the consequences for civilians when engagement does not take place'.[149]

3.5. *Improving armed groups' perceptions of the law's legitimacy*

The same dilemma develops out of the perspective of the logic of appropriateness and considerations of legitimacy. From the point of view of an armed group's command level, the logic of appropriateness might not exert a sufficiently strong compliance-pull since the group perceives international humanitarian law as not sufficiently legitimate. Such an empirical legitimacy, which describes the 'beliefs and attitudes of the affected actors regarding the normative status of a rule, government, political system or governance regime',[150] is an important element of inducing compliance since compliance as a law-abiding behaviour will often be based on an

[147] UNSC, 6790th meeting (25 June 2012), UN Doc. S/PV 6790, Statement of the Representative of Columbia, at 12; see also ibid. Statement of the Representative of India, at 25; 7019th meeting (19 August 2012), UN Doc. S/PV 7019, Statement of the Representative of Pakistan, at 18; ibid. Statement of the Representative of Columbia, at 44; ibid. Statement of the Representative of India, at 47; ibid. Statement of the Representative of Turkey, at 57.

[148] Ibid. 12 et seq.

[149] 'Report of the Secretary-General on the Protection of Civilians in Armed Conflict', above note 14, para. 45.

[150] Schmelzle, 'Evaluating Governance', above note 44, at 7; A. Cassese, 'The Legitimacy of International Criminal Tribunals and the Current Prospects of International Criminal Justice' (2012) 25 *Leiden Journal of International Law* 491, at 492 (in principle also distinguishing between empirical and normative legitimacy). Sometimes empirical legitimacy is also described as perceived legitimacy. S. Ford, 'A Social Psychological Model of the Perceived Legitimacy of International Criminal Courts: Implications for the Success of Transitional Justice Mechanisms' (2012) 45 *Vanderbilt Journal of Transnational Law* 405, at 407 et seq.

actor's perception that the rule has a high normative value. Research on governance in areas of limited statehood has identified various resources for the empirical legitimacy as a necessary prerequisite for the effectiveness, that is, compliance-pull of (normative) orders: effectiveness as output-legitimacy, the adaptability of norms, that is, the capability of international norms to be translated into the specific contexts of areas of limited statehood, participation of addressees and procedural fairness (input- and throughput-legitimacy), as well as the authority of the norm entrepreneurs.[151] From a legal perspective, the latter two criteria are particularly significant since they concern the process of norm-creation. Accordingly, they have also been highlighted in international legal theory. Thomas Franck, for instance, has identified some comparable preconditions for a compliance-pull of international norms. Franck starts from the assumption that the legitimacy of an international norm depends on the norm addressees' belief that it has 'come into being in accordance with the right process'.[152] As elements of the right process, Thomas Franck identifies, inter alia, symbolic validation. Accordingly, the legitimacy of an international rule also depends on its ability to communicate authority, that is, 'the authority of a rule, the authority of the originator of a validating communication and, at times, the authority bestowed on the recipient of the communication'.[153] He holds that a new rule will have a greater compliance-pull if it is introduced 'under the aegis of a particularly venerable sponsor'.[154] Both aspects – procedural fairness and authority of the norm entrepreneur – advocate a greater participation of non-State actors in inducing compliance with international humanitarian law.

From the perspective of armed groups, legitimacy is particularly deficient in terms of procedural fairness; armed groups must comply with rules whose creation they never consented to[155] since the law-making

[151] Sonderforschungsbereich 700, 'Governance in Räumen begrenzter Staatlichkeit – Neue Formen des Regierens?' Finanzierungsantrag 2014–2015–2016–2017, Freie Universität Berlin, 2013, at 29.

[152] Franck, *Fairness in International Law and Institutions*, above note 41, at 24; T. Franck, 'Legitimacy in the International System' (1988) 82 *American Journal of International Law* 705, at 706.

[153] Franck, 'Legitimacy in the International System', above note 152, at 725; T. Franck, *The Power of Legitimacy among Nations* (Oxford: Oxford University Press, 1990), at 91 et seq.; O. Schachter, 'Towards a Theory of International Obligation' (1968) 8 *Virginia Journal of International Law* 300, at 309–11.

[154] Franck, 'Legitimacy in the International System', above note 152, at 727.

[155] Lamp, 'Conceptions of War', above note 6, at 241; Sivakumaran, 'Implementing Humanitarian Norms through Non-State Armed Groups', Chapter 6 in this volume, at 130–31,

process is traditionally dominated by States. This lack of participation is increasingly seen as deficient.[156] However, the underlying idea of procedural legitimacy is that ownership of the norms is created[157] insofar as 'involvement in a process can lead to support for the results of that process'.[158] There are numerous suggestions on how to create ownership despite the limits of traditional international law. The approaches include considering the practice of armed groups and their *opinio juris* in the process of creating customary international law, inviting such groups to participate in treaty-making processes or bestowing ad hoc commitments and unilateral declarations by armed groups with legal force in the context of a particular conflict.[159]

Without evaluating the validity of these different proposals, what remains clear is that such efforts are more easily promoted by (other) non-State actors. They enjoy a high standing as norm entrepreneurs because organizations such as Geneva Call, or a neutral organization such as the ICRC, can act more independently from States' self-interests than UN organs.[160] They are not subject to certain (legal) limitations of the international order. Again, empirical research supports these findings. Jo and Bryant have shown on the basis of a case study from Sudan that political interaction among non-State actors – rebel groups and international humanitarian organizations – furthers compliance with international humanitarian law, and that, correspondingly, the most successful of the Sudanese rebel groups, the SPLA/M, followed a strategy of engaging with civil society as a means to attain status at the international level.[161] Here, symbolic validation is important. Both Geneva Call and the ICRC can claim considerable standing as norm entrepreneurs, which adds to

who describes the example of the Viet Cong, which explicitly stated in 1965 that it is not bound by the Geneva Convention since it did not participate in the norm creation process.

156 A. Roberts and S. Sivakumaran, 'Lawmaking by Non-State Actors: Engaging Armed Groups in the Creation of International Humanitarian Law' (2012) 37 *Yale Journal of International Law* 107, at 126 et seq.

157 Sassòli, 'The Implementation of International Humanitarian Law', above note 68, at 64; M. Sassòli, 'Taking Armed Groups Seriously: Ways to Improve Their Compliance with International Humanitarian Law' (2010) 1 *International Humanitarian Legal Studies* 5, at 6, 20 et seq.

158 Sivakumaran, 'Implementing Humanitarian Norms', above note 155, at 131.

159 Sassòli, 'Taking Armed Groups Seriously', above note 157, at 21 et seq.; Sivakumaran, 'Implementing Humanitarian Norms', above note 155, at 125–40.

160 Sassòli, 'Taking Armed Groups Seriously', above note 157, at 23; D. Zaum, 'International Non-Governmental Organizations and Civil Wars' (2009) 11 *Civil Wars* 22, at 27.

161 Jo and Bryant, 'Taming of the Warlords', above note 28, at 258.

the empirical legitimacy of the norms they are promoting.[162] Both institutions can rely on the so-called 'Swiss-factor' as actors coming from an internationally highly respected country'.[163]

The 'Swiss factor' adds to the general perception that these institutions are neutral and impartial actors and lack a 'State-bias'. At the same time, both can also rely on the expertise and standing of their personnel.[164] The often technical dimension of their advice, for instance, in the case of landmines, adds to their perception as neutral institutions.[165] Empirical research proves that such 'approaches to engaging armed actors are often viewed as being more sincere and dedicated to a sustainable resolution of the conflict based on the demands and preferences of the parties to conflict rather than being interested in the maintenance of the status quo'.[166] Unlike (powerful) State actors, they are unable to exert pressure to influence the behaviour of the parties to the conflict. Thus, the norm diffusion process appears to be (more) genuine and does not depend on pressure scenarios.[167] Accordingly, NGOs have become an essential part in the overall pattern of inducing compliance with international humanitarian law.

4. Turning to non-State actors as norm entrepreneurs inducing compliance

Empirical research has prompted a turn to non-State actors as norm entrepreneurs. For inducing compliance, diverging instruments[168] may be combined by different actors in order to overcome, at least to a certain extent, the limitations that State interests pose. Hierarchical coercive mechanisms by State-empowered international organizations might accommodate certain State interests while effectively ameliorating compliance using instruments of law enforcement (Section 4.1). Where State

162 See, in general, Finnemore and Sikkink, 'International Norm Dynamics and Political Change', above note 38, at 906.

163 Schneckener and Hofmann, 'The Power of Persuasion', above note 118, at 102, 107.

164 Ibid.; International Committee of the Red Cross: Ratner, 'Law Promotion beyond Talk', above note 40, at 491.

165 Zaum, 'International Non-Governmental Organizations and Civil Wars', above note 160, at 29.

166 Schneckener and Hofmann, 'The Power of Persuasion', above note 118, at 105–06.

167 Ibid.

168 Social sciences have identified four social mechanisms for inducing compliance: coercion, incentive structures, persuasion and capacity-building. See Risse and Börzel, 'Human Rights – The New Agenda', above note 1, at 3 et seq.

interests impede effective action, the responsibility of inducing compliance may be handed over to private non-State actors that act on the basis of non-hierarchical instruments such as persuasion and rewards (Section 4.2).

4.1. *Coercion: extending the responsibility of the international community*

Coercion can be defined as a hierarchical instrument to direct an actor's behaviour by leaving the actor no alternative but to comply with the norms. Thus, coercion is directly linked to law enforcement.[169] Law enforcement builds not only on actual coercion but also on the threat of sanctions as well. This is particularly apparent in international criminal law that relies on not only special but also general deterrence, each with a positive and a negative component.[170] And the punishment of the offenders is directed at stopping them not only from committing a specific crime but also from repeating criminal behaviour in the future. In addition, the threat of sanctions is also supposed to work as an incentive for others to remain law-abiding.[171] In law enforcement, the effectiveness of these sanctions relies heavily on the real threat of coercion, which a legal system with effective hierarchical instruments can exert.

Coercion as a means to enforce international humanitarian law is increasingly exercised by international institutions such as the ICC and the UN Security Council. These institutions have taken over responsibilities which traditionally lie with the State. In particular, experiences with conflicts in war-torn areas of limited statehood have pushed and prompted the creation of instruments that subsidiarily assume the responsibilities of States unable or unwilling to exercise them. This compensatory function of international organs is particularly evident in the case of the International Criminal Court.

4.1.1. Waning legitimacy of international criminal justice?

According to Article 17(3) of the ICC Statute, the ICC can intervene to replace the national judiciary if national judicial systems are ineffective.[172]

[169] Ibid.

[170] R. Cryer et al., *An Introduction to International Criminal Law and Procedure* (Cambridge: Cambridge University Press, 2007), at 20.

[171] On theories of deterrence Cryer, see 'The Role of International Criminal Prosecutions', above note 72, at 193–99, 205.

[172] Burke-White, 'Complementarity in Practice', above note 8, at 575.

However, efforts of the international community to take over a residuary responsibility by providing for international criminal justice will only work if these efforts are seen as legitimate by the communities affected.

What is needed is the creation of empirical legitimacy. Here, the criterion of adaptability of an institution to the context of local communities becomes important.[173] Efforts by international actors require clear strategies on how to communicate their activities to local communities. Otherwise, the actor's work may be undermined by processes of rejection.[174] Criteria for creating such empirical legitimacy include the court's location, the composition of the staff and the court's outreach efforts.[175] A particularly important criterion concerns the question of whom the court prosecutes, as decisions on prosecution might conflict with 'a group's dominant internal narrative about responsibility for the conflict'.[176] By perceiving the Court as biased, members of a group are able to maintain their own interpretation of the conflict.[177] The latter phenomenon appears to be part of the ICC's legitimacy problem in the DRC. Courts can counteract such perception if they are able to bring the 'internal narratives' in line with a more objective perception of the conflict in the long run.[178] The process of rejection might also be fostered if the court's activities are seen as biased and selective – a view which affects the procedural fairness.[179]

There is a perception in Africa that the ICC applies double standards in decisions concerning indictment and prosecution.[180] Indeed, as of 2014, all situations under investigation still concern African conflicts, although there are by now numerous preliminary examinations concerning States from other regions such as Afghanistan or Georgia. In the DRC, there appears to be a certain mixed or even negative perception of the ICC

[173] See above Section 3.2.3.

[174] Sonderforschungsbereich 700, 'Governance in Räumen begrenzter Staatlichkeit', above note 151; see also Bangerter, 'Comment – Persuading Armed Groups', above note 61, at 113 et seq.; A. Acharya, 'How Ideas Spread: Whose Norms Matter? Norm Localization and Institutional Change in Asian Regionalism' (2004) 58 *International Organization* 239, at 251–53.

[175] Ford, 'Social Psychological Model', above note 150, at 412; J. Stromseth, 'Pursuing Accountability for Atrocities after Conflict: What Impact on Building the Rule of Law?' (2007) 38 *Georgetown Journal of International Law* 251, at 268.

[176] Ford, 'Social Psychological Model', above note 150, at 410. [177] Ibid. [178] Ibid. 411.

[179] On the ICC and selectivity, see Cryer, 'The Role of International Criminal Prosecutions', above note 72, at 214.

[180] M. du Plessis, A. Louw and O. Maunganidze, *African Efforts to Close the Impunity Gap* (Institute for Security Studies, Paper No. 241, November 2012), at 2 et seq.

within the local communities. A majority of citizens in eastern DRC seem to prefer national over international prosecution,[181] notwithstanding the severe shortcomings of the national judicial system. However, this attitude might stem partly from a lack of knowledge. A population survey from 2008 stressed: 'While there is support for the ICC as a means of achieving justice in the DRC (26% of respondents), there is low awareness among the population of eastern Congo (27%) and in Kinshasa (28%) of the ICC or of the first scheduled trial against Thomas Lubanga in eastern DRC (28%) and Kinshasa (29%). Nevertheless a majority of those in eastern DRC who had heard about the ICC would like to participate in ICC activities (67%), but only 12 percent know how to access it'.[182]

To some extent, a process of rejection can also be observed on the State level. There are several initiatives on the regional as well as on the national level to reduce the impact of the ICC. A pertinent example on the national level involves the efforts in the DRC to improve the criminal justice system in regard of the prosecution of war crimes as described by Kumbu in the present volume.[183] Efforts on the regional level are more ambiguous. The relationship between the AU and the ICC apparently deteriorates: in 2012, the African Union Assembly Meeting adopted a draft amended protocol on the Statute of the African Court of Justice and Human Rights[184] which intended to extend the Court's competence to prosecute individuals for international crimes by establishing an International Criminal Law Section of the African Court with criminal jurisdiction over such crimes as genocide, war crimes and crimes against humanity.[185] In 2013, the 21st summit of the AU Assembly supported a request for a referral of the case against the serving Kenyan President Kenyatta back to

181 Kumbu, 'National Courts', above note 14, at 243–44; 'P. Vinck et al., 'Living with Fear: A Population-based Survey on Attitudes about Peace, Justice and Social Reconstruction in Eastern Democratic Republic of the Congo', August 2008, at 2–3, escholarship.org/uc/item/9738b4pm#page-1.

182 Ibid.

183 Kumbu, 'National Courts', above note 14, at 244–45; see, for such a prognosis, Cassese, 'Legitimacy of International Criminal Tribunals', above note 150, at 499.

184 On the role of the AU organs in inducing compliance, see Ntoubandi, 'Comment – Enforcement of International Humanitarian Law through the Human Rights Organs of the African Union', Chapter 13 in this volume, at 300–12; see also M. Löffelmann, 'The African Court on Human Rights and Peoples' Rights' (2010) 85 *Die Friedens-Warte* 161.

185 African Union, Meeting of Government Experts and Ministers of Justice and Attorneys General on Legal Matters (Addis Ababa, Ethiopia, 7–11 and 14–15 May 2012) Draft Protocol on Amendments to the Protocol on the Statute of the African Court of Justice and Human Rights, Exp/Min/IV/Rev.7 of 15 May 2012.

Kenya.[186] After an exchange of letters between the AU and the ICC, the AU adopted another decision at its extraordinary summit on 12 October 2013. Here, the Assembly requested inter alia that 'no charges shall be commenced or continued before any International Court or Tribunal against any serving AU Head of State or Government or anybody acting or entitled to act in such capacity during their term of office'. Moreover, it intends to 'fast track the process of expanding the mandate of the African Court on Human and Peoples' Rights (AfCHPR) to try international crimes'.[187] In July 2014 at its 23rd Ordinary Session, the Assembly amended the draft protocol to include an immunity provision for 'serving African Union Heads of State or Government, or anybody acting or entitled to act in such capacity, or other senior state officials based on their functions, during their tenure of office'.[188] At least no member State has so far withdrawn from the ICC Statute. The friction between African States and the ICC is partly based on their perception that the cases concerning Al-Bashir[189] and Kenya's post-election violence[190] formed a kind of 'top-down' intervention by the ICC, which prompted domestic rejections of prosecuting those responsible.[191] Other voices hold that the split between the African Union and the ICC over the Al-Bashir and Kenyatta cases serves interests of African heads of States because they are trying to protect themselves from the danger of prosecution.[192]

In the light of the ambiguous States' policy, there is interest in the involvement of NGOs. An example of such involvement is the South

[186] AU, Decision on International Jurisdiction, Justice and The International Criminal Court (ICC) 1 – Doc. Assembly/AU/13(XXI), Decision Assembly/AU/Dec.482(XXI) (26–27 May 2013).

[187] AU Decision on Africa's Relationship with the ICC, Ext/Assembly/AU/Dec.1 (12 October 2013).

[188] A. P. van der Mei, 'Impunity for African Heads of State', Maastricht University (20 August 2014), law.maastrichtuniversity.nl/newsandviews/impunity-for-african-heads-of-state/.

[189] S. Wedehaimanot, 'Arresting Al-Bashir: The African Union's Opposition and the Legalities' (2011) 11 *African Journal of International and Comparative Law* 208.

[190] C. Sriram and S. Brown, 'Kenya in the Shadow of the ICC: Complementarity, Gravity and Impact' (2012) 12 *International Criminal Law Review* 219; see on the crisis S. Sharma, 'The 2007–08 Post-Election Crisis in Kenya', in J. Hoffmann and A. Nollkaemper (eds.), *Responsibility to Protect: From Principle to Practice* (Amsterdam: Amsterdam University Press, 2012), 27–38.

[191] Plessis, Louw and Maunganidze, *African Efforts to Close the Impunity Gap*, above note 180, at 9.

[192] C. Jalloh et al, 'Assessing the African Union Concerns about Article 16 of the Rome Statute of the International Criminal Court' (2011) 4 *African Journal of Legal Studies* 5, at 8.

African legislation. Under Article 38 of the Constitution, NGOs have a standing 'to approach a competent court, alleging that a right in the Bill of Rights has been infringed or threatened'. They may request investigations and challenge the prosecution's refusal to do so before the courts.[193] This concept of NGO-standing was confirmed by South Africa's High Court in the *Zimbabwe Torture Docket* case. In the Case, which was launched by the South African Litigation Centre, the Court confirmed that South Africa had jurisdiction to prosecute crimes committed in Zimbabwe under the concept of universal jurisdiction, and that the South African ICC Act[194] removed immunity *ratione personae* for government officials.[195] Thus, while the ICC is a clear symbol for the International Community's willingness to take over responsibility for enforcing the laws of war where States fail to do so, it also demonstrates the limits of this approach. State empowered institutions remain subject to governments' interests, which may be constrained by international politics. There is a strong presumption that effective enforcement requires a multi-level system, involving not only the State, regional and international institutions, but also NGOs which help to limit sovereignty concerns.

On the basis of an empirical study, Reed Wood submits that threats of criminal prosecution might not direct armed groups' behaviour at all. Starting from his analysis that violence against civilians serves short-term interests to guarantee a group's survival, he argues that these interests and a group's strategy are hardly influenced by a threat of future prosecution.[196] Indeed, especially during an ongoing armed conflict, immediate reactions will be necessary in order to address actors that predominantly pursue short-term interests.[197] While international criminal law aims at creating a real threat of coercion, its partly retroactive nature consequently limits some of its effects. Thus, a system built on penal sanctions alone would indeed be defunct. Under the conditions of the present international system, with its strict limitations on belligerent reprisal, an immediate

[193] Plessis, Louw and Maunganidze, *African Efforts to Close the Impunity Gap*, above note 180, at 11.

[194] Republic of South Africa, *The Implementation of the Rome Statute of the International Criminal Court* (Act No. 27 of 2002), 18 July 2002.

[195] North Gauteng High Court: *Southern African Litigation Centre and Others v. The National Director of Public Prosecutions and Others* (77150/09) [2012] ZAGPPHC 61; 2012 (10) BCLR 1089 (GNP); [2012] 3 All SA 198 (GNP) (8 May 2012).

[196] Wood, 'Understanding Strategic Motives for Violence', above note 74, at 41.

[197] Dinstein, *The Conduct of Hostilities*, above note 96, at 253 et seq.

and real threat of coercion can, above all, be sustained by the UN Security Council.[198]

4.1.2. Shortcomings in the Security Council's effectiveness and legitimacy?

The UN Security Council has increasingly established its competence to enforce international humanitarian law. Although it has to be kept in mind that the Security Council is a political body with the primary responsibility of maintaining international peace and security, its competence is broad enough so that the Council can act as an enforcement organ of international (humanitarian) law if the violation of the law amounts to a breach of or a threat to peace. Efforts of the UN Security Council to enforce international humanitarian law began with its first thematic resolution on civilian and armed conflict.[199] Today, there are a number of measures contributing to the enforcement of international humanitarian law.[200] Important instruments include the Monitoring and Reporting Mechanism on grave violations against children in armed conflict according to UNSC Resolution 1612 (26 July 2005), as well as the so-called 'List of Shame', which is accompanied by targeted sanctions against persistent violators. In the case of children and armed conflict, the Secretary-General uses the so-called List of Shame annexed to his reports to the Security Council, wherein he lists those who persistently commit the six grave violations in relation to children and armed conflict.[201] The Security Council also imposes targeted sanctions against persistent violators of international humanitarian law, which are then integrated into existing sanction regimes. As of late 2012, six out of thirteen sanction regimes listed violations of international humanitarian law as relevant criteria. The sanctions impose travel bans and financial measures on individuals in Libya, the DRC, Côte d'Ivoire, Somalia, Eritrea and

[198] Oeter, 'Civil War, Humanitarian Law and the United Nations', above note 57, at 215.

[199] UNSC Resolution 1296 (19 April 2000); UNSC Resolution 1539 (22 April 2004); H. Krieger, 'Der Sicherheitsrat als Hüter der Menschenrechte: Grund und Grenzen seiner Kompetenz' (2006) 81 *Die Friedens-Warte* 107.

[200] G. Nolte, 'Practice of the UN Security Council with Respect to Humanitarian Law', in K. Dicke and J. Delbrück (eds.), *Weltinnenrecht* (Berlin: Duncker & Humblot, 2005), 487–502, at 489; M. Roscini, 'The United Nations Security Council and the Enforcement of International Humanitarian Law' (2010) 43 *Israel Law Review* 330.

[201] These six grave violations include killing or maiming of children, recruitment or use of child soldiers, rape and other forms of sexual violence against children, abduction of children, attacks against schools or hospitals and denial of humanitarian access to children.

Sudan.[202] Another response of the UN Security Council to persistent violations of international humanitarian law can be seen in the gradual changes in its peacekeeping system. Currently, a mandate for the protection of civilians is included in most of the UN Security Council's situation specific resolutions.[203] Civilian protection has become a central function of UN peacekeeping missions. In addition, the Security Council has also started to rely on the UN Human Rights Due Diligence Policy in its resolutions. In the resolution establishing the Intervention Brigade in the DRC, the Council authorized cooperation with the national armed forces 'in strict compliance with international law, including international humanitarian law and with the human rights due diligence policy on UN-support to non-UN forces (HRDDP)'.[204] Thus, the Council aims to prevent that UN forces contribute to grave violations of international humanitarian law.[205]

However, from an empirical perspective, the effectiveness of peacekeeping missions, as well as of targeted sanctions, is controversial. There are several studies which demonstrate that peacekeeping operations tend to lead to an increase in violence against civilians inflicted by armed groups.[206] In the present volume, Denis Tull has shown how MONUSCO failed to fulfil its protection mandate in the DRC.[207] Likewise, Reed Wood has demonstrated that partial and half-hearted foreign interventions may have reverse effects, prompting rebel groups to use more violence against civilians. He names the examples of interventions against the LRA in 2008 and Sierra Leone in 1998, both of which resulted in increasing numbers of civilian victims.[208] However, these findings do not imply that the UN should not intervene to end civil war and protect civilians; they require that planning operations and the corresponding strategies respond to

[202] Cf. 'Report of the Secretary-General on the Protection of Civilians in Armed Conflict', above note 14, para. 22.

[203] Ibid. para. 22; 'Report of the Secretary-General on the Protection of Civilians in Armed Conflict', above note 144, para. 43.

[204] UNSC Resolution 2098 (28 March 2013), para. 12 (b).

[205] H. Aust, 'The UN Human Rights Due Diligence Policy: An Effective Mechanism against Complicity of Peacekeeping Forces?' (2015) 20 *Journal of Conflict and Security Law* 61.

[206] M. Bussmann and G. Schneider, 'A Porous Humanitarian Shield: The Laws of War, the Red Cross, and the Killing of Civilians', Paper presented at the Pan-European Meeting of the Standing Group on International Relations (Stockholm, 9–11 September 2010), at 6 et seq., L. Hultman, 'Keeping Peace or Spurring Violence? Unintended Effects of Peace Operations on Violence against Civilians' (2010) 12 *Civil Wars* 29.

[207] D. Tull, 'Comment – UN Peacekeeping in the Democratic Republic of the Congo: The Travails of Civilian Protection', Chapter 17 in this volume, at 399–413.

[208] Wood, 'Understanding Strategic Motives for Violence', above note 74, at 41–42.

these dangers. Some studies submit that the operation's mandate is the decisive starting point and consider the extension of the mandates to protect civilians as a major step towards better compliance.[209] Other studies consequently view UN peacekeeping more positively.[210] Eventually, the UN peacekeeping missions will face problems similar to those faced by other actors involved in inducing compliance, like a lack of financial and material resources, as well as personnel, so that only insufficient numbers of troops with often insufficient equipment will be able to be deployed.

In the case of the sanction regimes, there are notorious examples of persistent violators that evade the UN sanctions system, with Bosco Ntaganda having been a particularly prominent case in the DRC.[211] Empirical research suggests that 'targeted sanctions are much more effective in signalling or constraining a target than they are in coercing a change in target behaviour'.[212] Although UN targeted sanctions appear not to be as efficient as anticipated, under certain conditions, they can still generate a change in behaviour. This is the case if they pursue a narrowly defined goal, such as turning over suspects, if they are immediately imposed as a reaction to a breach of a rule and if they are part of concerted actions including other actors. Thus, there appears to be a stronger compliance-pull if actions follow earlier sanctions issued by regional bodies[213] and if they are part of a larger pattern of enforcement, including the presence of peacekeeping missions and referrals to legal tribunals.[214] For effectiveness, actions need to target those responsible for decision-making,

[209] Bussmann and Schneider, 'Strategie, Anarchie oder fehlendes internationales Engagement?', above note 56, at 25.

[210] V. Fortna, 'Does Peacekeeping Keep Peace? International Intervention and the Duration of Peace After Civil War' (2004) 48 *International Studies Quarterly* 269; E. Melander, 'Selected to Go Where Murderers Lurk? The Preventive Effect of Peacekeeping' (2009) 26 *Conflict Management and Peace Science* 389; see also Lamp, 'Conceptions of War', above note 6, at 260.

[211] List of individuals and entities subject to the measures imposed by paras. 13 and 15 of UNSC Resolution 1596 (18 April 2005), as renewed by para. 3 of UNSC Resolution 2078 (28 November 2012); see www.un.org/sc/committees/1533/pdf/1533_list.pdf (last updated 30 June 2014); see also P. Wallensteen and H. Grusell, 'Targeting the Right Targets? The UN Use of Targeted Sanctions' (2012) 18 *Global Governance* 207, at 225.

[212] Targeted Sanctions Consortium (ed.), *Designing United Nations Targeted Sanctions* (April 2012), at 14; E. Shagabutdinova and J. Berejikian, 'Deploying Sanctions while Protecting Human Rights: Are Humanitarian "Smart" Sanctions Effective?' (2007) 6 *Journal of Human Rights* 59, at 70; Wallensteen and Grusell, 'Targeting the Right Targets?', above note 211, at 223.

[213] Targeted Sanctions Consortium, *Designing United Nations Targeted Sanctions* (April 2012), at 17.

[214] Ibid.; Wallensteen and Grusell, 'Targeting the Right Targets?', above note 211, at 222.

preferably listing few people, since monitoring will be more effective in such a case.[215] This observation corresponds to the finding that it is, normatively speaking, relatively expensive to rely exclusively on sanctions and rewards because, like governments, the international community has to spend meaningful resources on monitoring if it wants to make sanctions work.[216] Civil society exerting strong pressure for resolute international action is therefore a further prerequisite for UN sanctions' effectiveness.

Moreover, the legitimacy of these actions strongly depends on the general perception of the UN Security Council's legitimacy.[217] Quite like the ICC, the UN Security Council is often accused of selectivity. The selectivity reproach refers to the choice of situations in which the Council is prepared to determine that violations of international humanitarian law constitute a threat to peace,[218] as well as the choice of the law that it enforces. Thus, it has been suggested that the Council has promoted the enforcement of Geneva Law more than that of Hague Law.[219] However, even if the Security Council furthers law enforcement, the Council remains competent to act with a wide nearly unfettered discretion, and the maintenance of peace remains the primary goal of its activities, outweighing other goals and considerations like enforcing international humanitarian law.

The perception that the selectivity and inactivity of the Security Council in certain cases is not owed to a responsible exercise of its discretion – but is instead arbitrarily based on short-sighted national interests – is at the centre of present day international law. It has led to academic and political debates on how far the Security Council's and third States'

[215] Wallensteen and Grusell, 'Targeting the Right Targets?', above note 211, at 216.

[216] M. Levi, A. Sacks and T. Tyler, 'Conceptualizing Legitimacy, Measuring Legitimating Beliefs' (2009) 53 *American Behavioral Scientist* 354, at 355; Schmelzle, 'Evaluating Governance', above note 44, at 10 et seq.

[217] A. Peters, 'The Security Council's Responsibility to Protect' (2011) 8 *International Organizations Law Review* 15, at 26.

[218] UNSC, 6151st meeting (26 June 2009), UN Doc. S/PV 6151 Statement of the Representative of Australia, at 13: 'However, there is clearly a need for greater consistency in the Council's approach. Too often still, the Council appears unwilling to address the plight of civilians in many internal armed conflicts, notwithstanding the obvious destabilizing effects and regional consequences of such conflicts. In failing to do so, the Council falls short of its obligations under the Charter.[. . . What is lacking at times, as we know, is the political resolve of the Council to use those tools to protect civilians and of the broader membership to support such Council action.'

[219] R. Cryer, 'The Security Council and International Humanitarian Law', in S. Breau and A. Jachec-Neale (eds.), *Testing the Boundaries of International Humanitarian Law* (London: British Institute of International and Comparative Law, 2006), 245–75, at 274; Roscini, 'The United Nations Security Council and the Enforcement of International Humanitarian Law', above note 200, at 353.

discretion is curtailed by legal obligations. Although there is a competence (permissive authority) for the International Community to enforce international humanitarian law via the ICC and Chapter VII of the Security Council, what is in question is whether and under what conditions there is also a duty to act. The most prominent attempt is the development of the concept of the Responsibility to Protect.[220] States are legally responsible for their citizens' welfare. However, if they fail in this responsibility, whether out of sheer unwillingness or lack of capability, the international community obtains a – moral, political or even legal – responsibility to become involved or even to intervene.[221] However, at the present stage of international law, the Responsibility to Protect does not create an obligation of the United Nations, the Security Council or individual States to act if the national State has failed, let alone to intervene militarily. At best, the subsidiary Responsibility to Protect might be described as an emerging rule of customary international law,[222] the emergence of which is still disputed, given that the UN Secretary-General stated in his 2012 Report on Protection of Civilians in Armed Conflict that 'the responsibility to protect is a political concept'.[223] Moreover, the Responsibility to Protect is not identical with the enforcement of international humanitarian law. The latter is concerned with the most egregious violations of human rights, in particular genocide,[224] whereas the former might remain below this threshold. Moreover, international humanitarian law applies in times of armed conflict, while the Responsibility to Protect is applicable in times of peace and war alike.

For the enforcement of international humanitarian law in times of armed conflict, there is a more specific norm in Common Article 1 of the GC which obliges States 'to ensure respect for the present Convention in all

[220] See from the vast literature on the responsibility to protect: J. Hoffmann and A. Nollkaemper (eds.), *Responsibility to Protect: From Principle to Practice* (Amsterdam: Amsterdam University Press, 2012); H. Nasu, 'The UN Security Council's Responsibility and the Responsibility to Protect' (2011) 15 *Max Planck Yearbook of United Nations Law* 377; A. Orford, 'From Promise to Practice? The Legal Significance of the Responsibility to Protect Concept' (2010) 21 *Finnish Yearbook of International Law* 65; Peters, 'The Security Council's Responsibility to Protect', above note 217.

[221] A. von Arnauld, 'Souveränität und Responsibility to Protect' (2009) 84 *Die Friedens-Warte* 11, at 24 et seq.; A. Bellamy, *Global Politics and the Responsibility to Protect – from Words to Deeds* (Abingdon: Routledge, 2011), at 10; Risse and Börzel, 'Human Rights – The New Agenda', above note 1, at 15.

[222] Peters, 'The Security Council's Responsibility to Protect', above note 217, at 26.

[223] 'Report of the Secretary-General on the Protection of Civilians in Armed Conflict', above note 14, para. 21.

[224] Ibid. 5 et seq.

circumstances'.[225] However, whether these obligations entail an obligation for States parties which are not participating in a particular armed conflict to ensure respect by other States and armed groups is highly disputed. Likewise, it is far from clear which measures States would have to take in such a case. In this volume, Robin Geiß has suggested, on the basis of an analysis of the pertinent State practice, that Common Article 1 GC indeed possesses an external-compliance dimension,[226] including States as well as non-State actors.[227] He argues that the obligation to ensure respect 'in both its internal and external-compliance dimensions should be construed broadly to require positive steps whenever provisions of the Geneva Conventions are breached'.[228] In such a case, 'States are obliged to do what can reasonably be expected of them'.[229] This would include acting in cooperation with the United Nations according to Article 89 AP I. However, Common Article 1 GC would not impose a duty 'to vote positively for whatever resolution is contemplated in the Security Council as a response to serious violations of international humanitarian law'.[230] Thus, within a legal system still based on the consent of those who are bound by the rules, inertia can hardly be overcome by creating new legal rules.

[225] For an analysis of Common Article 1 GC, see F. Azzam, 'The Duty of Third States to Implement and Enforce International Humanitarian Law' (1997) 66 *Nordic Journal of International Law* 55; L. Boisson de Chazournes and L. Condorelli, 'Common Article 1 of the Geneva Conventions Revisited: Protecting Collective Interests' (2000) 82 *International Review of the Red Cross* 67; B. Kessler, 'The Duty to "Ensure Respect" Under Common Article 1 of the Geneva Conventions: Its Implications on International and Non-International Armed Conflicts' (2001) 44 *German Yearbook of International Law* 498; H.-P. Gasser, 'Ensuring Respect for the Geneva Conventions and Protocols: The Role of Third States and the United Nations', in H. Fox and M. Meyer (eds.), *Effecting Compliance, Armed Conflict and the New Law* (London: British Institute for International & Comparative Law, 1993), 15–21; U. Palwankar, 'Measures Available to States for Fulfilling their Obligation to Ensure Respect for International Humanitarian Law' (1994) 43 *International Review of the Red Cross* 9; C. Focarelli, 'Common Article 1 of the 1949 Geneva Conventions: A Soap Bubble?' (2010) 21 *European Journal of International Law* 125.

[226] R. Geiß, 'Common Article 1 of the Geneva Conventions: Scope and Content of the Obligation to "Ensure Respect" – "Narrow but Deep" or "Wide and Shallow"?', Chapter 18 in this volume, at 422–28; see also H. Brollowski, 'The Responsibility to Protect and Common Article 1 of the 1949 Geneva Conventions and Obligations of Third States' in J. Hoffmann and A. Nollkaemper (eds.), *Responsibility to Protect: From Principle to Practice* (Amsterdam: Amsterdam University Press, 2012), 93–110, at 95 et seq.

[227] Geiß, 'Common Article 1 of the Geneva Conventions', above note 226, at 428.

[228] Ibid. 433. [229] Ibid. 434.

[230] Ibid. 440. He suggests, however, that Common Article 1 GC could be a basis to require members of the Security Council to explain a veto or negative vote.

4.2. *Rewards and persuasion: the increasing role for non-State actors*

Therefore, international law might envisage a turn to alternative actors using an alternative instrument: persuasion by non-State actors. 'Persuasion and discourse' draws on the logic of consequences as much as on the logic of appropriateness. At first glance, it aims to induce voluntary compliance through arguing and learning, but without affecting the targeted actor's interests. In the practice of the international system, however, persuasion is often directly combined with incentive-based mechanisms, and both mechanisms depend on each other.[231]

As a soft compliance procedure, persuasion by institutions, such as Geneva Call and the ICRC, fits into the general compliance paradigm of international law. There is, among States in general, only a limited acceptability of hierarchical forms of compliance control. States prefer non-confrontational compliance mechanisms which rely on the fear of loss of reputation, since hierarchical law enforcement is considered to be too interfering.[232] More important, the ICRC and Geneva Call enjoy a greater flexibility than the State-empowered and dependent UN system. While the ICRC and Geneva Call can continuously adapt their line of argumentation to the exigencies of the particular conflict, UN institutions are forced to act with stricter coherence because they issue their findings publicly and also issue definite legal determinations.[233] At the same time, States will exert more political pressure within the United Nations in order to influence the context of such findings in their interest.[234] There is also greater flexibility from an organizational point of view in that smaller informal institutions can react more quickly, and they do not need to pursue their aims via administrative channels in the States concerned.[235] Correspondingly, there is no need for feedback to the hierarchical UN organizations through time-consuming processes of coordination. In addition, the low media profile adds to this flexibility since there is less pressure to succeed. Thus, these institutions can invest time in building up stable relationships.[236] On the other hand, if required, they have sufficient possibilities to mobilize public opinion.[237]

[231] Risse and Börzel, 'Human Rights – The New Agenda', above note 1, at 3 et seq.
[232] Bothe, 'Compliance', above note 2, para. 142.
[233] Ratner, 'Law Promotion beyond Talk', above note 40, at 489.
[234] Zaum, 'International Non-Governmental Organizations and Civil Wars', above note 160, at 26.
[235] Ibid. 28.
[236] Schneckener and Hofmann, 'The Power of Persuasion', above note 118, at 107.
[237] Mampilly, 'Insurgent Governance', above note 78, at 61.

Moreover, for institutions such as Geneva Call, instilling compliance is easier insofar as it can concentrate on a single or only few issues, unlike UN institutions, which promote a complex legal system. For some years, for example, Geneva Call had concentrated only on the banning of anti-personnel mines. Focusing on a clearly delineated goal makes compromise easier and dialogue less complex.[238]

However, empirical findings on the effectiveness of these approaches are contradictory. Bussmann and Schneider have suggested in an empirical study that the work of the ICRC does not induce compliance effectively, if at all:

> Even if we test for the possible endogeneity of ICRC activities, we cannot find evidence that the ICRC presence in conflict zones makes a crucial difference and that especially rebel leaders are not deterred from pursuing one-sided violence as an integral part of their military campaigns . . . training seminars which are provided by the ICRC do not have the desired effect and that the presence of the ICRC is associated with more rather than fewer killings.[239]

Still, the results of such empirical studies must be viewed with caution. While the Rwandan genocide seems to prove that persuasion is futile or idealistic,[240] these cases cannot and should not be generalized. Improvement in compliance as a consequence of the ICRC's involvement may be indirect and belated.[241] Its effects are difficult to prove, variables for empirical research difficult to determine. Accordingly, it will remain unclear whether a situation would even have been worse without the ICRC's intervention. This is partly a consequence of the ICRC's confidentiality, since few actors will be prepared to admit that they changed their behaviour due to the ICRC's intervention.[242] Finally, cases such as Bosnia-Herzegovina, on which many empirical studies are based,[243] can be seen as a turning point in the international community's approach to inducing compliance. Failure in these cases cannot be pinned to the ICRC alone. Many of the concepts currently being discussed, such as the role of Geneva Call, International Criminal Justice and UN Security Council activities, are a direct response to the experiences of the 1990s.

[238] Schneckener and Hofmann, 'The Power of Persuasion', above note 118, at 103–04.
[239] Bussmann and Schneider, 'A Porous Humanitarian Shield', above note 206, at 1, 17 et seq.
[240] Lamp, 'Conceptions of War', above note 6, at 257. [241] Ibid. 483.
[242] Ratner, 'Law Promotion beyond Talk', above note 40, at 483.
[243] For instance, Bussmann and Schneider, 'Strategie, Anarchie oder fehlendes internationales Engagement?', above note 56, at 24–29.

However, certain deficiencies in the work of NGOs cannot be ignored. Due to their limited financial and personal resources, NGOs' efforts might not be sustainable.[244] An organization such as Geneva Call has proven to be particularly successful in clearly circumscribed legal fields, such as a ban on anti-personnel mines, child protection or gender issues. It remains to be seen whether Geneva Call will face the same difficulties as State-empowered international organizations the more it broadens its activities. In addition, NGOs have become increasingly dependent on financial support from their seat States, impairing armed groups' perceptions of their impartiality.[245] This perception of impartiality has also been tainted by NGO contributions to peace-building efforts; their work appears to be increasingly political.[246] Moreover, unlike within the UN system, NGOs', and to a certain extent also the ICRC's, efforts to persuade and to use incentives cannot be directly backed by a threat of coercion, for instance, targeted sanctions.[247] There are no direct and intentional ways available to coordinate the effects of different compliance instruments. By contrast, the ICRC explicitly pursues a policy not to share its information and observations with the ICC. At the same time, armed groups might be reluctant to grant access because they might be anxious that violations will be detected and reported. A certain level of scepticism on the side of armed groups apparently remains.[248]

Moreover, what armed groups might perceive as independence and impartiality might be seen as instrumentalization by State actors.[249] Many States actively oppose efforts to engage more with armed groups. In particular, the criminalization of internal armed conflicts through the paradigm of terrorism restricts the wider legal margin which NGOs enjoy. The most striking example is US legislation, according to which 'it is a federal crime to knowingly provid[e] material support or resources to a foreign terrorist organization'.[250] Since material support encompasses

[244] Schneckener and Hofmann, 'The Power of Persuasion', above note 118, at 108.

[245] Zaum, 'International Non-Governmental Organizations and Civil Wars', above note 160, at 28.

[246] Ibid. 33 et seq.

[247] For the channels of NGOs' access to the UN, see S. Hobe, 'Non-Governmental Organizations', in R. Wolfrum (ed.), *The Max Planck Encyclopedia of Public International Law* (Oxford: Oxford University Press, 2010, online edition, www.mpepil.com), paras. 26 et seq.

[248] Jo and Bryant, 'Taming of the Warlords', above note 28, at 247.

[249] Zaum, 'International Non-Governmental Organizations and Civil Wars', above note 160, at 23.

[250] *Holder v. Humanitarian Law Project*, 130 S. Ct. 2705 (2010); 18 U.S.C. § 2339 B(a)(1), USA PATRIOT Act.

training and expert advice or assistance, activities of NGOs and efforts of the ICRC or Geneva Call to disseminate international humanitarian law, to provide legal advice or to assist with the disposal of landmines might be covered by the legislation. Groups classified as terrorists include(d) the Kurdistan Workers' Party (PKK) and the Liberation Tigers of Tamil Eelam (LTTE). American NGOs have challenged the prohibition on the basis that it violates their rights under the Fifth and First Amendment of the US Constitution, particularly because the regulation prohibits engaging with armed groups by training 'members to use international law to resolve disputes peacefully; teaching PKK members to petition the United Nations and other representative bodies for relief'. However, the US Supreme Court considered the statute to be constitutional.[251]

Such practice does not only hinder humanitarian organizations from engaging with armed groups, but also aims to reduce their reputation. Accordingly, the practice of the US has attracted international criticism. The UN Secretary-General has repeatedly expressed his concern about such measures[252] and 'urge[d] all Member States to refrain from adopting national legislation, policies or other measures that have the effect of inhibiting humanitarian actors in their efforts to engage non-State armed groups for humanitarian purposes, including to undertake activities aimed at promoting respect for international humanitarian law'.[253] His approach was supported by Switzerland in the 2012 Security Council discussion on the protection of civilians in armed conflict, where the Swiss representative called on

> the Council and Member States to take into account the potentially negative effects of certain measures and legislation adopted while pursuing the legitimate goal of fighting terrorism. It would be regrettable if those measures complicated or even prevented the establishment of a dialogue for purely humanitarian purposes, prevented access to vulnerable populations by humanitarian staff or weakened respect for international humanitarian law by armed groups.[254]

251 *Holder v. Humanitarian Law Project*, above note 250; see also K. Mackintosh and P. Duplat, 'Study of the Impact of Donor Counter-Terrorism Measures on Principled Humanitarian Action' (2013), at 40 et seq.

252 'Report of the Secretary-General on the Protection of Civilians in Armed Conflict', above note 14, para. 46; 'Report of the Secretary-General on the Protection of Civilians in Armed Conflict', above note 144, paras. 72–73.

253 'Report of the Secretary-General on the Protection of Civilians in Armed Conflict', above note 14, para. 76.

254 UNSC, 6790th meeting (25 June 2012), UN Doc. S/PV 6790, Statement of the Representative of Switzerland, at 32.

The 2013 Security Council's Presidential Statement recognizing 'the need for consistent engagement by humanitarian agencies with all parties to armed conflict' might be a step in the right direction.[255]

5. Conclusion

The international community responds to the challenges which conflicts in war-torn areas of limited statehood pose for compliance with international humanitarian law by allocating competences to actors other than the State concerned. In this respect in particular, international organizations increasingly contribute to enforcing international humanitarian law. However, these organizations remain dependent on their member States who, for various reasons, might be reluctant to accept engagement with armed groups. Here, activities of humanitarian non-State actors become important. Because armed groups in particular perceive these NGOs, including the ICRC and Geneva Call, as neutral, they can significantly contribute to inducing compliance by using the instruments of persuasion. In such cases, traditional motives rooted in the logic of consequences, as well as appropriateness, are still valid and must therefore be addressed by the corresponding compliance mechanism.

These compliance mechanisms are interdependent and mutually reinforcing. Persuasion apparently relies at least partly on a direct and real threat of coercion. Persistent violators in particular can hardly be reached by persuasion. As much as national law works on the basis of an intertwined system of coercion and persuasion, inducing compliance with international law requires a mix of instruments. Even if these instruments are not purportedly combined, they are mutually reinforcing insofar as persuasion and discourse are used by non-State actors that act under a shadow of hierarchy. The concept of a shadow of hierarchy has been developed in social sciences and describes the observation that, in national systems, public and private actors usually bargain and collaborate under such a shadow of hierarchy. The shadow describes the indirect influence that hierarchical enforceable decisions of the legislative, executive and judicial branches of government exert on private actors. The concept of shadow refers to threats of these institutions to adopt, enact or enforce adverse legislation or decisions if private actors do not change their behaviour.[256] Within the international community, persuasion and

[255] Statement by the President of the Security Council, above note 145, at 4.

[256] A. Héritier and D. Lehmkuhl, 'Introduction – the Shadow of Hierarchy and New Modes of Governance' (2008) 28 *Journal of Public Policy* 1, at 2.

incentives work more effectively if they are used under a shadow of hierarchy created by coercive legal enforcement instruments, such as international criminal justice, UN targeted sanctions and peacekeeping efforts. These instruments are in turn more effective if they are accompanied by a concerted effort and not used as isolated measures in an isolated context. Thus, it is not only a shadow of hierarchy which furthers inducing compliance in cases of persuasion. Legal enforcement will also be more successful if it is accompanied by persuasion. Inducing compliance is done through all of these different means, often applied concurrently. The choice of instruments will depend on the inducer using them.[257] The inducer's choice is determined by legal as well as social considerations, and the alternatives are delineated by legal competences and limitations, as well as by the anticipated impacts the instruments might have on the addressee's behaviour. Therefore, the inducer must take into account the special circumstances of conflicts in areas of limited statehood, as well as the special circumstances of the international system.

It needs to be borne in mind that, unlike other non-State actors, which are held captive by domestic rules, the behaviour of armed groups can, at least during an ongoing conflict, only be dealt with by international law since these groups are fighting the national (legal) system, which accordingly cannot be enforced against them.[258] If international humanitarian law shall be enforced, there is no real alternative other than to engage with the armed groups. Improving civilian protection in war-torn areas of limited statehood requires accommodating the interests of armed groups, as much as State interests. In particular, empirical studies demonstrate that efforts by the international community to protect civilians may entail serious consequences for civilians if these efforts work against the conflict dynamics and overturn political developments in the territory concerned.[259] Mechanisms for inducing compliance must respond to these findings.

[257] Ratner, 'Law Promotion beyond Talk', above note 40, at 493.

[258] Sassòli, 'The Implementation of International Humanitarian Law', above note 68, at 63.

[259] Wood, 'Understanding Strategic Motives for Violence', above note 74, at 42–43; Mampilly, 'Insurgent Governance', above note 78, at 61–62.

INDEX

CPSIA information can be obtained at www.ICGtesting.com
Printed in the USA
LVOW10*0006190915

454876LV00004B/15/P

9 781107 102057